# THE MODELMAKER'S HANDBOOK

Rio Grande
3801
3704

# THE MODELMAKER'S HANDBOOK

**ALBERT JACKSON**
**and DAVID DAY**



ALFRED A. KNOPF, NEW YORK 1982

**The Modelmaker's Handbook** was conceived, edited and designed by Dorling Kindersley Limited, 9 Henrietta Street, London WC2E 8PS

**Editor** Elizabeth Driver
**Art editor** Pauline Faulks
**Assistant editor** Jemima Dunne
**Designer** Nick Harris

**Managing editor** Amy Carroll
**Art director** Debbie Mackinnon

**Illustrations** Robin Harris
**Photography** David Strickland

This is a Borzoi Book
published by Alfred A. Knopf, Inc.



**Library of Congress Cataloguing in Publication Data**

Jackson, Albert, 1943–
The modelmaker's handbook.

Includes index.
1. Models and modelmaking. I. Day, David, 1944– joint author. II. Title.
TT154.J28 745.592'8 80–2702
ISBN 0–394–50788–6

Manufactured in the United States of America
Published March 18, 1981
Second Printing, October 1982

# Contents

# Introduction

Modelmaking today is a highly-developed, competitive hobby ranging over many subject areas. Figures, trains, airplanes, boats, cars, radio control, dioramas – each aspect has its own peculiar fascination. But each also has much to offer in terms of cross-fertilization from one field to another, stimulating ideas and providing techniques previously reserved for a specific interest.

Today's modelers have a seemingly inexhaustible supply of kits and equipment available to them, as well as a wealth of reference material. What they have lacked up until now was a single source for acquiring the skills and expertise necessary for producing successful models.

We hope that this book will introduce every reader to the "greater" world of modelmaking and that this discovery will be accompanied by pleasure and excitement. Moreover, we hope that by providing modelers with all the necessary technical information needed to produce more and more refined models, they will learn still other ways to enjoy this creative and satisfying pastime.

Ready-to-paint or easily assembled figures are available from every historical period. This Saxon chieftain is based on the famous treasure in the British Museum, London.

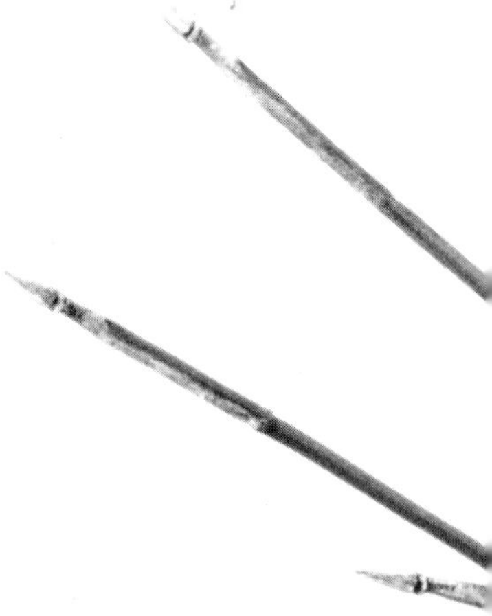

The poses of these pikemen have been modified to show them prepared to resist a cavalry charge.

Unusual subjects, such as this Westphalian lancer, can be devised from standard kits.

This standard military vehicle kit relies solely on skilful construction and painting for its realistic effect.

Extra detail has been added to this PZ KW1 tank by the modelmaker.

A cutaway involves extensive remodeling to create a highly detailed interior

With their fine detail and excellently simulated materials, scale model motorcycles are difficult to distinguish from the full-size originals. Information on producing extensive detailing for motorcycles is on page 110.

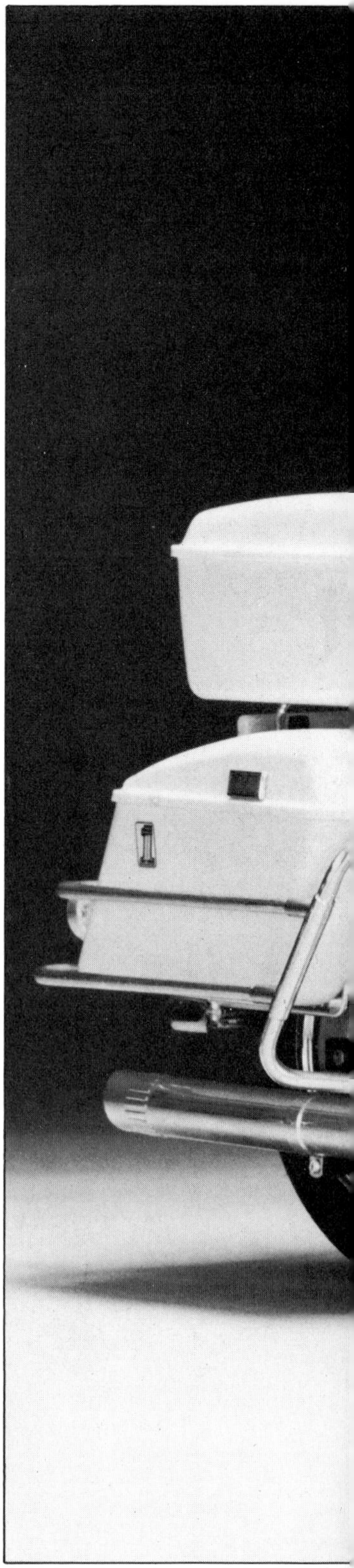

A railroad combines activities associated with many different areas of modelmaking. As these photographs demonstrate, not only can the railroad modeler enjoy the operation of a working model, but can also create landscapes and miniature buildings as well as construct, paint and weather vehicles. Railroads provide scope for those interested in setting up and operating electrical systems.

NORTHERN PACIFIC
NP
Rio Grande
1195

Here a Black Widow is being maintained by mechanics.

Nonflying airplane kits can be embellished with scratch-built items such as the pilot's safety harness in the cockpit of this Focke-Wulf FW 190.

This model of a Phantom shows the effectiveness of a simple diorama with figures.

Exact scale fidelity, enhanced by colorful insignia, makes aircraft the most popular subject for modelers of plastic kits. This is a Navy Grumman Tomcat.

An FE 8 pusher biplane makes an interesting subject for a semiscale free-flight model.

This gas-powered scale model of a De Havilland Tiger Moth has full-house radio control.

Most radio-control flying is done on a club basis.

Designed especially for radio-control flying, this monoplane is executing an unassisted take-off.

Sailing ships have been modeled for centuries. Modern kits enable even a beginner to produce highly detailed replicas like the Santa Maria.

This ancient Greek galley has been expertly weathered to disguise its origin as a plastic kit.

Some kits supply real fabric sails and wooden decking for great authenticity.

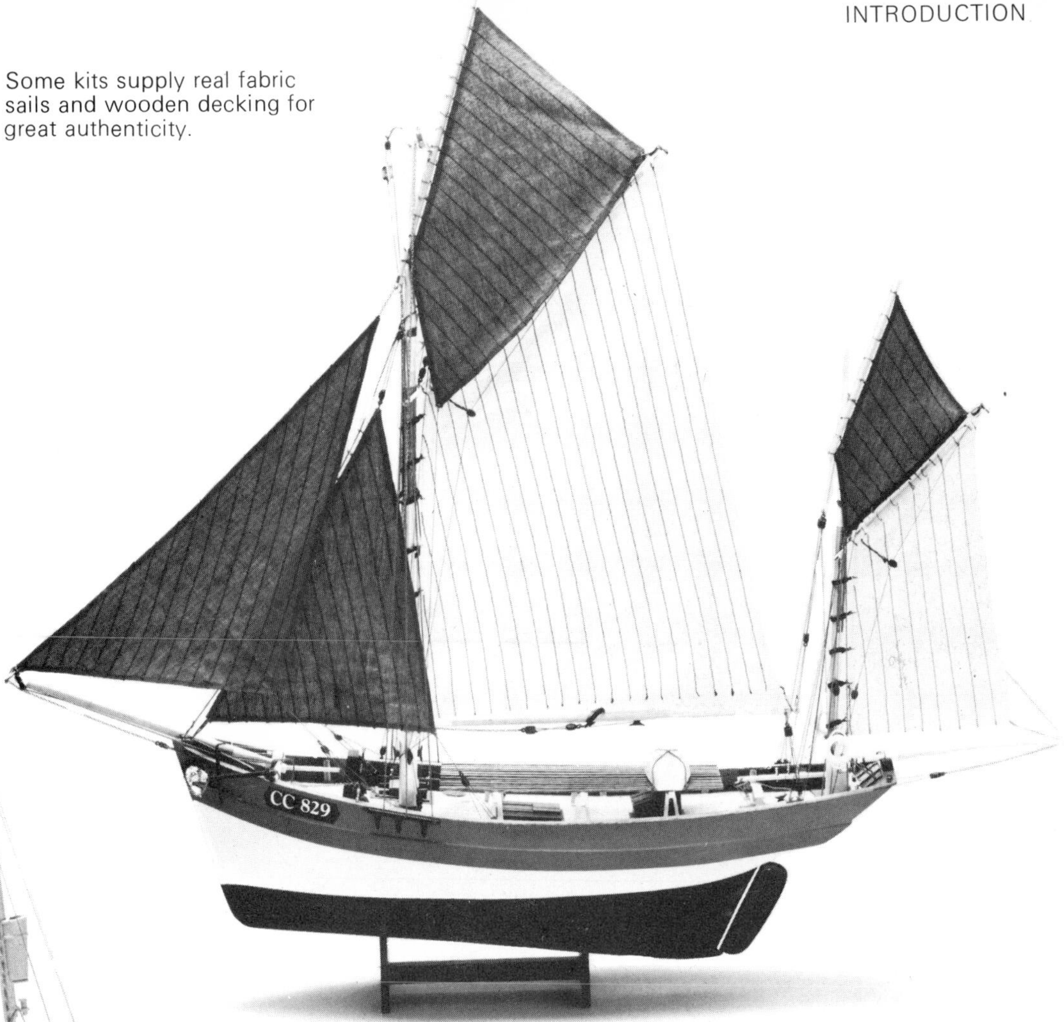


Even more detail can be added to modern warships like this 1:72 scale Corvette. For techniques see the chapter on improving vehicles.

Radio-control boats offer the modeler a wide choice of subject. The Bermuda-rigged yacht, above, is the most popular type of sailboat. The fishing boat seen negotiating a course marked with floats, above right, and the naval vessel, below right, are good examples of scale boats.

KY742

D80

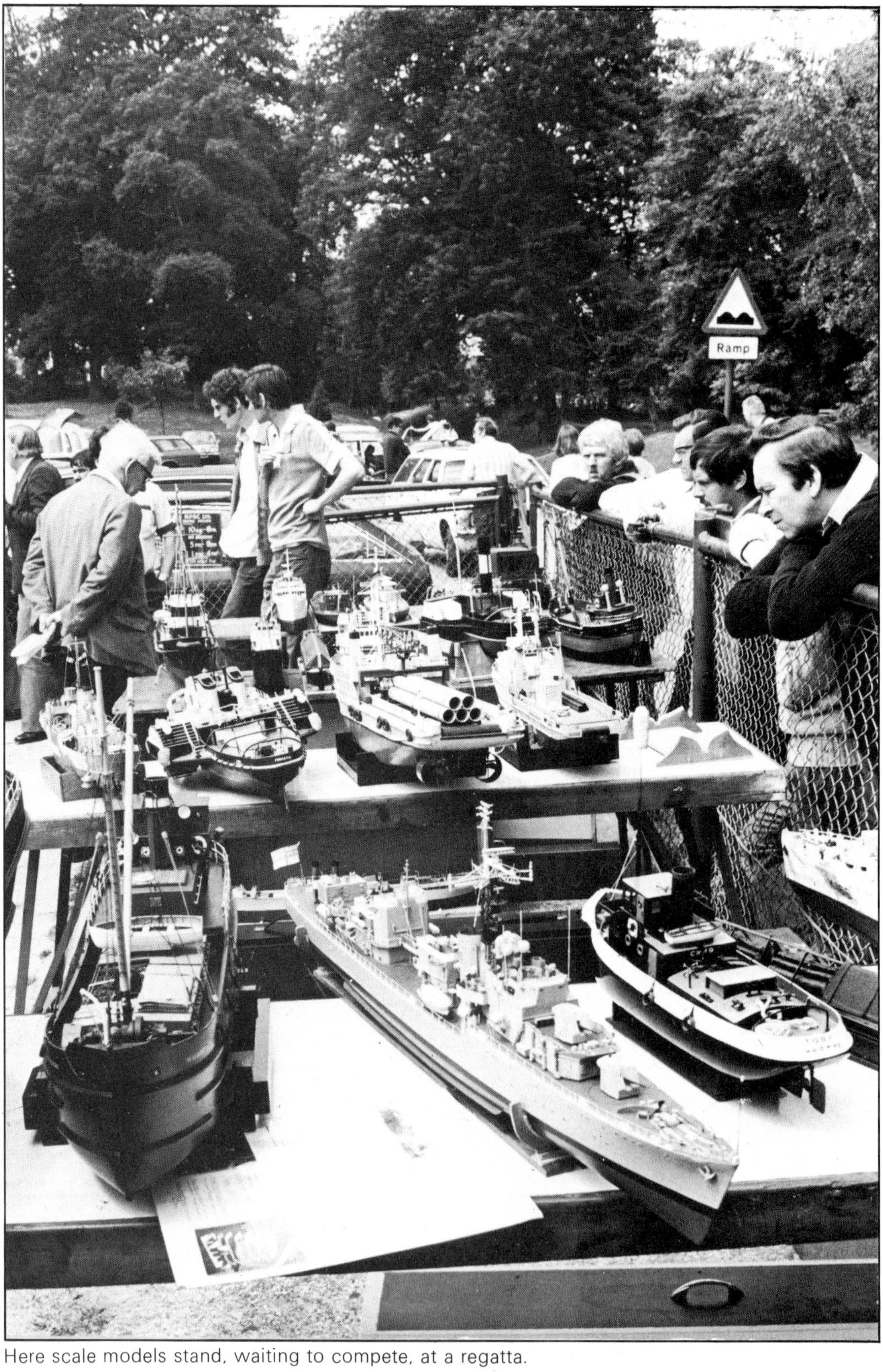


Here scale models stand, waiting to compete, at a regatta.

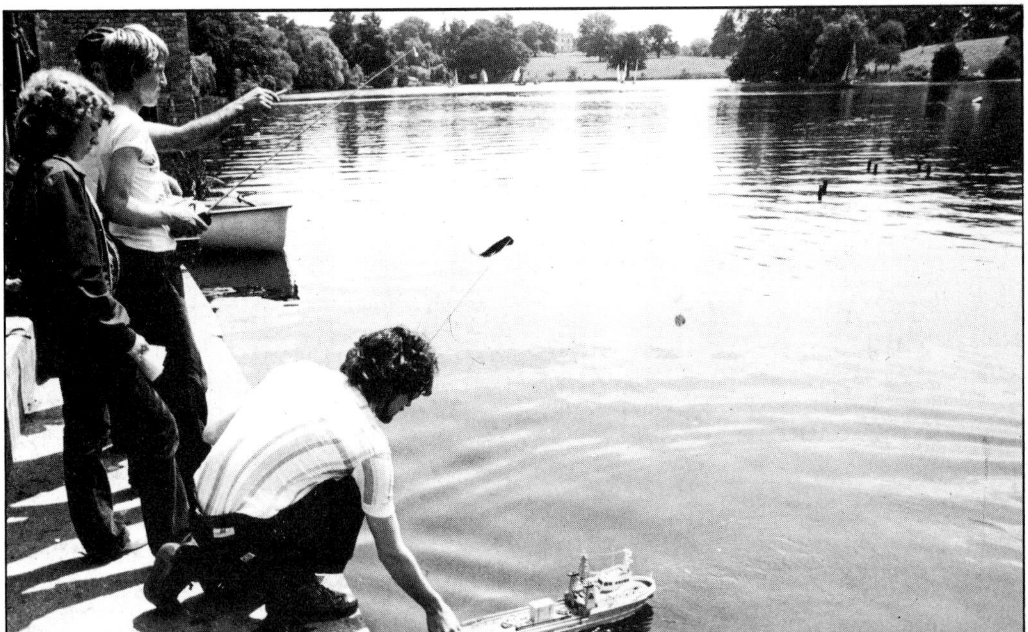

Launching a radio-control model of an oil-rig supply vessel.

The paddle wheels on this handsome scale steamer are controlled by radio.

This 1:8 scale gas-powered racing car has a beautifully finished Formula One body shell.

The same chassis can be given a completely new style by using a snap-on Sport/GT body.

A 1:12 scale electric-powered racing car has a Porsche turbo body shell.

# Basic techniques

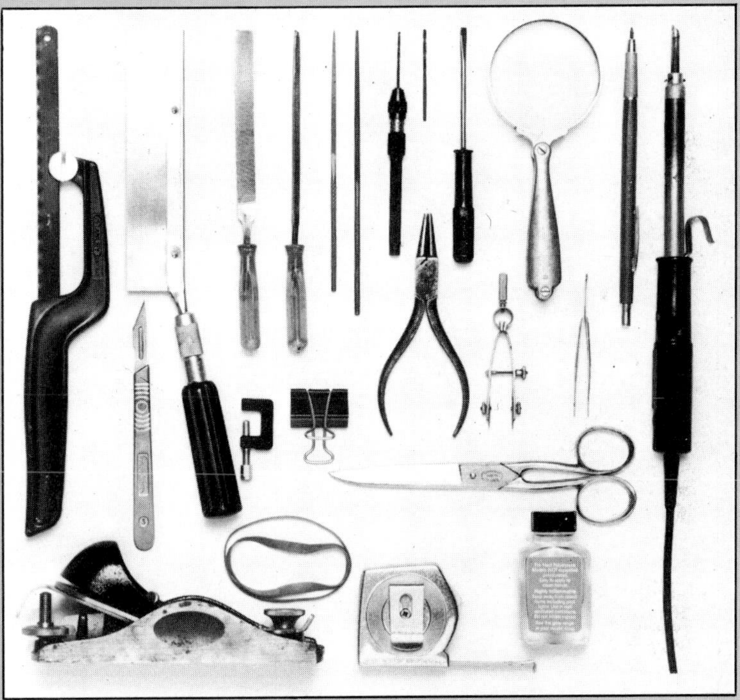

# Plans

Assembly instructions for static plastic kits come as a series of exploded drawings. Study them carefully before building the model and assess whether the suggested sequence of assembly is, in fact, the most convenient method. You may find it necessary to change the sequence to suit your painting technique, especially if you plan to add extra detail.

Plans for working models usually contain much more information and look more complicated since, in all but the most complete kits, each component must be made from scratch. Make yourself familiar with the sequence and study the main views and sections, noting how the components relate to one another. The full-size, true shape of each individual part will be included somewhere on the plan and will be keyed to the views and sections with letters and/or numbers. Some plans include sequential exploded drawings which are useful for modelmakers who are not accustomed to working from formal plans.

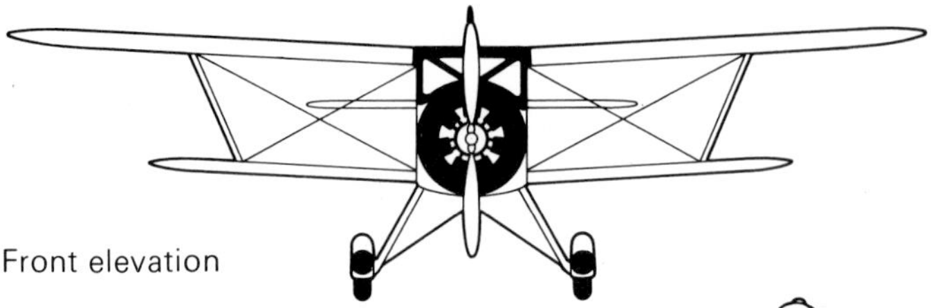

Front elevation

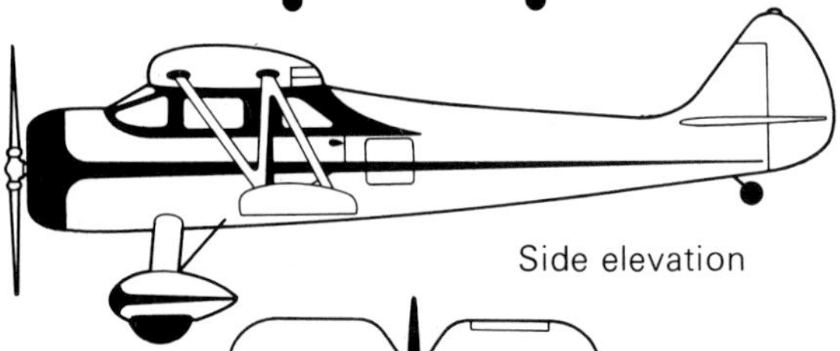

Side elevation

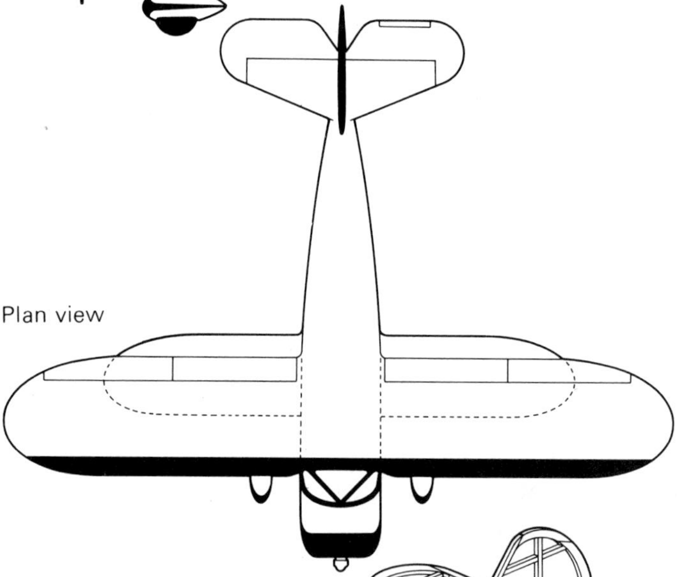

Plan view

Three-dimensional exploded view

Sectional plan view

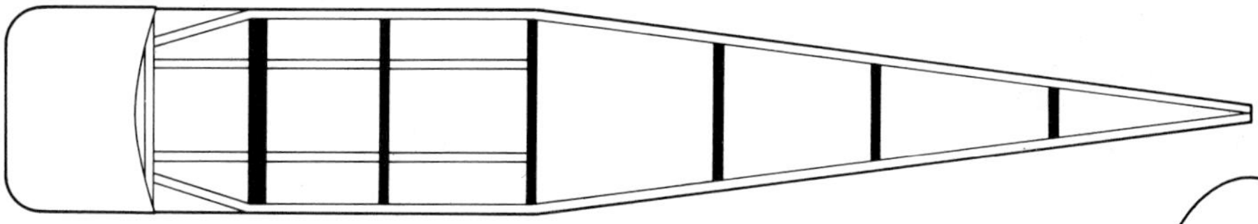

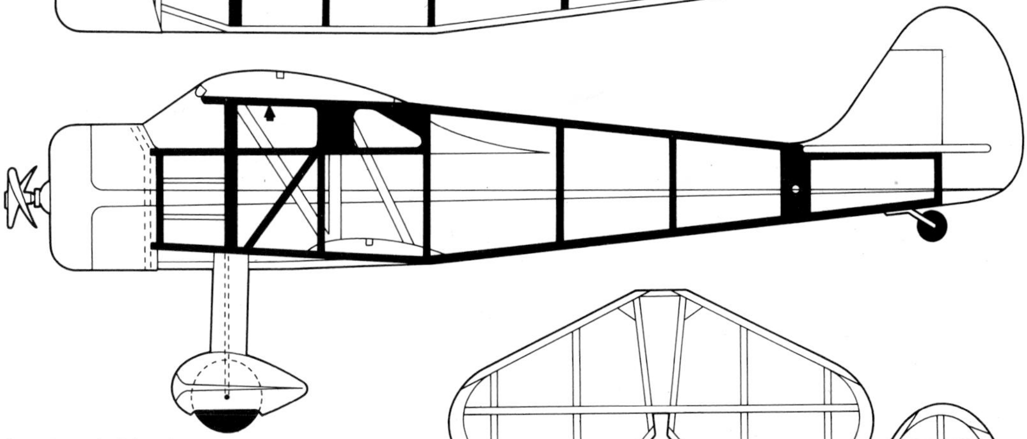

Sectional side view

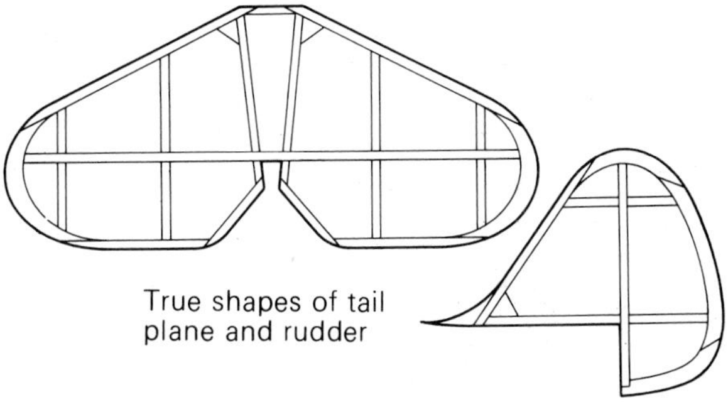

True shapes of tail plane and rudder

## Common symbols

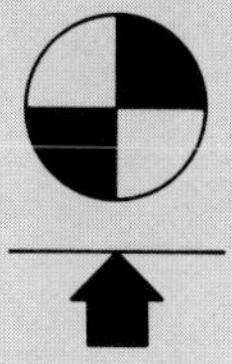

Center of gravity or balance point: the point about which the model is at rest; an airplane should assume the correct flying attitude when supported under its wings and in line with it (see page 294).

Centerline.

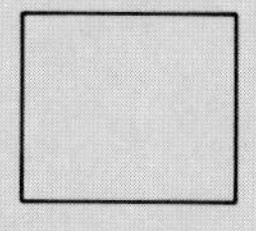

Solid line: indicates the outer edge of a component.

Dotted or chain line: indicates hidden detail.

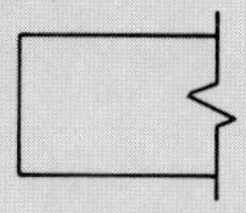

Break line: component continues past this line to be found elsewhere on the plan.

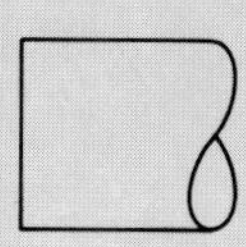

Break line for a shaft or tube.

Hardwood section: shape of a component when cut through at that point.

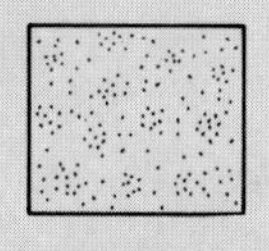

End-grain balsa wood section

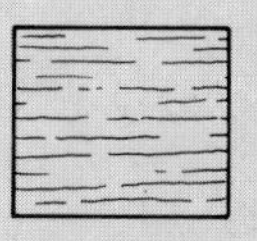

Side-grain balsa wood section

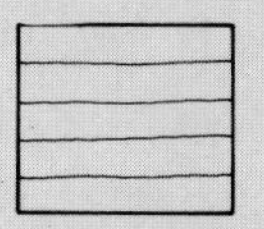

End-grain plywood section

Side-grain plywood section

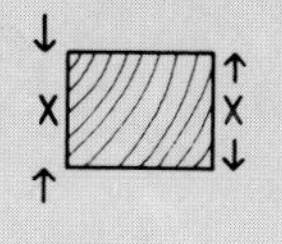


Dimension indicators: the size of the component.

# Scale

Scale is a description of the size of a model in relation to its full-size counterpart and can be expressed in a number of ways. A ratio of 1:72 means that one unit on the model represents 72 units on the full-size object. A fraction, such as $\frac{1}{4}$ scale, signifies that the original is exactly four times larger than the model. A measurement in millimeters of the model is often used to indicate the scale of figures, in particular. Model railroaders use letters and ratios. HO, for example, is 3.5 mm to 1 foot. (For a list of common railroad scales, see page 196.) Working models of aircraft, boats and cars are often not built to a true scale, unless they are replicas of a particular vehicle, in which case their scale is expressed as a ratio or a fraction, following the system described above.

Some modelmakers collect subjects in one scale only, so that their relative sizes are obvious. Others construct the same subject in a variety of scales, each model more detailed as the size increases. Small-scale models are popular because they are cheaper, and they have the additional advantage that a large collection can be displayed in a small space.

Kits are made in a range of standard scales so that models from different manufacturers are compatible. Figures and vehicles of closely related scales can also be used together. For example, vehicles in 1:86 scale and 20-millimeter figures can be incorporated in the same diorama or in an HO model railroad layout, and the most common figure scale, 54 millimeters, corresponds with 1:32 or 1:30 vehicles.

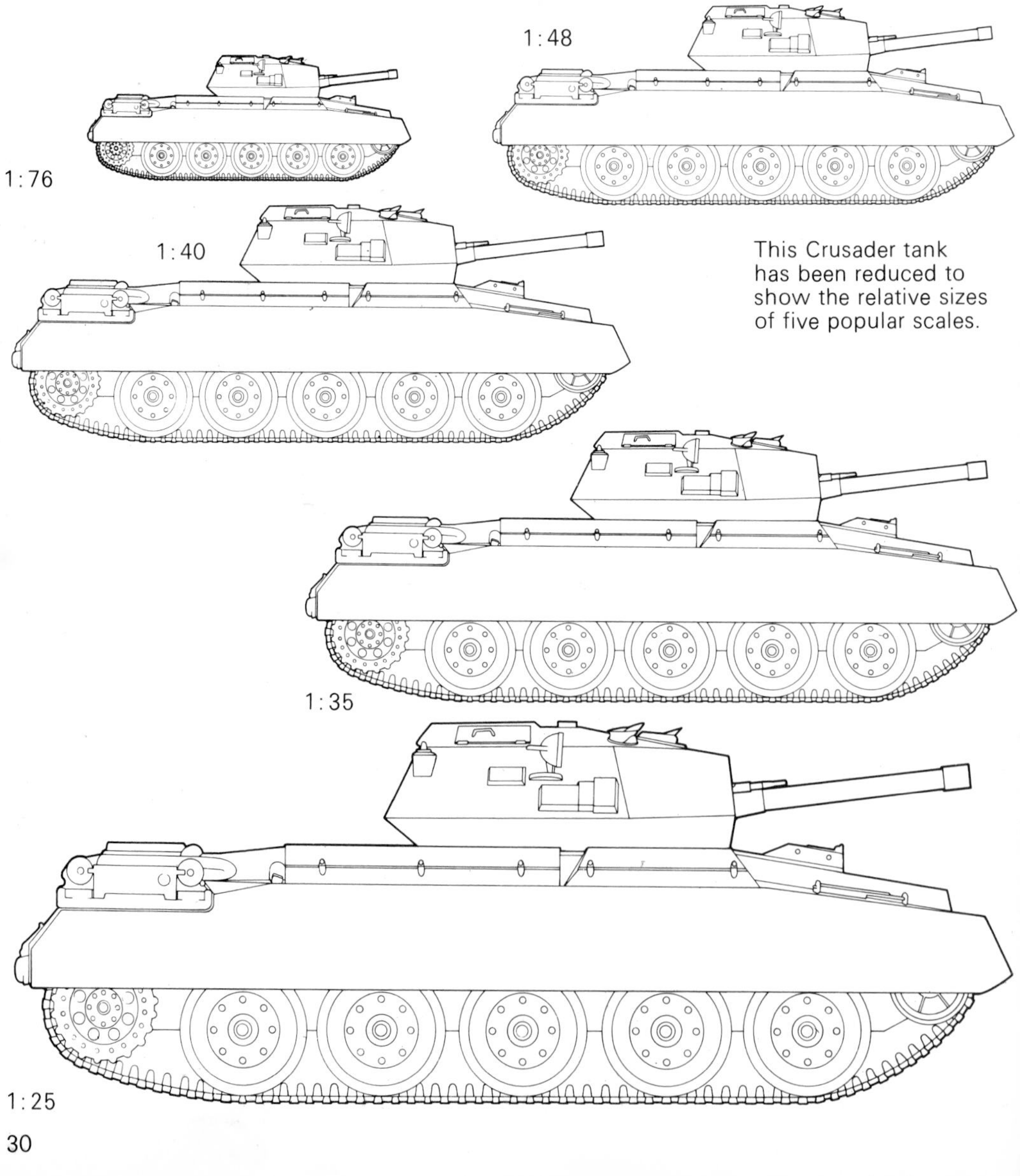


This Crusader tank has been reduced to show the relative sizes of five popular scales.

# The work space

Ideally every modelmaker would like a room entirely devoted to his hobby; a railroad modeler may need one to house a working layout.

Most people, however, work on a kitchen table or desk. A desk with a rolled top or hinged flap makes a good modeling surface. It has ample drawers and pigeonholes for storing things, and it can be closed after use, leaving half-finished models undisturbed inside. Line the desk with a sheet of hardboard to protect it from knife cuts and spilled paint or glue.

If a permanent surface is not available, work on a portable building board. You can use a tray or make one out of a sheet of hardboard, particle board or plywood. The size depends on the type of model you are building. Nail or glue strips of wood to three sides.

An aeromodeler's board should be absolutely flat, so make it out of particle board – materials such as plywood may warp. It should be large enough to accommodate your biggest frame. Seal both sides with polyurethane varnish and glue a $\frac{1}{2}$-inch-thick (12-mm) piece of woodfiber board to one surface to take either pins or thumbtacks. Do not cut on this board, but have a small plywood cutting board which hooks over the edge.

Adequate lighting is vital. Work in daylight, if possible. Otherwise, use an adjustable desk lamp, as well as overhead lights. Avoid throwing your own shadow over the work.

Store small components in the cardboard boxes supplied with plastic kits; paste a paper label on one end of the box to note its contents, and store it on a shelf or in a cupboard. Coffee jars and plastic food containers are particularly useful for storing materials for diorama and scenery building, such as sand.

Tools should be stored carefully if they are to remain in good condition. A small toolbox is useful if you do not have a permanent workshop. Always take special care to protect the cutting edges of tools.

## Building boards

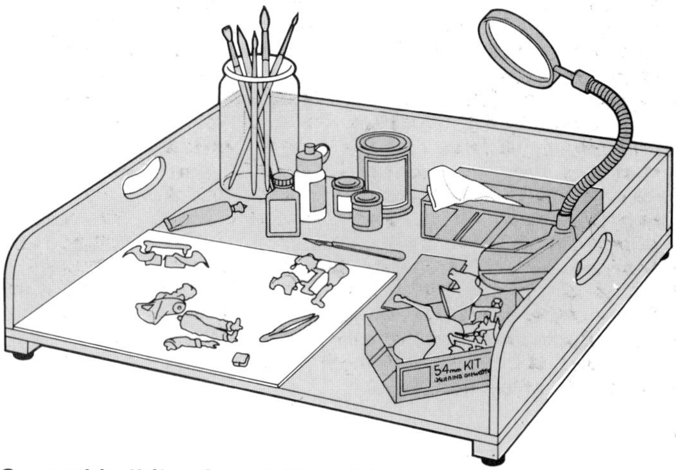

**General building board** Make it large enough to carry a few basic tools and kit parts, with sufficient room for constructing the model.

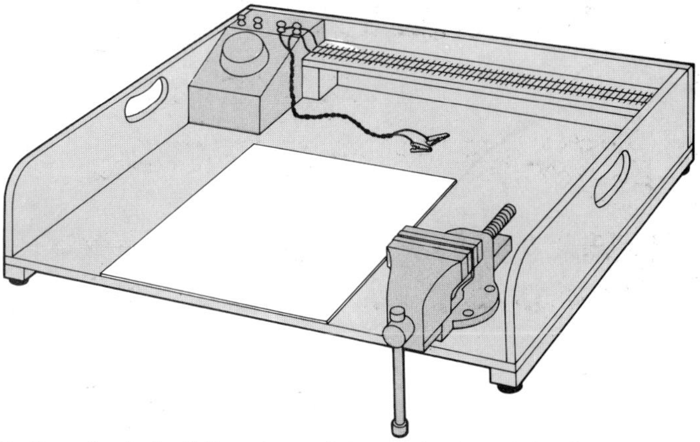

**Railroader's building board** A length of track is often attached to the board, to which a power pack can be coupled for testing locomotives. Attach a pair of clips to the power pack for connecting to the rails.

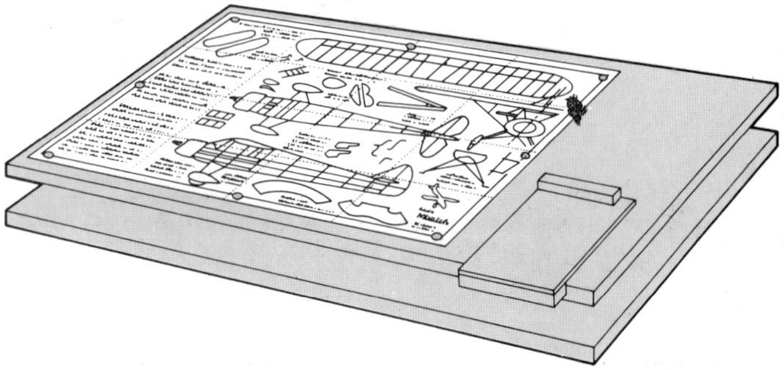

**Aeromodeler's building board** Pin the plan to the board with thumbtacks. Protect the plan from glue by rubbing a candle over those areas to which the frame will be pinned, or pin a sheet of polyethylene or wax paper tightly over the board. This type of board does not need a wooden lip.

# Tools

All modelmakers need a selection of tools, but what those tools will be depends on the type of model being made.

An assortment of tools is described below which all modelers will find useful, if not essential. Painting equipment is included in a separate chapter; see pages 68 to 73.

## Marking tools

### Pencils and pens

Use a number 2 pencil to mark paper, cardboard, plastic sheet and most types of wood. A fine felt-tipped pen is best for balsa wood and special felt-tipped markers are available for drawing on clear acetate sheet. Another way is to use a chinagraph which can be easily wiped off. See page 84 for ruling pens.

### Scribers

To mark lines on metal, use a sharp, pointed metal scriber. A double-ended scriber with a knife blade at one end can also be used for wood.

### Compasses

Any inexpensive version can be used to mark curves on cardboard or paper, but always make sure that the hinge is secure and the point is sharp to avoid inaccuracies.

### Dividers

Use a pair of dividers with hardened steel points to scribe circles and arcs on a metal surface. Spring dividers are the most useful as they can be finely adjusted.

### Center punch

Made of steel, this tool is used to make a starting point in metal for a drill or a pair of dividers.

### Steel rule

This is used for measuring and cutting straight edges.

### Try square

Use this for marking up and checking right angles during construction. The smaller, all-metal ones are generally the most useful.

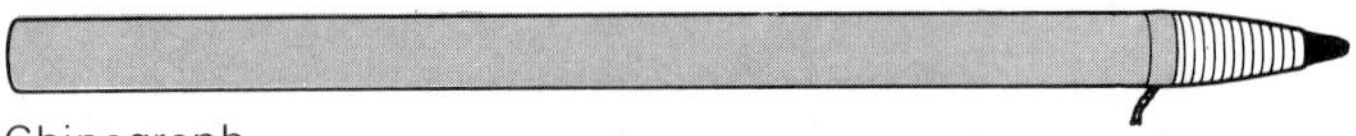

Chinagraph

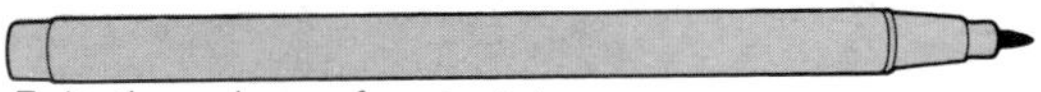

Felt-tipped pen for acetate

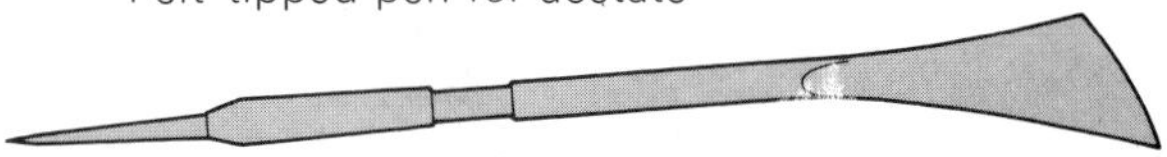

Double-ended metal scriber

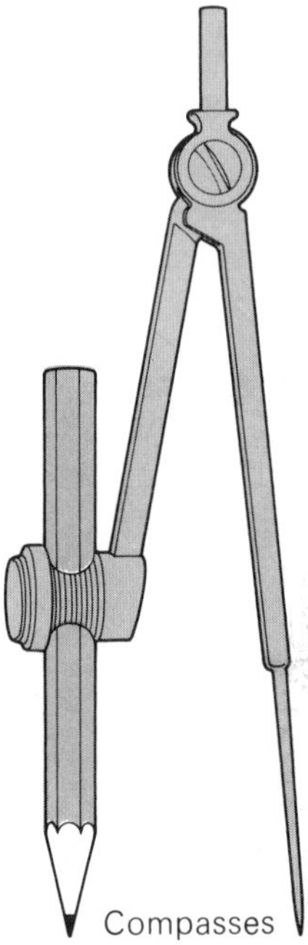

Compasses

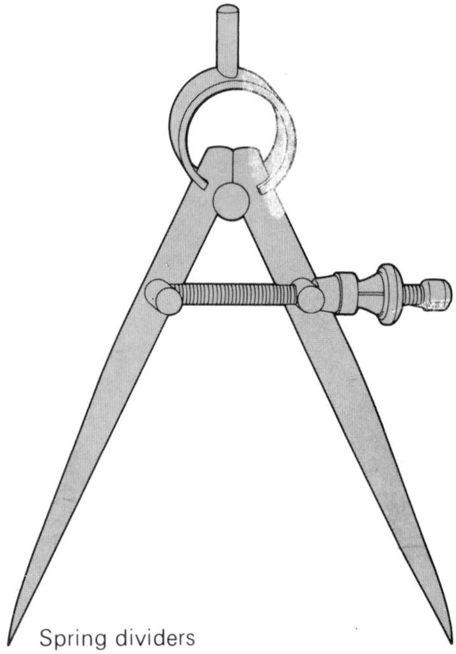

Spring dividers

Center punch

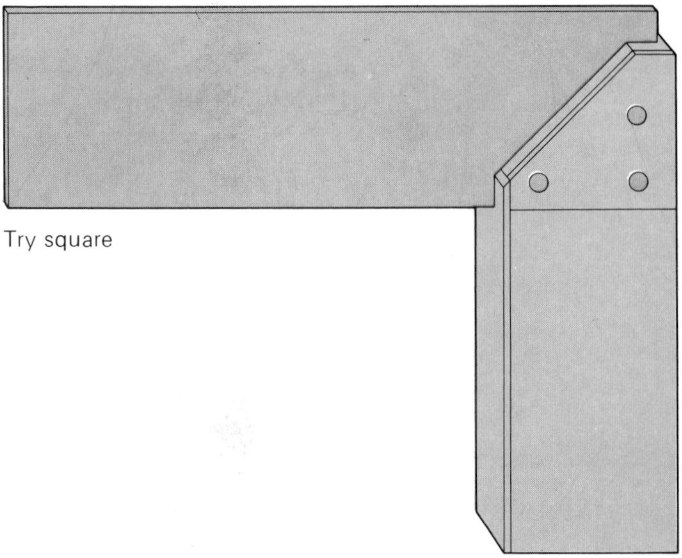

Try square

## Cutting tools

These are an important part of the tool kit. Always work with sharp tools; most blades can be sharpened on an oil-stone or replaced when dull.

### Modeling knives

A good quality knife, especially one with interchangeable blades, is one of the most useful tools a modelmaker can own. Many modelers find it more convenient to have two knives in their kit, one with a slim handle for delicate work, and another with a large grip for heavier cutting. A good knife set will provide several handles and a range of differently shaped blades.

### Razor saw

This blade fits in the heavy-duty modeling knife handle. It is capable of making fine cuts in wood and plastic.

### Single-edged razor blade

A traditional and extremely useful modelmaking tool, it has a very thin, sharp blade which is ideal for "chopping" balsa wood. The metal strip along the back edge provides a safe grip.

### Scissors

A sharp and sturdy pair are indispensable for trimming paper, cardboard and thin pieces of plastic.

### Tin snips

Use tin snips to rough-cut sheet metal to size. Double-cutting snips can be used to avoid distortion on both sides of the marked line.

### Balsa stripper

This tool holds a blade in a jig. It allows you to cut accurate strips from sheet balsa and make the most economical use of the wood. It is good for cutting identical strips for aircraft construction, where consistency of weight and strength is essential.

### Razor plane

This lightweight, miniature plane has an adjustable razor blade for shaping balsa wood accurately.

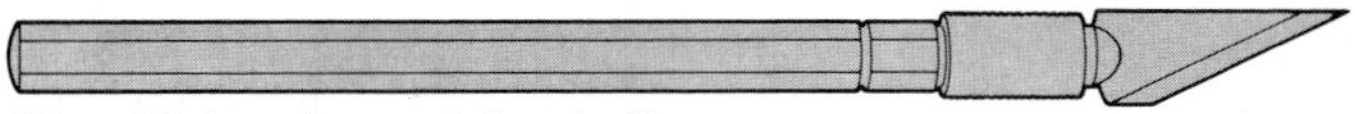

"Pencil"-handle modeling knife

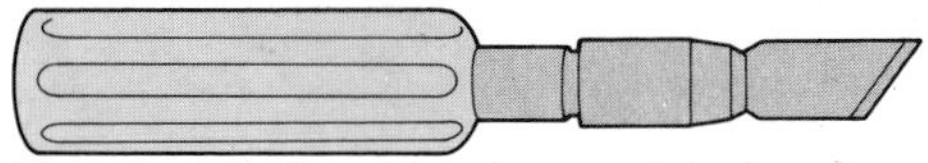

Modeling knife with a heavy-duty handle

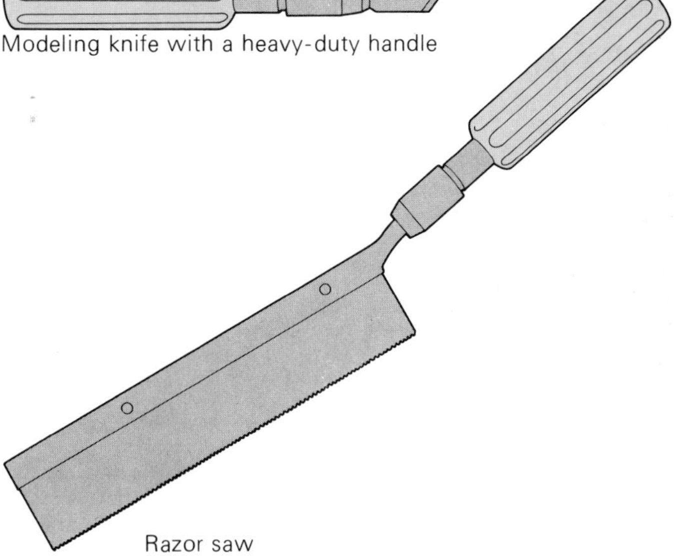

Razor saw

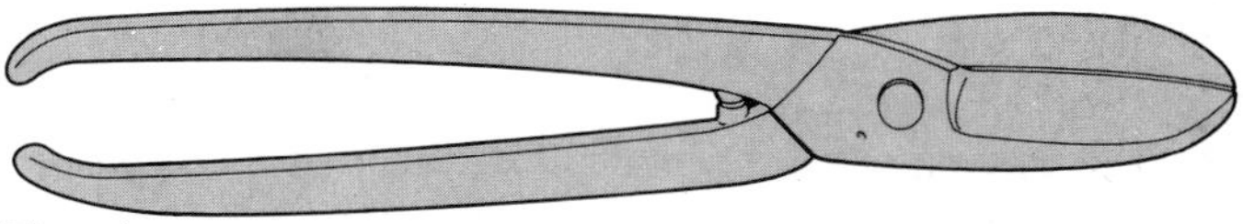

Tin snips

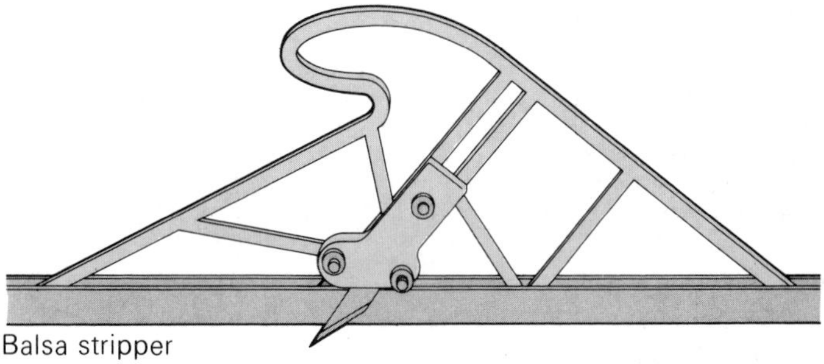

Balsa stripper

Razor plane

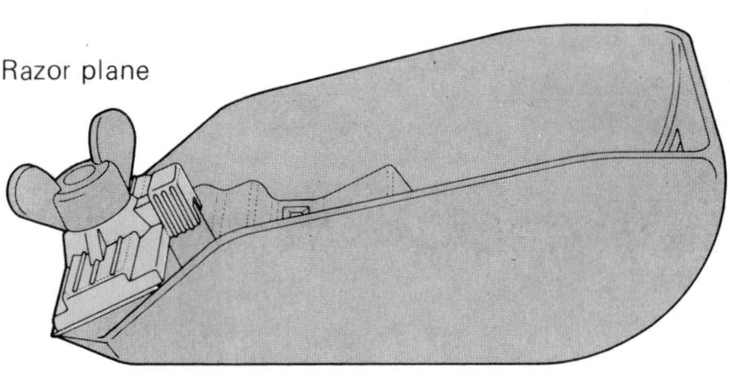

**Files**
You will need a selection of small fine files to shape and finish wood, metal and plastic. Buy 4- to 6-inch (100- to 150-mm) flat, round and half-round files for general use, and a set of needle files for precise work in metal and plastic. A surform file which can be used in any direction, both with and against the grain, is ideal for shaping wood.

**Deep-bladed backsaw**
This has small, finely set teeth and a brass or steel reinforcing strip along the back edge. It is used for cutting larger sections of wood.

**Fret and coping saws**
These are used to cut curved shapes from the edge of a wooden panel. Both blades can be adjusted to cut at any angle. The fret saw will cut tighter curves, and further in from the edge because of its deeper bow. The coping saw has coarser teeth and cuts thicker pieces of wood.

**Compass saw**
This has different handles to take an assortment of blades. Use it to cut holes in a panel.

**Piercing saw**
Use this to cut tight curves in sheet metal.

**Hacksaws**
There are several types of hacksaw. A junior hacksaw cuts small metal tubes, rods and bars. One with a deeper blade allows you to cut the end of a section square, and both cut plastic easily. Use a standard hacksaw for cutting large sections of metal and a mini-hacksaw in confined spaces.

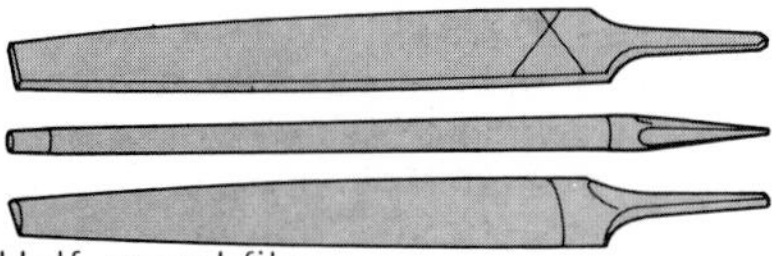

Flat file
Round file
Half-round file

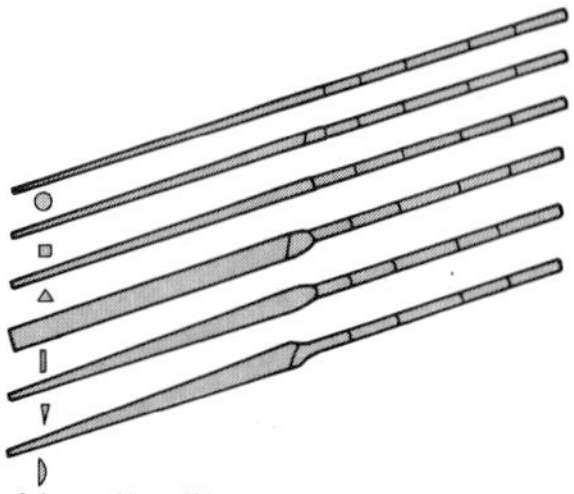

Needle files

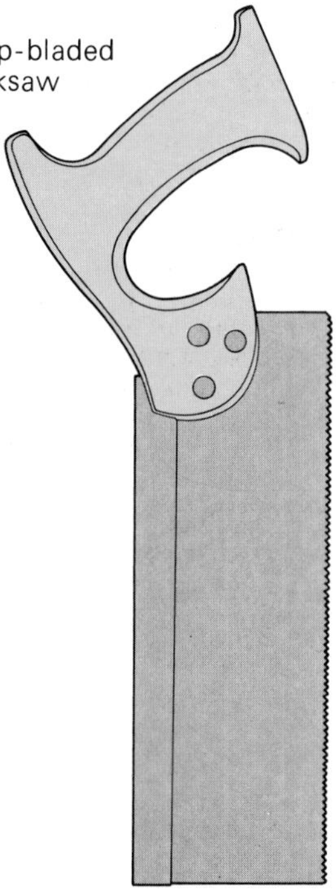

Deep-bladed backsaw

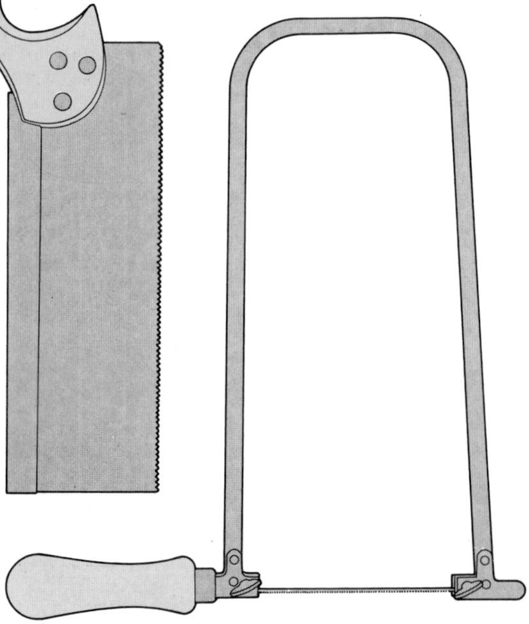

Fret saw

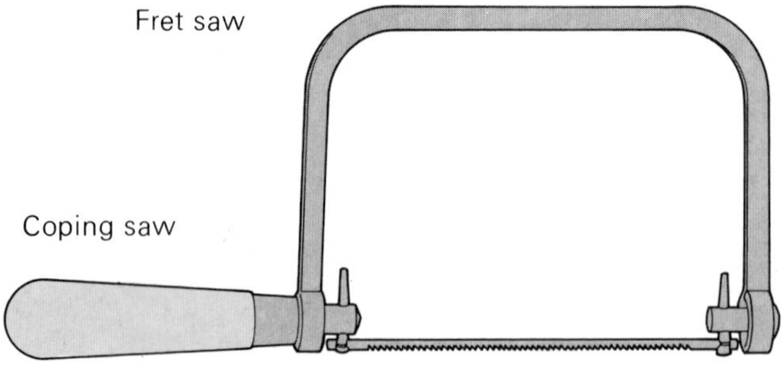

Coping saw

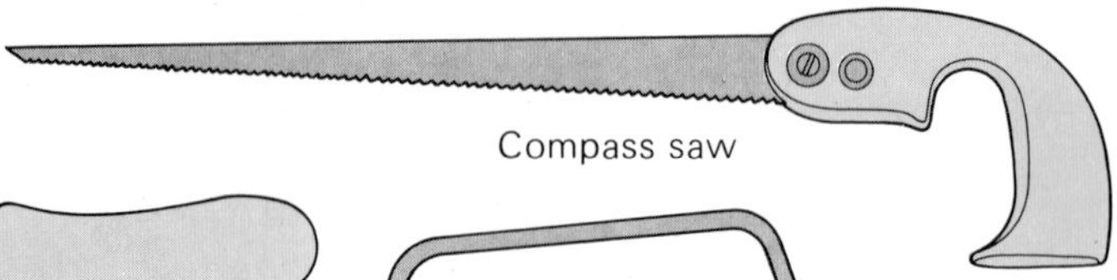

Compass saw

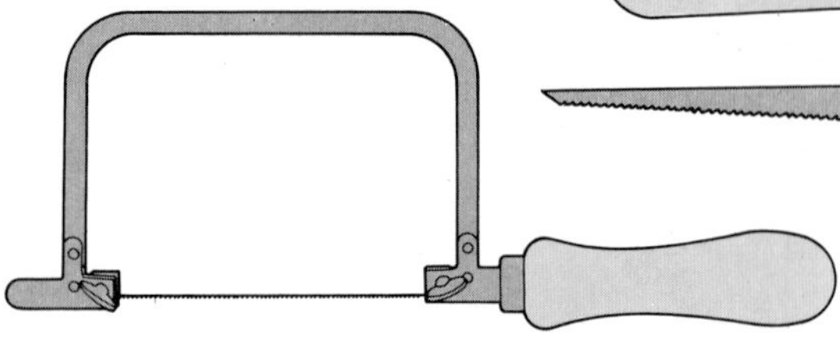

Piercing saw

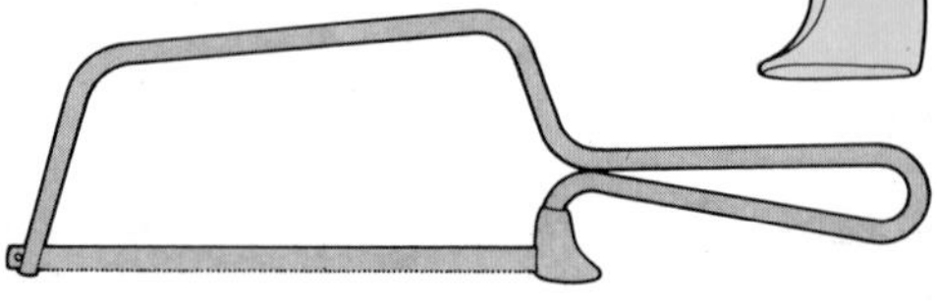

Junior hacksaw

## Power drills

A miniature power tool with a suitable range of accessories and a power drill for large-scale work make a model-maker's power workshop. You can work quickly with these tools and it is possible to perform not only accurate, but very delicate work. The action of a hand drill produces a sideways movement of the bit whereas a power drill can be held steady. One with a variable motor speed is preferable.

Many different tools can be mounted in a vertical drill press or in a bench stand, leaving both hands free to apply the model to the tool.

## Hand drill

You will need this drill for slow, controlled work on large-scale models. Buy a set of high-speed steel twist drills from $\frac{1}{16}$ to $\frac{1}{4}$ inch (1 to 6 mm) in size to drill metal and wood.

## Pin vise

An invaluable tool for drilling holes $\frac{1}{16}$ inch (1 mm) or smaller, it is revolved between the fingers of one hand.

## Punches

Large holes are difficult to drill in balsa. Buy punches for this job or make your own from thin-walled metal tube by filing the inside edge sharp.

Wad punch

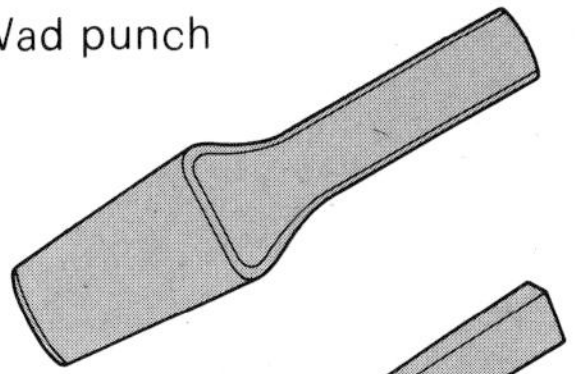

Crew punch

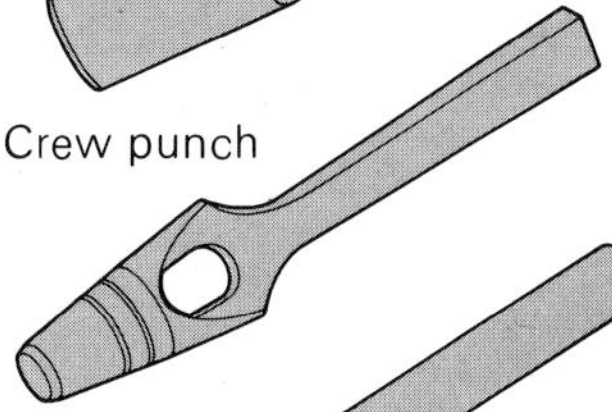

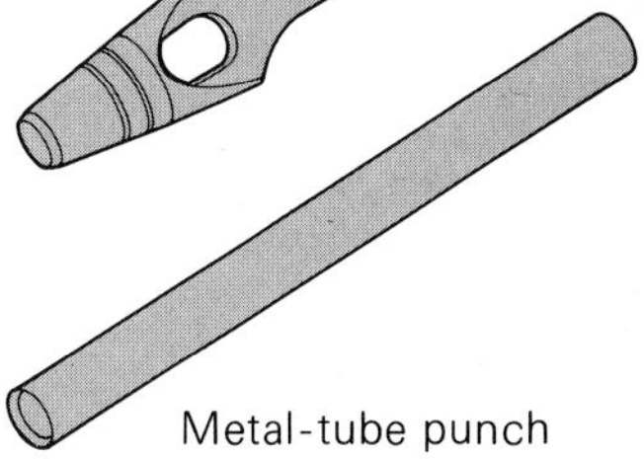

Metal-tube punch

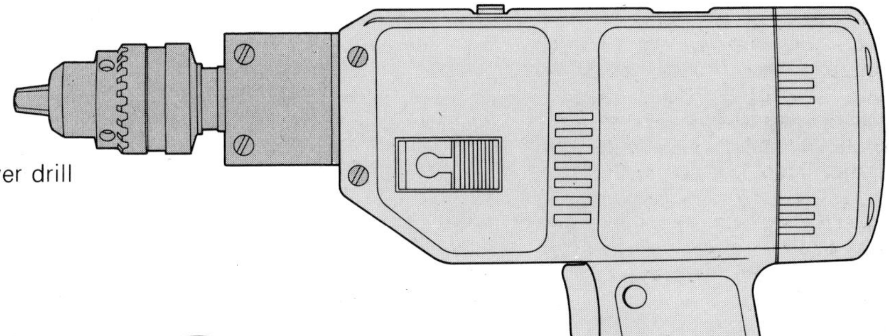

Power drill

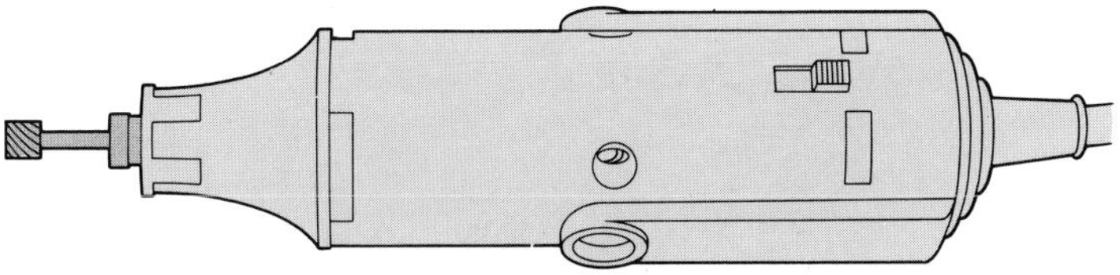

Miniature power drill

Hand drill

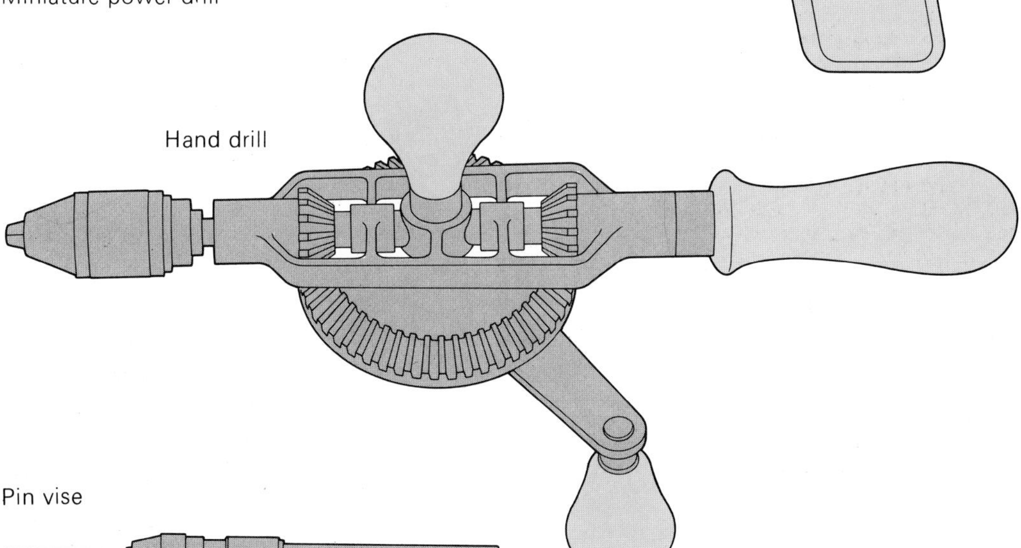

Pin vise

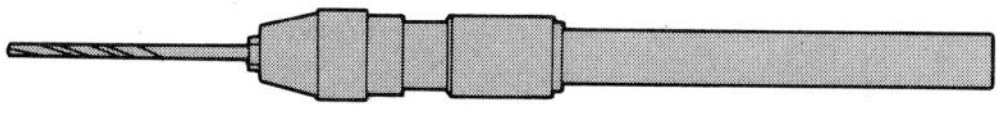

# Holding tools

### Pliers
A pair of standard, engineer's pliers which incorporate a wire cutter is useful for manipulating wire and metal sheet and rod.

### Needle-nose pliers
These have tapered jaws and are invaluable for handling small items. Round-nose pliers are necessary for making loops in wire.

### Tweezers
Those with fine, tapered points are useful for assembling small components, but flat-bladed tweezers are better for holding sheet material.

### Clamps
Small, nylon, sliding clamps, which have rubber bands to pull the jaws together, are produced especially for model-makers. You can also use miniature "C" clamps.

Clothespins make good, quick-action clamps. You can use adhesive tape or rubber bands to hold two halves of a model temporarily together or rubber bands to hold a model on a board. Straight dress-making pins are also used to hold work while the glue sets.

### Vises
Use a small machinist's vise or a woodworking vise which clamps to the worktable, to hold a model so that you can work on it with both hands. Make sure the jaws are soft if clamping a soft material.

Alligator clips mounted on a base hold small components at convenient angles. You can use a pair of clips to hold two pieces for gluing.

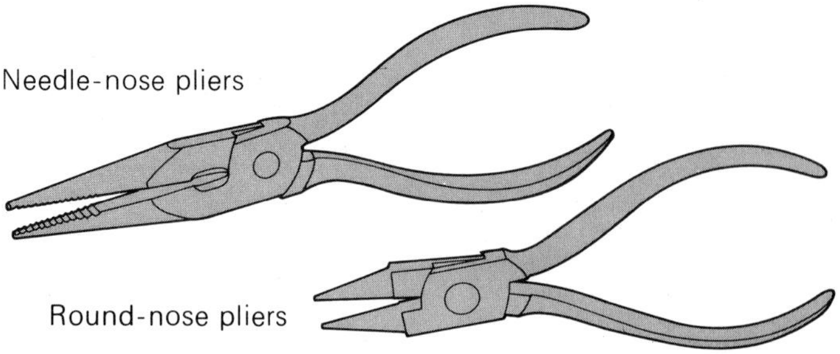
Needle-nose pliers

Round-nose pliers

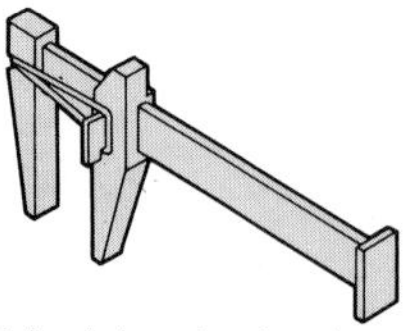
Modelmaker's clamps

**Securing a model with rubber bands** Lay the model on a piece of foam rubber. Use rubber bands, held down with thumbtacks, to pull the model into the foam.

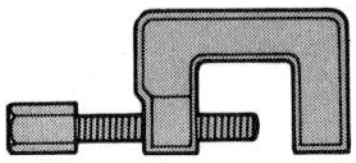
"C" clamp

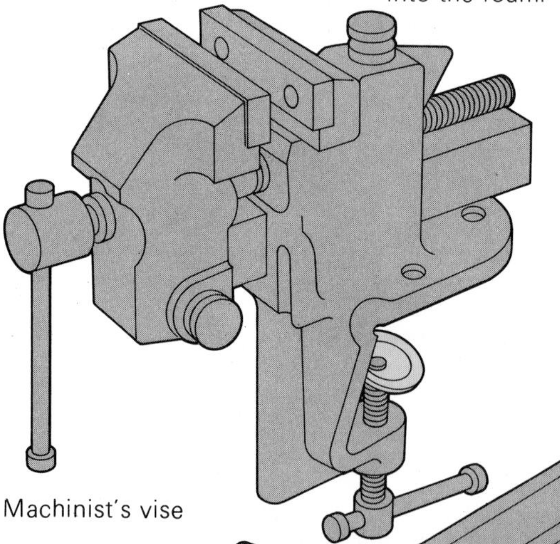
Machinist's vise

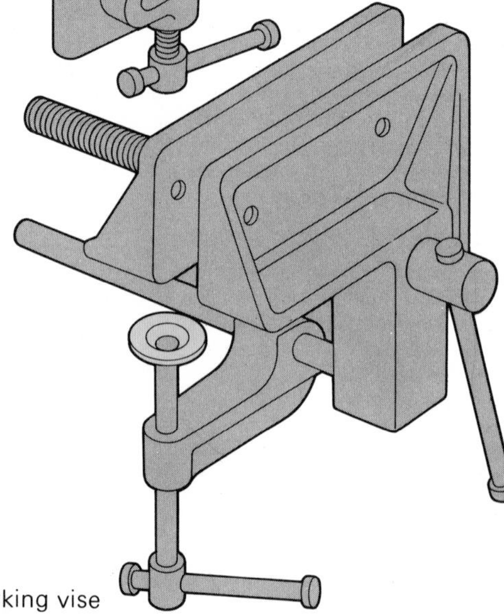
Woodworking vise

## Other useful tools

### Magnifying glass
There is a wide range available, from the common hand-held variety to those mounted on adjustable bench stands. Magnifying glasses can also be attached to a headband by a hinge so that they can be moved away from the face when not in use.

### Heat gun
This has two settings: the hot setting is used to shrink plastic film onto an airplane; the cold to cool it down.

### Heat-sealing iron
This tool has a variable heat setting and is used to tack plastic film onto airplane wings and fuselages.

### Soldering irons
Irons have different capacities. They must be able to heat the object to a temperature at which the solder will flow. To solder a brass fuel tank, for instance, you will need a large soldering iron, while a cooler iron and a lower temperature solder are necessary for white metal kits which have a lower melting point than normal solder. To control the temperature of a soldering iron, wire to a household dimmer switch.

Alternative bits are available for these tools.

### Pyrogravure
Although similar to a soldering iron, this heats to a low temperature only and is designed specifically for engraving plastic. Its very fine tip makes it useful for producing hair and fur textures on figures.

### Screwdrivers
An electrician's screwdriver is a valuable addition to a modelmaker's toolkit. A set of jeweler's screwdrivers is useful but not essential.

### Toothpicks
These can be used for stirring, applying glue or modeling and shaping fillers.

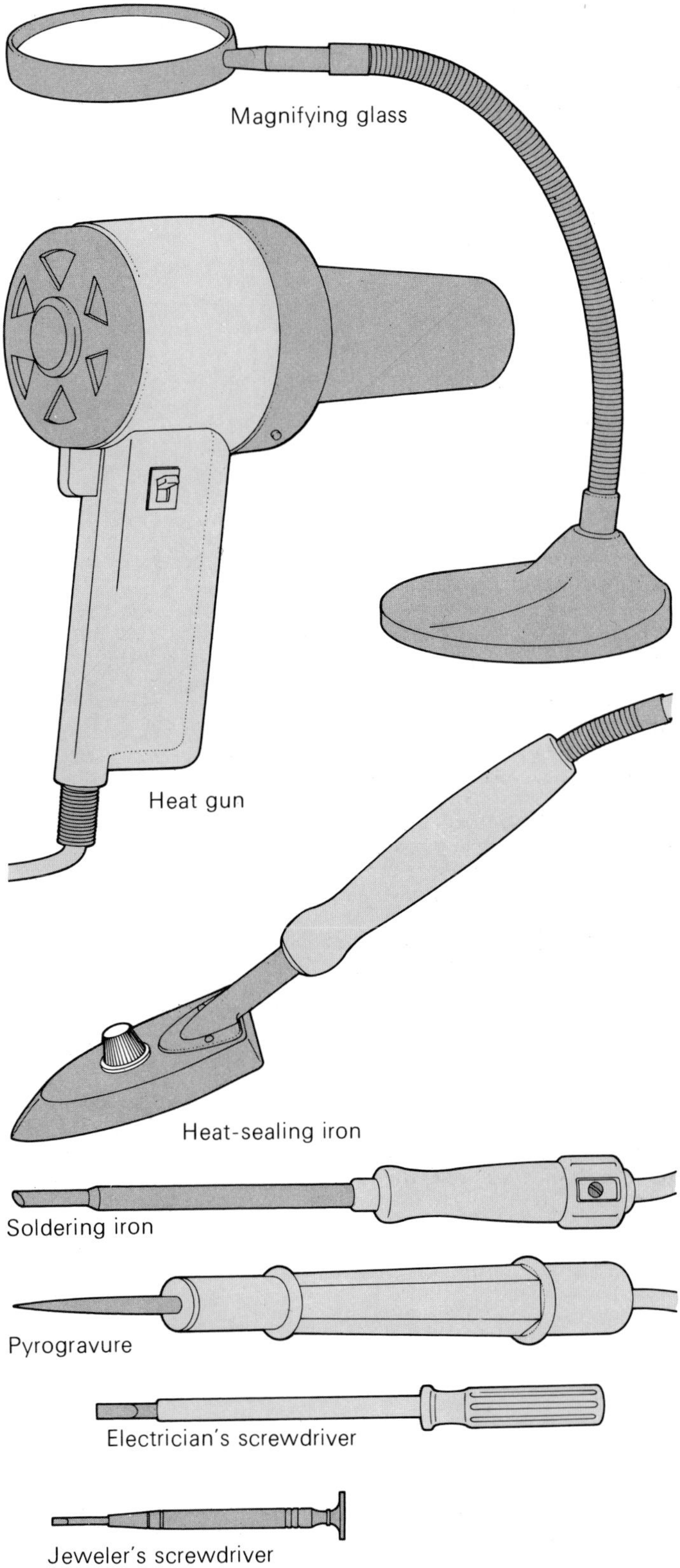

# Abrasives

These are used in all fields of modelmaking for shaping as well as finishing surfaces. Different products suit different materials, but all are graded according to the size of the particles on the paper or cloth backing material. The usual grades are: extra coarse, coarse, medium, fine and extra fine, with subdivisions within each category. Abrasives can also be selected for the spacing of the particles on the backing. A "closed coat" abrasive has the grains packed tightly together for fast cutting. It becomes clogged quickly. Widely spaced or "open coat" abrasives are more suitable for smoothing painted objects.

Abrasives can be glued to shaped pieces of metal, wood or thick cardboard, or wrapped around a block of wood, as shown right, to suit different situations, especially when you need to avoid producing hollows.

### Sandpaper

True sandpaper no longer exists, although the term is widely used to describe other abrasives such as flint (glasspaper) and garnet paper. Flint paper, which is yellowish in color, is a cheap abrasive paper used to shape lumber. Garnet paper has a harder, red-colored grit and gives a finer finish. Any of these can be used to shape balsa wood and soft- and hardwoods, as well as plywood.

### Emery paper and cloth

This natural, black grit is glued to a paper or cloth backing and is used to finish metal. The paper is particularly suitable for flat areas. Emery cloth is very strong and can smooth even tightly curved pieces of metal.

### Wet-and-dry paper

This dark gray abrasive consists of synthetic silicon carbide particles glued with waterproof adhesive to a paper backing. The material can be used wet or dry for fine shaping of plastic or wood. The water acts as a lubricant to produce an even finer finish on plastics and paintwork. The sanding action produces a fine slurry which should be wiped from the surface, and the abrasive itself should be dipped in water periodically to wash the clogging material away from the grit.

A pale gray silicon carbide abrasive is available for dry use only. It is glued to an ordinary paper backing and coated with a fine zinc oxide powder which acts as a dry lubricant. The finer grades make excellent abrasives for plastics especially as they cut for longer without a great deal of clogging.

There are even finer grades of silicon carbide abrasives, which are particularly suitable for use with plastic models. In this case, the grit is backed with a plastic sheet which can be bent and folded without cracking for working around contours and fine detail. This type can be used wet or dry. It is relatively expensive but it is also long-lasting.

## Finishing a surface

Sanding gradually reduces marks and scratches and makes an extremely smooth and blemish-free surface, when progressively finer grades of abrasive are used in sequence.

To smooth a piece of wood, always sand in the direction of the grain. If you sand across the grain, you will make scratches that may only show up after you have painted the model. To finish wood which is to be clear varnished, dampen it with clean water to encourage the fibers to rise. When dry, sand it again with the finest grade of paper. Before painting an open-grain wood such as balsa, brush on a sanding sealer to fill the grain; allow the sealer to soak in. When dry, sand it smooth with a fine-grade paper. Seal and sand once or even twice more using a finer grade of paper each time.

Plastic has no grain and can, therefore, be sanded in any direction. After removing all the scratches from a plastic component, polish it with a liquid metal polish, if you wish to have the best possible surface.

**Sanding a small component** Pick it up on the tip of a wet finger and move it over the abrasive. If it is plastic, use wet-and-dry paper with water.

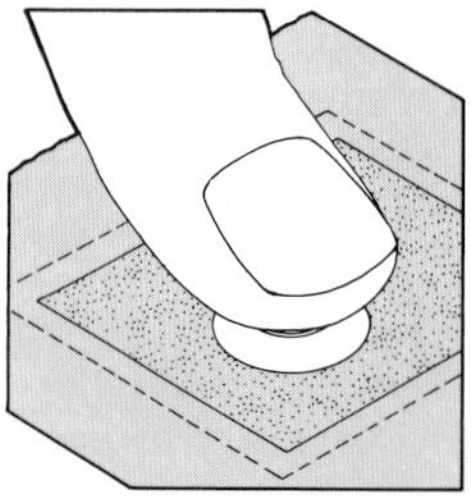

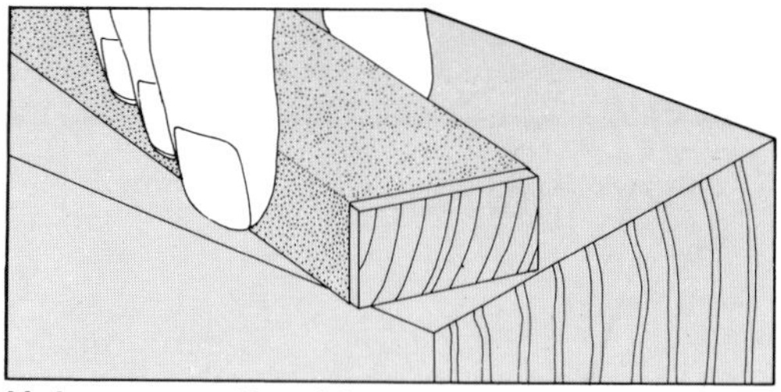

**Using a sanding block** Wrap a strip of abrasive paper around a block of wood for sanding flat surfaces to avoid the hollows produced by using fingers alone. When sanding up to an edge, keep the block flat so that you don't round off sharp corners.

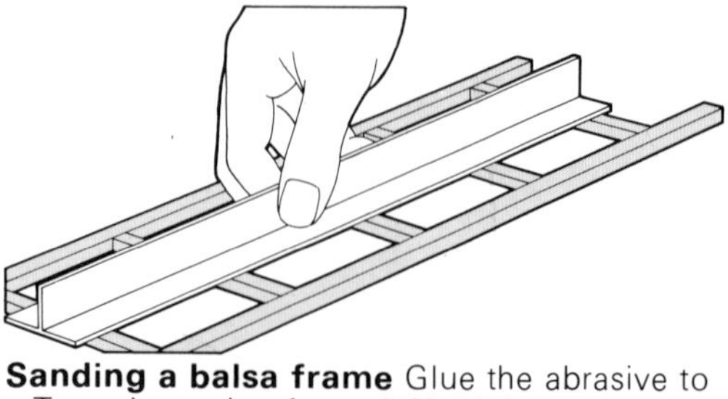

**Sanding a balsa frame** Glue the abrasive to a T-section strip of metal. Hold the tool parallel to the long edges and sand across the frame using diagonal strokes.

# Bonding materials

Choose the adhesive to match the material or materials being bonded. The characteristics and uses of the adhesives below are described on the following pages. Information about polyester resin and dope is on pages 51 and 56, and 288 to 290, respectively.

| | Balsa wood | Softwood and hardwood | Plywood | Tissue | Polystyrene | ABS | Acrylic | Cardboard | Paper | Fabric | Polystyrene foam | Polyurethane foam | Metal | Cork | Glass | Rubber | Fiberglass |
|---|---|---|---|---|---|---|---|---|---|---|---|---|---|---|---|---|---|
| Fiberglass | LN | LN | LN | | L | L | L | LN | | JN | EK | LN | LN | JL | LN | IJ L | LN |
| Rubber | J | J | J | | K | IL | IL | IL | J | J | K | JN | IL | JL | JL | IJ | |
| Glass | L | L | L | | IL | IL | IL | IL | | J | EK | JL | IL | JL | L | | |
| Cork | JL | JL | JL | | L | L | IL | IL | EK | JK | EK | EK | JL | EJ N | | | |
| Metal | L | L | L | | IL | IL | IL | IL | EK | J | EK | JL | IL | | | | |
| Polyurethane foam | EK | EK | EK | | EK L | EK L | EK L | EK | EK | EK | EK | EJ KL | | | | | |
| Polystyrene foam | E | E | E | | EK | EK | EK | E | E | EK | EK | | | | | | |
| Fabric | JK | JK | JK | | J | J | J | JK | EK | | | | | | | | |
| Paper | E | E | E | EF | E | E | E | DE F | DE F | | | | | | | | |
| Cardboard | DE | DE | DE | EF | EI L | EI L | EI L | DE | | | | | | | | | |
| Acrylic | IL | IL | IL | E | BI L | BI L | C | | | | | | | | | | |
| ABS | IL | IL | IL | E | BI L | BI L | | | | | | | | | | | |
| Polystyrene | IL | IL | IL | E | AI L | | | | | | | | | | | | |
| Tissue | FG M | FG M | FG M | EF | | | | | | | | | | | | | |
| Nylon and silk aircraft covering | FG M | FG M | FG M | | | | | | | | | | | | | | |
| Plywood | EH | EH | EH | | | | | | | | | | | | | | |
| Softwood and hardwood | EH | EH | | | | | | | | | | | | | | | |
| Balsa wood | DE | | | | | | | | | | | | | | | | |

**Key**

- A Polystyrene cement
- B ABS cement
- C Acrylic cement
- D Balsa cement
- E White glue
- F Tissue paste
- G Tissue cement
- H Synthetic resin glue (UF glue)
- I Cyanoacrylate glue
- J Rubber-based contact glue
- K Latex glue
- L Epoxy glue
- M Clear dope
- N Polyester resin

# Adhesives

The wide selection of adhesives now available have largely superseded mechanical fastenings and can often be used instead of a welded or soldered joint. General-purpose adhesives produce very strong bonds between dissimilar materials, and special-purpose cements are formulated for cold welding a specific material.

Cements are made of plastic dissolved in a solvent. They are normally designed to suit one particular plastic and will only bond plastic to plastic. The solvent softens the meeting surfaces, which fuse as it evaporates. The two components become welded together without a film of adhesive between them. You can use the solvent by itself if the joint is close fitting as the plastic simply adds body to the cement for filling gaps. The solvents are highly volatile and produce fast-setting cements: lightweight components will be self-supporting after a few minutes, large ones need light pressure only. Many plastics can be bonded using compatible cements but not all of them will readily dissolve and fuse, for instance nylon and polyethylene.

Mechanical adhesives work when the glue forms an interlocking bond with the surface of the material. This type is very effective on porous material. If you are gluing a nonporous surface, roughen it to encourage the adhesive to bond. Some adhesives are specially formulated to bond smooth, nonporous surfaces.

Even in a successful bond the joint is only as strong as the adhesive film and, depending on the nature of the glue, this film may be rigid or elastic. The latter type is normally needed for flexible materials, even though it may "creep." Rigid structures usually require a rigid adhesive which is stronger. However, if the structure will be subjected to vibration or any impact which could result in the breakdown of the film, an elastic adhesive may be a better choice.

## Polystyrene cement

This is the principal glue used in the construction of plastic kits, so much so that it is often referred to as plastic cement. It is, in fact, a solution of polystyrene in chlorobenzene or acetone, which will only dissolve polystyrene.

Polystyrene cement is available in two forms: a transparent, viscous fluid sold in tubes (tube cement) and a clear liquid (liquid cement) which is the solvent on its own. Both forms are powerful solvents, especially the tube cement which, if squeezed from a joint, is not only capable of removing all the surface detail from a molding but could even make a hole in it. Moreover, if too much tube cement is applied to the inside of a model it can distort the molding, even after it has been painted as the dissolving process continues for a long time. Use tube cement for bonding structural components or similar, loose-fitting joints only. Use the less volatile liquid cement wherever there is a possibility of damaging the surface. Neither type should be used on polystyrene foam as it will dissolve it. Use white glue instead.

## Using polystyrene cement

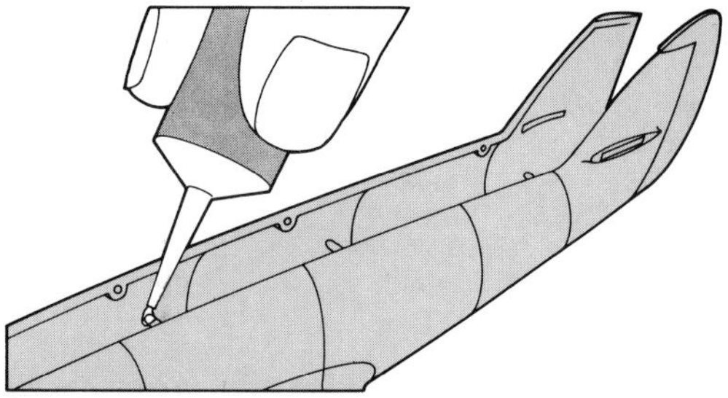

**Joining two halves of a model** Apply a tiny drop of tube cement to the locating pins and join the two halves. Temporarily secure them with self-adhesive tape or rubber bands.

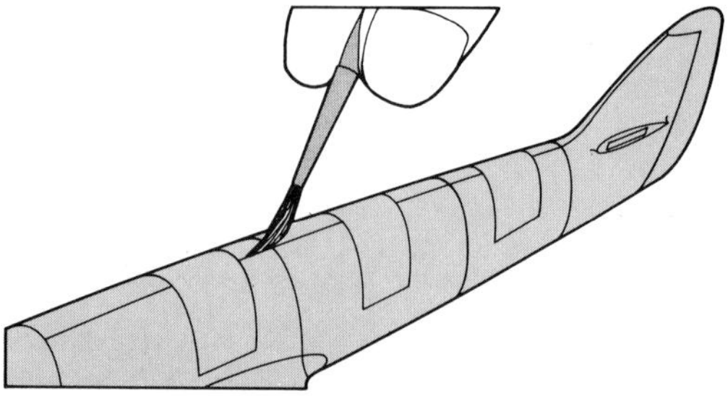

Using a pointed brush, carefully apply liquid cement to the join (do not paint up to the tape). Remove the tape and go back over areas where there is no glue.

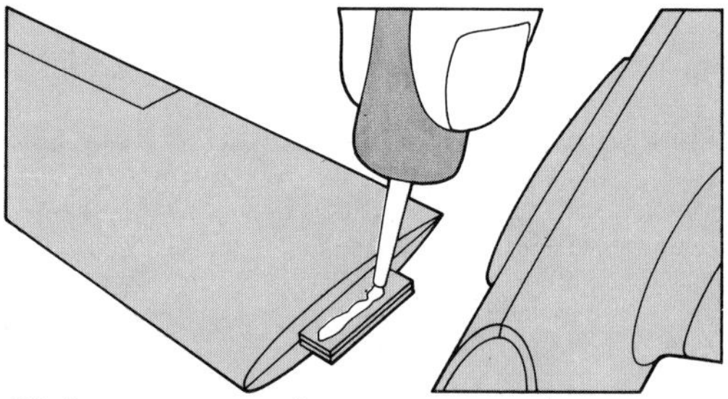

**Gluing structural components** Use tube cement to attach a wing to the fuselage of an airplane. Apply just enough to do the job. Seal the joint line with liquid cement.

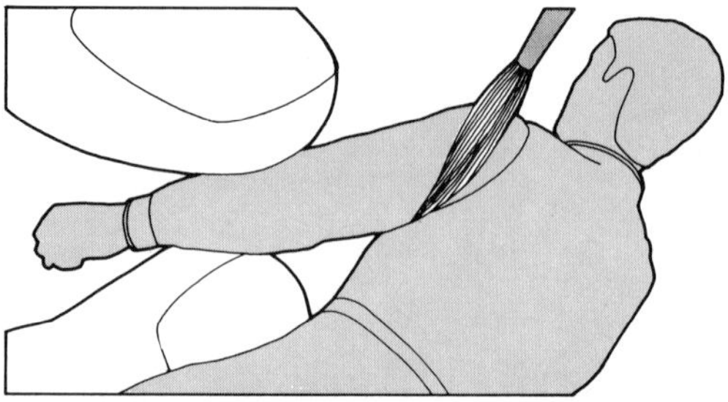

**Attaching small items** Tack them in position with liquid cement. Then, run the cement around the item to secure it. Another method is to apply solvent to both surfaces to soften them before pressing them together.

## ABS cement

Acrylobutyl styrene (ABS) can be bonded with a solvent marketed by Plastruct called Plastic-Weld. It contains ABS plus additives and, unlike most cements, is capable of bonding other plastics, namely polystyrene and acrylic. Apply it the same as polystyrene cement.

## Acrylic cement

This cement contains acrylic dissolved in dichloromethane, and is available in different viscosities. The most useful for modelmaking is an extremely thin type which is brushed on. Take particular care when joining clear acrylics which can be fogged by the cement and watch out for air bubbles trapped in the joint.

To apply the cement, first clean the joint with lighter fuel then wash it in clean water. Mask up to both edges of the joint with masking tape and make a hinge with another strip. Open up the joint and apply cement to both surfaces. Leave for about 30 seconds, then close it. Leave it to set for at least 3 hours; it will not reach maximum strength for about 3 weeks.

## Balsa cement

With balsa wood, as well as other porous materials, the cement sticks by mechanical adhesion, and is, therefore, not strictly speaking a cement.

Balsa cements contain synthetic resin additives for strength and to improve their gap-filling properties. The additives also slow down the setting speed but not enough for gluing large areas where white glue is more effective.

Always apply balsa cement to both surfaces. For end-grain butt joints which tend to soak cement away from the glue line, use the technique known as double-gluing. Spread the cement evenly on both surfaces, press the joint together and take it apart; leave the cement to dry but not set. Apply a second layer of cement and rejoin the surfaces.

Do not use balsa cement on marine structures as it is not waterproof.

## White glue (PVA or polyvinyl acetate)

This is a general woodworking adhesive ideal for mixed wood construction. It will bond many other materials, both rigid and flexible, producing a slightly flexible film which does not creep under load. It is ready to use straight from the bottle or it can be thinned with water, if you find it necessary.

Spread white glue evenly over both surfaces with a brush. Join the two components and clamp the joint for 24 hours to allow the glue to set. Corner braces do not need clamping, just "rub" them into position – the suction alone is sufficient to hold them in place. Wipe off excess glue with a damp cloth and wash the brush in water.

White glue will soften if you immerse the model in water.

## Tissue paste

This is a dextrin adhesive used to apply tissue covering to aircraft wings and fuselages (see pages 289 to 290). Tissue cement or dope can be used for the same purpose.

## Synthetic resin glues

These are woodworking glues. There are several types available but the most common is urea formaldehyde, sometimes called UF glue. Its waterproof properties make it ideal for boat modeling. It is an excellent gap-filling glue and produces a very rigid film.

The glue has two constituents: the resin itself and a catalyst or "hardener." When they are mixed together a chemical reaction takes place which sets the adhesive. The glue is sometimes supplied as a powder which is mixed to a paste with water. The setting time varies. On a hot day a UF glue sets within 2 to 3 hours, but it takes longer in low temperatures and should not be be used in temperatures below 50°F (10°C). Paint glue onto both surfaces and leave it to penetrate the wood for a while before joining the components. As a rule, the joints should be clamped and left overnight to set thoroughly.

## Cyanoacrylate glue

CNA glues, such as Krazy glue, are almost universal adhesives and as such have many applications in modelmaking. Their main advantage lies in their extremely fast setting time (10 to 15 seconds under finger pressure alone). They are expensive, but only a tiny amount of the clear, liquid adhesive is required to make a good joint; too much will give a poor bond to the work.

Cyanoacrylate glues have no gap-filling properties so the joints must be close fitting. Otherwise, use the glue to tack the components together and reinforce the joint later with a gap-filling glue, such as an epoxy one.

Make sure that the joining surfaces are clean and grease-free. If the job is large enough, apply the glue sparingly, direct from the tube. For small items, apply the glue with a toothpick or squeeze a little onto a scrap of cardboard and dip the item into the glue. To glue porous materials, dampen the surface with water first to prevent too much glue soaking into it. If a joint will not stick, take it apart, leave it to dry for about 10 minutes, then try again applying less glue.

Contact with fingers and eyes should be strictly avoided. When removing the cap, and especially when unblocking a sealed nozzle, point the tube away from you. If your fingers become glued together, use a spoon handle to pry them apart. Keep cyanoacrylate glues out of the reach of children.

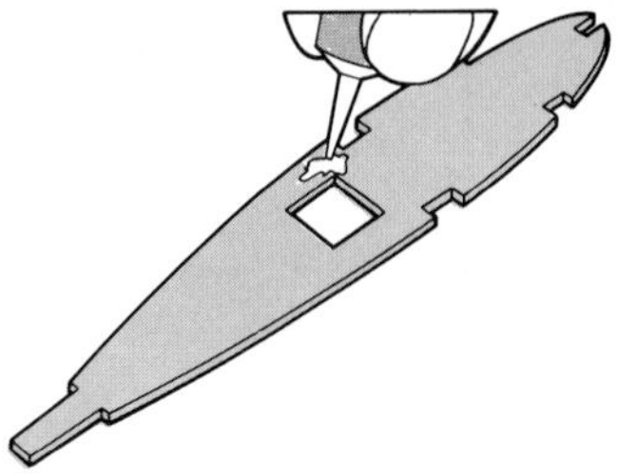

**Soaking with cyanoacrylate glue** You can repair a crack in very porous material such as balsa, or strengthen weak, short-grain sections, by adding a few drops of cyanoacrylate glue.

## Rubber-based adhesives

There is a large family of adhesives based on natural or synthetic rubber in solution. They are good, general-purpose adhesives, and because they produce a flexible film, they are useful for bonding flexible materials to each other or to more rigid ones. They can be softened with a variety of chemical solvents.

So-called rubber cements are rubber solutions with resin additives to improve gap-filling and increase strength.

Rubber-based adhesives fall into two main groups: those dissolved in spirit, and those emulsified in water, which are commonly known as latex adhesives. Spirit-base glues are flammable and viscous; latex ones are white and more fluid, and can be applied to the material with a brush.

Many rubber-based adhesives are contact glues. Spread this type thinly and evenly over both surfaces and leave until tacky or dry to the touch. When the two surfaces are joined, they will bond immediately. The strength of the bond increases as the solvent evaporates, so do not apply a full load to the joint for about twenty-four hours.

## Epoxy glues

These are extremely versatile, general-purpose adhesives with excellent gap-filling properties which bond porous and nonporous materials alike. Two constituents are mixed together to form a paste which, when it sets, makes a very strong water- and fuelproof bond. The setting time ranges from four minutes to twenty-four hours, depending on the type, although it can usually be accelerated by warming the "job." Fast-setting glues, unfortunately, have correspondingly short pot lives.

A good epoxy joint is as strong as a soldered one and, although it normally produces a rigid film, its elasticity varies according to the additives. It is not suitable for gluing flexible materials and it will not shrink as it sets.

# Paper and cardboard

Apart from the more specialized products listed below, paper and cardboard are readily available as newsprint, packaging materials, stationery items and artist's materials. Brown wrapping paper, manilla envelopes and folders in particular are cheap and useful for modelmaking purposes.

### Lining paper

This is a cheap, off-white paper produced in rolls and used to line walls before applying wallpaper. It is one of the few easily available sources of an uninterrupted length of paper and is especially useful for drawing large plans or full-size railroad layouts.

### Tracing paper

A translucent paper, it is supplied in pads, separate sheets or rolls. Depending on its thickness, it is more-or-less see-through, and is often used by modelmakers to simulate other materials. Its most common application is for tracing plans in order to transfer them onto a structural material such as balsa or other wood.

### Artist's paper

Cartridge and watercolor paper are made in many qualities, some of which are expensive. They accept paints well, especially watercolors, and their textures are often used for effects in modelmaking.

### Tissue paper

Ordinary household tissue paper can be used to make all kinds of accessories for model figures or to mask the interiors of vehicles when painting. Make sure you use special high-quality tissue paper for covering the balsa wood frames of flying models.

### Crepe paper

Although this thick, crinkled tissue paper does not have many applications in modelmaking, its coarse texture and ability to stretch make it a suitable material for clothes for large-scale figures.

### Corrugated paper and cardboard

This is available in three forms: single- or double-skin and multicore. The single-skin type folds and rolls easily, while the others make strong, lightweight, flat structural members.

### Mounting board

Produced for picture framing, it is available in a variety of thicknesses and a range of colors. The color is usually on one side only.

### Illustration board

This board is surfaced with a smooth, coated paper which is ideal for pen line work. It is expensive but you can economize by buying the paper separately and backing it with cheap carton board.

## Folding paper and cardboard

To produce a sharp crease, especially in thick paper, run your fingernail up and down the fold. It is easier to fold thin cardboard or thick paper if the line is first scored with a knitting needle or a blunt needle in a pin vise. Run the tool along a straight edge to mark the fold; the crease will automatically follow the scored line.

To fold thick cardboard, first score part way through the material with a knife, using a straight edge to guide the blade and making light cuts (for thinner material, the weight of the knife itself may be sufficient). Next, align the scored line with the edge of the worktable and gently press down on the overhanging section.

To induce a curve in a sheet of paper, hold a straight edge firmly on the sheet with one hand, then pull up the sheet with the other. Every time the paper is drawn under the edge, a tighter curve is produced. For thick cardboard or a large sheet of paper, draw the piece over the edge of the worktable. Keep the pressure light and even to avoid a sharp crease. If you wish, you can straighten the curve by turning the material over and repeating the very same process.

## Cutting cardboard and paper

Use a sharp knife and work along the length of a straight edge to make a straight cut in paper. Use the same method to make a straight cut in thick paper or cardboard, but first establish the cut in the material with light cuts, then apply more pressure and cut right through.

Gentle curves are best cut freehand with scissors or a knife. If you use a knife, make very light cuts to establish the line and make the cut as continuous as possible to prevent the knife slipping off-line. To cut a tight curve, see below.

Small holes can be cut in paper and cardboard with a commercial stationery punch or a leather punch, but to cut a hole between $\frac{1}{4}$ and $\frac{3}{4}$ inch (6 and 20 mm) in diameter, you will need to make a punch from a metal tube. File a sharp edge on the inside of the tube, then follow the instructions below. If you want to keep the cut-out disk, file the sharp edge on the outside. Cut a large hole in thin material as shown below, or use a modeling knife clamped in a compass.

To cut a square hole, first mark the corners then make all the cuts working away from them to avoid knife marks. If the hole has curved corners, punch out the corners with a tube punch, making sure that it is aligned with your marks, then join up the holes neatly with a straight edge.

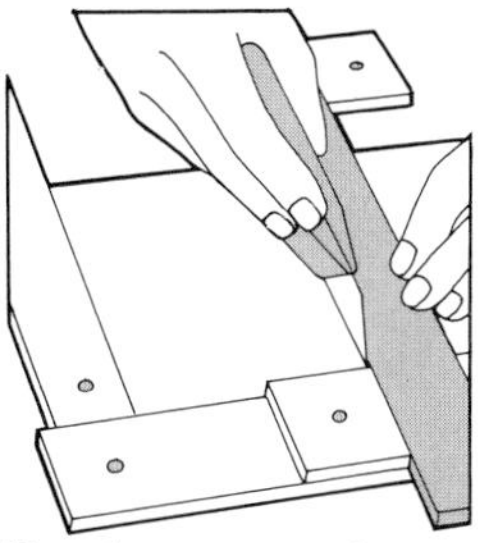

**Cutting several pieces to the same shape** Attach scraps of thick cardboard to a building board to make a jig. Hold each piece of cardboard in the jig as you cut.

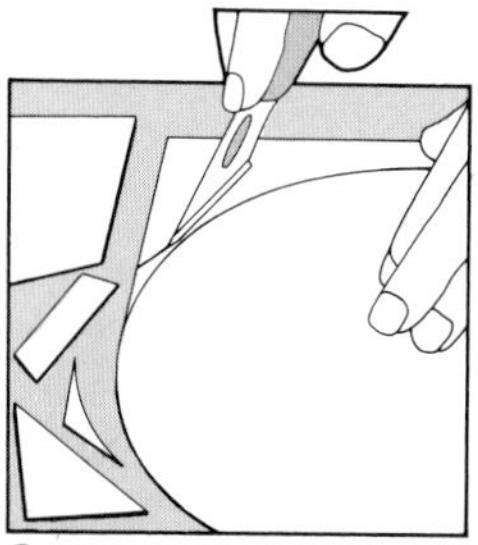

**Cutting a tight curve or disk** Draw the curve, then make straight cuts at a tangent to it, gradually removing the waste material. Finish a curve in cardboard with an abrasive paper.

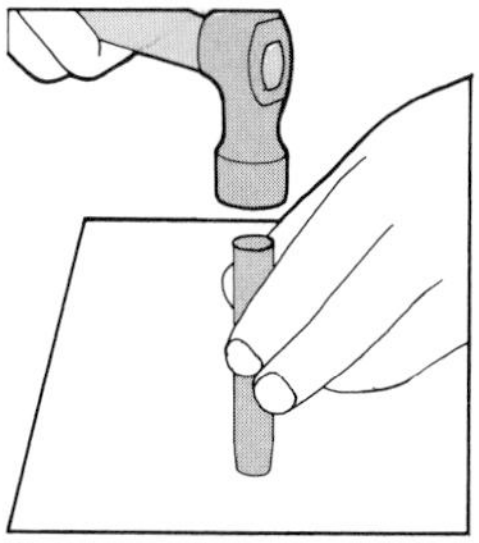

**Using a homemade hole-punch** Center the punch on the paper or cardboard, then strike a sharp blow on the end with a hammer.

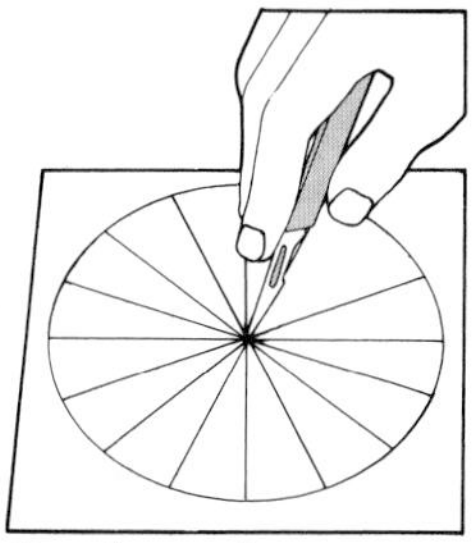

**Cutting a large hole** Make several radial cuts, then remove the waste with freehand cuts. Smooth the edge of cardboard with an abrasive paper wrapped around a wooden dowel.

## Joining paper and cardboard

Lap one piece of paper over another to make a strong joint. Use glue or single- or double-sided self-adhesive tape to secure the join. If you wish to align the pieces, draw a line parallel to the edge of one piece and butt the edge of the other up against it. To butt joint paper, lay both pieces facedown on a board and hold them in place with pieces of adhesive tape, then run a piece of tape along the join.

Butt joint cardboard like paper but, if necessary, reinforce the join with a strip of cardboard glued over the seam. Reinforce a corner butt joint by gluing a strip of balsa into the corner or running extra glue down the inside.

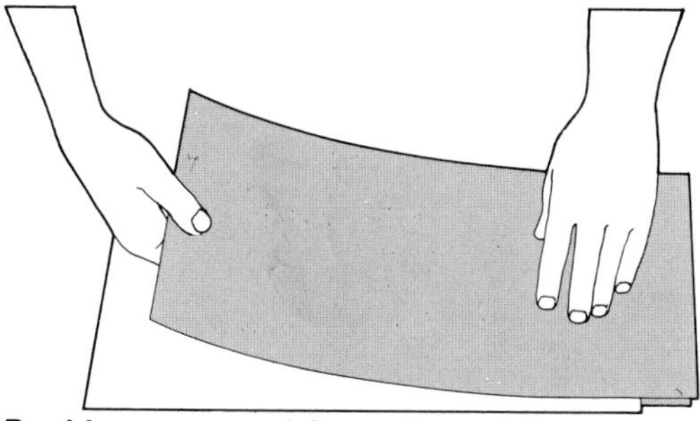

**Backing paper with cardboard** Spread rubber-based contact glue on both surfaces; let them dry. Lay wax paper over the cardboard, leaving a narrow strip of cardboard exposed at one end. Rub the paper down onto the exposed section. Pull the wax paper out a little at a time and rub the paper down.

**Making a pattern continue over a butt joint** Overlap the edge of the paper with another piece, aligning the visible part of the pattern. Cut through both pieces down the center of the overlap. Remove the waste.

## Papier-mâché

This is a mixture of pulped paper, water and a cellulose-base wallpaper adhesive which sets hard when the water evaporates. Tear the paper into smallish pieces to make a thick paste for modeling solid shapes. To form a hard shell for a hollow structure, cut the paper into larger strips or squares, then overlap the pieces on the framework and brush adhesive over the top. By changing the color of each complete layer, you will find it much easier to keep the layers even.

When the papier-mâché has set hard, seal the surface with paint or varnish.

**Making papier-mâché**
Tear the paper into small pieces. Put them in a bowl or bucket and add hot water from a kettle.

Knead the mixture to an even consistency with a stick; leave it to soak for about one hour.

Gradually add the wallpaper adhesive, mixing it to a homogenous paste.

# Balsa wood

This type of wood is light, soft and easy to cut and shape; it can be glued with balsa cement as well as other glues. Due to its particular strength/weight ratio balsa is the principal material for making all kinds of flying models. Although there are lighter materials, such as polystyrene foam, they are not as strong. Balsa is also widely used to model finely detailed, small-scale static vehicles, such as ships. Moreover, it is used for railroad buildings and bridges, because it is so easily worked.

Balsa wood is supplied in three main forms: sheet, strip and block. For the aeromodeler, there are leading and trailing edge sections. Special shapes, such as round dowel or triangular sections with a right angle, are also available.

Balsa varies in density more than any other wood and the denser the wood, the stronger it is. It is graded as light, medium and hard with further subdivisions – ultra-light, light, light-medium, medium, medium-hard, hard and extra-hard – for aeromodeling where the selection is more critical. Color is not an accurate guide to strength.

Aeromodelers also choose their balsa by the "cut" which is determined by the direction of the grain within the section. Tangent-cut sheet bends easily across the width, making it suitable for covering curved surfaces. Smaller sections can be identified by gently squeezing the sheet to see if it bends easily crosswise.

Quarter-cut sheet, also referred to as quarter-sawn or quarter-grain, is rigid across the width and will crack longitudinally if you try to bend it. It is ideal for ribs and other sections which need to be stiff. Although this cut is often difficult to identify, especially on thin pieces, you will recognize it by its speckled surface or by the manufacturer's mark.

Random-cut is a general-purpose balsa. Thin or small sections bend reasonably well; larger, thicker pieces, however, are fairly stiff.

## Transferring plans to balsa wood

Trace the shape onto tracing paper; reverse the paper and lay it on the balsa. Trace over the shape again to offset the pencil mark. (This is not suitable for soft balsa.)

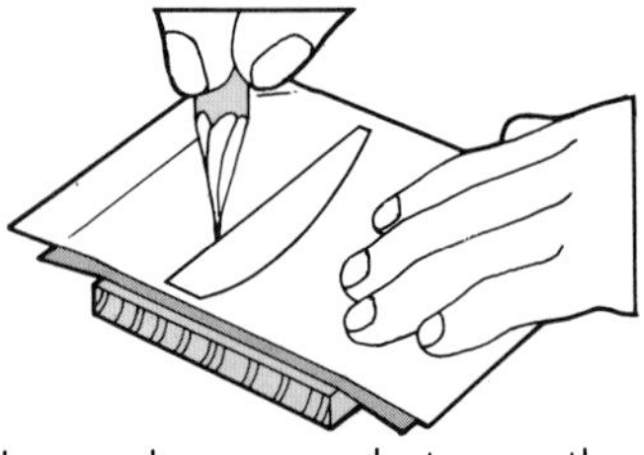

Lay carbon paper between the balsa and the plan so that the shape only has to be drawn once, reducing inaccuracies. The resulting thick line, however, can be a disadvantage.

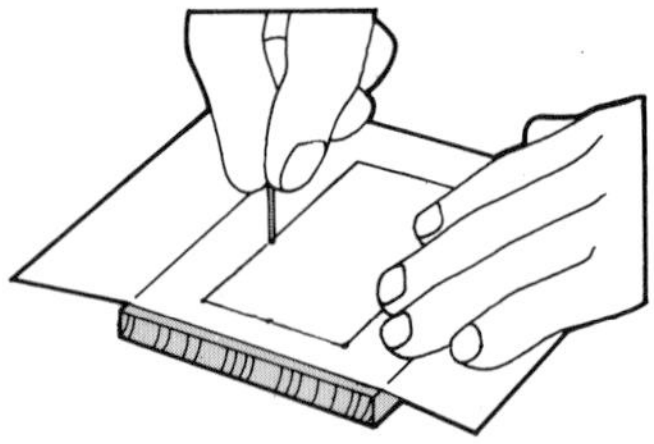

For straight-sided shapes, prick through the plan with a pin, then join up the marks with a steel rule. For curved shapes, plot the curve carefully with close pin marks. Join the marks by eye.

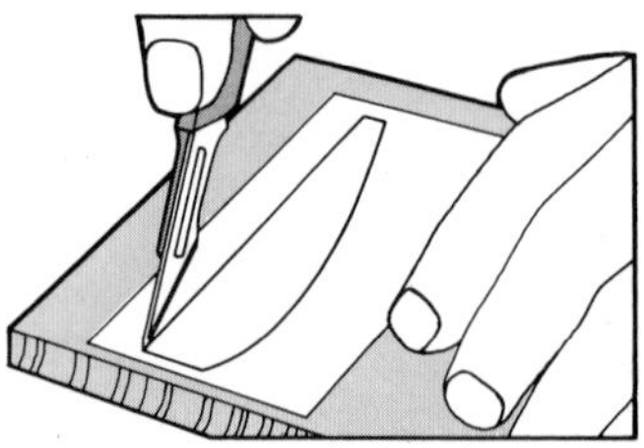

Glue a tracing of the shape on the balsa with a rubber-based adhesive, then cut around the shape with a knife. Peel off the paper.

## Marking up balsa

Right angles can be marked on sheet balsa with a triangle but it is better to use a try square, marking from a long edge (the long edges are always accurately cut by the manufacturer). Hold the stock of the try square against the edge and press the blade firmly onto the wood face. Draw along the edge of the blade with a pen or pencil to mark the line or, for very thin sheet, just use a modeling knife. If you are working with soft balsa, make marks at strategic points along the line with a pin. Join up the marks with a steel rule when you make the cut.

To mark block balsa which is to be sawn square at one end, use a try square and mark a line all around. You can use a pen or pencil, but a knife cut will prevent any grain breaking out when you saw.

Curves and circles can be drawn with compasses or freehand with a template. To avoid marking or crushing soft balsa with a compass point, stick a small piece of cardboard to the center of the circle with double-sided tape.

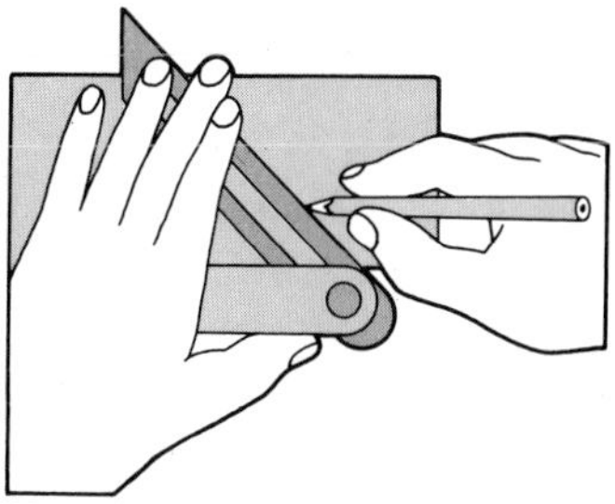

**Marking an angle on sheet balsa** Use an adjustable bevel, or mark the angle on a piece of cardboard with a triangle of the appropriate angle. Cut it out and use it as a template. Use a try square to extend the mark down the side of a block of balsa wood.

## Cutting strip balsa

This is best cut to length with a chopping action; slicing is not as accurate. A modeling knife is adequate, but a single-edged razor blade, which is extremely thin and sharp, is a better tool. Use a razor saw for cutting large pieces.

## Cutting sheet balsa

Use a modeling knife or razor saw for all the techniques described below. To cut holes or disks, use a metal-tube punch. Twist the tube into the surface or drive it with a hammer as described for cutting holes in paper or cardboard on page 43.

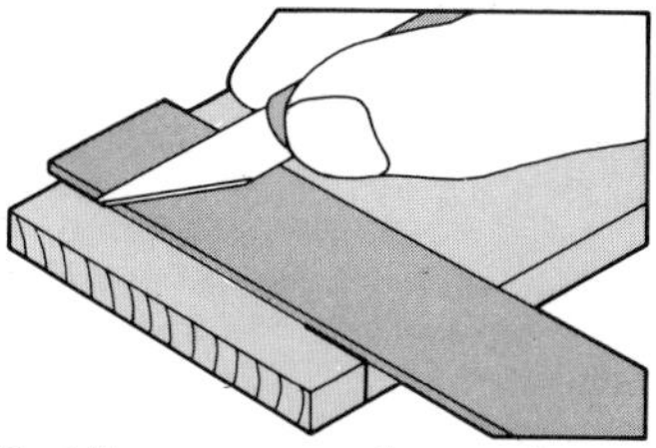

**Cutting across the grain**
Use a modeling knife to cut sheet balsa less than $\frac{3}{16}$ inch (5 mm) thick. Guide the blade with a steel rule or a try square and cut from both edges to avoid splintering. Cut thicker sheet with a razor saw.

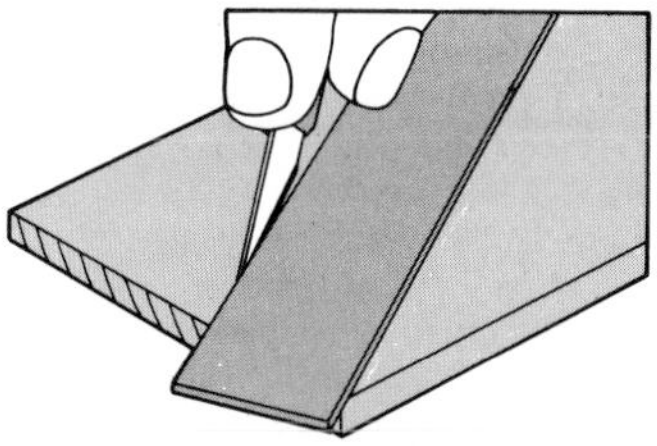

**Making diagonal cuts**
When using a modeling knife, position the steel rule so that the grain of the wood holds the knife blade against it. This is easier on one side of the sheet than the other so check before you mark the cut. Use a razor saw to cut thicker sheet and cut the wood in either direction.

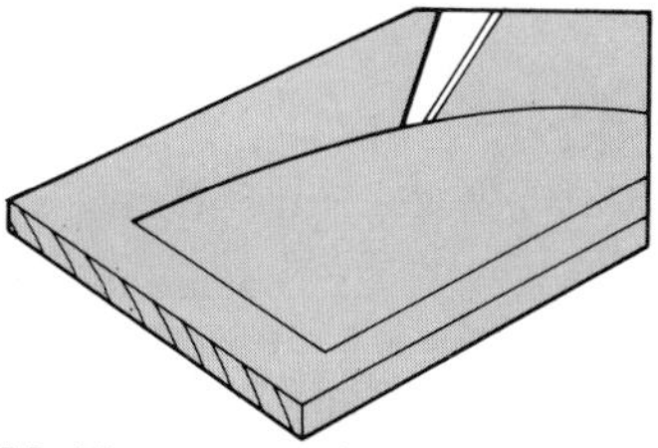

**Making curved cuts** Hold the modeling knife so that the grain leads the blade away from the cutting line rather than into it. To cut thicker sheet, clamp it so that it overhangs the edge of the worktable and use a fret saw.

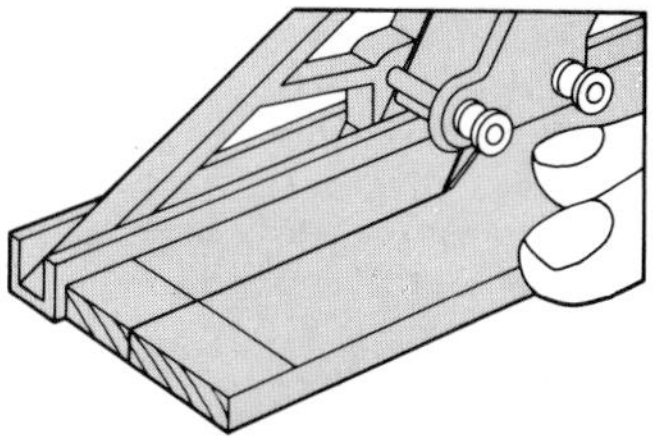

**Cutting matching strips**
First mark a line across one end of the sheet so that the strips can be aligned accurately later. The best tool for making the cuts is a balsa stripper. If you use a knife, be sure to hold it upright and against the edge of a steel rule for accuracy.

## Cutting block balsa

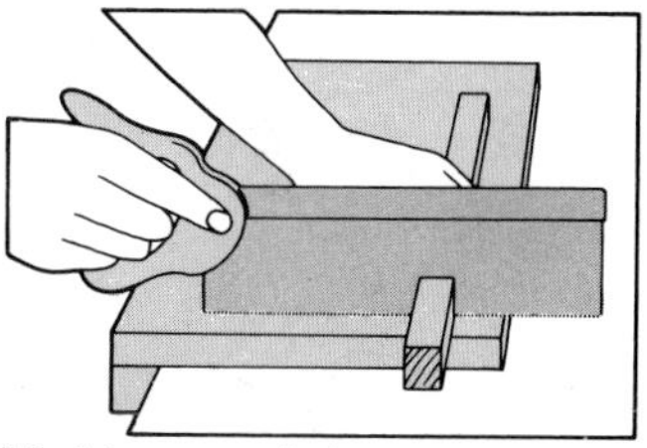

**Making straight cuts**
Support the balsa on a bench hook. Using a fine-tooth saw or a razor saw, start the cut with backward strokes, guiding the blade with your thumb until the cut is established.

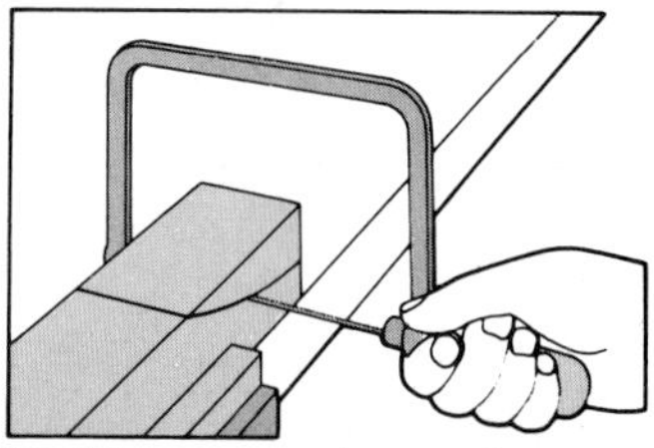

**Making curved cuts** Support the block in a vise, or clamp it to the workbench. Make the cut with a coping or fret saw.

## Shaping balsa

Balsa wood is easily carved for rough shaping but use a very sharp knife or it will crumble.

Most balsa can be shaped exclusively with abrasives. Large sections may need to be filed first; use a surform file which can be used both with and against the grain. Finish smoothing the wood by using a fine abrasive paper.

## Bending balsa

Although balsa wood has a degree of natural flexibility, it can be bent further using the following techniques.

For thin sheet balsa it is usually only necessary to wet it on the outside of the bend with a damp cloth, but if you want to form a sharp bend, thoroughly soak the sheet in water, preferably hot. Apply weights to keep it submerged, being careful not to damage the surface of the wood. A more effective way of bending balsa, particularly strip balsa, is to play steam from a kettle onto the wood and gradually form it with your fingers. Let wet balsa strips dry out pinned to a building board, as shown below.

You can also bend balsa by laminating very thin strips with white glue. Pin the strips on the plan as described for making a laminated wing tip on page 279.

Balsa has a tendency to spring back slightly when it dries so, unless you are going to attach it to a framework, bend it more than you require.

To bend thick balsa, cut notches in the vicinity of the bend with a hand saw, then attach it to a frame.

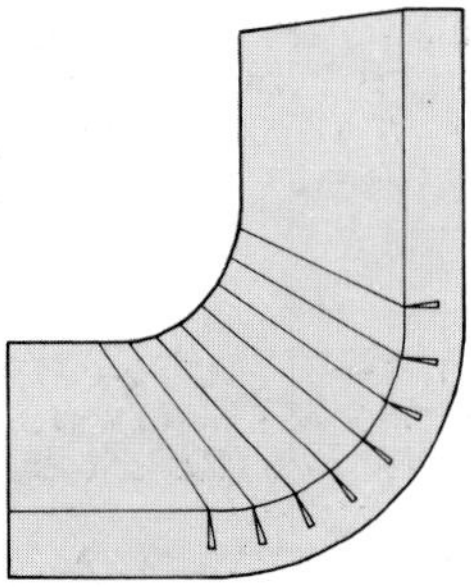

**Bending thick balsa** Cut straight-sided or "V"-shaped notches with a hand saw about half to three-quarters of the way through. The closer the cuts, the tighter the bend.

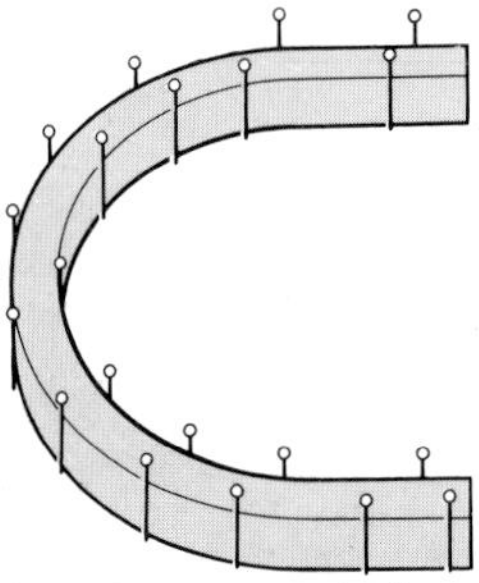

**Pinning a wet balsa strip** Secure the strip on the building board with straight pins to hold it in shape while it dries.

## Joining balsa

Most joints suitable for balsa are variations on the butt joint. Use balsa cement or other woodworking adhesives – nails and screws can crush the wood. Bolts can be used to join large sections of block balsa so long as wide washers are used to spread the load. Always protect balsa wood from being damaged by the jaws of a clamp by inserting extra wood blocks between the jaws and the workpiece.

To guarantee a close fit when joining thick balsa edge to edge, first clamp the two edges together and plane across them (they do not have to be square).

Reinforce a right-angle corner by gluing a balsa strip or triangular gussets into it. For a neater appearance, make a miter joint. This joint can also be reinforced with gussets.

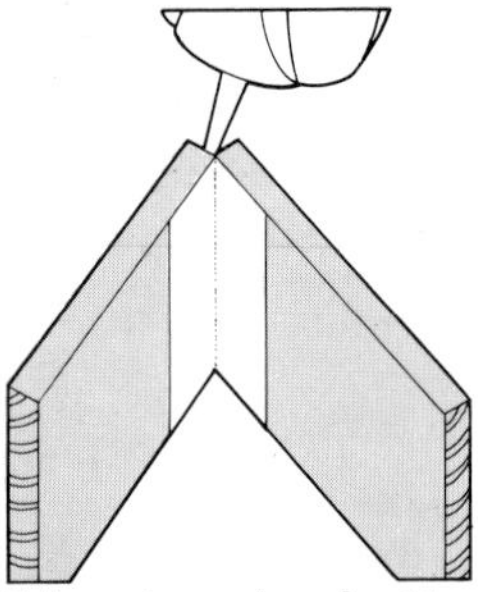

**Edge-to-edge butt joint** Lay the edges together and tape them along one side temporarily. Open up the joint, run white glue along it and close it again.

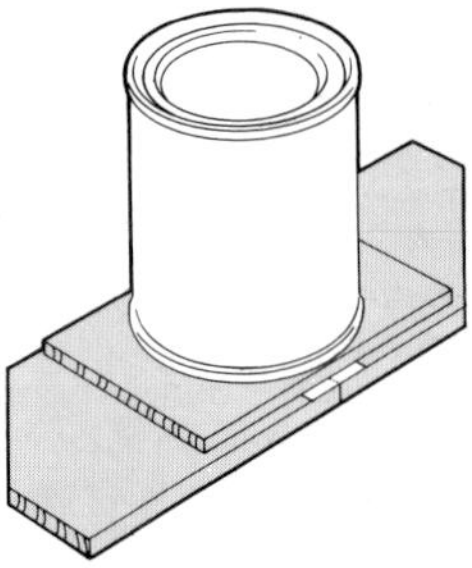

Wipe off any excess glue. Weight the sheets on a flat surface to hold the joint until it sets.

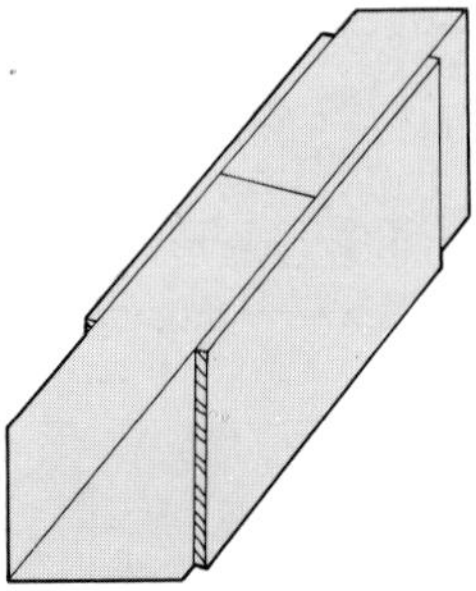

**End-to-end butt joint** Reinforce balsa cement by gluing a "plate" of plywood to both sides of the wooden joint.

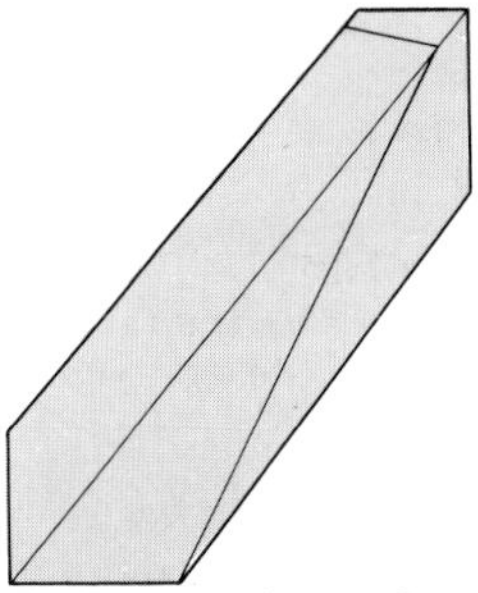

**End-to-end scarf joint** This joint is used to enlarge the gluing area and avoid true end grain butting. Hold both sections together and make an angled cut which is four times the width of the section in length.

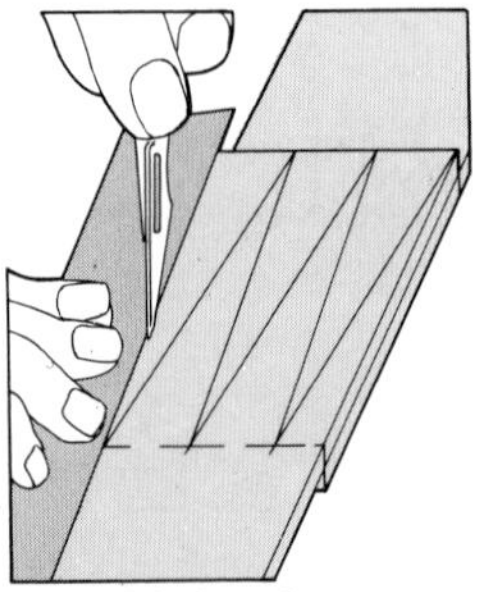

**Scarf joint for sheet balsa** To enlarge the gluing area even more, overlap the ends by about twice the width of the sheet and make "V"-shaped cuts through both.

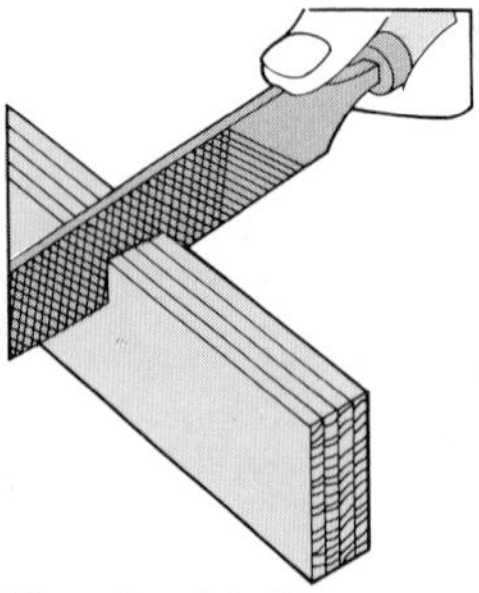

**Notched joints** These are used for joining wing ribs and spars. Make two parallel saw cuts and chop out the waste, or use a file of the correct width to make the notch.

# Softwoods and hardwoods

Although modelmakers often refer to any wood harder than balsa as a "hardwood," in this book we are following the normal convention. The characteristics and uses of several common softwoods, hardwoods and composite woods, such as plywood and blockboard, are described below.

Wood sizes quoted at a lumber yard are often referred to as "nominal" because they only approximate the actual size of the wood. A nominal 2×1 inch (50×25 mm) sawn board, for example, may vary slightly from the quoted size, and a nominal 2×1 inch (50×25 mm) planed board has an actual size of about $1\frac{7}{8}\times\frac{7}{8}$ inch (47×22 mm). Sizes specified in model catalogs, however, are the actual sizes.

### Spruce

This is a strong, straight-grained and flexible softwood, ideal for modelmaking. It is easily worked and takes nails and screws well. It is used by aeromodelers for critical components, such as main wing spars, and by boat modelers for spars, chines, masts and stringers.

### Hemlock

Sometimes used instead of spruce, it is evenly textured with an uninteresting grain pattern.

### Obeche

This hardwood has a soft, even texture. It is easily carved and shaped and is about twice the weight of balsa wood. It is widely used by boat modelers for decking and planking, and is also suitable for making bread-and-butter hulls (see pages 309 to 310).

### Birch and beech

Both are extremely strong, short-grained hardwoods used extensively as engine bearers. Beech is preferred for heavy engines, although it is in limited supply. Model suppliers may stock these woods; otherwise, consult a specialist lumber dealer. Ash or maple, also hardwoods, can be substituted for birch and beech.

### Ramin

This is a cheap hardwood sold in small sections and many different moldings. It is a tough, even-grained wood which is easy to shape.

### Mahogany

Its attractive reddish color makes it a popular hardwood for skinning boats. Although it is not really strong enough to be used for bearers, it is occasionally employed for aircraft propellers. Some mahoganies are easily worked while others have a wild grain which makes carving and finishing difficult.

### Jelutong

An extremely even-textured hardwood with virtually no grain pattern, it is ideal for carving molds or boat hulls. It is normally only available from specialist lumber yards.

### Plywood

This is a composite wood made from laminated veneers where the grain of each layer runs at right angles to the next. Plywood is a strong material which is less likely to warp than solid wood of the same thickness.

Birch or mahogany plywood is the most suitable for modelmaking. Birch ply is tougher although mahogany is sometimes used for its decorative properties. Marine plywood, which is laminated with waterproof glues, is essential for building boats; any other plywood will separate into layers if immersed in water for any length of time.

### Particle board

Cheap and readily available, this is the most stable of all manufactured boards. It is made from small chips of wood and glue compressed into a sheet. It has no dominant grain direction and is, therefore, unlikely to warp. However, its edge may crumble unless protected by a solid wood edging.

### Blockboard and laminboard

These boards are used where stability is important, such as for a diorama base. They are made from strips of solid wood glued together and sandwiched between layers of veneer. Laminboard has thinner sections of core material for greater stability.

## Marking up wood

All wood can be marked up with a try square and sliding bevel as described for marking block balsa on page 45. If you want to scribe a line parallel to the edge, use a marking gauge.

To find the center of a strip of wood, set the point of a marking gauge to approximately half the thickness of the wood, then mark the wood from both sides. If the marks are short of or overshoot each other, adjust the tool.

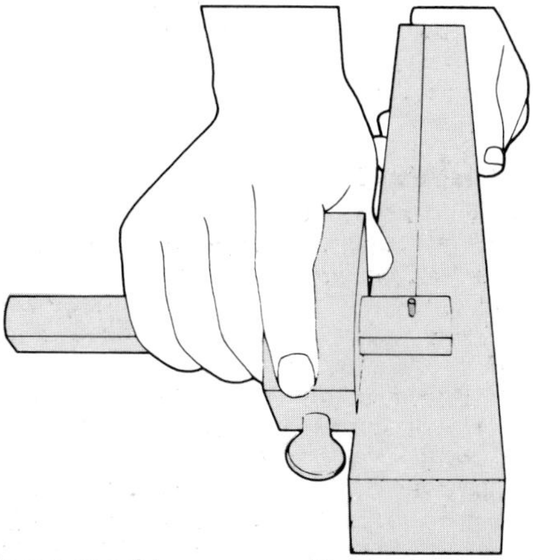

**Using a marking gauge** Hold the stock of the tool against the edge and lean it away from you so that the pin touches the surface at an angle. Push away from you to scribe the line in the piece of wood.

## Cutting wood

Most softwoods and hardwoods cannot be cut with a modeling knife, but should be sawn. Use a razor saw or fine backsaw for cutting strips, sheets and small blocks of wood as described for cutting balsa on page 45. Make slow, firm strokes using the full length of the blade and extend the forefinger in line with the blade to help steady the saw. Miniature power table saws can be used to make square and angled cuts in softwoods and hardwoods, both with and across the grain, but they are not essential.

Very thin plywood can be cut with a heavy-duty modeling knife with a strong blade. Do not use a delicate blade as it will wander off line or even break.

Use a fret saw or a coping saw for making curved cuts, following the method for cutting balsa on page 45. There are miniature power fret saws available which make this job easier. They cut thin boards and sheet materials easily, but can also be used to saw thick sections of solid wood.

When drilling holes of less than $\frac{1}{16}$ inch (2 mm) in diameter, use a pin vise to hold the drill bit. Some modelers prefer to use the bit between the fingers alone, but a pin vise provides a more comfortable means of holding bits as well as better control. When drilling the holes, twist the bit back and forth using only as much pressure as necessary to make the hole – too much pressure may bend the bit.

Use a hand drill to drill holes up to $\frac{1}{4}$ inch (6 mm) in diameter. Rotate it at high speed with light pressure to drill a hole cleanly. A hand drill can be used vertically or horizontally, whichever is the most convenient. Use a try square as a guide to keep the bit at a right angle to the work.

For larger holes in thick sections of wood, use a brace and bit. Brace bits normally have a lead screw at the end to pull the drill into the work. To prevent the wood splitting, as soon as the lead screw starts to emerge, remove the drill and complete the work from the reverse side. For deep holes, use an auger bit. This bit has spiral twists which help keep it central and clear the waste.

You may need a full-size power drill if you are making large-scale models. A set of power bore bits, capable of drilling large holes, is useful. Bits with a long lead point are ideal for locating the center when drilling holes at an angle. Use a vertical drill stand to hold a power drill steady where accuracy is important.

Over a certain diameter, holes cannot be drilled in the conventional way, but must be sawn out of the material. Special hole saws which fit into the chuck of a power drill are available for holes up to 4 inches (100 mm) in diameter. A normal twist drill centers these saws. They can also be used to cut out a wooden ring (see right).

Larger holes in softwoods and hardwoods must be cut with either a power saber saw or by hand, using a compass or coping saw as shown right. Always drill a starter hole for the saw before you begin cutting.

Whatever type of model you are making, the saw-cut hole will need to be cleaned up when the sawing is finished. Use a fine round file or a piece of abrasive paper wrapped around a dowel to smooth the edges.

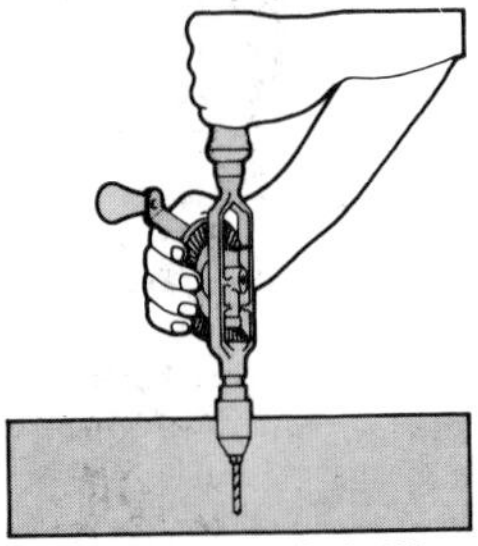

**Using a hand drill** Start the hole by rotating the gear wheel back and forth with your hand. Then use the handle to drive in the drill bit.

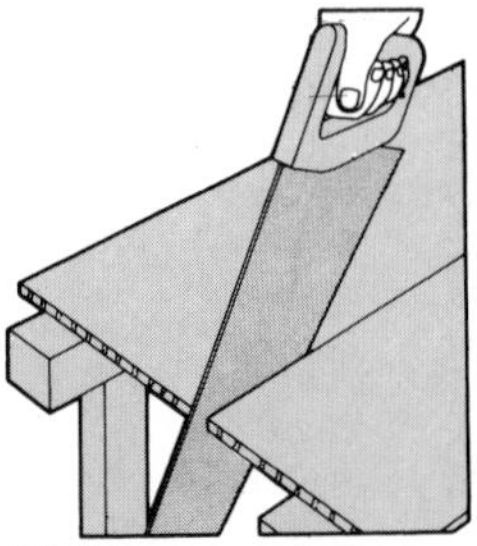

**Making straight cuts in panels** Use a panel saw which has a long blade and can pass right through the wood. Support the work on each side of the cut to prevent the saw jamming.

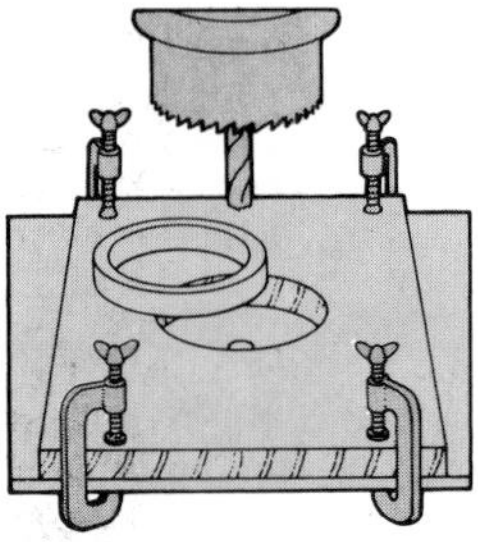

**Cutting a ring** Clamp the work to a sheet of waste board. Drill a smaller hole with a hole-saw blade. Replace the blade with a larger one and, without moving anything, recenter the drill and cut the outer edge.

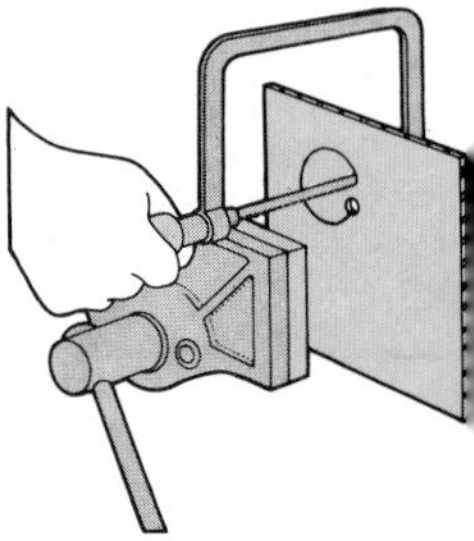

**Using a coping saw** Drill a hole inside the cutting line and pass the blade through it; reconnect the blade to the saw frame. Make the cut on the inside of the line, adjusting the angle of the blade to accommodate the sweep of the curve.

**Cutting a square hole** Drill a hole through each corner for the blade. Use the widest blade possible to keep the cut perfectly on line.

## Shaping and smoothing wood

Any wood which is harder than balsa is best smoothed by a slicing or planing action. Even ready-planed surfaces can benefit from skimming with a very sharp plane. Bench planes are best for truing up large pieces, but you may find a block plane more convenient for small-scale work. Originally designed for cutting end grain, this small, lightweight plane can be used to finish the face and edges of wood.

When planing an edge, keep the plane from rocking by guiding it along with your other hand. Hold the tool at an angle to plane a bevel along one edge. Use a try square or sliding bevel to check the accuracy of the work.

Shape small curves with a rasp and file. Use the rasp to reduce the roughly sawn edge to more-or-less the finished shape, then use a fine file to smooth the wood.

For more complex shapes with several curves, use chisels and gouges or surform planes. When shaping large sections of wood, such as when making a wooden boat hull, the work must be held firmly on a strong, rigid bench. There are special clamps available but a simpler method is to screw a piece of softwood to the underside and hold it in a woodworking vise or the jaws of a workmate bench. You can start by removing as much waste as possible with a saw, or rough-shape the work with carvers, gouges and chisels immediately. Follow the carving stage by using surform tools to shape the required curves approximately, and finish with files and abrasive papers.

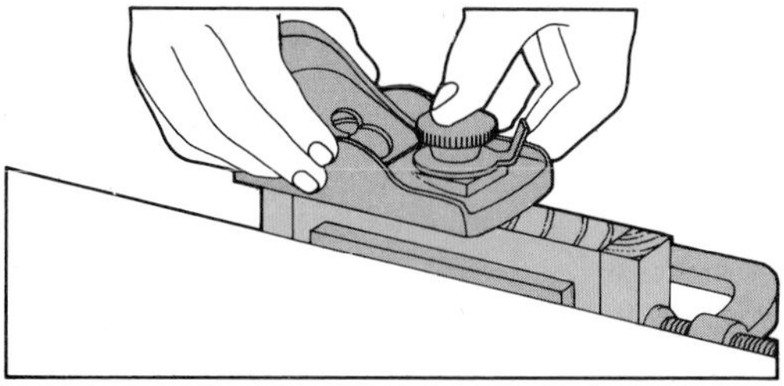

**Planing end grain** Support small pieces in a vise with scrap wood clamped on each end to prevent the wood from splitting when you plane, and work from one direction. Large pieces can be planed from both directions.

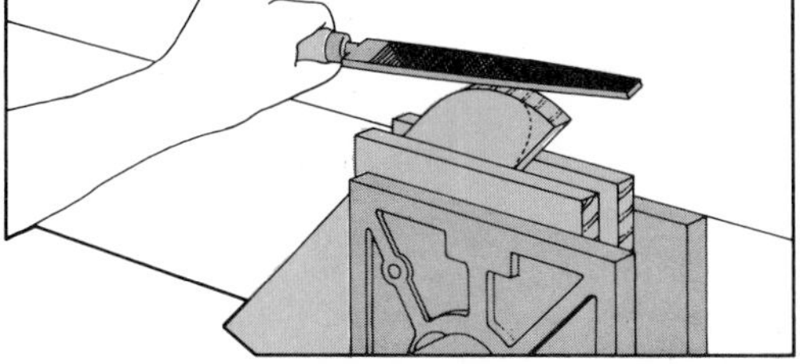

**Filing a convex curve** Hold the wood in a vise and, using a flat file, work in the direction of the grain. Turn the work around to complete the curve. Another method is to shape the wood on a power sanding disk.

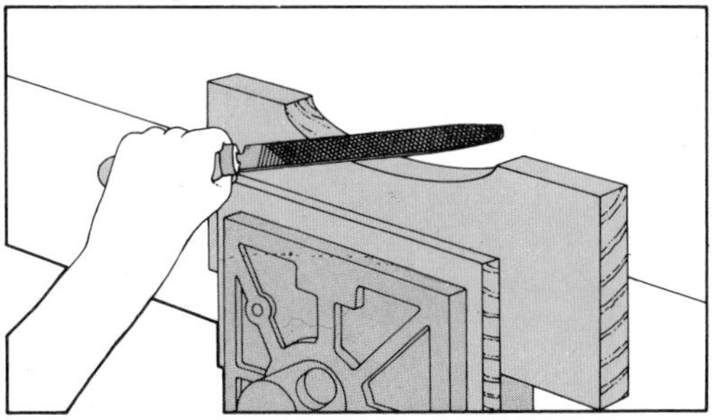

**Filing a concave curve** Using half-round or round rasps and files and working from both directions with the grain, make a combined sideways and forward movement. To remove coarse file and rasp marks, hold the file in both hands across the work and draw-file.

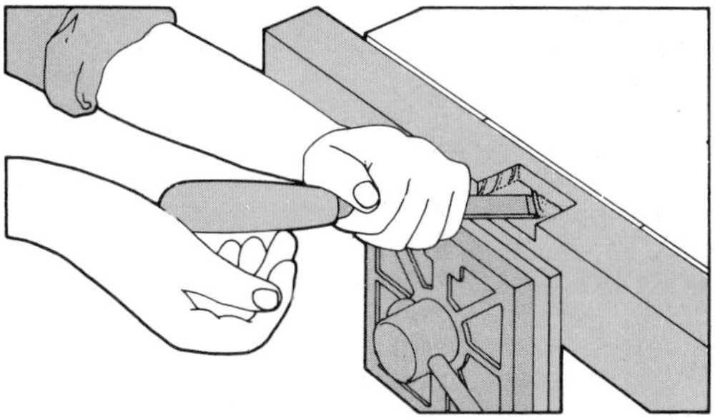

**Hand-driving a chisel** For softwoods, strike the chisel handle with the ball of your hand to drive it through stubborn sections of grain. Use a mallet to drive the chisel through harder wood.

## Bending wood

Solid wooden strips and sheets can be bent by soaking in water or steaming. Plywood will shape more easily if you make the bend parallel with the grain of the surface veneer. Larger sections of wood need notches cut in the inside of the bend beforehand.

Individual veneers or very thin pieces of plywood can be laminated. Small laminations can be held in place with pins as described on page 281 for making a laminated wing tip. Large laminations need to be held in place on a former with clamps while they dry (see below).

**Clamping large laminations** Screw softwood blocks to a piece of thin metal to make a strap. Clamp this over the laminations.

# Joining wood

Joints for softwoods and hardwoods are basically the same as those described on page 46 for balsa wood. Unlike balsa, however, these woods can be joined with mechanical fastenings as well as woodworking adhesives. Where possible clamp a glued joint while it sets and, if necessary, insert a protective softwood block between the work and the clamp.

Some joints need to be reinforced. Glue plywood plates to each side of an end-to-end joint and secure them with screws or small bolts. Strengthen a corner butt joint by gluing a strip of wood into the corner; glue and nail a plywood plate across the top. Mitered corner joints can be reinforced with nails or in either of the two ways shown below.

**Reinforcing mitered joints** For a narrow-sectioned corner, clamp the work and cut angled grooves across the corner. Glue strips of veneer into them; let the glue set and plane the surfaces flush.

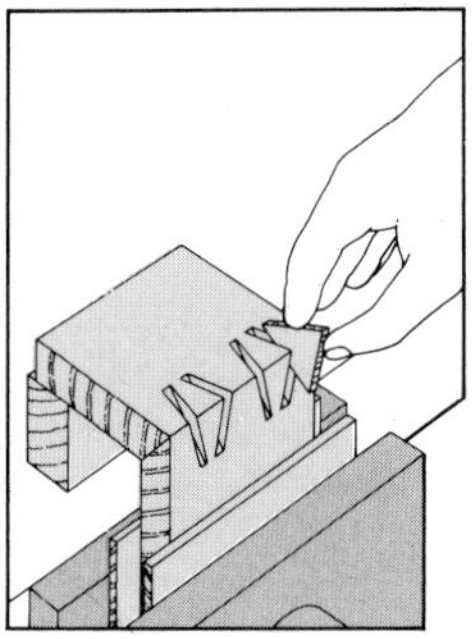

You can also set the glued joint in a vise or miter clamp and drill holes across the corner. Tap dowels covered in glue through the holes. Leave the glue to set and plane flush.

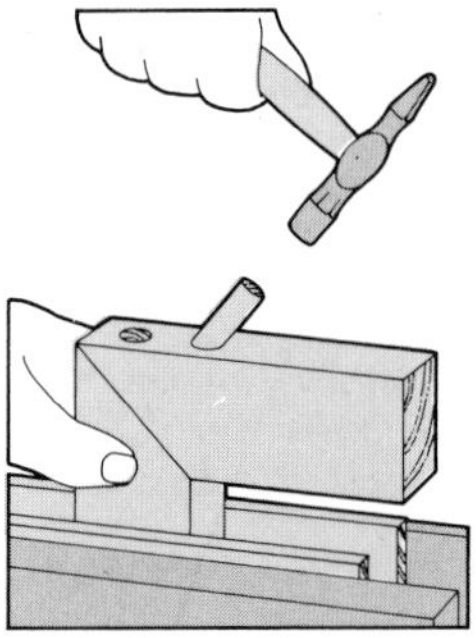

## Mechanical fastenings for wood

These can be used as a means of holding a joint while the glue sets, or as a permanent fastening in their own right. When making small models it is rarely necessary to use anything larger than brads. Use a lightweight hammer to drive them in.

The small wood screws used in modelmaking can be easily damaged. Make sure the screwdriver blade is in good condition and that it fits in the slot. Drill pilot holes when nailing or screwing hardwoods and countersink the holes where applicable. Brass screws are much softer than steel ones; drive a matching steel screw into the hole first, then replace it with a brass one.

Use nuts and bolts to make a stronger fastening than is possible with wood screws or if you want to dismantle the components later. For small-scale work, use a slotted-head machine screw (see below). Lock the nut in position by tapping the end of the bolt with a center punch. For some other methods of locking nuts, see Mechanical fastenings for metal, page 62.

To align the bolt holes accurately, clamp the two pieces of wood together and drill right through them both. In order to match the drill size to the bolt, simply lay the drill over the bolt's threaded section and judge the size by eye.

**Nailing a right-angled corner** Angle the nails to produce a dovetailed effect.

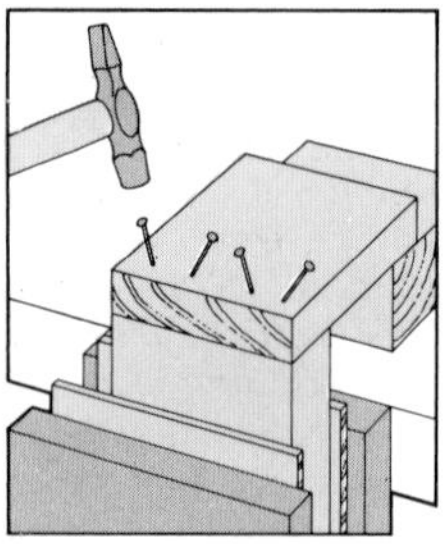

**Nailing overlap joints** Stagger the position of the nails to avoid splitting the grain. Trim the overlap afterward.

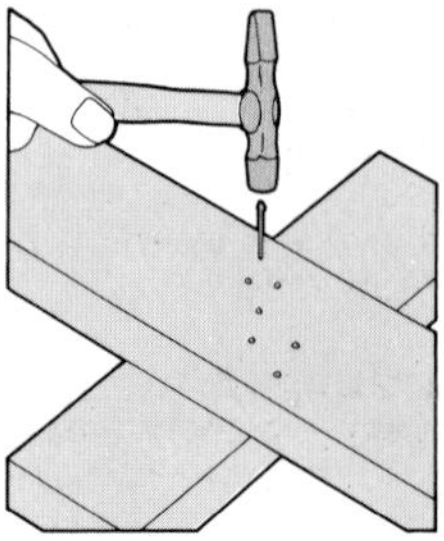

**Slotted-head machine screws** Use these with screwcups or washers for a neat finish and to protect the wood face by spreading the load when a nut is tightened. Flat and ovalhead screws are used with screwcups which can be either surface-mounted or countersunk; round ones are used with surface-mounted washers.

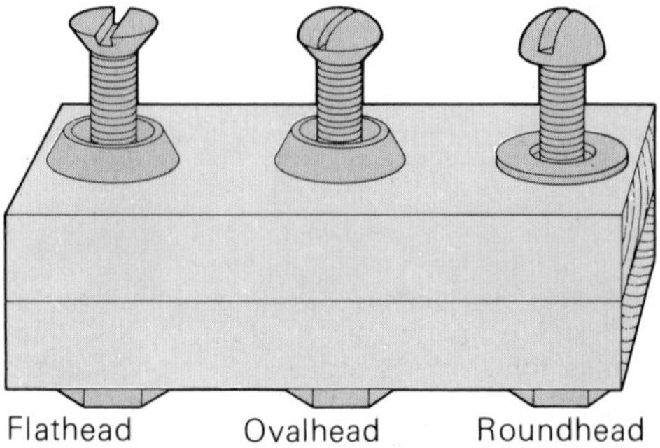

Flathead with screwcup — Ovalhead with screwcup — Roundhead with washer

# Plastics

These are widely used in modelmaking. Thermoplastics, which include polystyrene, acrylobutyl styrene, acetate, acrylic, polyethylene, PVC, nylon and polycarbonate, can all be heated and remolded any number of times.

### Polystyrene

This is used almost exclusively for injection-molded kits, although it is also available as plain and embossed sheet, rod and strip for modelers who prefer to scratch build.

Unmodified polystyrene is a hard brittle plastic which is used for making cockpit canopies and vehicle windows, but it is unsuitable for most kit production. Rubber is added to the basic material to soften it, forming what is generally known as high-impact polystyrene, the material with which all kit builders are familiar. It is produced in a wide range of colors but it cannot be produced as a transparent plastic in its modified form.

Polystyrene is also available as a foamed plastic (see opposite).

### Acrylobutyl styrene

Sometimes referred to as ABS, this is a much-used plastic, second only to polystyrene, for injection- and vacuum-formed moldings. It is more expensive than polystyrene but has extremely high impact strength which allows for thinner shell moldings. Plastruct Incorporated produce sheets of acrylobutyl styrene as well as a wide range of moldings such as miniature beams, H-shaped columns, angle strip, and square, round and rectangular tubing.

### Acetate

Sold in transparent sheets, cellulose acetate can be used for making windows, car windshields and cockpit canopies. It is sometimes used for making injection moldings.

Cellulose acetate butyrate has high impact strength, making it less likely to crack. In its liquid form it is the basis of the butyrate dopes used for painting and shrinking covers for flying aircraft.

### Acrylic

Better known by its trade name, Plexiglass, it is available in transparent, translucent and opaque form, in a wide range of colors. It is very brittle but can be readily bent and remolded with the application of heat. Acrylics are more expensive than most other plastics so they are generally only used to make display cases or flat bases for static models.

### Polyethylene

This is a soft, greasy plastic used to mold bottles and other plastic containers, such as fuel tanks for working models. It is difficult to cut and virtually impossible to glue and finish. Polyethylene is used to make cheaper scale models which are painted or even remodeled by some enthusiasts.

### Silicone rubber

This is most commonly used as tubing for exhaust pipes and flexible fuel lines for working models. It is both heat- and chemical-resistant and will not harden with use. Cold-curing silicone rubbers are available to modelers for making molds for plaster, resin, and low-melting-point metal castings.

### Polyvinyl chloride

Known as PVC, it is available as flexible tube and is used for making fuel lines. You can also buy PVC molds for resin and plaster castings. They are not suitable for metal castings.

### Nylon

This is an extremely tough, durable material used to make components such as wheels and bellcranks for working models. These components run silently and need no lubricating.

Nylon fabric is used for covering the wings and fuselages of flying aircraft.

### Polycarbonate

This is another tough plastic sometimes used instead of nylon for small components. It is also used to vacuum-form body shells for power racing cars, where its high impact strength is an advantage. Polycarbonate rejects many paints; they flake off if the shell is flexed. This can be overcome by using specially formulated acrylic paints on them.

### Laminated plastic

Mainly used in sheet form to make boat decks or mounting boards for electrical equipment and engines, it is a tough material made by bonding reinforcing fibers and synthetic resins. Laminates can also be used to make small fittings such as cleats, bowsies and control horns for working models.

### Foamed plastic

Flexible foamed plastic, sometimes called foam rubber, is used by modelmakers as shock-absorbing packing for radio-control equipment. Its rigid form – expanded polystyrene and polyurethane foam – has more varied uses.

Expanded polystyrene is used a great deal for landscaping but it can only be cleanly cut using a "hot wire" or very sharp knife. It is also used to make wings both for kit as well as scratch-built flying airplanes.

Polyurethane foam is more rigid and is used in sheet or slab form. It is easy to cut and shape and can be used for making smoothly contoured landscapes. Although not strong enough to be used as a structural material, it is often employed in powerboat hulls in order to add strength and buoyancy.

### Casting resin

Many synthetic resins are available but polyester resin is the most common. It is used with fiberglass to make a molding, or on its own to simulate water.

## Marking plastic

A soft pencil is adequate for marking a cut or bend line on opaque plastic but use a chinagraph, felt pen or a scriber to mark transparent plastic. Acrylic sheet is usually covered with a layer of paper to prevent its surface being scratched. You can mark cutting lines with a pen or pencil directly onto the paper or use a scriber to mark the actual surface.

To mark up a cylinder for a square cut, wrap a straight-edged piece of paper around the cylinder, as shown in step 1 of Extending a fuselage on page 131. Guide your pencil, pen or scriber along the edge of the paper.

If you have to mark a cut line on an irregular three-dimensional shape, work freehand with a pencil or scriber before making the cut, or stick masking tape along one side of the cut line, removing it only when the cutting and filing process is complete.

## Cutting plastic

Very thin plastic can be cut freehand with scissors or a modeling knife as described on page 43 for cutting paper and cardboard. Use the method described right for making straight cuts in thicker polystyrene or acrylobutyl styrene. This method can also be used for curved cuts as long as they are not too tight.

Brittle plastics, such as acrylics, plastic laminates, or acetate may break off-line with this method and should be cut with a knife or, as in the case of most acrylic sheet, sawn with a backsaw. Clamp the sheet to the edge of the workbench with a piece of wood over the plastic to protect the surface. Make the saw-cut, working on the waste side of the cut line. Plane and polish the edge afterward. Use a fret saw or piercing saw to make a curved cut, holding the work on a bench hook as shown right.

Cut holes in thin, paper-like plastic in the same way as for paper (see page 43). You may also use a pair of dividers to scribe a circle in the plastic. Thick sheets are too tough for such methods so use a drill. For very small holes use a pin vise; a hand drill can be used on larger holes. Clamp the work over a piece of scrap wood and protect the top surface with cardboard. When drilling acrylic, lubricate the work with light oil. This polishes the hole at the same time. For a larger hole, use a hole saw (see Cutting wood, page 48) or a fret saw, or drill small holes around the edge and remove the center. Finish the edges with fine files and abrasive paper. To avoid rounding the sharply cut edges, wrap the abrasive paper around a wooden dowel of the appropriate size.

Cut small plastic strips, rods and tubes to length with a knife or razor blade. Cut a large flexible tube by piercing the plastic with a pointed blade, then cut through it gradually, turning the tube as you cut. Use a saw on brittle plastics or large work. Hold the tube against a bench hook and revolve it away from you as you cut.

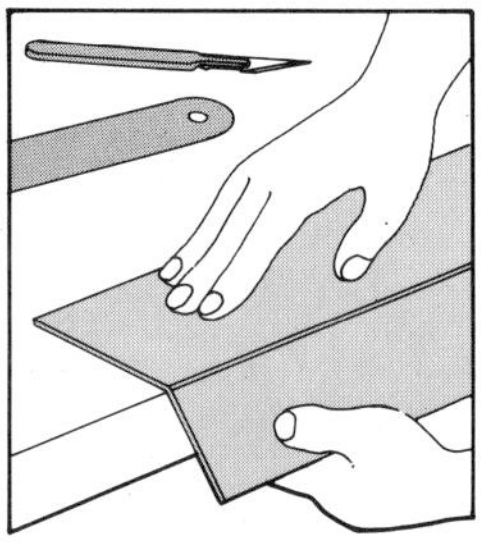

**Cutting sheet plastic** Score a straight line with a knife and snap the plastic over the edge of a bench. The break will be perfectly clean along the scored line.

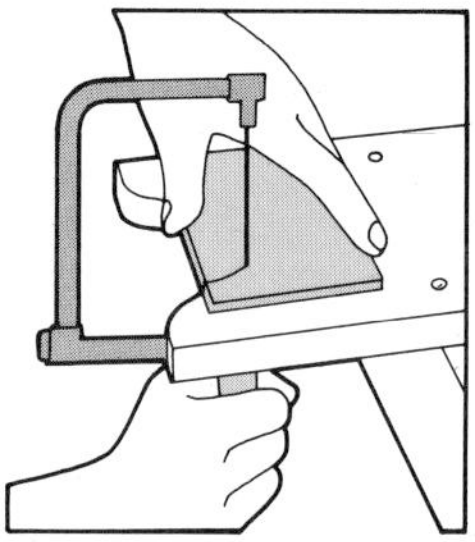

**Cutting curves in acrylic sheet** Support the plastic on a "V"-shaped plywood bench peg clamped or screwed to the workbench. Position the cut line close to the peg and turn the plastic as you cut.

## Cutting molded components

Separate each component from the sheet with scissors or a sharp knife. Cut off the excess plastic close to the edge of the component. Finish by rubbing carefully on abrasive paper glued to a board. Check the fit of each component constantly as you work.

**Cutting parts from sprue** Support the "tree" on a block of wood and cut off a piece of sprue, leaving a small stump on the component. Pare this away once it has been separated from the "tree."

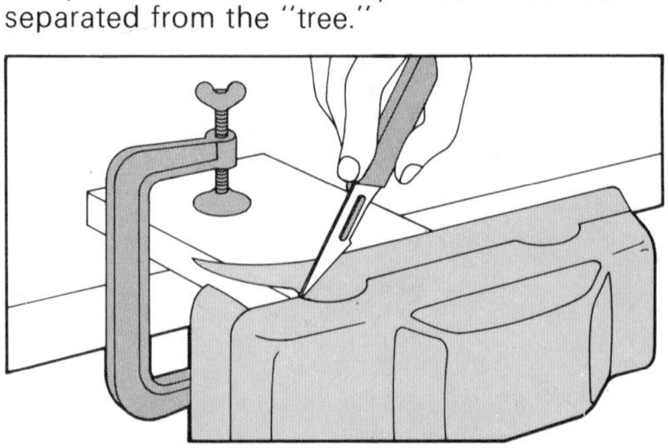

**Trimming large vacuum-formed components** Support the body shell on a board overhanging the workbench and score along the cut line. (The scored line must be continuous.) Tear away the waste.

## Cutting foamed plastic

Expanded polyurethane and thin, sheet polystyrene can be cut with a knife. Large pieces of expanded polyurethane can be cut successfully with woodworking saws. To shape large pieces of expanded polystyrene, use a hot-wire foam cutter which is a nickel-chrome wire cutter under tension. A small electric current is passed through the wire to heat it and the wire melts the polystyrene, making a fine "cut." See Foam wings, pages 282 to 284 for how to use the wire cutter.

## Joining plastic

Almost all plastics are joined using plastic cements (see pages 40 to 41). Polyethylene, however, does not glue well. Small pieces should be welded together with a hot knife; larger pieces can be joined with epoxy glues, but be sure to reinforce the joint with a straight pin.

Once a polystyrene joint has set, scrape away the excess cement with a knife. Smooth the joint with wet-and-dry paper, then rub some liquid metal polish over it with a soft cloth to replace the shine.

## Laminating plastic

Small components, such as a gun turret for a boat, can be made by laminating several layers of plastic to build a small block and then filing this to shape when set. Use liquid cement to bond the layers and clamp the block until dry to make sure all air is excluded from the joints. To hold the block for filing and sanding, leave an extension attached to the component and make the final cut after it has been shaped, or temporarily attach the component to a piece of balsa with double-sided tape.

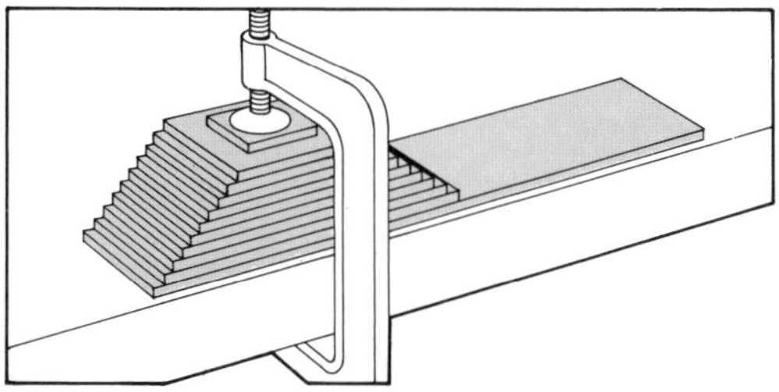

**Making a plastic block** Bond layers of plastic sheet using liquid cement. Clamp the block and leave it to set hard.

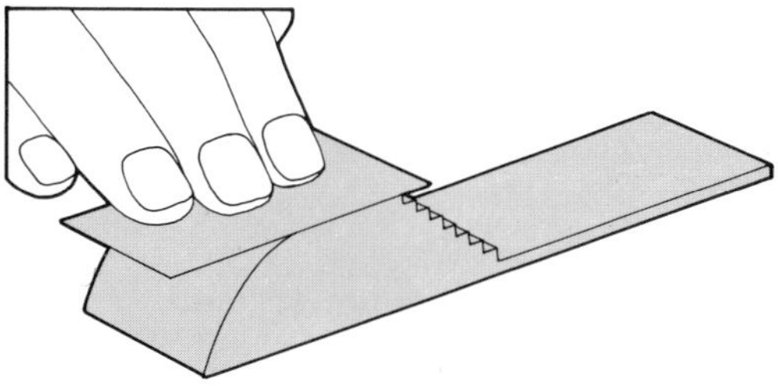

Smooth the block to the required shape using files and fine abrasive papers.

## Filling plastics

Even the best modelers find it difficult to make invisible joins in a rigid material such as polystyrene or acrylobutyl styrene. Fine gaps can be filled by brushing matt enamel paint into them. When the paint has set hard, rub it down with wet-and-dry paper.

For larger gaps use a special epoxy paste for filling plastic, sold ready-to-use or in two parts for mixing. Only a very small amount of filler is used at any one time and it shrinks very little so work the filler as close as possible to the required shape. Press it down hard into each joint with a spatula of some kind (the best tools are discarded dental instruments but an old knife blade and darning needle are adequate), then dampen the tip of a finger and wipe along and across the joints lightly to smooth it flush. Leave to harden overnight before lightly sanding with a piece of very fine abrasive paper.

Epoxy paste is also useful for filling dents. You can simply smooth paste into them but it is better to follow the method illustrated below.

The paste can also be used to build up sections of a model. Be sure to mold it as close as possible to the finished shape, then smooth it with water to achieve a good finish. If necessary, the filled area can be sawn, filed and sanded in the same way as the surrounding plastic. The instructions for modeling a fender flare on page 132 use epoxy paste to build up the correct profile.

Liquid plastic, which is extremely useful for filling gaps as well as building up small details and textures, can be made by dissolving scrap polystyrene in liquid cement or artist's paint remover (trichlorethylene). Cut the scrap into small pieces and drop them into a screw-top jar. Pour in the solvent, then replace the lid and leave overnight to dissolve. The consistency of the liquid can be modified by adding more solvent or sprue. Use a thick consistency for gap filling, a medium one when adding small detail and a thin one when coating tissue paper for making clothing for model figures (see pages 147 to 148).

Liquid plastic is particularly useful for filling the large gaps produced when converting models. Not only does it fill the joint but it bonds the components. Simply brush the liquid into the gap, building it up little-by-little, and let each application harden before adding the next. Sand flush when hard. Wash the brush by dipping it in liquid cement.

**Filling dents** Drill shallow holes in the depression from different angles to anchor the filling. Overfill very slightly, leave to harden and sand flush.

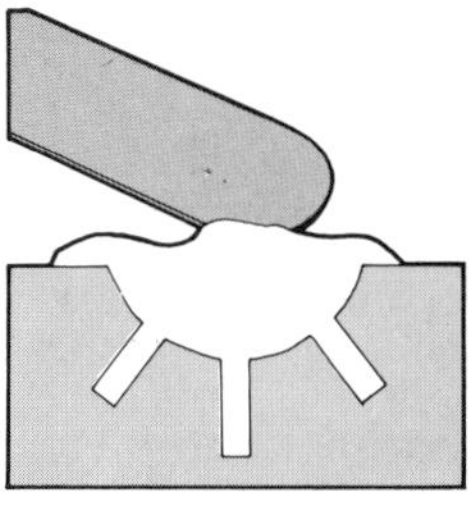

## Smoothing plastic

All the rigid plastics mentioned so far, with the exception of polyethylene, can be smoothed with fine needle files and suitable abrasives. Flash (the thin film of plastic which results from badly fitting molds) can be removed in this way or with a sharp knife. Plastic tends to clog fine files but it is easily cleaned from the teeth with a soft wire brush. Most plastics can also be trimmed with a finely set, sharp plane.

Larger components and thick acrylic sheet can be successfully shaped and smoothed on a bench-mounted disk sander. Use light pressure to avoid overheating the plastic.

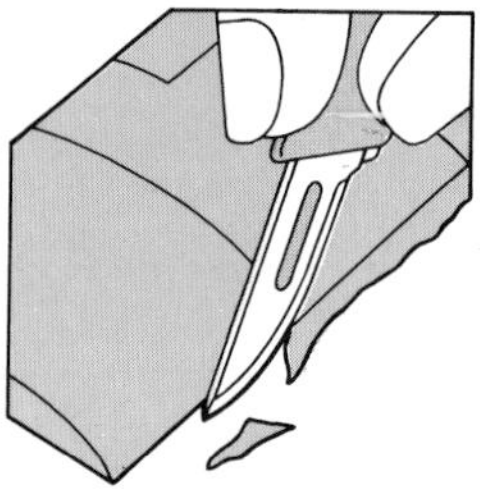

**Removing flash** Cut the flash away with a sharp knife, working as close to the edge as possible. Smooth the edge with a needle file or abrasive paper.

## Engraving and embossing plastic

A thermostatically-controlled, electrically- heated needle, known as a pyrogravure, is the ideal tool for engraving plastic. For detailed descriptions of some of its uses see the chapter on figures, pages 136 to 154.

You can also emboss small features such as rivets or panel lines for static vehicles on the reverse side of plastic. First, mark out the position of the embossing with a pencil. Then tape the sheet face down on a piece of thick cardboard and press the design into it with a dry ruling pen or an empty ballpoint.

## Heat-stretching plastic

When softened by heat, lengths of plastic can be stretched into hair-like filaments which can be used to simulate such features as rigging on a model sailing ship. Even plastic tubes can be stretched in this way to reduce their diameter but sprue – the waste material to which most plastic injection-molded components are attached – is ideal for this purpose. Heat the sprue evenly over a candle flame. To produce a fine filament the sprue must be stretched immediately after removal from the heat. Keep the action smooth or the sprue will break, and allow it to hang vertically for a few seconds until it cools and hardens.

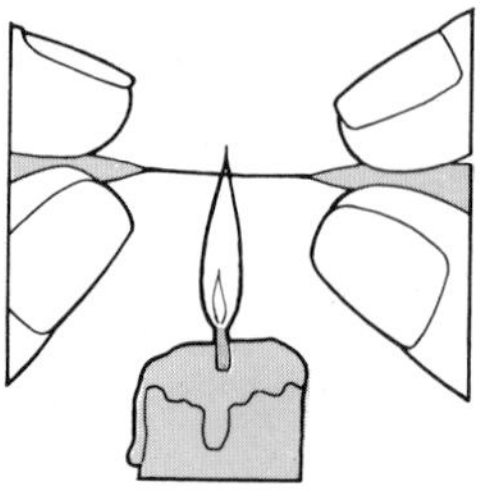

**Heat-stretching sprue** Revolve the sprue about 1 inch (25 mm) above a candle flame. When it becomes soft and shiny, remove it from the heat and stretch it to the required diameter.

## Bending plastic

You can bend plastic strip or rod by pulling it under a rounded tool held on a flat surface or by rolling a dowel across the top of the strip or rod held on a piece of cardboard – the firmer the pressure the greater the curve. Very thin plastic sheet can be curled around a paintbrush handle.

A more accurate method is to apply a drop of liquid cement to the area you want to bend; leave to soften for a few minutes then bend gently to avoid stretching. To bend several components to the same shape, use a simple jig made of nails positioned in a plywood board at the angle you require. Begin by taping one end of the rod to the board up against one of the nails. Apply a little solvent to the outer edge of the bend and, when it softens, bend the component around the next nail, holding it against the nail under slight tension – do not stretch. Tape once more just behind the bend and repeat the softening and bending procedure.

Water and heat can also be used to bend plastic. For the water method, tape the component over a former and plunge it into very hot water; leave to soften, then cool in cold water while still attached to the former.

See below for using heat to bend large components or sheet material. Wear protective gloves and use an electric burner, if possible – gas may scorch the material. For small pieces, use a soldering iron. Support the tool so that both hands are free and hold the plastic directly over the tip but not touching it. As soon as the plastic softens, make the bend around a wooden former for accuracy.

Thick, brittle plastic such as acrylic needs to be heated to a temperature of 300 to 340°F (150 to 170°C) to make it bend. Depending on its size and thickness, it may take up to 15 minutes in a heated oven to soften plastic to a rubbery state when it can be bent. Do not use a cold former or the plastic may cool before the bend is made. Hold the shape until the plastic cools enough to be rigid, then cool it completely by immersing it in cold water.

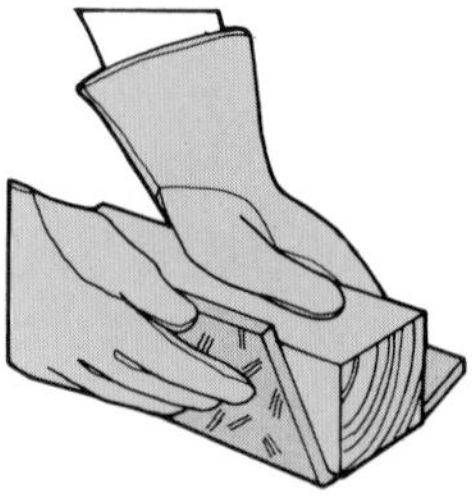

**Making a right-angle bend** Wrap foil, shiny side out, tightly around the plastic sheet; leave a band of acrylic exposed along the line of the bend. A $\frac{1}{8}$-inch (3-mm) gap will produce a sharp angle.

Hold the plastic over an electric burner and keep it moving. When it has softened, make the bend around a block of wood which has a slight curve planed along one edge. Hold it in position until cool.

## Plug-molding plastic

This technique can be used to replace an off-scale kit item or to add a part not supplied in the kit. Polystyrene, acrylobutyl styrene and acetate sheet can all be plug-molded, though the methods for working with transparent and opaque plastic differ.

Follow the procedure illustrated below when molding transparent sheet. It can be painted to make it opaque, if you wish. For opaque plastic, glue the wooden stops to the underside of the former to lift it off the bench and give clearance for the plug. When the plastic is heat-softened, push the plug in from above.

A plug can be made from wood such a jelutong or balsa, or acrylic, and should be finished well because surface grain or blemishes may be reproduced on the molding. Do not include returns or undercuts or the plug may become trapped in the mold of the sheet or the detail may not reproduce. Coat the surface of a wooden plug with sanding sealer before sanding to remove all irregularities. If surface detail is required, add it to the finished molding.

A simple shape, such as an aircraft canopy, can be molded in one piece. A complete fuselage, however, needs to be molded in halves using two mirrored plugs. To make the plugs, glue two pieces of wood together with a thin piece of paper in between; the joint represents the junction between the fuselage halves. Carve the shape using cardboard templates, then split it to form two separate plugs. The overall size of the plug should be slightly smaller than the finished component to allow for the thickness of plastic. This will vary depending on how much the plastic will be stretched in the molding process.

## Plug-molding an aircraft canopy

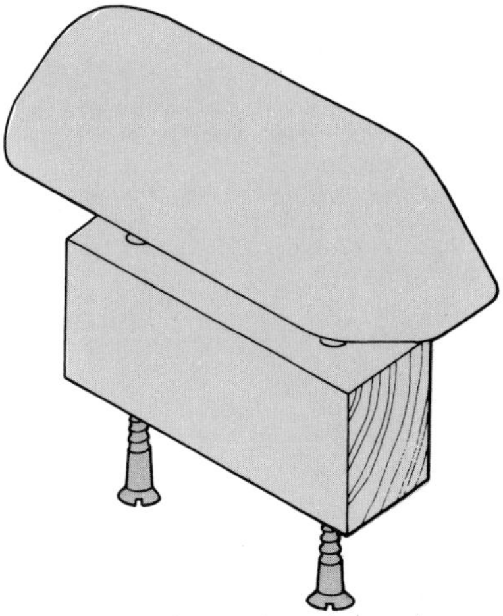

**1** Carve a block of wood to shape then screw on another block for a handle. Make the plug deeper than the molding so the component can be cut out without damage.

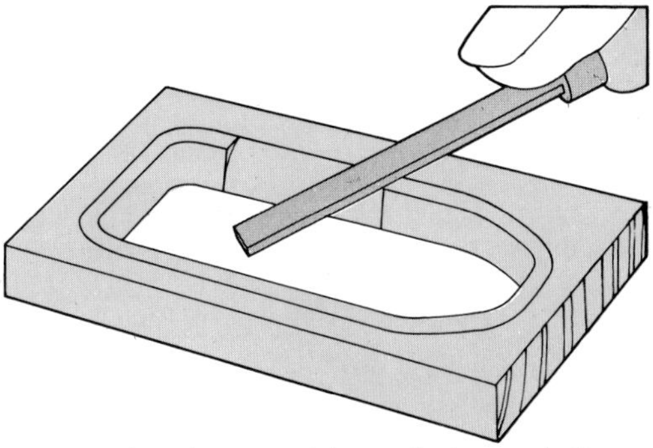

**2** Place the plug on a piece of plywood. Draw around the plug, enlarging the shape by slightly more than the thickness of the plastic to be used. Cut out the shape. Curve one edge of the hole and sand all the edges smooth. Rub graphite from a lead pencil over the curved edge to lubricate it.

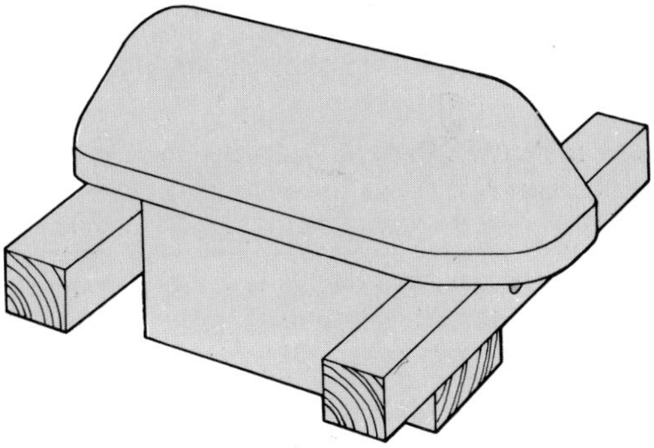

**3** Mark the cut line on the plug then place the plywood former straight over the plug, curved edge first, so that the line is just below the top surface. Glue a balsa wood stop to each end of the handle to keep the plug in the correct position during the molding procedure.

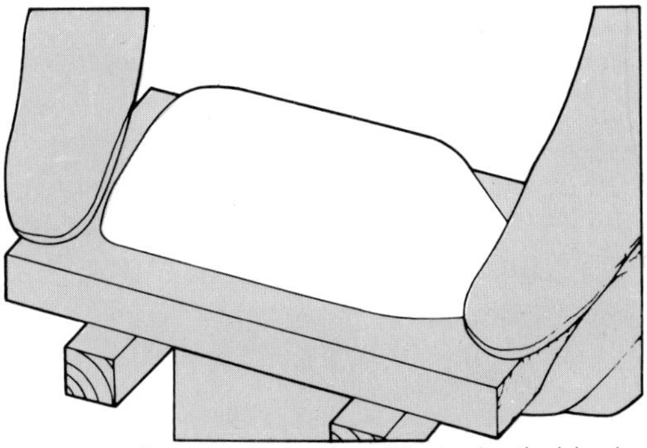

**4** Set up the plug in a vise. Fix a plastic blank to the curved side of the former with double-sided tape. Heat the plastic over a burner until it wrinkles then, at the moment the plastic pulls tight again, push the former down over the plug. Hold it in place for a few seconds until the plastic becomes rigid. If the plastic is not hot enough to shape, reheat it over the burner and try again.

## Polishing plastic

To polish polystyrene, acrylobutyl styrene or acrylic, use liquid metal polish on a cotton ball and lightly rub the surface. Change the cotton ball regularly and do not let it dry. Finally, polish the surface to a high-gloss finish with a clean cotton ball.

Fine scratches can be polished out with a polishing wheel attached to a miniature power drill, using a polishing compound. Having removed the scratches, polish it by hand with a clean cotton ball as described above.

Deeper scratches must be removed by using progressively finer grades of wet-and-dry paper to reduce the blemishes until they are shallow enough to be polished out.

Polish large sections of plastic, such as acrylic sheet, by holding them against a 6-inch (150-mm) buffing wheel treated with polishing compound. Press the plastic firmly against the lower part of the wheel, with the wheel revolving down onto it; keep the plastic moving as the action of the wheel can quickly round off the edges. Finally, polish with a soft cloth.

# Fiberglass

This covers a group of materials made up of strands of fiberglass embedded in one of a number of plastic resins. This combination produces a strong, light material which can be molded into complex shapes and can be colored so that painting is unnecessary.

Fiberglass is sold either in solid form as moldings such as boat hulls, aircraft fuselages, or flat sheet, or as separate components for making your own molding: fiberglass mat or cloth, liquid resin, catalyst and accelerator.

The fiberglass most commonly used is in the form of a coarse, felt-like material made from randomly laid short fibers and referred to as chopped-strand mat. Various fiberglass cloths and continuous fibers (rovings) are also available; these are stronger than chopped-strand mat but not as cheap or easy to use. Fiberglass tissue can be used to reinforce the surface of moldings and to hide the texture of the mat. The glass used for making fiberglass varies in composition and properties, and is graded accordingly. Where water resistance is important, for example when molding boat hulls, grade E (electrical) fiberglass should be used.

The resin used for making fiberglass moldings comes as a syrupy liquid. There are many different types available, each having slightly different properties. However, a general-purpose resin will fulfill most requirements. There are tough resins intended for use as a gel coat (surface layer) only but they are not essential and have a tendency to remain tacky unless covered with a sheet of cellophane while setting.

The catalyst is a liquid which is added to the resin to trigger the setting. Add it to a small batch of resin just prior to use. Very small amounts are used and it is important to follow the instructions carefully.

The accelerator is a liquid added to those resins which do not already contain it to speed up the setting rate when the catalyst is added. It is important that the accelerator and catalyst never mix directly because a violent reaction can result. Always mix one or the other with the resin first.

Release agents are applied to the pattern or the mold to prevent the fiberglass from sticking. Although there are several different release agents on the market, a good method is to apply a layer of nonsilicone wax to the pattern or mold and coat it with polyvinyl alcohol; the wax can be peeled away or washed off the molding when it has set.

Specially formulated pigment pastes can be mixed in with the resin to color the molding. Add the color to each resin layer or just to the gel coat. The pigment allows you to see the distribution of the gel coat, but if added to each layer of resin, it makes it difficult to judge when the fiberglass mat is sufficiently saturated. Moreover, too much pigment may have an adverse effect on the resin.

## Making an object in fiberglass

This can involve three stages: making a pattern for the mold, making the mold and making the actual molding.

An existing object can be used as a pattern for the mold as long as the resin is compatible with the material. Avoid those thermoplastics which are distorted by the heat produced by the resin as it cures (a list of thermoplastics is found on page 51). With simple shapes it may be easier to build a wooden mold than to make a pattern, and to take a mold from it. The hard-chine boat hull on page 314 is a good example of this procedure.

It is sometimes possible to eliminate the mold-making stage altogether if you can find an object that will serve as a mold. Bowls, food containers and aerosol caps make good, simple molds, particularly if they are made of polyethylene because it does not require a release agent. Flat sheets for decks or bulkheads can be molded directly on a sheet of polyethylene or cellophane stretched over a board.

Whatever you use as a pattern or a mold, if you want a smooth finish on the molding, the matching surface on the mold or pattern must have a good finish.

### Making the pattern

This can be made from materials such as clay, modeling clay, plaster, wood, or cardboard. Modeling clay is attacked by the resin so it should be sealed first with shellac or polyurethane varnish. Clay or plaster must be completely dry before making the mold. Use balsa, pine, obeche or jelutong for constructing wooden patterns.

Several methods for making patterns are described on pages 314 to 315. Use templates made from the plans to check the shape of the pattern while you build.

### Making a mold from a pattern

Treat the pattern with a release agent, then mix up a small quantity of resin and paint the surface of the pattern and a strip of the baseboard adjacent to it. If you are using a thermoplastic object as a pattern, work very slowly and make sure that the resin does not have too much catalyst or accelerator Leave this layer to dry then mix up more resin and apply another layer but do not leave to dry.

Cut or tear a piece of fiberglass mat to size and lay it in position on the wet resin. Stipple the mat with a short-haired, stiff brush or roll it with a special roller until it is thoroughly saturated with resin – the fiberglass changes from white to transparent as the resin soaks in. Cover the pattern with more pieces, overlapping them by about 2 inches (50 mm) and work the fibers together. Extend the fiberglass onto the baseboard to make a flange. This will stiffen the edge of the mold and make a guide for trimming the molding. (Another method is to scribe a trim line around the edge of the pattern beforehand; it will appear on both the mold and molding.)

When the mold has set, remove it from the pattern, place it flat on the workbench with the flange overhanging, and carefully trim the edges of the flange with tin snips or a hacksaw (see Cutting fiberglass, page 58). Finally, smooth the edges with files.

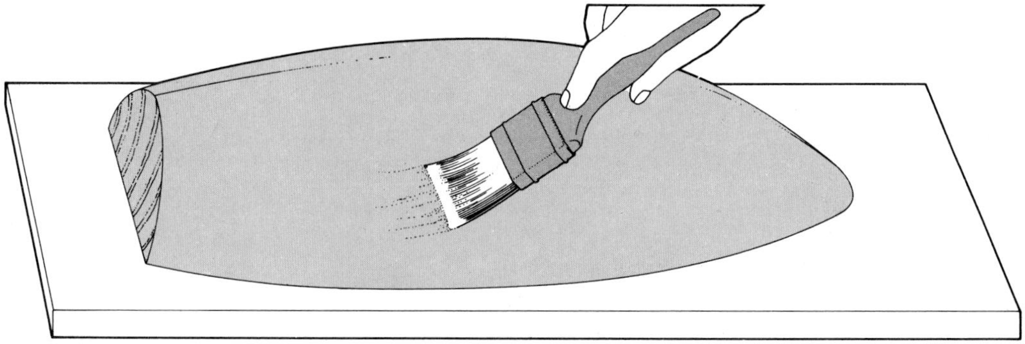

Stage 1: Painting on the gel coat

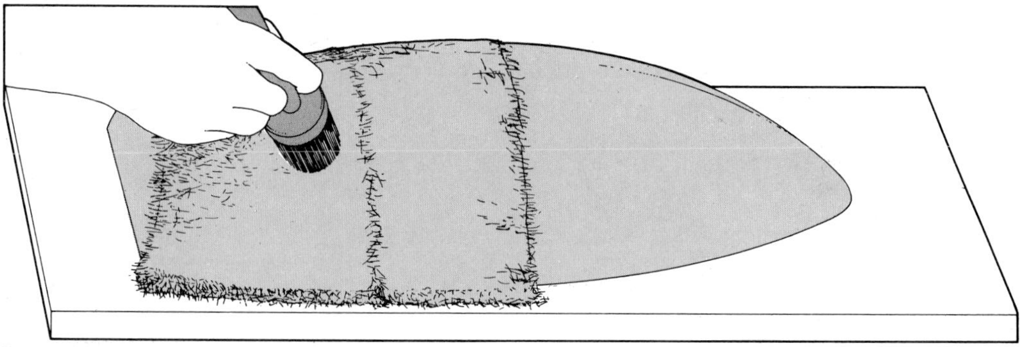

Stage 2: Laying the fiberglass mat

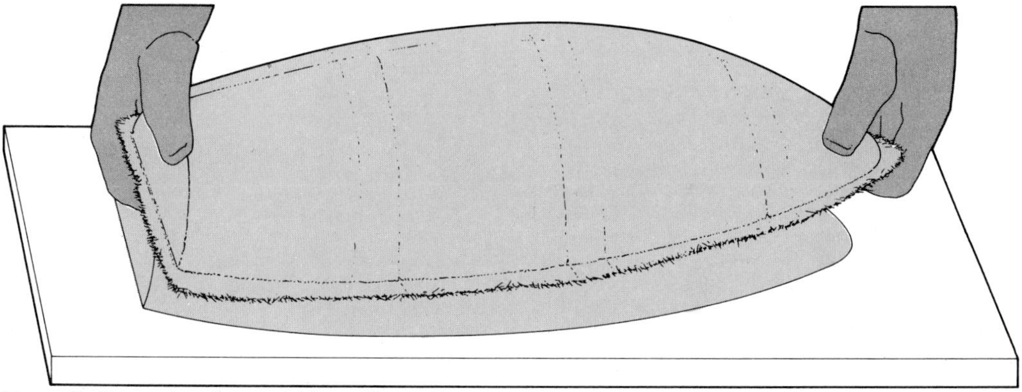

Stage 3: Removing the mold from the pattern

### Making a split mold

When a pattern has a shape which would trap the mold, make the mold in two halves. Begin by building a temporary cardboard wall along the dividing line on the pattern and support it on one side with modeling clay. Lay fiberglass over one side of the pattern and up the wall. When set, remove the wall, treat the exposed fiberglass and pattern with release agent and build the second half of the mold. When set, drill holes in the flanges and bolt them together.

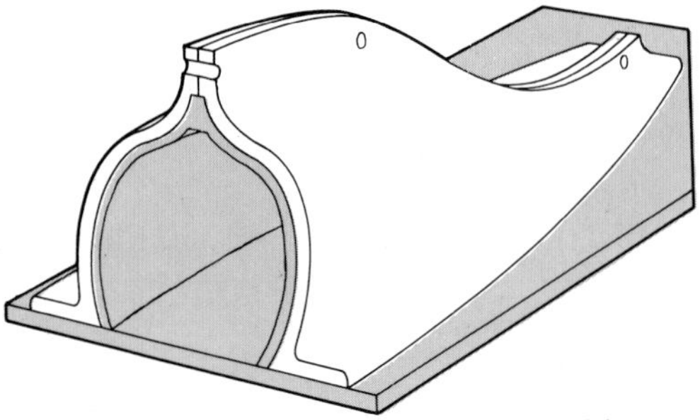

Drill the bolt holes before taking the mold off the pattern.

### Making the molding

Apply release agent to the mold and lay the fiberglass following the procedure described on page 57 for making a mold from a pattern. Carry the fiberglass beyond the trim line. Edges, and any fixing points, should be reinforced with extra pieces of mat. If necessary, glue a balsa strip or paper rope to the finished molding and lay the extra fiberglass mat over the top. This technique makes a very strong structure.

## Cutting fiberglass

It may be possible to cut a molding with scissors shortly after gelling while it is still soft. But when it has set completely, you will need to use a coarse file, tin snips or a hacksaw. Curves can be cut with a file or abrasive disks.

High-speed, steel twist drills should be used to make small holes. Cut larger ones with a hole saw, or make a series of small holes and remove the center; finish the edge with a half-round file. Always work from the gel coat side of the fiberglass molding.

## Joining fiberglass

Before joining the surfaces, roughen them with a mild abrasive, then paint them with resin. Lay fiberglass mat or woven glass tape across the join and use a stippling brush to impregnate it with resin. You may need to apply several layers of tape to make a strong joint. Self-adhesive tape can often be used to hold the parts together while the resin sets.

Joins can be made with aluminum or laminated plastic held in place by self-tapping screws or bolts. If necessary, waterproof the joint by laying pieces of fiberglass mat over the top or by applying epoxy adhesive to the surfaces beforehand.

## Repairing damage

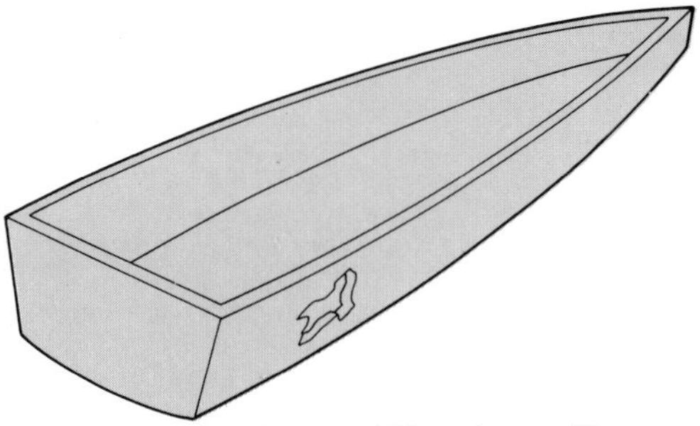

**1** Cut away the damaged fiberglass with a hacksaw, drill or file.

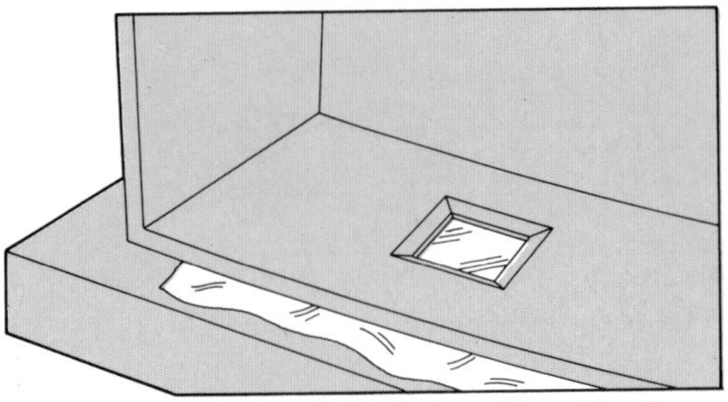

**2** Bevel the edges of the hole with a file. Tape a piece of cellophane over the outside of the hole; pull it taut and, if possible, support it on a flat board.

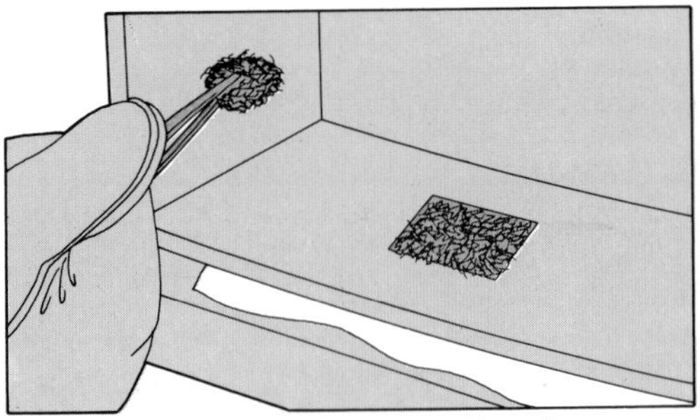

**3** Working from the inside, brush resin onto the cellophane and leave to set. Lay pieces of fiberglass mat in the hole to build up the thickness, then cover the hole completely with a larger piece.

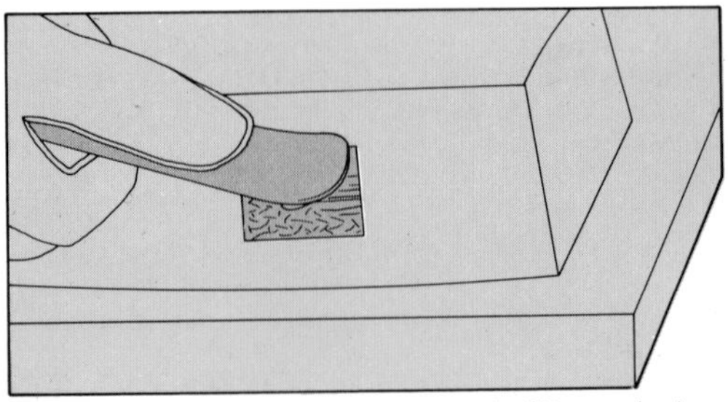

**4** When the repair has hardened, fill any holes on the surface with a resin-based filler. When dry, smooth the surface with wet-and-dry paper and polish it.

# Metals

These fall into two categories: pure metals such as copper or tin, and alloys (mixtures of two or more metals) such as brass or steel. The properties of pure metals are constant, whereas the properties of alloys are affected by the proportions of the different metals which are used to make them.

The techniques and materials described in this section will be most helpful to boat and aeromodelers and, to some extent, modelers who cast metal figures.

### Copper

This is a pure metal which is red in color and oxidizes to brown or green. It is quite soft, although it hardens quickly with bending or hammering. Copper has the highest thermal and electrical conductivity of all common metals. Pieces of copper can be joined with soldering and brazing alloys.

Copper is available in sheet, rod, square bar and tube form, or as electrical wire and cable in a wide range of thicknesses. It is used to make steam pipes and fuel lines and tanks for all kinds of working models.

### Lead

Also a pure metal, lead is silvery in color, oxidizing to black or gray. It is a soft metal with the highest density of common metals and it has a low melting point, making it easy to cast. For these reasons it is an ideal material for keel weights. Miniature figures, although now made of casting alloy, were once molded in lead.

It is available as foil, sheet and slab and is widely used in alloys, solder being one of the best known.

### Aluminum

This can mean the pure metal or one of the many alloys made with this metal. Pure aluminum has a low density, is silver in color, oxidizing to white, and is soft. The alloys (referred to as light alloys) resemble pure aluminum except that they are stronger. Although some alloys bend easily, others need to be softened by heat. Aluminum and its alloys are difficult materials to solder and weld.

### Tin

Another pure metal, tin has a low melting point, is corrosion resistant and silver-colored. It is used as a protective coating for other metals and is a constituent of solder and bronze. Pieces can be joined by soldering.

A combination of tin and lead is used for metal figures and is available as bar and casting ingots for making your own castings.

### Tinplate

This is a thin sheet of steel with a coating of tin on each side which makes soldering easy. This material is suitable for making fuel tanks and boat hulls. The cut edges can rust because the steel is exposed.

### Zinc

This is a silvery-gray, corrosion-resistant metal with a low melting point. It is often used to protect other metals which corrode more easily. Zinc-coated metals are called galvanized metals. Zinc can be soldered and will bend easily if it is first heated.

### Brass

This term refers to a wide range of alloys consisting mainly of copper and zinc. Brasses are of moderate weight and yellow, oxidizing to brown or green. Strength and hardness vary greatly, depending on composition and treatment during manufacture. Brasses make good bearings and machine well. They can be joined by soldering, hard-soldering and brazing.

Brass is available as round or square tubing, sheet, square, hexagon, round and half-round bars and angle strip.

### Bronze

This term covers a range of alloys made from copper and tin. They are similar in color and consistency to brass. They resist corrosion well and are used extensively for marine fittings and equipment. Most bronzes can be joined by soldering and brazing.

### Cast iron

This substance contains a relatively high proportion of carbon; in its most common form it is weak in tension and brittle. However, it has good machining and bearing qualities and is used extensively to make parts for engines. It is available in rod form.

### Steel

This refers to a range of alloys of iron and carbon with other metals. By varying the proportion of the constituents and heat treatment, widely differing properties can be achieved. Mild steel contains a small amount of carbon, is silvery-gray and relatively soft. It can be soldered, brazed and welded easily. It is a general-purpose steel used where weight is critical and stress is not high, and is available in a wide range of sections as well as plain and galvanized wire.

Carbon steel has a higher carbon content than mild steel. It is a very hard, brittle metal which can be toughened by tempering (reheating at a controlled temperature). It can be soldered, brazed and welded, and is used to make tools and highly stressed components.

Silver-steel is another high-carbon steel, sometimes with some chromium added. It is sold in accurately ground lengths of round and square sections. Alloy steels are carbon steels with additives to improve strength and corrosion resistance.

Stainless steel has nickel and chromium added. It can be soldered and welded, but heating may reduce the resistance to corrosion. Some types of stainless steel are more difficult to machine than others.

## Marking metal

To mark a straight line, use a steel rule and a hardened steel scriber. Rub graphite in the line to make it stand out against new metal. A simple way to mark parallel lines, is to run a pair of spring dividers along a steel rule positioned on the first line.

Compasses or dividers can be used to mark curves on metal. Mark the center with a punch, or stick a piece of masking tape on the metal to hold the point.

To mark square stock, use a scriber and try square as described for balsa wood on page 45. Mark round stock as in step 1 of Extending a fuselage, page 131, or place the work on a board and position the scriber on a block of wood as shown below. Small adjustments in the height of the block can be made with strips of cardboard or metal.

Use a sharp pencil, felt pen or chinagraph to mark a bend line because a scored line marked on the outside of a bend may crack when the metal stretches.

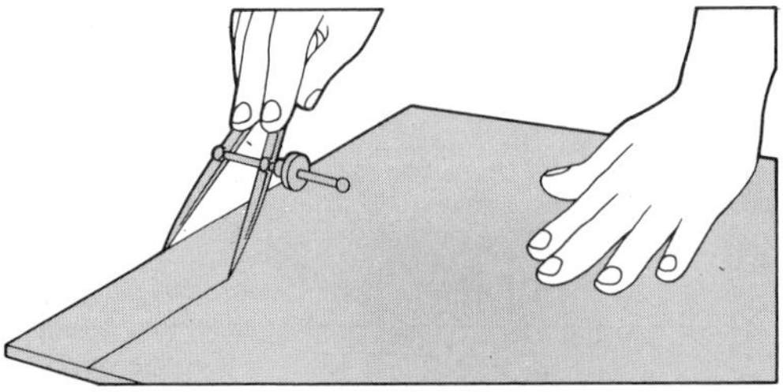

**Marking a line parallel to an edge** Run one point of a pair of spring dividers against the edge and scribe a line with the other.

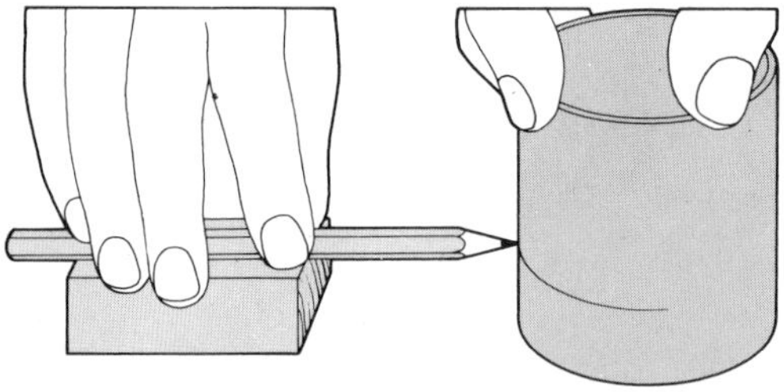

**Marking round stock** Holding the scriber firmly with one hand, rotate the work against it.

## Bending metal

To make a sharp, right-angle bend in sheet metal, set it up in a vise, clamped between two stout wooden formers aligned with the marked line. Ideally, you should use a mallet to tap the metal over, flattening the bend against the former. If you do not have a mallet, however, you will find that you can do the job with a block of wood and a hammer.

To bend a long piece of metal, clamp the work in the same way using "C" clamps where necessary. Starting at one end and working backward and forward along the length of the metal, tap it over gradually, bending the metal a few degrees at a time.

If the angle is anything other than a right angle, or if the bend is to be curved, plane or shape a former accordingly. If you are bending "springy" metal, be sure to make the angle slightly larger than required to allow for a certain amount of springback.

Thin wire can be bent successfully with a pair of pliers. If the wire is long enough, hold it in one hand and bend it with the pliers held in in the other. For short pieces, which are often needed for modelmaking, you will need two pairs of pliers: one for holding, one for bending. Apply pressure as close to the jaws as possible to produce a tight bend.

When bending thick wire or thin rod, clamp it in the soft jaws of an engineer's vise. Use a hammer to make the bend around the end of the jaws so that you can see the angle of the bend from above.

If a particular curve is required or if you want to repeat a bend, make up a bending jig. Tap a metal peg, with a diameter slightly smaller than the inside diameter of the bend, into a hole drilled in a hardwood or plywood base. Draw the required angle on the base beforehand so that you can match the bend to it. If a series of bends is required, make the first bend, then insert another peg and make the second bend. To keep the bends in the same plane, sight along the work and twist it back in line by hand, if necessary. If the wire is too stiff, clamp it in a vise and use a block of wood to lever the other section into line.

Make a coil by winding the wire tightly around a single metal peg several times.

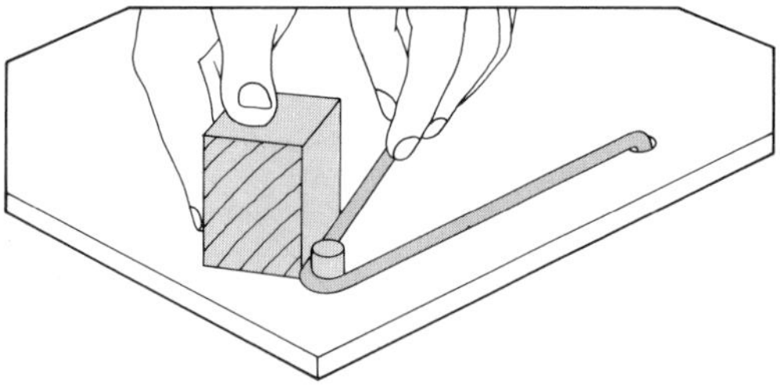

**Using a bending jig** Drill a hole at one end of the base and hook one end of the wire in it. Leave the wire as long as possible to provide good leverage and use a block of wood to hold the wire tightly against the metal peg.

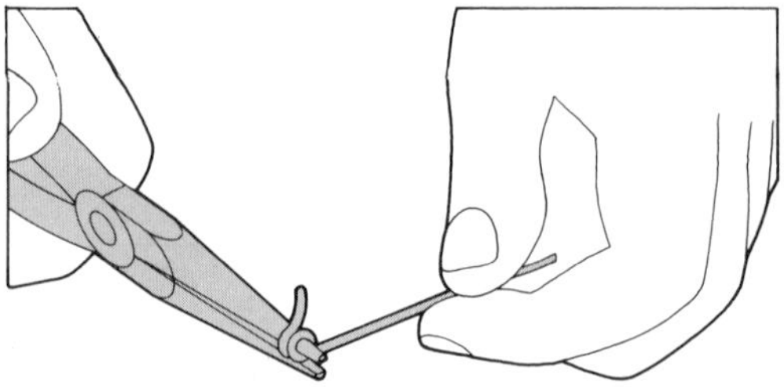

**Forming a loop** Use long-nose pliers, keeping tension on the wire with one hand while twisting the tool away from you with the other. Trim the ends with pliers.

## Cutting metal

It is advisable to wear protective gloves when cutting sheet metal. Very thin sheet metal can be cut with tin snips. Follow the marked line closely, keeping the jaws upright. Use the length of the blades but avoid closing them completely – it produces a ragged edge. For thicker sheet metal, support the tin snips in a vise as shown right. Double-cutting snips cut a narrow strip right out of the metal, leaving the material flat on each side. Remember always to cut on the waste side of the marked line when using this tool.

Thick metal should be cut with a hacksaw. Clamp the work in a vise, sandwiched between two sheets of wood as close to the cut line as possible. Choose a fine-toothed blade to cut thin sheet metal and, if necessary, hold the saw at an angle to get at least three teeth in the cut to prevent the saw jamming. Saw steadily, applying pressure on the forward stroke only. When you have finished the cut, smooth the edge with a file.

To make deep cuts, turn the blade sideways so that the frame is out of the way. Support the frame with one hand to keep the cut straight. Use more than one blade in the hacksaw if you want to cut a wide notch.

To cut square tube or rod, establish the cut on all four sides: rotate each cut face away from you in turn, picking up the line on the next face. Cut away the metal in the center using your first cut to guide the blade. Position metal angle-strip in the vise so that you can follow the line across one face and down the other.

When cutting small aluminum tube, rest the tip of a knife blade on the work and roll the tube away from you under the palm of your hand until the cut line joins up. Having established the cut line, simply snap the tube with your fingers. The end will be rough or even jagged so trim the edges with the knife or use a file.

Most wire can be cut with pliers. Use the side cutters just in front of the pivot or open up the handles to align the croppers. Some wire, such as piano wire, is too stiff to be cut with pliers. Clamp it in a vise as close to the cut line as possible and cut it with a junior hacksaw. Very thin wire can be cut with a knife or even a pair of nail clippers.

The best method of cutting holes in thin sheet metal is to use a punch. Lay the work on the end grain of a block of wood – do not use the side grain as it allows the metal to distort too much. Mark the center of the hole with a center punch, then use a hollow punch as shown right. If the hole is over $\frac{1}{4}$ inch (6 mm) in diameter, scribe the circle with a pair of dividers first.

A lever punch with interchangeable punches will cut small holes without distortion.

To cut large holes, use a hole saw in a power drill, set at a slow speed. You may also use a piercing saw or a saw file if you first drill an access hole on the waste side of the cut line for the blade. Pass the blade through the hole and reconnect it to the saw frame.

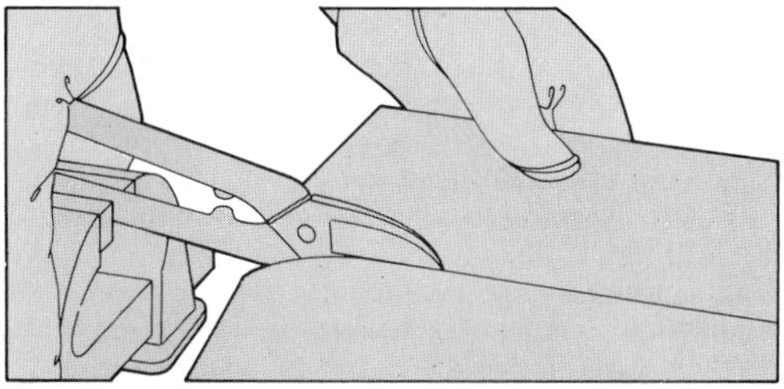

**Cutting sheet metal with tin snips** If extra pressure is needed, clamp one handle in a vise and apply pressure with one hand while guiding the work with the other.

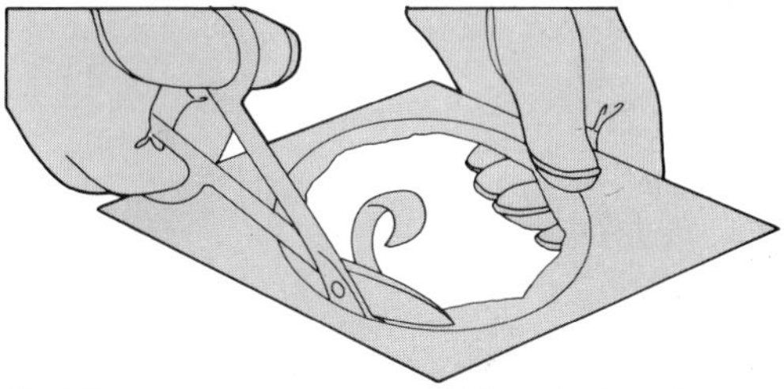

**Cutting concave curves** Use circle snips which have curved jaws, or clamp the metal in a vise and use a piercing saw or a saw file inserted in a hacksaw frame.

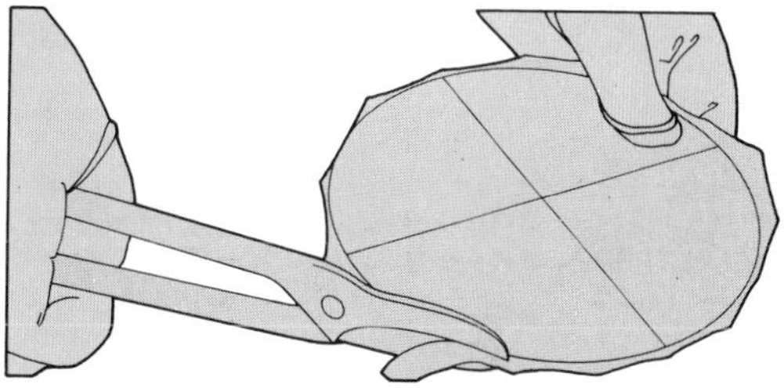

**Cutting convex curves** Trim away as much of the waste as possible, then cut to the line with tin snips. Try to keep the waste in one continuous piece as this will help to produce a smooth edge.

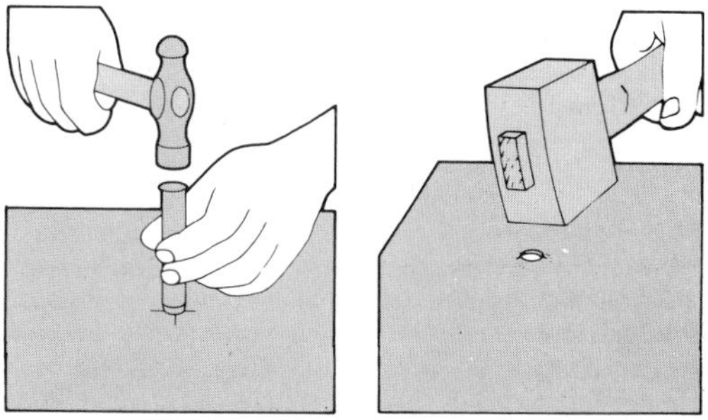

**Using a hole punch** Center the punch on the mark and tap it with a hammer; make sure the mark is accurate, then strike one hard blow to cut right through.

The metal will be distorted around the hole. Turn it over onto a hardwood surface and flatten it with a mallet or a block of wood and a hammer.

## Drilling holes in metal

Always use high-speed drill bits for metal. Use a twist drill bit in a hand drill or power drill to drill holes in sheet metal but be sure to grind the point to 140° to prevent it from catching as it emerges.

Before drilling a hole, mark the center to keep the drill in place: scribe intersecting lines to mark the center, position the center punch on the mark, and strike it with a hammer. If your first mark does not correspond with the intersection, angle the punch toward the center and strike it again. Punch the exact center again to hold the drill bit in position.

Clamp the workpiece either in a vise or a "C" clamp. If you are using a power drill, set it at a slow speed. While drilling, lubricate aluminum with kerosene and all other metals with light oil except brass, which does not need any kind of lubrication.

To drill a large hole in a thick section of metal, drill successively larger pilot holes, lubricating the work well to avoid overheating. If a pilot hole is off-center, correct it with a round file before drilling the final hole.

## Mechanical fastenings for metal

**Screws, nuts and bolts**
Self-tapping screws are designed specifically for joining sheet metal. Drill a pilot hole through both sections of metal at the same time; the screw will cut its own thread as it is driven. Another method is to punch a hole with a sheet metal punch to distort the side of the hole and give the screw thread more material to bite into.

If you want to be able to dismantle a joint later use nuts and bolts. Hexagonal-head screws are shown below; machine screws are illustrated on page 50.

There are several different ways of locking a nut in position. You can paint the exposed thread, or put a spring lock washer under the nut to grip the metal and keep the tension on the thread. Use a split pin through a hole in the bolt to secure a castle nut. Another method is to screw two nuts up against each other on the same thread. You can also buy special lock nuts with nylon or fiber inserts which bind against the thread.

**Rivets**
These are made from soft, malleable metals and are used to join sheet metal. They are available with flat heads or round heads. When joining metal with the flat-head type, use the method described below for round-head rivets, but countersink the rivet and file it flush. You can also buy special "pop" rivets which are installed using a rivet gun. Drill a hole through both components and put the shank of the rivet into the gun; insert the rivet in the hole. Press the gun against the work and squeeze the handles until the shank breaks, expanding the rivet head. The distance between a rivet and the edge of the work should be no less than twice the rivet's diameter.

Drill out the head of a pop or flathead rivet to remove it; chisel off a roundhead one. Remove the shank with a center punch.

**Joining with roundhead rivets** Clamp the sheets together and drill a hole for the rivet. Insert the rivet, making sure that it projects approximately one and a half times its diameter.

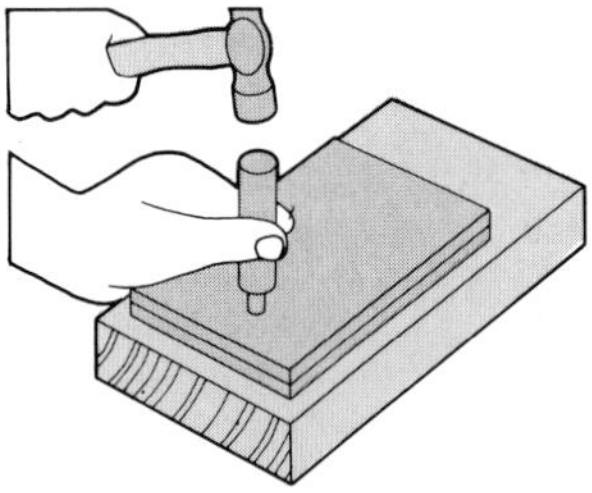

Turn the work over and support the head on a block of hardwood. Place a tube over the shank and tap it with a hammer to set the joint.

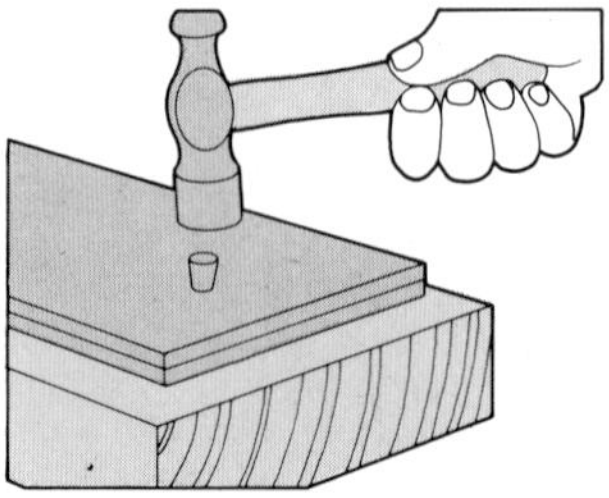

Swell the rivet with a flat-face hammer.

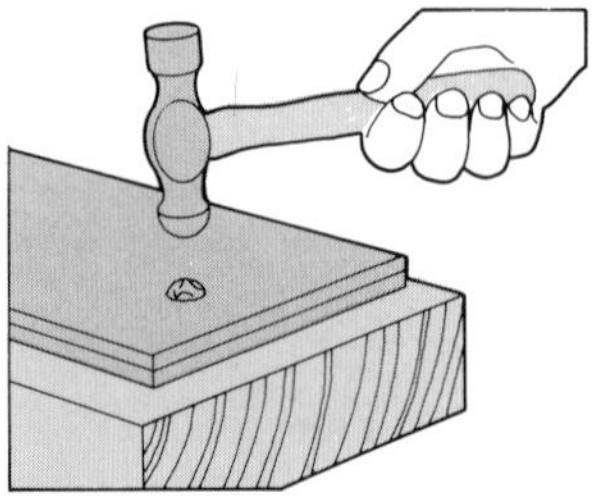

Shape the rivet with a ball-pein hammer.

## Soldering metal

This term refers to the joining of metal components using a liquid metal alloy (solder) which has a lower melting point than the pieces to be joined. Solders are composed mainly of lead and tin. They are suitable for joining brass, copper, steel and tinplate but, because they are relatively weak, the joints should have as large a surface area as possible.

Use a soldering iron to melt the solder; it must be large enough to heat the work sufficiently for the solder to flow. Most are electrically heated and they range in size from 15-watt models intended for electrical work up to 240 watts. Some gas-heated irons are also available, as well as ones for use with propane torches.

To keep the metal oxide-free while soldering, you must apply a flux to both surfaces beforehand. There are two types of flux: active and passive. Active flux, which is available as a liquid or paste, cleans the surface and dissolves the oxide. It should be washed from the surface after soldering, or it may corrode the metal. Passive flux excludes the oxygen and should be used on delicate work, such as electrical connections, where the joint cannot be washed after soldering. It is available as a resin core in the center of a wire solder, or separately in liquid or paste form. Always clean the joint before adding the flux coating and, if you are using a passive flux, take special care: rub the surface with emery cloth and avoid touching it with your fingers afterward.

After applying the flux it is necessary to coat the tip of the soldering iron and both meeting surfaces with a thin application of solder before assembling the joint. This process is known as "tinning."

When the two surfaces are joined, reheat the solder with the iron, making sure that a continuous bead of solder appears along the seam. If the iron cannot produce sufficient heat, the solder will not melt and will look crystalline. Play the flame of a propane torch over the joint to melt the solder. If the solder collects in beads, the work is probably dirty.

Leave the work clamped while the joint cools, then scrub it under running water to remove any remaining active flux.

## Soldering a joint

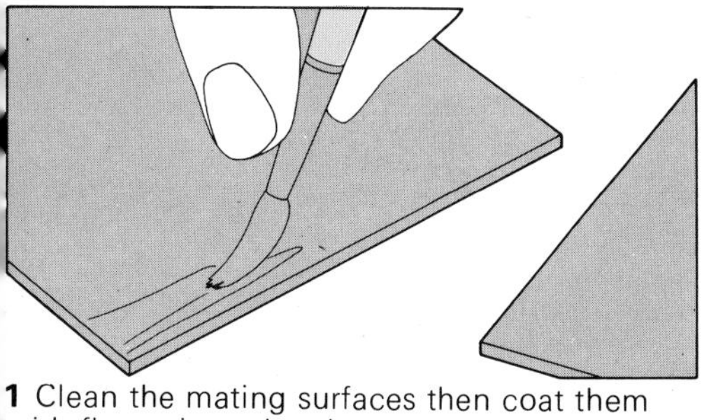

**1** Clean the mating surfaces then coat them with flux using a brush or a metal rod.

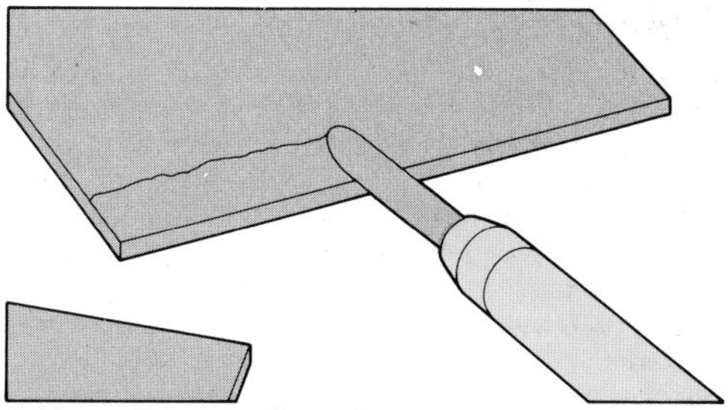

**2** Next, "tin" both surfaces. Dip the hot soldering iron in flux and apply solder to the tip. Spread an even coating of solder over the surfaces with the soldering iron, adding more solder to the tip, if necessary. Assemble the joint and clamp it together.

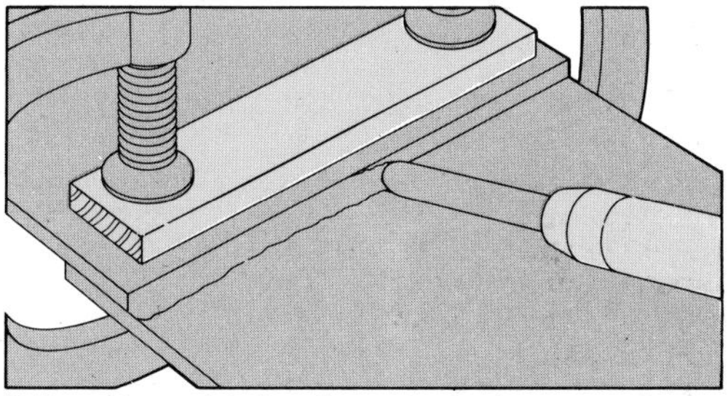

**3** Run the soldering iron along the seam, or down the center of the overlap, to remelt the solder. Leave the joint to set under pressure.

## Soldering a wire landing gear

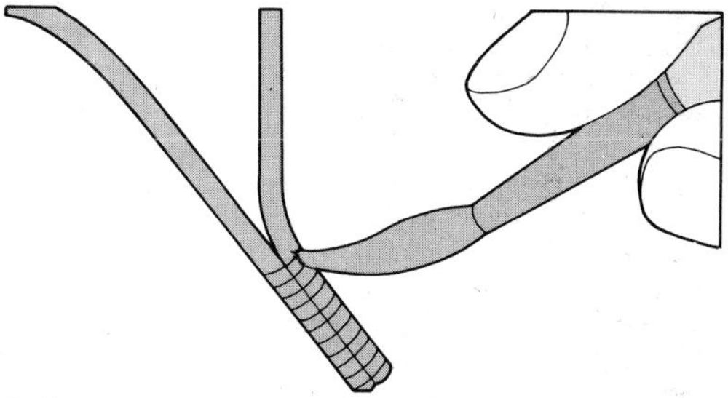

**1** Clean the undercarriage wire and a length of electrical wire with emery cloth. Bind the joint with the wire. Apply active flux.

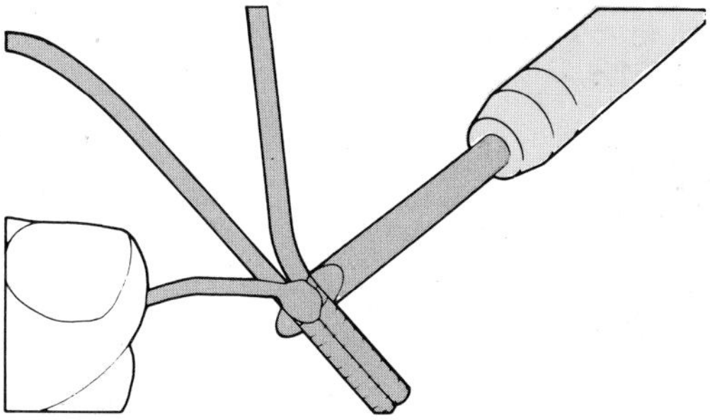

**2** Press the hot iron on one side of the joint and apply solder to the other. Only use enough solder to join the components. Wash the joint with hot water.

## Hard soldering and brazing

These processes are similar to soldering, except that higher-melting-point alloys are used and, therefore, a propane torch is needed to apply the heat. Stronger joints are possible than with ordinary solder. The actual techniques are the same but brazing involves using brass as a joining medium, whereas soldering alloys are used in hard soldering. There is a range of alloys giving a choice of melting points. Silver solder, for example, may have up to 60% silver and melts at around 600°C. The fluxes for these alloys are usually the active type. Always use the recommended flux and make sure that the alloy has a lower melting point than the work or you will damage your model.

Begin by cleaning the joint thoroughly, then mix the flux to a paste with water and apply it to the joint. Assemble the joint. It should be as close-fitting as possible and clamped or wired together, if necessary. Next, it is advisable, and with some jobs essential, to enclose the work with fire bricks to reduce heat loss. Heat the job with a propane torch. When the flux has melted and flowed, touch the joint with the brazing or soldering material. The tip should melt so that metal flows into the joint. Remove the heat and, when the solder has set, quench the work in cold water. Finally, scrub the surface to remove the flux.

An alternative method is to cut small pieces of solder and lay them on the joint before heating the work. Dip the work in water and scrub as before.

## Casting metal

Metal castings of small-scale figures or sailboat keel weights are well within the scope of the average modelmaker. You can reproduce a wood or clay object in metal or a number of metal figures. Simple shapes can be cast using relatively cheap molds made from plaster or wood. More complicated moldings, which incorporate fine detail, are better cast in silicone rubber.

### Making a silicone rubber mold

The first stage is to make a box from plywood or even children's plastic linking bricks, which is open top and bottom. Press a ½-inch-thick (12-mm) slab of modeling clay into the bottom and press the object you wish to reproduce – the pattern – into the clay. Carefully work the clay up to the edge of the pattern, making sure that exactly one half of each part of the pattern will be included in each half of the mold. To form a tapered opening in the mold through which the metal can be poured, press a cut-down golf tee or a piece of clay into the base of the pattern. To make sure the molten metal fills the mold, run narrow rolls of clay, known as "runners," from the base of the pattern to its outer extremities. Make indents in opposite corners of the box with the point of a pen top or a similar tool to guarantee correct alignment of the finished molds.

The next stage is to make the mold. Make up some release agent from 5% petroleum jelly mixed with 95% turpentine or mineral spirits. Stand the container in hot water and stir until the jelly dissolves. (The mixture can be stored in a screw-top jar, if you wish, but redissolve the jelly before you use it.) Paint the release agent evenly over the modeling clay, the pattern and the inside of the box. Mix a cold-curing silicone rubber according to the manufacturer's instructions. Brush a layer over the mold to prevent air bubbles from being trapped, then slowly pour the rubber into one corner of the mold, letting it fill to a depth of ½ to ¾ inch (12 to 20 mm) approximately.

When the rubber has set, turn the box over and peel away the modeling clay. Take the rubber mold and pattern out of the box and clean them. Put them back in the box. Rebuild the opening and runners as before then apply release agent and rubber to make the other half of the mold. When set, separate the two halves and clean them thoroughly with a nailbrush and remove any flash with a knife.

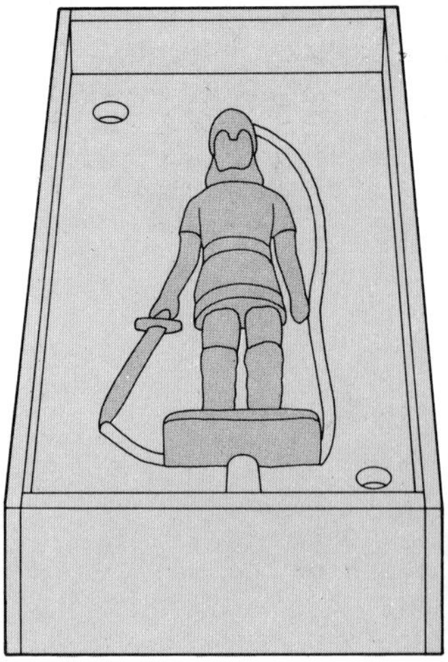
Stage 1

Stage 2

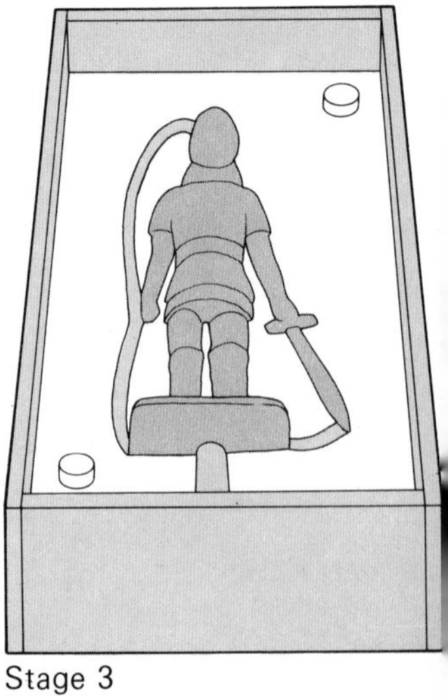
Stage 3

### Casting in the rubber mold

Prepare the mold by dusting the inside with talcum powder. Use a cotton ball to make sure the deeper crevices are coated. Then, clap both halves together to remove the excess. Set the mold up in a bench vise between pieces of hardboard. Make sure there are no gaps and use additional "C" clamps, if necessary; molten metal will flow out of the smallest gap.

Cut the metal casting alloy into small pieces and put the pieces in a ladle, preferably one with a lip. Heat the alloy over a gas stove. When the metal turns to liquid, pour it into the mold. Leave it to cool for one or two minutes, then take out the casting. After three castings, leave the mold to cool before using it again.

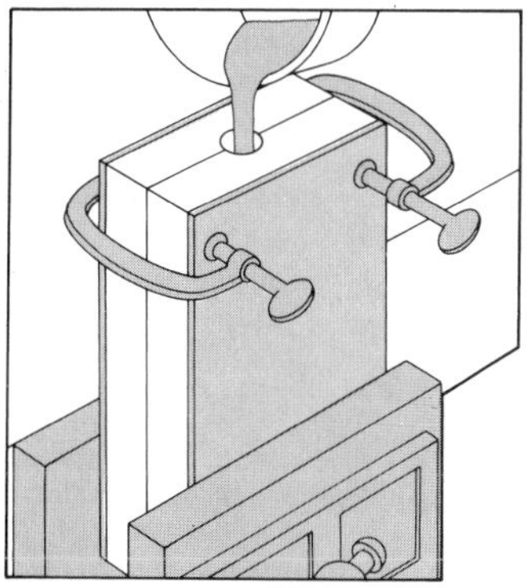

**Using a rubber mold**
Carefully pour the hot metal into the mold; tap the sides to encourage the metal to flow into the corners.

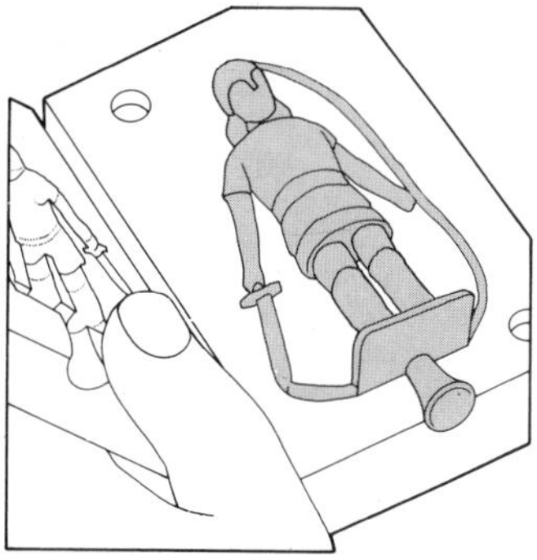

Take the mold apart and lift the casting out with pliers, flexing the rubber to help release it. Cut off the metal runners as close to the model as possible with a hacksaw.

### Casting in plaster molds

Large, simple objects, such as lead keel weights for sailboats, or airplane nose weights, are cheaper to cast in plaster molds. Follow the procedure for making a silicone rubber mold, opposite, to make a plaster mold from a pattern. As well as an opening for the hot metal, include a second hole, called a "riser," at the highest point of the casting to allow air to escape so that the metal fills the cavity.

It is essential to dry the plaster mold thoroughly before using it; otherwise, the remaining water may turn to steam when the hot metal is poured in and form "blow holes" in the finished casting. It may also blow molten metal out through the holes in the mold, possibly shattering the mold. To reduce the risk of this happening, mix 50% dry sand with the powdered plaster, and add a small amount of gelatin to the water before mixing the plaster to delay the setting time – this will result in a stronger mold. Dry the mold in the oven at a temperature of 300°F (140°C) for about 2 hours. The mold can be considered dry enough when it can be placed on a cold surface and no moisture condenses. Be certain to let the mold cool to room temperature before using it. This will not take long.

Set up the mold in a "C" clamp between two pieces of wood. No release agent is necessary when using a plaster mold to cast lead. Cut up scrap lead or lead pellets and put them into an old iron saucepan, preferably one with a pouring lip. Heat the lead to approximately 650°F (400°C). (Always remember to wear protective gloves when handling hot casting equipment.) Make sure that it is the correct pouring temperature by watching the color of the oxide forming on the surface of the molten metal. At 650°F (400°C), lead does not oxidize fast, and if you skim the surface with an old spoon, it will remain uncolored for some time. If the metal is too hot, the surface rapidly turns colors ranging from pale green to red and purple. Carefully pour the metal into the opening in the mold and watch for its appearance in the riser hole which indicates that the mold is full; stop pouring.

Open the mold a few seconds after the riser has solidified to avoid contraction of the metal casting between the openings which would grip the mold. Use pliers to handle the casting – it will still be hot. Any small holes can be filled with an epoxy filler.

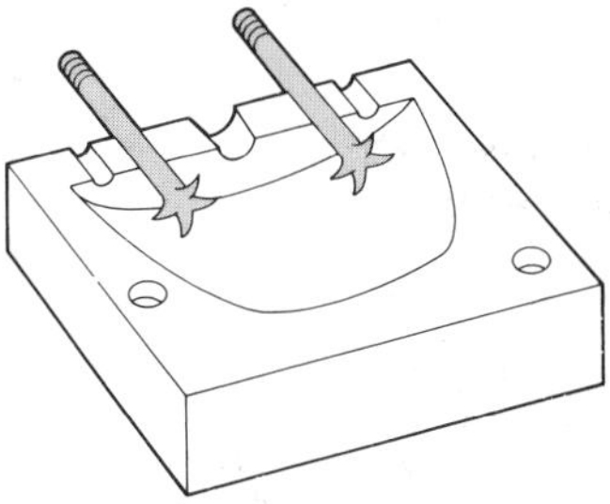

**Casting bolts in a keel weight** Cut two indents in each half of the mold to take the bolts. Position them in the mold and pour in the metal.

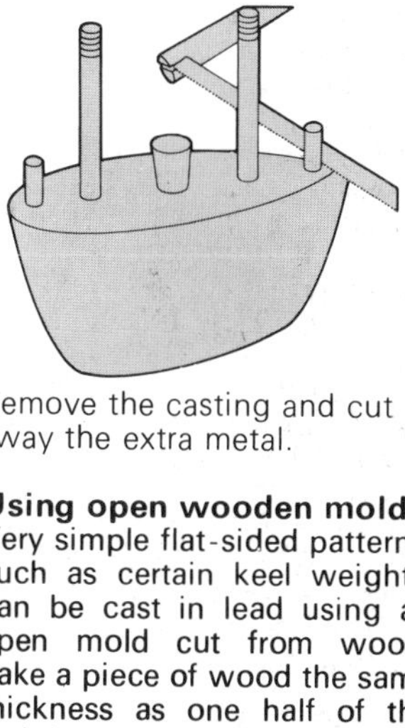

Remove the casting and cut away the extra metal.

### Using open wooden molds

Very simple flat-sided patterns, such as certain keel weights, can be cast in lead using an open mold cut from wood. Take a piece of wood the same thickness as one half of the weight and cut out the shape of the component twice. Screw the mold to a baseboard. Pour molten lead into the hollows and allow it to cool. There will be a certain amount of charring of the wood which should not affect the castings. To remove the castings, tap the mold on the bench to tip them out or, if necessary, dismantle the mold so that they can be pushed out easily from one side.

## Filing metal

Use a flat file to file an edge square and a half-round file for concave curves. Make sure that the file teeth are not clogged with metal before you start. If necessary, clean the file with a wire brush. Rub chalk into the file to prevent metal becoming packed into the teeth.

To remove "burrs" – the splinters which occur on the edge of a piece of metal after cutting with a hacksaw – place the metal on a workbench overhanging the edge. Hold the file at an angle, and push it along the edge. For safety always remove burrs immediately after sawing metal.

To file a surface flat and square, clamp the work in a vise set low in the jaws to prevent vibration. Hold the handle of the file in one hand and steady the point with the other hand. Working across the metal, apply pressure on the forward stroke of the file and ease off on the return. If the face of the file does not cover the area being filed, it is necessary to file with a combined forward and sideways movement, periodically reversing the direction of the stroke. This action is more likely to cover the whole area of the work evenly. Next, draw-file the metal to remove any marks: hold a smooth file across the work with both hands and draw the file toward you, maintaining an even pressure. Finish the surface with emery cloth wrapped around a file.

When filing round stock, clamp the work in a vise, and rock the file throughout the forward stroke to keep the face of the file in contact with the surface. Keep the pressure even to avoid producing flat areas.

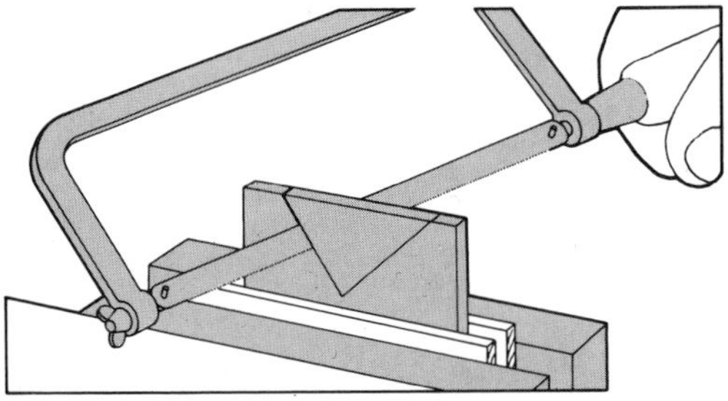

**Making a concave curve in metal** Remove as much waste as possible with a hacksaw.

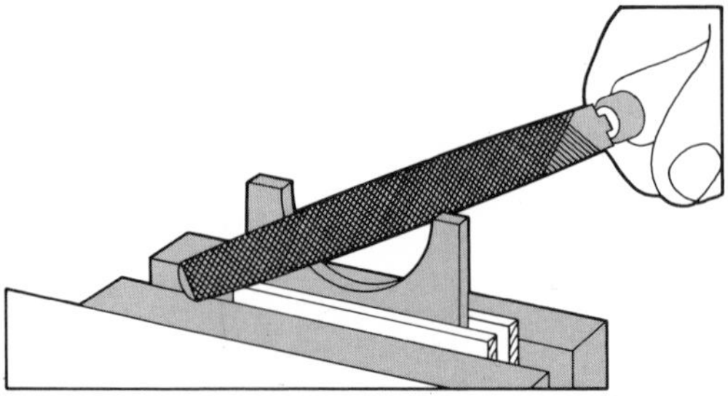

File the curve roughly to shape with a coarse file, then complete the curve with a smooth file. Finish the edge by draw-filing with emery cloth or paper wrapped around a file.

### Cleaning up metal figures

Even the best metal kits or figures will require a certain amount of cleaning up to remove the seam line or "flash" produced along the dividing line of the mold. The line is sometimes quite marked but on a well made piece it may only be noticeable when turned into the light. It will, however, be obvious through a coat of paint if it is not removed.

White-metal castings are soft enough to be scraped with a sharp knife but where the surface is highly contoured use needle files. Follow the line, carefully tracing its path across textures such as hair or fur, and watch out for an unexpected change in direction. Check against the light to make sure that there are no file marks showing. If there are, carefully remove them with fine emery paper wrapped around a file to complete the job.

## Finishing metal

Rotary wire brushes are used to clean up metal or to roughen it before gluing or soldering. A wide range of sizes is available which will fit into a bench-mounted drill for larger work or into a miniature power tool for cleanir.g up small components. A steel brush can be used on hard metal, but use a brass brush on softer metal, such as brass or aluminum which is easily scratched by a steel brush.

Always wear protective goggles whenever you are working with a rotary wire brush. Fix the power tool in a bench stand so that the wire brush revolves toward you and down onto the work. Hold the work against the brush slightly below center. Be sure to grip it firmly to prevent snatching and do not position any sharp edges against the wheel's direction of rotation.

Remove scratch marks made by a wire brush or file by using successive grades of abrasive paper or cloth.

Metal can be polished quickly using a calico buff or mop mounted in a power tool. Once again, large versions are installed in a bench-mounted drill, while miniature buffing wheels fit into a modeler's power tool. Use the buff as described for using a wire brush. Although the wheel is soft, too much pressure will round edges and can even make a hole in thin metal. Finally, polish the component by hand with a soft cloth and liquid metal polish.

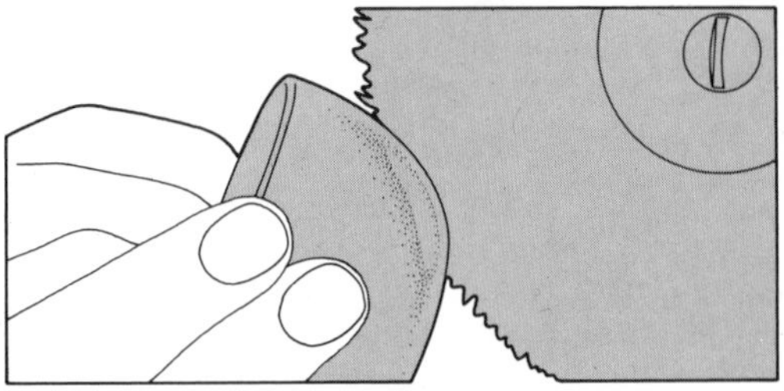

**Buffing a metal nose cowl** Run the tool at high speed and apply a polishing compound to the wheel. With the wheel revolving down onto the work, hold the cowl against it.

# Painting and finishing

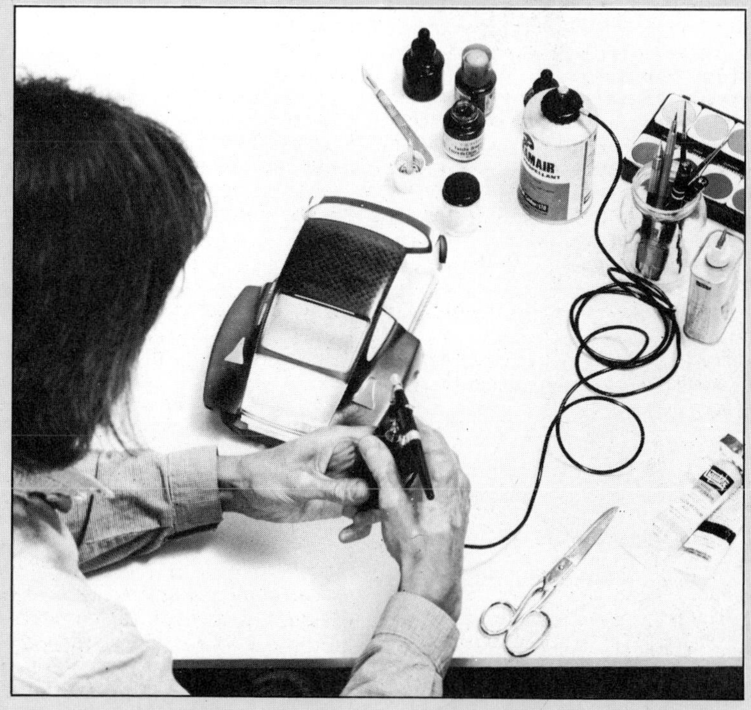

# Using color

Painting is crucial to the success of your model and there are several factors which affect the appearance of color that you should bear in mind.

No object appears as one color overall and light plays a major part in this illusion. It emphasizes the contours of an object by throwing some parts into shadow while highlighting others. Colors viewed in bright sunlight are richer than those in shadow. An object also reflects other colors in the environment and to make your model look natural, you must reproduce these effects.

Color is changed by the effect of distance: near subjects are brighter than those further away. Atmosphere diffuses color, neutralizing it so that it appears paler and grayer. To make your model look the same close up as the full-size original seen at a distance, add white or pale gray to its basic shade. Finish, too, is modified by the effect of distance. Smooth surfaces are glossy because light is reflected into the eyes of the viewer; matt surfaces are rough and scatter light in all directions. Atmosphere also scatters light so that a gloss finish may appear semigloss or even matt as the distance from the observer increases. To scale down the finish of a model, use matt paint or varnishes to produce the required sheen, or add a flatting agent to the paint to vary the finish.

Color is also affected by age and wear. Blue denim clothes, for instance, bleach to a lighter color after washing; tanks rust when exposed to the elements. To make your models true to life, you must paint them accordingly. See pages 90 to 99 for weathering vehicles.

Although there are no formulas for achieving a realistically painted model, there is one rule of thumb: if it looks right, it is right. Bear in mind, too, that you must always begin with a well prepared surface.

# Paintbrushes

Paintbrushes are an essential part of modelmaking equipment and different types and grades are required for specific tasks, from finely detailed work to the application of glue. Whatever the purpose, always buy the best quality available. A good brush will last a lot longer than a cheap one. A poor brush will not keep a point and will shed hairs.

A good quality sable brush is the best brush for general-purpose painting. It has the right amount of spring and flexibility and is suitable for use with oil- and water-base paints. Good quality brushes are also made in nylon or mixed sable and hair. Stiff hog-bristle brushes are required for some weathering and highlighting effects, and even small household paintbrushes are useful for large areas. As your best quality brushes become worn, use them for rougher work.

Your choice of shape and size of brush is a matter of personal preference. Detailed work is usually carried out with a 00 or 01 brush, but a large brush will point equally well if you find it more convenient. It is best to apply a flat coat with a large brush. Some people prefer a chisel-edged brush for flat areas; however, a round brush will form a wedge shape and performs well in any direction.

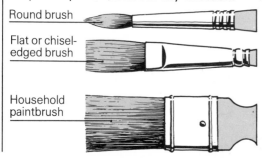

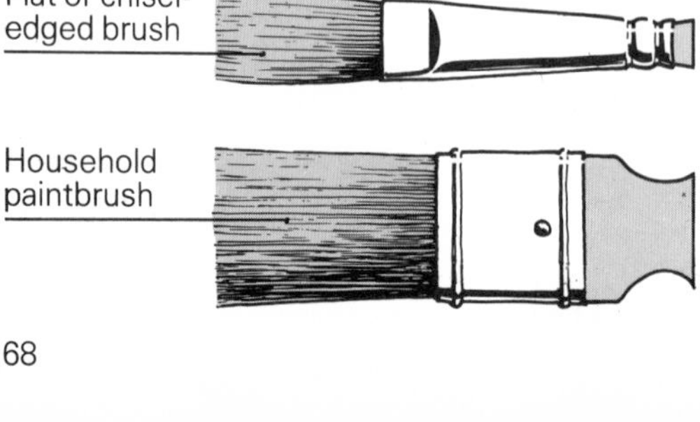


## Cleaning and storing brushes

Rinse brushes between applications of paint in a jar or saucer of thinner, carefully blotting the bristles on a soft rag before picking up more paint. At the end of a painting session, each brush should be very carefully rinsed in a generous amount of thinner to remove all traces of paint. Then, wash the brush in warm water containing liquid detergent, flexing the bristles gently between your fingers. Dry it on a rag before drawing it between your lips to repoint it.

Protect best quality brushes in a transparent plastic tube when not in use. Carefully guide the brush into the tube steadying the ferrule on your finger.

**Storing brushes**
Protect the ends in a plastic tube; store on their handles in a jar, or flat in a box.

## Palettes

A palette is a surface on which to mix and blend colors. A traditional artist's palette is a thin, oval or rectangular board. Although several types of palette are commercially available, it is cheaper to improvise with materials at home. If you are working with thick paints such as oil paints, choose a thin, flat board with a smooth, non-absorbent surface. A piece of plastic-laminated wood or a glazed tile is ideal. If you are working with thin paints use small foil or ceramic bowls or saucers.

# Spray-painting equipment

Applying paint to a model using a spray device has several advantages: the paint can be applied finely and evenly on the most detailed model; it can be done quickly once the basic preparation is carried out; the paint dries in a short time and there is no danger of touching the painted surface as you work. There are three types of tools for spraying paint: aerosol cans, miniature spray guns and airbrushes (see next page). They vary in price and sophistication so first read the descriptions, then choose one to suit your needs.

## Aerosol cans

The simplest spray applicators are aerosol cans which are cans of paint under pressure. As a valve is pressed, paint is forced out as a fine spray. There is no control over the amount of paint or pressure. Because you cannot refill an aerosol can with your own paints, you are limited to the colors offered by the manufacturer.

Aerosol cans do not need cleaning. When you have finished painting, simply turn the can upside down and spray onto an old newspaper until no further paint emerges. This will clear any paint out of the nozzle. Sometimes a nozzle becomes clogged during use. If it does, remove it and leave it in a container of thinner to clear. As a precaution, keep spare nozzles from used cans.

Store aerosol cans away from a direct source of heat. When you dispose of empty aerosols, take care not to puncture the can and do not throw it onto a fire.

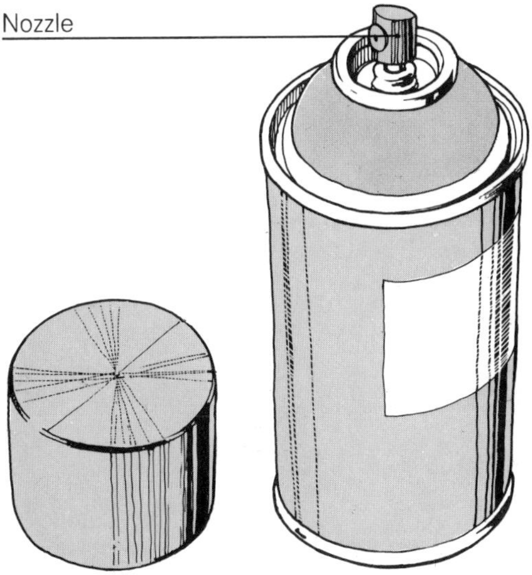


**Aerosol can**

## Miniature spray guns

A spray gun mixes paint and air externally. A stream of pressurized air from one nozzle passes over another which leads to the paint reservoir. This action draws up paint from the reservoir which is atomized into a very fine spray as it emerges from the nozzle. The spray pattern can be adjusted from about $\frac{3}{4}$ inch (20 mm) to 2 inches (50 mm) by turning the paint tip. The flow of air is controlled by pressing a button on the handle.

A spray gun is extremely cheap and easy for a beginner to operate. It can produce a wide range of effects when combined with various masking techniques (see pages 80 to 83). Although it is excellent for spraying flat coats of paint, it is not adjustable for fine line work or free-hand patterns. It can apply as good a finish as an airbrush, but unless the paint nozzle is adjusted accurately, a scatter of coarse drops will occur at the outer edges of the spray pattern.

### Cleaning spray guns

A spray gun should be cleaned immediately after use. Empty any remaining paint from the reservoir; wipe it clean with a rag or tissue, then fill it half-full with some clean paint thinner. Press the trigger to blow the thinner onto an old newspaper; the thinner will clean the passages as it is forced through. Finally, unscrew the paint nozzle and wipe any paint from the screw threads.

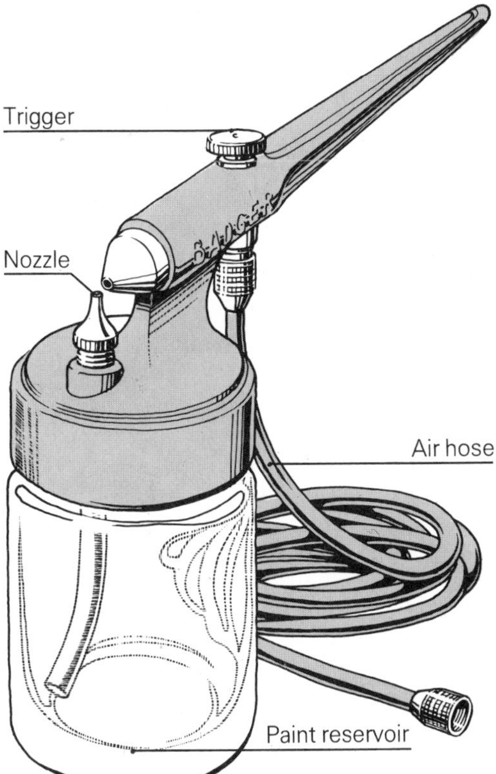


**Miniature spray gun**

# Airbrushes

An airbrush mixes paint and air internally. This means that, unlike the less sophisticated spray gun, it is capable of much finer atomization and creates very accurate patterns. A wide variety of effects is possible because you can make fine adjustments of both the air and paint supply. Normally airbrushes have interchangeable paint tips for different spray patterns. There are two types of airbrush, single action and double action.

## Single-action airbrushes

A single-action airbrush is the most popular kind. It has a button to release the flow of air and a separate control, usually in the form of a screw found below the paint tip or at the rear of the handle, to pre-set the spray pattern. It is relatively easy for a beginner to use as a constant volume of paint means he can concentrate on controlling the air supply. The paint supply can be adjusted with the free hand while spraying, but this takes considerable practice. With experience, a single-action airbrush is capable of extremely fine work. There is a wide range of these brushes available in price and quality.

## Double-action airbrushes

On a double-action airbrush, both the paint and air supply are controlled by one trigger mounted on top of the tool. You press down on the trigger to supply air, and slide it backward to release the paint. Because the double-action airbrush allows you to adjust paint and air with one finger, it is extremely versatile. A means of pre-setting the pattern width is also supplied. The brush costs more and requires more practice than a single-action airbrush, but the extra expense can be justified if you feel that its versatility is essential, and if you are prepared to practice sufficiently to exploit its greater potential.

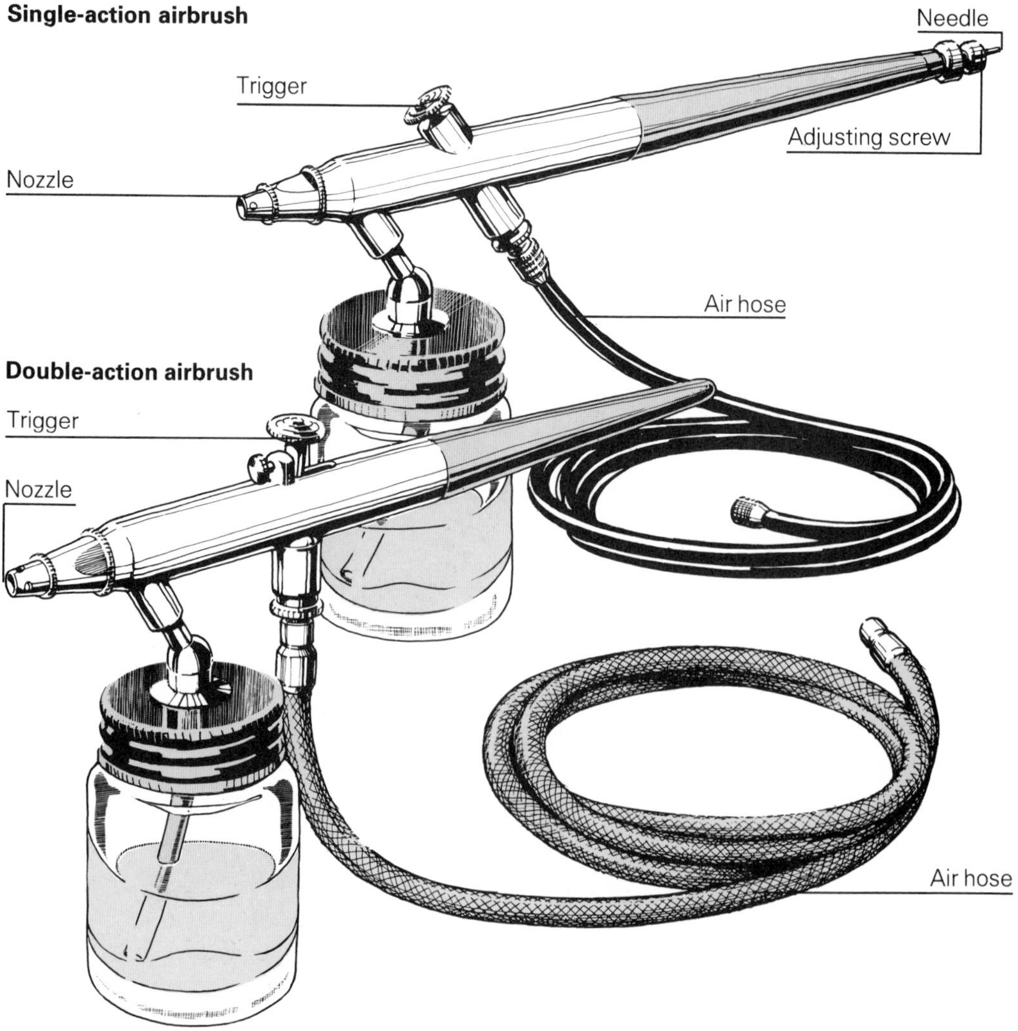

## Holding an airbrush

Control an airbrush like a pen or pencil, with your index finger held in a relaxed position on the trigger. Position your finger on the trigger differently for each type of brush (see below). Wrap the air hose around your wrist to make sure that it cannot accidentally pull the brush from your hand.

**Holding a single-action airbrush** Place the second joint of your index finger on the trigger, and pivot your fingertip for control.

**Holding a double-action airbrush** Place the first joint of your finger on the trigger so that you can press and pull back all at once.

**Using an airbrush clip** Hold your brush in a clip when you are not working to prevent it being damaged. Buy one or make one from copper pipe; glue it to a heavy tile or clamp it to your workbench.

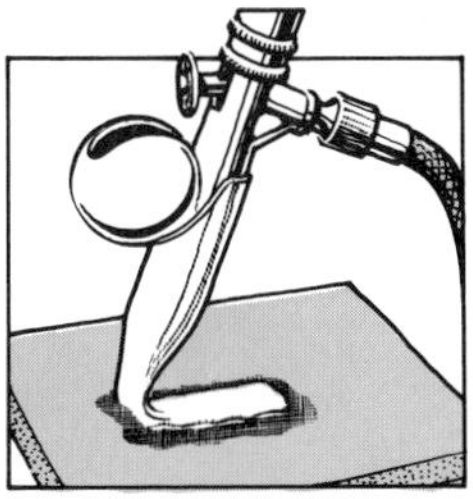

## Cleaning airbrushes

It is very important to clean an airbrush as soon as possible after use, as even the smallest amounts of dried paint can impair its performance. Wipe out the reservoir with a rag or tissue; half-fill with thinner. Blow the thinner through the brush until it contains no paint particles, then hold a rag over the paint tip so that air is forced down into the paint reservoir and bubbles back through it to clean the passages.

Repeat this procedure after each painting session to keep your airbrush in good working order. After it has been in use for some time, however, you should strip it down and soak the needle and head in thinner in a shallow bowl overnight. Do not stand the needle on its point in a jar.

**Repairing a bent tip** Hold the needle against a flat surface at the angle of the point; run your fingernail across the point while revolving the needle.

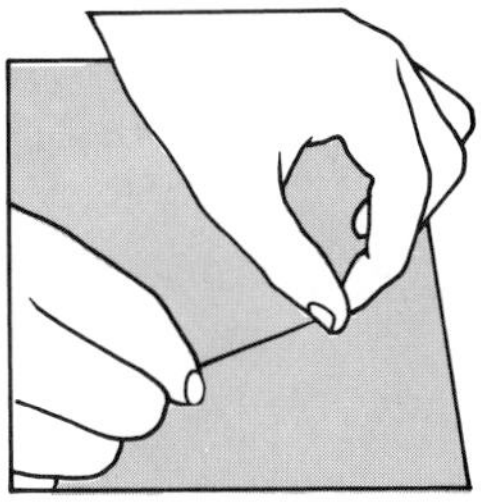

# Reservoirs for spray guns and airbrushes

Paint reservoirs hold the paint supply for spray guns and airbrushes. The different types include glass jars which plug into the brush from below, or fixed or interchangeable cups for small quantities of paint. Airbrushes can have any type of reservoir; spray guns are normally available with jars only. Being able to change reservoirs is a great advantage: once you have sprayed one color, you simply attach a reservoir containing thinner to clean out the brush, then replace it by another containing a new color. Colors can be stored in jar reservoirs with screw tops.

Fixed cup

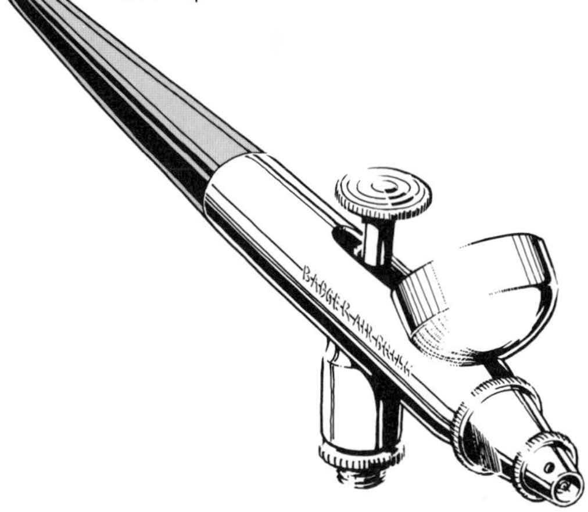

Glass jar with screw top

Interchangeable cup

# Air supply for spray guns and airbrushes

Both miniature spray guns and airbrushes require a supply of compressed gas. There are several different ways of providing it.

## Liquid propellant

Cans of liquid gas propellant are the most popular form of air supply. They are highly portable, safe as long as they are not punctured or subjected to direct heat, and economical for intermittent use. (Compressors, however, are cheaper if you make a lot of models.) Propellants are also used to clean the spray gun or airbrush, so always keep a spare can on hand.

Contrary to popular belief, a new can of liquid propellant does not deliver gas at a higher pressure than a half-used can. If a can is used intermittently, the gas pressure will recover as long as there is some liquid gas remaining. A noticeable pressure drop does take place, however, when the valve is held open for a long time. It is unlikely to happen but if you can foresee a prolonged spraying session of 20 minutes duration, stand the can in a bowl of lukewarm water while you work; this will slow down the fall in pressure. If the pressure drops in the middle of a job, gently shake the can in your free hand to warm it.

## Propellant regulator

A regulator can be attached to the top of a propellant can in order to adjust the gas flow. It not only economizes on the propellant, but is needed for certain techniques that require fine adjustment. A full gloss finish needs a medium pressure flow as full-can pressure tends to dry out the solvents in the paint. For a grainy effect, set the pressure at a minimum so that the paint is not atomized well.

The screw thread on the top of cans is universal so that a regulator will fit any brand of propellant. With some airbrushes, regulators are supplied as standard equipment.

Propellant regulator

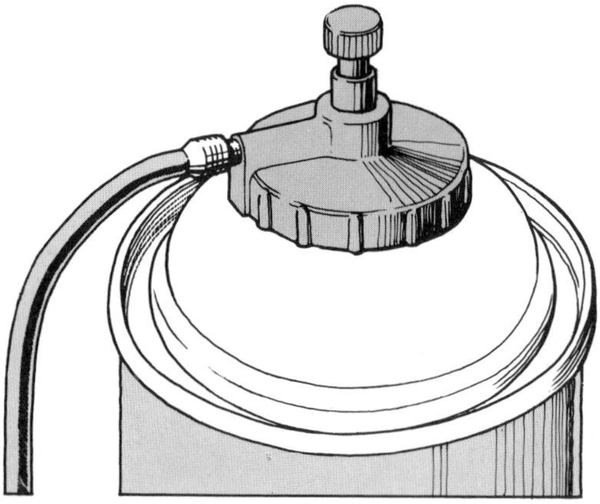

## Compressors

In the long term, a compressor is the most efficient means of supplying air to an airbrush. The initial cost is high but there is no further expense involved and the supply of air is limitless. There are many types but the most suitable for modelmakers is an electric-powered, oil-free diaphragm compressor which delivers air at 25 to 30 psi (1.5 to 2 bars). It is small and lightweight and usually quiet when running.

A foot-operated switch is a necessary accessory: it provides a convenient way of operating the machine and prevents it from running continuously, prolonging its life.

## Moisture trap

A problem in a humid atmosphere is that water vapor present in air condenses in the hose and is sprayed out as drops with the paint. A moisture trap can be used to filter out the moisture in the air. Install an in-line filter or a wall-mounted model with some hose between it and the compressor. Do not put a filter directly on a compressor as heated air containing water vapor can pass through it to condense afterward.

## Air regulator

Air regulators are used in conjunction with a moisture filter and, like a propellant regulator, they allow you to adjust the air pressure.

## Car tire adaptor

A car tire adaptor allows you to use pressurized air from a car tire – a cheap, supplementary form of compressed air. Although not very convenient, it is useful for completing a model or cleaning an airbrush when stores are closed. Simply screw a propellant regulator onto an adaptor attached to a tire valve. The tire must be in reasonable condition and on the wheel rim so that it can be safely pressurized to 40 psi (2.5 bars). Pressure decreases as the air is used and the regulator must be adjusted to compensate.

Car tire adaptor

## Compressor and accessories

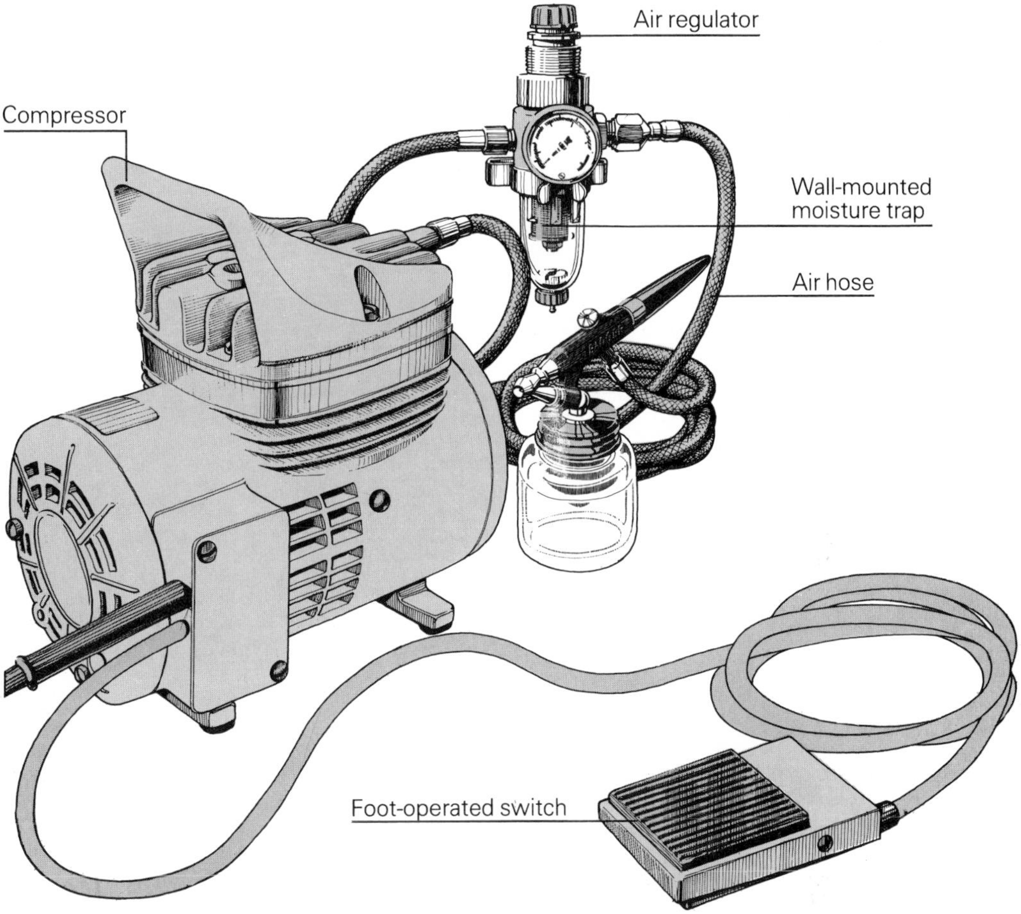


## Foot-operated compressor

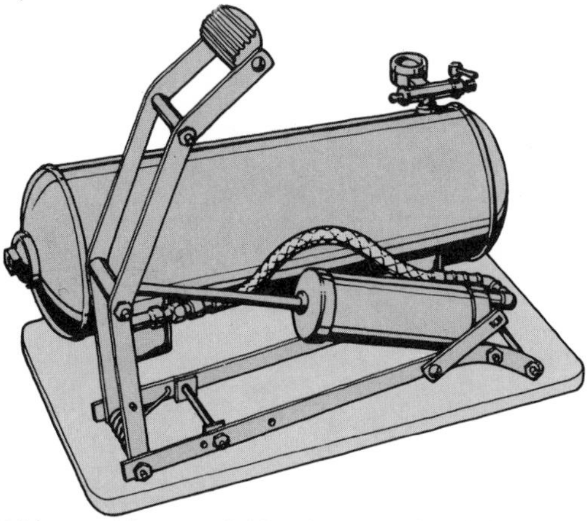

This machine, useful for the occasional airbrusher, works on the same principle as the car tire adaptor. Pump it up, then use the brush until the pressure drops. Pump again to replenish the supply of compressed air.

## Air hoses

Air hoses connect the airbrush to the air supply. They come in various lengths and are made in lightweight plastic or heavy-duty rubber covered with cotton braid. Plastic hoses, some of which are not recommended for use with a compressor, are very flexible and can be conveniently wound around the wrist during use. Some people find the braided hose too rigid and, because it is heavier, it may accidentally pull over the propellant can while you work.

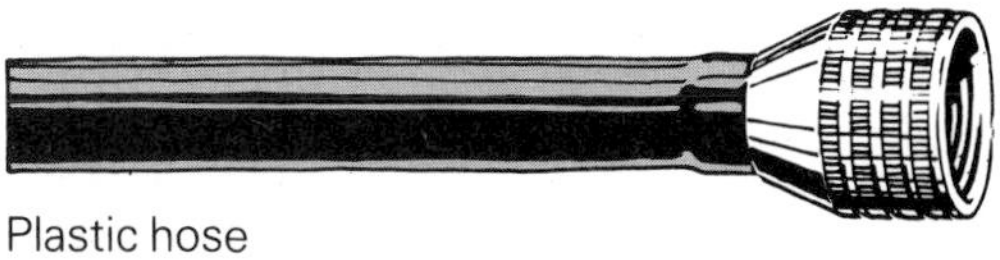

Plastic hose

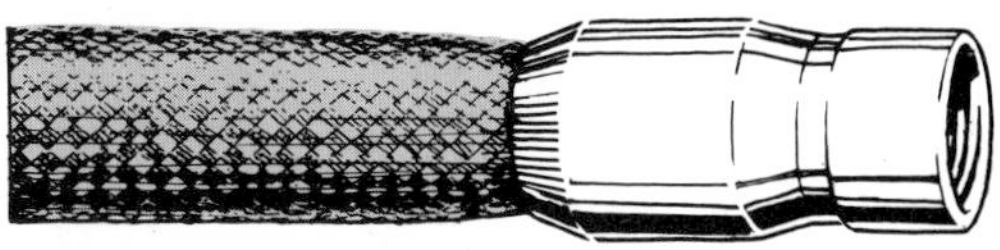

Rubber hose

# Types of paint

Paints are classified according to the medium which binds together the pigment or color; for each type of paint there are specific solvents and thinners. Oil paint, for example, belongs to the group of oil-base paints because the color is suspended in linseed oil; it is dissolved and thinned by liquids such as turpentine. The chart below gives you the different types of paint and their characteristics. Some of the paints are intended for canvas, some for household use, others for modelmaking and some for vehicles, but all can be used for modelmaking depending on the material you are painting and the effect you wish to create.

A varnish is a transparent liquid applied as the last layer to protect the paintwork below or to provide a luster or shine to the surface. Most of the paint groups include varnishes. Shellac is a resin-base varnish.

| Water-base paints | Characteristics |
|---|---|
| **Watercolor** | Available in blocks or tubes; blocks give very weak wash only. Applied in transparent washes; picks up color from previous coats; matt finish. Use on absorbent surface.<br>Thinner and solvent: water. |
| **Poster color*** | Available as paste, powder or blocks. Applied in opaque coats; picks up color from previous coats; matt finish.<br>Thinner and solvent: water. |
| **Tempera*** | Available as paste, liquid, powder or blocks. Picks up color from previous coats; matt finish.<br>Thinner and solvent: water. |
| **Gouache*** | Available in tubes. Applied in opaque coats or transparent washes; picks up color from previous coats; matt finish. Less durable than watercolor, oil or acrylic.<br>Thinner and solvent: water. |
| **Ink** | Available as liquid. Transparent; picks up color from previous coats; matt finish.<br>Thinner and solvent: water. |
| **Water-resistant ink** | Available as liquid. Transparent; semigloss finish. Resists dissolving in water when set.<br>Thinner: water.<br>Solvent: ethyl alcohol, washing soda and water, or soap and water. |
| **Acrylic** | Available in tubes. A water-base resin. Slight gloss to matt finish.<br>Thinner: water.<br>Solvent: ethyl alcohol; not water soluble. |
| **Latex** | Available in liquid or gel. Opaque color; matt finish.<br>Thinner: water.<br>Solvent: ethyl alcohol; not water soluble. |

*PVA medium can be added to increase water resistance.

| Oil- and resin-base paints | Characteristics |
|---|---|
| **Oil** | Available in tubes. Semigloss finish. Thinner: linseed oil, turpentine or oil copal medium; the latter speeds drying time. Solvent: paint stripper*. |
| **Enamel** | Available as gel or liquid in cans and in aerosol form. Gloss or matt finish. Thinner: turpentine. Solvent: paint stripper*. |
| **Polyurethane** | Available in cans; the best quality, with a high resin content, comes in two parts and requires mixing. Fuel proof; tough finish. Do not apply over oil-base paint. Thinner: use thinner recommended on label. Solvent: paint stripper*. |
| **Epoxy** | Available in cans; comes in two parts, the paint and the hardener, and requires mixing. Apply over cellulose base or own filler only. Quick-drying, therefore, best sprayed. Fuel proof; tough finish. Thinner: use thinner recommended on label. Solvent: paint stripper*. |
| *When base is plastic, use stripper safe for plastics. | |

| Cellulose-base paints | Characteristics |
|---|---|
| **Cellulose** | Available as liquid and in aerosol cans. Quick drying; gloss and matt finish. Attacks some plastics, particularly polystyrene. Thinner: cellulose thinner. Solvent: acetone or amylacetate. |
| **PVC** | Available as liquid. Gloss finish. Flexible; does not crack easily. Thinner: cellulose thinner. Solvent: acetone or amylacetate. |

| Wood stains | Characteristics |
|---|---|
| **Water-base** | Available as powder or liquid. Picks up color from previous coats; matt finish. Thinner and solvent: water. |
| **Spirit-base** | Available as liquid. Matt finish. Thinner: solvent naphtha. Solvent: solvent naphtha or turpentine. |

# Preparing and priming

All materials need some preparation before painting so as to create a smooth, clean surface; some need priming to make the paint adhere.

## Plastic

To prepare a plastic model, fill and sand it to produce a smooth surface, then dust it with a soft paintbrush, working systematically from top to bottom. A gentle flow of air from an airbrush while dusting helps to remove any loose particles. Next, wash the model in lukewarm water containing a small amount of liquid detergent, scrubbing it gently with an old, soft brush; blot dry with clean tissues. Do not touch the surface once it has been washed. Either hold the model with a tissue or wear soft cotton gloves.

Polystyrene, the most common plastic for models, does not need a primer. Polyethylene, the soft, greasy plastic, must always be coated with diluted white glue or it will reject paint. Apply two thin coats so as not to obscure detail with thick glue.

## Metal

Once you have neutralized any flux used for soldering, wash the metal model in warm water containing a little liquid detergent. Scrub fine detail with an old toothbrush. Rinse and blot dry.

Prime metal models to prevent oxidation. Non-ferrous metals are best treated with a chromate primer. Cellulose acetate or polyurethane varnish are also suitable for white metal models. Treat steel and tinplate with a general metal primer.

## Wood

Wood, including balsa, must be sanded and sealed before painting. After sanding, dust the surface as described for plastic, then apply a wood primer to prevent the paint soaking in. When the primer has set, sand to provide a surface for the undercoat.

## Cardboard

Cardboard models should be sealed with a coat of varnish. The varnish will raise the surface of the cardboard which should then be sanded. If necessary, spray a second coat of primer to make a smooth surface for painting.

## Fiberglass

Fiberglass should be cleaned and primed. Wipe the surface with a rag soaked in thinner then apply a primer sealer to counteract the porousness of any filler and provide a good base for undercoating.

## Polystyrene foam

Polystyrene foam should be coated with a primer to protect it from thinners and paints which destroy the material. This is particularly important for a foam airplane to prevent it being damaged by spilled fuel. Lightly sand the surface after priming, taking care not to penetrate it. For aircraft, use one of the specially formulated lightweight primers available in cans or aerosols.

# Undercoating

An undercoat serves several purposes. It provides a surface for the following layers and is applied to prevent the base color of the model from showing. Choose a color related to the top coat. Where several colors are involved, use a neutral gray or white coat. For metallic paints, use white for silver or steel, and yellow for gold, brass or bronze. Normally the undercoat is the same type of paint as the top coat.

The first undercoat will show up any blemishes on the surface of the model. Fill or rub them down then add the top coat or a second undercoat.

Undercoats are also used to build up layers of paint to produce a high gloss finish on a yacht hull, for example. Lightly sand each undercoat layer before adding the final gloss top coat.

# Painting by hand

Always paint in a clean, dust-free environment to protect the model. Before you begin, clear your worktable, wipe it and lay down newspapers.

It is essential to plan ahead to avoid touching a painted surface. Decide on the order in which you will paint the model and make jigs to hold the various parts. For small items, make jigs from toothpicks; for large items, use stiff wire. Some people like to paint small pieces while still on the sprue; however, it is impossible to paint the patches where they join the sprue and you may ruin the paintwork if you have to modify the parts later.

**Jigs for small parts** Glue a toothpick or piece of trimmed sprue to the part; use a pin for small wheels. Hold jig in modelling clay. Some items can be held directly in the clay.

**Jigs for large parts** Make a jig from stiff wire; the spring of the wire holds the jig in place.

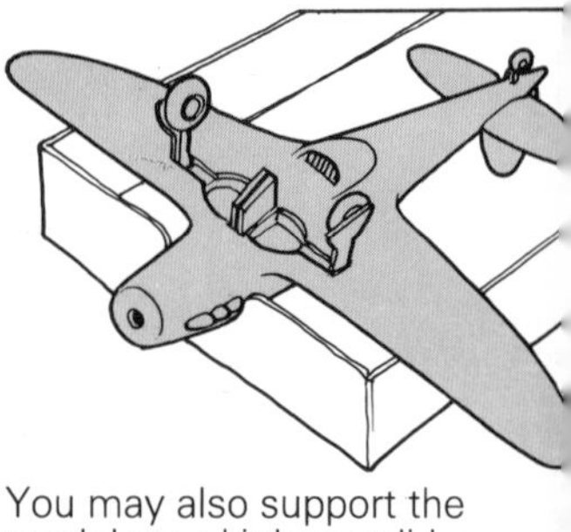

You may also support the model on a kit box or lid.

## Mixing and thinning paints

Sometimes you will want to use paint straight from its tube or can; other times you will want to thin it, either to lessen the intensity of color or to make it flow more smoothly over the surface of the model. A very diluted paint is called a wash.

Oil paint is the most popular paint in tubes. Squeeze pea-size amounts of the required colors around the edge of your palette, mixing them in the center, little by little. To thin the paint slightly, mix the pigment with linseed oil; for a wash, use turpentine. The amount of thinner picked up on your brush is enough for most situations, but to make a wash to cover a large area, squirt thinner from a dropper into a small bowl and add paint to produce the required intensity.

Use very small amounts of oil paint at one time: it will remain fresh on the palette for several days. If a skin forms on the surface, puncture it to reach the paint underneath. When it is no longer usable, scrape the palette clean with a flat-bladed knife.

Watercolors which come in tubes are mixed like oil paint but use water to thin the pigment. They are usually applied as transparent washes.

Enamel paints come in cans. Always stir them before use or the color and covering power will be diminished and matt paint will dry with glossy streaks. Do not mix colors in a can but deposit a little of each color around your palette, then mix them with a brush in the middle. Mix metallic paints on a separate palette.

Enamel paint is too thick to flow well. Mix a batch to a thinner consistency or mix it on your palette with a little turpentine from a brush.

Replace the lid on a can of enamel paint as soon as possible, wiping the rim beforehand to guarantee an airtight seal. If a skin forms on the paint, lift it off with a stirring stick and discard; filter the rest before using it.

## Applying a flat coat

Two coats of thinned paint are needed to achieve a flat finish. Load the brush so that only about half of its head is immersed in the paint and touch off any excess onto the edge of your palette. Apply the paint as shown below, working systematically and filling in the area as quickly as possible. Use light strokes so you don't pick paint off the surface and create streaks.

Once the first coat has set, the second can normally be applied directly, but if specks of dust or runs mar the surface, rub it down very lightly with fine wet-and-dry paper and water.

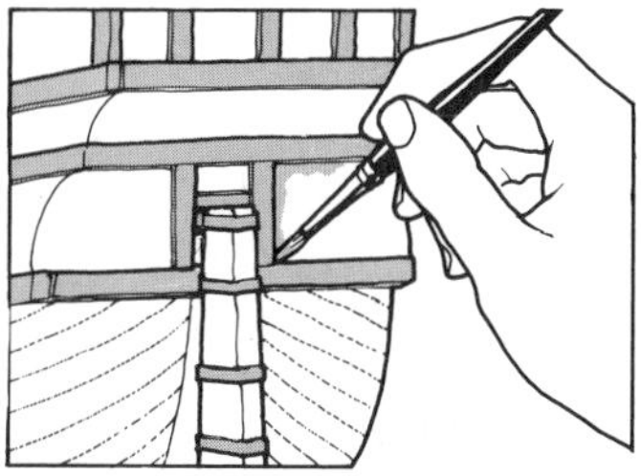

**Applying a flat coat** Begin by painting details, into corners and along boundaries.

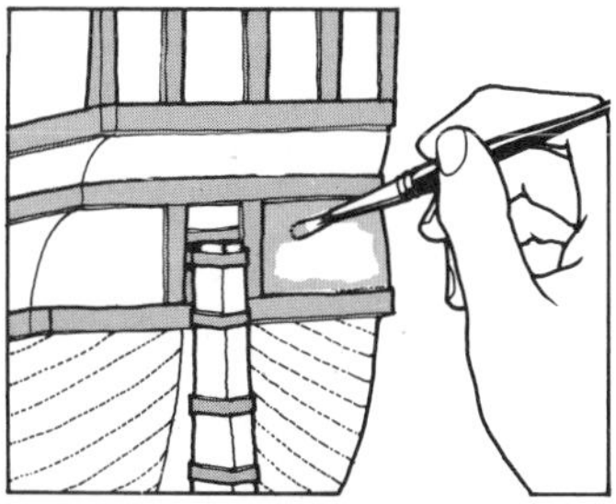

Now fill in the area, picking up the edges of the paint before they begin to set so that brush strokes flow out naturally.

Never stroke against an edge or you will inadvertently scrape excess paint off the brush.

## Blending colors

By blending colors on your model you can produce a gradual transition from one color to another. You will need to blend colors extensively on figures to make flesh tones and model clothing, but the technique is also useful to accentuate shadows or to create subtle colors. Oil paints are perhaps the easiest to blend although some people achieve equal results with watercolors. Apply the paint in very small quantities and work the edge of one color into another.

**Painting a shadow** Add a small amount of a darker color and, with the brush dressed to a wedge shape, blend in the edge of the dark color.

## Highlighting

Highlighting is used to emphasize edges and to pick out small details and textures. Choose a pale tone of any color although white is often all that's needed as only minute amounts of paint are used. Take a very small quantity of pure paint onto the tip of a brush and brush most of it onto the edge of a palette. Next, drag the brush lightly across the surface.

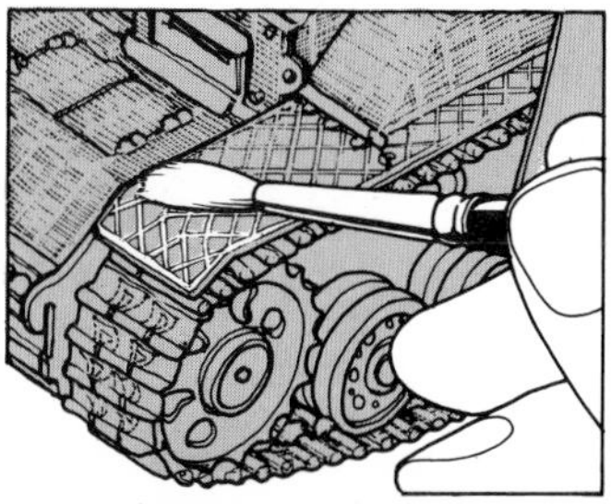

**Highlighting a textured surface** Drag a brush, very lightly loaded with pure pale-colored paint, across the surface.

# Spray-painting

When you spray paint, it is important to take certain precautions because most paints are flammable and dangerous to inhale. Therefore, never spray near a naked flame or smoke while spraying or in the same room afterward, and always provide adequate ventilation by opening a window. For extra safety, wear a lightweight gauze face mask.

Before you begin to paint, put down newspaper to protect your work area from paint spray. Be sure to tape some paper on the wall behind your worktable as you may need to spray directly at the side of the model. You may also find it useful to spray the model in a spray booth made from a cardboard box. The box will catch the paint and protect the drying model from dust. Position the model on a turntable to allow you to spray all sides.

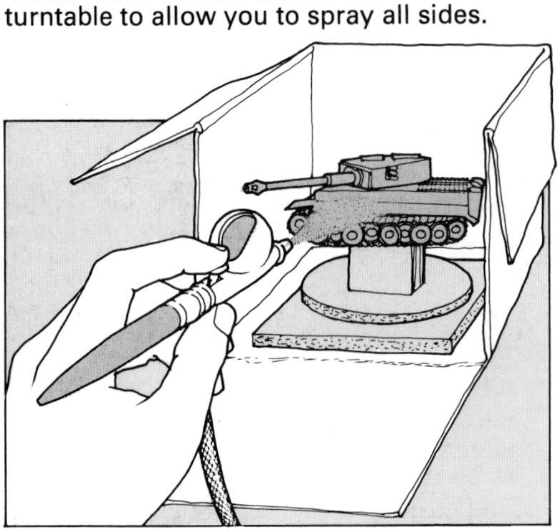

**Using a spray booth** Spray the model in a cardboard box with one side open; moisten the interior with water beforehand to prevent dust falling on the model. After spraying, close box and allow paint to dry.

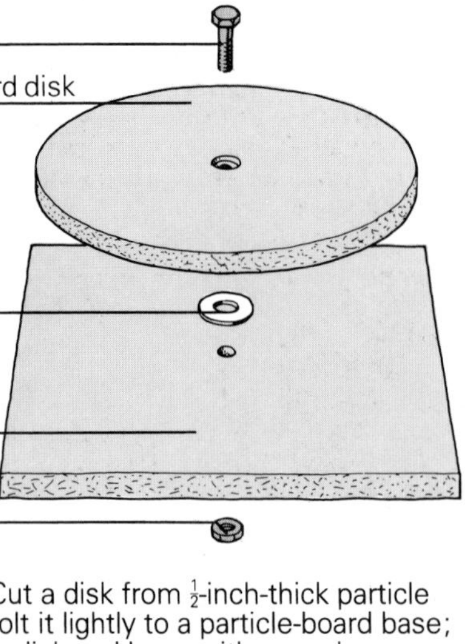


**Turntable** Cut a disk from ½-inch-thick particle board and bolt it lightly to a particle-board base; separate the disk and base with a washer.

## Thinning paint

All paints can be sprayed except for poster colors which are too coarse. The paint must be thinned down to the consistency of milk either in the jar reservoir or in a palette. Transfer it to the spray cup with a brush or dropper. If the paint is too thin it will run as soon as it hits the surface of the model; if it is too thick, the airbrush will splutter and spray unevenly. Too thick paint may also cause a wrinkled surface; rub it down with wet-and-dry paper and water. If there are lumps in the paint, strain it through a fine nylon mesh.

## Spraying a flat coat

Whether you use an aerosol can, spray gun or airbrush, the procedure for spraying a flat coat is basically the same. Hold the tool at a constant distance from the surface, 6 to 8 inches for an airbrush, a little more for an aerosol can, and keep it moving at a steady pace straight across the surface with nozzle pointing directly at the model at all times. Swinging the airbrush across the model in a curve makes an uneven coverage. Begin each pass well before the model, triggering the spray as you approach it. Release the trigger when clear of the surface on the other side.

This technique produces an even coat on a flat surface but on a three-dimensional model, to make sure that the paint covers the corners, edges and hollows, spray them first then make overall passes.

If runs or sags appear, too much paint is being applied. Make sure you move the brush at a steady pace, not too slowly, and that you are not holding it too close to the model. Let the paint set hard, then rub down the blemishes with a piece of fine wet-and-dry paper and water.

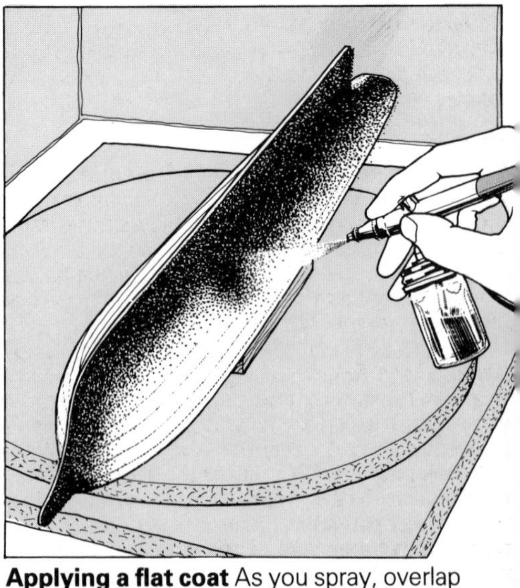

**Applying a flat coat** As you spray, overlap each previous stroke by half by aiming the nozzle at its lower edge.

# Metallic finishes

Many models, such as airplanes or figures holding weapons, require metallic finishes. Use paint, paste or pieces of foil.

The realistic finish on the F100D Super Sabre (above) and the RF 101C Voodoo (below) was made by covering the body with thin metal foil.

## Paint

Metallic paint which comes in gold, silver, aluminum and copper, is extremely versatile as it can be mixed or used with other colors to produce a wide range of hues. Several techniques for painting different types of armor and weapons are described on pages 102 to 105 but these methods apply equally to other small components. For a smooth finish over a large area, on a plane or a car for example, it is best to spray rather than brush on the paint.

## Paste

Metallic paste such as Rub-n-Buff is useful for an overall finish on a vehicle. It is sold in craft stores for use on picture frames and is available in gold, copper and silver in a variety of finishes. You can mix different pastes to vary the color, for example to indicate where heat from a jet engine has darkened the surface.

To apply the paste, squeeze some onto a scrap of cardboard and add a little at a time to the model using a soft cloth wrapped around your finger or a piece of sponge. Spread the paste thinly but evenly over the surface. Apply a second thinner coat, gently buffing it to the required sheen. Small parts can be finished in the same way or you can thin the paste with turpentine or turpentine substitute and apply it with a brush. Remember to remove any paste from locating pins before gluing the parts together.

## Foil

Thin foil applied in individual panels can produce a very realistic effect. You can use foil specifically for modelmaking such as Bare Metal which is self-adhesive and designed to bend around most curves without creasing, or ordinary kitchen foil. To make kitchen foil adhere, use a foil adhesive or apply matt varnish to the surface of the model and add the foil when it becomes tacky.

Foil has a grain and if you lay the panels in different directions the tone and color will vary from panel to panel just as on the full-size vehicle. You can also vary the color by spraying areas of the foil with metallic paint before cutting it into panels. To avoid a patchwork appearance, weather the surface as described on page 92.

If you are finishing the whole model in foil panels, you may find it easier to cover the main parts such as wings and fuselage on a plane, before assembling them. Conceal the joints between the components with foil. Remember to paint the interior of wheel wells and cockpits before applying the foil and if the rivets and panel lines are badly molded, file them off and inscribe new ones in the plastic. Lift off a badly applied panel with a knife and try again using smaller panels: a good joint will not show after it has been burnished. Any small creases can be rubbed out with a paintbrush handle.

## Applying a foil panel

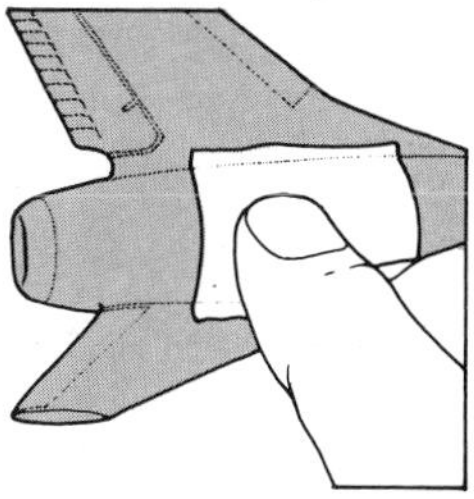

**1** Position a piece of foil slightly larger than the area to be covered, on the model. Press it down with a finger working from the center outward.

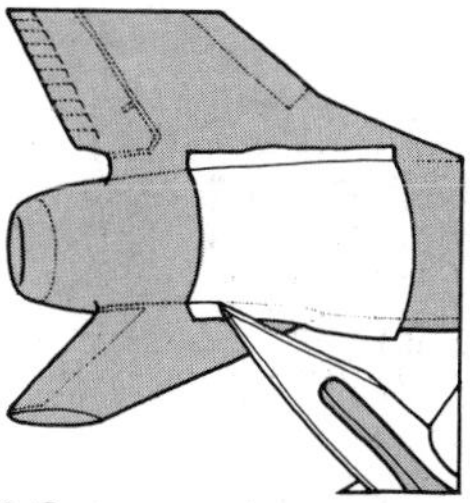

**2** Cut away the excess foil following the panel lines. Use very gentle pressure to avoid tearing the foil.

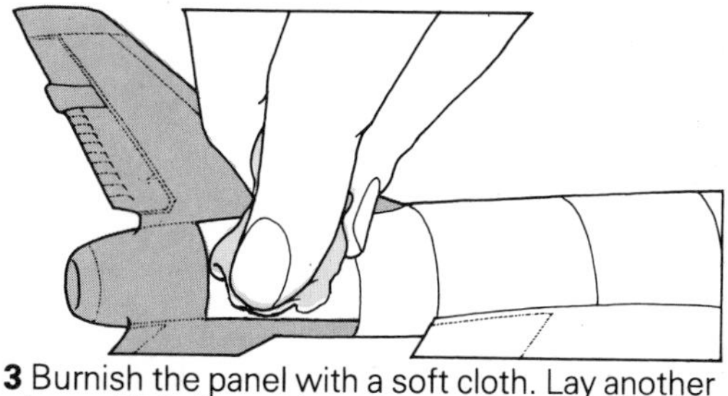

**3** Burnish the panel with a soft cloth. Lay another piece of foil alongside and repeat the process to cover remaining panels.

# Masking techniques

A mask is a covering used to prevent an area from being accidentally painted while an adjacent part of the model is being worked on. It is used in conjunction with an airbrush or a paintbrush, either to protect a finished area or to make patterns and decorative effects. A stencil is a mask where the design is cut from the center of a piece of paper, cardboard or film. Masks are used extensively for customizing vehicles and can be made from a wide variety of materials, from tape and tissue paper to liquid masks and net material.

## Tape

This is the most common and practical means of painting a sharp edge of color, for both straight and wavy lines. It is often used by airplane and boat modelers for applying camouflage (see pages 85 to 87).

Paper masking tape is flexible and has the right kind of adhesive quality. Although the edges are a little rough for models you can cut the tape down the center to make two straight edges. Plastic tape, such as electrical insulation tape, has a much better edge. Test it beforehand to make sure that it peels away easily and does not leave adhesive on the model. Narrow drafting tapes, such as those produced by Letraset, are ideal for painting lines or stripes on model custom cars (see page 84).

**Painting a straight edge** Paint the entire surface of the model one color, generally the lighter color; leave 24 hours to dry completely.

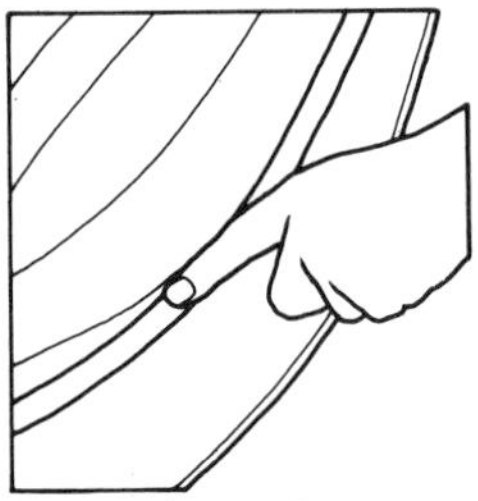

Lay a piece of tape along the edge of the area to be painted the second color; rub down well. Cover the rest of the model with paper taped in place.

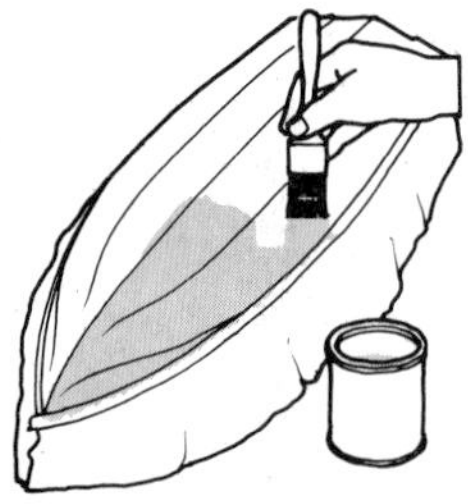

Spray or brush on the second color. If you brush it on, stroke away from the tape to avoid making a thick edge. Let it dry.

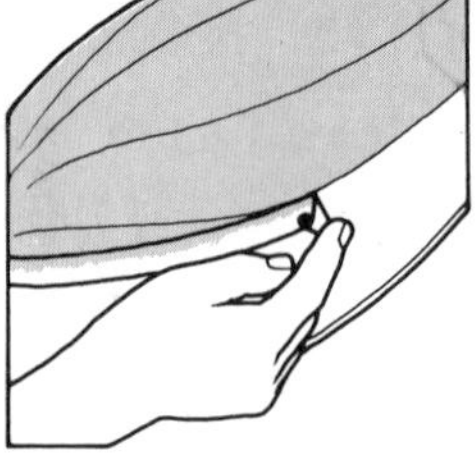

To remove the tape, peel it back at a slight angle to the painted edge, rolling it underneath your fingertip.

## Film

Low-tack masking film in sheet form is widely used for decorative techniques which require the mask to be lifted and reused, such as stenciled patterns or the three-dimensional ribbon below. It is semitransparent, making it easy to position, and thin which prevents a build up of paint against the edge. It can be used to cover large areas although it is difficult to use on a contoured surface. Cut out the shape on the model with a knife, but take care that the knife does not damage the paintwork.

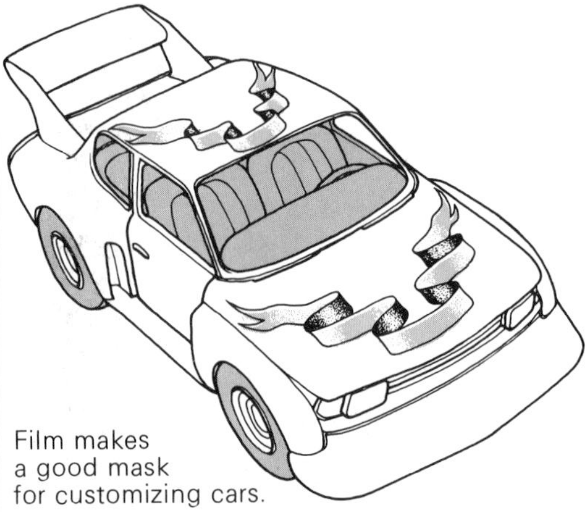

Film makes a good mask for customizing cars.

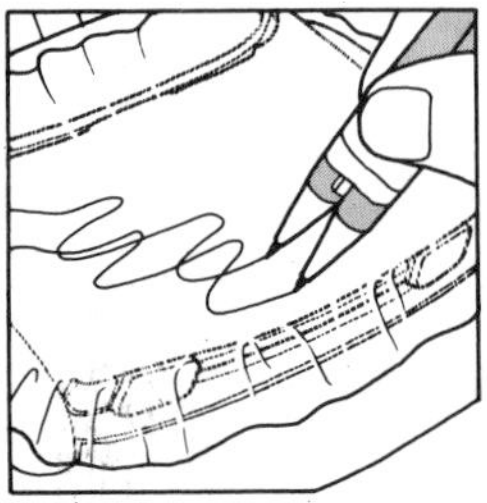

**Painting a ribbon** Lay film on the surface. Holding two pens together, draw a ribbon. For a wide ribbon, tape a spacer in between.

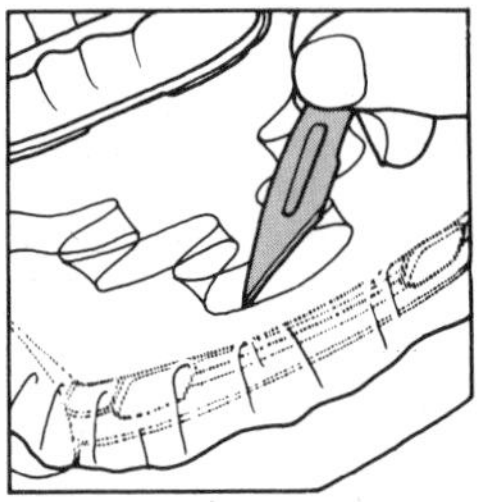

Score through the lines with a sharp knife. Be careful not to cut into the paint.

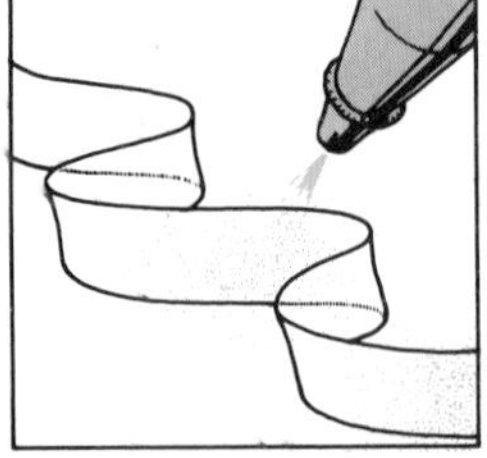

Remove the front sections of the ribbon. Spray, letting more color fall in some areas for a three-dimensional effect.

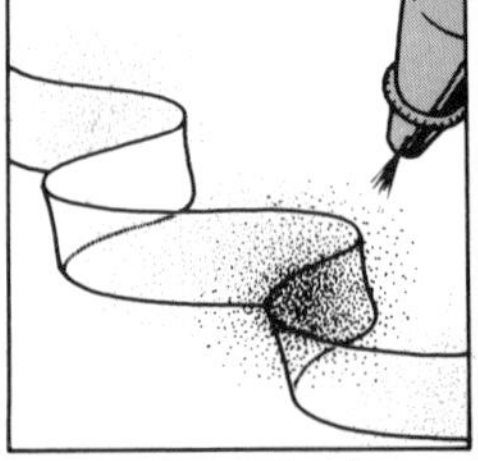

When the paint is dry, replace the front sections and remove back pieces. Spray using a darker tone or a different color.

## Paper and cardboard

Masks made from these materials can be used in place of masking tape or film. Simple to make and easily repositioned, paper and cardboard masks are a convenient method of repeating a decorative motif. A hard edge will result if the mask is held firmly on the surface of the model, but if you lift it slightly as you spray, some of the paint will fall underneath to create a soft edge.

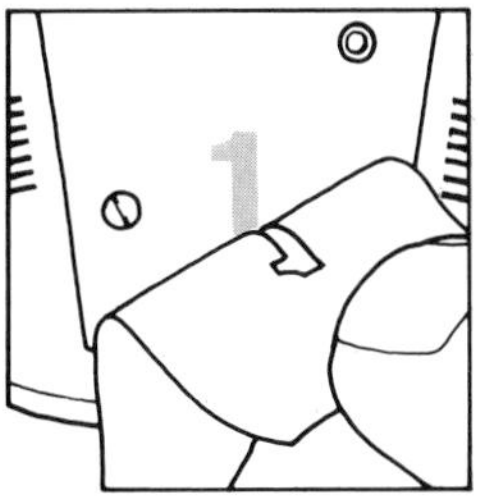

**Using a stencil** Cut the design from the center of a piece of paper. Paint through the opening for a positive image.

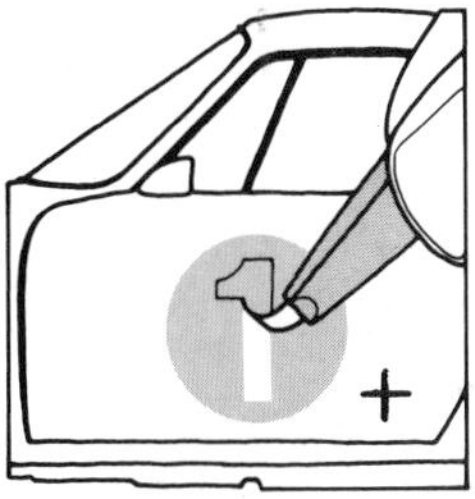

For a negative image, paint over the cut-out paper shape.

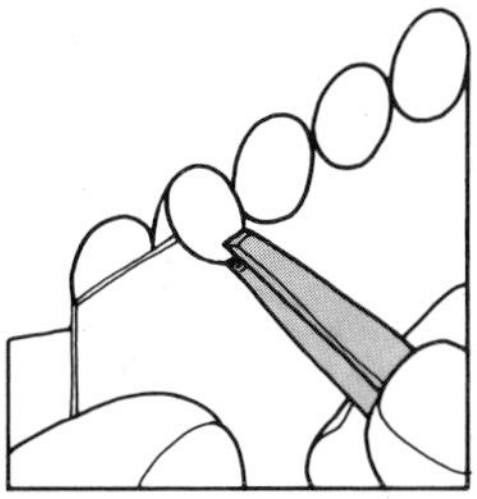

**Making fish scales** Stick round, self-adhesive labels onto a strip of paper, letting them overlap the edge. Repeat row of labels on other side, with gummed sides facing each other.

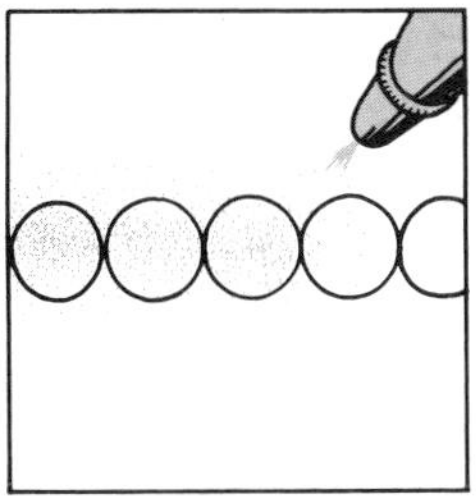

Position mask. Spray along the line of the scales, concentrating the paint on the mask, so that only a little falls onto the surface of the model.

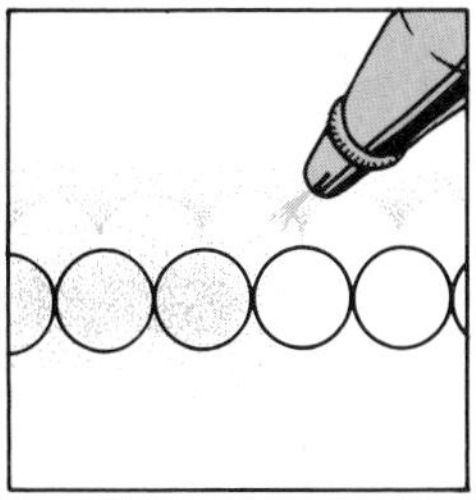

Move the mask down and across by half a circle. Spray again. Repeat to cover the area. You can use the same color throughout or vary the tone to create a three-dimensional effect.

**Painting flames** Cut out flame shapes along the edge of a piece of cardboard. Hold mask on the model and spray, concentrating the spray on the mask. Move it down, repeat.

## Liquid masking materials

Brand-name liquid masks are useful for protecting small areas, such as train windows, from being painted. White glue is particularly effective as a mask on metallic paint which is easily marked by other materials.

Brush the liquid onto a clean surface. When it is dry, you can cut the mask with a knife to remove a section or shape the edge. After painting, carefully remove the mask with adhesive tape or by lifting the edge with a knife point or a pair of tweezers. It will soften if brushed with warm water.

## Tissue paper

This is only used to mask interior areas of models, such as engine air intakes or wheel wells. Dampen it with water and push it into place with tweezers or a paintbrush handle.

## Other materials

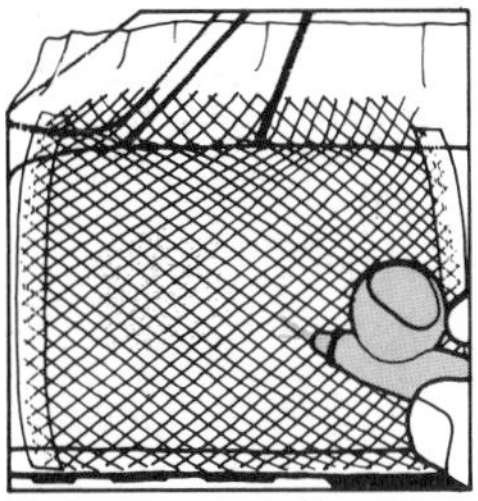

**Painting snakeskin** Stretch a piece of net material over the model and secure it with tape; spray.

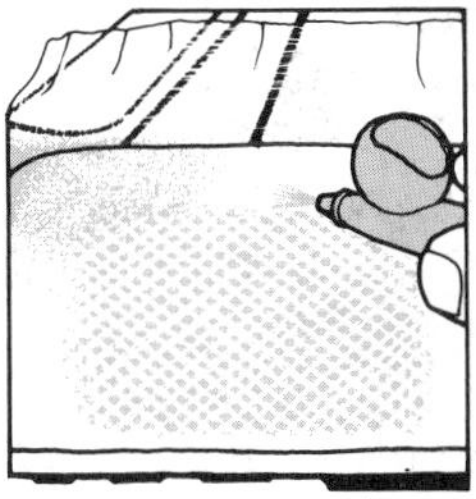

Remove the material, then spray to blend in the edge of the snakeskin pattern.

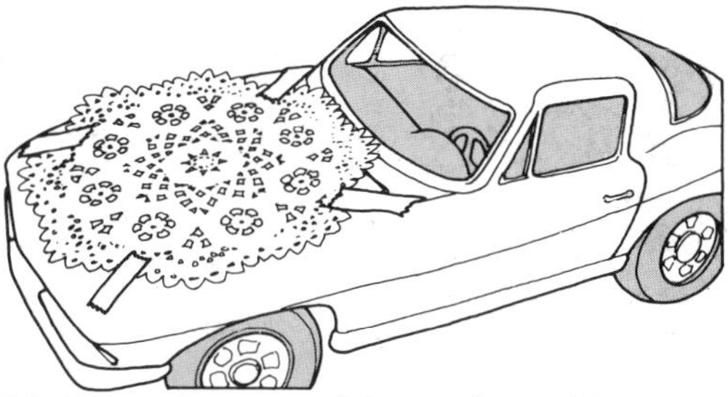

**Making a lace panel** Lay a piece of lace or a doily on the model; tape it in position.

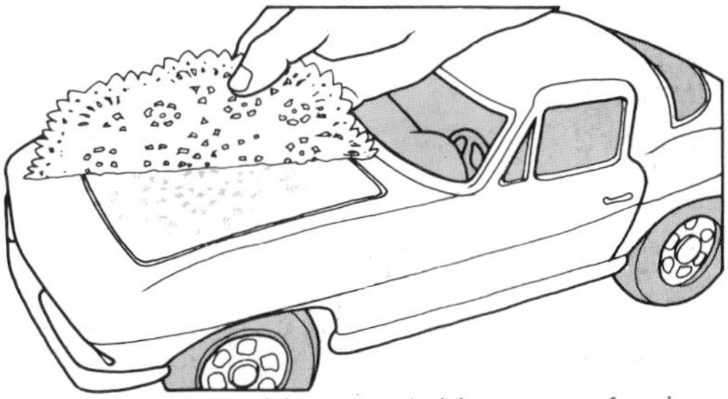

Spray the area with several thin coats of paint to build up color without clogging up the lace. Lift off the mask when the paint is dry.

## Painting custom cars

Any effect found on full-size custom cars can be reproduced on a model by combining free-hand painting and the masking techniques on pages 80 to 81. Always paint the design over a smooth surface. To build up the finish, apply several layers of undercoat to the vehicle, sanding each layer lightly before adding the next one. Spray on the top coat, then complete your design. Finally, paint the vehicle with gloss varnish, if you wish. The Corvette shown right was sprayed with a red-tinted varnish to give depth to the colors.

To make the strip of film on the Corvette, right, use an air-brush and masking film, and follow the method for painting a ribbon described on page 80. Dry-transfer letters were used for the name. If you cannot find the style of lettering you want, make a stencil and spray on the inscription.

This pattern was made by spraying paint onto netting stretched over the surface.

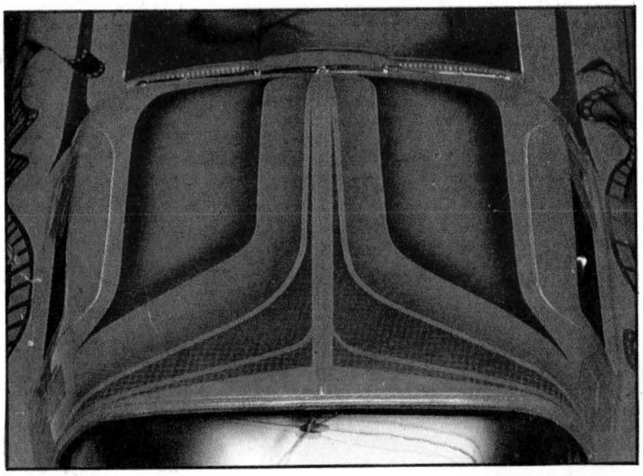

To make these soft black edges, aim the air-brush along a piece of tape, letting the paint fall to one side.

Masks were used to paint the hard edges in the designs, left and above. The rest was painted freehand.

# Stripes and lines

Stripes and narrow lines used to outline panels or features are an essential part of the decoration of many vehicles. There are several ways of applying them.

Tape itself can be used for stripes as long as its thickness is not obtrusive. Narrow, colored drafting tapes ideal for this purpose are widely available in widths from about $\frac{1}{64}$ inch (0.4 mm) to $\frac{1}{2}$ inch (12.7 mm). Providing the surface is smooth, they can be lifted and replaced. There are some tapes which are specially designed to go over curves.

Stripes and lines are also available as decals in both the water-slide and dry-transfer type. Apply them as described on pages 88 to 89, being very careful to avoid any distortion or creasing.

## Painting stripes and lines

Stripes and lines can be painted using narrow tapes and a variety of masking techniques. The drafting tapes mentioned above are particularly useful. Make negative or positive stripes as shown below. An interesting variation of a negative stripe is to spray down the center of the tape letting the paint fall to either side. Remove the tape, leaving a clearly defined stripe with color fading gradually from its edges. This type of negative stripe is an effective decoration on customized cars.

## Painting a positive stripe

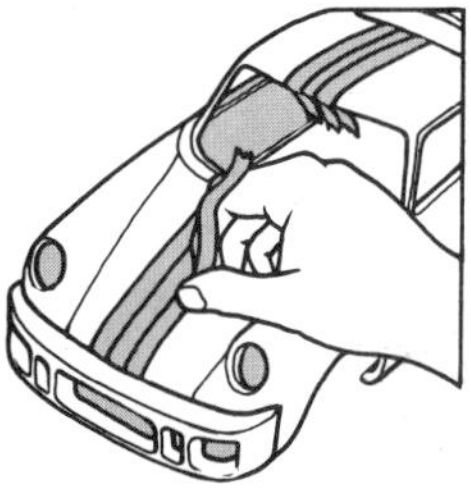

**1** Lay masking tape the width of the stripe on the model. Place another piece of tape up against each side.

**2** Remove the center tape and spray paint down the stripe. Remove remaining tape.

## Painting a negative stripe

**1** Paint the model the color of the stripe, then position tape in place of the stripe.

**2** Spray the model its overall color, then remove tape to reveal the stripe.

## Drawing lines

Drawing lines on a model takes more skill than other methods. It is often the best technique for outlining panels and numbers; tapes tend to bunch around corners. It's easier to draw on a matt surface so if you want the vehicle to have a shiny finish, paint the base color with matt paint, draw the lines, then coat the surface with glossy varnish. For best results, before you draw secure the model with rubber bands on a layer of foam rubber on a piece of wood (see Basic techniques).

There are two types of pen for drawing lines: the old-fashioned adjustable ruling pen and the modern ruling pen. The traditional pen is adjusted by means of a screw to draw lines of different widths. This type of pen is cheap and can be used with any kind of paint or ink, but a lot of practice is required to use it. Fill it with a dropper or paintbrush. The modern pen has a tubular point with interchangeable nibs to draw lines 1 mm to 2 mm in width. This pen is easy to use, but it is expensive and will only take special inks.

You will need a bevel-edged ruler for drawing straight lines. If you are using a traditional pen, place the ruler bevel downward. If you are using a modern pen, place the ruler bevel upward and hold the pen vertically.

For curves you need a compass. Always rest the point of the compass on a piece of masking tape to protect the paintwork. A set of French curves is useful for drawing curves which do not have a constant radius and thin plastic templates are available for drawing circles or ovals, though the latter are only suitable for use with a modern pen.

Traditional ruling pen

Modern ruling pen

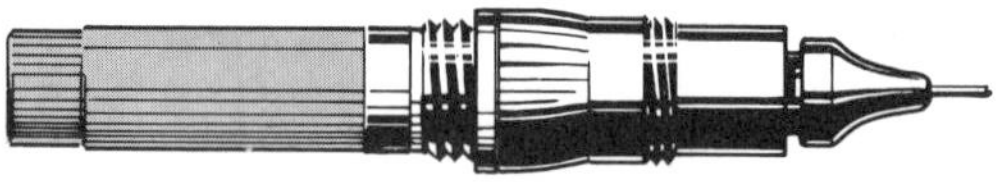

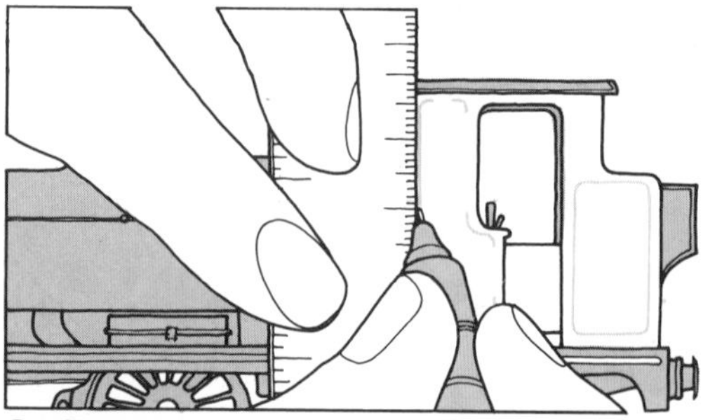

**Outlining a panel** Draw the corners with a compass, then join the corners with straight lines using a ruler as a guide.

# Camouflage

The purpose of camouflage is to make a subject difficult to recognize, either by painting it a color which is close to that of the terrain, or by breaking up its outline. In the case of aircraft which have to operate over various backgrounds including directly against the sky, this is quite difficult. Such problems are responsible for the many experiments in color, shape and finish.

Some schemes feature a single color but the majority involve a minimum of two colors in order to break up the outline. The colors can meet at a hard or soft edge. The patterns are carefully specified by military authorities; however, local availability of materials, method of application or, in some cases, misinterpretation of regulations, produce countless variations. Although the detail varies widely, certain basic techniques can be modified to suit any subject.

## Straight-edged camouflage

Second World War planes and battleships often employed a two- or multi-colored pattern where the areas of color met at hard, straight edges. Never attempt to paint this type of camouflage freehand. Always mark the color boundary with tape and follow the masking technique on page 80.

If you are hand-painting, the simplest method is to paint the lightest color over the whole surface, then paint the darker-colored patches over the light undercoat. In very small scales the thick coat of paint applied to the dark areas is unacceptable. In this case, mask off the dark areas first and paint the lighter; let dry, then reverse the process so that there is an even coat of paint over the whole surface. The fine spray of an airbrush allows even the smallest scale model to be painted using the first method.

## Single-color camouflage

One method of camouflage is to paint the vehicle a color which approximates that of the landscape. The model can be sprayed or hand-painted in the normal manner unless the method employed on the full-size vehicle dictates otherwise. Some tanks, for example, were painted with brooms, the only suitable tool available at the time. This method resulted in a rough finish which is best simulated with a coarse paintbrush.

The same principle of using an overall color can be observed on some planes although, in fact, two colors are used: one for the upper surface seen against the ground or sea, and another for the bottom of the plane viewed against the sky. The boundary between the two can be a straight or wavy line with a hard or soft edge. Follow the basic masking technique on page 80, painting or spraying the lighter color first.

This type of camouflage with hard, straight edges, is sometimes called splinter camouflage on German, World War Two planes.

This Messerschmitt has straight-edged camouflage on its wings and tail plane.

## Wavy-edged camouflage

Corsair II jet

Mirage 5J jet

A curved or wavy boundary of color may have a hard or soft edge depending on the scheme or the scale of the model. Even if the full-size prototype was painted with a soft edge, at a small scale, 1:48 or less, the edge may appear hard.

For a hard edge, paint the lightest color overall, then mark out the pattern with a pencil, or draw the edge freehand with a brush; fill in the color working from the edge toward the center. Alternately, mask the edge with a sheet of masking film or with tape which is wide enough to encompass the wavy edge. Mark the pattern lightly on the masking material before rubbing it down. With a knife, lightly cut along the marked line taking care not to damage the paintwork. Strip off the unwanted portion of masking and rub down the new edge.

The only satisfactory way of achieving a soft-edged line is to spray it. Use an airbrush adjusted to a very fine setting and simply draw the edge freehand, following a pencil guideline if necessary, then gradually move back to fill in the solid area of color. If you are using a spray gun which cannot be adjusted finely, spray over a cardboard mask cut to a wavy edge. Hold the mask just above the surface of the model to create a slight under-spray of paint.

## Mottle camouflage

A common method of camouflage is to apply an overall pattern of small patches of color with a spray gun. The most realistic scale representation of mottle camouflage is produced by a finely set airbrush.

If you do not have an airbrush, use a mask and spray gun. Punch or tear irregular holes in a piece of cardboard cut fairly small for easy positioning. Hold the mask just above the surface and turn it after each burst to avoid obvious repetition. You can also stipple on the color with a trimmed stiff-bristle paintbrush, but keep the thickness of paint to a minimum to avoid a noticeable texture. Alternately, apply the paint with a small piece of sponge held in tweezers.

This mottle camouflage was reproduced with a finely set airbrush.

## Lozenge camouflage

One of the most difficult of camouflage schemes to reproduce is the German World War One lozenge pattern where quite small, irregular patches of color were printed on the plane's covering fabric and sometimes painted over the metal and plywood parts. Rather than hand-painting this design, use a Micro Scale decal sheet for 1:72 scale aircraft. Separate sheets are available for lower and upper surfaces.

## Winter camouflage

Land-based vehicles and aircraft were camouflaged specifically for winter conditions. Methods ranged from spraying the vehicle as it left the factory to emergency measures in the field which might be as crude as pouring buckets of water-soluble paint over a tank. Spring thaw gradually reduced the camouflage to streaks and patches.

To reproduce winter camouflage, paint the original color scheme or camouflage on the model before spraying on a light coat of pale gray rather than white. Make a patchy coating by concentrating the spray pattern in the center of panels to suggest wear on exposed edges and surfaces. Hand-applied camouflage can be simulated by streaking on some thinned paint.

## Other spray patterns

Numerous spray patterns consisting of narrow bands, crosshatching, squiggles and meandering lines are found as camouflage on all types of vehicle. All can be reproduced by drawing freehand with an airbrush.

Panzerjäger Tiger with sprayed-on crosshatch camouflage.

# Decals

The colorful insignia, serial numbers and letters for models are supplied in the form of decals. There is a wide variety of designs available. Moreover, you can adapt decals to create original symbols. There are two types of decal. Their names, water slide and dry transfer, refer to their different methods of application. Both, however, should be applied to the model on top of the finished paintwork but before any weathering is carried out, so that they are included in the weathering process and lose their starkness.

The water-slide decals on this Tyrrell Ford are well applied. Note especially the number 2 on the side of the car which has been made to curl around a panel. Setting agents make such precise applications easier. The insignia are always supplied in the kit, but if you want to create a different scheme, choose from the wide range of special decals available.

## Water-slide decals

These are the most commonly used type. The symbol is printed on a layer of varnish which is coated on the reverse with water-soluble glue. They are supplied on a paper sheet which must be soaked in water to soften the glue and release the decal.

Although water-slide decals can be used as supplied by the manufacturers, it is better to apply them using softening and setting agents such as Micro Set and Micro Sol. Micro Set is applied to the model before positioning the decal to improve adhesion and eliminate air bubbles. Micro Sol is applied to the surface of the decal after positioning it to soften the carrier film and draw the decal onto the surface of the model encouraging it to follow the contours.

If you are not using the setting agents, the carrier film may shine on the model so first dull the decal, then trim away that part of the carrier film which exceeds the area of the symbol, leaving rows of small letters in one piece. To dull the decal, rub the sheet with very fine sandpaper using a circular motion to create an overall even texture. White decals should be trimmed first otherwise they are difficult to read: trim away as much of the letter as possible leaving a strip on one side; then, hold the strip on a flat surface and stroke away from you with the sandpaper to avoid tearing the decal.

If the decal is accidentally torn at any stage, carefully rejoin the pieces on the surface of the model; paint in any cracks when it is dry. If the edge of the decal lifts after it has dried, reglue it with a little varnish or diluted white glue. Providing you have not used softening and setting agents, you can move an incorrectly positioned decal up to 30 minutes after applying it, by brushing the edge with water to soften the glue.

**Lifting a floating decal**
The decal may float off the backing sheet if it is left too long in the water. To lift it, slip a piece of shiny plastic sheet or cardboard under it, lift out and apply in the normal way.

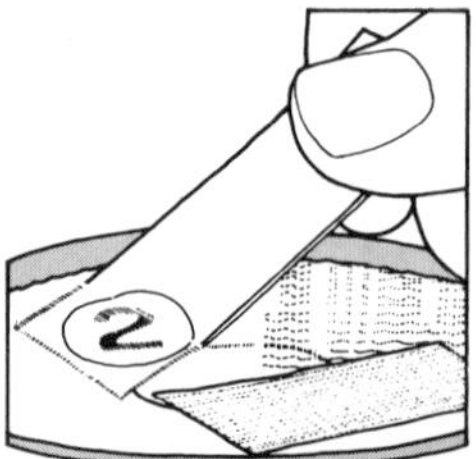

## Applying a water-slide decal

**1** Spray the whole model with gloss varnish to make a smooth surface. Let it dry.

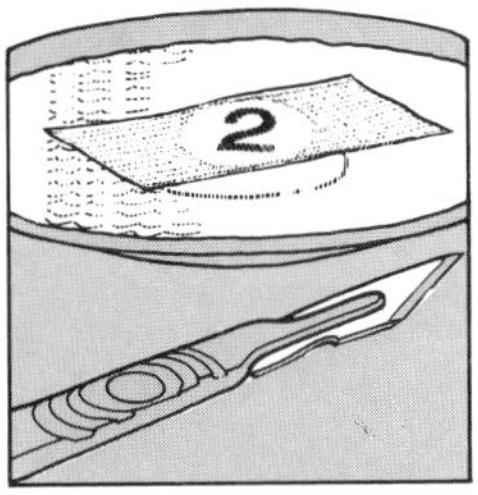

**2** Cut decal from the backing sheet and float it in a bowl of water for a few seconds.

**3** Remove from bowl; lay on a tissue for 1 minute to allow water to soak into backing sheet.

**4** Meanwhile, apply a few drops of Micro Set on the model.

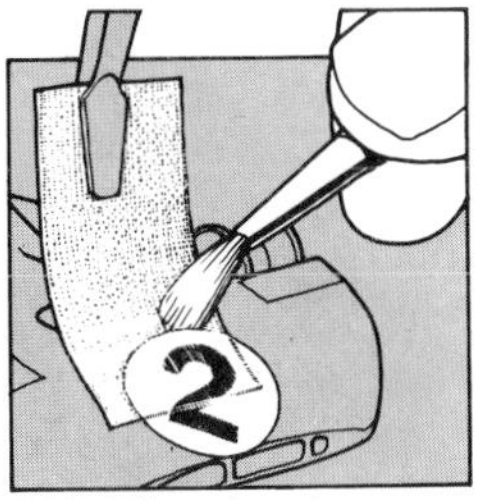

**5** Holding the sheet with tweezers, slide decal off and onto the model with a dry brush. Press gently to make it adhere.

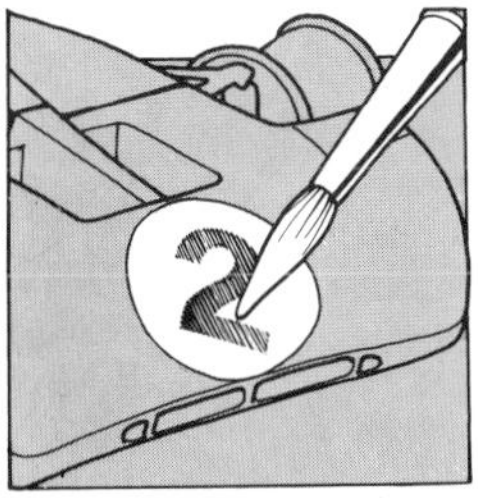

**6** Apply a few drops of Micro Sol to the decal. Ignore any distortions. Let dry.

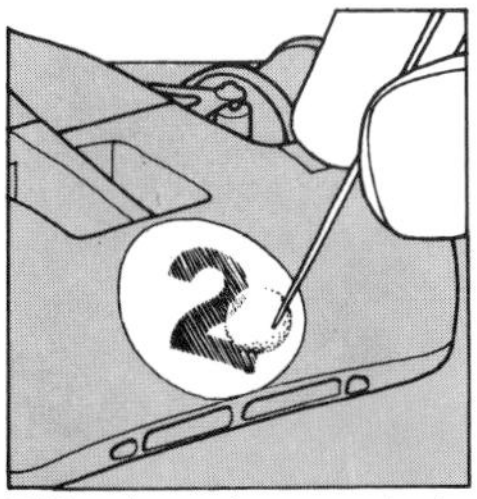

**7** If, when dry, any bubbles or blemishes remain, puncture them with a needle and add a little more Micro Sol. Leave overnight.

**8** Wash the decal with a soft, wet brush to remove excess glue. Finally, seal it by spraying with gloss or matt varnish.

## Dry-transfer decals

With this type of decal, the symbols are printed on a transparent sheet and protected by a separate backing paper. They are transferred to the model by placing the carrier sheet, symbol-side down, on the model and rubbing the back of the sheet with a blunt tool. This type of decal, unlike a water-slide decal, is very thin and leaves no film on the model. Apart from the standard range of lettering, companies such as Letraset produce sheets of symbols, lines and textures. There are also a growing number of dry-transfer symbols specially for modelmakers.

## Applying dry-transfer decals

To avoid damaging the paintwork, apply the symbol using the pre-release technique. Before positioning it on the model, lightly rub over the carrier sheet with a blunt tool such as a ballpoint pen, keeping an even pressure over the whole symbol to avoid distorting it. The symbol will change tone as it begins to release from the carrier sheet. Now position it on the model and lightly rub over the sheet with the tool or your fingertip; remove the carrier sheet, lay the backing paper over the symbol and burnish firmly with a finger. If the symbol breaks up during this process and you are unable to reposition it, remove it from the model with a piece of masking tape.

Sheets of lettering are printed with marks below each letter for easy positioning. Use a piece of masking tape on the model as a guideline and position the marks against it to make sure that each letter lines up. You can also use the marks to space each letter but it is just as easy to space them by eye. When it is not convenient to use the whole sheet of lettering, cut it into blocks or strips, but not single letters which are difficult to align.

Seal dry-transfer decals with a coat of varnish after checking on a spare piece that the varnish is compatible.

## Improvising insignia

If you wish to show something which is not available commercially there are various ways in which you can adapt existing material. You can cut spare decals into single numbers or letters and reassemble them in the required sequence. Alternatively, convert one letter into another, for example a capital E into the letter F or the number 8 into a 3, by lightly cutting through the figures on the reverse side of the sheet and flicking off the unneeded portion. Try combining letters or symbols: one letter can overlap another without any apparent difference in thickness.

If you require insignia of a different color, you can either paint over a spare water-slide decal with thinned enamel paint, or paint any symbol onto the transparent margin of the decal sheet. For large-scale models, cut the insignia from masking film (page 80) and spray any color.

# Weathering vehicles

Weathering is the term used to describe any process which gives a model an old or worn appearance. By using good reference material and common sense you can bring a model to life by the application of just a few techniques. On the following pages are methods for weathering both tanks and military vehicles, aircraft and trains. The same ideas can be modified for use on other vehicles.

How a vehicle weathers depends on its construction and shape, its age, environment and degree of maintenance. Water, for instance, will run down certain areas to cause rusting. Cars can rust right through, whereas armored fighting vehicles show surface rust only, and aluminum airplanes do not rust at all. Airplanes are regularly maintained but tanks often function with a minimum of maintenance and are exposed to a high degree of wear.

All types of vehicle should be washed to remove any grease, sprayed with the appropriate color or camouflage, and decals added, before doing any weathering. If you are only going to apply a coat of dust, paint all the details beforehand. However, if you are weathering a vehicle extensively, you may find it easier to paint the details while weathering.

For the most realistic result, apply the effects of weathering in the order they would occur naturally: if you start with a vehicle in its factory finish, first break down its overall color, then apply the effects of wear and exposure on the paintwork, proceed to show metallic effects where the paint has almost worn through and finally, indicate bare metal in those parts which take the most wear. If you intend to set your model on a base, do so before you weather it.

**"Opel blitzed"** The areas of rust, bare metal and faded paintwork on these army vehicles contribute to the realism.

# Weathering tanks and military vehicles

Tanks, army trucks and jeeps experience more wear and tear than most vehicles. The example and instructions below concern a vehicle which has fought in wet conditions. To simulate the effects of wear on a tank in a desert, see page 95.

Observe the discolored surface on this battle-worn American Lee tank.

## Stage 1: Breaking down the color

As vehicles age, they become dirty and discolored. To break down a factory-fresh finish, simply apply washes of white, burnt umber and pale yellow oil paint to the vehicle in no particular order, judging by the changing effect how much to put on.

Begin by coating the top of the vehicle liberally with clean turpentine, allowing it to run freely down the model (as long as the base coat has been left to dry for two to three days the turpentine will not affect it). Take a little color on the brush and touch it off across the top edge so that it flows down the side in streaks. Do not drag the brush along the surface leaving brush strokes. When the turpentine evaporates only slight stains of color remain. Lettering will still show through.

Work down the model applying a fresh wash of turpentine before adding the color. Mix your colors, darkening or lightening them as you think appropriate. Use pale, almost white streaks, to suggest splashes of muddy water. If one color looks too strong or the edge shows up too much, apply a little more turpentine. Try not to treat the whole surface uniformly, but break it up with different colors and apply less streaking in some areas. Allow the model to dry thoroughly overnight before proceeding to stage 2.

## Stage 2: Rust

Strictly speaking, rust should be applied at a later stage in order to follow the natural process; however, the method described here requires quantities of turpentine and may disturb the paintwork applied later.

Make a very light wash of chrome orange oil paint. For older rust, mix a darker color. Working from top to bottom, touch off the paint in the appropriate areas. Rust occurs in channels and in grooves where rainwater would run and collect, and where one sheet of metal is riveted or welded to another. Don't apply it to every detail but be selective for maximum effect. Let it run around bottom edges, pushing it along with the brush to encourage it to flow, but do not apply brush strokes. Allow it to run down channels and seams and collect around the base of details. Touch out any residue leaving a subtle orange color. If, as the turpentine begins to dry out, the stain is too obvious, soften the edge with a little turpentine. Let the rust dry overnight. It will turn a realistic brown.

To simulate rust on a truck or a car where it blisters the paint from beneath, before spraying the vehicle with the base coat, paint the area with thin white glue and lightly sprinkle on powdered Spackle. Blow off any excess powder. Add rust as described.

## Stage 3: General wear

General wear dulls paintwork. To simulate this effect, take a small amount of pure white or pale yellow paint on a cut-down stiff bristle brush. Apply it to the vehicle using a light scrubbing action and small circular motions. Do not stipple on the color but keep the brush on the model. Vary the intensity of the color, concentrating the effect on exposed areas – ribs and ridges, tool boxes, around hatches and especially the drive wheels of tanks. For contrast, scrub the high points of wheel moldings, nuts and rims. If part of a decal breaks away, make it work to your advantage by weathering the area heavily to suggest that the paint has been chipped away. Use this technique also to accentuate the form by highlighting one area against another.

## Stage 4: Areas of bare metal

Continuous use wears through the paintwork in places to give a metallic sheen to the surface. Concentrate this effect on the most exposed areas which in tanks are track-guards, the front section of the hull and turret, the wheels and tracks.

First apply a light wash of metallic steel paint to the appropriate areas. Feather out the paint so that the effect is only apparent when the vehicle is turned into the light. As the turpentine evaporates, it leaves a very thin film of metallic particles which highlights the texture without being obvious. Make sure the steel wash does not run into joints or channels where this kind of wear would not occur. If it does, lift it out with a dry brush and dull the metallic effect by applying a dark brown or gray wash.

While the turpentine is still damp, add very small highlights of pure silver paint on a dry brush to the steel areas. The turpentine will encourage the silver to blend in. Use the silver sparingly on raised areas such as the edge of shackles, worn nuts or rivets, grab handles, hinges, rims of wheels. Lightly brush across the edges of slight moldings such as the cover on a driver's view panel or a tool box lid. Bear in mind that silver is difficult to remove if too much is applied.

Graphite can be used in place of steel and silver paint to simulate areas of bare metal. It looks particularly good on the exposed areas of a tank turret and can also be used to burnish gun metal on machine guns after a normal coat of gun metal gray or matt black enamel. Graphite can be applied over any color but it is best to add it as the final stage of painting.

Scrape some graphite from a soft lead pencil into a powder on a palette. Dip a finger in the powder and rub it on the model. As you rub, the graphite will take on a sheen and pick out pitting on the molding. Blend in the edges of the graphite with a clean finger. Wrap a tissue on the end of a paintbrush handle to get at points you cannot reach with a finger.

## Stage 5: Tracks and tires

If you are painting a tank, washes will have stained tracks and tires the color of the body. The tracks now need to be painted to look like unpainted metal and the tires like rubber.

First paint areas of rusted metal on the tracks using a rust-colored paint, then apply a wash of burnt sienna adding very small amounts of orange in places. While it is still wet, run a steel wash along the exposed surfaces of the tracks. Let the turpentine dry for a while, then use very small amounts of pure silver to highlight the edges and those parts which come in contact with the ground.

Now paint the rubber tires using shades of gray – they will never be black, especially after extensive use. You can add interest by varying the shades of gray from wheel to wheel as some may be newer than others. Lighten the surfaces which come into contact with the tracks and pick out the edges with a pale color. Don't forget to paint any spare tires that may be fixed to the body of the vehicle and treat the rubber shoes found on some tank tracks in a similar way.

Paint truck, jeep and motorcycle tires like tank tires but be sure to pick out the texture of the rubber tread.

Motorcycle tires have a distinctive tread. Paint them gray then highlight the surface that comes into contact with the road with a pale color to emphasize the deep texture.

## Stage 6: Details and equipment

The next stage is to go over the vehicle bringing out the smaller details in relief and treating various pieces of equipment specially. To pick out the details, draw a thin line of raw umber paint under a grab handle or tool box lid, for example, then blend it in with a brush which has been squeezed dry. A little turpentine can be used.

**Exhaust stains** Paint inside of exhaust pipes matt black, then spray on the paint to stain the surface. Run diluted black paint into the holes of grilles.

**Kit bag** Stipple on cream paint to give the fabric a subtle texture. Model folds.

**Jerry cans** Give cans a wash of burnt sienna or black then age the surface with white paint.

**Hawser, spare tracks and bucket** Paint hawsers with a burnt sienna or black wash, then run a hint of steel over the edges leaving dark paint in the grooves to emphasize the texture. Treat spare tracks in a similar way. Paint a bucket with steel, then highlight the edge with silver.

## Stage 7: Mud or dust

The final stage is to depict the immediate effects of the environment. For a tank moving through a muddy landscape, for example, take a dark earth-color paint and mix it with some Spackle into a smooth paste. Stipple it onto the tracks, wheels and bottom of the tank. Build it up under the front edge of the trackguards and on the front of the hull. Let dry overnight. Dry brush a lighter tone of paint onto the mud to vary the color. Then, simulate thin, sprayed-on mud by dragging brown paint along the lower edges of the tank with a stiffer bristle brush. When the paint has dried out a little, highlight certain areas with a soft brush and very small quantities of pure white paint, allowing the paint to pick up color from underneath.

To portray a vehicle in a dry environment, apply a light coat of dust with an airbrush. Concentrate the spray on the bottom, allowing only a light overspray to creep up the sides. Another method is to stipple on powder scraped from a white pastel.

**Muddy tank** Stipple mud onto the front of the hull and tracks but don't apply an even cover.

**Dirty windshield** Mask the window with tape before spraying on dust with an airbrush.

**Dried mud** Dry brush a pale color along the side of the tank to simulate dried mud.

**Desert conditions** Increase the effects of general wear in stage 3 and the areas of bare metal in stage 4. Omit rust. Apply dust all over.

# Weathering airplanes

Most planes are well maintained and few show signs of wear, but in wartime, those areas of a plane which do not affect its performance often become dirty, chipped or streaked with oil, as the ground crew are too busy on essential maintenance to deal with them. Maintenance itself can wear down the paintwork in specific areas, and sunlight can bleach and discolor it.

## Old paintwork

To simulate worn or faded paintwork, break down the color with washes of varying tones. Then, emphasize the areas suggested by the washes using small amounts of pure paint on a cut-down, stiff-bristle brush and a scrubbing action. The base color should still show through. Concentrate on the upper surfaces of wings and around hatches and make sure you tone down any bright decals.

To show areas of wear on metal-skinned planes, you can also use the metallic effects described on page 93. For an even more realistic effect, apply metallic paint to the areas before painting the base color. Either paint up to these areas stippling around the metallic paint, or spray, then carefully rub with fine wet-and-dry paper until the metallic paint begins to appear.

Silver paint can be dulled down to an aluminum color by applying a coat of matt varnish over the surface. Pick out polished areas afterward with more paint.

Areas of fabric-covered aircraft which are constantly handled by ground crew can be dirtied by applying brown-gray paint.

**Aged paintwork** Break down the color with washes, then emphasize areas with pure paint.

**Sun-bleached paintwork** Weather the upper surfaces of a desert plane with pure white paint for a faded effect.

**Worn paint on wing** Show bare metal on the upper surface of the wing where the pilot enters the cockpit.

**Chipped paint around cockpit** Dry brush metallic paint over the base color to show worn areas on the cockpit entry flap.

**Metal ladder** Be sure to weather equipment and accessories like this mechanic's metal ladder for a realistic effect.

## Stains

Oil and hydraulic fluid stains can be shown running from the edges of engine cowlings and wheel flaps. Apply clean turpentine liberally to area, then touch off diluted brownish-black paint. Let it flow down for a parked plane, or streak the paint straight back with a turpentine-dampened brush to show stains distributed by the slipstream. Use dirty turpentine to simulate a stain running down from a fuel cap.

**Gunport and exhaust stains** Indicate the black stains that run from gunports by adding a drop of diluted black paint behind the port and streaking it back with a turpentine-soaked tissue. Show brownish-black exhaust stains in the same way or spray on with a finely set airbrush.

## Mud and dust

Planes which operate from a grass field may be slightly muddy. Treat wheels like other vehicles (see page 93), and apply the same effect to undercarriage struts, wheel flaps and along the underside of the fuselage, especially around a tail skid or wheel. A light layer of dust can be applied to any aircraft, especially desert planes.

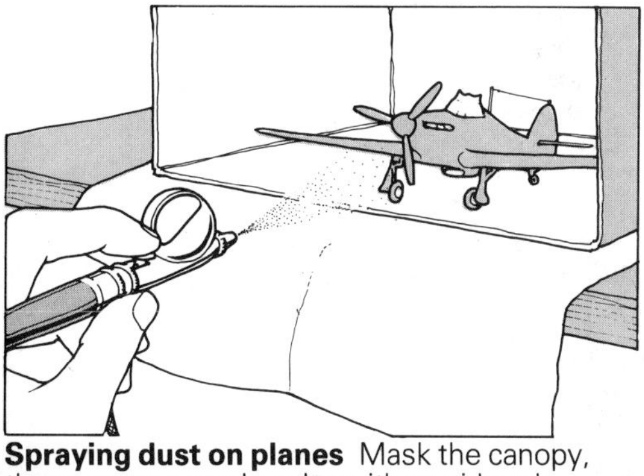

**Spraying dust on planes** Mask the canopy, then spray on a pale color with an airbrush. Position the brush slightly below and some distance ahead of the model so that the paint is almost dry when it lands.

## Repairs

A few patches can give a plane a weathered appearance but keep the effect restrained. Paint small patches on fabric-covered aircraft or apply small patches of foil on metal-skinned aircraft, before aging the paintwork. To indicate a new control flap, paint it a color that does not quite match the original or only use a primer coat.

**Tail wing repairs** The tail of this Hawker Hurricane has painted patches to simulate various emergency repairs.

# Weathering trains

The beautifully detailed trains available today can be transformed into realistic miniatures merely by weathering; rolling stock, like military vehicles, is bleached by sun and sand or rusted and streaked by water. Almost any degree of weathering can be applied, from a light coat of dust on a passenger car to dirt and wear on an old freight car. After weathering a working locomotive, always clean any paint from the wheels so that good electrical contact with the track is maintained.

## The chassis and wheels

The chassis and wheels of every model are treated in the same way. Almost without exception this part of a model is molded in black plastic which benefits from an overall coat of a mixture of rust-colored paint and thick pigment from the bottom of a can of steel paint. Apply the paint with a controlled stippling action so that it dries with a slight texture. Next, dry brush the chassis and wheels with burnt sienna oil paint using a stiff bristle brush, and highlight the details.

**Passenger car** For well maintained passenger stock, dust with an airbrush (see page 97) and lightly streak the roof with "sooty" deposits by dry brushing with black oil paint. Concentrate dirt around vents and smoke stacks.

**Steam locomotive** Steam engines are ideal subjects for weathering. You can suggest water, oil, rust and coal deposits as well as the normal dirt and grime.

**Diesel locomotive** Break down the color with washes, then weather the lower part to match the trucks, dry brushing the paint along the side in one direction. Dry brush black paint around vents and along the roof.

**Freight car**
Apply color washes, then emphasize the deposits further by dry brushing with pure oil paint. Bleach the upper surfaces using white and continue dirty deposits up from the chassis with burnt sienna. Show wear on the metal steps.

**Wooden coal car**
Even such an attractive car as this one can be enhanced by weathering. Apply charcoal-gray washes to the top of the vehicle. Streaks and deposits will run down the sides, simulating coal dust washed down by rain. Use steel and silver sparingly on the metal reinforcing ribs in those places which receive most wear.

**Tank car**
Apply color washes to indicate where the dirt and stains will collect naturally, then exaggerate the deposits by dry brushing burnt sienna up the side of the tank, blending it into white paint bleaching the upper surfaces. Using pure turpentine on a fine brush, apply streaks to the sides of the tank to show where rain has washed through dirt.

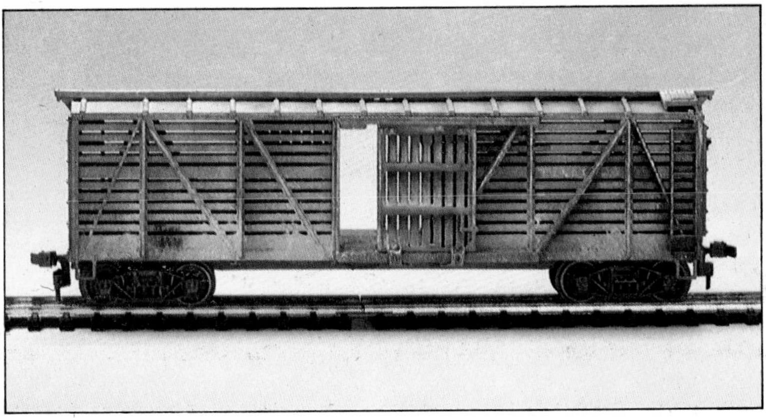

**Stock car**
Undercoat this car to cover the black plastic, then paint it with oil paint. Mix up a color approximating "box car red" using virtually no turpentine. Vary the color on the model by applying other colors to blend and shade the wooden planking. Stipple on white oil paint to build up thick deposits of "lime." Add touches of steel to the various metal parts.

# Painting figures

The techniques described here are for oil paint although many are applicable to other paints. Oil paint is uniquely suitable for painting figures as it can be blended in subtle ways which are difficult to achieve with other paints. Most painters prefer to use sable brushes for figures, especially for blending colors. Nylon brushes are a little stiff and tend to drag off too much paint, though the stiffness is useful for painting details.

Complete the figure before painting as you will have a better idea of the overall color scheme. However, it is sometimes more helpful to paint small pieces of equipment such as weapons separately to avoid having to reach into crevices. There are no strict rules about the order of painting, but you are less likely to spoil the paintwork if you work from top to bottom. Most modelmakers agree that the face sets the character and once completed is a spur to further work. After undercoating a figure the procedure is the same whether it is metal or plastic.

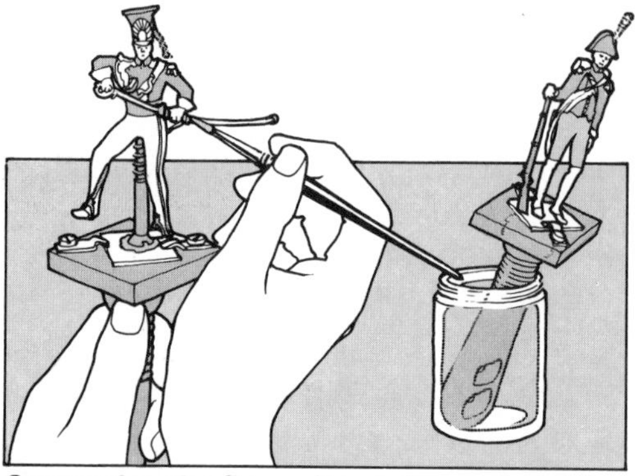

**Supporting the figure** Attach the model's temporary base to a dowel rod handle or a clamp such as an Andy clamp. For a mounted figure which does not have a base, glue a wood screw to a base to support the model. Store figures on a handle in a glass jar.

## Undercoating

Figures, like other models, need undercoating and sometimes priming before being painted (see Preparing and priming and Undercoating, page 76). A white undercoat unifies a figure and shows up detail for further painting, but gray is a better base for darker shades of paint. To preserve the fine detail, spray on the undercoat. Apply several coats leaving a couple of hours between each, and 24 hours after the last coat.

Aerosol car matt primer is particularly suitable for figures. Its coarse texture not only adds character to fabric and leather but is ideal for horses. You can apply enamel primer on both plastic and metal figures but use cellulose primer on metal only. If you want to smooth flesh areas of metal figures, rub the dry undercoat lightly with a toothbrush.

## Painting faces

A figure's face is its focal point and it should show as much detail and character as possible. Paint should be applied to the face as an actor applies make-up; it should accentuate the molding and emphasize details. All too often figures have over-made-up, clown-like appearances. At normal viewing distance the features should be obvious, but not the painting technique.

Some modelmakers prefer to treat all the flesh areas at the same time, but the hands may become smudged and are best left until later. If the figure is not fully clothed, continue the face color down to a natural break.

## The base color

Take pure white oil paint and lay a little naples yellow and burnt sienna on either side of it on your palette. Gradually add small amounts of color to the white to achieve a natural skin color. If anything, make it a little darker than normal because it will be brushed out and highlighted later which will lighten it. For brown- and black-skinned people, use the same mix, but add more burnt sienna; for orientals, use more naples yellow.

Brush the color into all the details such as eyes, nose, mouth and ears, working up to the hairline and the collar. Concentrate on an even cover so that there is no undercoat showing. Now squeeze any excess paint from the brush onto the palm of your left hand, by drawing it under the finger of your right hand into a wedge shape; do not use a cloth or tissue or any thinner. Brush off all the excess paint from the face. Do not scrub, but smooth off the paint, squeezing it from the brush as you work. Remove as much paint as possible until the face is virtually stained with color rather than painted. Brush marks will not show and even though you have not deliberately left paint in the details, natural highlights will show up. Leave the model to dry overnight. Repeat to build up a body of color. After brushing out the second time, add shadows without allowing it to dry.

## Shading and highlighting

Shade the areas where shadows would show up the modeling. (Imagine that the face is lit from three quarters above unless you've planned your diorama differently.) Use pure burnt sienna; it will blend in with the base color to form a skin tone.

First, draw a very thin line all around the hairline. Clean the brush on your hand as before and lightly brush out the brown line working into the face and removing color until it blends into the skin tone leaving a hint of shadow at the hairline.

Place the point of the brush in the corner of the eye and draw a tiny line down the side of the nose; painting both sides makes the bridge of the nose stand out. Blend the color into the cheeks.

Hollow out the eye sockets by drawing a thin line from the corner of the eye below the eyebrow and under the eyes. Blend in lines.

Add shading under the lower lip, the chin, the nose and in the ears blending the paint gradually into the lighter areas. Finally, shade the creases running from the nose to the corners of the mouth.

You now need to highlight the bone structure and upper surfaces of the face. Use pure white paint in small amounts; the base color will show through and tint it.

Begin by running a narrow line down the bridge of the nose and adding a spot on the bridge of each nostril. Delicately blend these areas into the shade so that not too much color is removed. Highlight the forehead, the chin and cheekbones. Now take a close look at the face to decide which areas need further treatment to add depth to the shadows and high points to the lighter areas.

Add color to the cheeks by placing a minute spot of red below the cheekbone. Brush out into a triangle between the sides of the face, cheekbone and crease from corner to the mouth. Only the smallest amount of red is needed to add warmth to the face.

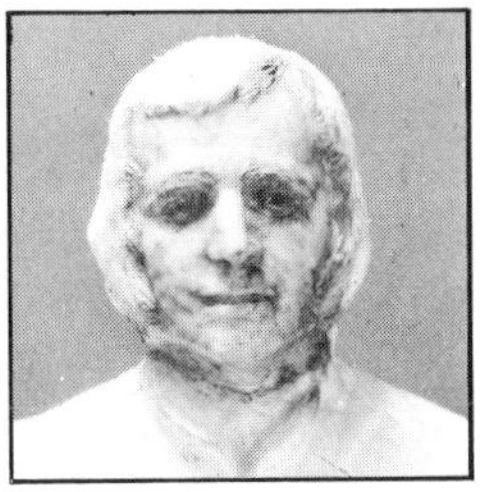

Base color

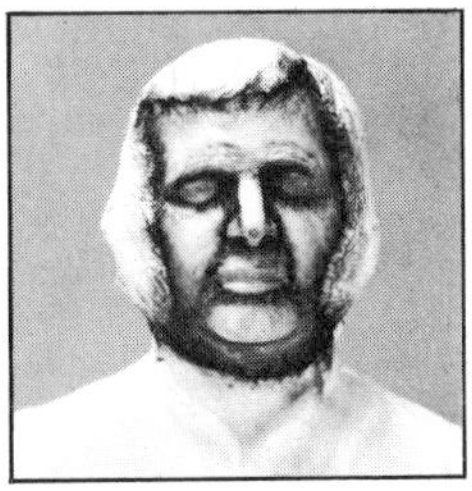

Shading

Highlighting

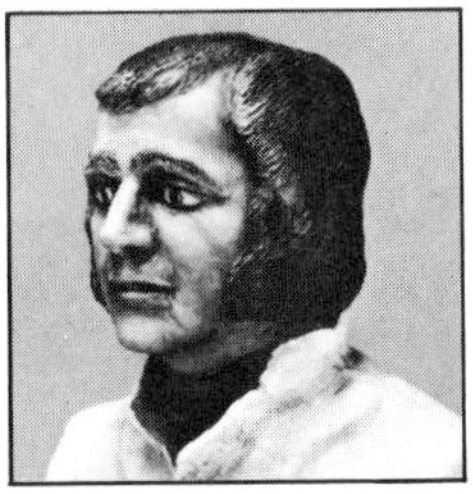

Completed face

## Eyes

Pick out the almond shape of the eyes with white paint, then paint a light brown or blue iris: place the point of a fine brush on the eye and revolve it; the iris should touch at top and bottom, slightly high of center. Put a dot of raw sienna in the center of the iris to form a pupil. On a large scale figure, the eyes can be highlighted by a small dot of white. Clean out the corners of the eyes with small touches of white and paint a fine burnt sienna line over the top edge of the lid and another halfway along the bottom, blending the bottom one in. Highlight the outer edge.

## Lips

Mix red and dark blue to make a dark plum red. Put the point of the brush between the lips and wobble the tip as you move across the mouth. Allow the lips to guide the tip of the brush rather than trying to paint a line. Now shape the corners a little up or down depending on the character. Wipe the brush dry and blend the color on the lower lip, shading it out from the upper lip until a stain of color remains; the lower lip should be slightly darker in the corners. Leave the upper lip as a dark line, but add the smallest highlight to the front of the lower lip.

## Hair

Mix your base color and brush it onto the hair making sure that it penetrates into the deeper engraved areas and aiming for an even cover. Stop short of the hairline around the face: this area will be highlighted later.

When the hair is covered, brush out as much paint as possible. The color will stain the hollows accentuating the molding. Emphasize the shape of the hair using a slightly darker tone of the basic color, perhaps adding a touch of blue or red to the shadows to add character. Shade any curls to add greater depth to the modeling.

Highlight the hair with a light tone of the base color. Even white will be toned down by the base color, and it is particularly suitable for an older man. Brush the paint back from the hairline rather than drawing a line along it, preserving the darker skin tone applied earlier. As you work further back, brush across the growth of the hair so that only the top edges are painted. Highlight the crown picking out the individual hairs.

Treat facial hair in a similar way adding very small touches of paint as it is difficult to blend it properly in these small areas. Add some stubble to the face by stippling on black or brown paint.

Lift off any paint that accidentally stains the face with a turpentine-dampened brush. If the turpentine goes through to the base color, carefully retouch the face after the turpentine has completely evaporated.

## Painting the body

Treat other exposed areas of the body in a similar way to the face. Build up a base color, then emphasize the shadows and highlight the bone structure blending the colors as described previously. Sunburned skin can be simulated by adding a red tinge, blending it in as described for painting cheeks. The effect can be heightened by painting shirt marks on the body to define the area.

Paint the hands with the same base color, darkening the color between the fingers and around the cuff. Use tones of the base color to emphasize the different planes of the fingers. Highlight the knuckles to indicate a tightly gripping hand.

# Painting clothes and equipment

**Below and on the following pages you will find methods for producing a wide variety of colors and textures. Metallic finishes require special attention as metallic enamel paints alone do not always reproduce the range of subtle colors found on real metal.**

**Buttons and belts** Even small details can be made more realistic with subtle modeling.

**Leather coat** To simulate polished leather, apply the paint smoothly and pick out highlights with a pale color. For a real sheen, cover the surface with semigloss varnish.

**Epaulets, fur backpack and hat** Emphasize these heavily textured surfaces. Drag pale paint across the fur leaving dark paint in the hollows. Pick out the strands of the epaulet.

**Musket** Accentuate the contours of the butt and highlight parts of the metal trim.

**Samurai armor** This type of armor requires meticulous attention to detail. Outline each section of armor in gold paint and pick out the stitching that holds them together with blue. Paint the decorative design in the center of the panels with silver.

**Chain mail** Use several colors to show up the texture of this armor (see page 104).

**Bronze shield** Washes of metallic powders create this bronze finish (see page 105).

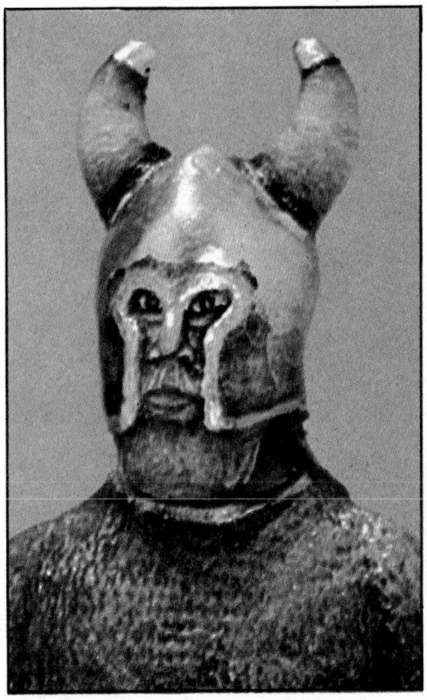

**Plate armor** For a polished appearance, highlight with silver paint (see page 105).

## Procedure for painting clothes

Shade the depths of the folds in fabric garments with a darker shade of the basic color.

There are no set rules for painting costumes as so much depends on the nature of the model. For large-scale metal figures, it is helpful to apply a wash of basic color to an area and then leave it to dry overnight. This defines the molding well and gives a good background color for further painting. Small scale figures can be painted with the base color and brushed out as described for faces (page 100), then worked on right away unless a deeper body of color is required; never apply a thick coat of paint to build up color. Work right up to and even over the edge of adjoining areas to guarantee a proper cover at the junction.

Once you've applied the basic color, add darker tones of the same in the depths of folds and creases. Blend the edges out well so that the shading enhances the model without being obvious. Highlight the upper surfaces of clothing, particularly the upper edges of creases, with a light tone. Be careful not to overdo the highlighting, especially on matt fabrics. Determine the creases on which light would be falling and emphasize these only.

Now model braid, buttons and belts. Use shadows and highlights to indicate where a strap passes over another, or add the tiniest highlight for a polished button. Define some of these features further by picking out an edge with a thin, dark line; this line should not be obvious as it only indicates the thickness of the material and the direction of the light falling on it. A very thin line around a button, for instance, gives the illusion that it is being pulled into the material. Concentrate on the shaded side of straps and where they fit loosely, fading the dark line out to almost nothing with your brush.

## Fur, sheepskin and leather

Dry brush materials like fur and sheepskin with a pale tone lightly across the top of the texture to make it stand out against the darker base color. Soft leather and suede or buckskin can be textured with paint. Apply the base color and model the leather in the normal way, but blend the paint with a soft brush using a light stippling action in one direction to give a very fine texture. Add highlights in the same way. Keep the texture fine and do not pull it out from the surface or it will resemble hair or fur.

Polished leather should not be textured. Use darker tones and greater contrast in the highlights. For highly polished leather, you can add a coat of semigloss varnish when the paint is dry.

## Chain mail

This type of armor was made from hundreds of interwoven links and it requires special care to show up its metallic qualities and depth of texture on a model. Begin by painting the chain mail with a coat of black ink; leave it to dry for 24 hours. Ink dries to a dense black and will resist the turpentine which will be used extensively in further painting stages.

Using turpentine, mix up some of the thick sediment from a can of steel and silver paint to a very runny consistency; brush it all over the armor working quickly to flood the entire area. Keep it moving, encouraging it to flow into the deeper textures. Let it dry, gently blotting excess turpentine from the surface with a brush to prevent an excess of steel from building up in the crevices. After 5 to 10 minutes you will see a subtle sheen where fine particles from the metallic paint are spread thinly over the surface.

While the surface is still damp, but not wet, paint the main highlights of the armor, which are apparent as you twist the model in the light. These will be on the shoulders, center of the breast and so on. Use pure silver in tiny amounts, working from the center of the highlights and then fading toward the edges. Brush lightly across the surface letting the highlight appear gradually. There will be just enough turpentine on the surface to allow the silver to flow under control.

Add some dark color to shaded areas and pick out the edges of belts or other details with fine lines. You can use a deep blue or even a green, but brown adds warmth to the metal and will dry with a greenish tinge. If the turpentine on the figure is beginning to dry up so that the color will not blend in, slightly dampen the brush. Careful shading of the small details at this stage greatly adds to the success of your model.

The armor will benefit from a wash of very diluted blue. Apply the wash lightly to small areas underneath the highlights to give only the barest hint of color.

## Plate armor

Treat smooth metal armor in a similar way by undercoating with black ink, then adding a generous wash of steel to give it a luster. Add a small amount of darker paint to shaded areas and pick out the re-inforcing on the edge of the plates, rivets and so on with fine lines. A thin wash of blue or even green will add character to the darker areas.

Special highlights are required for a polished appearance: just touch the model letting a small drop of runny silver paint flow onto it. Do not brush it on for the paint will develop a smooth shiny surface as it dries giving just the right effect. If the edge of the highlight does not blend in of its own accord, touch it lightly with a turpentine-dampened paintbrush. Let armor dry.

## Brass and bronze

For brass, use metallic powders such as Rose rich gold or light antique gold. A medium is supplied to mix with the powder, but you can use turpentine. Put a touch of powder onto a palette and add the medium to make a fairly runny consistency. Run the wash over the surface; keep it moving for an even, smooth finish. Do not brush it out or the metallic powder will lift off.

Add shadows with raw umber oil paint while the surface is still wet. Blend in the edge of the color by dabbing with the point of the brush. Add highlights with silver as described for plate armor, again blending in the color with small dabbing touches. You can simulate reflected light behind a highlight on brass with a touch of steel; use a touch of green wash instead of steel for bronze, and a little yellow for gold.

## Weapons

Paint the blades of cutting weapons with a black undercoat and steel wash. Hold the model in the light to see where the highlights occur naturally; touch them in lightly with silver. Darken the channels in the blades with small amounts of brown with perhaps the tiniest touch of gold paint in the shadows to add warmth. Add a blue wash to the metal near the hilt and add a white highlight to the cutting edge at the curve of a saber or axe head. The weapons on metal figures can be polished and varnished to retain their natural brilliance.

Paint the barrels of firearms in the same way but add more blue or brown wash depending on the weapon. Paint the lock plates and brass trim as described adding highlights and carefully picking out the edges with fine lines. Add a glaze of brown ink to wooden parts for sheen and depth of color, or simply apply a varnish to the stock when the paint is thoroughly dry.

Add a realistic shine to machine guns by rubbing them with graphite on the end of a finger (see page 93).

## Reflecting the environment

These maintenance men at work are shown realistically smeared with grease and dirt.

A figure should fit in with the situation in which it is depicted. An officer on parade would be smartly turned out with polished metal and leather equipment. If a soldier is shown marching or in battle, however, his clothing should show the effects.

A figure in a dry environment might have dusty boots. Dry brush a pale color sparingly onto them as you paint the ground. Gradually fade out the effect up the boots. A figure marching in a column behind horses, could have dust settled on the front of his body. Scrape a white pastel with a blade to create some dust. Pick a little up on a cotton ball and lightly rub or press the powder onto the figure. The powder will adhere to the uppermost surfaces, exactly how the dust would settle. The paint must be thoroughly dry before applying dust in this manner. Do not overdo this effect, and avoid the face.

To depict a figure in a muddy landscape, dry brush an appropriate color onto his boots. It may also be thrown up in very fine splashes onto the back of the pants. Stipple on this mud sparingly.

Rain darkens fabric on the upper surfaces of the shoulders and hats and splashed trouser bottoms will also appear darker. Fade out this effect quite quickly at the edges. Use a darker tone, too, to simulate sweat if a man is working hard, especially in a hot climate.

For an injured soldier on the battlefield, show the fabric soaked with blood around a wound. Do not apply too much or use a bright red. Real blood stains the fabric almost black around the wound itself fading out to a reddish brown around the edges.

Don't forget the effect of wear on clothes. In most cases, for instance, a soldier's uniform will have become worn and faded with time.

# Painting horses

Paint a white horse following the techniques described opposite. Use gray for the base color.

The Dutch lancer's horse below has been carefully highlighted and shaded to show up the muscles.

The breed of horse and its setting determine the way it is painted. On a parade ground a horse will be well groomed with a slight sheen to its coat, its saddlery impeccably clean and highly polished. On the other hand, if a horse is on campaign or working in a field, it may be dusty or spattered with mud.

To give the coat a sheen, paint the horse as described opposite and let it dry thoroughly, then apply a wash of linseed oil and turpentine mixed in equal proportions, with a large, soft brush. To simulate the effects of mud and dust, follow the same procedures as described for painting figures (see page 105).

Always paint the horse and rider separately. The reins and other equipment can be attached to the horse after it has been painted, otherwise they will only obstruct your brush.

The horse opposite has a dark brown coat but the painting instructions can be adapted to suit any color. You can also vary the expression on a horse's face if you wish.

## Adding the base color

Apply pure burnt umber oil paint liberally to the horse. Use older brushes as this task tends to spoil the bristles. Now take a small piece of dry sponge and wipe off any surplus paint. The paint will come off the high points and remain in the hollows showing up the natural modeling. Leave dark paint where you want deep shadows, such as under the mane, but brush it well out of the mane itself to show up the fine engraving. To reach between the legs and under the tail, attach a piece of sponge to a paintbrush handle with a rubber band, or use a stiff brush. The model tends to look better if the final strokes follow the direction of the hair on a real horse.

## Painting the hair and hooves

On most horses the mane and tail are darker than the body. Paint them a dark tone of the base color (black is too stark), then brush out leaving dark paint deep in the engraving. Finally, brush a light tone across the hair to pick out the texture.

Paint the hooves a light ocher color if the horse has white ankles, but if the legs are dark above the hooves, paint them the base color.

## Highlighting and shading

The next stage is to accentuate the modeling. First highlight the high spots with naples yellow, lightly brushing on very small amounts of color with a clean piece of sponge. Pick out the muscles, veins, bones and sinews especially. Any paint which gets into the shaded areas can be removed with a brush and the area touched up later.

Next, emphasize the dark areas using small amounts of pure base color on a soft brush. Pick out the veins on the belly of the horse with a fine line, blending in the edges of the color. Darken the front of the neck to show up the horse's face which will be painted in detail at a later stage.

This horse has white "stockings." Paint the ankles white and the hooves a light ocher; shade them at the top and highlight the front. Give the horseshoes a very light wash of chrome orange followed by a steel wash. Highlight the edges with very small amounts of silver paint.

## Painting the face

Darken the hollows on each side of the face and pick out the hairline at the forelock with fine lines, blending in the color. Highlight the bone down the axis of the face, veins, the tip of the muzzle and over the eyes with pure white paint. Model the nostrils with white and burnt umber.

The lips of a horse are a dark, warm gray without a definite edge. Brush the undercoat out of the mouth, then apply a very dark purple to the mouth blending it out over the lips. If the mouth is open, it will be a yellowish pink inside with a darker tongue and light yellowish brown teeth.

Paint the almond of the eyes a yellowish white. Paint a large brown iris so that it touches at the top and bottom. Add a dark pupil and a tiny white highlight on the eyeball. A touch of varnish when the paint is dry will give the eye a realistic watery appearance. Pick out the eyes with a dark brown line under the upper lid and at the outer edge of the low lid; blend it out from the lower lid into the face.

If the horse is marked with a white patch, stipple it on.

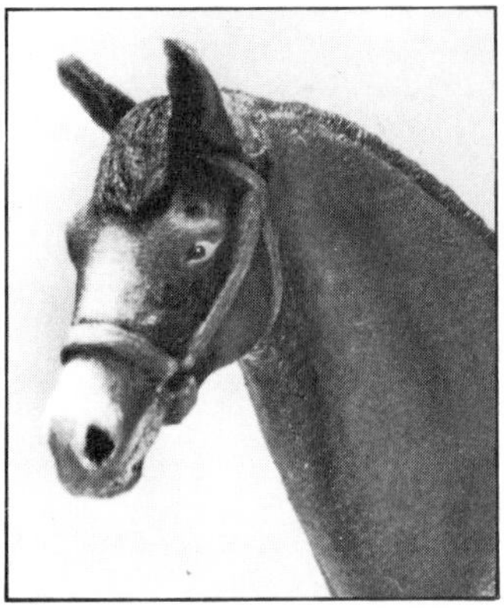

Paint a blaze on the horse's face to add interest.

This galloping horse is painted with a wild look in its eye.

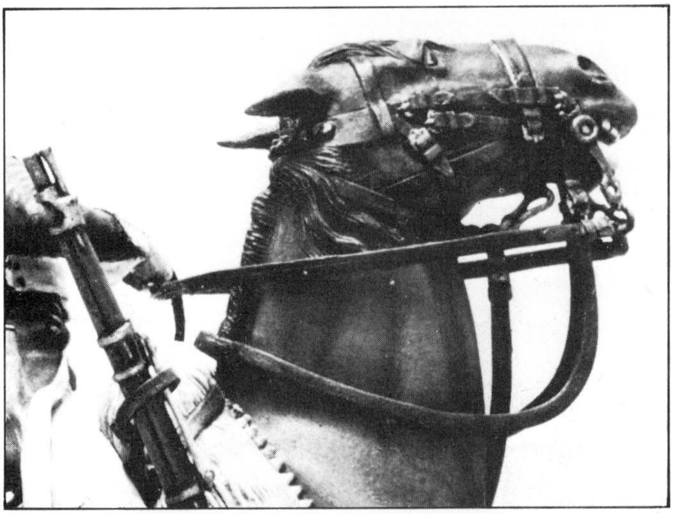

To show a startled expression, paint the horse with a more open, staring eye.

## Dappling

This sometimes occurs all over a horse though it is more often only on the flanks and haunches of gray and bay horses. Paint the horse with the base color; then, using a cut-down brush apply slightly irregular, closely packed spots which fade out at their edges. This effect should not be applied in thick layers but built up gradually. Fade out the dappled areas at the edges.

On large-scale horses, dappling can be applied with an airbrush for a realistic effect. Use the method described for mottled camouflage (page 87).

The dappling on this gray horse is concentrated on the side of its head and around the top of its legs.

# Improving vehicles

# Improving a kit vehicle

Below you will find techniques for improving upon the basic kit model which are aimed at constructing true-to-scale detail. Many molded kit parts are oversized, and the manufacturer does not always provide all the details and accessories which would be found on the real vehicle. Not only can you correct or replace the molded detail to produce a convincing miniature, but you can add new features to make the kit vehicle into a unique model. Every aspect can be improved from the engine to parts of the external structure. The body can also be cut and reshaped to change its character or convert it to another style.

The techniques below are not limited to the type of vehicle they describe, as suggestions for detailing plane parts may work equally well on either cars or tanks.

## Engines

Exposed engines, most notably in the case of motorcycles, are a focal point of many vehicles. Almost every component can be improved in some way. On small-scale early planes the engine is partly visible and as the scale increases, panels, cowlings or hoods can be removed from all kinds of vehicles to exhibit the engine. Even when the power source is hidden, extensions such as the exhaust can be seen.

An engine must be painted with care to make it look realistic. If possible, take notes and color photographs of the original engine compartment. Otherwise follow the various common features adopted by many manufacturers.

**1 Brakes** If present in the first place, these are often too large. Replace each lever with a piece of soft wire hammered flat, filed into shape and bent to the correct angle.

**2 Wiring or control cables** Only large-scale models can include all wiring. For small scales, show only the most obvious. Use heat-stretched sprue, wire or nylon thread.

**3 Fuel line** Make fuel lines from soft wire. For transparent fuel lines, use nylon thread, heat-stretched transparent sprue or empty ballpoint pen refills. For a realistic yellowish tinge, paint plastic with varnish mixed with a little paint.

**4 Rubber hose** Use thick wire for hose and paint it matt dark gray. For hose clips, leave a small section unpainted at each end or paint a silver band. For large scales, thicken wire with tape and use strips of metallic tape for clips.

**5 Springs** Shape springs from wire by winding it around a pin. Real springs can sometimes be used, but if they are glued in a stretched position they may be too strong for a plastic model.

**6 Exhaust pipe** Drill out kit part or replace the last section with aluminum or plastic tube painted to match the rest of the system.

**Truck engine**
Larger engines, such as on trucks, are also easy to improve. The plastic exhaust stack can be drilled out and covered with foil or the chrome finish toned down with varnish. Alternately, replace the stack with a metal tube.

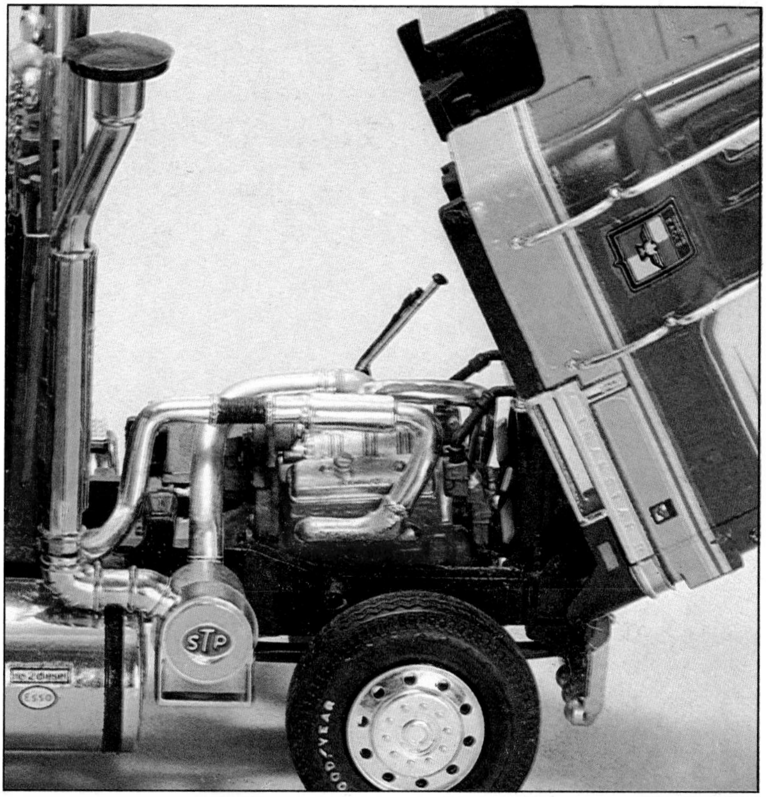


**Steam traction engine (below)** The success of this type of model depends on careful painting. Each part of the engine including the flywheel and the furnace, should be embellished in bright colors and gold or silver.

# The interior

The cockpit of a vehicle provides an opportunity to incorporate fine detail which can give the model a sense of completeness. Small-scale models in particular have very little interior detail. Because it is impossible to incorporate every feature, it is important to select those which add character and charm without creating a cluttered look. Always complete all interior details before assembling the main body.

## Instrument panels

The instrument panel or dashboard is normally supplied as a separate molded piece except in very small-scale models. There are several ways you can improve upon the kit part.

Always begin by checking it for accuracy. Important instruments may be misplaced or even omitted and you may need to correct the panel by adapting the techniques for making a new panel or recessed instruments. Planes, for instance, often have a secondary dashboard set slightly below the main panel and modern jets have consoles on both sides of the cockpit; if the panel or consoles are missing, shape them from plastic sheet and apply decals for instruments. The transparent display screen situated in front of the pilot in a modern jet plane can be made from clear plastic.

On small-scale models the dials may be set too deeply. Make a new panel by drilling through the dials of the original, then tracing the panel's shape onto thin plastic. Cut out the shape and glue it on a thicker backing sheet to stiffen the plastic. For more recessed instruments and an exceptionally realistic panel, drill through the dials and add a second panel behind the first as shown below.

Most instrument panels can be improved by the addition of metal rims around the dials and painted or three-dimensional switches (see right and opposite).

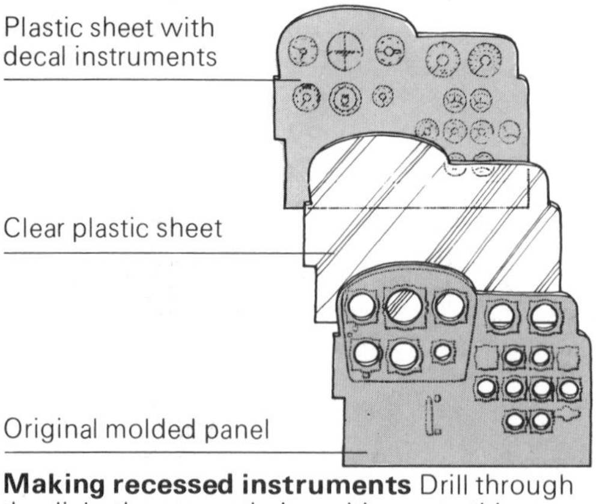


**Making recessed instruments** Drill through the dials, then trace their position onto thin plastic. Stick decal intrument faces on plastic. Paint panel, then glue plastic and panel together, sandwiching a very thin clear plastic sheet in between for glass. Trim any excess material from panel edge.

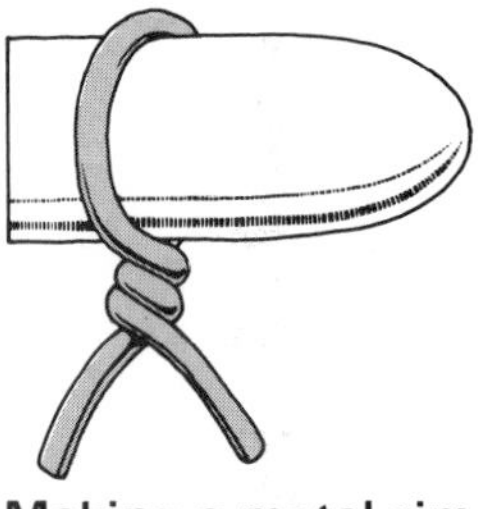

**Making a metal rim** Wrap thin, soft wire around a tapered paintbrush handle and twist the ends. Remove from handle.

Carefully tap the wire ring with a hammer to flatten it slightly. Trim twisted ends down to the joint.

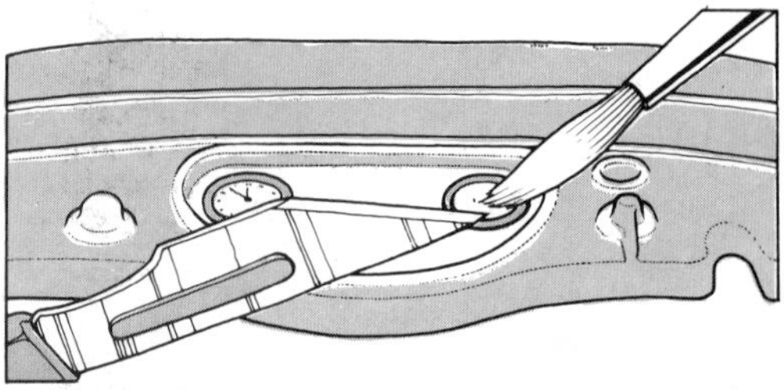

Join the ends with a touch of cyanoacrylate glue and attach the ring to the instrument panel with glue or the gloss varnish used for glass on the instrument face.

## Painting instrument panels

The color of the instrument panel may provide a touch of drama to the interior of a vehicle. Take care to paint the panel accurately by maintaining the correct scale and using authentic colors for all of the switches and instrument faces in the vehicle.

Always follow the same procedure: paint the whole panel, including the instruments, one overall color before touching in the faces and the rims surrounding them. To paint the raised molding around instrument faces, simply brush across the high points using very little paint and avoiding a build up of paint on the edges.

It is usually best to use decals for the instrument faces as they are far more detailed than hand-painted ones. Some kits include a decal sheet. You can also buy complete sets of decal instrument panels for specific vehicles and these can be cut up and used on models for which they were not intended.

Cockpits often contain painted instructions to remind the pilot of procedures and safeguards. Indicate these with thin lines or dots of paint. They will give an impression of fine detail and add color.

After painting the panel and adding any decals, lay the panel flat and drop small amounts of gloss varnish onto each dial for glass. Do not brush on the varnish, but merely encourage it to flow with the tip of the brush until it completely fills the dial. Cover the panel until the varnish dries to prevent dust settling on it and marring the surface.

## Wooden instrument panels

Wooden dashboards are common on early planes and cars. On a small-scale plastic dashboard you can simulate the wood grain with paint. Use a brush squeezed almost dry and spread it to a wedge shape. As you draw the brush over the surface, the bristles will separate marking a parallel grain.

Real wood veneer can be used to construct an instrument panel on large-scale models. First glue the veneer to a backing board so that you can thin it by sanding with fine sandpaper wrapped around a block. Use rubber-based contact cement so you can remove it later. Punch the instruments from the thinned veneer, then remove the veneer from the board by dissolving the glue with lighter fluid. Rub the back with a fingertip to remove any last traces of cement. The advantage of using wood veneer is that it can be stained and varnished to reproduce the finish of a classic car dashboard. Apply several coats of varnish to make a highly polished surface.

## Rearview mirrors

Automobiles and some airplanes have rearview mirrors. On modern jets they are situated on the leading edge of the canopy. Additional mirrors can be fixed to the dashboard on some cars to add a personal touch. Make the frame from plastic sheet and sprue, and the mirror surface from thin metal foil.

Rearview mirrors made from plastic have been added to the canopy of this Corsair II.

## Switches and controls

All dashboards have switches of various kinds, most of which can be indicated by spots of paint or dry-transfer dots. On larger-scale models, and in particular those of early cars and airplanes, switches can be modeled in three dimensions from wire. For large controls on the instrument panel such as those for the choke or pump on early vehicles, file the head of a pin flat. Hold the pin in a vise with the head on the jaws to hold it securely as you file.

Although the main control levers and pedals are usually included in many kits, they should be examined for accuracy and scale and then rebuilt if necessary. Column gear shifts and control stalks are easily replaced with fine wire. Build up a round knob on the end with layers of white glue. For more complicated shapes, use the end of the kit control or cut one from plastic.

A throttle lever is normally situated on the lefthand side of a cockpit. Use any of the methods described for making switches.

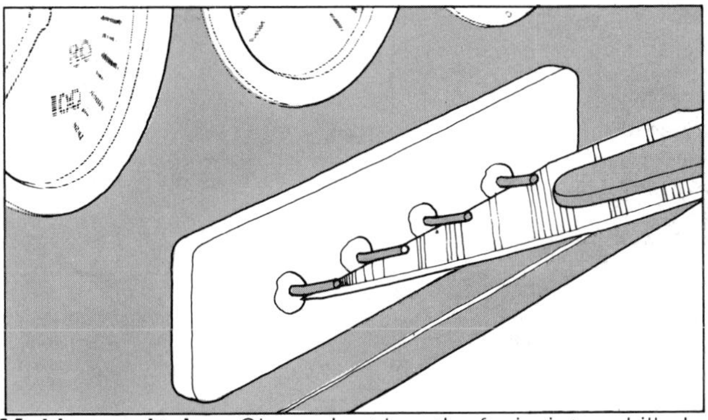

**Making switches** Glue a short length of wire into a drilled hole and add a touch of white glue on the end of the switch for a round knob. To set a row of soft-wire switches to the same angle, stroke all of them at once with a knife blade.

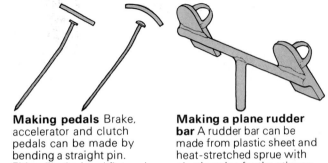

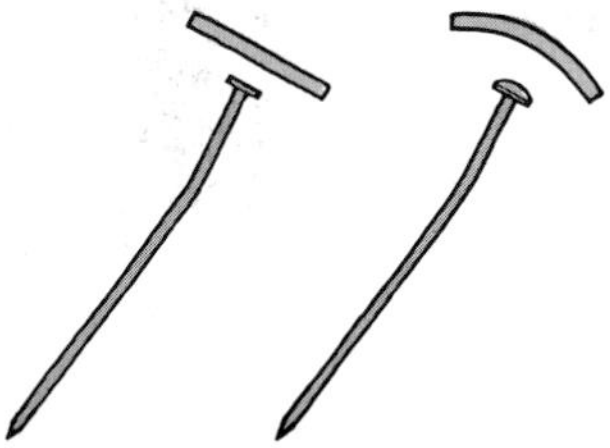

**Making pedals** Brake, accelerator and clutch pedals can be made by bending a straight pin. Either file the head flat and glue on a plastic foot plate or use the original pin head to hold the plastic plate in a curve.

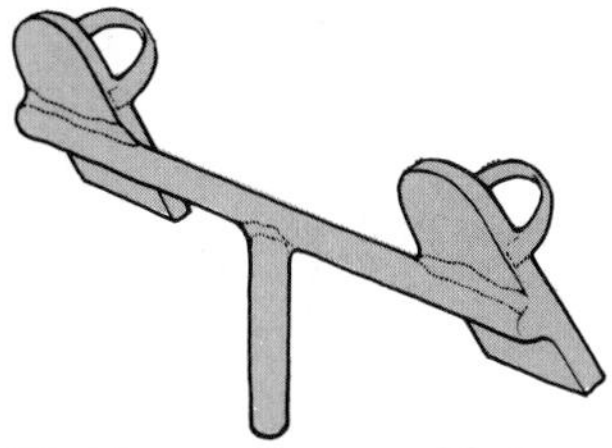

**Making a plane rudder bar** A rudder bar can be made from plastic sheet and heat-stretched sprue with plastic strips for the stirrups. Dry brush metallic paint on the bar and on the floor where the pilot's feet operate the controls.

## Seats

Make sure that safety straps hang or lie naturally on the seat like those on this Grumond A6 Intruder. Note, too, the hand-made ejector seat loop.

Most kits contain a seat in the cockpit or cab. Some of them are very good reproductions; however, there, are common omissions of detail and inaccuracies in scale which can be corrected.

Some kits, for instance, purposely distort or omit the seat cushions to allow the weight of the driver or pilot to be more realistically simulated. If you are not including a driver, build up the kit part with modeling putty or make a new one out of plastic sheet.

Safety straps or harnesses are important details which are often missing. Those which are molded on the seat look fine if well painted; however, fully three-dimensional straps are more convincing. Cut strips of paper, plastic or toothpaste tube foil, bend them into shape and glue in place. They need not be all the same length or lie at the same angle. Seat belts, for instance, can be left casually on the seat or even hanging over the edge of the cockpit or out of the car. Clips and buckles can be modeled from thin wire or painted on with a fine brush.

Ejector seats in modern jets are usually operated by pulling on a loop or handle fixed above the pilot's head. It is normally out of scale in kits. Cut it off and drill a small hole to take a thin wire substitute. Paint the new loop or handle the usual distinctive colors.

# Wheels, tracks and suspensions

All vehicles should stand convincingly on the ground. By modifying the suspension and the wheels you can simulate the weight of the original car, airplane or tank. Furthermore, attention to all the individual parts – the valve and tread pattern of a tire, the tension on a tank track or the profile of the mudguards – will enhance the look of the model.

The tires on this Corsair II have been filed so that they appear depressed by the weight of the body of the plane.

### Simulating weight on a tire

You can file the bottoms of solid plastic tires flat to show them depressed under the weight of the vehicle. With the wheels on, drag the vehicle across a piece of sandpaper fixed to a board; or, file each tire in turn, checking them together on the model for accuracy.

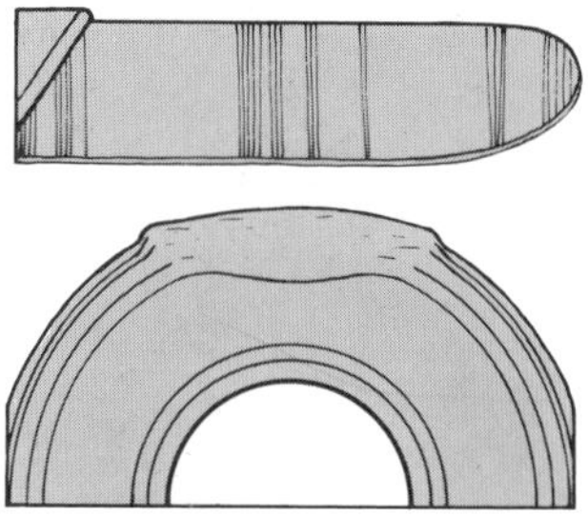

To make a soft-walled tire bulge, heat a knife and press it on the tire. Practice on spare wheels until you can distort all the tires equally. This method does not work well with hollow wheels.

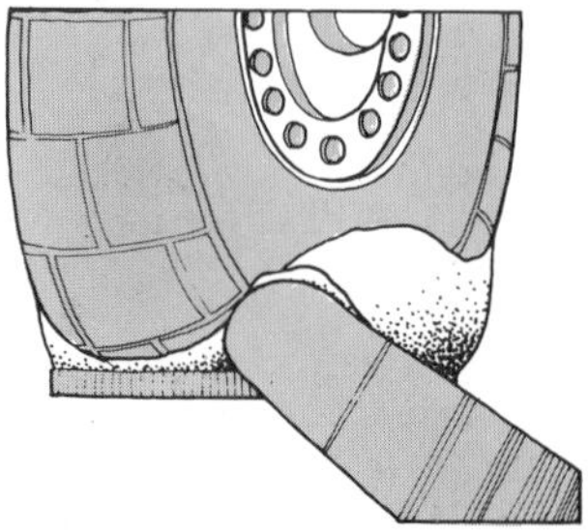

Another way of making a soft-walled tire bulge is to file the tire flat, then glue a piece of thin plastic to the base and build up the bulge with filler. This technique is not practical with small wheels.

## Standing the vehicle on the ground

One of the most important aspects of modeling a wheeled vehicle is making sure that it stands firmly and squarely on the ground. Creating the correct balance involves very careful checking at the critical stages of construction.

The chassis of a road vehicle must be built without a warp to prevent a wheel from lifting up. Sight across the chassis members or floor of the vehicle to line up both long sides when gluing it. If necessary, weight it or tape it down in position on a board until the glue sets. Check the vehicle for symmetry again when you add the suspension, first with all the wheels assembled dry, and again after gluing them.

The plastic body of a road vehicle with a working suspension may not be heavy enough to depress the spring sufficiently. It may be possible to weight the body as for a plane with a tricycle landing gear as described below, but if necessary, glue the suspension in the correct position. Loose wheels which can revolve may prevent the model standing properly. In most cases, there is little to be gained from working wheels and they, too, can be glued in place.

Planes need special care as the landing gear of most models is not strong enough to support the plane while the glue is setting. Support the aircraft on blocks, then adjust the landing gear so that it is at the correct angle.

A plane with a tricycle landing gear may need a weight in the nose to hold the nose wheel on the ground. Tape the main parts of the plane together and weight the nose with modeling clay until it sits properly. Weigh the modeling clay and replace it with small metal weights such as lead shot plus enough clay to hold it in place. Polystyrene cement should be used with discretion to secure the weights as it can dissolve the plastic.

Older model planes were often molded with the landing gear suspension in an extended position as it would be just after take-off and landing. If the plane is on a stand this is acceptable, but an extended suspension tends to make the plane ride too high when standing on the ground. Make sure that your kit is modeled in the appropriate position; if it is not, remodel the suspension.

An effective way to simulate the weight of almost any vehicle is to show the tires depressed (see opposite).

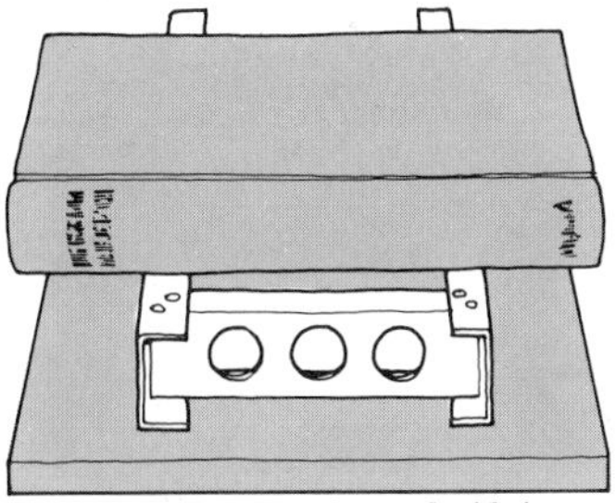

**Assembling a chassis** If the parts will not stay symmetrical, weight the chassis down on a flat board until the glue dries.

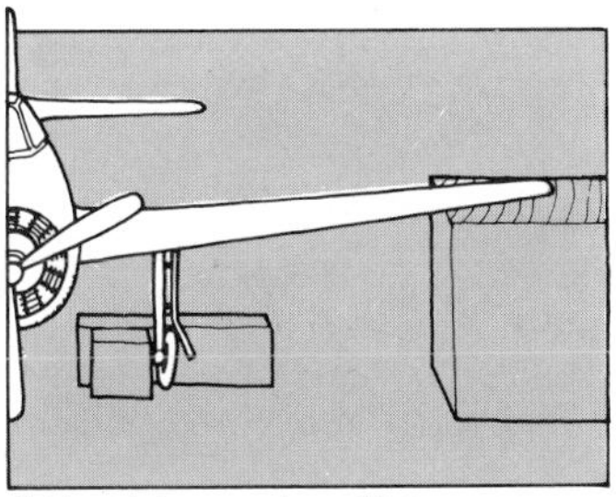

**Attaching a landing gear** Support the plane on blocks so that the wheels are just above the ground. To stop any movement as the glue sets, place small weights against the wheels.

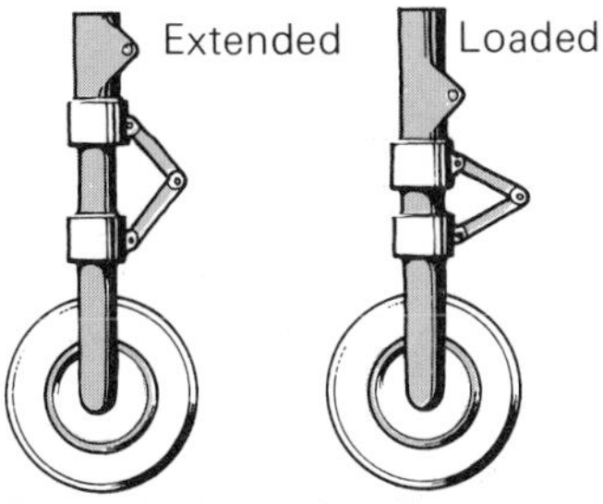


**Remodeling a landing gear suspension** Cut and remodel the suspension in the loaded position if the plane is to stand on the ground.

## The suspension

Only modify the suspension if it will be sufficiently visible to make it worthwhile. Leaf springs are usually molded in one piece and, therefore, the separate strips, clamps and "U" bolts may not be sharply defined. If you cannot improve it enough by careful scoring and trimming, rebuild the unit using the kit part as a guide.

Cut away the clamps and "U" bolts, and if the main part of the spring is satisfactory, add self-adhesive tape, heat-stretched sprue or wire replacements. To replace the spring unit itself, cut individual strips from plastic sheet. Check their combined thickness against the kit part and sand the cut edges smooth. Cut the longest strip longer than required and tape it to a wooden former. Mark the center with a pencil. Cut the other strips to length and mark their centers. Assemble the strips with liquid cement.

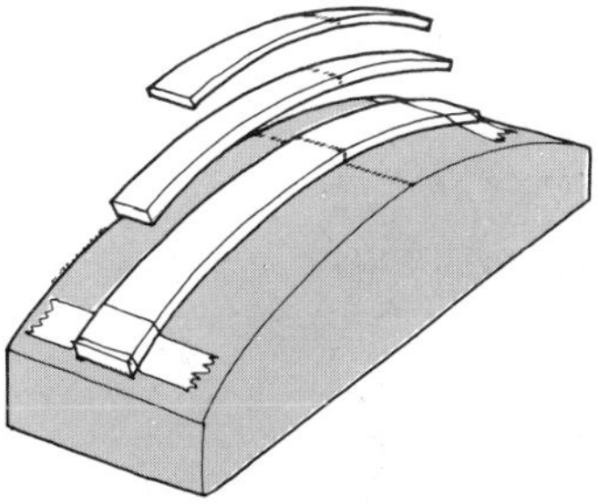

**Assembling a spring unit** Glue the strips together on the former with liquid cement, carefully aligning the center marks. When set hard, cut the longest strip to length and remove unit.

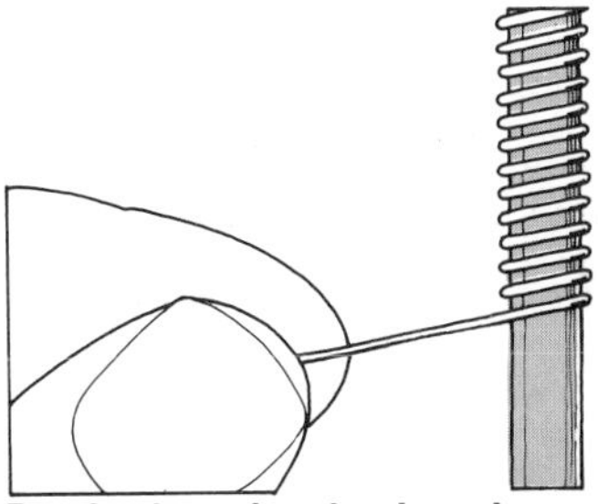

**Replacing shock-absorber springs** The coil of a spring may not be well enough defined. Cut off the molded part and replace it with wire wound around a plastic rod.

## Wheels and tires

Some large tires are molded with a joint down the center of the tread and even some of the smaller solid wheels often have a flash line in the same place. Always sand or scrape away this junction with a knife, even at the risk of losing some tread. Recut the tread of solid tires if you wish, using the techniques shown right.

You can use any areas of lost tread to suggest a worn tire. File away more tread if necessary and don't forget the spare wheel – it might show more or less wear than those on the car depending on its age. To indicate badly adjusted steering, just file the tread slightly off center.

The soft plastic tires which resemble real rubber tires in large-scale kits are very convincing. Sometimes, however, they can be a little too shiny to be realistic and look much too new on a weathered vehicle. To alter their appearance, after cutting off any flash line, roughen the tread and the side walls with fine sandpaper to dull the shiny surface.

If you wish, you can emphasize the tread on the wheels of showroom-condition models with paint. Run a dark wash onto the tire letting it settle into the tread. When dry, carefully dry-brush the top surface with a lighter tone of gray to highlight the tread.

The "chromed" parts of plastic wheels rarely look authentic, even on showroom models. The imitation chrome looks particularly odd and unsuitable on weathered vehicles. Apply a very light wash of black or brown paint to dull the plastic as well as emphasize the details. Pick out parts of the wheel in different metallic finishes, perhaps some foil on the hubcaps and steel-colored paint on the wheel nuts. The rims can be painted a color to match the body of the vehicle. A final coat of clear varnish will age the chrome a little, while a light coat of "dust" from an airbrush (see page 97) will tone in the wheels with the rest of a weathered vehicle. Use a pale color for the dust.

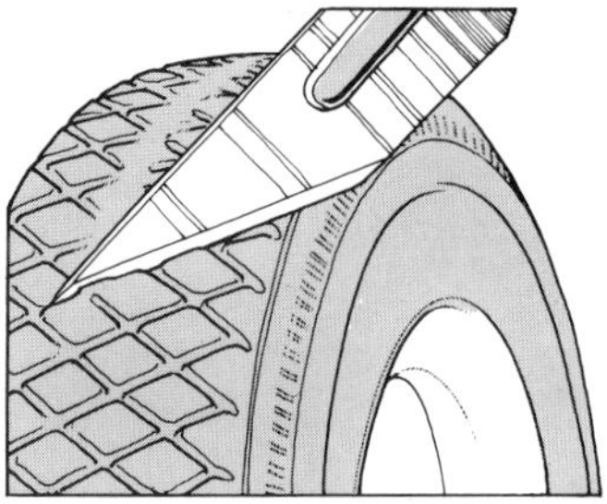

**Scoring tread across the tire** Match up the lines by eye with a sharp knife.

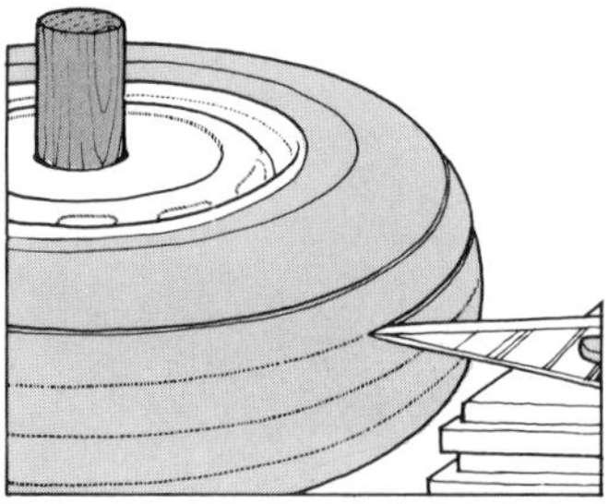

**Scoring tread around the tire** Set wheel on a rod so that it can revolve. Support knife on cardboard strips. Revolve wheel against knife point.

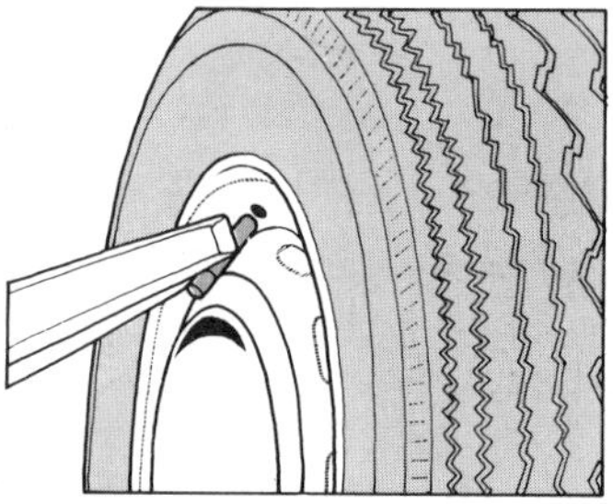

**Adding a valve** Drill a small hole in the wheel and glue in a piece of heat-stretched sprue. Or, paint a length of fine wire matt black leaving a tiny metal cap at the end; glue wire in the hole.

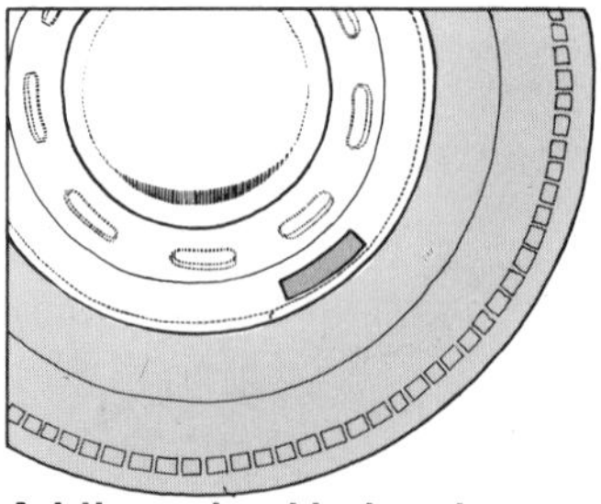

**Adding wheel balancing weights** Glue small strips of plastic sheet to the rims to make wheel balancing weights.

## Airplane wheel doors and wells

The doors which seal the wheel wells on planes with a retractable landing gear are normally too thick in 1:72 scale kits. Use the kit doors to trace replacements on thin plastic.

The wheel wells themselves should be lined with plastic walls around the opening. Tape the two halves of the wing together to gauge the size and shape of the walls. Cut pieces of plastic to fit the contour of the upper wing surface leaving enough plastic to project out of the opening. Glue the plastic wall pieces to the edge of the lower wing half; trim the wall flush when the glue has set. Next, trace the shape of the wall on the upper wing half and separate the wing. Add plastic strips or heat-stretched sprue for ribs, and thin wire or sprue for hydraulic lines, on the inside of the wing. To complete the assembly, glue the wing halves together and the wall to the upper surface of the wing.

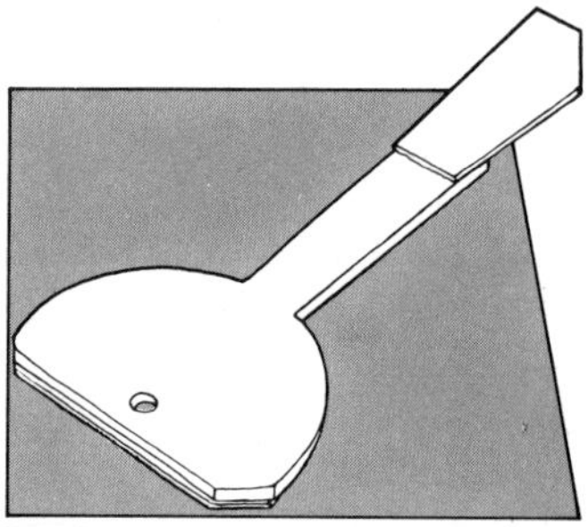

**Making a wheel door** Some doors are made of more than one piece of metal. Construct the model door in the same way to make it look authentic.

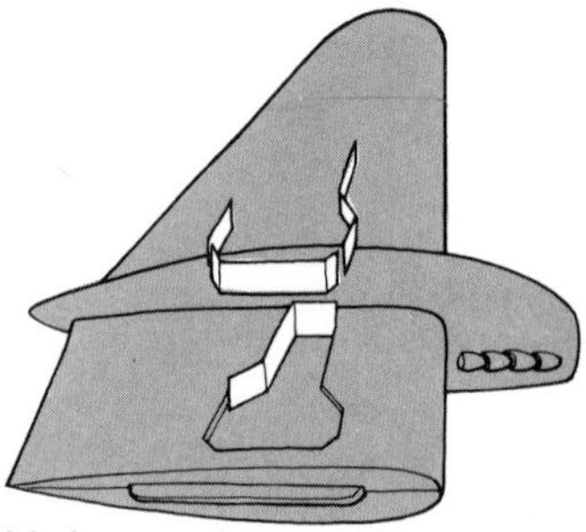

**Lining a wheel well** Use pieces of thin plastic to line the wheel wells of a plane with a retractable landing gear.

## Tank tracks and tires

The tracks on tanks are heavy and sag under their own weight. When the track on a model is made from individual links, as in large scales, it can normally be encouraged to hang realistically. Tracks in smaller scales, however, are often molded as one continuous plastic strip which tends to stay taut over the guide wheels. Tie down this type of track with thread, or glue it down with white glue wedging tissue between the track and mudguards to hold the track in position until the glue sets.

Tank wheels have hard rubber tires. To improve a model, round off the edges of the tires slightly and even cut a few nicks to indicate wear.

The plastic tracks on model tanks should be shaped to sag over the guide wheels, as on this Panzer, so that they imitate those on the original vehicle.

## Motorcycle mudguards and license plates

It is often necessary to reduce the thickness of mudguards so that they look as thin as sheet metal. Use a knife with a curved blade to scrape away the inside. On small-scale models, the mudguard is sometimes molded so that a straight edge of plastic shows across the width of the guard on the inside. Take a small round file and file a depression to match the outer curve. When the inside is painted any small difference in thickness will not show.

Mudguard support brackets are not always well molded on small-scale motorcycles, yet they can often add character. Make new ones from plastic or wire depending on the shape. Plastic brackets can be shaped on the mudguard with liquid cement. Wire brackets should be shaped over a rod as wide as the guard, then attached.

Motorcycle license plates are often too thick when molded in one piece with the mudguard. Cut it away and smooth the mudguard with wet-and-dry paper. Cut a replacement from plastic sheet. Use the decal as a guide to its shape and size, but cut the inside curve to fit on the mudguard before cutting out the rest of the plate; cut the outer curve to match the inner one.

This model has homemade wire mudguard support brackets and license plate. The mudguard itself has been pared down on the inside to make it look more like thin sheet metal.

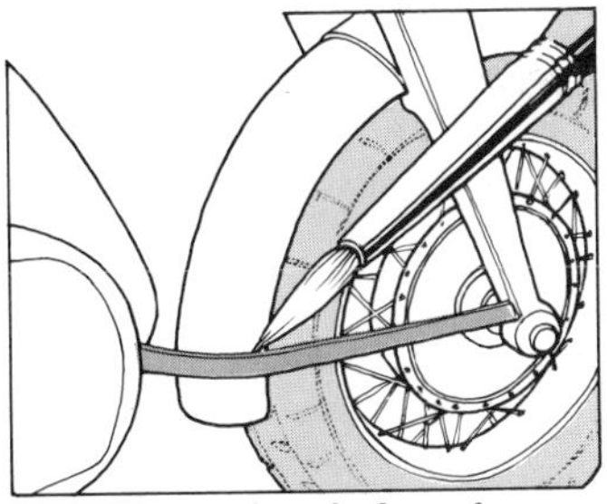

**Shaping a plastic bracket**
Shape a plastic bracket on the mudguard by softening it with liquid cement.

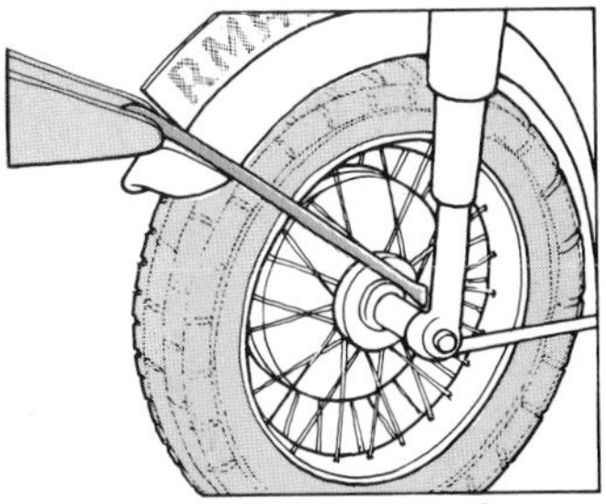

**Attaching a wire bracket**
Add a touch of cyanoacrylate glue to the forks and position the bracket with tweezers.

# Wings and propellers

Always check that the trailing edges of wings, tail plane and rudder are true to scale, especially in 1:72 scale, and correct them, if necessary. Wings which are molded in two halves and which join along the trailing edge, never have a sufficiently thin edge. Even when the trailing edge is molded as part of one half or the wing is a solid piece of plastic, the edge is often too thick. Propellers also need careful attention.

## Wings

To correct the type of wing that joins along the trailing edge, sand each of the sections on the inside as shown below, assembling the two halves frequently to check the thickness. The major advantage of this method is that the surface detail is undamaged.

If the wing is a solid piece of plastic or its construction makes this method impossible, reduce the thickness from the outer surface of the complete wing piece by scraping and sanding both sides of the trailing edge in turn. Make sure that the edge still matches the rear wing fillet where it attaches to the fuselage. You will almost certainly need to rescore the control surfaces and the panel lines afterward (see page 120).

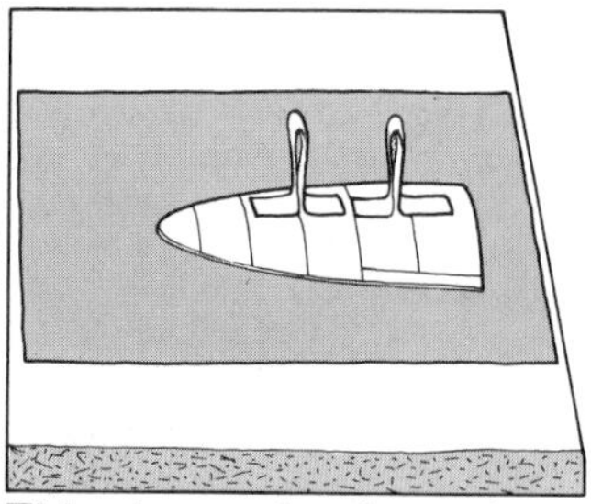

**Thinning a wing from the inside** Glue a piece of fine wet-and-dry paper to a board. Cut off any plastic locating pins from inside wing half and stick adhesive tape "handles" to top surface. Move wing in a circular motion, holding it flat on the paper with your fingertips and keeping an even pressure over the entire wing.

## Propellers

The edges and tips of a kit propeller are almost always too thick. To thin them, support the blade on a flat surface and scrape down the edge with a knife, followed by a fine file and wet-and-dry paper. Alternately, make a new propeller entirely from scratch.

Early two-bladed wooden propellers can be carved from thick plastic or built from alternating layers of light and dark wood veneer for an attractive striped effect. Each veneer must first be sanded to reduce its thickness. The blades of more modern metal propellers can be carved individually from a strip of thick plastic then glued into a center boss, as shown opposite.

The rotor blades on this Puma helicopter were scraped to a sharp edge to reduce them to scale thickness. They were then gently heated and bent into a slight curve to imitate the original blades bending under their own weight.

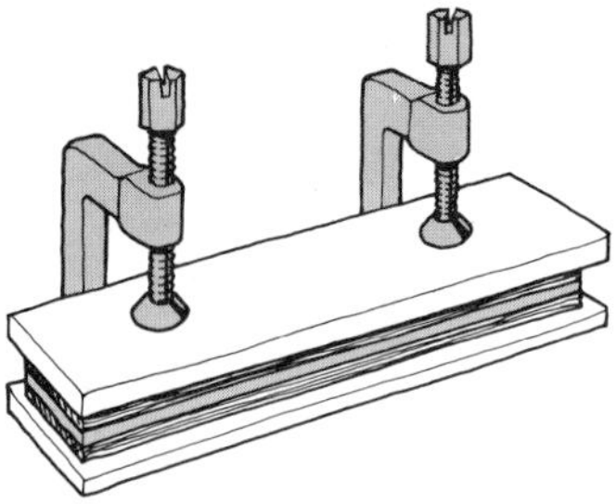

**Making a wooden propeller** Glue alternating light and dark veneers into a block; clamp the block overnight to guarantee a good bond.

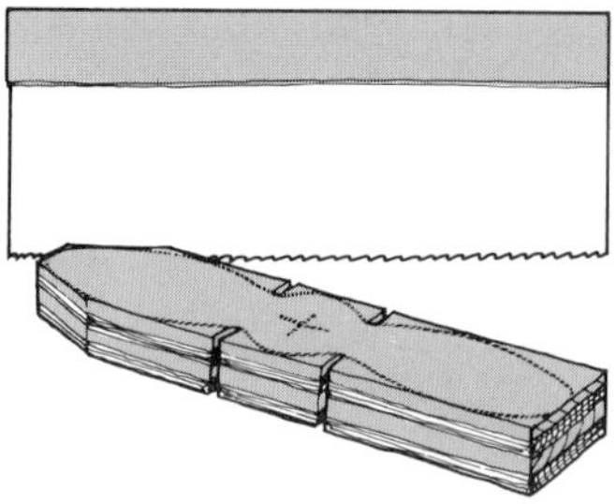

Mark the propeller's shape on the block and cut around the outline with a saw and a knife.

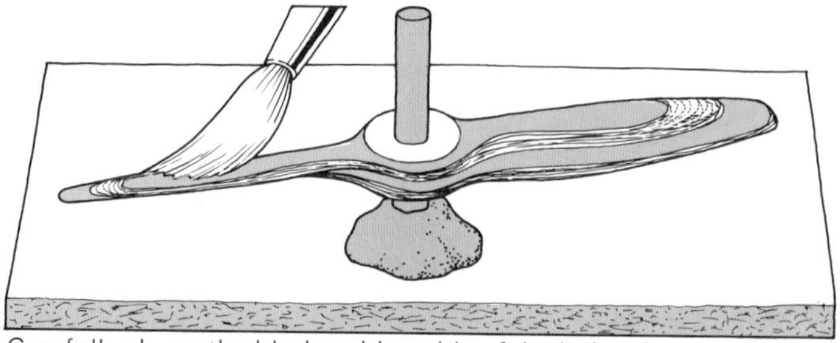

Carefully shape the blades either side of the hub using a knife or file to create the correct profile, then smooth the surface with wet-and-dry paper. Finally, stain and varnish the propeller to produce an authentic finish.

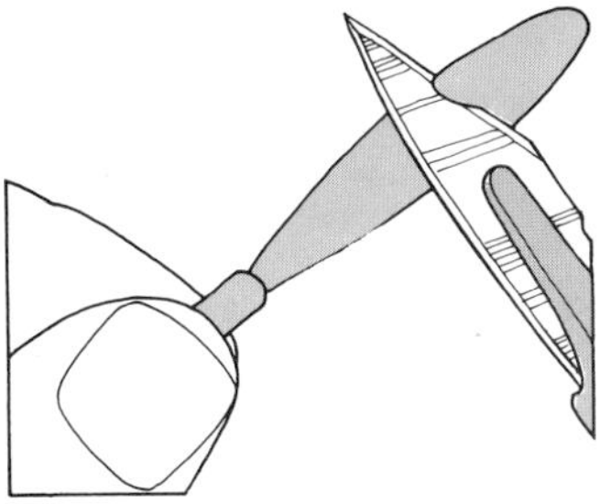

**Making a metal propeller**
Shape three blades from a strip of thick plastic using a knife, a file and wet-and-dry paper. File a peg on end of each blade.

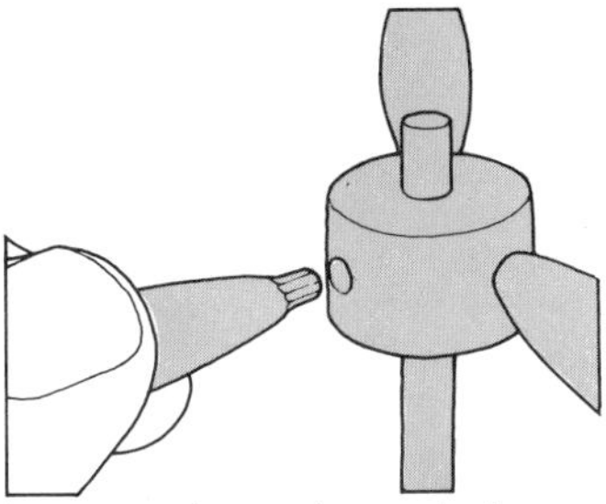

Insert each peg into a hole drilled in a center boss made from sprue. Run liquid cement into base of each blade; twist them all to the same angle.

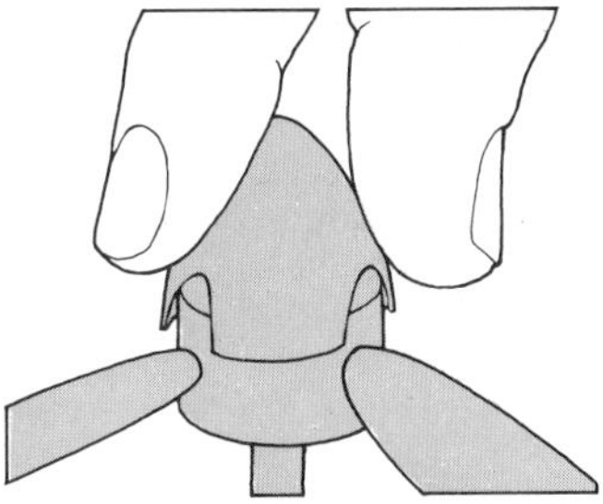

To complete the metal propeller, cover the center boss with a spinner made using the plug-molding technique described on page 55.

## Ship superstructures

**Like airplane wings and propellers, the screens, bulwarks and overhanging decks on model ships are often too thick and should be corrected. Scrape the oversized section to scale, or make up blocks of plastic to form the main parts of the superstructure and glue pieces of thin plastic sheet to the edges.**

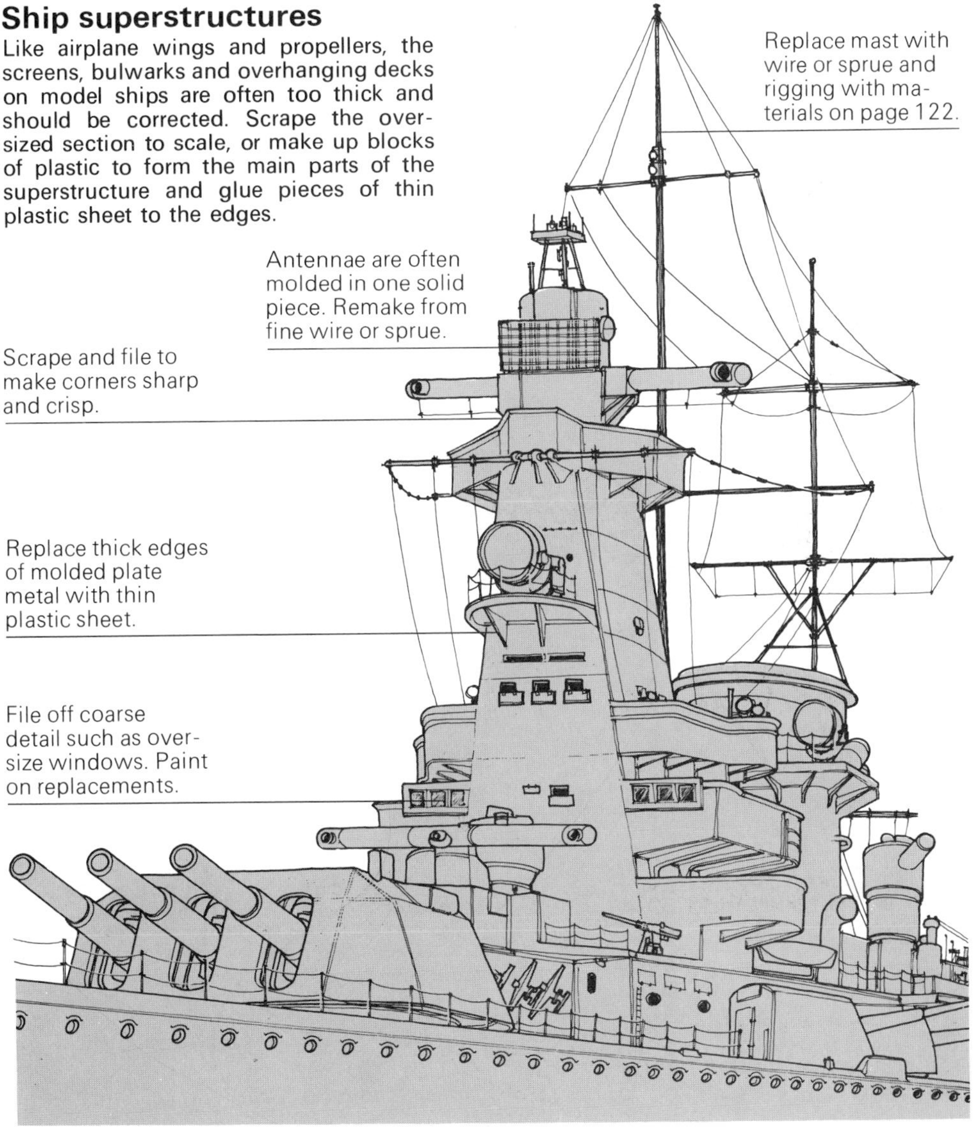

Replace mast with wire or sprue and rigging with materials on page 122.
Antennae are often molded in one solid piece. Remake from fine wire or sprue.
Scrape and file to make corners sharp and crisp.
Replace thick edges of molded plate metal with thin plastic sheet.
File off coarse detail such as oversize windows. Paint on replacements.

# Scribing surface detail in plastic

All kits have molded surface detail such as panel lines, planks, rivets and, in the case of early planes, a fabric weave. In many cases this detail is inaccurate. On planes and ships lines are often raised where they should be sunken, and rivets are oversized. The woven fabric effect is particularly unrealistic on small-scale planes as the original fabric would have been stretched and painted with dope for a smooth finish. Consider each detail individually and decide whether it should be left as is, scribed anew or removed altogether. Certainly, if some detail has been removed during construction, to make a good joint between components for instance, it must either be replaced or any remaining detail sanded away.

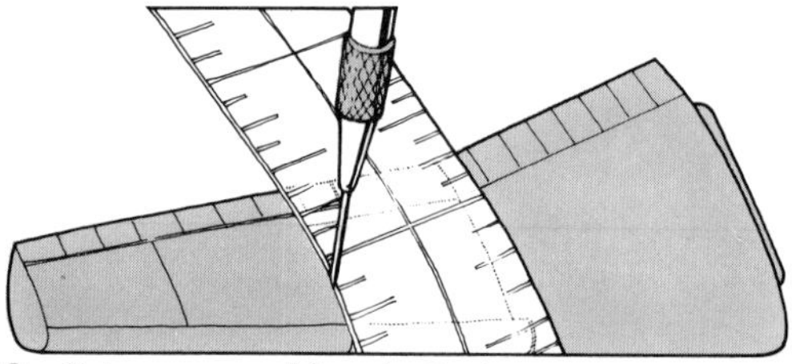

**Scribing a panel** Sand off raised panel lines and mark new ones with a pencil. Scribe new lines with a pointed tool or the back edge of a knife blade held against a flexible ruler. Sand surface very lightly to remove burr produced by scribing.

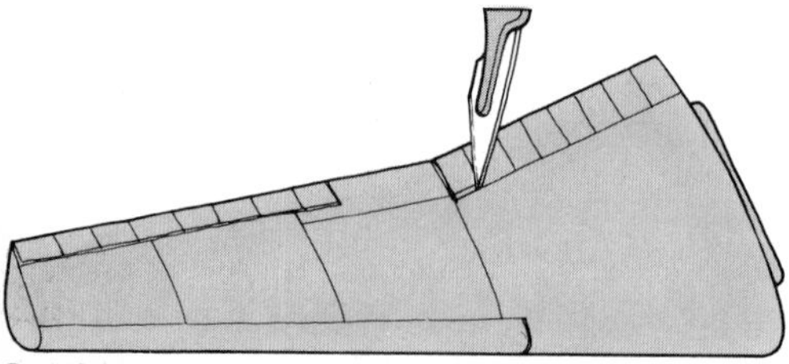

**Scribing a joint** Use the side of a pointed blade to mark the joint between a flap and wing: the blade will cut a square edge on the wing and an angled edge on the flap.

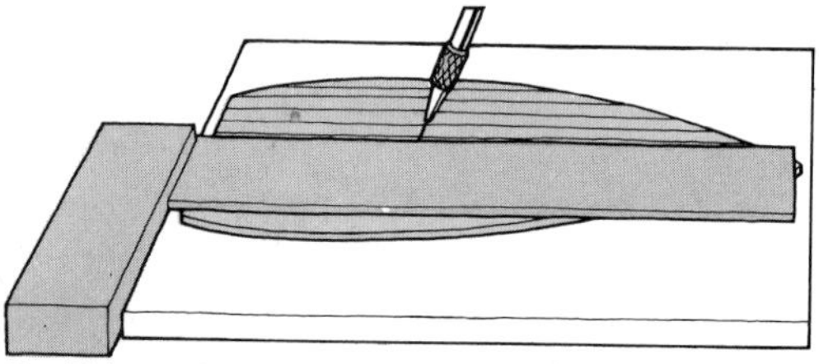

**Scribing planks** Note the position and shape of molded details on ship deck; cut them off. Sand deck smooth and stick to a board with double-sided tape, aligning it with a straight edge. Use a try square to mark, then scribe, new lines. Remake raised detail from scratch. Alternately, cut a new plastic deck; scribe.

# Windows and lights

Most model vehicles have windows or canopies molded in clear polystyrene. These items are often called transparencies. They are easily scratched or damaged by solvents, so remove them from the kit and store in a safe place.

Before attaching a window or canopy to the model, wash it in warm soapy water and dry with a soft cloth. Scratches can be removed by polishing with liquid metal polish, followed by a little toothpaste on a fingertip. Finally, rub with a cotton ball.

A window or canopy can be glued with polystyrene cement, but it is safer to use white glue which can be washed off with water if necessary. Use only enough glue to hold it in place and take care that it does not squeeze out into an area from which it cannot be removed such as the inside of a cockpit.

Fill the joint between the canopy and fuselage of a plane with epoxy putty on a knife blade. Smooth it down with water on your fingertip, as it is very difficult to rub down excess filler after it dries without damaging the canopy. When it has set hard, smooth the filler with water and fine wet-and-dry paper, carefully working away from the canopy.

## Replacing kit parts

A kit window or canopy may fit so poorly that no amount of cutting or filing will improve it. Flow lines or discolored plastic may obscure the interior of the model. The window or canopy may also be too thick, especially where the edge is visible such as a windshield on an early airplane, open car or jeep.

New flat windows can be cut from clear acetate using the kit part as a guide. Three-dimensional shapes can be molded from acetate using the plug-molding technique described on page 55.

If a vehicle such as a train passenger car needs a frosted glass window, sand the back of an acetate panel with very fine paper until the scratches produce a milky-white surface.

Small windows or portholes may be molded as part of the body or omitted altogether. Drill or cut out a tapered opening from the inside and glaze the window with Kristal-kleer, a milky-white liquid which will span a hole up to $\frac{1}{4}$ inch (6 mm) in diameter and dries clear.

Molded beacons and lights can be painted the appropriate color and varnished but a handmade one made from Kristal-kleer or clear plastic is superior to the kit version. For a raised beacon, file down the molded light to a flat base and paint it the appropriate color. You can drill a slight hollow for a round beacon, if you like. Apply a drop of Kristal-kleer to the base: a round beacon will form naturally, but for a tear-drop shape, leave the liquid until a skin forms then push it into shape with a toothpick. To make it larger, apply a second drop on top of the first. Let it dry thoroughly, then coat the beacon with some gloss varnish to make it shine realistically.

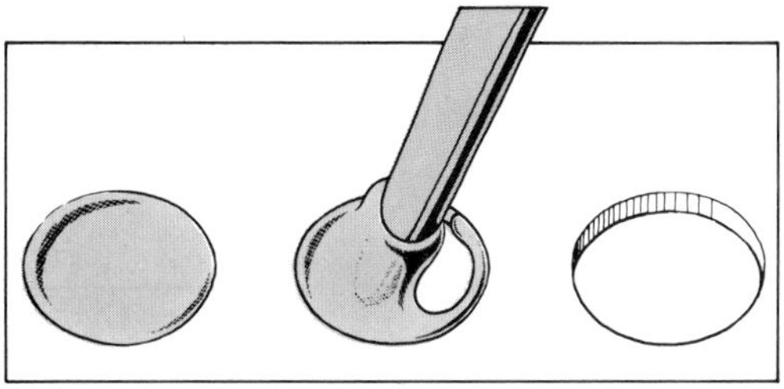

**Glazing a porthole** Touch a drop of Kristal-kleer on the inside edges of the hole. Work it in a circular motion with a toothpick until the liquid spans the porthole opening. Leave the porthole to dry.

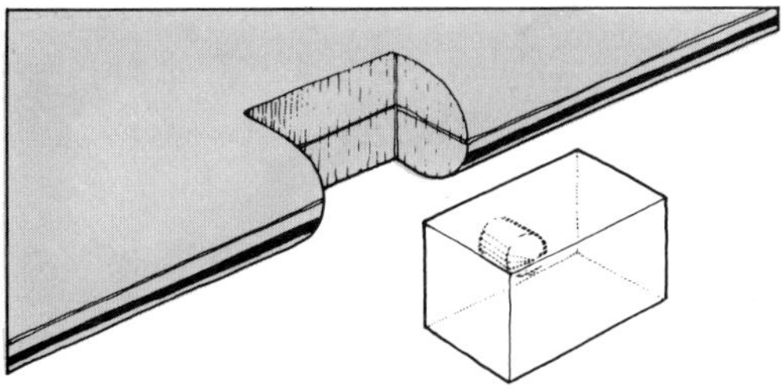

**Making an airplane landing light** Cut a notch in the edge of the wing, then cut a block of clear plastic to fit notch. Paint face of notch white or silver and drill a shallow hole in the block to represent a light bulb.

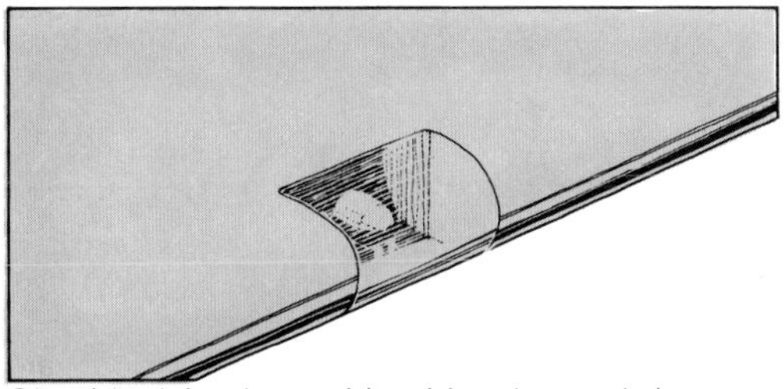

Glue block in place with white glue and shape it to match the wing section with a file and fine wet-and-dry paper. Finish with liquid metal polish and a coat of clear varnish.

## The canopy frame

The appearance of a model plane can be greatly improved if you carefully pick out the canopy frame with color. If it is molded on the canopy as it is in most cases, paint it with a fine brush using paint thinned enough to flow easily without becoming translucent when dry. Start with the widest section of the frame then paint the finer sections. Concentrate on painting one edge of the frame straight; if this stroke does not cover the complete width, turn the model around to paint the other edge and fill the space in between. The thinner used to erase any mistakes will fog some plastic. To protect the canopy from thinner, spray it beforehand with clear gloss varnish. The varnish will also give it a realistic shine. Alternately, paint the canopy glass with clear varnish after the frame is dry to restore its transparent quality.

Where the canopy frame is not marked clearly, apply strips of painted clear adhesive tape or spare decal sheet in place of the frame. To prepare the tape, stick it to a ceramic tile, paint it and when dry, cut it into thin strips. Use a decal sheet for small-scale planes where tape would be too thick: paint a piece of the clear margin, cut it into strips and apply it as a normal decal (see Decals, pages 88 to 89).

The best method of painting a canopy frame, however, is to mask the glass with clear adhesive tape and spray it with an airbrush. The paint will form a perfect edge against the tape. Hand-paint the inner frame first – this is particularly important if the canopy is to be displayed open. Stick tape over the entire outer surface to protect it while painting the inside. It will be cut to mask the frame later. Paint just inside the edge of the frame so that the paint on the outside will cover the hand-painting.

Cut and peel away the tape from the frame and glue the entire canopy closed with white glue, even those parts which are to be modeled open, to protect the interior. The canopy can be removed when finished and reglued in the open position. Spray the entire fuselage and the frame at the same time. This way the color will match and disguise the joint between the canopy and the fuselage.

Canopy frames must be painted with care. The masking technique described above works equally well for the fine old-fashioned frame on the Hawker Hurricane (above) and the modern canopy on the North American T28 (below).

# Rigging

Fine rigging is an essential element of early planes and ships and can be modeled from transparent nylon thread, heat-stretched sprue, fine wire, twine or cotton thread. Whichever material you choose, make sure that it suits the scale of the model for overscale rigging is worse than omitting it altogether. It is impossible to rig a small-scale vehicle fully, but by following good reference material you can choose the important features which give the model its specific character.

It is necessary to plan carefully from the early stages of construction so that the other components can be attached and painted before the rigging is in place, and to determine the most practical order of assembling the rigging itself. Interplane struts and landing gear and control horns supplied in plane kits, especially, should be examined to see that they are sufficiently fine in scale. Sharpen the edge of struts by scraping with a knife and, if necessary, replace control horns with new ones cut from thin plastic.

On small-scale sailing ships dead-eyes and blocks can be simulated by adding a touch of white glue after rigging the model. Paint the glue after it has hardened completely in the appropriate colors.

## Nylon thread

Unpainted transparent nylon thread is an excellent material for rigging as it is barely noticeable until it catches the light; its fine highlights give it the delicacy needed in a scale model. The disadvantage of nylon thread is that it must be held under tension until the glue sets. On sailing ships or early monoplanes this can be done by passing a single thread from point to point, holding it in a small groove cut into each point. The groove can be filled with a touch of paint afterward to disguise it. Glue each end of the thread and in the grooves, with cyanoacrylate glue. If possible, leave the thread overnight, then trim the ends as close as possible.

## Heat-stretched sprue

Heat-stretched sprue is a practical alternative to nylon thread as gray or transparent plastic takes on almost the same quality when it is stretched to a fine filament over a small flame. You may have to experiment to find sprue which will stretch conveniently to the required width because not all types react equally (see page 54). Its main advantage over nylon thread is that it does not need to be held under tension. This makes sprue useful for biplane interplane rigging which cannot be done with nylon thread without too many holes having to be drilled in each wing. Heat-stretched sprue also eliminates the strain on fine masts and booms on ships.

To apply this material, first measure the distance between points with a pair of dividers and cut accurate lengths of stretched sprue. Position each length of sprue with a pair of flat-ended tweezers (pointed tweezers tend to distort the plastic), and add a minute amount of glue at each end. Liquid cement dries quickly but can dissolve the plastic altogether; white glue is safer but takes a little longer to set and must be used sparingly.

Once the glue has set hard, any slight sag can be taken out of the rigging by holding a pyrogravure close to one end for a second. Do not touch the filament or it may melt.

**Rigging a ship with sprue** For longer sections of rigging, glue a length of heat-stretched sprue at one end and let harden before stretching it to the second point. Liquid cement will soften it locally at the second point allowing you to take it to a third point in one single piece.

## Fine wire

Very fine wire can be used to rig large-scale biplanes. Cut a piece of wire slightly too long and straighten it as shown below. Next, measure the length on the plane and cut the wire to the exact measurement. Apply it to the model with white glue. Because wire is a rigid material, it is particularly easy to position.

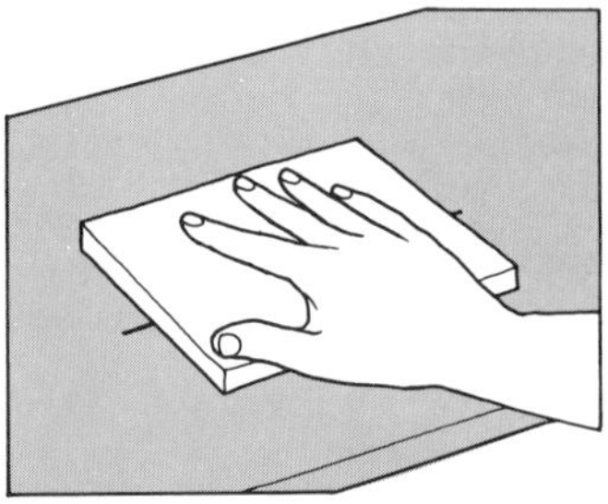

**Straightening wire** Roll the wire under a block of wood on a smooth, flat surface to straighten it.

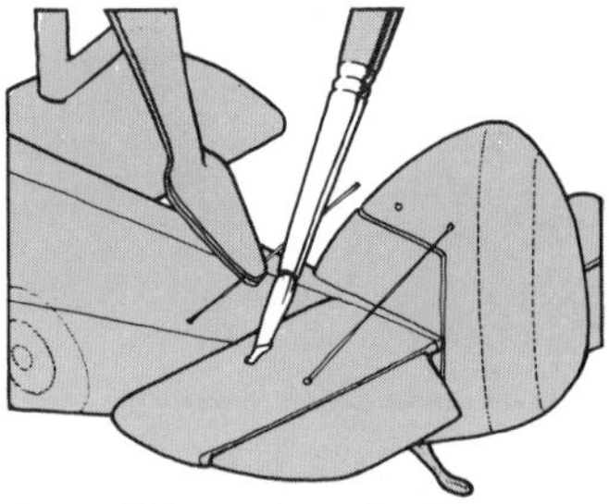

**Attaching wire rigging** Holding the wire with tweezers, fix it in place with white glue.

## Twine or thread

Large-scale sailing ships are traditionally rigged with twine or cotton thread and many kits supply the material. Fix it on the model with glue to avoid overscale knots.

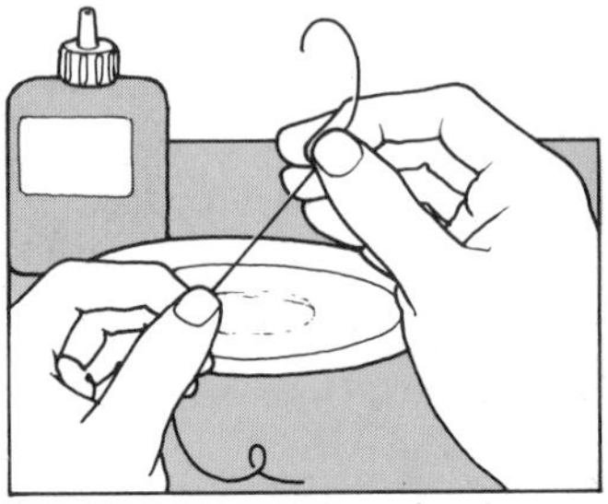

**Smoothing twine** Apply thinned glue to the twine before fixing it on the model.

## Radio antennae

Although the radio mast is usually supplied in an airplane kit, the wire running from it to the fin is not. Use nylon thread or heat-stretched sprue for the wire. The method for attaching it is similar to that described on the opposite page.

Drill a small hole in the fin to take the thread or sprue. Glue one end of an overlong piece of "wire" into it. Let the glue set hard. Next, glue the other end to the mast (this should have a flat tip to hold the "wire" and be firmly glued in its socket on the fuselage). Sprue will normally hold its position as soon as a skin forms on the glue, but nylon thread is best wound around the propeller spinner or another convenient point to hold it under tension. Trim off excess "wire" after the glue has set.

Circular antennae can be made from thin metal foil or thin wire. Wrap the foil or wire around a paintbrush handle to make the circle, twisting the ends together tightly to form a pin-shaped end. Glue the end into a hole drilled in the body of the vehicle.

A kit Pitot tube is often too thick or bent. Replace it with a fine wire or, if the tube tapers to a point, use a needle or pin glued into a drilled hole. On the ground, Pitot tubes are sometimes covered to prevent accidental damage.

Whip antennae like those on this Churchill Crocodile should be made from heat-stretched sprue. A bent antenna gives an air of authenticity to a model.

Rub down the blade antenna on a modern jet to make a sharp edge, or build it from scratch with plastic.

Moving parts and weaponry are locked with a pin while the airplane is on the ground to prevent their accidental use. Each pin is marked with a colored tag called a "remove before flight" tag. Make the pin and tag from twisted wire and painted tissue paper.

# Artillery

The most important improvement to carry out on any gun is to drill out the barrel especially main guns on tanks and armored cars, but even machine guns and cannons on AFVs and airplanes should be drilled out when scale permits. Paint the inside of the barrel with matt black paint.

Very small-scale guns may be too small to drill out. Cut the tip of the barrel straight off and paint it matt black, then paint the barrel letting the color overlap the black slightly to suggest the width of the rim.

Blast bags are often molded on a tank where the gun barrel meets the turret. On large-scale tanks you can improve the texture by painting diluted white glue onto the molding and applying coarse tissue over it. Encourage the tissue to follow the contours with a brush and more glue, but do not apply so much glue that the texture is lost. Blast bags can also be added to a ship's gun using epoxy putty.

Gun barrels are sometimes protected with muzzle covers when not in action. Blank off the barrel and wrap strips of fine linen or tissue, depending on the scale, around the muzzle; fix it in place by painting with diluted white glue.

This model of an American half-track has several small guns, each of which has been drilled out.

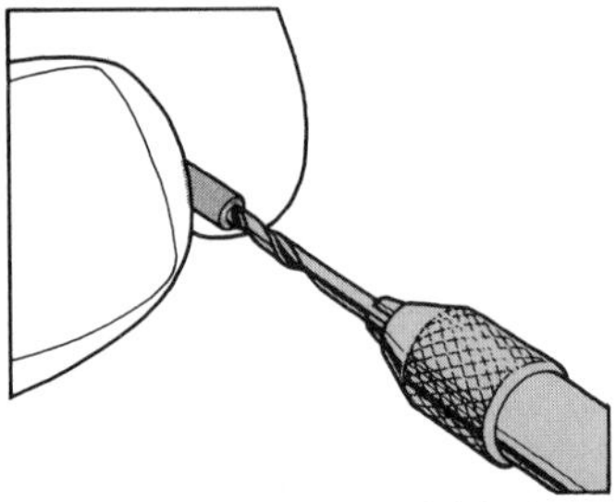

**Drilling out a barrel** Mark the center with a pin or pyrogravure. Use a very small drill to enlarge this center; check it for accuracy then drill to the full diameter. Correct an off-center hole by scraping to one side of it with the point of a knife.

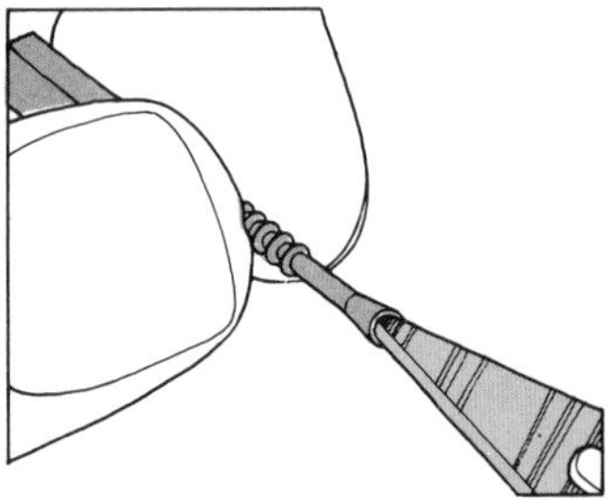

**Drilling a flared muzzle** Drill a hole in the center, then revolve a pointed knife blade in the barrel to form a tapered hole.

A thermal sleeve has been added to the gun barrel of this Chieftain tank. Made from an open-weave bandage wrapped around the barrel, it is fixed in place with diluted white glue and painted when the glue has set completely.

# Additional equipment

Many model vehicles benefit from the inclusion of extra detail such as personal effects left casually on the driver's or back seat, or cargo carried in a truck or freight car. Military vehicles, more than most, can carry all manner of additional articles. Apart from the basic equipment which the model manufacturer normally supplies, vehicles in the field can be festooned with personal items. These include tent and blanket rolls, crates of food or toiletries, clothing, packs, kit bags and handguns. The best way to attach them to the model is with glue, but they must appear to be strapped or tied securely as they would be on the real vehicle. Equipment which cannot be bought as spare parts can be built.

Recovery vehicles carry spares and fuel for other vehicles. On this model the tool rack is fully equipped and includes an extra hammer and roll of wire. Spare fuel drums lie against the bulkhead.

Souvenirs hang from the turret of this tank. The German jacket is assembled from pieces of plastic and white glue, then molded by heating with a cigarette. Buttons, collar and epaulets are added last.

# Extra protection for AFVs

Throughout World War Two armored fighting vehicles were modified to give greater protection to the crew and the vulnerable parts of the vehicle. Sometimes temporary measures were taken in field workshops or by the crew itself, such as welding on patches of armor plate or positioning sandbags on the vehicle. Other measures, such as Zimmerit or protective side skirts, were added to existing vehicles in the factory to counteract particular developments in enemy weapons during the war.

## Sandbags

Sandbags were often piled up against the thin armor plate as emergency protection against an air attack. They are easy to reconstruct and make a model appear more authentic.

Shape sandbags from modeling clay and cover them with coarse fabric for texture. Paint the bags with white glue to seal them, and position them before the glue sets so that they can be molded to suit the shape of the vehicle. Make sure that you do not place them so that they restrict the view of the crew or the travel of guns or turret.

## Armor patches and spare tracks

Patches of armor plate were welded to the vehicle in the field to add extra thickness to vulnerable areas of the turret or hull. This is easily simulated on a model by cutting a patch from thick plastic and gluing it to the model with liquid polystyrene cement. If glue squeezes from the edge, texture it with a needle to look like a crude welded joint. A pyrogravure can be used where there is insufficient or no glue.

Spare tank tracks were often welded to the body to protect it in the same way. If they are not supplied in the kit, use tracks from a scrapped model – they do not have to be from an identical vehicle. Glue them in position on the model.

## Zimmerit

Zimmerit was an anti-magnetic paste applied to the near vertical surfaces of German AFVs from 1943 onward. Its purpose was to prevent magnetic anti-tank weapons from adhering to the surface. It is possible to ascertain the particular patterns applied to specific vehicles.

One application method used by some modelmakers is to apply a thin coat of Spackle to the model and then texture it with a fine saw blade. This method is similar to the way the real material was added but it is difficult to apply the paste thinly and evenly. The best technique for adding this finish to a model is to engrave the plastic surface with a pyrogravure or a hot needle. It is easy to control the tool on very small-scale models which are difficult to texture with paste. Check to see if some components can be worked on before assembly as the pattern is easier to apply on a flat surface and it can be touched up after construction if necessary. Mark the parts where they meet so that the engraving will match on both sections.

Paint and decals should be applied over Zimmerit. The Micro decal system is the only practical method of guaranteeing that the decals follow the texture (see pages 88 to 89).

**Simulating Zimmerit** Mark grid of parallel lines. Engrave between lines with a pyrogravure allowing the melted plastic to pile up alongside. If you wish to apply radial lines around rivets, engrave them first then add horizontal lines.

## Protective side skirts

To protect tracked vehicles from anti-tank missiles the Germans hung steel plates from a metal framework along both sides. Kit side skirts should be sanded down to reduce them to scale thickness, or used as a guide for cutting new ones from plastic. The framework, too, may need to be carefully rubbed down to make it thinner, or replaced with wire and heat-stretched sprue. You can individualize your model by leaving a space on the framework where one or more plates have been shot away, or by painting one a slightly different color.

This STUG III assault gun has side skirts. Use decals or dry-transfer numbers for insignia, or paint them by hand with a fine brush.

# Damaged metal and broken glass

Altering vehicles to show wear-and-tear is a popular pastime for modelmakers. Military vehicles especially show effects of combat, but heavily worked commercial vehicles and railroad rolling stock, racing cars and motorcycles are also worthy subjects. Even models of private cars can be shown as less than perfect.

One technique for simulating dented metal on a plastic model is to hold the tip of a soldering iron close enough to a component to soften it, to allow for shaping with a tool. Avoid touching the plastic with the hot iron or it will melt rather than soften. Try to imagine how the damage would occur. If a vehicle has collided with the corner of a brick wall, the edge of a block of wood could be used to push in the dent. If pushed-out dents were caused by crates falling against the thin metal body of a van, truck or freight car, distort the plastic with a suitable tool from the inside. Small components like airplane landing gear legs and propeller blades can be bent by first heating them over a soldering iron or pyrogravure.

If a mudguard or fender is torn, or airplane paneling is damaged by flak, the jagged edges must be to scale thickness. It is often necessary to reduce the thickness of the plastic component before you shape it. Mudguards can be scraped or sanded from the inside, then cut with a knife, softened and shaped. For a flak-torn fuselage, pierce holes with a pyrogravure, then drill from the inside with a countersink bit and sand away any thickness built up around the hole by the heated needle. Open up the hole and create a jagged edge by twisting a knife blade in it. Bear in mind that if a panel is opened up so that you can see inside, you may need to build in ribbing or a framework made from pieces of plastic sheet or heat-stretched sprue.

Another way of simulating dented metal is to replace the plastic part with a piece of thin metal which can be crumpled and holed in a more realistic way. For example, substitute a trackguard panel made from toothpaste tube foil for the original kit part.

To make a shattered windshield, cut the plastic kit part or homemade replacement to the required shape, breaking it along the cut line to create a jagged edge. Score cracks in glass with a knife. Drill bullet holes, if you wish.

The damaged trackguards on this tank were made by cutting the plastic part with a heated knife blade.

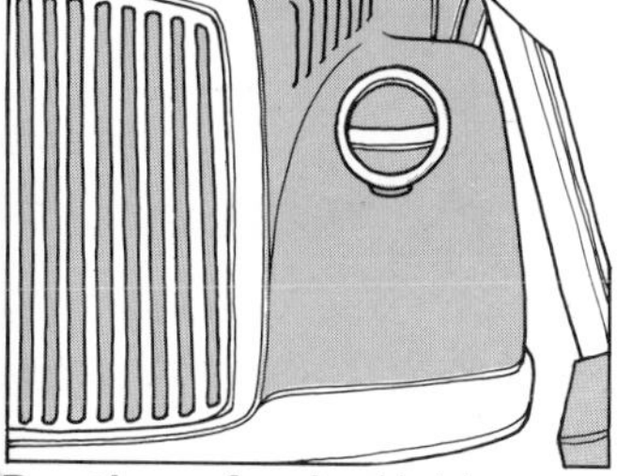

**Denting a fender** Hold a soldering iron close enough to the fender to soften the plastic. Do not touch the surface of the model or it will melt.

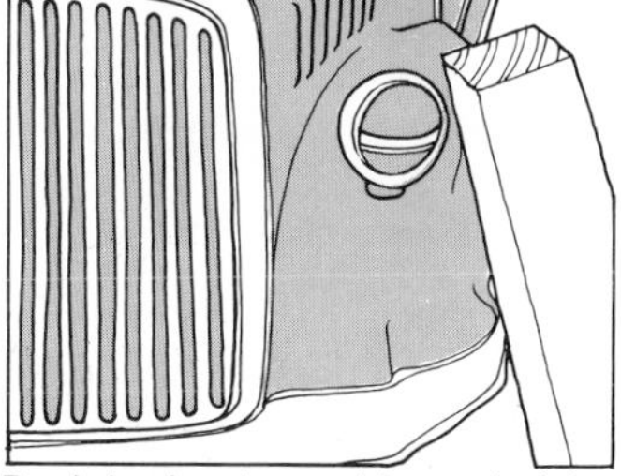

Push in the dent with a suitable object. You can use the sharp edge of a piece of wood to indicate that a vehicle has crashed into the corner of a wall.

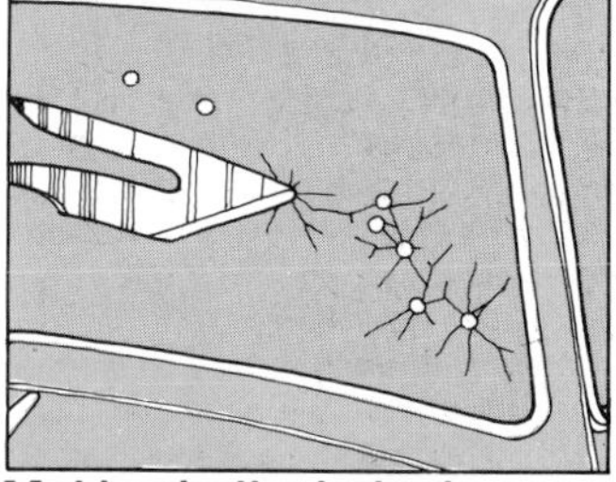

**Making bullet holes in windows** Drill holes in plastic then twist a pointed knife blade in hole to shatter the edge. Score cracks in surface.

# Simulating moving parts

Many of the best kit vehicles have moving parts, or parts which can be repositioned. This is a great advantage as moving or open doors, canopies and engine covers, for instance, allow the onlooker to view interior detail and the engine compartment. Moreover, by simulating moving parts on a vehicle you can bring it to life. An open canopy or inspection hatch may suggest that the pilot or mechanic will return at any moment to close it. A plane modeled with drooping flaps will give the impression that if the flaps were tested they would move. Even the way a vehicle is parked can imply human activity by the angle of the front wheels or by the driver's door left ajar. If the kit does not provide these options, cut and re-model the working parts yourself.

## Airplane control surfaces

Although the control surfaces on the wings, tail plane and rudder are often modeled in a neutral position, parked planes are likely to have drooping flaps or elevators and the rudder cocked to one side. If these items are molded as one piece with the fixed surface, they can be cut out and repositioned. Alter the position of the elevators and rudder as described for wing flaps, right.

Leading edge slats on the wing are extended to provide greater lift when landing. They are often molded onto the wing in a retracted position. To model them extended, cut out the leading edge of the wing and fill it with new slats as shown opposite.

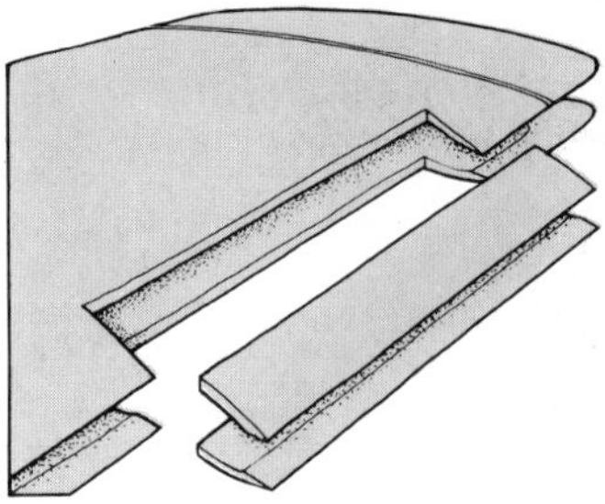

**Repositioning a flap** Cut out wing flaps before gluing the wing halves together, using a razor saw to make the short cuts and a knife to cut along the length. Make light cuts to establish the line, then cut right through the piece. Unless the joint is well defined, use a ruler as a guide.

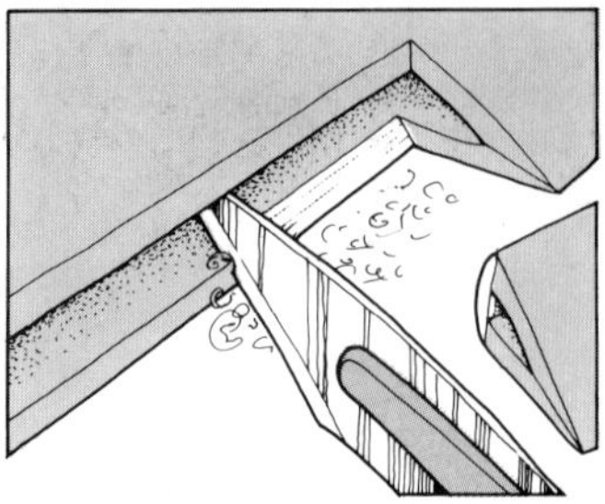

Assemble the wing halves and scrape a "V"-shaped notch in the back edge. On large-scale planes, fill in edges if they will show with flap in new position. Glue the flap halves together and stick a piece of thick plastic or sprue to the inner edge; round it off with a file and sandpaper.

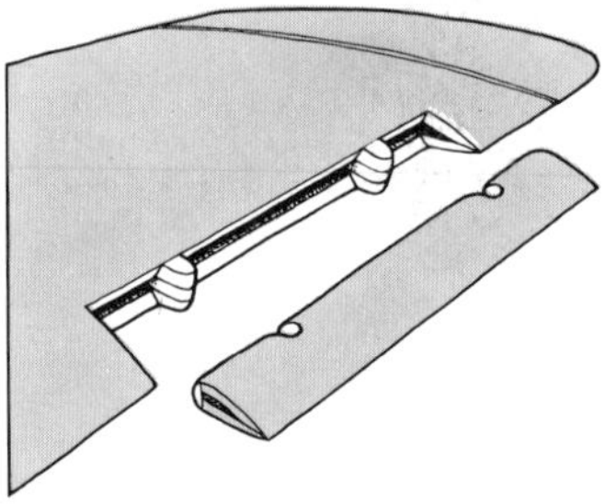

For prominent hinges, glue small blocks of plastic to the wing. Round off the hinges with a file and sand them on top to make sure that they are flush with the wing surface. Cut corresponding slots in flap, finishing the bottom of the slot with a round file.

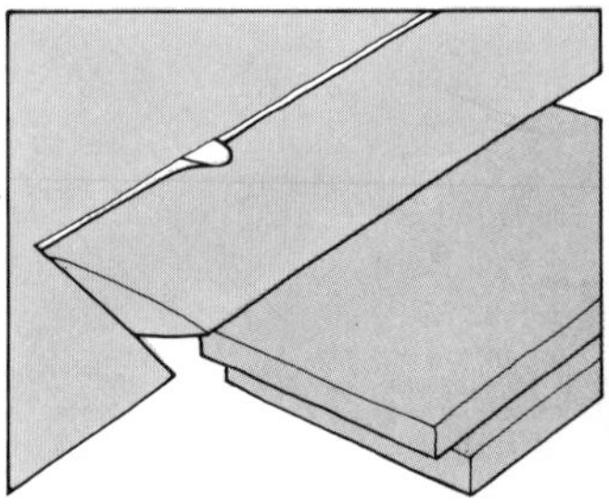

Position flap in wing and apply liquid polystyrene cement to the joint. Make sure that the flaps on both wings are at the same angle. You may need to support the flaps while the glue dries.

**Folding wings (right)** Cut wings at joint; add ribs cut from plastic and a folding mechanism from fine sprue, to the cut ends. Shape the weapon pylon to suit the open wing section and "wire" it with fine sprue or painted wire. Make wing props from heat-stretched sprue.

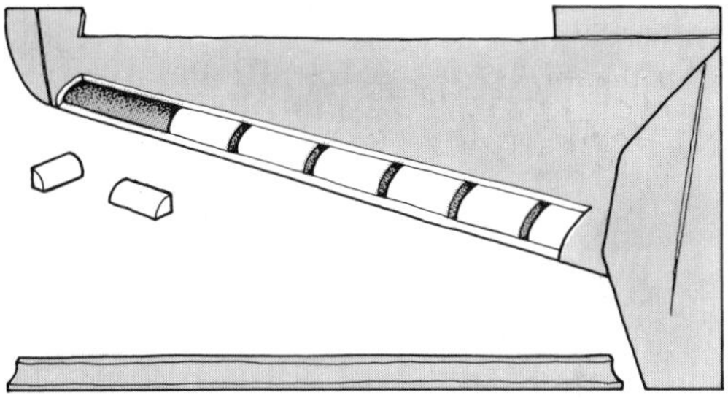

**Making extended slats** Cut out leading edge; set aside. Round off a piece of thick plastic and cut it into sections. Glue them in place leaving a gap between each for a rib.

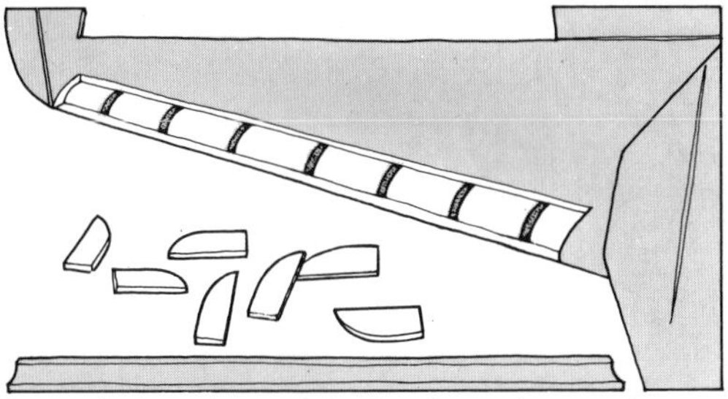

Smooth the edges of the leading edge cut from the wing and make ribs from plastic sheet to fit its inner curve.

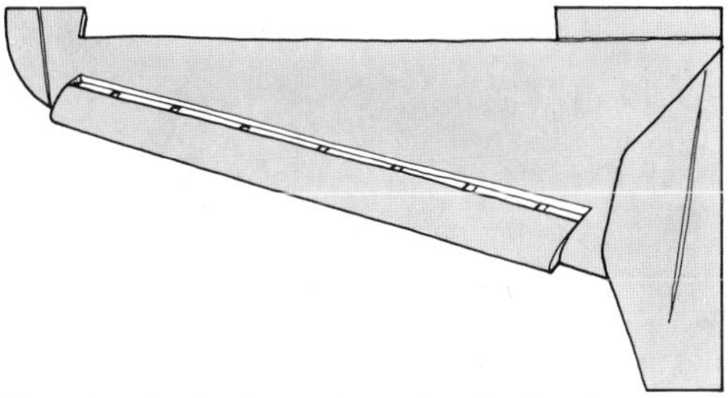

Glue the ribs in place, then glue the leading edge to the front of the ribs.

## Hatches, doors and canopies

There are various inspection hatches or access panels molded on the surface of planes and tanks which can be modeled open. Cut them out and replace with a new, open hatch door as shown right. Plane canopies which have been molded in one piece can be cut out and glued in the open position.

If a vehicle is supplied with a moving hood, trunk or doors, adjust them carefully with a file and wet-and-dry paper to make a perfect fit. Allow a sufficient gap all around for the thickness of paint.

If a door is not designed to open, buy two identical kits and combine them. Cut out the door from one body as described for a hatch, right. Saw the door out of the other kit and file it to fit the opening. Fill in or build up the edge of the door and door frame, if necessary. After assembling and painting the vehicle, glue the door in the open position.

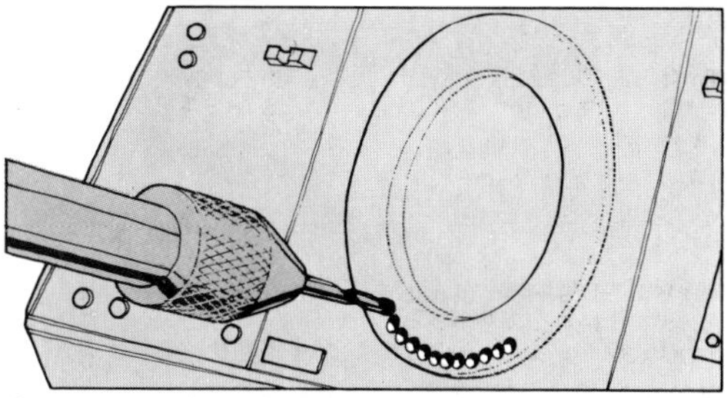

**Opening a hatch** Remove the molded hatch door by drilling holes inside its boundary.

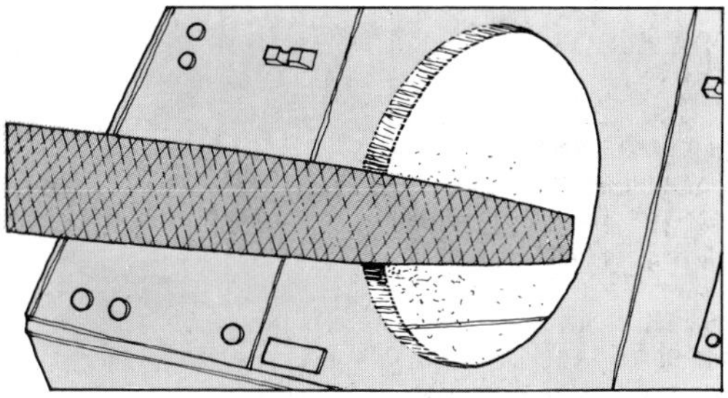

Smooth the edge with fine files and reduce the thickness of the edge by scraping the plastic from the inside.

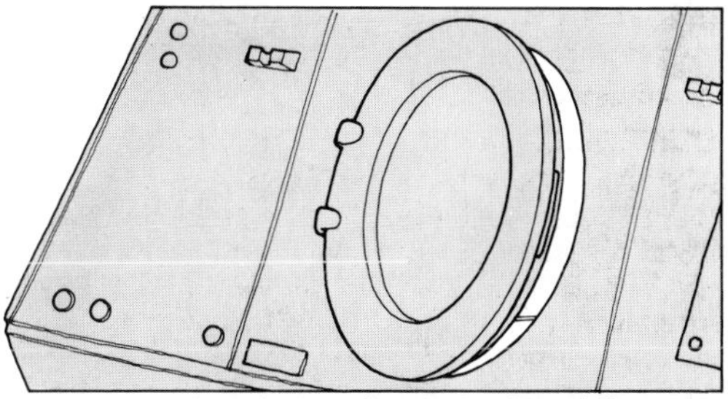

Make a new hatch door from plastic, adding any ribs or re-inforcing made from plastic strip or rod. Glue door in open position. Add any hinges or hydraulic jacks.

**Opening a canopy**
Stick clear tape over the plastic canopy to protect it. Cut along the line of the frame with a razor saw. Smooth the cut edges.

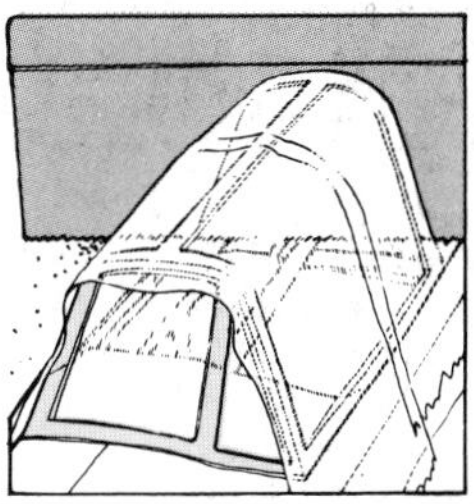

Glue canopy in open position on model. The thickness of paint will make up for any material lost by the saw cut.

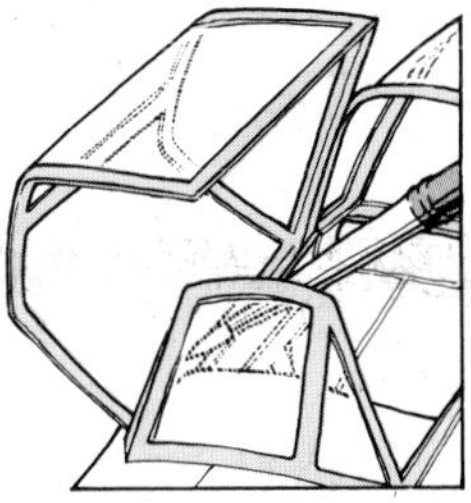

# Conversions

Many modelmakers combine the components of two or more kits to produce a vehicle which is not available as a standard kit. Any components which cannot be found in kits can be built from scratch using any form of scrap, from packaging material and old plastic toys to sprue. However the parts are obtained, the process of converting one vehicle into another will almost certainly involve extensive cutting and reshaping. Although each conversion is unique, the following techniques will supply solutions to some of the common problems.

This kit truck with its standard cab and chassis has been successfully converted into a vehicle transporter by the addition of ramps.

## Converting a ship hull

Most model ships are molded with a full hull but you may wish to show a ship as it would look fully loaded and floating in the water. To do this, simply saw off the bottom half of the hull at the waterline which is normally molded as a raised line on the outside. Each hull half can be sawn separately before assembly, but to guarantee perfect alignment of the hull parts, it is best to glue the hull into one solid piece before sawing it.

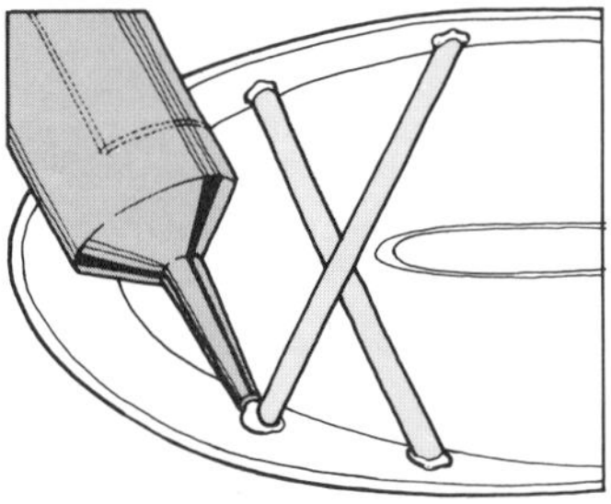

**Cutting a ship hull at the waterline** Glue cross bracing made from sprue inside the hull above the waterline using small amounts of tube cement.

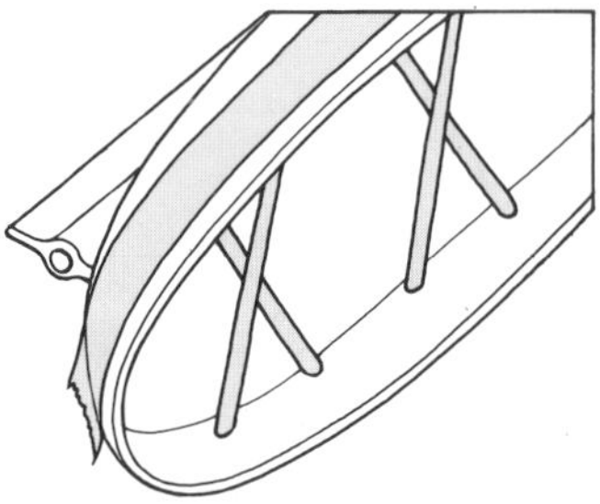

Apply masking tape above and to the edge of the waterline. The tape acts as a guide for the saw and also protects the upper part of the hull.

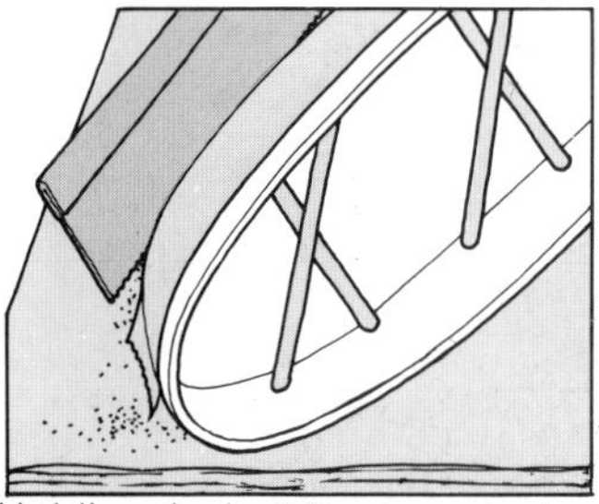

Holding the hull firmly against a cloth pad or wooden block so that the waterline is uppermost, establish the cut at the far end with a razor saw. Work backward with slow, steady strokes. Do not cut through both halves of the hull at once.

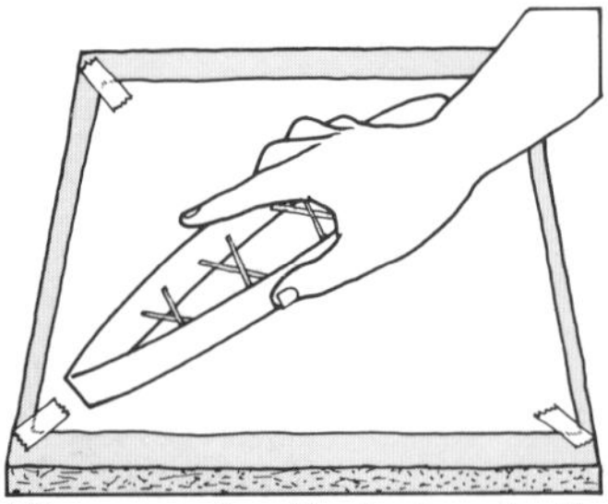

After removing the bottom half of the hull, smooth down the edge of the remaining part with a fine, flat file. Then, to guarantee an even edge all around, tape a piece of fine wet-and-dry paper to a flat board and rub the hull over it.

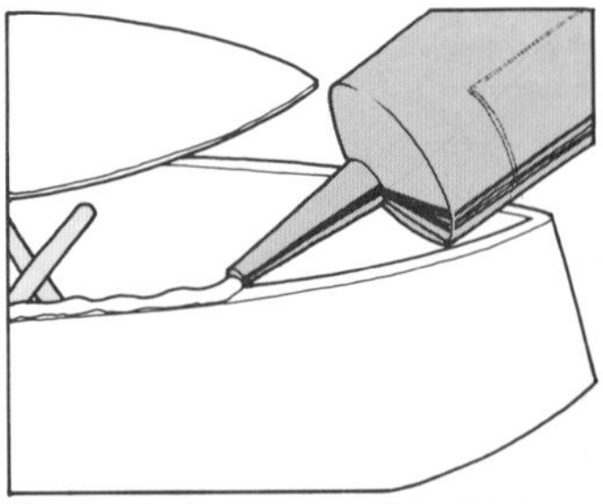

The cross bracing will hold the hull together, but a plastic base can be glued to the bottom to make a neater job. Allow for the thickness of the base beforehand by sticking the masking tape the equivalent distance above the waterline.

## Extending or shortening a plane or train

There are often several variations to the basic design of a commercial airliner. The different styles incorporate longer or shorter cabin sections. Sometimes, too, there are longer versions of a passenger train or freight car. Although you will almost never find a complete range in kit form, it may be possible to convert a standard model into another style by, for instance, cutting a piece from the fuselage to shorten the cabin, or by incorporating a section of fuselage from a second kit plane to lengthen it. Always examine the original vehicle very carefully to decide the exact place to insert or take out a section in order to produce correct window spacing.

Whether you want to alter an airplane or a train, you will need to know how to mark up and cut a cylindrical shape. To mark the cutting line, wrap a piece of paper with straight edges around the body of the model and carefully align the edges where they meet. Draw around the cylinder with a sharp pencil following the paper. Use a sharp razor saw to cut through the plastic. Make slow, deliberate strokes and revolve the model away from you as you cut.

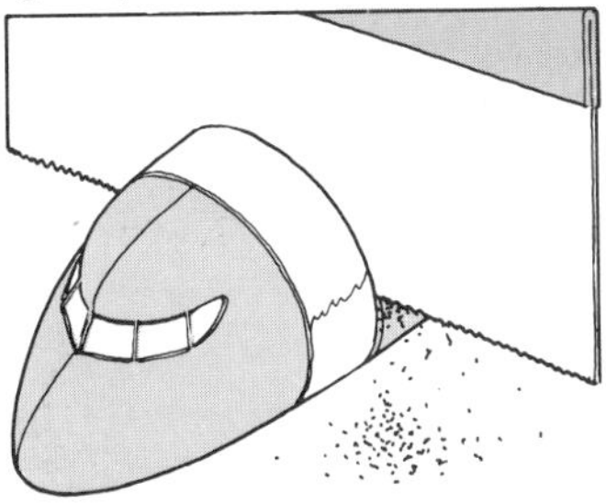

**Extending a fuselage** Mark the cutting lines and place masking tape along each side to protect the model and guide the saw. Cut through the fuselage with a razor saw, making slow, steady cuts in the plastic.

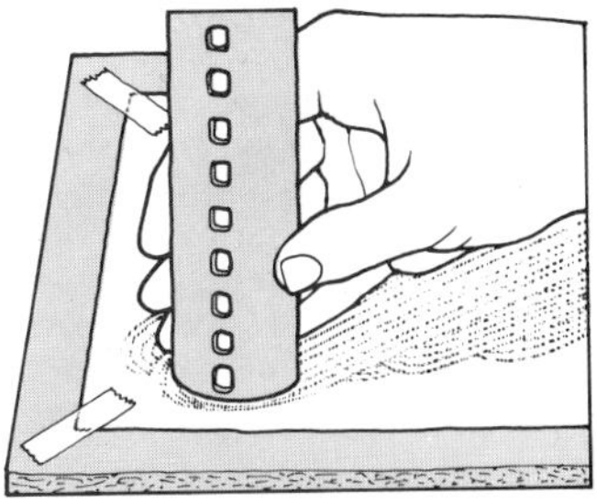

Carefully smooth the cut edges on wet-and-dry paper taped to a board. Make sure you wet the paper and keep the sections upright throughout.

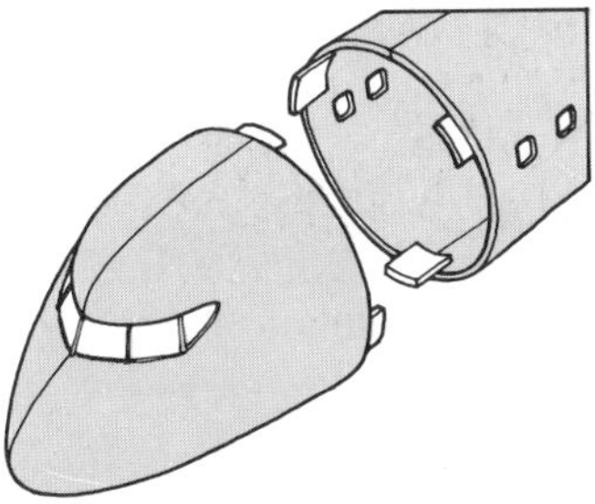

Glue small tabs of plastic onto the inside of the fuselage to help align the sections properly during assembly.

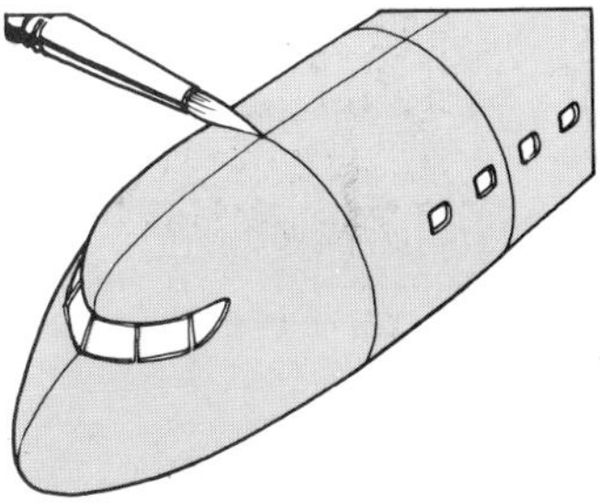

Glue together a second fuselage and cut it in the appropriate places. Cement the sections from the two kits together aligning the longitudinal joints; sight along the row of windows to check the alignment.

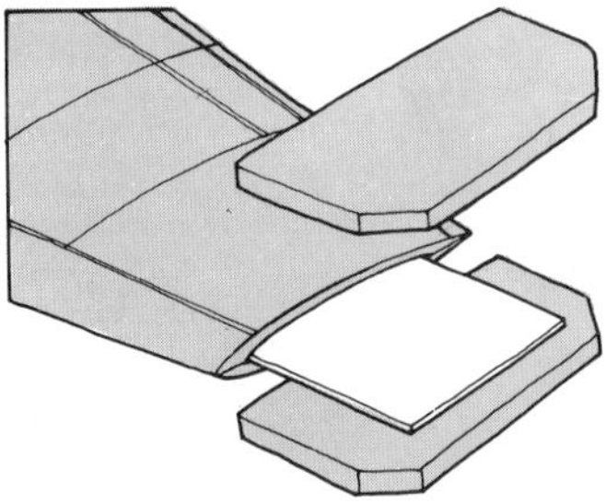

**Extending a wing or fin** Cut the tip off straight across and add a tongue of thin plastic in between the parts. Stick plastic roughly to the new shape to either side. Shape it with files and wet-and-dry paper.

The nose and tail housing of the Harrier (right) were extended in a similar way to the fuselage (above) by cutting a spare drop tank to length and gluing it onto a center plug.

# Customizing cars

Customizing is the term used to describe the process of cutting and reshaping the body and/or chassis of a car to convert it into a unique vehicle. Much of this kind of work depends on the type of vehicle as well as current fashion, but there are standard techniques employed by those who customize full-size cars which can also be applied to model kits. The most common techniques, including modifying both the headlights and fenders, are described below.

## Lowering the body

Models of early cars are often customized by cutting away part of the body or by modifying the chassis to produce a low, stylish profile. Choose the method according to the construction of the model vehicle.

"Stepping" is cutting the frame so that its central portion can be lowered taking the body with it. It may involve modification of the suspension and the wheel wells to provide adequate clearance but the body itself remains unchanged. Stepping can, of course, only be performed on a vehicle with a separate chassis.

"Chopping" involves the removal of a section of each window post so that the roof of the car is lowered, reducing the size of the windows at the same time. The windows will have to be recut to match the new openings or replacements made from transparent plastic (see pages 120 to 121).

"Sectioning" is the most difficult of these techniques as a section of body is removed altogether which involves reshaping the engine compartment, trunk, front grille and interior panels. Try to make the cuts where the body panels are mostly vertical and will rejoin along the line of any chrome trim. Make the cuts in a similar way to that described for cutting a hull at the waterline (page 130), using masking tape at the side of the cuts to protect the plastic. Stick small plastic tabs on the inside of the body halves to strengthen the joint and aid realigning.

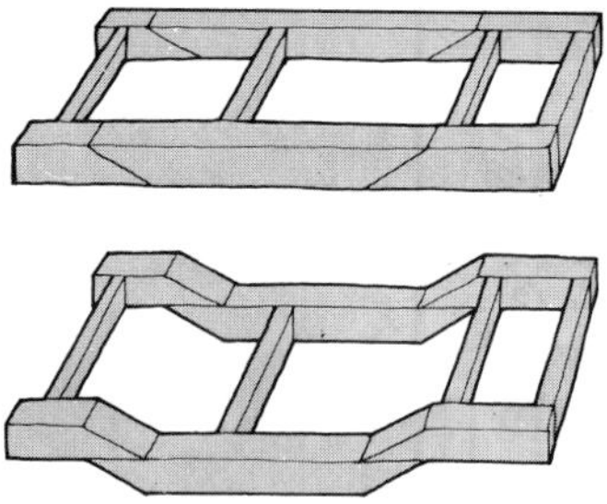

**Stepping** Remove the center section of the frame by making a 45° cut just behind the front suspension unit and in front of the rear one. Glue this piece underneath the frame.

**Chopping** Make one cut all around to remove the roof.

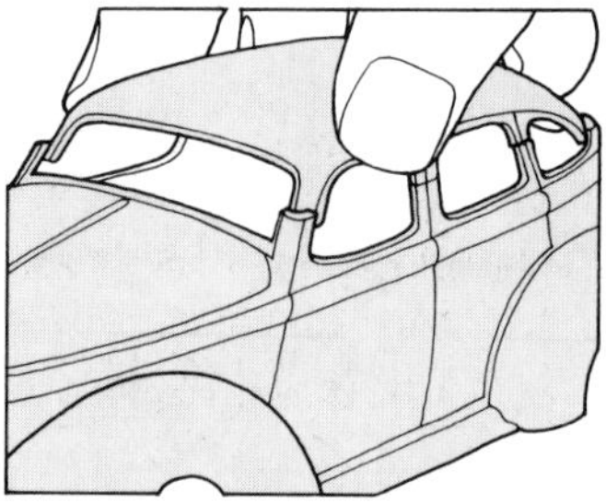

Cut the required amount from the two center posts only and position the roof temporarily to check the location and angle of the cuts on the corner posts.

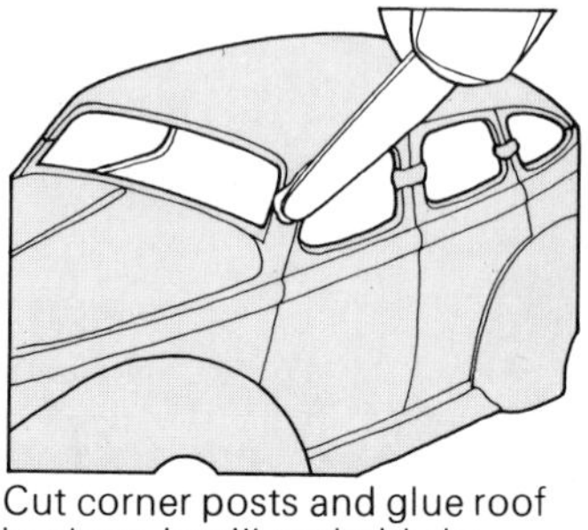

Cut corner posts and glue roof in place. It will probably be necessary to soften the corner posts with gentle heat in order to align them, adding filler to make them fit.

## Recessing headlights

Moving the reflector and lens back into the fender involves the removal of the chrome trim. When the chrome surround is molded with the fender, saw it straight off from the body. Fill the resulting space with a piece of thick plastic with a hole drilled in the center to take the light. Use a file and wet-and-dry paper to smooth it into the shape of the fender and fill any obvious gaps with some model filler.

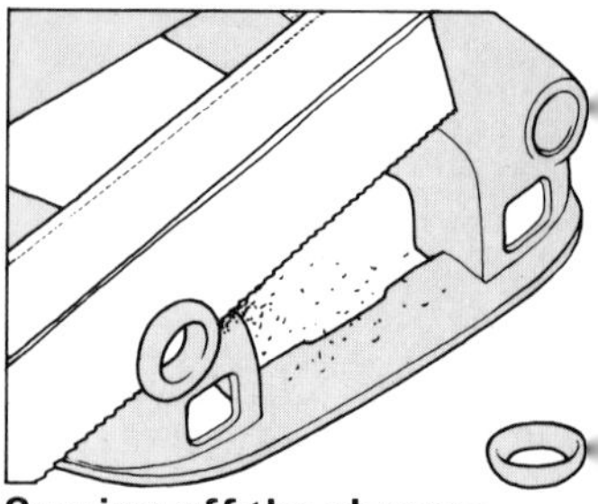

**Sawing off the chrome trim** Use a razor saw and, keeping it upright, make a straight cut against the body of the car.

## Fender flares

You may wish your model car to have fender flares to accommodate tires which are too wide for standard wheel wells. It may be possible to modify flares from another kit, but if this means buying a whole kit merely for the fenders, it would be cheaper to mold a set using the plug-molding technique described on page 55. Carve a wooden plug to fit the wheel arch so that two flares can be cut from a single molding. Sand off any rough spots.

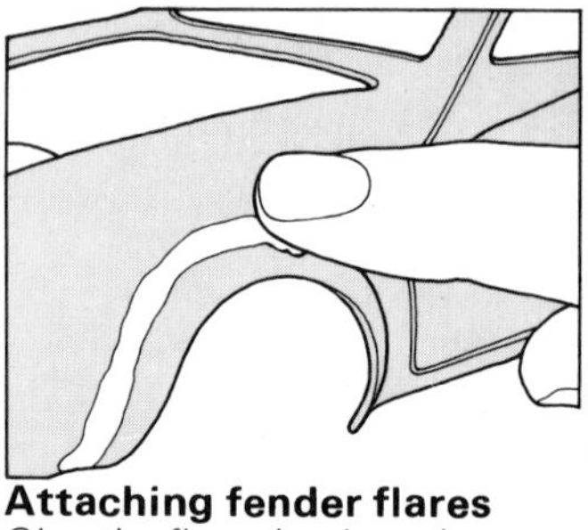

**Attaching fender flares** Glue the flares in place then use epoxy putty to create the correct profile, smoothing it with a wet finger.

# Figures

# Assembling figures

Plastic and metal figures are supplied in kits and both types are easy to assemble with a set of basic techniques. You can improve figures by adding detail, or even by changing their pose and costume.

Plastic figures are extremely versatile and their pose and costume can be easily altered. Beginning modelmakers should practice construction techniques on plastic figures; they are relatively cheap and you can experiment with them without the fear of spoiling a finished model. It is worth constructing two or three figures completely, adding as much detail as possible. Paint each model all one color; this will show up any fault in construction and finish, and the quality of the model will be seen in the basic pose and detail. The practice figures can be used at a later date when you are experimenting with different painting techniques.

Metal figures are usually made from fewer pieces. They can, therefore, be constructed quickly, and, in the case of the best metal miniatures, they are superbly modeled and rich in detail making them ideal subjects for the skilled painter. They normally cost more than plastic ones and, although their pose can be adapted to new uses, they are less easy to cut and shape. Instructions for altering metal figures are on page 142.

## Assembling a metal figure

**Materials**
Before you assemble a metal figure always make sure that all the pieces are present and clean each one. Cyanoacrylate glues such as Krazy glue rather than epoxy glues or solder are the most popular for assembling metal figures. Use very small amounts.

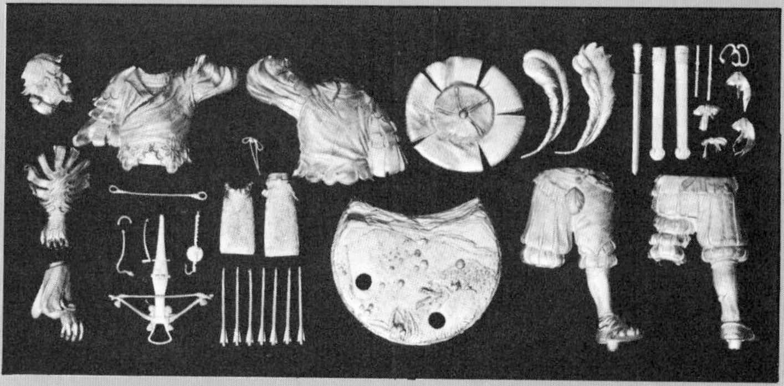

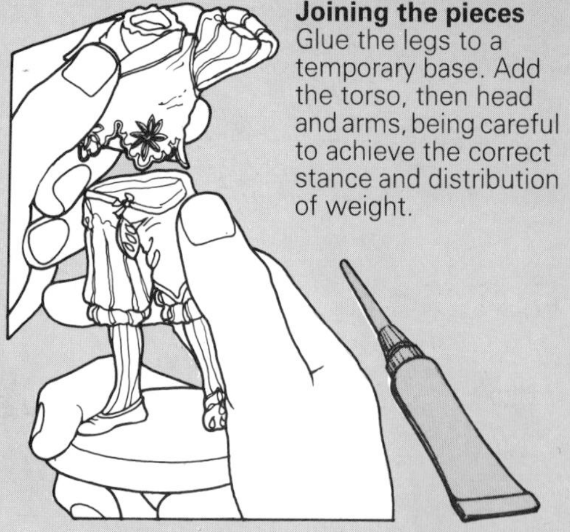

**Joining the pieces** Glue the legs to a temporary base. Add the torso, then head and arms, being careful to achieve the correct stance and distribution of weight.

**Cleaning up the model** Pare away the flash lines; smooth creases with a round needle file; reduce any lumps with a flat file; use steel wool or fine emery to finish smooth surfaces. Fill all joints and blemishes. When dry, file and smooth with fine wet-and-dry paper.

**Sharpening any weapons** Sword or knife edges may be blunt or damaged so remember to sharpen the cutting edge of any weapons by scraping with a knife, then finishing with wet-and-dry paper.

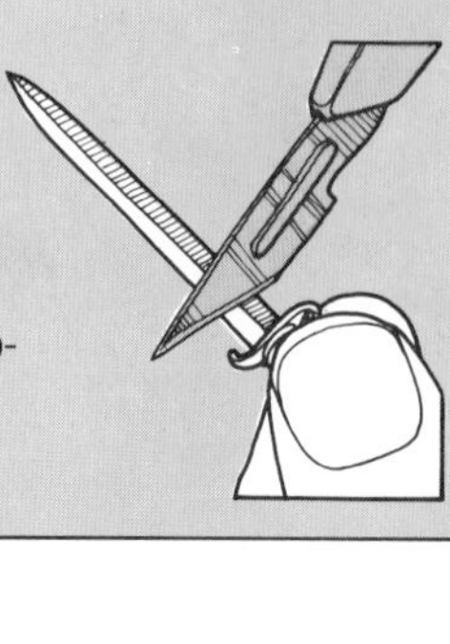

**Washing the figure** Add any accessories, then wash the figure in detergent solution. Blot dry with a tissue. Do not rub; small pieces of tissue can get caught. It is now ready for undercoating and painting.

## Assembling a plastic figure

**Materials**
Before assembling a plastic figure, make sure that all the pieces are present and clean each one well. Plastic cement in liquid form is the most useful adhesive for plastic figures.

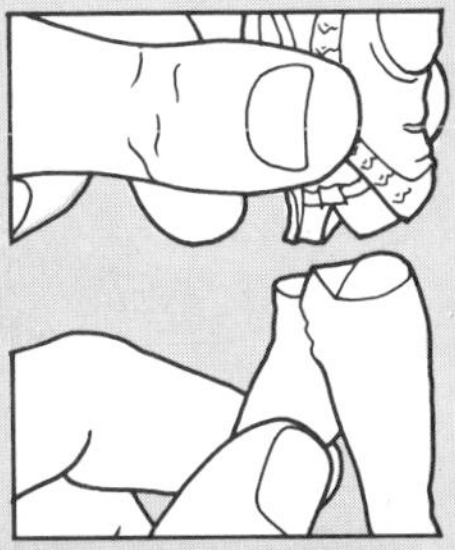

**Joining legs and torso** Glue the legs to the torso making sure that the body balances convincingly.

**Attaching the head** Some kits allow the head to be fixed at different angles. Make it suit the character.

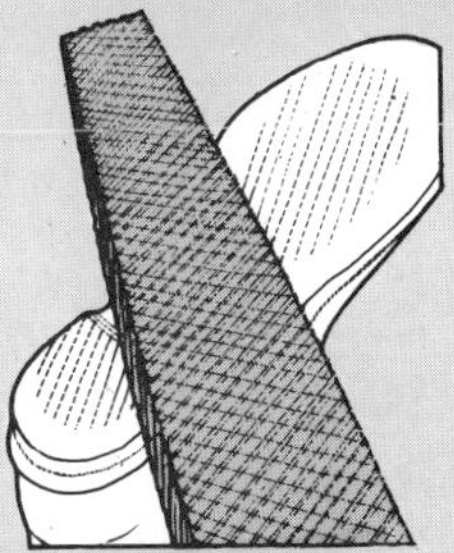

**Filing the feet** If needed, smooth the soles of the feet so they meet the ground at a realistic angle.

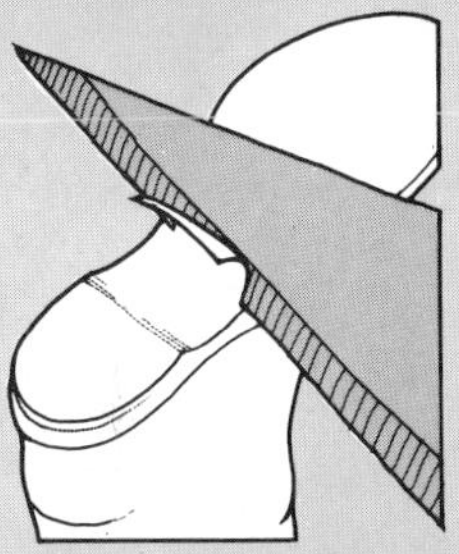

**Paring the instep** Carve the plastic to make an arch under the foot and a clearance under the toe.

**Fixing the model to a base** Temporarily attach the figure to a base of thick plastic; clamp the base to a bench or in a vise to free your hands for the next stages. If the figure is standing on one leg, drill a hole in the underside of the foot and glue a short section of straight pin in it to help attach the figure firmly.

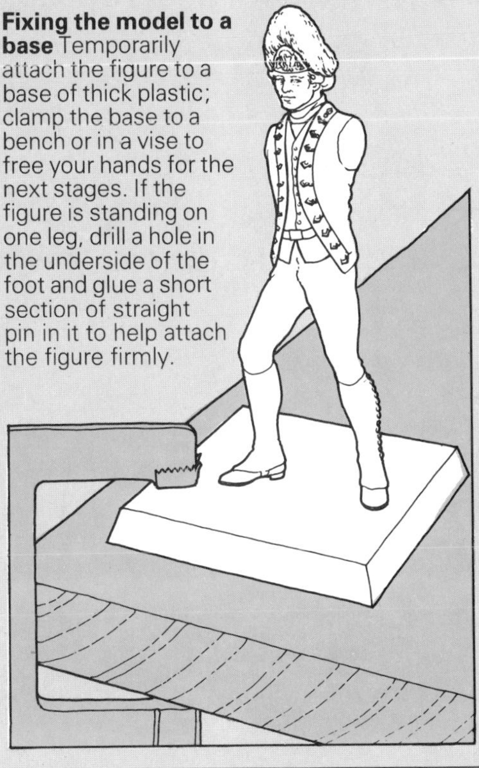

**Adding straps and arms** Add any straps, then the arms. The shoulder joints may need to be filed to position the arms correctly, especially if the model is holding a weapon.

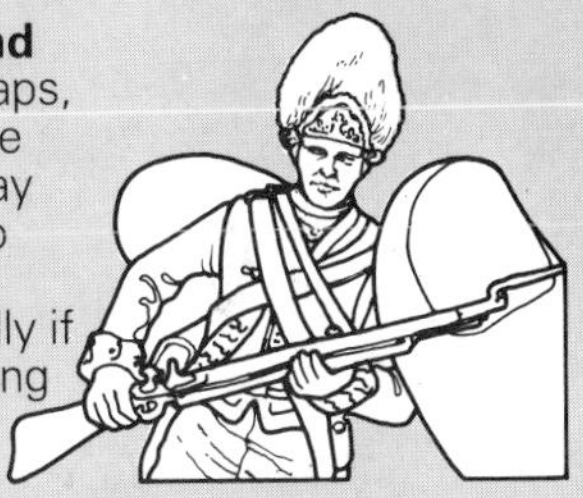

**Cleaning up the hands** Trim the ends of the fingers with a knife; fold fine wet-and-dry paper to form a crease and clean between the fingers.

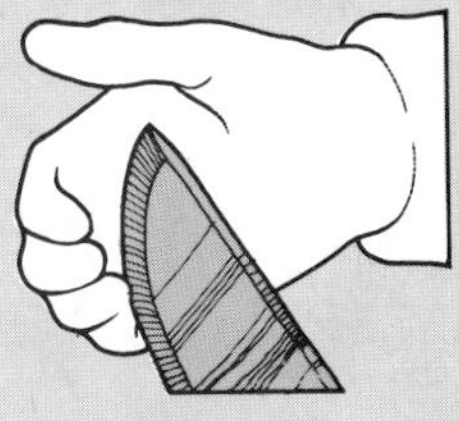

**Making hands grip** If the figure holds a weapon and the hands aren't pliable enough to bend around it and make contact with the glue, soften them in hot water or score on the inside to make them bend. Now paint the model.

# Adding detail to plastic figures

Plastic figures can be greatly enhanced by the addition of detail. This may involve improving any molded-in features or adding extra articles.

## Hair

Molded-in hair can be improved by using a pyrogravure to accentuate the flow and add very fine texture. Engrave in the direction of growth starting at the neck and overlapping previous engraving as you work. Then, gently rub to remove any projecting hair.

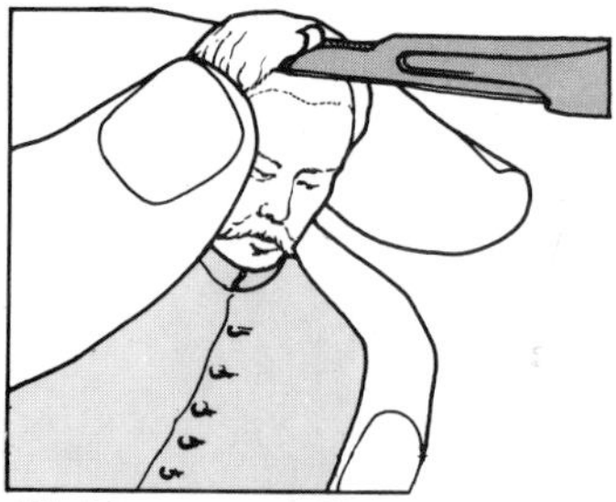

**Making a receding hairline**
Cut away part of the hair then rework the receded hairline with a pyrogravure.

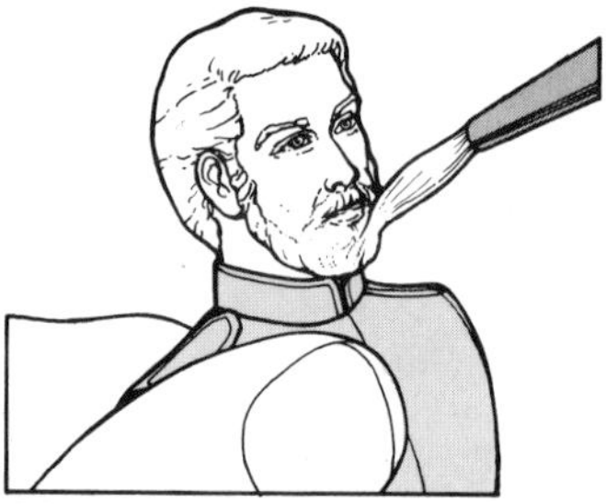

**Making a beard**
Paint on thin liquid plastic to the required shape; when set hard, work it with a pyrogravure.

## Headgear

The fit of headgear is important; a loose hat placed at the wrong angle often makes a figure look comical. After fitting a hat you may need to rework the hair.

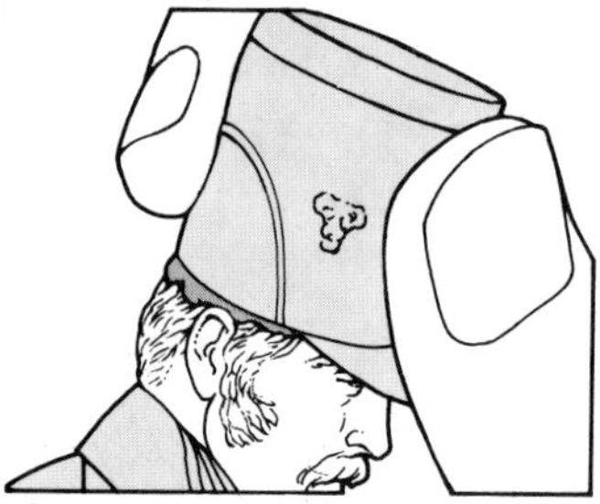

**Attaching a hat**
Paint a small amount of liquid plastic at the hairline; press on the hat. The plastic will spread out giving the realistic appearance of the hat depressing the hair slightly.

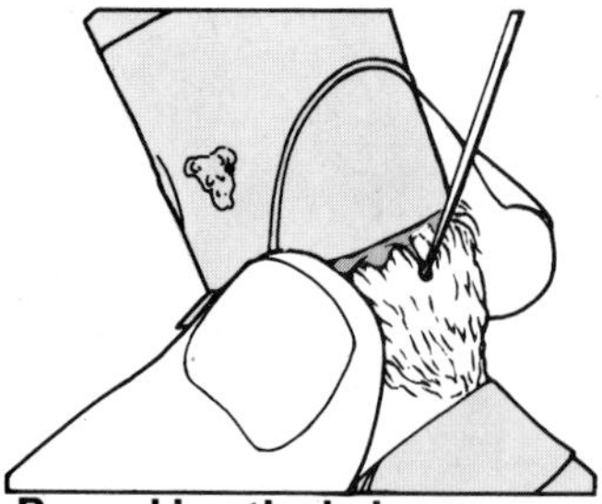

**Reworking the hair**
Let the plastic set and work with a pyrogravure; or, work it as a skin forms, picking up the surface with a cold needle and drawing out strands. Alternately, form a new hairline with filler; add texture to the filler with a cold needle.

Unlike most headgear, World War One and Two steel helmets should be loose fitting. Do not allow the plastic to spread out under the edge of the helmet.

Incorporating a hat is a simple device for adding interest and drama to a figure. George Washington doffs his hat, left.

## Fur hats and plumes

Treat a fur headdress like hair, working it with a pyrogravure. Kit plumes can be improved (see below) or replaced. To replace a plume, pare a piece of sprue roughly to shape, then paint it with liquid plastic to add fine detail. Use a pyrogravure for the finest textures. Or, make a natural looking plume from a real feather.

A pyrogravure has been used here to create the fine texture on this bearskin.

These officers are both wearing headdresses with plastic plumes. Note the lightness of the feathers.

**Improving a plastic plume**
Pare the sides to give a lighter appearance. As you make each cut, the feather below will fan out. Finally, touch up individual feathers with a pyrogravure.

The headdress worn by this Zulu warrior incorporates a real feather at the front.

## Chin straps or scales

You may want to attach chin straps or scales while the new hairline is still soft. The hairline will be depressed by the strap and the hair can be worked to curl over. Or, after the strap is in place, paint on liquid plastic up to the edge then work it to curl realistically over the strap.

**Adding a chin strap**
Cut a long plastic strip and hold it near a gentle source of heat to soften. Bend it to shape and glue one end to the hat. Positioning it carefully, trim and glue the other end in place. Run a little glue underneath the strap and press it to the face.

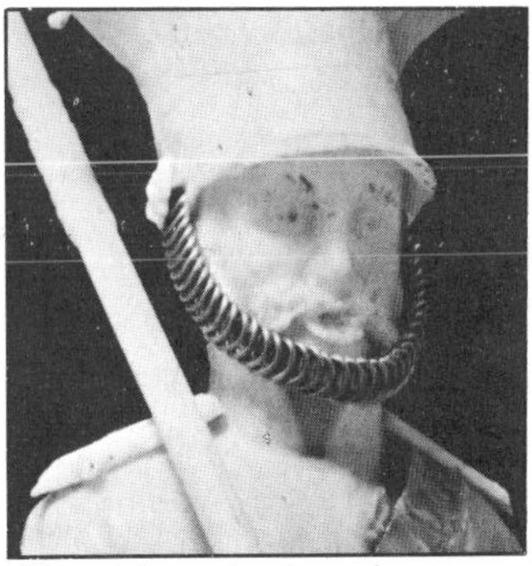

Wire chin scales have been added to this figure to replace molded scales.

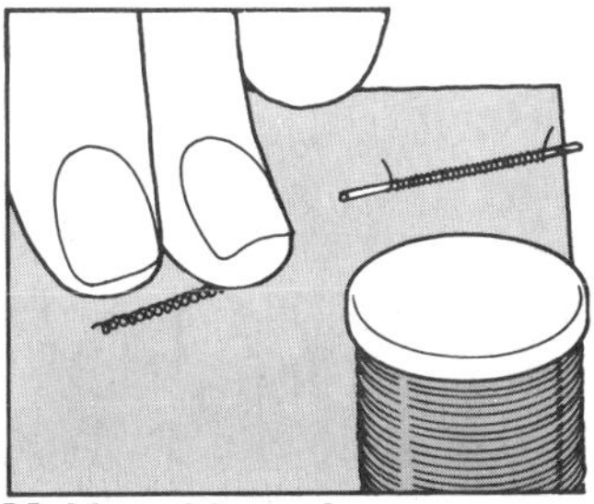

**Making chin scales**
Wind thin wire around a needle. Slide off the coil and flatten it. Glue the chin scales on the figure with cyanoacrylate glue.

## Fabric edges

A simple way to improve a figure is to lift the edges of pocket flaps, cuffs and collars with a sharp knife. Edges of garments can also be treated this way or they can be undercut to give the appearance of thin, light fabric. Use a curved blade and push it steadily.

**Lifting fabric edges** Support the figure against something solid and push the blade away from you controlling the pressure carefully. The cutting action will curl the edge.

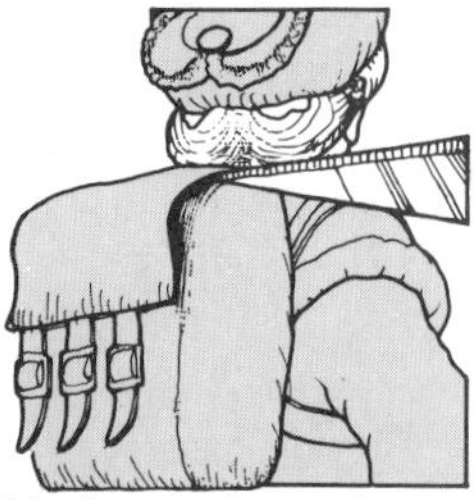

**Undercutting edges** Make a straight cut as for lifting edges, then make an angled cut to slim the fabric. Scrape out any waste with a pointed blade.

## Straps and belts

Some figures have straps and belts molded onto them. Molded straps are adequate but for a single set-piece figure, custom-made straps are always preferable. If necessary, first pare away the molded strap. Cut new straps from thin plastic, paper, ribbon or thin metal foil. Plastic is used in the following methods, but the method of attachment is applicable to all materials.

## Cross belts

Cross belts must lie flat on the shoulder and pass under the epaulet. To help with the fitting, first soften them near a light bulb.

**Adding a cross belt** Cut a long plastic strip and form a loop. Slip the loop over the head. Pull ends to check fit. If the strap gapes, cut or file away the molded detail underneath until it hangs naturally. Glue strap to shoulder; let set. Glue strap across the back cutting off the end where the accessory will be attached. Glue and trim strap across chest. Glue on accessory.

A more realistic figure can be achieved by using the techniques for adding detail on pages 136 to 141. Note especially the handmade straps and belts and the fine texture of the hair, hat and pack of this soldier.

## Packs and pouches

When adding a backpack to a figure, first attach the straps following the method described opposite for cross belts. Backpacks are heavy and there are techniques for emphasizing the depression made by the strap on the shoulder. Before gluing the pack in place, lift the ends of the fixing straps and undercut the flap as described opposite.

**Attaching the strap** File a depression in the cloth for the strap or run some liquid plastic along the shoulder and, as a skin forms, pull the strap into it to create bunched fabric.

**Making the pack fit** Feather the ends of the straps and hollow out the pack with a round-tipped blade to make the pack sit snugly on the figure.

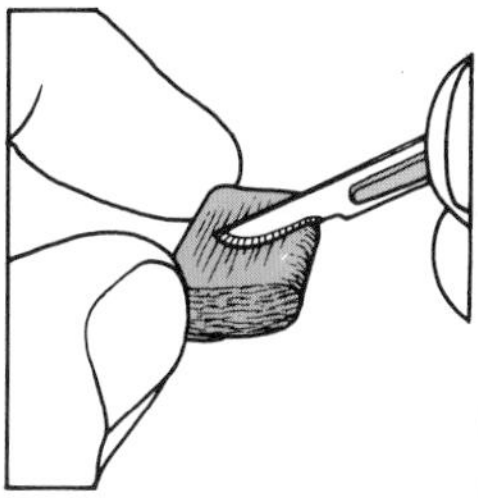

## Buckles

Some companies supply individual buckles which can be glued on homemade belts or straps. Position them as shown below. To complete the belt and buckle detail, cut belt loops from tiny strips of plastic.

**Positioning a buckle** Pick the buckle up on a modeling-clay-topped toothpick and hold it in place while applying the glue with a brush.

## Epaulets

Epaulets should fit snugly on the model. Scrape away the underside of molded epaulets or make new ones from plastic.

**Making an epaulet** Cut out the shape and glue it to the outer edge of the shoulder. When set hard, smooth the joint with wet-and-dry paper. Glue the other end only where it is attached by a button. Cut the button from a plastic rod.

## Blankets

Figures often carry rolled blankets. Molded plastic ones can be exchanged for more realistic versions made from tissue, fine linen or even fabric-backed bandaids.

**Making a rolled blanket** Roll up a strip of material and hold it in position by gluing the edge. To retain the individual folds, do not glue the ends.

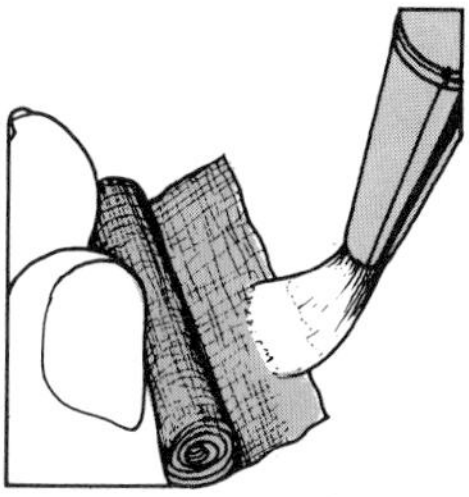

Next, tie the roll tightly with thread then, using a light application of thin liquid plastic or white glue, shape the roll exactly as required. Attach the roll to the figure with glue.

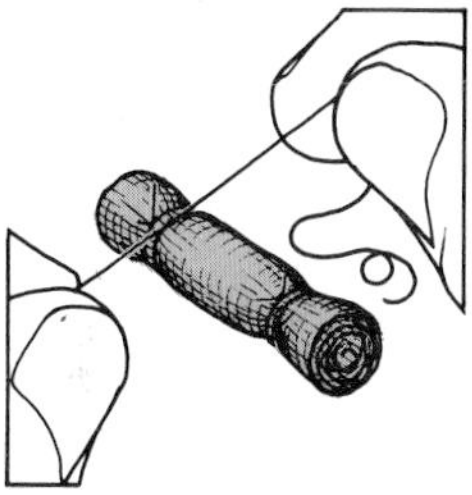

**Making a blanket with straps** Tie the roll with two strands of thread at each end. Glue plastic straps over the thread before attaching the roll to the figure.

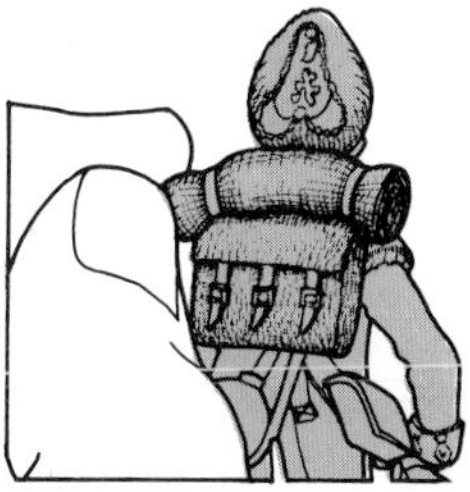

## Kit bags

Kit bags are easy to make with modeling clay and tissue. Begin by forming the basic shape of the bag in clay.

**Making a kit bag** Using thin white glue, stick a circle of tissue to the bottom and a piece around the outside of a modeling-clay shape, leaving the tissue long at the top. Work the edges of the tissue together with glue.

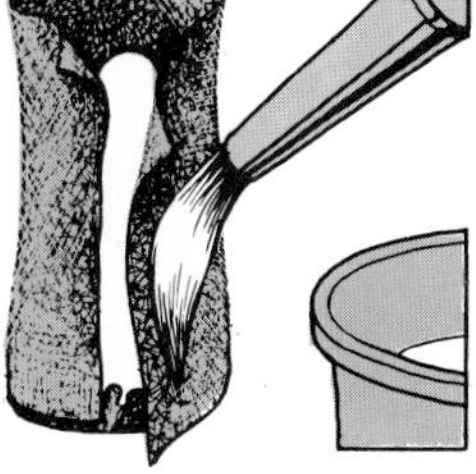

Tie the top with thread allowing the clay to fill out the shape.

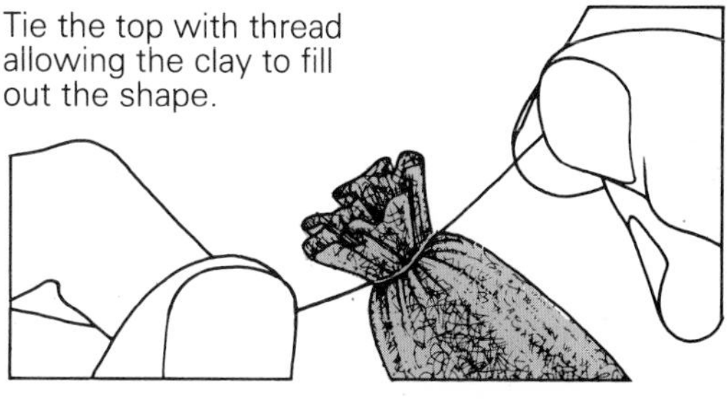

## Flags

Different materials are suitable for making flags. Small flags or pennants can be made successfully from foil, paper or thin softened plastic; larger flags are often made of fabric. The instructions below right are for making a larger flag from fine linen. To make a fringed linen flag, simply fray the edge before pinning the flag to the board. You can paint the design with waterproof paints before forming the flag but if you paint the design after, you can model shadows at the same time.

A flag draped over a tank for identification from the air adds color to a diorama. Make the flag by soaking the linen shape with glue, laying it on the vehicle and molding it in situ.

The flag above is from a plastic kit. Always paint shadows in the folds of a kit flag to emphasize them.

The deep folds in this linen flag were formed by lifting the wet fabric with a pencil.

## Making a linen flag

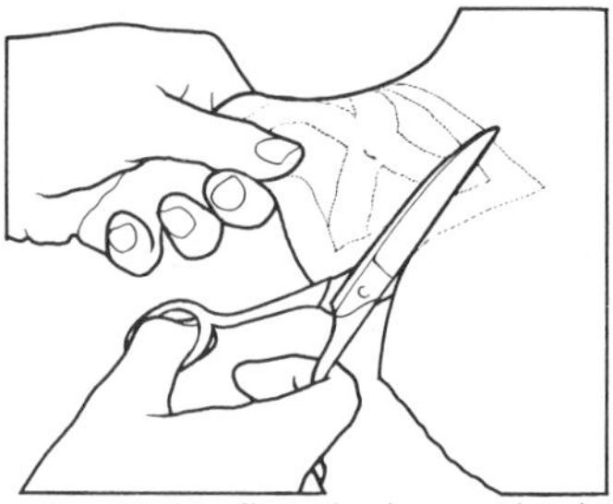

**1** Draw the flag design on both sides of a piece of linen, then cut out the flag with scissors $\frac{1}{2}$ inch larger all around.

**2** Pin it to a polyethylene-covered board, shaping it into folds. If the flag is to be attached by the corners, pull them out to apply tension; if it will be wrapped around a staff, hold edge rigid with a sliver of wood.

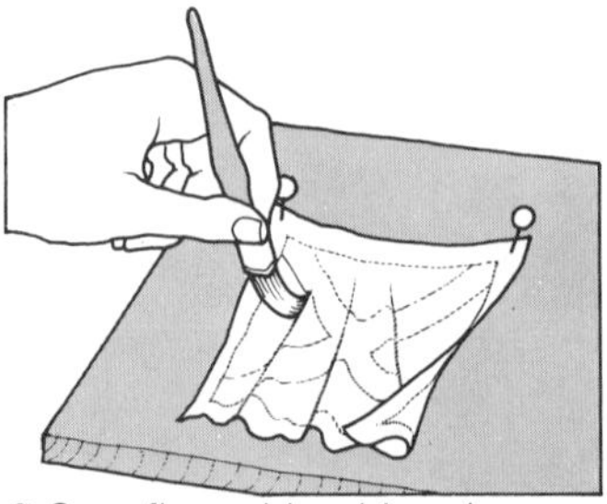

**3** Coat flag with white glue diluted 50% with water. Work the glue into all the folds; it must soak through to the other side. When it is wet, shape it by pulling and brushing the folds. Let it set hard.

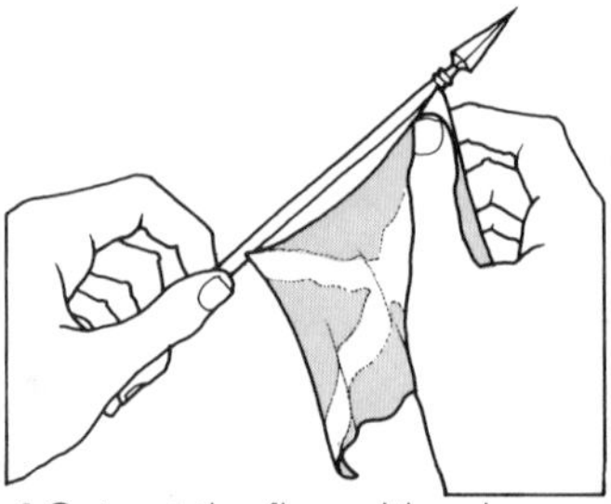

**4** Cut out the flag with scissors and attach it to the staff with glue. Paint the flag with oil or enamel paints following the drawn design. Darken the inside of the folds to indicate deep shadows.

## Gun barrels

Many of the firearms carried by kit figures have the barrels blanked off, but there are several different ways you can make the weapons look more realistic. While small caliber weapons are too small to be drilled out, you can cut the tip of the barrel perfectly square and paint it matt black to represent the hollow end of the barrel. You may also be able to touch up the end with the tip of a pyrogravure. Muskets, on the other hand, can be drilled out successfully. Use the technique for drilling gun barrels on tanks (page 124). A musket with a bayonet is particularly easy to drill out because of its wider diameter.

Not all models carry muskets with bayonets but a bayonet can easily be added. An alternative to drilling out a musket barrel is to replace it with a section of heat-stretched plastic tube.

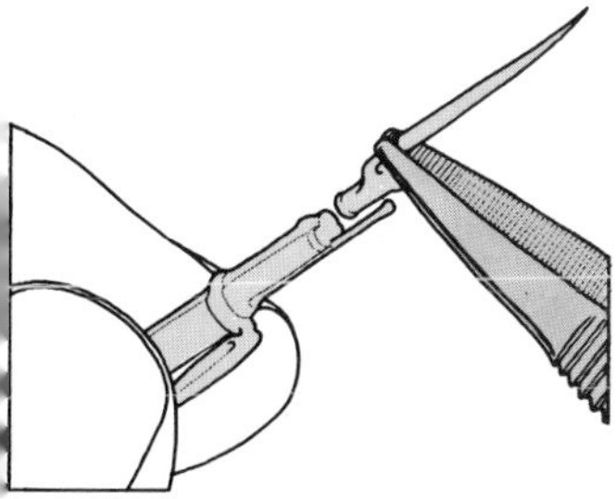

**Adding a bayonet**
Cut off the part of the barrel which would be covered by the bayonet, then glue the bayonet in place. You will probably need tweezers to position it correctly.

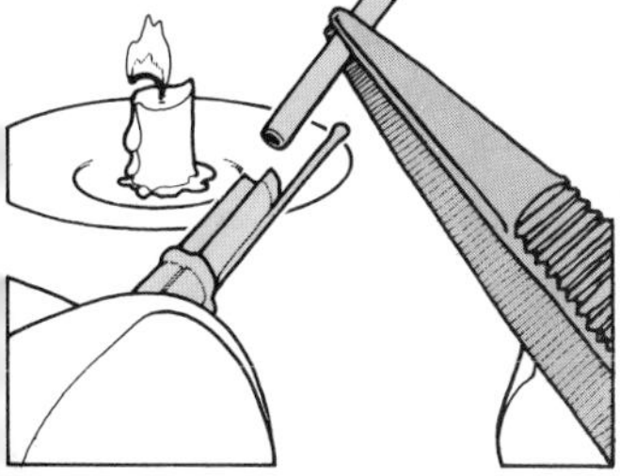

**Making a barrel from tube**
Cut off the barrel at the first ring and glue a section of heat-stretched plastic tube in its place. Heat the tube over a flame, then stretch it to the required diameter.

The muskets in this military scene have been made to look more authentic by adding handmade slings and wrapping the lock.

## Musket or rifle slings

Many kit firearms will need slings. A sling can be cut from the same materials used for straps and belts. Cut the sling to length and fold the ends over to form loops. Glue the ends down, fixing them according to how loose the sling is to be. Add slide buckles, swivels and loops from spare parts, thin wire or plastic. Glue one end of the sling to the weapon leaving the other end free so that you can shape the sling to hang at the correct angle. You may want to twist the sling, particularly if it passes over an object or if the weapon is lying on the ground. Foil can be twisted cold, but it is best glued in place to hold its shape. Shape plastic slings by applying touches of liquid cement on appropriate places to soften the plastic before twisting it. Finally, attach the other end of the sling to the weapon.

## Flintlocks

Flintlocks were often wrapped in rags to keep the lock clean and dry while on campaign. This can be simulated on a model by wrapping the lock with thin strips of tissue. Wrap the lock in two stages. Paint it to look worn.

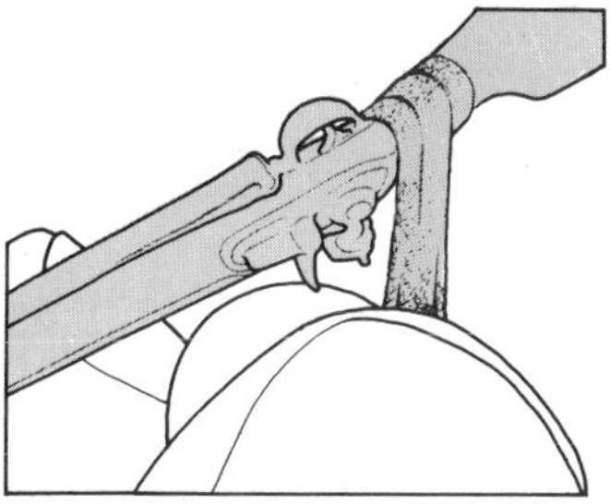

**Wrapping a flintlock**
Paint thin liquid plastic onto the lock and bandage it with tissue. The plastic will soak into the tissue to form a pad of the required shape.

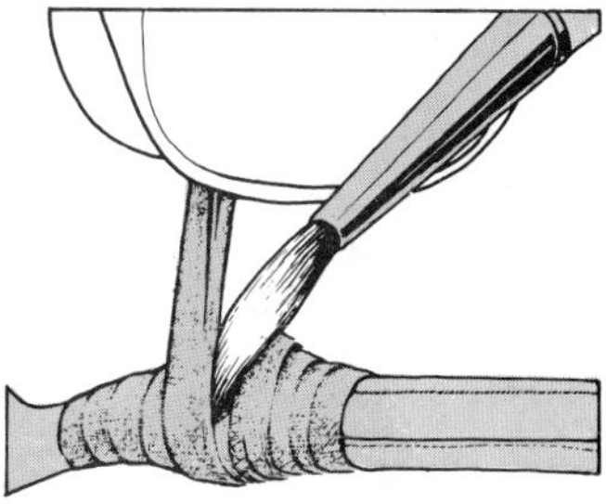

**Adding the second layer**
When the plastic has set hard, coat with thinned white glue and wrap with a final layer of tissue. To maintain the texture, do not apply too much tension.

# Changing the pose

Using all the same figures in a diorama is obvious and unrealistic and although some manufacturers supply interchangeable body parts, there are numerous occasions when you will need to cut and reshape a figure. For best results, any changes to the model should be planned and researched carefully. Each new action must be anatomically possible and should be reflected through the whole body. Check the pose in the mirror yourself or ask a friend to take it up and, if possible, take several photographs from different angles. Observe the way in which clothing stretches or bunches to form creases, and reproduce them on a figure with liquid plastic.

The instructions which follow are for plastic figures. Metal figures can be converted in a similar way, but use a fine jeweler's saw for making most cuts. Slight changes to the limbs or hands of metal figures can be made by bending the pieces carefully in a pair of pliers with padded jaws. When you bend the figure in pliers, take special care not to over-stress the metal part.

The poses of these kit soldiers have been adapted by the modelmaker to create an accurate representation of an army ration party.

## Head

A simple turn of the head can be made by cutting the head off evenly and gluing it in a new position. To tilt a head backward or forward use the technique described below. For a combined movement, cut the head off evenly at the collar. With a round-tipped blade, scrape a hollow inside the collar; then, add a drop of thick liquid plastic and when it achieves a putty-like consistency attach the head, twisting it into position. Leave it supported overnight to harden. Pare away excess plastic and fill where needed.

## Tilting a head back

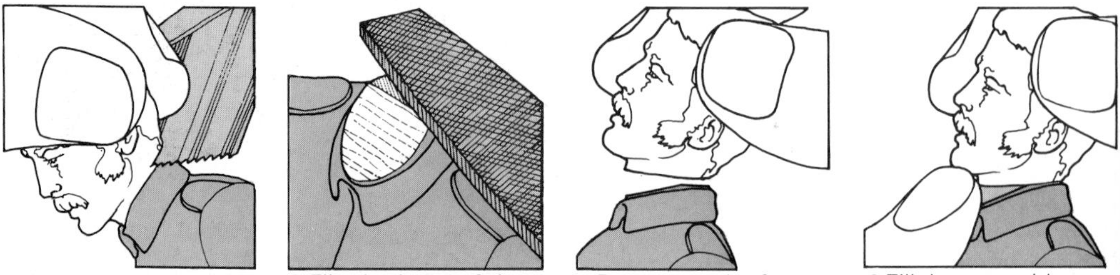

**1** Saw off the head. Be sure to make the cut at an angle, sloping from back to front.

**2** File the base of the neck flat to allow the head to sit at the required angle.

**3** Pare away the front of the neck to suit the new angle, then glue on the head.

**4** Fill the gap with a plastic wedge. When set, cut and file away any excess plastic.

## Features

The character of a figure can be changed by remodeling the features. You can pare away or build up the nose with touches of liquid plastic. Cheeks can be hollowed by scraping with a curve-tipped blade, or thickened with filler along with the jaw to make the figure look several years older.

A shouting figure is sometimes required in a military scene. The simplest method is to open the mouth by working it with a pyrogravure. Shape the opening very carefully for a realistic effect. Any melting plastic forms a good foundation for the lips which can be further shaped with a knife when the plastic has cooled. Finish by painting the small creases at the corners of the eyes and from the nose to mouth. For a more realistic set-piece figure, more extensive work is needed. Follow the instructions, right.

## Making a shouting figure

**1** With a knife, pare away the figure's lower jaw leaving the upper lip intact.

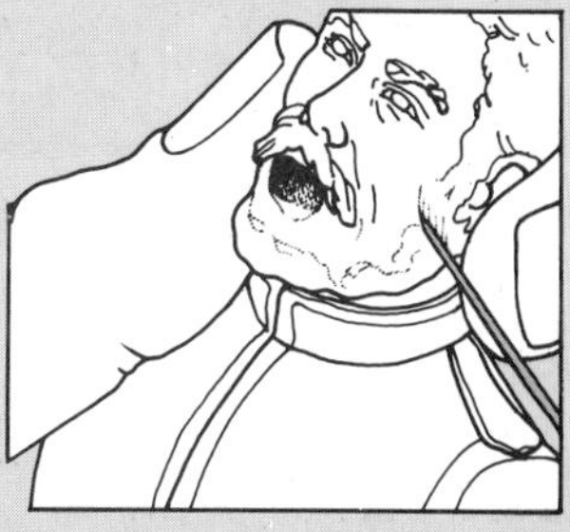

**2** Rebuild jaw with filler shaping it with a cold needle. Deepen creases in cheeks.

**3** When the filler has set hard, shape the lower jaw with a file and fine emery paper. Shape the upper lip to suit the open mouth.

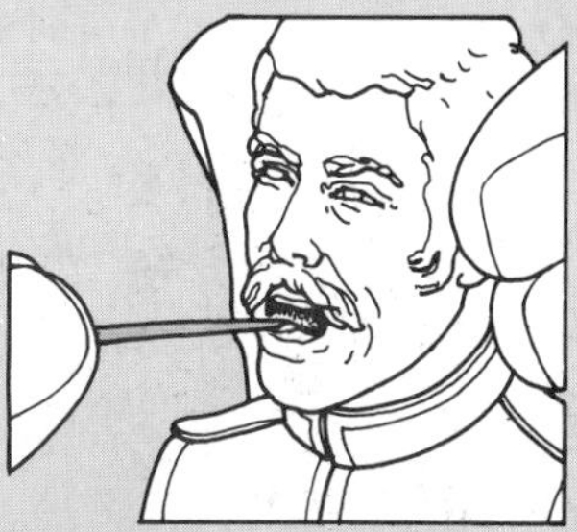

**4** Form teeth and tongue with touches of liquid plastic. A continuous band of teeth looks better on smaller figures than individual teeth.

## ɨands

\ hand can be moved sideways and up and ɨown by following the method described ɔelow. While humans twist their forearms vhen turning over their hands, to turn over a nodel's hand, simply cut it off square at the :uff and glue it on at the new angle. The :lothing usually hides the forearm on the nodel. To make a hand grasp, use the techɩique described on page 135.

**ɜending a hand to the eft** Cut a wedge from he left side of the wrist. Лake a straight cut ɔpposite. Bend the ɪand to the left and glue ɩ position. Fill and eshape with liquid plas-ɩc or filler.

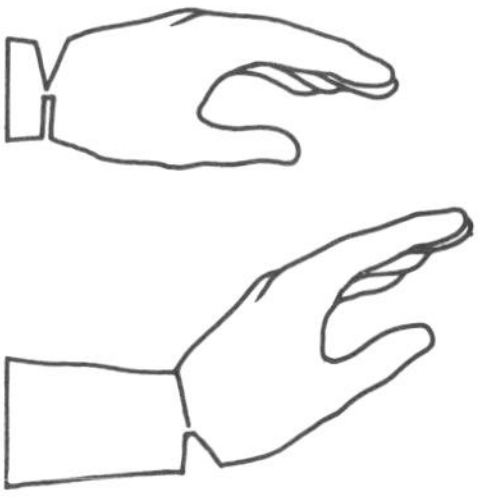

**Bending a hand up** Cut a wedge from the top of the wrist. Make a straight cut opposite the wedge. Bend the hand up and glue it in position. Fill and reshape the hand with liquid plastic or filler.

A variety of new hand positions can be created by using spare parts, or by altering kit parts as described left.

## Arms

Kit arms can be easily assembled at different angles. Sometimes, however, you will need to cut off an arm to reposition it. Arms can also be bent or straightened. To straighten an arm, make a cut on the inside of the elbow and open it to its new position. Remember that fabric creases at the elbow even when an arm is straight. Add these creases to clothing using liquid plastic.

These Napoleonic soldiers are depicted shaking hands. The arms of both figures were repositioned to create this pose.

**Bending an arm**
Cut a wedge from the inside of the elbow. Make a short, straight cut on the outside.

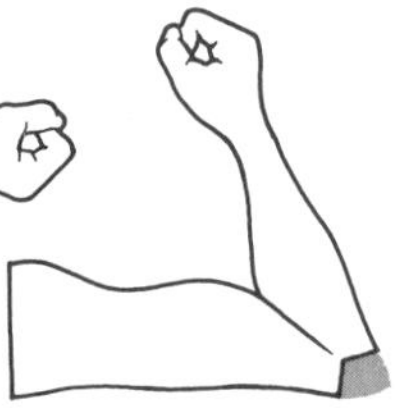

Bend arm into position. Glue and fill.

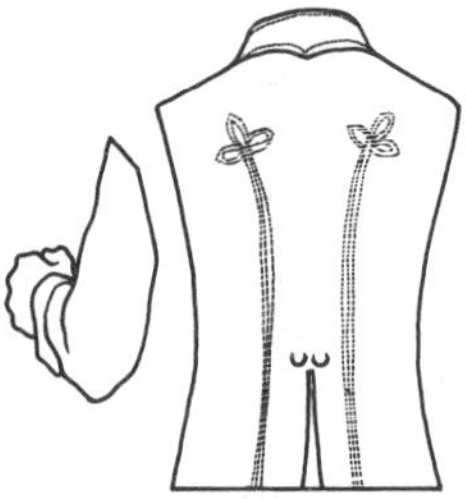

**Raising an arm**
Cut off the arm. Bevel the joint with a file so that the arm will fit in position.

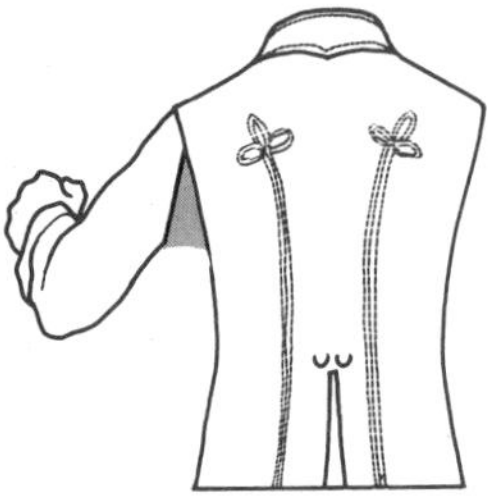

Glue it in place and fill the gap.

## Legs and feet

The toes should always bend on the rear foot of a walking or kneeling figure. Boots will show pronounced creases across this point which helps to disguise the joint. Legs move from the hip. Hinge the knees like elbows, and the feet like hands.

The legs, knees and toes of these World Wa Two soldiers were repositioned to show them running over rubble.

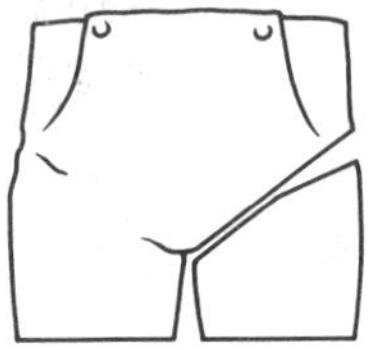

**Moving a leg**
With a razor saw, make an angled cut from the hip joint to the crotch. Bevel the joint with a file so that the leg will fit in position.

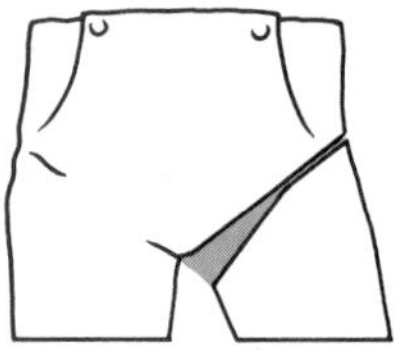

Glue the leg in place in corporating some thin plastic in the joint to re place plastic removed by the saw. Fill.

**Bending a leg**
Cut a wedge from behind the knee. Make a straight cut in front.

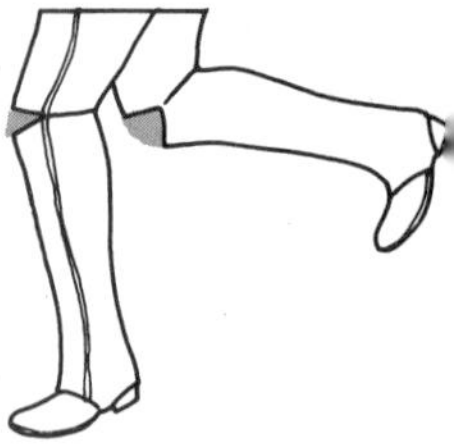

Bend the leg into position. Secure it with glue, then reshap with filler.

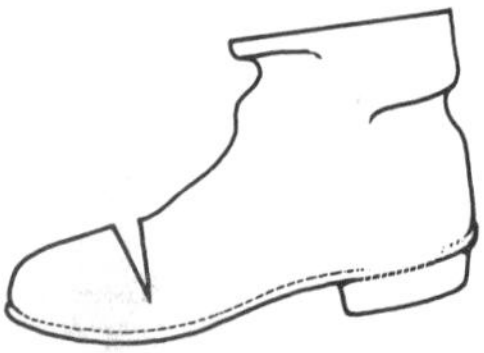

**Bending toes**
Cut a wedge from the top of the foot, at the base of the toes.

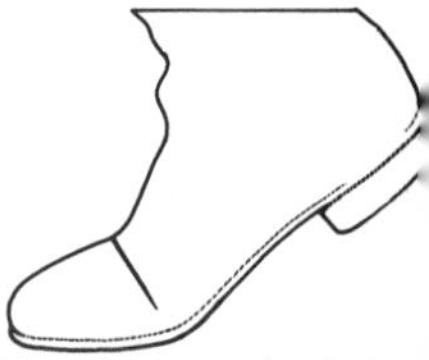

Glue the toes into the new position.

## Torso

Some dramatic and interesting actions are achieved by altering the position of the torso. To make a torso pivot at the waist, cut right across the waist and glue the two parts at the required angle. To bend a torso either forward or backward or from side to side, follow the method of wedges and cut low. Occasionally an action will body to bend in an "S" shape; th movement can be created using simple method. Below you can see of some of the poses possible.

Soldiers playing cards

Soldier passing canteen

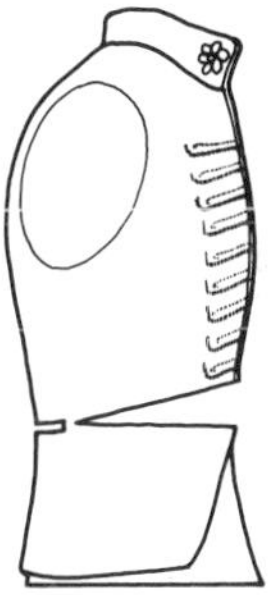

**Bending a torso forward** Cut a wedge from the front. Make a straight cut in back.

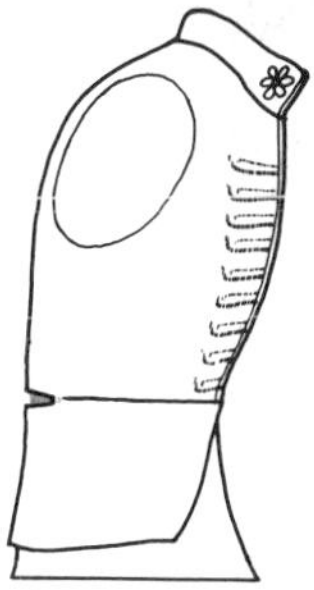

Bend the torso into position. Glue. When set, reshape with filler and file.

Soldier climbing

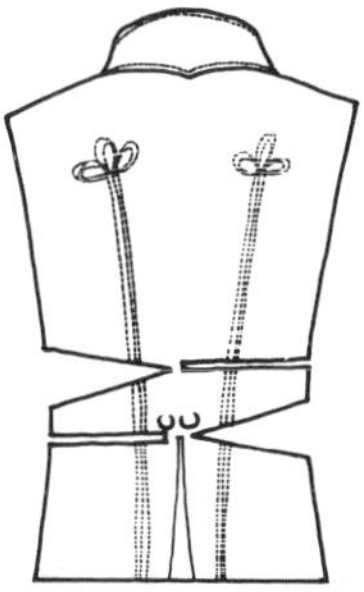

**Making a complex bend** On each side of the figure make a wedge and straight cut as shown above.

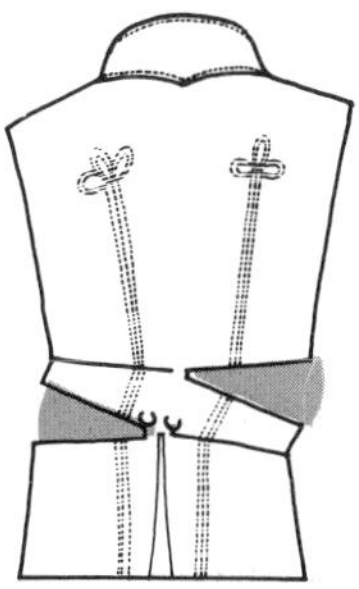

Bend the torso into an "S" shape. Glue in place. When set, reshape the torso with filler and file.

# …ostume

…uy a figure in a …u can always …st to adapt …acter you …away all the …ired, such as

…can be made with …cloth caps are particu-… molded from this ma-…shape the filler; smooth it

**Making a peaked hat**
Cut a peak from plastic. With a fine saw, make a cut in the forehead of the figure; glue the peak in place.

Mold filler over the peak and head, then smooth the hat with water and let set.

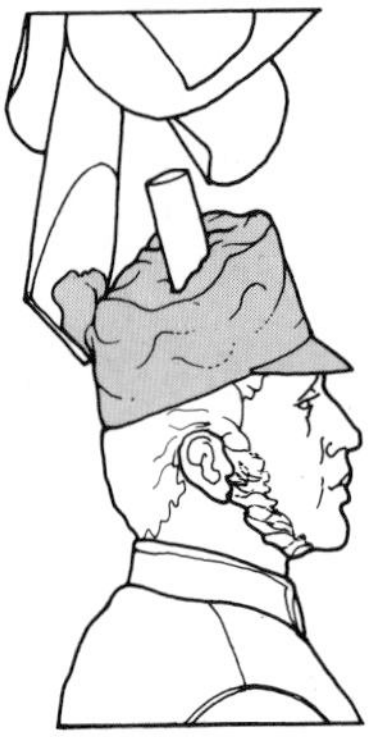

**Making a tall hat**
Drill a hole in the head. In the hole glue a short length of sprue. Build up the shape of the hat around the sprue support with filler. When set, shape with a file. For fur, add liquid plastic and tease it out as a skin forms. Use a pyrogravure to make the fine texture.

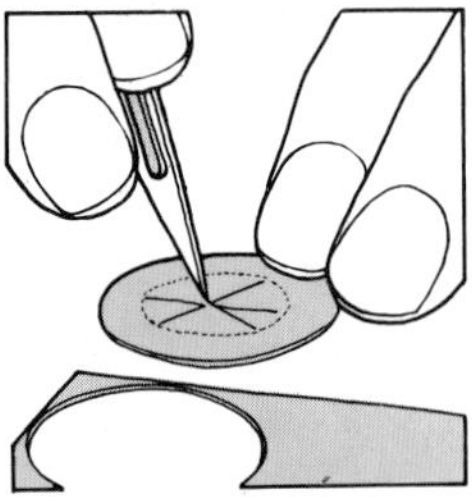

**Making a top hat**
Mark a circle (the head diameter) within a disk cut from notepaper or thin plastic. Make star-shaped cuts within the circle; bend the tabs upward.

Slip the brim over the head and glue it in place. Form a crown with filler or with a paper or plastic cylinder. Add a hatband or ribbon separately, if you wish.

pockets, buttons, braid and medals, until a basic figure remains. The exact method of building up the new clothing depends on the nature of the garment. New clothes can be made from scratch or you may be able to combine spare parts.

## Scarves and shawls

A scarf or shawl is a useful accessory for converting a female figure to a peasant. Always try to make the material hang naturally.

**Making a scarf**
Fold over one corner of a square of tissue to form a triangle. Add a touch of glue to the crown of the head; fold the scarf over the head.

Paint the ends under the chin with diluted white glue; form a knot with a small, glue-soaked ball of tissue. Finally, brush over the scarf with thinned glue to make it hang.

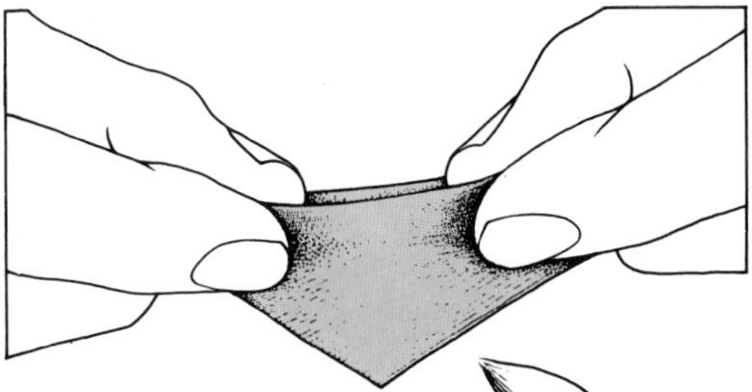

**Making a shawl**
Cut out a long tissue triangle and turn under the long edge. Form one pleat along the long edge to encourage it to hang naturally.

Apply glue to each shoulder, then drape the shawl on the figure crossing the points in front. Glue the points.

Add a tissue knot or brooch where the points cross. Coat the shawl with thinned glue to make it hang.

## Skirts, dresses and coats

Skirts, dresses and coats can be made from thin plastic, linen, tissue or silk depending on the intended finish. Build up these garments in parts. A dress is made from a skirt and bodice. A man's jacket or coat is made from a back and a front of two pieces.

Leave an excess of material on the meeting edges when you cut out the pattern pieces. For fabric and tissue garments, overlap this excess at the seam. (The seams of a tissue garment will be almost invisible if you tear rather than cut the edges.) For plastic garments, use the excess to pull the piece into position; trim and butt edges.

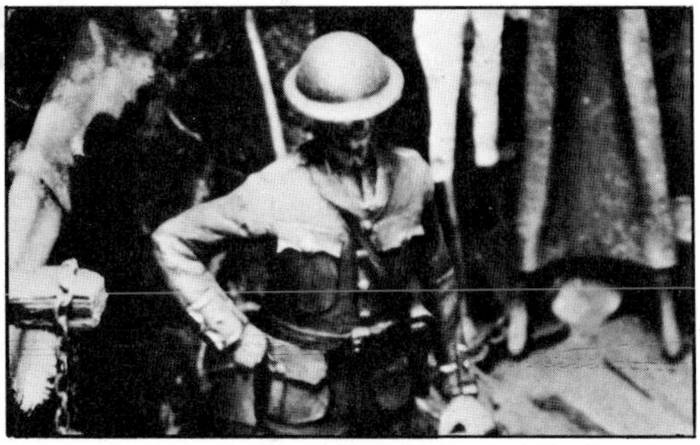

The jacket on this World War One soldier is constructed from pieces of thin plastic.

This peasant woman's dress, shawl and apron are made from tissue to simulate coarse fabric.

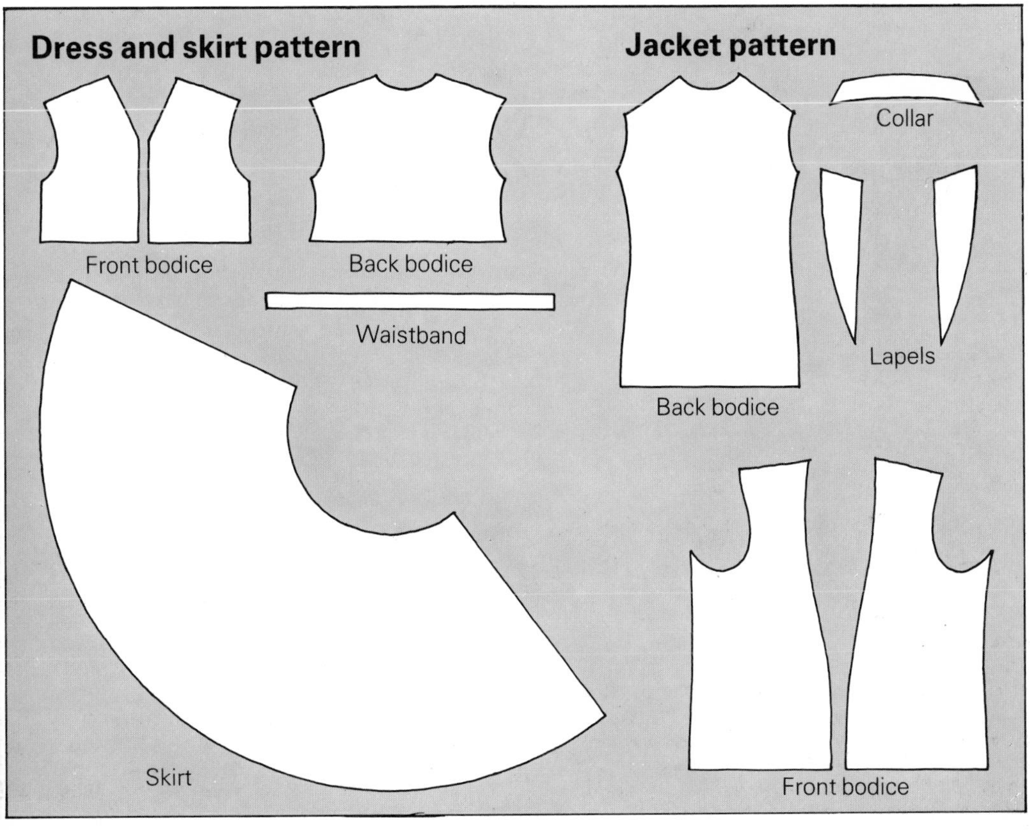

## Making a skirt

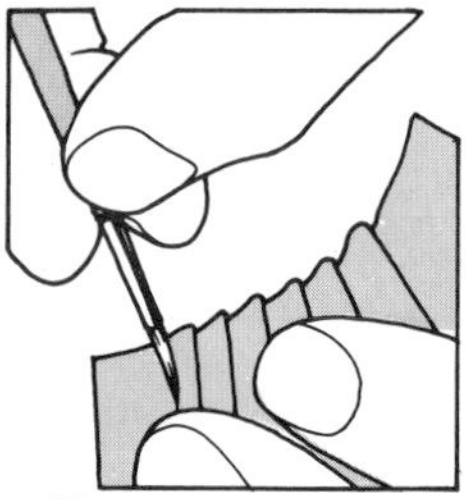

**1** Pleat the waist, carefully holding each pleat in position with a touch of glue.

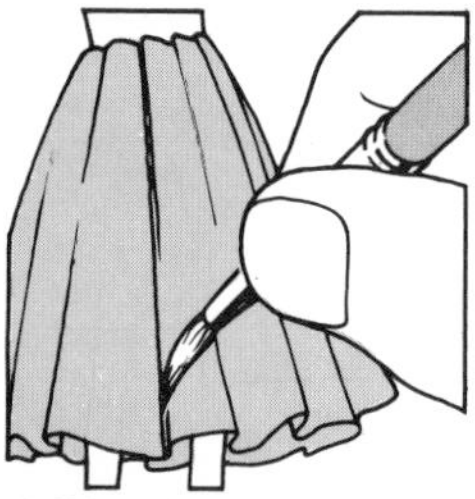

**2** Glue the skirt around the waist of the figure. Mold it to fit by soaking the material with glue, and join the edges at the depth of a fold.

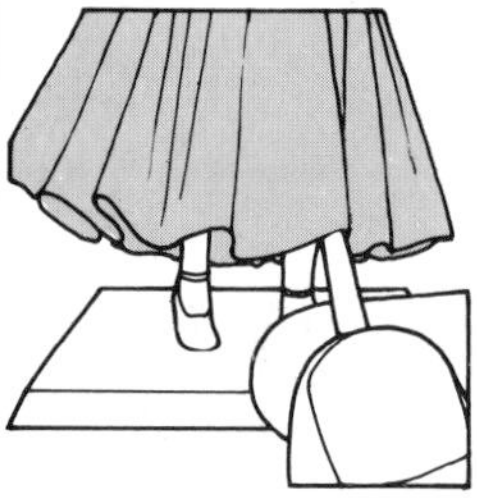

**3** Gently coat the skirt with glue or liquid plastic and emphasize the folds by lifting them from the inside with the handle of a paintbrush.

**4** To finish the skirt, glue a waistband over the pleated top of the garment.

## Making a dress

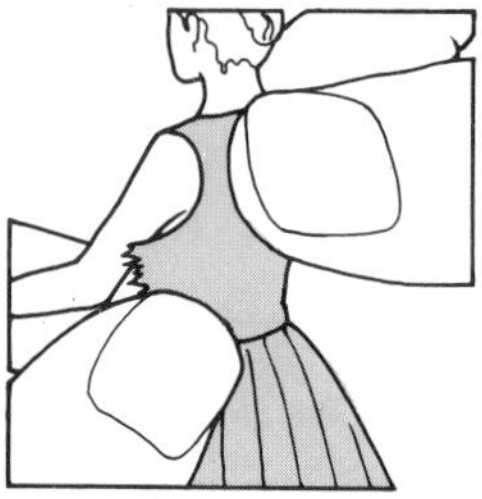

**1** Fit the skirt then glue the back bodice just below the neck. Pull it into the model pasting it under arms and on shoulders.

**2** Add the two front pieces in the same way, overlapping the edges down the sides and crossing them in front.

**3** Finish dress with a waistband. If you wish, add a bow separately.

## Making an apron

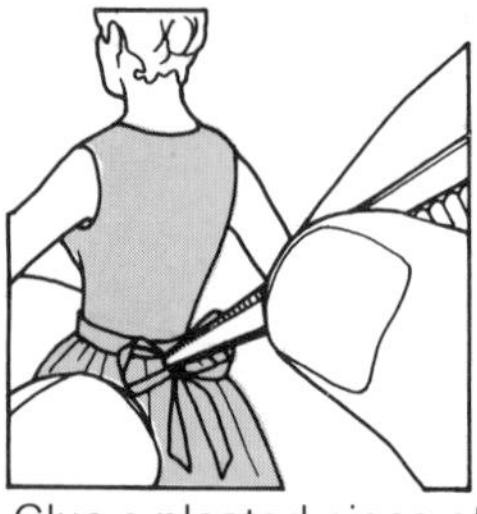

Glue a pleated piece of material to the model as described for a skirt. Add a waistband of thin tape.

## Making a plastic jacket

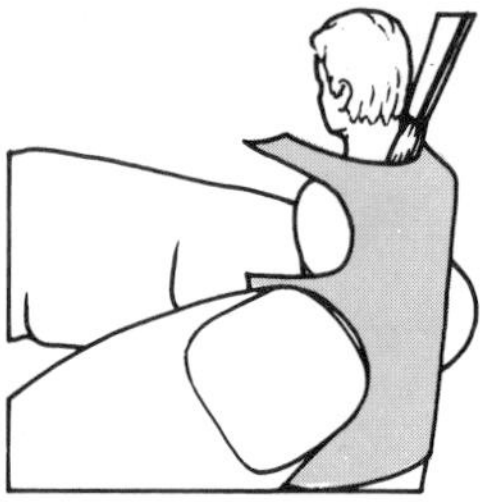

**1** Stick on back piece between shoulders. Shape it from center, adding liquid polystyrene cement underneath to soften it.

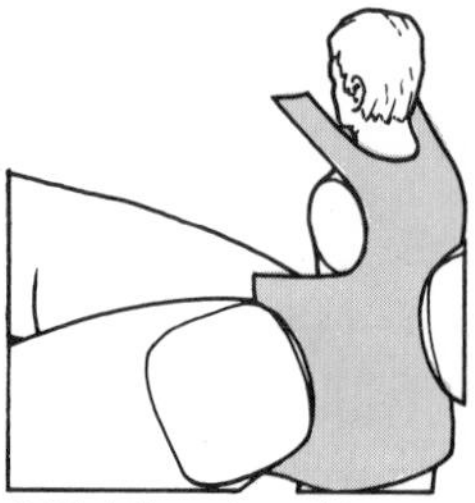

**2** Holding the sides, pull it into the figure. Cut off any excess plastic on a line down from the armpits and along the shoulders.

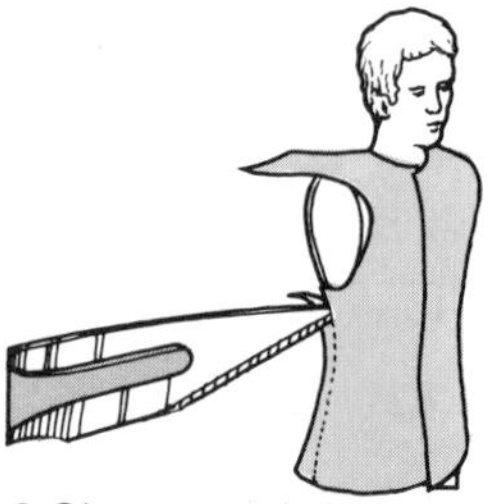

**3** Glue on and shape each front piece letting them overlap. Trim the sides and shoulders so the edges butt.

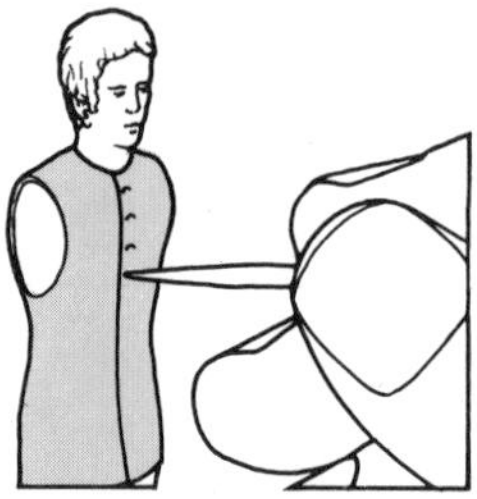

**4** While the plastic is still soft, press the button positions with a toothpick to indicate a pull on the fabric.

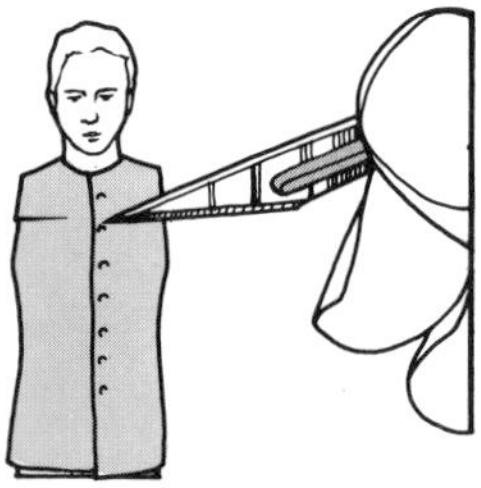

**5** Make a small cut from chest to armpit on each side. Overlap the plastic along the cut to take out any fullness. When it has set, file flush.

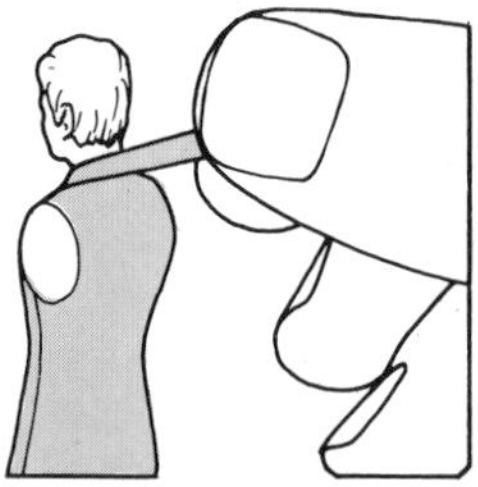

**6** Cut an overlength collar and trim one end to shape. Fix this end to the jacket, then glue the collar around the neck. Trim other end when glue has set.

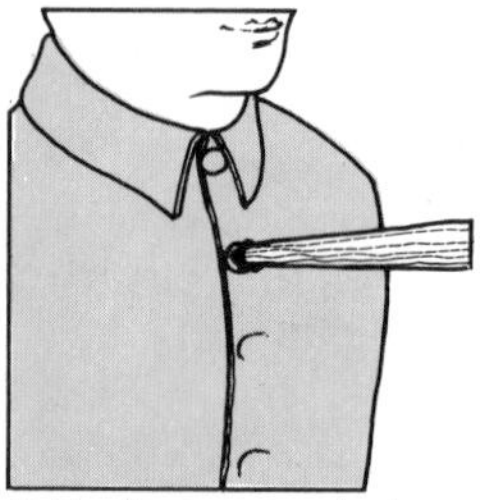

**7** For buttons, glue on disks cut from thin plastic rod.

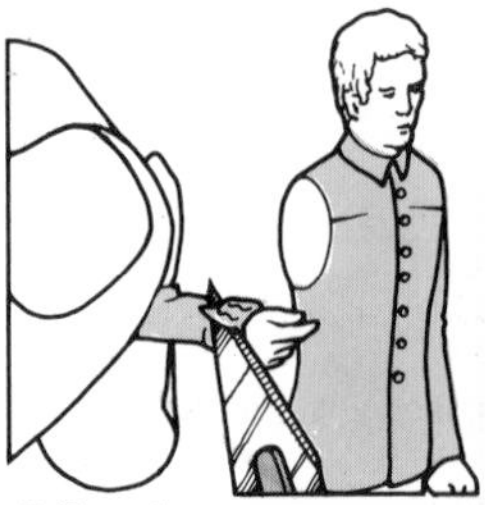

**8** For sleeves, use arms from a spare kit. Alter cuffs, if needed.

## Pockets

There are several different types of pocket and all are easy to make. For a patch pocket, simply glue on a square or rectangular piece of plastic. For an inset pocket with a flap, just glue a plastic flap in place. Add interest to pockets by incorporating details such as buttons or button holes. Buttons can be cut from thin plastic rod or they can be painted on later with thick oil paint.

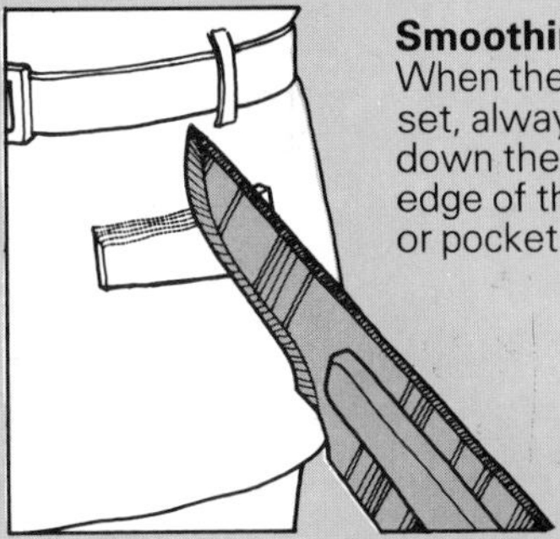

**Smoothing seams** When the glue has set, always scrape down the "sewn" edge of the flap or pocket.

**Making a button hole** Pierce the flap with a knife to indicate a button hole.

## Pants

When making pants, often only the part below the knee is added; the section covering the thigh is shaped from the original leg. Wrap plastic or paper around the leg attaching the tube at the knee with glue.

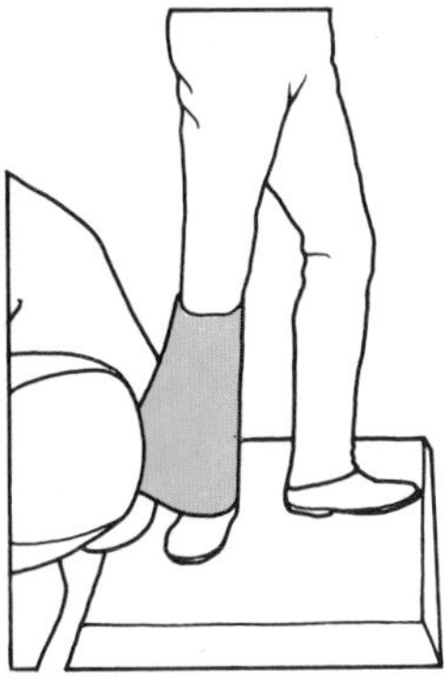

**Shaping the pant leg** Use excess material to pull the pant leg to shape trimming it off carefully with a knife after the glue has set completely.

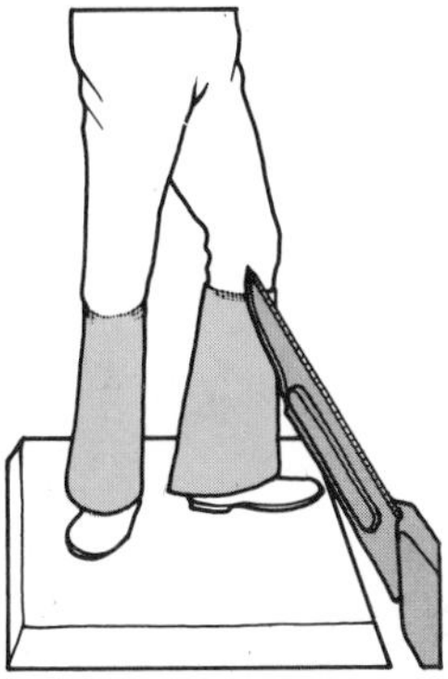

**Finishing the pants** Scrape down the joint or leave as a seam depending on the style. Build up the pants around the knee adding creases to the fabric.

## Boots and leggings

Many military figures are depicted with high boots, puttees or fur leggings. Leather boots can be adapted by carving away or adding to the original with filler or plastic. For spurs, glue a short length of wire into a hole drilled in the heel. Make straps from plastic. Puttees can be realistically depicted by binding the leg with a long strip of thin plastic and gluing it at intervals with liquid glue. Make fur leggings by applying thick liquid plastic to the legs and teasing it out just before it sets with a cold needle, as for fur hats (see page 137).

The texture of the leggings (left) was made by engraving the fur with a cold needle.

World War One soldier in puttees (below)

**Making puttees** Pull the plastic strip tight around the leg, but not perfectly even. Make sure the edges are not obscured by glue; they will give an impression of fine detailing after the figure has been painted.

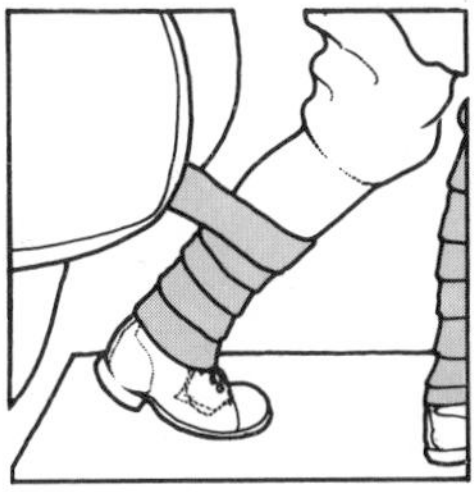

# Horses

Military dioramas often feature horses and even single figures are often depicted mounted, so it is especially important to master the techniques for modeling horses. Each part must be assembled in order and care should be taken to recreate correctly the detail of the saddlery and harness. A more realistic horse can be achieved by making some equipment yourself. Like model figures, horses can also be changed in pose. Horses often carry a rider and on the following pages are tips for mounting him.

## Assembling horses

**1** Begin by gluing the two main body halves together, making sure there is a good bond. Check that legs designed to touch the ground do so firmly.

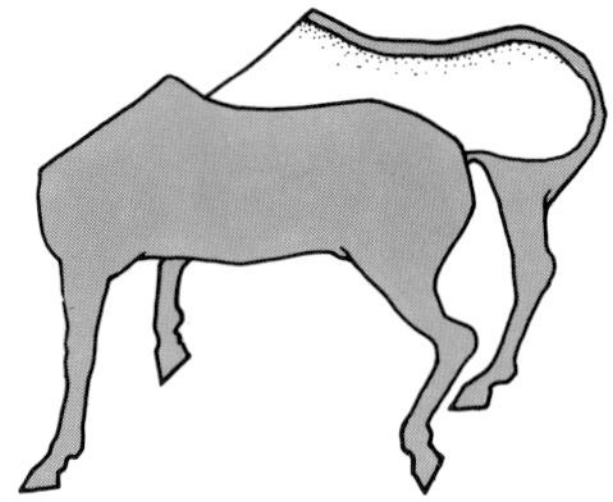

**2** Fit the head to the body so that there is an uninterrupted surface between neck and body, then scrape and file off flash lines and glue squeezed from the joints. Fill any gaping joints. If the ears are not molded into the head, glue them on at the required angle and fill the joints.

**3** Hold the mane on the horse, adding touches of liquid cement until it is fixed in position; then, run glue along the whole length, pressing the mane onto the neck to close up the joint. Trim and secure the forelock so that it fits snugly between the horse's ears.

**4** Glue on the tail. You may need to trim and file it to fit the rump. If the tail curls back on itself or hangs straight down and you intend to touch it up with a pyrogravure (see right), it will probably be easier to engrave the underside before attaching it.

**Fitting horseshoes**
First file a rough "V"-shaped indentation in the rear of the hoof and texture the underside by picking out a slight hollow with a knife, then glue on the shoes.

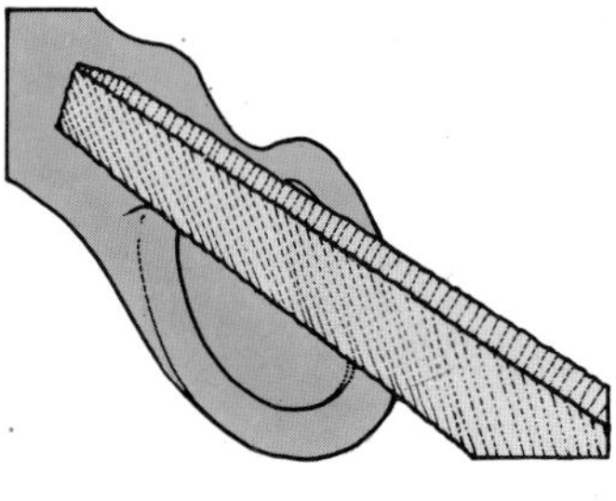

## Improving the hair

The mane, forelock and tail can be made to look more realistic with a pyrogravure in a way similar to that for improving human hair (see page 136). Always work in the direction of growth so that new engraving overlaps previous work and use the tool to create fine texture only – it is important to keep at least some of the molded form to retain depth and movement.

Begin by engraving the tail as shown below. Next, where the mane hangs to touch the body, string the hair out continuing the engraving slightly onto the body so that the mane no longer looks like a separate piece of plastic. Similarly, where the hair grows from the center line of the neck, hide the joint by finely engraving over it. Engrave fine hair onto the top of the head merging it gradually with the forelock. Work on the hair around the ankle, too.

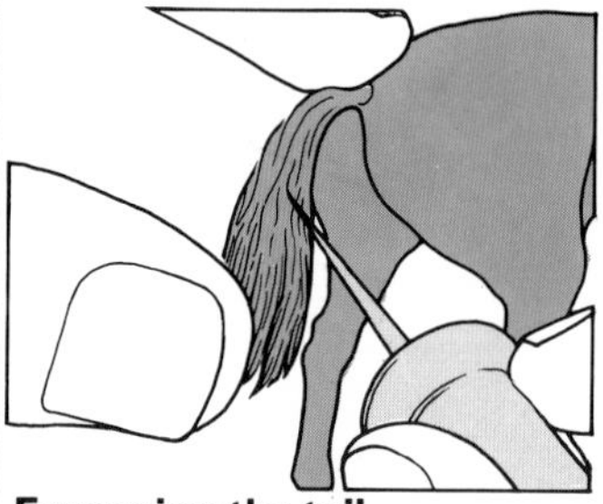

**Engraving the tail**
First, string out the plastic at the very tip to break up the rigid outline; then, add fine texture to the surface and deepen any hollows molded into the tail.

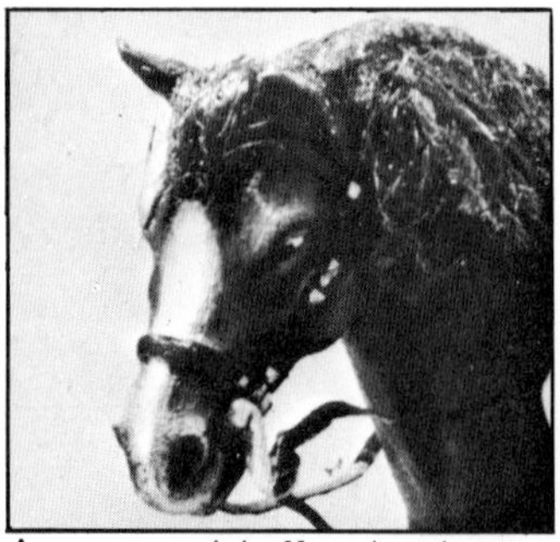

A very special effect has been created here by replacing the plastic part with a mane made of real hair.

## Assembling the saddlery and harness

Before you assemble the saddlery and harness, decide in what order you will paint the model. It is often easier to paint the horse first before attaching any equipment.

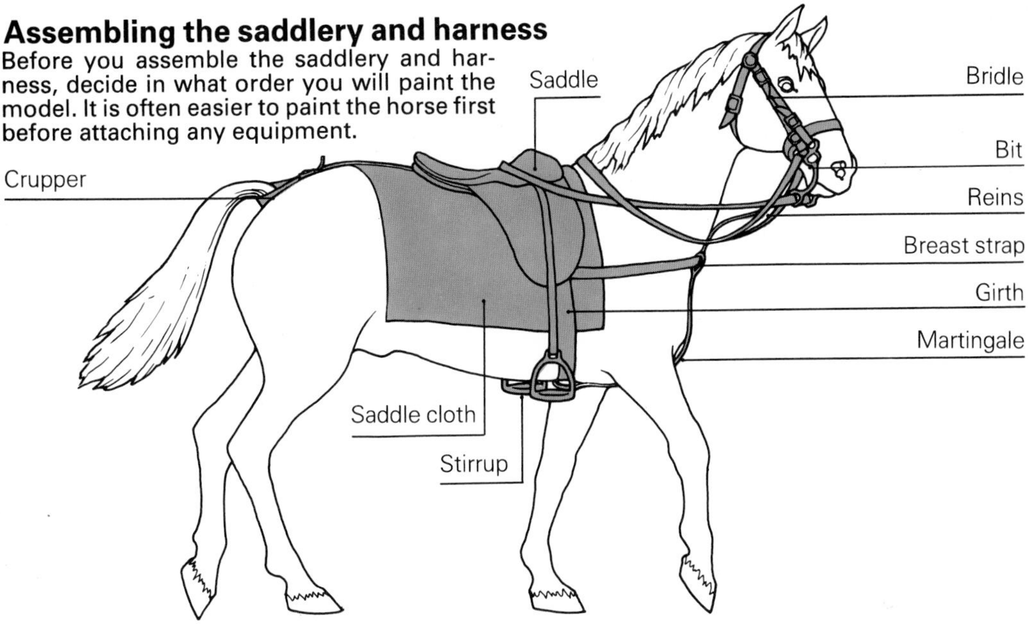


## The saddlery

Glue the horse to a temporary base. The saddle cloth, the first item to fix on the horse, should fit snugly. Scrape and sand the underside to make a close fit or, if necessary, remake it from tissue paper or thin plastic. You may need several layers of paper.

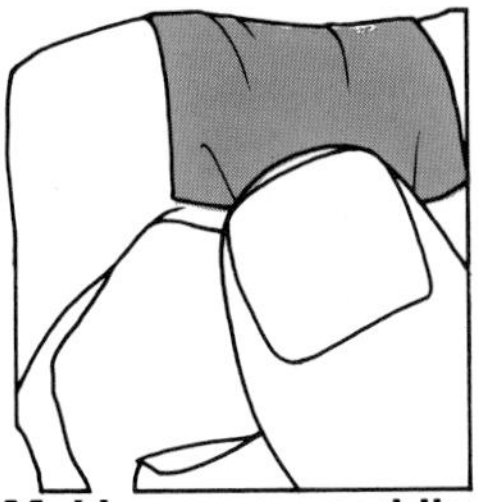

**Making a new saddle cloth** Attach tissue paper to the back with thin white glue, shaping it to hang naturally down each side.

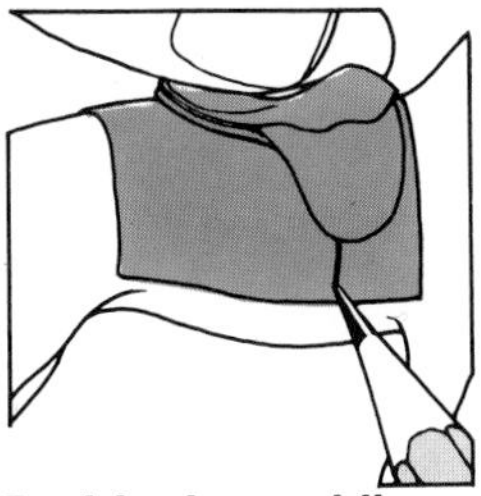

**Positioning saddlery and harness** Mark their position. Coat cloth in diluted glue; impress strap marks and press saddle into cloth; set saddle aside.

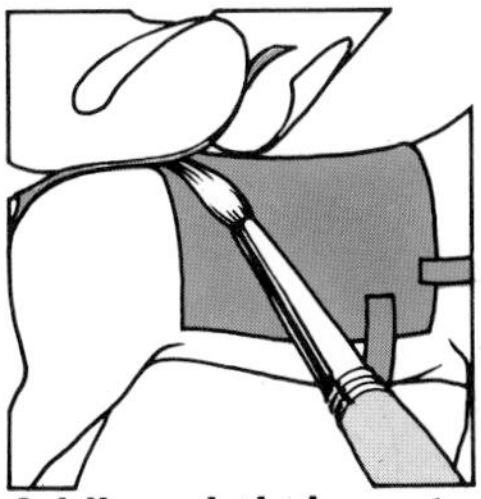

**Adding girth, breast strap and crupper** Attach these straps, taking the excess under the saddle. Feather the ends of the straps when the glue has set.

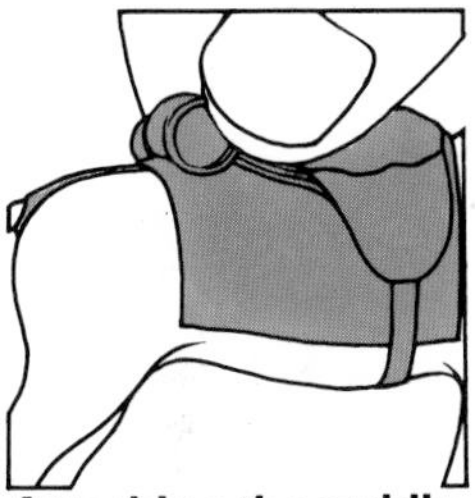

**Attaching the saddle** Glue on the saddle and any pouches, blankets or other baggage.

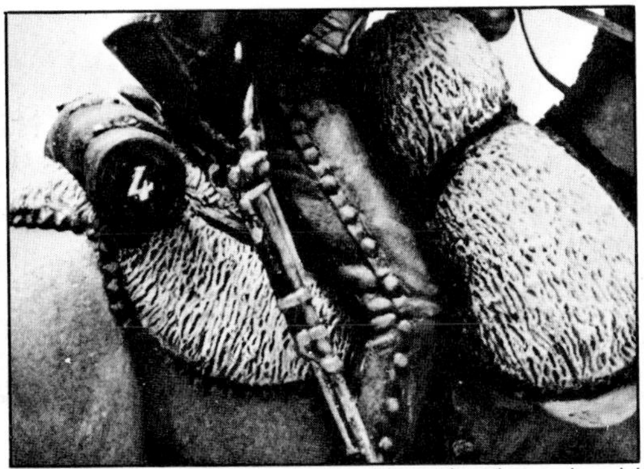

All saddles, whether sheepskin or leather, should fit snugly on the horse like this one.

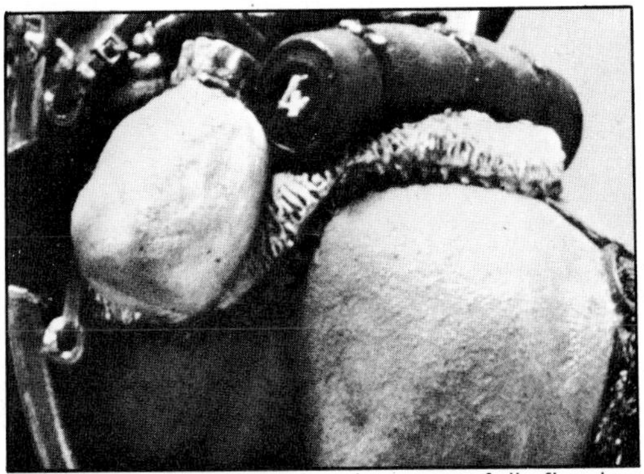

Each item of baggage has been carefully fixed to the back of the horse.

## The rider

Remember always to make the horse before the rider; you can then adjust the figure to sit convincingly.

Assemble the rider except for the arms and sit him on the horse to check his fit. Scrape and file the saddle and the inside of the rider's legs to indicate the weight of the figure pressing into the saddle. Hold the figure temporarily in the saddle with some small pieces of double-sided adhesive tape, and position the riding arm as described below. Glue on the other arm in the appropriate position – some figures may be firing a gun, while others may have their arm by their side if on parade. Now paint the figure and horse separately before gluing them together.

If the horse carries a lot of baggage you may find it easier to change the order of assembly. Do not glue the saddle to the horse but attach first the rider, then the baggage, to the saddle. Paint this unit and the horse separately.

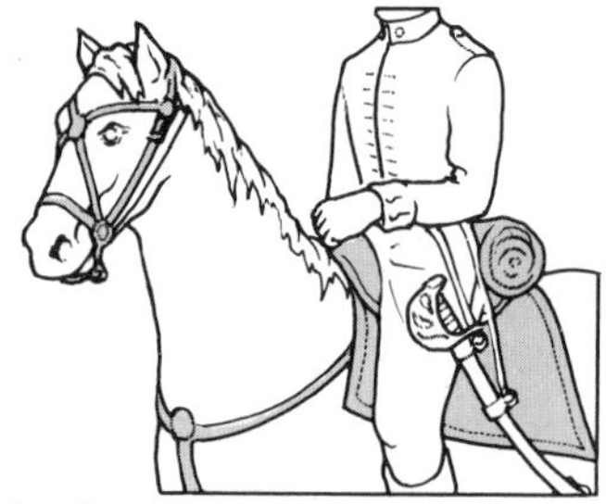

**Positioning the riding arm**
Glue the arm onto the figure so that the forearm is in line with the horse's mouth.

Note how this mounted figure sits very convincingly in the saddle.

## Bridle and reins

The bridle is normally molded to the horse. If it isn't, you may need to attach it before the mane and forelock are added. Only attach the reins, however, once the horse is painted or the painted figure has been glued to the horse. Attach them following the principles described for making musket or rifle slings (page 141). Always secure the reins at one end first, then soften and twist them to shape before gluing them in place at the other end.

Where the reins should go through the fingers of the rider's hand, trim them straight across and glue them into the joints. This will create the impression of continuous reins. If the glue discolors the paint, retouch with fresh paint.

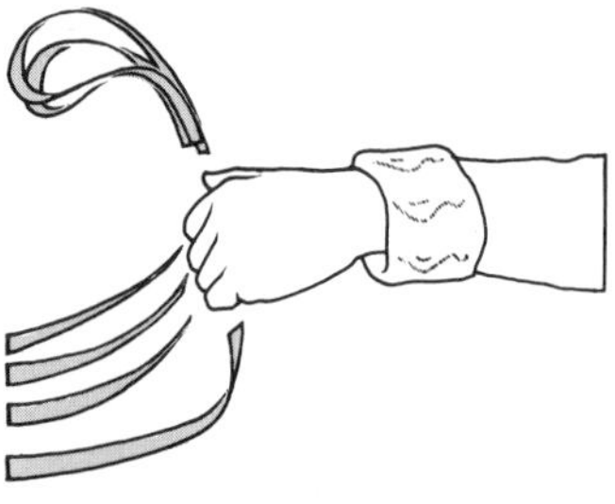

**Attaching reins to the hand**
To give the illusion of continuous reins passing through the rider's hands, cut off the ends of the reins straight across, then glue the ends in between the fingers and thumb.

Note the careful detail and correct positioning of the reins on this model.

## Stirrups

There are two methods of attaching stirrups. One is to fix them to the rider before gluing him in the saddle. If the rider is dismounted, attach the stirrup strap to the horse's saddlery.

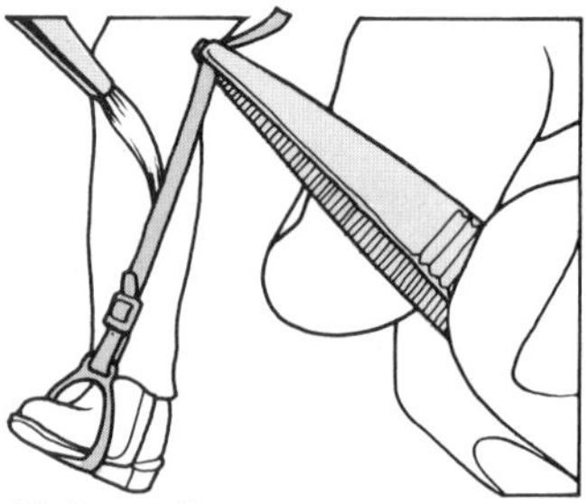

**Fixing stirrups to the rider**
Glue the stirrups to the ball of the rider's foot. Glue the straps to the stirrups, then under tension to the inside of the leg so they will not show. Feather the ends of the straps when the glue has set.

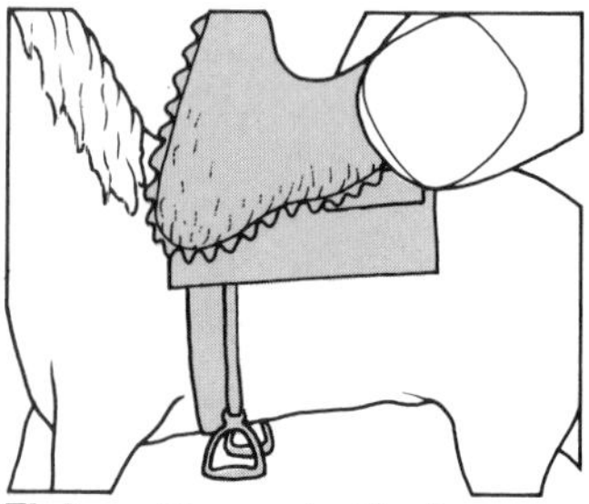

**Fixing stirrups to the horse**
Glue the stirrup strap to the saddlery in its correct position. Make sure the stirrup appears to have weight pulling on it.

The rider's leg should be slightly bent with the foot at an angle in the stirrup.

## Changing the pose of a horse

Horses, like figures, sometimes have to be altered to take a new pose. When you change the pose of a horse, take note of the way a horse's limbs move as it goes through the stages from a walk to a trot, a canter and a full gallop.

The main difficulty with changing the pose of a horse is that muscles and sinews must be reworked. Furthermore, most modelmakers do not have much opportunity to observe a horse in action. Nevertheless, by combining the various parts produced by kit manufacturers a wide variety of poses can be built up without extensive reworking. More poses are possible if body halves are cut into fore and hind quarters and recombined. Use a fine craft saw for this kind of work.

On page 154 you will find some basic techniques for changing the angle of the head from being reined in to the position for a full gallop. The neck can also be twisted to show a horse that has been turned quickly or has fallen to the ground or one that is trying to get up. Legs can be moved slightly using the method for twisting the neck, but for more extensive movement, cut the joints and reposition as for changing a figure's pose (pages 142 to 145).

The head and neck have been altered here to show a restless horse with his head turned and chomping at the bit.

The body position of this horse has been reworked to make it look dead. Note especially the angle of its legs and head.

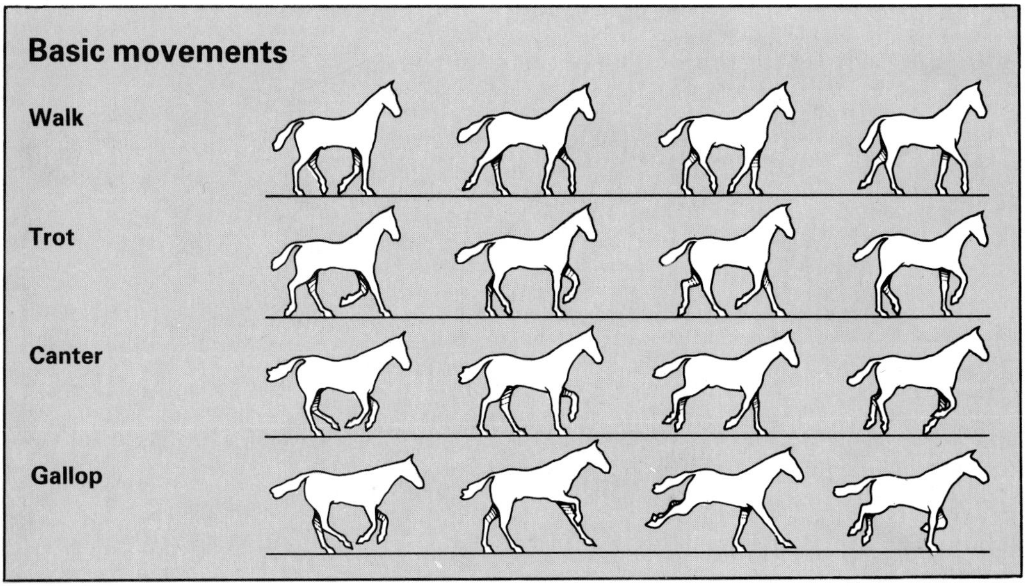

## Changing the angle of the head

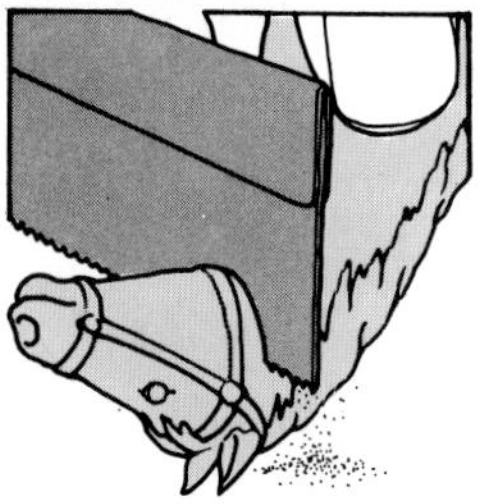

**Extending the head**
Cut the throat toward the back of the ears.

Soften the head and neck by holding it in a bowl of hot water.

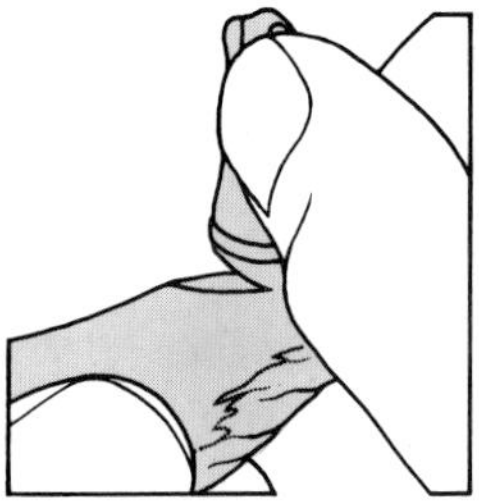

Stretch the head into its new position.

When the plastic is cool, fill and remodel the throat.

The horse's legs left have been fully extended to show it charging into battle. Note the raised mane and tail.

The horse's head below has been pulled in toward the chest and turned by the reins.

**Reining in the head**
Cut a wedge behind ears. Soften the head and neck in hot water.

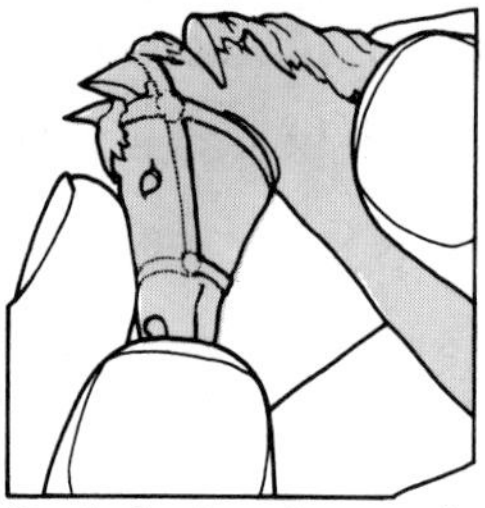

Push the head toward the chest. When cool, remodel the neck.

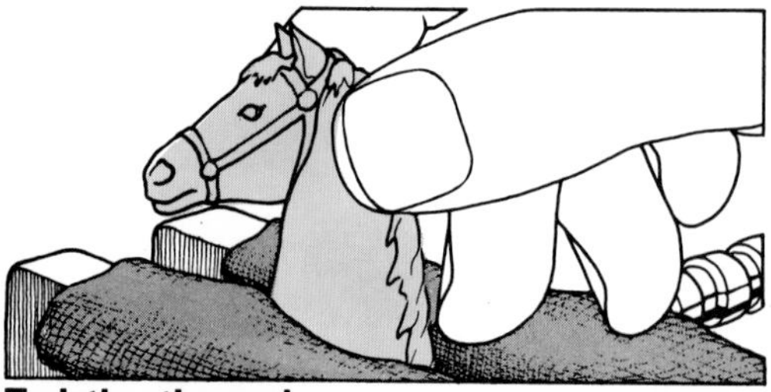

**Twisting the neck**
Soften the head and neck in hot water, then place in a vise. As you twist the neck, the muscles will stretch or bulge realistically.

# Dioramas and landscapes

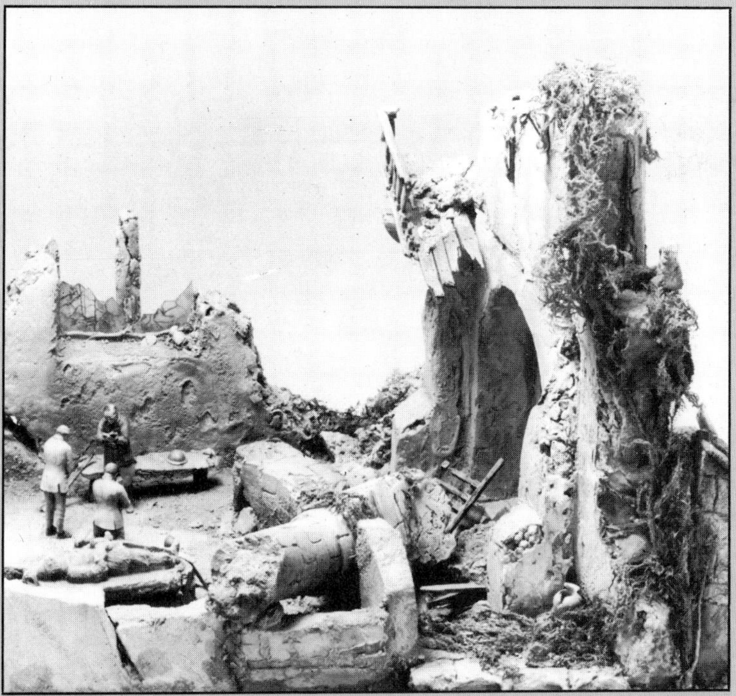

# Types of diorama

A diorama is a miniature scene, wholly or partially three-dimensional, depicting figures or objects in a natural setting. A diorama is normally built in a box and viewed through a window in the front, forming in effect a three dimensional picture. Boxed dioramas are used to display a scene which would be difficult to model on an open base. For battles, for instance, a few key figures can suggest a larger scene if displayed in a boxed diorama using the illusion of perspective and a painted background. Numerous figures and scenery on a vast scale might be required if it were modeled in the round. Boxed dioramas can be lit by colored lights to produce such effects as sunlight or moonlight.

A more common type of setting for models, however, is an open base, also known as a diorama but more accurately described as a "scenic base." Here the models are displayed on a base without walls and with a minimum of background detail; they rely on realistic groundwork to substantiate the scene. Most models benefit from being displayed on an open base because they are so highly detailed or well posed that it would be a pity to view them from one angle only. Furthermore, they may appear cramped if confined in a boxed diorama. Open bases are widely used to display non-working models of all kinds.

In this chapter we show how to plan and construct both types of diorama. We include examples of different varieties of landscape with building and painting instructions, as well as a catalog of individual effects from which to choose, from ice and snow to bushes and trees. These effects can be used equally well for model railroads.

Open bases are often used to exhibit highly detailed single figures or small groups.

Many non-working models like this one look most convincing when displayed on an open base.

Use the illusion of perspective and a painted cardboard background in a boxed diorama to recreate a large scene such as this one.

# Planning a diorama

Both types of diorama require careful planning before any building is undertaken. Accurate or subtle characterizations demand thought and research. First decide on the exact nature of the scene. It can be full of action, such as a battlefield, or it can be peaceful and relaxed, with figures cooking, playing cards, washing clothes or engaged in conversation. The finished diorama will be a frozen moment in time like a still photograph, but it should convey what has happened immediately before or what is about to happen. If you are depicting an incident which is well documented, the diorama must work even harder to convey an actual time and place. Every detail should add to the mood or atmosphere. Remember that it is often worth creating a humorous incident in a diorama. It might be the center of attraction, or it may be a quite insignificant part of the scene.

Consider the size and shape of the base or box. It should be strong enough to be handled with confidence but, at the same time, attractive. It should offset the model in the way a frame does a picture. If it is too large, and the elements of the scene widely spaced, the diorama will look empty and lack drama. A closely grouped scene provides a focus and always looks better as long as the subjects appear to be able to function normally if they were full-size.

Avoid aligning the main elements of the diorama with the edge of the base. You will create a more dramatic effect if you position figures or vehicles at an angle to destroy the symmetry. Make them move up or down a slope or place them slightly off-center. Alternatively, raise one figure in relation to another by gluing a piece of balsa wood underneath it.

The diorama will also look more interesting if the ground is rough or irregular so that it doesn't echo the shape of the base. On pages 160 to 161 you will find instructions for building simple contours as well as high and low hills out of Spackle or plaster.

## Attaching the model to the base

Before you start, you should also decide on the order in which you will assemble the diorama. If you are displaying a single figure on a simple landscape, it is usually best to finish the figure, attach it to the base, then build up the landscape around the figure. Trim the temporary base to which the figure is attached to be as small as possible and experiment with different positions before fixing it to the base with glue.

If you want to fix a figure to hard ground such as pavement or concrete, you will have to complete the landscape and figure separately. When you assemble the figure itself, remember to drill a hole in each foot and glue in a pin (see page 135). To fix it to the base, peel away the figure's temporary base and glue the pins into holes drilled in the ground.

For a diorama with several vehicles and figures or with a vehicle moving over very rough ground, both the models and base should be developed together to achieve the best results. For instance, you may need to attach a vehicle to the half-completed landscape so that you can arrange the wheels to relate to the shape of the ground.

## Making a boxed diorama

The box itself should be built from plywood or particle board so that it is strong and will not warp, and it must be tall enough so that the top cannot be seen through the window at the front. Before you begin to build it, consider the composition of the scene.

Think of the space contained in the box as three quite different areas, the foreground, middle distance and background. The main action is normally placed in between the foreground and the middle distance, although you can arrange several groups of figures ranging from the foreground to the background if you choose figures in diminishing scales. It is helpful to experiment. Arrange the main elements of the diorama on a table and look at the scene through a frame made from two L-shaped pieces of cardboard temporarily taped together so that you can try out differently shaped windows. When you have built the box, experiment again with the figures in it. Make sure the foreground features are spaced so that you can see through them to the main action.

To create the illusion of distance, model the foreground in three dimensions and in fine detail but leave all the background features less defined and paint them in softer hues. Make a thin cardboard backdrop and bend it in a curve to hide the corners of the box. You can paint a landscape on the backdrop but an easier and equally effective technique is to paint a simple skyscape, then build up the ground in front to hide the bottom of the backdrop. Rocks, trees or other features can be positioned along this horizon to contribute to the illusion of a receding landscape and to provide a more interesting skyline.

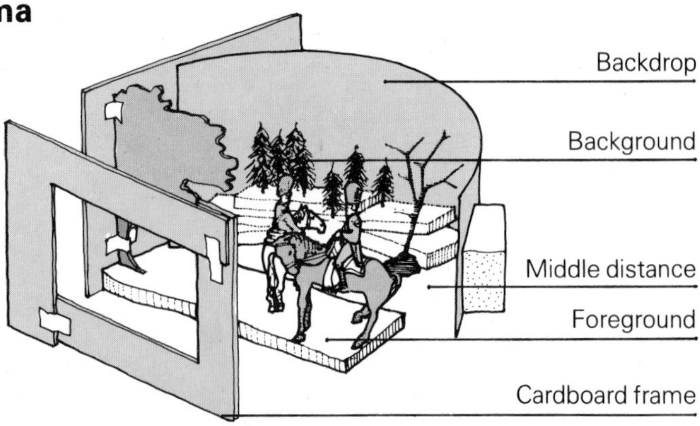


**Planning the composition** Experiment by viewing the composition through a temporary cardboard frame. Adjust the frame to try differently shaped windows.

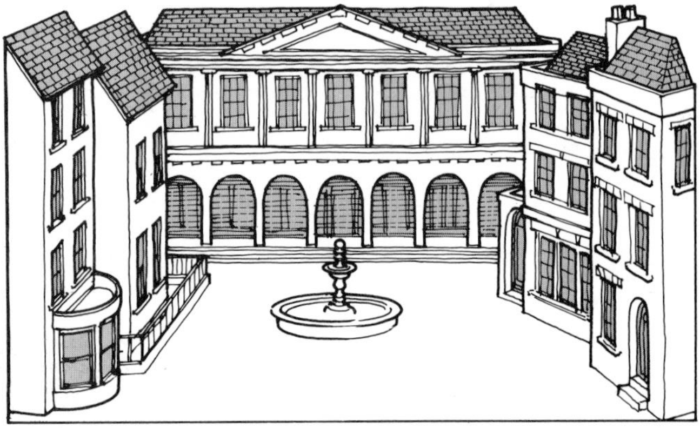

**Modeling a street scene** Make the buildings in low relief so that they fit against the backdrop without throwing unnatural shadows. Roofs and walls will recede according to the laws of perspective to create the illusion of depth. This technique can be used to dramatic effect.

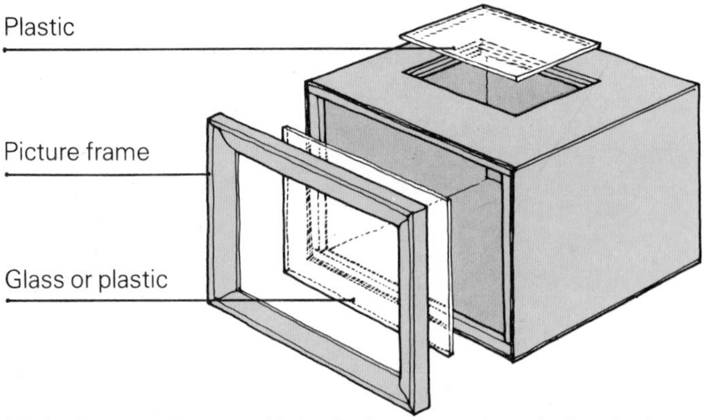


**Finishing the diorama** Light the box through a window in the top sealed with translucent plastic to diffuse the light and prevent unrealistic shadows on the backdrop. Seal the front window with plastic or glass and surround the front with a picture frame to finish the diorama.

# Choosing a base

A single figure or a simple group looks good on a round base as no single viewpoint is dictated by the shape of the base. Although a square or rectangular base can be viewed from any direction, the straight edges invite you to look at the model from certain angles. This makes a rectangular base an appropriate choice for displaying models which have one particularly good side. A rectangular base also provides more space in the corners to position additional models or detail to enhance the principal subject.

Natural materials such as flat rocks, irregular pieces of slate or pieces of bark-covered or driftwood also make interesting bases.

n this diorama the shape of the driftwood reates the contours of the terrain.

Use a round base if you wish a single figure or simple groups to be viewed from all sides.

Jse a base with straight edges if you wish your nodel to be viewed rom one angle only, or you want more room or additional detail.

## Making a base

The base on which you build a diorama must be strong and stable. You can buy bases in a variety of shapes and sizes. The simplest are made from solid wood. Also available are small landscapes cast in plaster which can be used as bases on their own. It is often best to make your own base, however, because you can design it exactly as you require.

Wooden bases are easy to make. Choose a piece of particle board, blockboard or plywood and follow the directions below. To make a large base easier to lift, attach a thin piece of hardboard cut $\frac{1}{2}$ inch (10 mm) smaller than the base all around to the bottom. Nail or glue on the hardboard piece before covering the bottom of the base with felt. The gap created between tabletop and base allows you to grip the edges.

If you want to set your model on a thin base, use a piece of metal or plexiglass. Transparent plexiglass makes an effective base because its edge is virtually invisible. Be sure to roughen the surface of both metal and plexiglass so that any other materials you add will adhere to it. Avoid using hardboard; it is unstable and will eventually warp. Likewise, do not use unsupported polystyrene.

## Making a wooden base

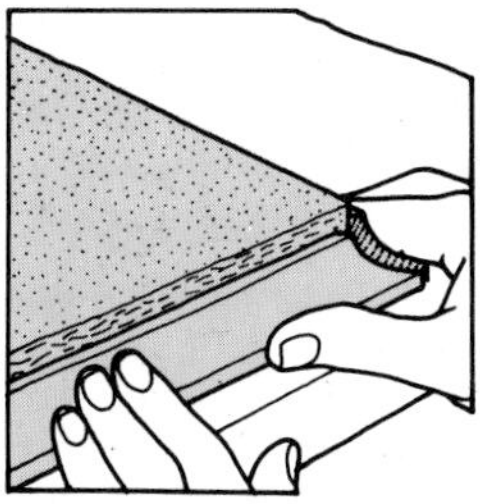

**1** Cut the shape from particle board, blockboard or plywood, then finish the corners with iron-on veneer or a picture-frame molding glued all around and mitered at the corners.

**2** Coat the base all over with clear polyurethane to preserve its finish and prevent water soaking into the base from other materials.

**3** If necessary, roughen the surface to help materials adhere. Apply another coat of polyurethane over the surface to seal it.

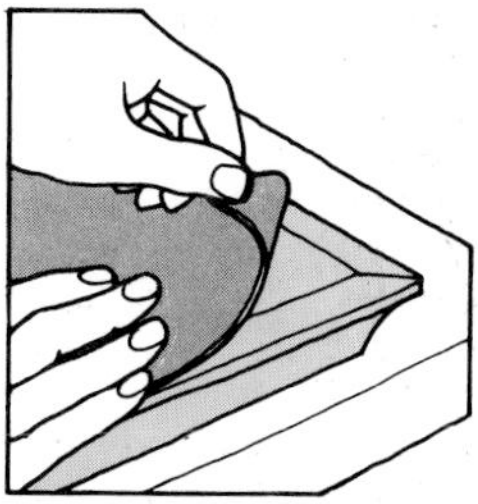

**4** Finally, cover the bottom of the base with a piece of baize or felt; this will prevent it from scratching any polished surfaces.

# Building contours

Sometimes you will want to display your model on a flat base, on pavement or concrete, for instance; but most often you will need to build contours on the base.

Weight is an important factor if you want your diorama to be portable. The methods described on this and the following page all employ lightweight materials. If you are making a large diorama or one with a mountainous landscape you should consider using hollow-shell scenery.

Add any features such as trees or rocks to the contours while they are still soft, pushing them into the modeling material and securing them with a touch of white glue. Then apply the surface texture such as grass, earth or sand to the landscape.

## Simple contours

To make simple contours, just shape any soft modeling material directly on the base. Some of the best materials to use are modeling clay, Spackle or fireclay cement. These are all very simple to shape with your hands or a tool.

**Making simple contours**
Shape the modeling material directly on the base.

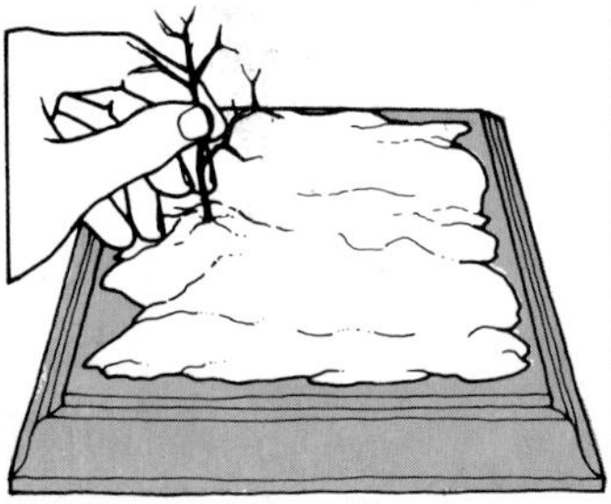

**Adding detail to a landscape**
Push stones, plants or other features into the modeling material while it is still soft.

## Hills

Build up hills in layers using sheets of polyurethane foam or polystyrene. For low hills, use only one or two layers of material; for high hills, build up several layers. Both of the materials are light and will not add unnecessary weight. Saw polyurethane foam to shape with a coping saw. You can use a saber saw but if so, wear a face mask to avoid inhaling dust. Cut polystyrene with a sharp knife or with a hot wire. Glue the layers to the base and to each other with white glue. When set shape the corners with a surform or coarse file, or texture them with a blunt tool such as a screwdriver. To finish, coat the layers with Spackle (see below, in steps 2 to 4 for making low hills).

## Making low hills

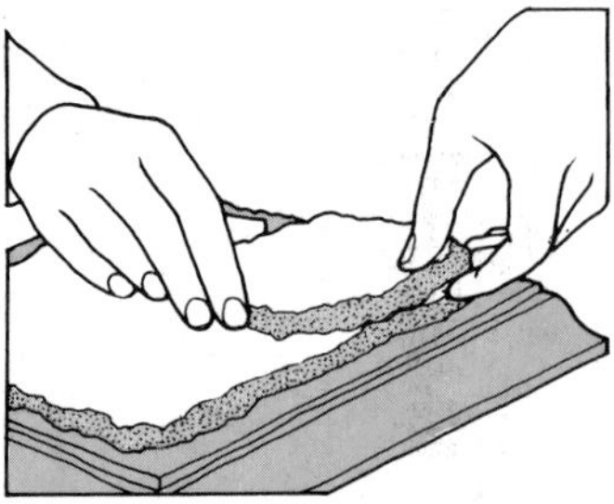

**1** Cut sheets of polyurethane foam or polystyrene roughly to shape and fix them to the base with white glue. Use nails, if necessary.

**2** Spread Spackle, mixed to the consistency of soft butter, roughly over the contours without concern for the finished texture. Don't take the Spackle up to the edge of the base.

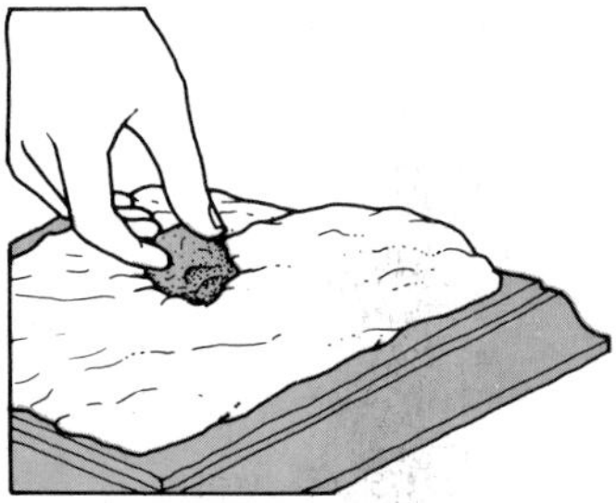

**3** Before this coat sets, half bury any large rocks or other large features in the Spackle.

**4** Let dry, then apply a final thin layer of creamy Spackle or thick white glue. Add surface texture and fix any small features into this layer.

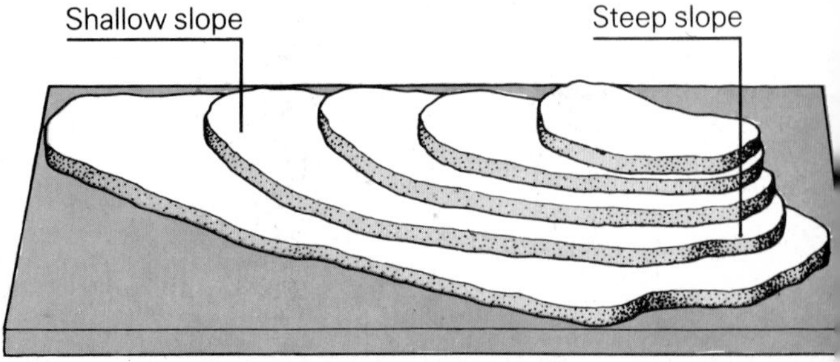


**Making high hills** Build up several layers. For a steep slope, make narrow steps; for a shallow slope, make wide steps. Carve roughly to shape.

## Hollow-shell scenery

Hollow-shell scenery is made by forming a thin shell over an open wooden frame. It is very light and it is a suitable technique to use if you are modeling a large landscape or one with a high terrain. Although it is most often used for model railroads, it can be used for dioramas and in combination with other techniques for building contours.

The shell itself is made of pieces of fabric or brown paper soaked in plaster and laid over a lattice of wire or cardboard strips. A lattice of chicken wire or window screen makes very strong scenery but cardboard strips, the method shown right, are cheaper and lighter. They are very flexible and, therefore, easier to shape into contours. Although a cardboard lattice is not as strong as a wire one, once the plaster has set, it is self-supporting. Another advantage is that it is easier to cut through cardboard if you wish to replace a section.

If you are interested in incorporating specific railroad features such as tunnels and bridges, see pages 210 to 214.

## Making hollow-shell scenery

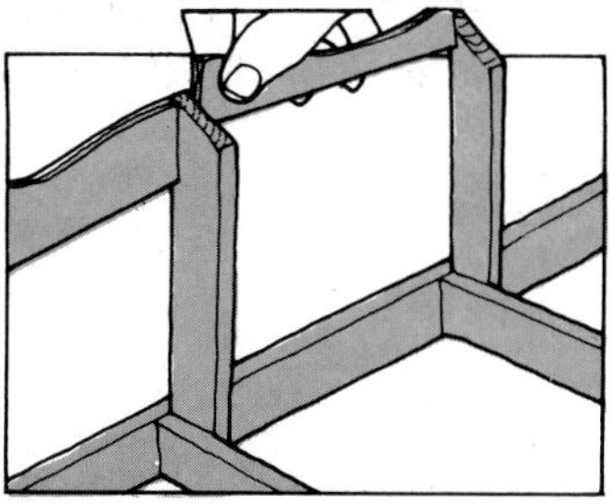

**1** Build an open wooden frame. To the frame, fix plywood pieces sawn roughly to the shape of the contours.

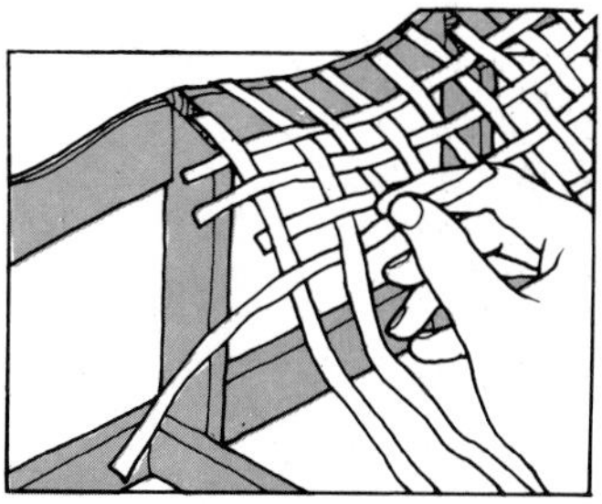

**2** Staple $\frac{1}{2}$-inch-wide (10 mm) cardboard strips vertically to the frame; press into shape, then weave in strips. Temporarily support lattice with balls of newspaper, if needed.

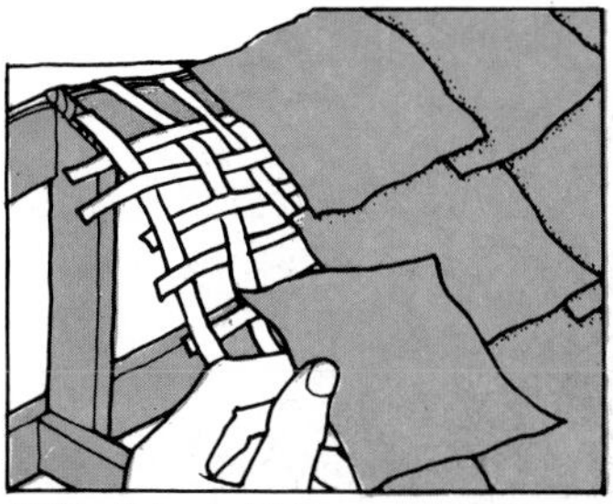

**3** Dip 6-inch (150 mm) fabric or brown paper squares in thin plaster and overlap on lattice; smooth. When set, if needed, add another layer for strength.

**4** With a spatula and paintbrush, apply a $\frac{1}{8}$- to $\frac{1}{4}$-inch-thick (3 to 5 mm) layer of plaster. Add any surface texture such as grass to the wet plaster.

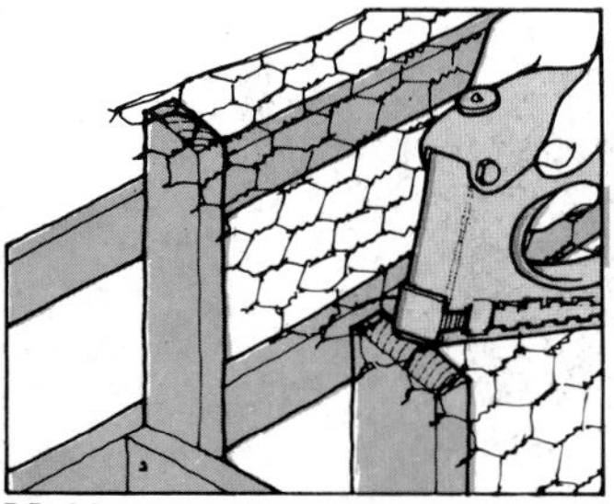

**Making a wire lattice** Screw pieces of softwood to the open frame to approximate the high and low points of the contours. Tack or staple pieces of chicken wire or window screen to the wood, pressing and pulling them into shape.

Hollow-shell scenery is most often used for the landscapes of model railroads because it is very light.

Instructions for making and painting the diorama are on pages 164 to 165.

Made in 1:72 scale (H0/00 railroad scale).

Spackle and grass powder for the ground and steel wool for the bushes are the main materials used in this landscape.

# Pastureland

**This kind of landscape is often required for both dioramas and model railroads, and the various elements of grass, shrubs, trees and bare earth can be recombined in many forms. Every item in the scene can be translated with ease to a larger scale.**

## Procedure for making pastureland

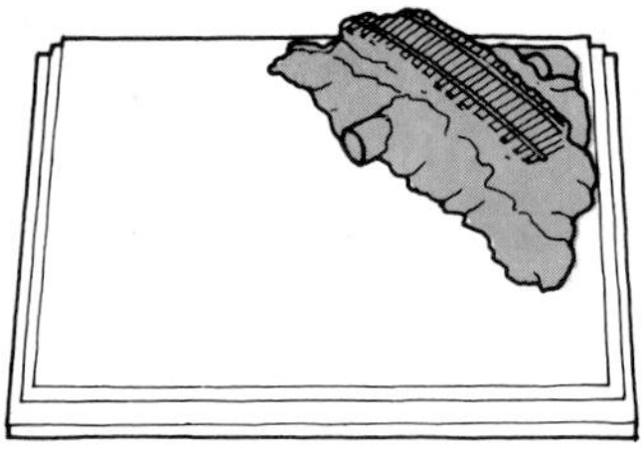

**1** Build embankment including culvert; fix railroad track.

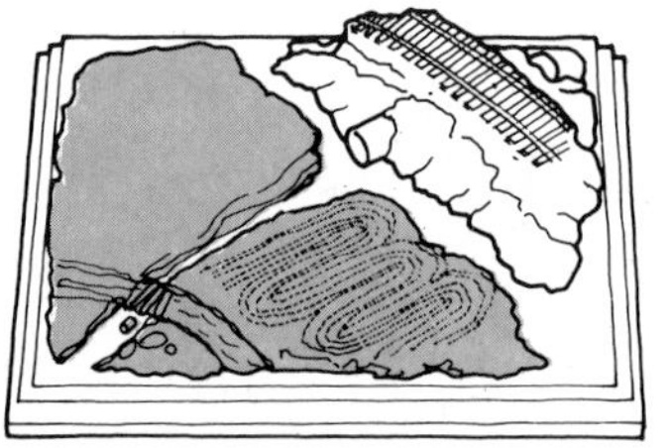

**2** Build pasture and plowed field, muddy path and dirt road including small culvert.

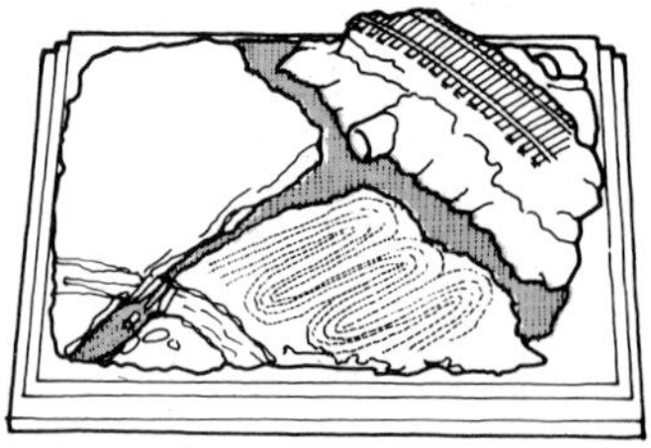

**3** Cover ditch beds with sand.

**4** Make the tree, bushes and weeds and glue them into place.

**5** Build wall and gate.

**6** Add reeds then build up around bottom of reeds and sides of ditches with Spackle.

**7** Age abandoned car, then glue onto base.

**8** Paint scene, then add water to main ditch and run gloss varnish along smaller ditch to simulate a wet bottom.

**Key**

**1 Railroad embankment** Polystyrene core covered with Spackle. To simulate bare earth and grass, see page 181.

**2 Large culvert** Made from two short lengths of plastic tube set into each side of the embankment. Make sure that they align.

**3 Railroad track** The track is glued onto a hardboard track bed set in the Spackle bank. Sprinkle with fine granite chips for the ballast. For realism allow some of the chips to fall down sides of the bank.

**4 Pasture** This field is built on a layer of hardboard which raises the ground level to form ditches. Shape contours with Spackle. To make grass, see page 181.

**5 Plowed field** Spackle on a hardboard base like the pasture. To form furrows, see page 181.

**6 Muddy path** To form the ruts, run a paintbrush handle through wet Spackle.

**7 Dirt road** Make ruts but brush a little water on the edges to soften them. Sprinkle with fine sand.

**8 Small culvert** A small plastic tube. Press railroad ties into the Spackle on top.

**9 Drainage ditch** The hardboard base for the fields forms the banks. The diorama base is the ditch bed; coat with white glue and sprinkle with sand.

**10 Tree** Steel wool on a twig (see page 186).

**11 Bushes and weeds** To make, see pages 181 to 182.

**12 Stone wall** Stone chips glued together and grouted with Spackle.

**13 Gate** Carved wooden matchsticks glued together. The hinges are made from toothpaste tube foil.

**14 Reeds** Clumps of bristles from a brush (see page 183).

**15 Abandoned car** A plastic H0 gauge model. To age car, take off wheels. Cut around one door; glue it open and remove glass. Fog inside of other windows with liquid polystyrene cement.

**16 Water** Clear casting resin poured along the ditch (see page 188).

## Painting pastureland

A real field of earth or grass is made up of many different colors. Your model landscape can be greatly improved by applying thin washes of oil paint and turpentine to all the groundwork. Subtle changes of color will be produced as the washes merge.

Undercoat the *railroad embankment* with a dark earth colored wash before adding grass or bushes. Apart from this undercoat, paint each side of the embankment differently. Tint the side with the dense foliage in washes of olive-green, brown and lighter green, and highlight with white and yellow. Run dark washes under the bushes. Paint the drier side in warm browns and use dark olive-green washes to suggest thin grass cover. When the paint is almost dry, highlight the textures with white.

Coat the *railroad track* and ballast with gray washes, merging the edge of the ballast with the ground; then highlight the shoulders of the road bed. To suggest rust, run a light wash of raw umber and chrome orange along the sides of the rail. Paint a brown wash between the ends of some of the ties and highlight some of the ends. Finally, run a dark gray wash down the center of the track to simulate oil stains and clean the running surfaces to replace the metallic shine.

Next, apply green and brown washes to the *pasture grass.* Also use these washes to paint *shadows* under the tree and bushes. Apply them with a stippling action to avoid brushing off grass powder. Highlight some areas with white or pale yellow. Add only light touches of paint to the *tree* for contrast.

Add interest to the *plowed field* using a variety of earth colors. Highlight some of the furrows. Pick out weeds around the field with greens and yellow.

Paint the *drainage ditches* with dark brown and green washes. Apply dark green paint around the reeds. Highlight the edges of the banks.

Instructions for making and painting the diorama are on pages 168 to 169.

Made in 1:35 scale.

This diorama is made almost entirely of natural materials such as sand, rocks and shaving brush bristles.

# Desert scene

A desert scene is a suitable setting for a variety of subjects from Indians, cowboys or cavalry of the American West to the North African campaigns of the Second World War. Desert tribesmen such as Australian aborigines and the nomadic people of Africa also make interesting subjects.

## Procedure for making desert scene

**1** Position rocks in corner of base and glue in place.

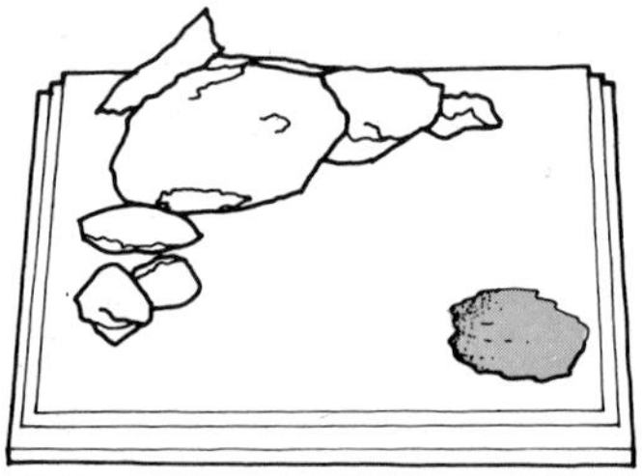

**2** Carve depression in base for the waterhole.

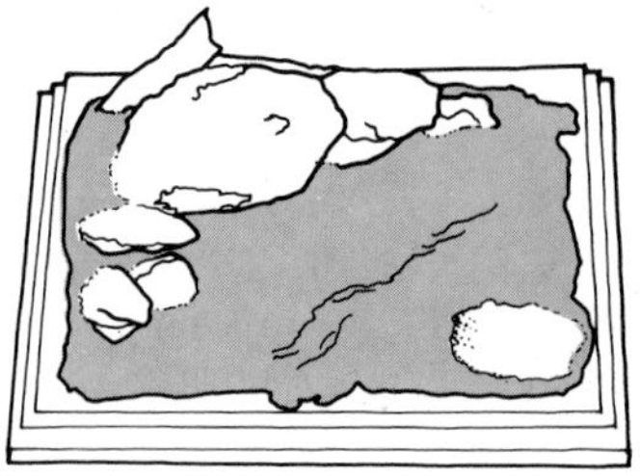

**3** Add sand and make contours, burying rocks realistically.

**4** Add small rocks, plants and coarse desert grass.

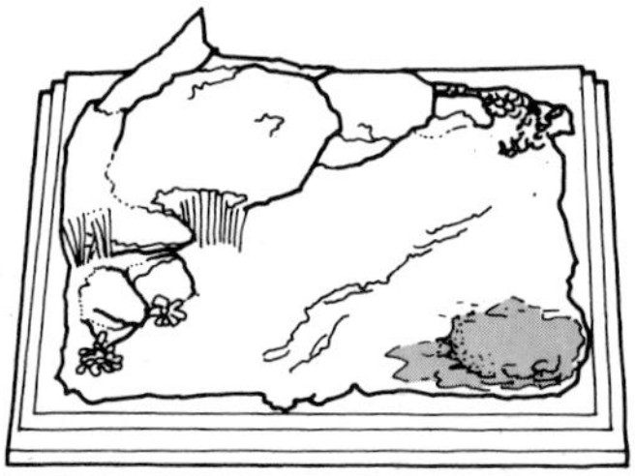

**5** Make dried out waterhole with flaking mud.

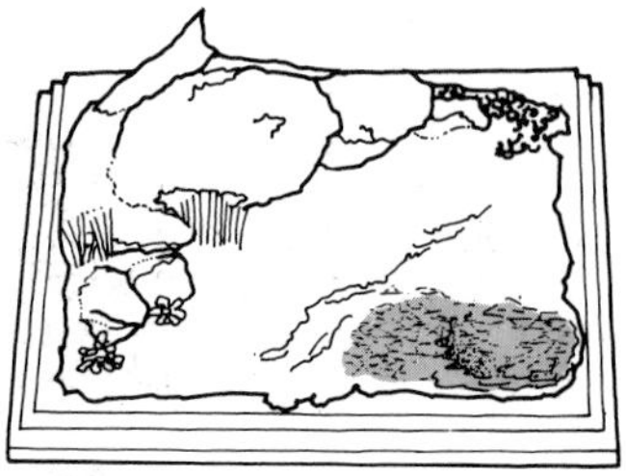

**6** Score surface cracks in waterhole 24 hours after adding sand to hole.

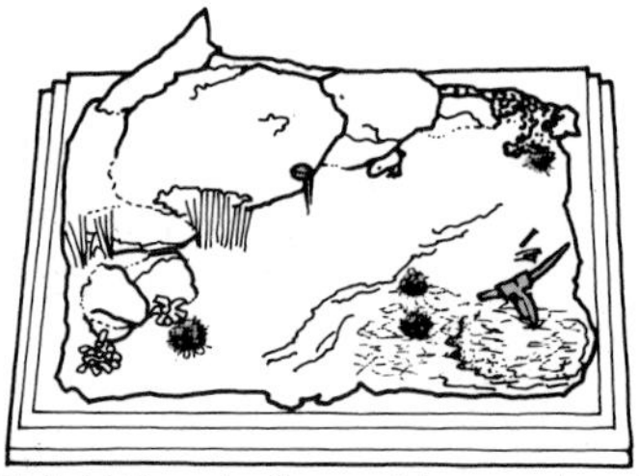

**7** Add the skull, tumbleweed and canteen.

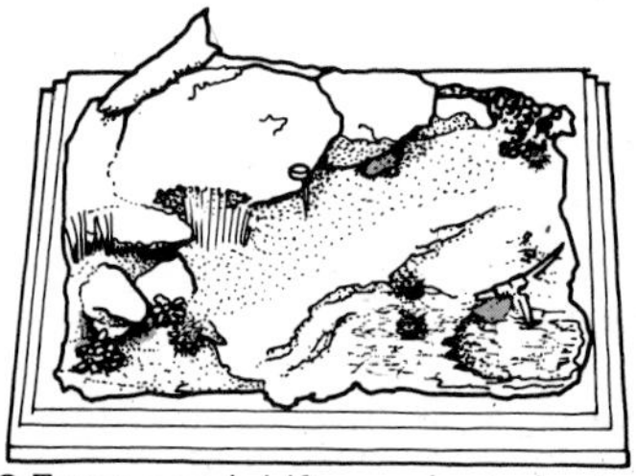

**8** Form sand drifts against plants and skull. Paint scene. Paint gila monster separately then glue it into position.

**Key**

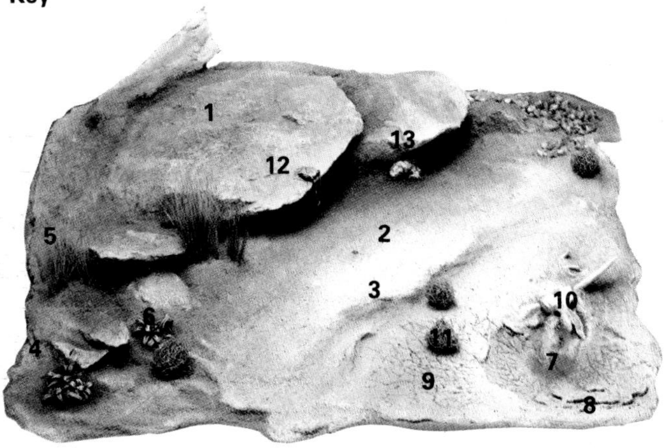


**1 Rocks** A rock with pieces chipped off; the pieces are set to either side at the same angle to suggest stratified rock. Fix the rocks on base with a layer of Spackle; hold them temporarily in place with small stones while the Spackle sets.

**2 Sand** Fine sand trickled freely over a thick layer of white glue (see page 180).

**3 Sand contours** These are formed by the base coat of glue flowing beneath the sand while it is still wet (see page 180).

**4 Sand drift** Thin layers of white glue and sand built up on the windward side of features such as skull or plants. Let each layer dry for 15 minutes before adding the next.

**5 Desert grass** Clumps of bristles from a shaving brush (see page 183).

**6 Desert plants** Carved from sprue (see page 182).

**7 Dried out waterhole** A shallow depression carved in the base. Coat with glue, then sprinkle with sand. Smooth surface.

**8 Flaking dry mud** Paint on a thin layer of thick glue; sprinkle the glue lightly with sand. Repeat. While the glue is still soft press with your fingertip, and as you raise your finger flakes will lift up.

**9 Surface cracks** Score cracks in the sand with a sharp knife.

**10 Skull of steer** Made from the back of a plastic soldier's vest. The horn, carved from sprue then bent into a curve, fits into an armhole. Drill eye sockets. Add nose of thin plastic. Smooth over the joints with Spackle; when dry, scrape the surface with a blade to simulate the bone texture.

**11 Tumbleweed** Lightly roll a small piece of steel wool between fingers and thumb. Glue it in place.

**12 Canteen** This bottle is from a plastic kit. The straps are made from strips of toothpaste tube foil.

**13 Gila monster** Carved from a block of dental plaster. Run water on the dry plaster to prevent it from crumbling while you carve.

## Painting desert scene

The first stage of painting the desert scene is to run clean turpentine over the entire surface, then add washes of white, burnt sienna, burnt umber and pale yellow oil paint with a large sable brush. Let the washes flow naturally, mixing tones and blending the edges of one color into another. It may take several applications to build up the required base tone.

Use white to highlight the *sand* and light browns and yellows to emphasize the contours. To suggest bright sunlight, paint deep *shadows* under the rocks and around plants. Pick out the details in the *rock* surfaces by running a dark brown wash over them, then dry brushing with a pale tone. Highlight areas such as the extreme front edge of the rocks to exaggerate the contrast with the shadows.

Run a dark wash into the cracks in the *waterhole* and continue the faint cracks at the edge with paint alone. To show a last patch of damp ground, mix a little gloss varnish and dark green oil paint and add to the bottom of the depression.

When you have painted the surface of the landscape, treat the smaller items on it. Blend the roots of the *desert grass* into the ground using a dark wash. Add shadows under the leaves of the *desert plants*, again with a dark wash. Accent the flower in the center of each plant with bright color. Dry brush the *tumbleweed* with burnt umber making sure that thick paint does not clog the fine mesh. Wash a pale shadow under the tumbleweed and highlight the top surfaces with white.

The *skull* requires special treatment. Run a wash of burnt umber over it to accentuate its form. Allow the wash to dry, then scrape through in places to indicate bleached animal bone.

Paint the *gila monster* completely before attaching him under the rock. Make sure you create a realistic skin pattern with bright colors.

Use paint to simulate the bleached blue denim cover on the *canteen*.

Instructions for making and painting the diorama are on pages 172 to 173.

# Beach scene

**A beach is an imaginative and atmospheric setting for a variety of models from fishermen mending nets to military figures. Many of the features can be used individually in other contexts and the basic elements of rock, sand and water made for any scale.**

Made in 1:35 scale.

## Procedure for making beach scene

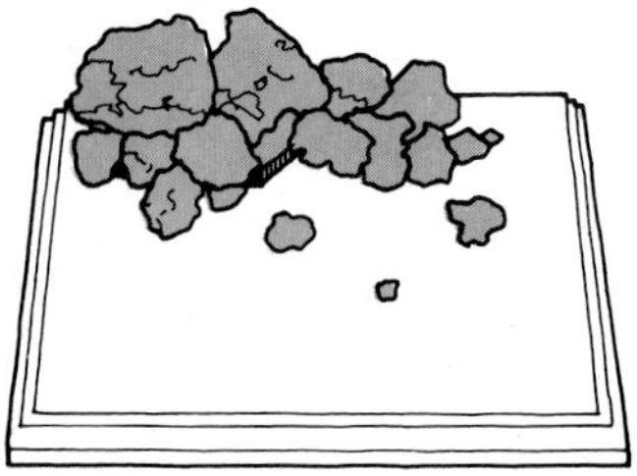

**1** Build rock outcrop on polystyrene wedge.

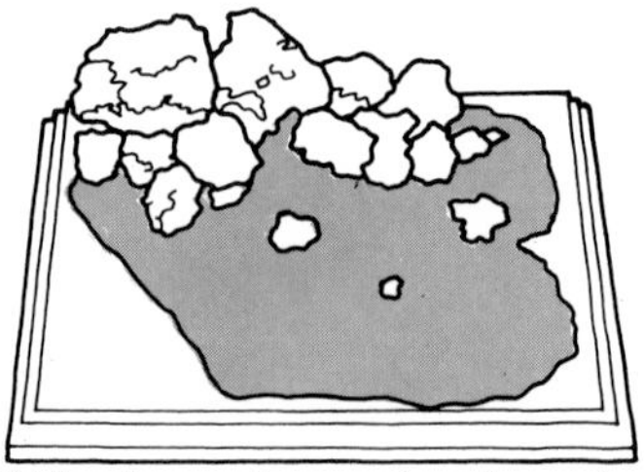

**2** Apply sand around rocks and on the beach.

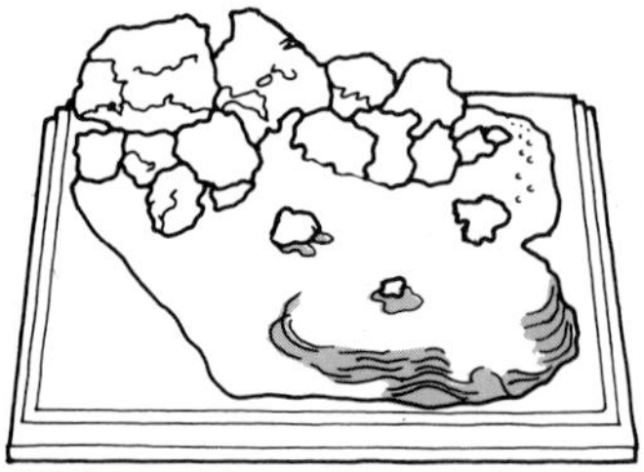

**3** Make ebb marks and depressions for pools in sand.

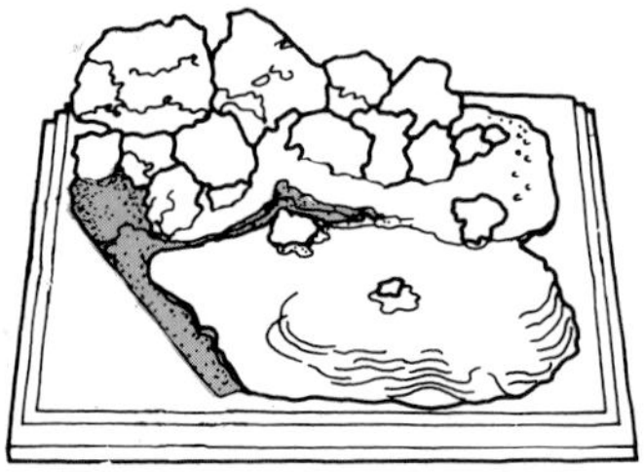

**4** Form course for stream and cover bottom with sand.

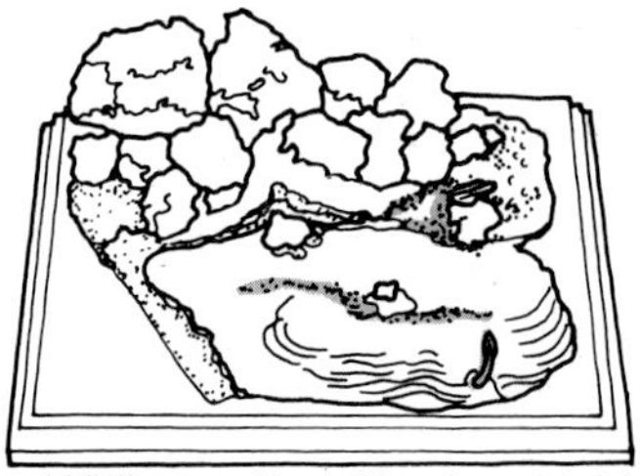

**5** While sand is still soft, add tide mark, the rusty anchor and any small rocks.

**6** Add vegetation along the back of the rock outcrop.

**7** Build breakwater and sand drift against it.

**8** Add seaweed, pail, shovel and sandcastle. Paint scene, adding water to stream and pools.

Key

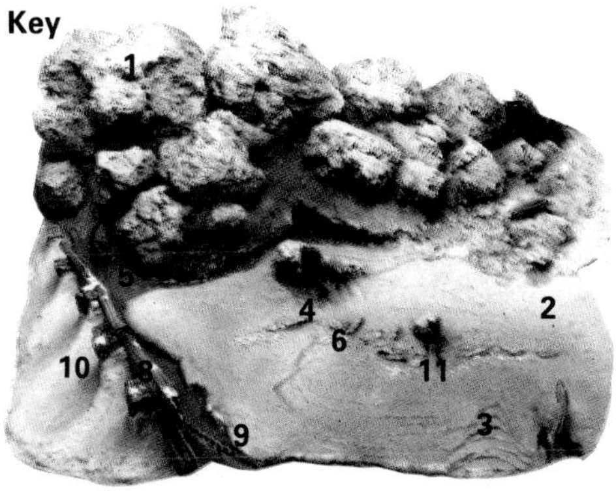


**1 Rocks** Lumps of mortar supported on a wedge-shaped piece of polystyrene. Secure the wedge; spread on Spackle; set in rocks.

**2 Sand** Sprinkle sand over a layer of Spackle. Let it form a natural edge.

**3 Ebb marks** Bend thin cardboard to make a wavy edge; press into setting sand to form ridges. Gently drag paint scraper over ridges.

**4 Pool** A shallow depression made in the sand and painted with gloss varnish.

**5 Stream** Make the stream course by clamping a piece of wood in the position of the breakwater and pouring water along the course, letting it deflect off the wood. Paint stream bed with white glue; sprinkle with sand. Paint on water (see page 188).

**6 Tide mark** Bury a small piece of particle board core and pieces of old wood in sand, then wash sand away until bits appear. For shells, sprinkle some finely chopped egg shell onto white glue.

**7 Vegetation** Moss pressed into white glue (see page 183).

**8 Breakwater** Made from old wood split into pieces. First glue posts to the base, then secure rails with small pins and glue. Leave pin heads to simulate bolts.

**9 Chain** A model railroad accessory. Attach it to a screw eye set in the wood.

**10 Sand drift** Spackle over wedges of polystyrene. As Spackle sets, pinch to shape. When hard, scrape to exact contour, cover with diluted white glue and sprinkle with fine sand.

**11 Seaweed** Use weed from a pond or painted pieces from a cotton ball.

## Painting beach scene

The *ground* and *rocks* of the beach scene are tinted all over with washes of olive-green, pale yellow, white and the occasional touch of warm brown. Using a large brush, give the rocks a generous wash of clean turpentine and apply a wash of olive-green over it. It will take several applications to build up a body of color because the wash becomes paler as it dries. Tint the landward side of the rocks with brown to indicate drier conditions away from the sea. After applying these basic washes, treat the crevices with extra color to add depth, and highlight the edges of the crevices for contrast. Use yellow and white washes on the sandy areas around the rocks, blending them into the greens with plenty of turpentine to produce subtle shades. Highlight the tops of the rocks with a mixture of yellow and white, again blending the edges.

Apply dark washes to the *beach* to accent the ebb marks. Paint the sand darker near the water's edge to indicate dampness, and drag white paint across the surface for the drier areas. Highlight detail in the sand.

Apply dark brown washes under the edges of the *vegetation*, then highlight the texture by brushing a pale mixture of white and raw sienna lightly across the surface with a fairly stiff brush. Indicate flowers on the moss by highlighting with yellow, and enrich its overall color by small additions of red-brown.

Darken the wooden *breakwater* by staining it with washes of oil paint; olive-green will give the impression of slime on old, damp wood. Highlight the wood to bring out textures. Apply rust-colored paint to bolts and run rust streaks from the lower ones. Also apply rust to the chain and add some rust stains to the sand. Paint gloss varnish on the lower sections of the breakwater to simulate very wet wood.

The effect of water in the *stream* is made solely by paint and varnish. Begin by painting the sand on the stream bed a deep amber color. Then, pick out the water course by running a darker wash under the banks, blending the color out into the stream bed. Highlight the top edges of the sandbank for contrast with almost white pale yellow. Add weeds to the stream by painting green stains in the direction of the water flow. When the paint is dry, coat the stream bed with 7 or 8 coats of gloss varnish, waiting until each is dry before applying the next. The texture of the sand on the bed will give the surface of the varnish a slight ripple, ideal for a running stream. Finally, paint the underside of the rocks by the stream with gloss varnish.

Add water to the *pools* and around the anchor in a similar way. First, paint the bottom of the depressions with gloss varnish. When this coat is dry, paint semigloss varnish around the edges of the gloss, blending it out into the dry sand.

Pick out the *seaweed* with color, blending the roots into the rock and adding fine weed with green oil paint alone. Paint the finished seaweed with gloss varnish so it appears wet.

Instructions for making and painting the diorama are on pages 176 to 177.

Made in 1:35 scale.

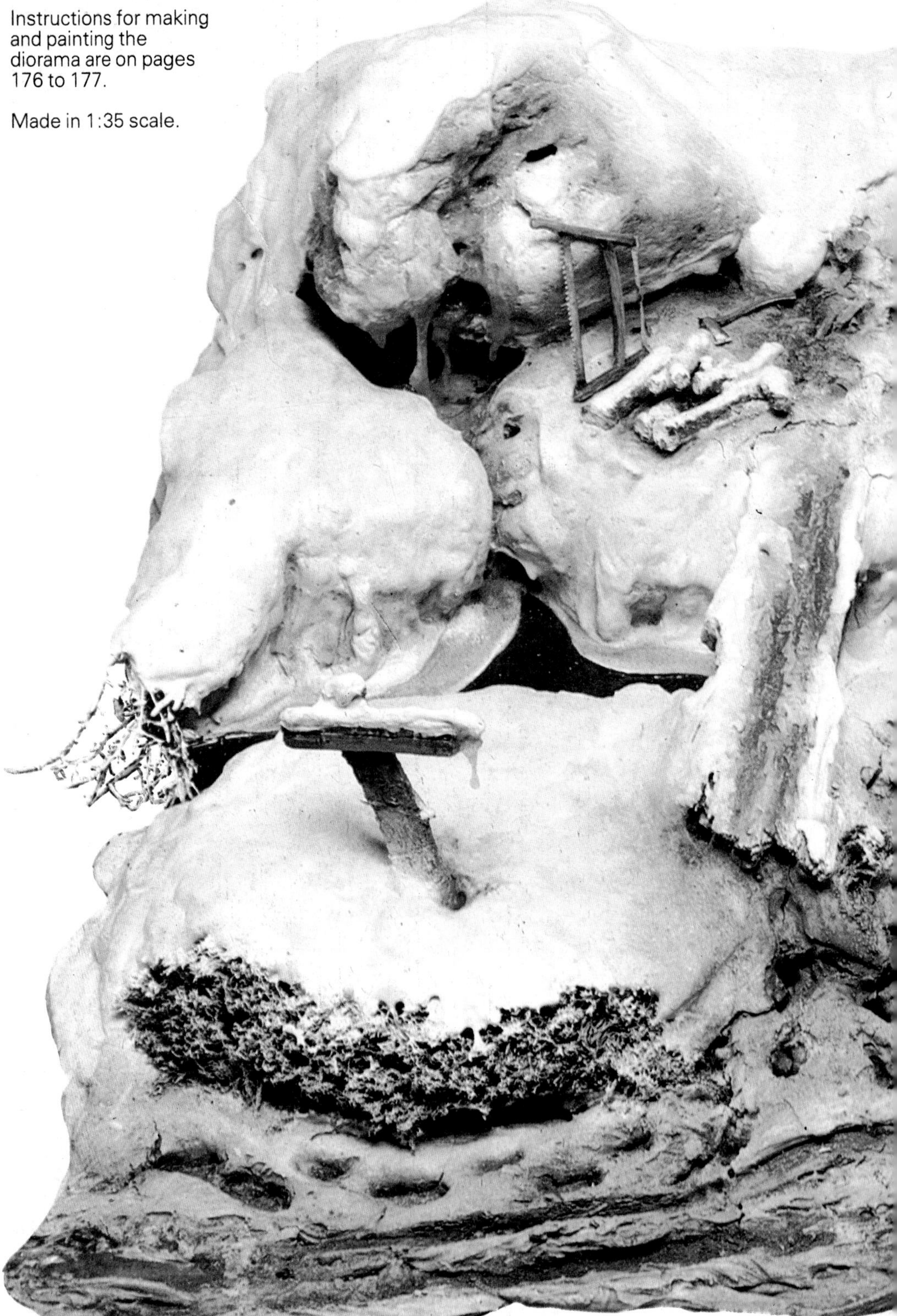

# Winter scene

A winter scene is one of the most attractive to model and provides a dramatic setting for figures and trains.

## Procedure for making winter scene

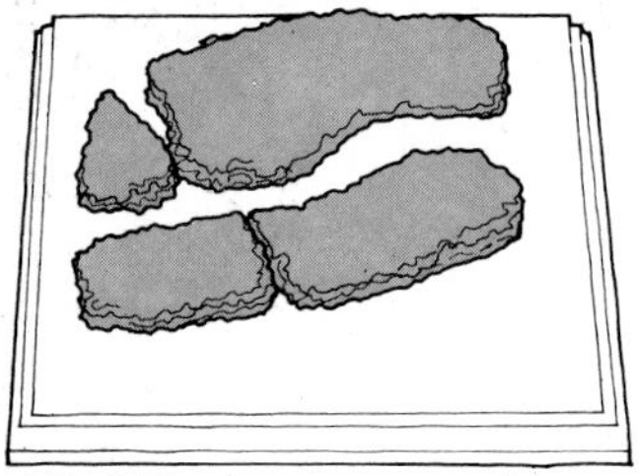

**1** Build basic structure with pieces of polystyrene.

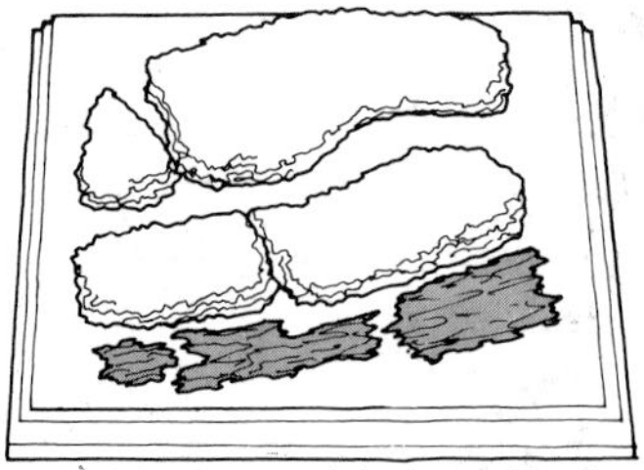

**2** Add split particle board as base for cart track.

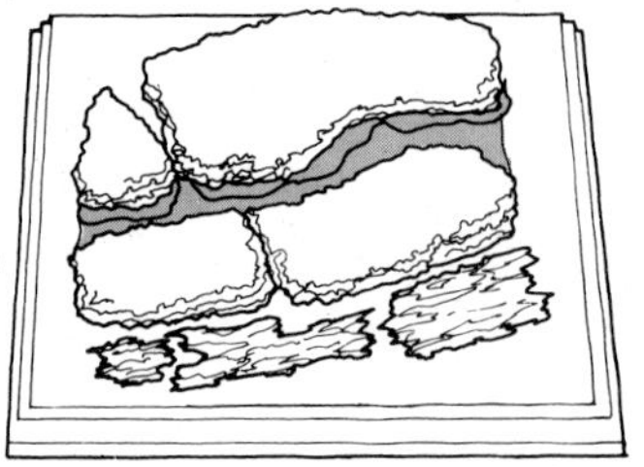

**3** Paint the stream bed and lay the plastic sheet for ice.

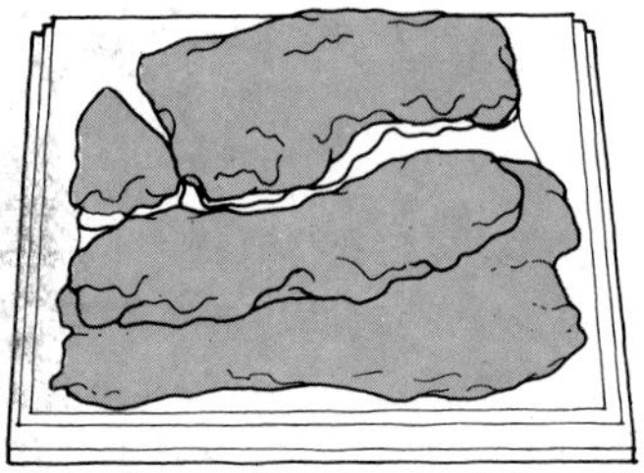

**4** Apply the first layer of Spackle snow to the surface.

**5** Fix moss, rushes, rocks, fallen tree, bridge, cart and signpost in place in the snow.

**6** Add more layers of snow to incorporate features in drifts. Make melting snow on rock.

**7** When the Spackle forms a crust in about 1 hour, create areas of slush and cart track with ruts and footprints.

**8** Paint scene. Add small details such as tools and icicles.

**Key**

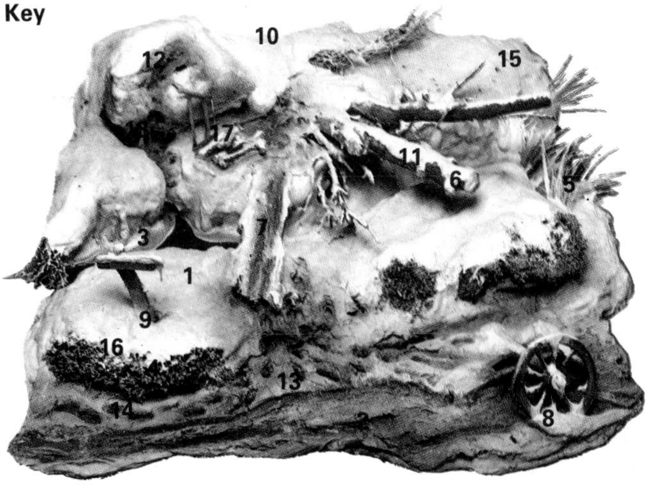


**10 Snow drift** Formed from layer of Spackle (page 188).

**11 Snow on branches** Built up by dragging Spackle on a brush along branches. For very small branches, use white paint alone.

**12 Melting snow** Build up snow (page 188) to a definite edge, then soften it with water on a brush. Wash out the snow under the rocks.

**13 Slush** This effect is created by the ruts and footprints; sprinkle earth into the depressions and paint.

**1 Banks and stream** Shaped from pieces of polystyrene.

**2 Cart track** Spackle on a piece of particle board, split to provide surface texture. Score ruts in soft Spackle.

**3 Ice** Thick plastic over a painted base (see page 188).

**4 Vegetation** Moss (see page 183) fixed to first layer of Spackle with white glue.

**5 Rushes** Made of bristles cut from an old shaving brush (see page 183).

**6 Fallen tree** Made of small twigs and roots of plants.

**7 Bridge** A split branch.

**8 Abandoned cart** Spare parts from a kit.

**9 Signpost** Twig for the post; veneer for the sign.

**14 Footprints** Formed by rocking a paintbrush handle in half-set snow.

**15 Animal footprints** Marked in partially set snow with tip of paintbrush handle.

**16 Light snow cover** Matt white paint sprayed from one direction.

**17 Tools** Kit accessories.

**18 Icicles** See page 188.

## Painting winter scene

The first item to paint is the *stream bed*. This must be done just after building the basic structure of polystyrene and particle board and before adding the plastic sheet for ice. Cover the stream bed with matt black paint. Allow it to dry, then apply dark olive-green and brown washes to simulate the dark tone which water takes on in contrast to the snow and ice around it. Now finish building the landscape before painting the ice and all the other features.

Treat some areas of the ice with light washes of blue-gray and pick out the edge with minute amounts of white paint. While the paint is still wet, apply matt varnish to soften the edges of the color and to give the ice an overall smooth surface.

A coat of ordinary white undercoating paint on the *Spackle snow* is all that is needed to provide a base color and achieve a smooth finish. If, when it dries, it has an unnatural sheen, dull it down with matt varnish. Add pale washes of brown-gray and a little blue-gray to the snow in places to give form to the drifts and to make branches and rocks stand out. In particular, make a blue-gray shadow under the edge of the *melting snow* on the boulder and run faint white washes down the rock to collect in the crevices. Apply deep brown and blue washes in the hollow underneath the boulder.

Use matt white paint alone to indicate snow in some places. Apply it thickly along the very *small branches and roots*. Paint the tips of some *rushes* with it so that they appear frozen together. Dry brush the *fallen tree* with white paint to bring out the texture of the natural wood. For the *light snow cover* on the *vegetation* on the earth bank, use spray paint. If you spray from a distance and from one direction only, it will look as if it's been driven by the wind. Be sure to mask off the other parts of the landscape before you spray.

Areas of *slush* on the *cart track* and *bridge* where the snow is mixed with mud, require a different range of colors. Add some dark brown washes to these areas. Let them settle into the ruts and footprints where they will pick out the texture of the earth. Lightly dry brush the top surface of the ruts with white to contrast with the darker tones. To create the impression of icy slush on the bridge, give it a light coat of matt varnish.

# World War One trench scene

The trench scene below illustrates a wide-scale use of the techniques for modeling mud and water. Such techniques are essential for recreating a World War One scene but they can also be applied to other subjects: a mud track and pond in a country landscape or another military scene, for instance. Turn to page 181 for instructions on modeling mud from Spackle and to page 188 for modeling water from clear casting resin.

**Mud** Made from Spackle (see page 181).

**Retaining wall** See opposite.

**Rusting tank**

**Pool** See below.

**Rusting iron** This is made from corrugated paper painted to look like rusty iron.

**Stagnant pool** Incorporate brown washes in resin layers for muddy color (see page 188).

**Sandbag retaining wall** The bags can be made by wrapping linen around a piece of modeling clay pressed into shape; glue the fabric at each end.

**Wooden retaining wall** Use pieces of wood and twigs.

**Retaining wall** See right.

**Wire fence** To make, see below.

**Barbed wire fence** The barbed wire is fixed to wire posts set into the soft Spackle mud.

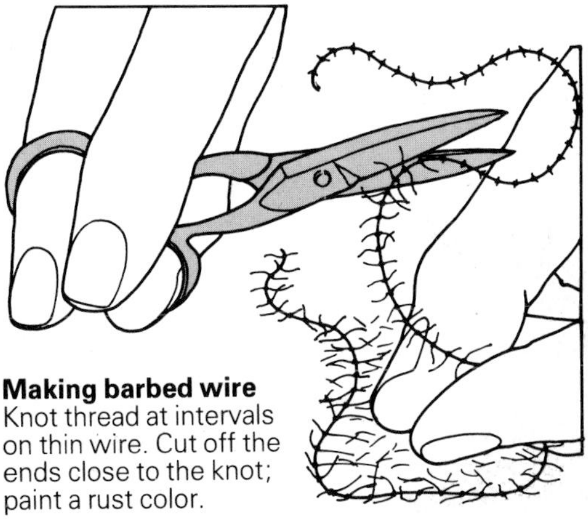

**Making barbed wire** Knot thread at intervals on thin wire. Cut off the ends close to the knot; paint a rust color.

# Rocks

Real rocks create a natural effect with little effort. Simply set them into a layer of soft Spackle on the base, or attach the smaller ones with glue. They can be used in almost any scale, larger ones for cliff faces, smaller ones for boulders, gravel or granite chippings to line a railroad track. There are alternatives to using real rocks, including lightweight ones of cork or molded plaster.

## Mortar rocks

Lumps of mortar have an interesting texture but they are a featureless gray and require painting. Find them on a building site or mix your own.

## Cork rocks

Cork makes extremely lightweight rocks. Use large irregular pieces for outcrops and small pieces for individual stones and boulders. When painted, cork looks natural but it lacks the subtle texture of the real material.

## Molded rocks

Lightweight molded rocks are made from plaster formed in a latex rubber mold. Materials are available from hobby stores. The homemade mold reproduces the texture of real rock. Choose the rock from which you wish to take a mold, wash it and brush away all loose particles. Make the mold and rock as shown below; follow the manufacturer's instructions for mixing the latex.

## Making a molded rock

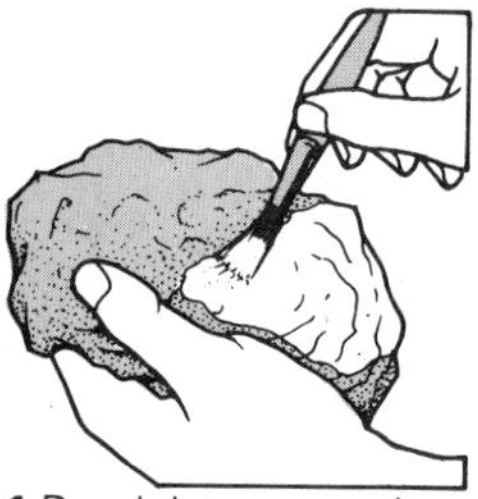

**1** Brush latex on a clean rock. Add one or two more layers, including a layer of gauze if recommended. When set, peel off mold.

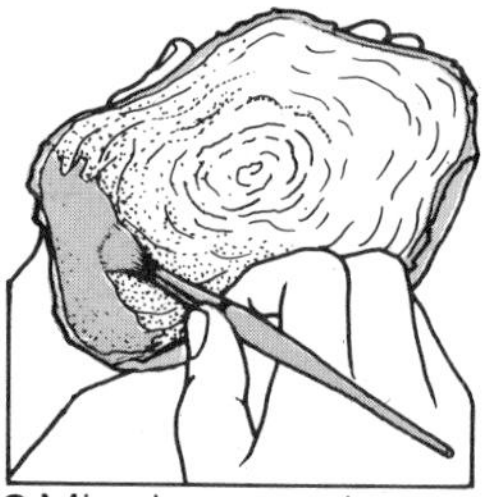

**2** Mix plaster to the consistency of thick cream and brush it inside mold, pushing it well into the texture.

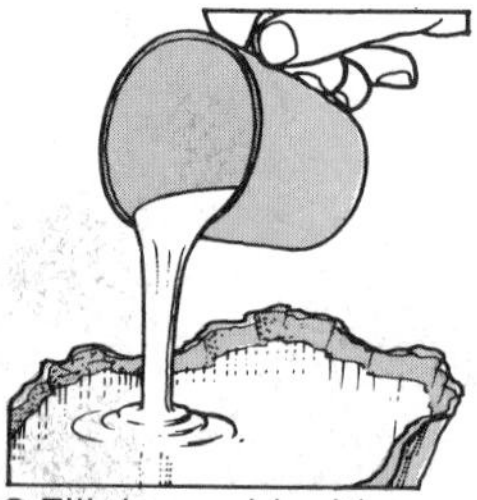

**3** Fill the mold with plaster. Let it set.

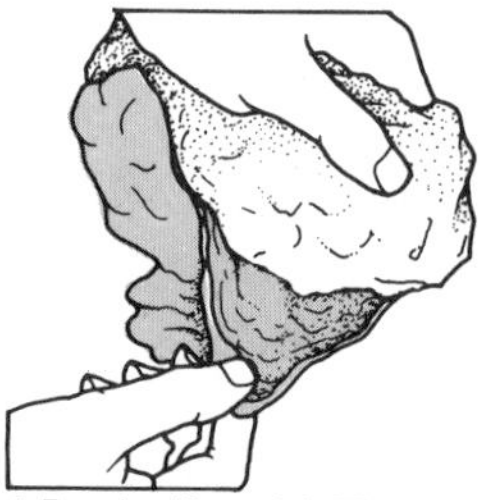

**4** Peel off mold. Fix the rock on base. Paint.

# Sand

If you have no local source, sand is available in various grades and colors from hobby and hardware stores. Fix it to the base by sprinkling it over a layer of white glue. Whatever type of landscape you create, whether a beach or desert, let the sand form a natural, soft edge on the base.

## Contours

To make simple contours, sprinkle sand over a thick layer of white glue. As the glue sets, it will form a skin and flow under the weight of the sand into rivulets and contours. This technique is particularly effective when the sand and glue bank up against other features such as rocks. Emphasize the contours later with paint.

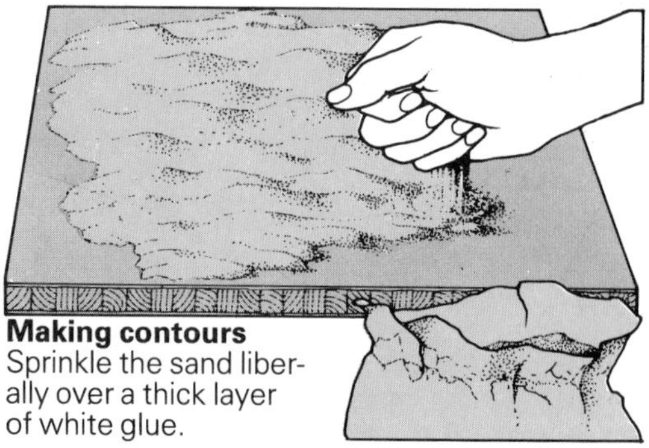

**Making contours**
Sprinkle the sand liberally over a thick layer of white glue.

## Sand drifts

When making sand drifts, always build all drifts in any one model on the same side of rocks, plants or other features; this would be the windward side in reality. There are two ways of making sand drifts. To make a small one, spread white glue on the windward side of the feature, sprinkle on sand and blow off any excess. Leave 15 minutes and add another very thin layer. Build up the drift in this way to the required height. Large sand drifts are best made by applying Spackle to wedges of polystyrene glued to the base. As the Spackle sets, pinch it to shape. When hard, scrape it to its exact contour, then cover with a light coat of white glue and fine sand.

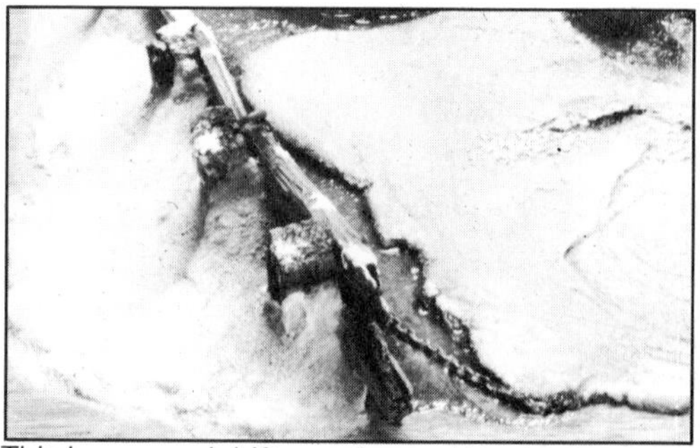

This large sand drift was formed by shaping Spackle over a polystyrene wedge.

# Earth

To make an area of bare earth, sprinkle potting compost liberally over a layer of wet Spackle, thick white glue or plaster on the base. It is the extra texture provided by the potting compost that makes the area look more like earth than mud. Remove any residue by tipping it back into a container. If the base is very large, vacuum it from the landscape carefully.

When set, paint the potting compost with a dark earth color. Large areas of bare earth require extra washes of different tones of brown to add interest. Highlight the texture.

## Plowed field

Powdered Spackle mixed to a thick, creamy consistency is the best material to use for a plowed field. With its slight grain, it is better than ready-mixed Spackle. Spread it as evenly and thinly as possible. File teeth in the edge of a $\frac{3}{4}$-inch-wide (20 mm) piece of plastic and drag this comb through the Spackle to make furrows. Sprinkle potting compost only around the edges of the field. Let the field dry, then paint it with a variety of earth-colored washes and highlight the tops of the furrows.

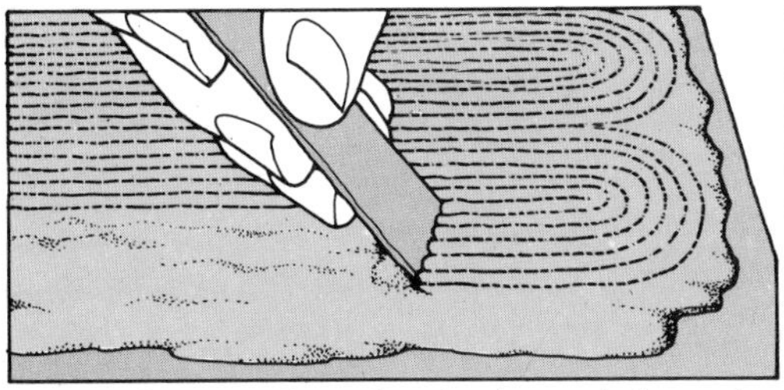

**Making furrows** Drag the plastic comb through the Spackle to form furrows. Sweep the comb in a curve at each end and return in a parallel line.

## Mud

Areas of mud can be simulated by applying a generous layer of Spackle to the base. More than one layer may be needed in some areas to achieve the correct profile, but be sure to blend the edge of the top layer into the one below with a wet brush. For mud banks or other raised features, it is best first to roughly form the ground in polystyrene, then apply the Spackle. You may wish to half-bury objects such as old logs or sandbags in the mud while it is still wet. Impress any footprints or cart tracks at this stage too.

Mud does not have as rough a texture as earth. To create the smoother surface of mud, sprinkle potting compost on the Spackle just before it sets so that only some of the compost adheres. Tip any residue back into a container. For smooth wet mud at the edge of pools, lay on more wet Spackle over the potting compost. When the surface is dry, paint the mud with a dark earth color, then add brown washes, using very dark tones to show the wettest areas.

# Grass

To make grass, spread a layer of Spackle or plaster on the base with a palette knife; this forms the ground. While wet, sprinkle with potting compost, if you wish. Although this is not necessary, it softens the contours. If you do not use potting compost, be sure to paint the Spackle or plaster brown to prevent white patches showing through the grass. Now paint the potting compost or brown-colored ground with very thin white glue. Sprinkle on finely ground foam, commonly called grass powder, which is available in hobby stores. Allow the glue to soak into the material and harden before removing any excess. Finally, to add interest to the grass powder, paint it with different greens and perhaps some brown, and highlight with white and yellow.

## Lawn

To make a well-kept lawn, lay the Spackle or plaster flat and cut straight edges with a knife where it meets a path or driveway. After sprinkling on the grass powder, press it flat and when it has set, blow off any excess.

Note how the edges of the lawn have been cut straight where they meet the path.

## Weeds

For weedy areas, sprinkle sawdust onto small patches of matt varnish applied over the original grass. Run drops of varnish from the tip of a brush onto the sawdust; the varnish will soak into it and bind it together. Sprinkle the sawdust with grass powder. Let dry and paint an appropriate color.

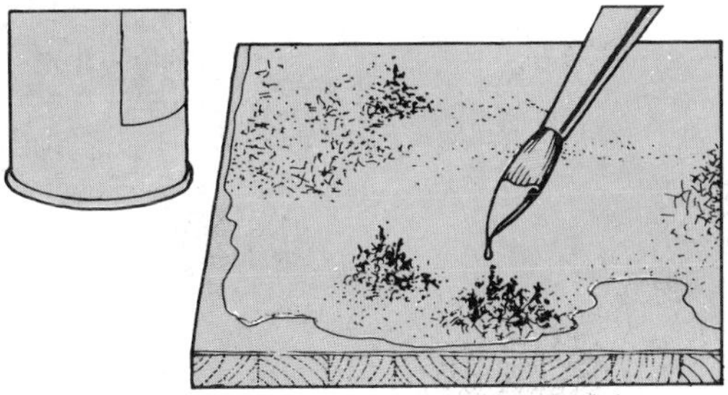

**Making sawdust weeds** Drip matt varnish onto the sawdust to secure it to the grass.

# Plants and bushes

Strategically placed low-lying plants and bushes provide a natural transition between such features as a river and plowed field or a grassy area and forest. There is a variety of materials and types of vegetation from which to choose, from reeds made of shaving brush bristles to bushes made of steel wool. Real plants such as grass and moss can also be used to good effect. They provide natural-looking textures and are readily available.

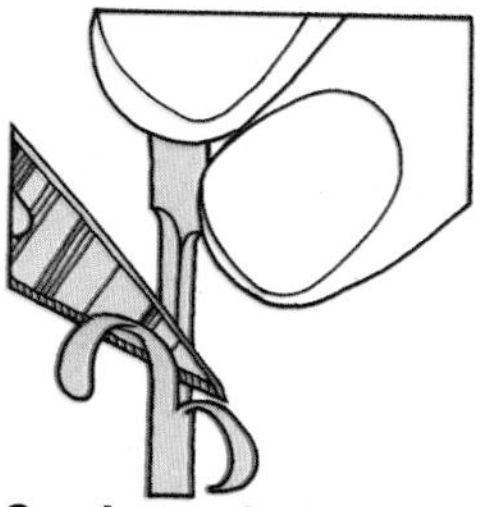

**Carving a plant**
Pare slivers of plastic around the base about $\frac{1}{4}$ inch (5 mm) from the bottom. Repeat to make one or two more rows of leaves.

Cut off the tip of the center section, then divide center finely to form a flower.

**Plants**
These plants are made from sprue (see left). Vary them by shortening the leaves, omitting the flower or painting a different color.

**Daffodils**
Carve daffodils from wooden matchsticks. Make a row of leaves as for plants (left). Bend over the head for the flower and divide to make petals.

**Bushes** You can make bushes from small clumps of steel wool. Before gluing them on base, spray matt black and sprinkle with grass powder while the paint is still wet.

These bushes are made from pieces of lichen. To add leaves spray matt dark green or black; let dry, then spray with glue and sprinkle lightly with some grass powder.

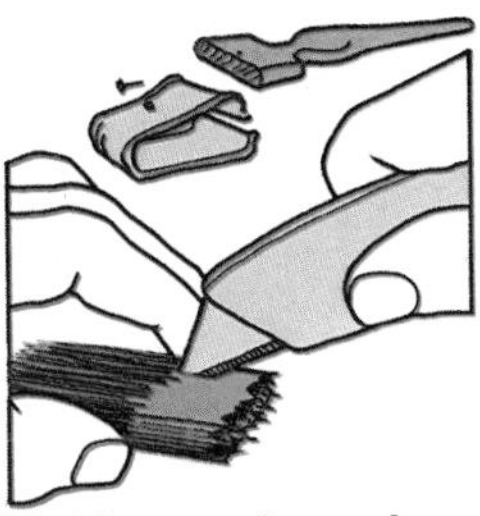

**Making reeds, rushes and coarse grass** Break off the handle of a brush and split the resin to separate the clumps of bristles. Cut to size allowing $\frac{1}{4}$ inch (5 mm) for planting. Dip ends in cyanoacrylate glue to secure them.

Holding a clump in tweezers, glue it in a hole drilled in the baseboard or push it into the soft ground. Position the clumps of bristles in several irregularly spaced groups.

**Reeds** Note how these clumps, made from shaving brush bristles, are grouped irregularly in the stream.

**Desert grass** This grass, made from light brown shaving brush bristles, needs no painting.

**Rushes** These are real pieces of dry grass chosen for their fine texture.

**Undergrowth or general vegetation** Moss can be used in a variety of situations, from earth banks to forest floors. Remove most of the roots and earth and press it into white glue with the tip of a paintbrush to avoid damaging the surface. An occasional drop or two of water will keep the moss fresh.

# Trees

There is a variety of trees you can model to add interest and authenticity to your diorama. For trees in the background, make simple versions from lichen. If you require more detailed trees, choose from coniferous trees made of wire and sisal fibers or deciduous trees made using the method for pines or those constructed from steel wool and twigs. To evoke a particular season, use the techniques described on page 187.

Whichever type you make, take great care with the finished texture. Grass powder is the best material to use for leaves. Don't use sawdust – not only is it too coarse but it is too brightly colored.

## Background trees

Trees made from lichen are useful for positioning in the background or in the middle-distance of a model landscape. Traditionally used by railroad modelers, they are easy and extremely quick to make in quantity.

For a background tree, select a piece of lichen which looks like a complete tree in silhouette. Cut a piece of wire of medium thickness to the length of the tree plus enough for planting. Plastic-covered garden wire is ideal for this job. Coat the wire with white glue and push it into the base of the lichen, interlacing it till it supports the soft material. Set the tree aside for a few minutes to let the glue dry.

The lichen sold in stores is usually bright green. This is a very unnatural color and to create a realistic effect, it is necessary to paint the tree and add some finer texture. First, spray the tree with matt dark green, brown or black paint. Lay the tree aside a few minutes, then spray it all over with aerosol glue. Immediately sprinkle it lightly with grass powder. A greater concentration of powder on the top surface will add form to the tree.

For a tree in the middle-distance, choose a twig which resembles a trunk with lower branches and attach small lichen cuttings to the twig as shown below.

This tree has enough detail to be positioned in the middle distance of a model landscape. It is made from several small pieces of lichen attached to a twig and has been carefully shaped to look like a large deciduous tree.

Plant groups of lichen trees closely together to form a wooded area. Mix their size and shape to add interest.

**Making a middle-distance tree** Attach lichen cuttings to a twig with white glue. Color and sprinkle with grass powder as for background trees. Scrape the twig in places with a knife and apply washes, to create a more subtle color.

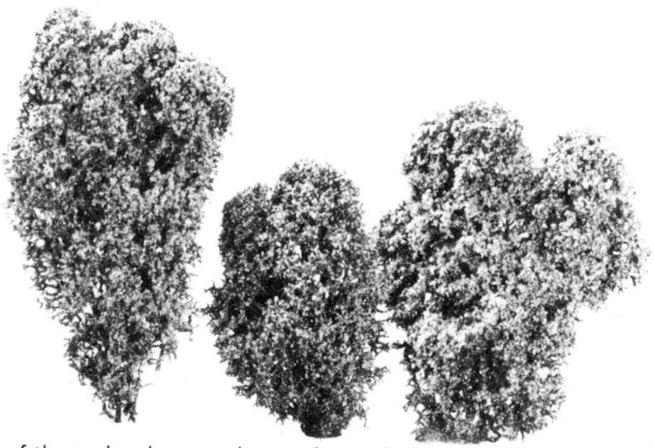

Each of these background trees is made from a single piece of lichen selected for its silhouette.

## Pine trees

Pine trees are appropriate for northern or mountainous landscapes. They are particularly effective dusted with snow.

## Making a pine tree

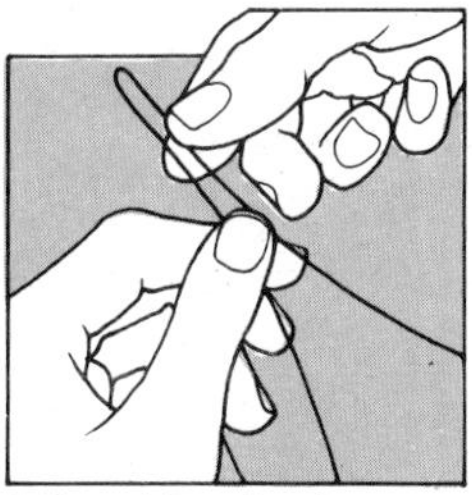

**1** Cut thin wire four times the tree's height; fold in half.

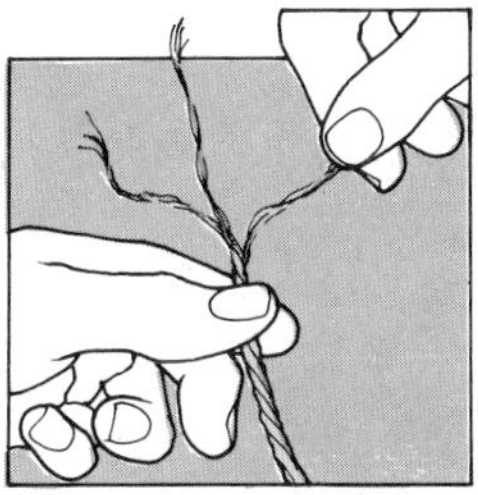

**2** Cut pieces of sisal string to the width of tree's base; unravel. Twist the fibers between your fingers to stop them curling.

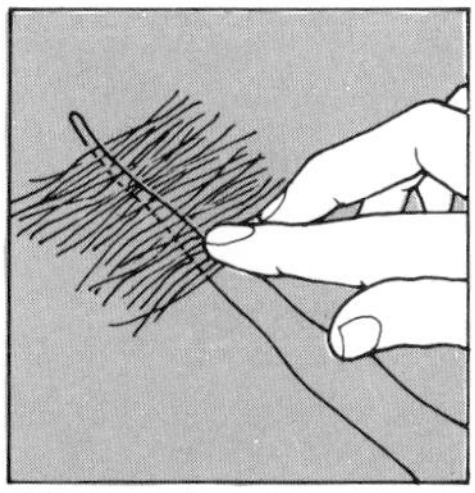

**3** Run polystyrene cement along inside of one half of wire. Starting $\frac{1}{2}$ inch (10 mm) from fold, lay fibers closely together; press into glue.

**4** Twist wire ends together clockwise then insert tip in a vise. Insert other end in a hand drill and wind into a tight spiral making a brush shape.

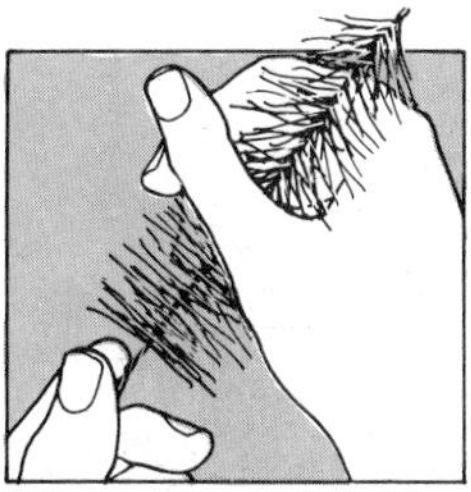

**5** Separate and distribute the fibers with a pointed tool, then run tree through your fingers to make the branches grow down.

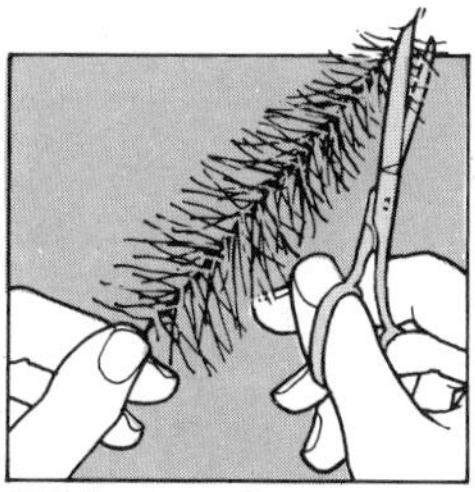

**6** Trim tree to taper from top to bottom. Crop the wire at the top leaving $\frac{1}{4}$ inch (5 mm). Spray tree matt black. Let it dry.

**7** Dip tree in matt varnish. Lift it out letting the varnish run off, then hold it in a box and twist back and forth to throw off any drips.

**8** Roll wet tree in grass powder to form needles on ends of the branches. Sprinkle some powder on inside for color. Let dry.

Mix several different sizes of pine tree for an attractive grouping.

## Tall pine trees

Tall pine trees made with thin wire as shown above, are easily bent and the base of the trunk must be thickened with masking tape or filler before painting. For a sturdier and better proportioned tree, glue a top section made from thin wire to a lower section made from thicker wire. To join the two parts, dip the meeting fibers in varnish and add a drop of polystyrene cement to the tip of the lower trunk. Position the sections, encouraging the varnished fibers to intertwine. Let set, then trim and add needles.

**Making a tall pine tree**
Glue together a top section made from thin wire and a bottom section made from thick wire. Support in a block of polystyrene overnight to harden, then trim to shape. Spray black and add the needles.

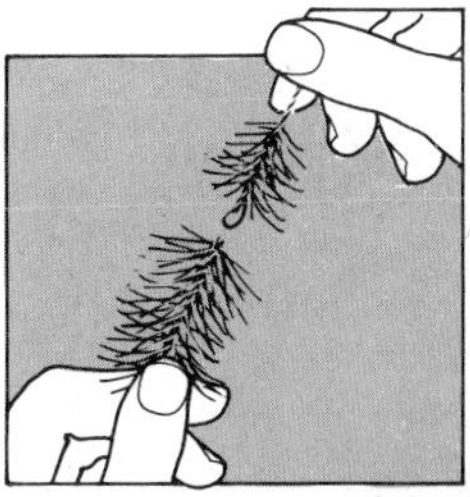

## Deciduous trees

Deciduous trees can be made by adapting the technique for making pines (see page 185). Another method is to construct them from twigs and steel wool.

**Short tree**

Make a section of sisal fibers as for a pine tree, steps 1 to 4 (page 185) using thick wire and letting the wire extend equally at both ends. Cut in half to make two trees. Coax the fibers to cover the cropped end, trim to shape and spray black. Add leaves as described for pine needles. For thick foliage, first roll the tree in sawdust, let dry, then redip in varnish and roll in grass powder.

**Tall tree**

Make as pine tree, steps 1 to 4, using thick wire but space the fibers at less regular intervals. Shape the branches to show gaps and spray black. Add leaves as for short tree (left).

**Poplar**

Make as pine tree but substitute teased out steel wool for sisal fibers at the top. Shape the branches to grow upward to a point. Dip the tree lightly in grass powder for fine leaves.

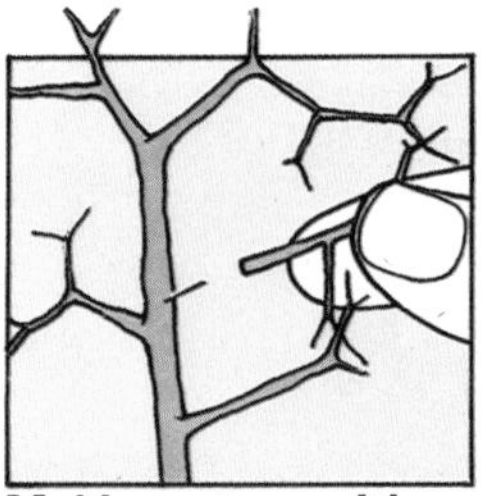

**Making a tree with an irregular shape**

Build a framework of branches on a twig. Attach smaller twigs on a cropped pin with white glue and make the upper branches from very fine wire glued to their ends.

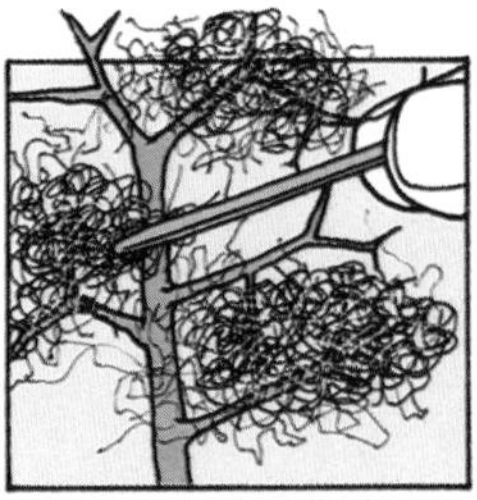

Tease out small pieces of steel wool, avoiding obvious bunching and swirling, and attach to the framework. Spray matt black and trim to shape, if necessary. Spray with glue and sprinkle with some grass powder.

**Small tree with an irregular shape** Make as shown below opposite, using a single twig to support the steel wool, or make a framework by twisting together fine wire.

**Young tree or bush**
Tease steel wool to lie in one direction, then bind one end with wire and fan out the other. Add leaves as for adding pine needles (page 185) to the top two-thirds only. Plant tree in ground up to base of branches.

**Vine** Use the roots of a plant for a vine, attaching small lengths of teased out steel wool for the finer branches.

**Ornamental bush**
Cut the tip from a tall or short tree, opposite. Shape and trim into a bush. Coat the length of the branches evenly with grass powder to produce the fine texture of small leaves.

## Seasonal changes

**Spring**
Add only light touches of grass powder. Apply small touches of pure oil paint for the blossoms.

**Autumn**
Spray tree in autumn colors with an airbrush or use chopped tea leaves or finely ground orange-brown foam.

**Winter**
Build a skeleton from twigs and teased out steel wool as shown opposite. Paint the tree matt black.

# Water

You can use mirrors or ripple glass for water but the most effective materials, by far, are varnish and clear casting resin. They are usually applied after painting the landscape. Gloss varnish on a painted ditch bottom or pool edge will indicate wetness; semi-gloss will indicate dampness. For larger bodies of water, use clear casting resin, mixed with hardener following the manufacturer's instructions. To create depth, build up the resin in layers, no more than $\frac{1}{4}$ inch (5 mm) at a time and let each layer dry before adding the next. Brush or tilt the base to make an even layer. For ripples, blow the final layer with a hair dryer until it holds its shape. When working with resin, make sure it cannot leak from the base and always cover each layer as it dries to prevent dust from settling on top.

To enhance the illusion of depth or to create the effect of algae or mud in water, incorporate oil paint washes in the layers. Apply the color to the dried resin, then add the next resin layer; the wet resin will float the color and distribute it.

## Lakes

Paint the bottom of a lake dark green or deep blue, then build up the resin in layers, incorporating color washes to create the illusion of depth. Remember to secure features such as docks or piers before adding the resin.

Add green color washes to the resin layers to create the effect of algae in a pond.

## Streams or rivers

For a small stream, pour resin along a stream bed which has been sprinkled with sand then painted in appropriate color washes, perhaps brown and green. If the stream runs to the edge of the base, fade out the resin at the edge. Paint groundcover over the side of the stream to disguise the curved surface of the resin. Several coats of gloss varnish alone will suffice for a very shallow stream. The sand under the varnish will create a realistic rippled effect.

Make a river like a stream but paint the river bed much darker in the center using cold greens and deep blues fading out to warmer sandy colors in the shallows, and build up the resin in layers.

## Frozen water

An ice-covered lake or river is made from translucent thick plastic. This should always be constructed before building the surrounding ground; banks or snow drifts can then be built over the edge of the plastic.

First paint the bottom of the lake or river matt black; then apply dark olive-green and brown washes. Stick down the plastic sheet with white glue. Paint the ice with light washes of blue-gray in parts and while still wet, soften the edges of the color with matt varnish. For melting ice, cut the plastic with a wavy edge.

## Icicles

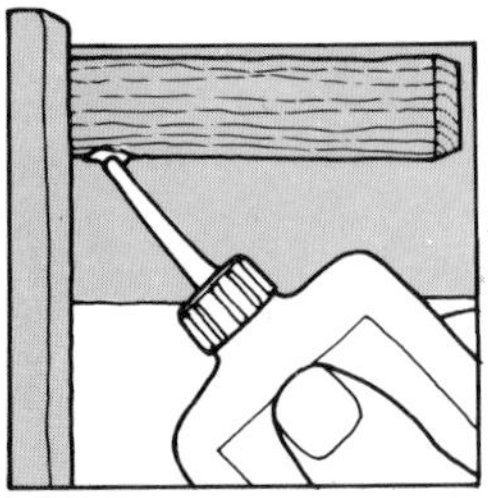

**1** Touch white glue at intervals along the bottom of a wooden strip clamped in a vise. Let dry for 15 minutes.

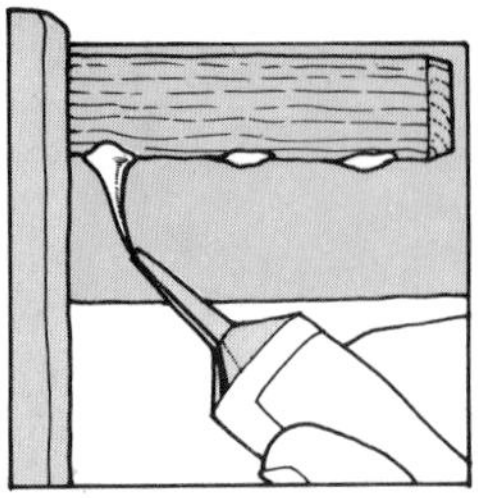

**2** Touch polystyrene cement from a tube onto the white glue letting it run down into an icicle shape.

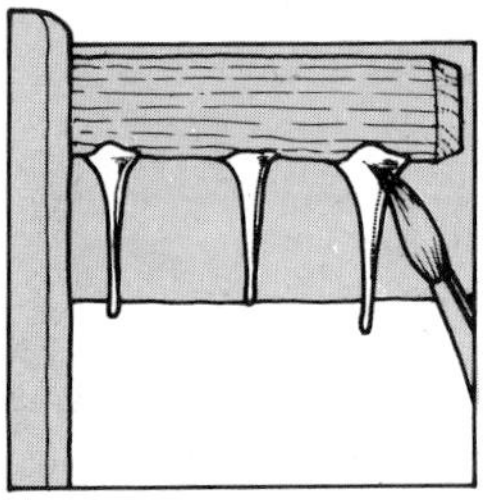

**3** Run liquid polystyrene cement over the icicles to encourage them to lengthen. Let them set hard. Cut individual icicles from the wood keeping base intact.

**4** Attach to model with tube cement. When set, run a little more liquid cement from the top to secure it realistically. Paint with gloss varnish to add sparkle.

# Snow

Matt white paint applied by brush or from a spray can and Spackle are the materials used to simulate snow. For tall snow drifts, build up layers of Spackle, blending the edges together with a wet brush. Half bury trees and other objects in the Spackle while it is still soft. Coat large tree branches with Spackle and paint the tops of smaller branches white. Paint the Spackle white, dulling it with matt varnish if it is too shiny. Apply light washes of brown-gray and blue-gray to give form to the drifts. Spray paint on objects from one direction to simulate wind-driven snow.

# Man-made surfaces

The old-fashioned surfaces such as cobblestones are not only essential for a period piece, but also make attractive backgrounds for contemporary subjects. Modern surfaces such as asphalt or concrete are useful for displaying vehicles.

Many readymade surfaces, from cobblestones to brick walls, can be bought in the form of printed papers or embossed plastic sheets from HO/OO model railroad stores. They can also be used in 1:72 scale models. There are, however, fewer examples in larger scales. All the man-made surfaces shown on this and the following pages can be modeled from scratch in both small and large scales. Some of the techniques for making buildings for model railroads on pages 216 to 226 can be adapted for use on dioramas.

## Stone slab sidewalk

Build up the level of the sidewalk with plywood. Coat it and the gutter evenly with $\frac{1}{16}$ inch (1.5 mm) of fireclay cement. Let dry for about $\frac{1}{2}$ hour, then shape stones as shown below. Leave to dry overnight, then lightly sand the stones with fine sandpaper.

## Shaping the stones

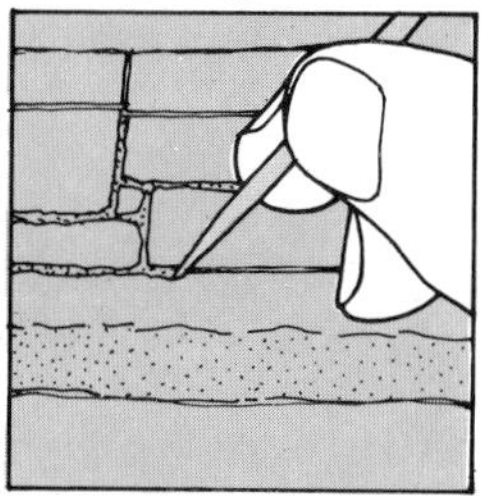

**1** Cut stones in the cement with a knife, then widen the gaps and round edges with a toothpick. Sections flaking off give a worn look.

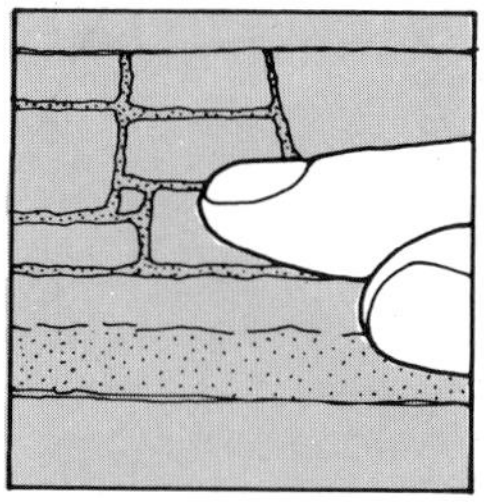

**2** To show wear, gently press the center of the stones along the middle of the sidewalk with a finger.

**3** Cut small stones in gutter then brush with water to soften edges. Cut curb stones.

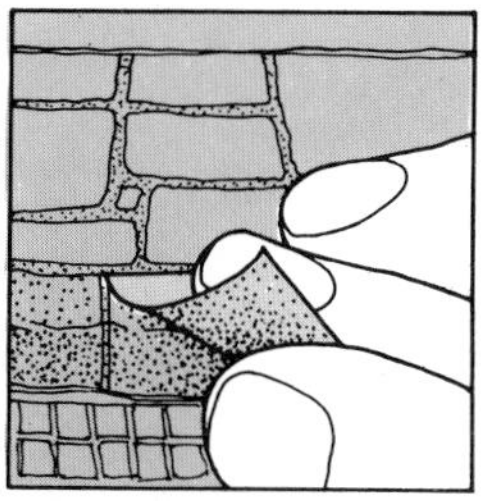

**4** Press coarse sandpaper onto curb to create texture.

## Flagstone path

Make the stones in fireclay cement as for sidewalk above. Paint white glue between the stones and sprinkle with grass powder.

## Cobblestones

Mix up about $\frac{1}{2}$-inch-diameter (12 mm) ball of epoxy putty – any more will set before you have finished. Roll it into a thin rope and cut into small pieces which will roll between finger and thumb to produce balls of $\frac{1}{8}$ inch (3 mm) diameter. Make balls and position on the base. Moisten a fingertip with water and smooth over them applying a slight pressure to secure them and create a worn appearance. When set hard, grout as shown below. Finally, wipe very lightly across the tops with a damp finger to smooth them.

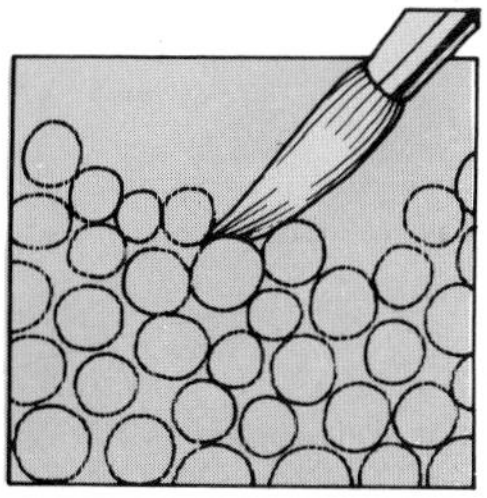

**Positioning cobbles**
Roll the balls into position with the tip of a brush. Group them closely but do not press them together.

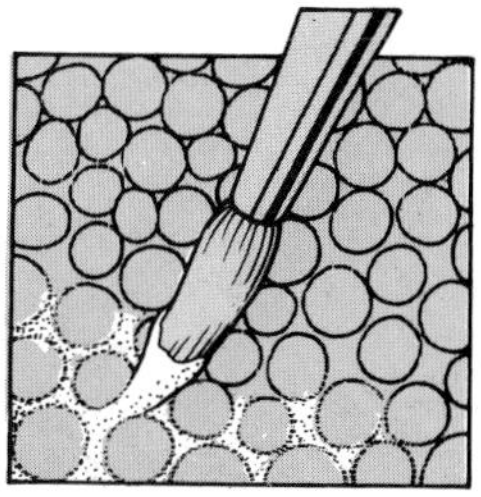

**Grouting cobbles**
With a stippling action, apply Spackle mixed to the consistency of thin cream, between each of the cobbles.

Use effects such as this stone slab sidewalk and cobbled road in period pieces.

## Asphalt road

Build a flat base for the road. A small scale road will not need a camber built into it. Paint the tar surface directly onto the road using a flat enamel paint as a base color. Apply any dry-transfer lettering over the base coat. Use oil washes for shading in the gutter and highlights on the crown. Wash dirty turpentine down the center of lanes for oil stains. To make soft shoulders, sprinkle fine sand or granite chips over white glue painted onto the shoulder.

## Concrete road or sidewalk

Simulate a concrete road or sidewalk with paint in a similar way to asphalt roads. To add texture, apply the paint over very fine sandpaper. Place the pieces of paper end to end to create expansion joints in the concrete.

## Ruined buildings

A ruined building is an evocative setting for all types of military scenes, from battles to peaceful occupations. To make one, build the walls from polystyrene as shown below and assemble them on the base. The walls of both the church, below, and the house, opposite, are constructed in this way, only the surface treatment differs. The church walls are covered with fireclay cement to imitate stone, while the house walls are coated with Spackle to look like stuccoed brick. See also page 192 for making a brick wall. Once the walls of the building are in place, add the small detail to create atmosphere and authenticity.

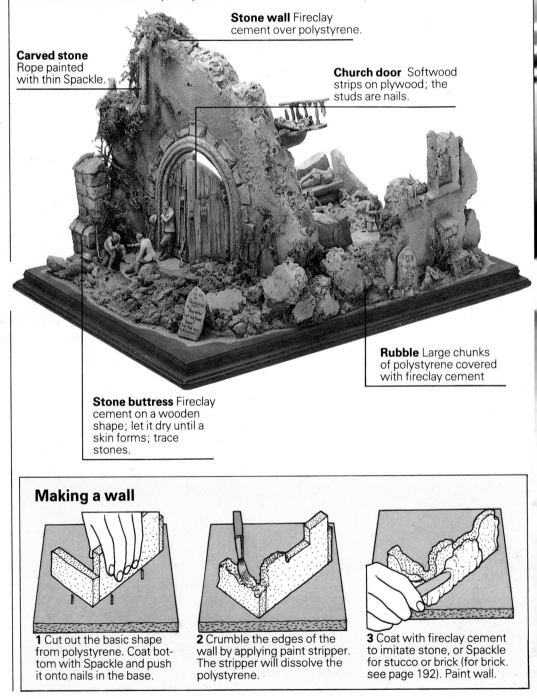

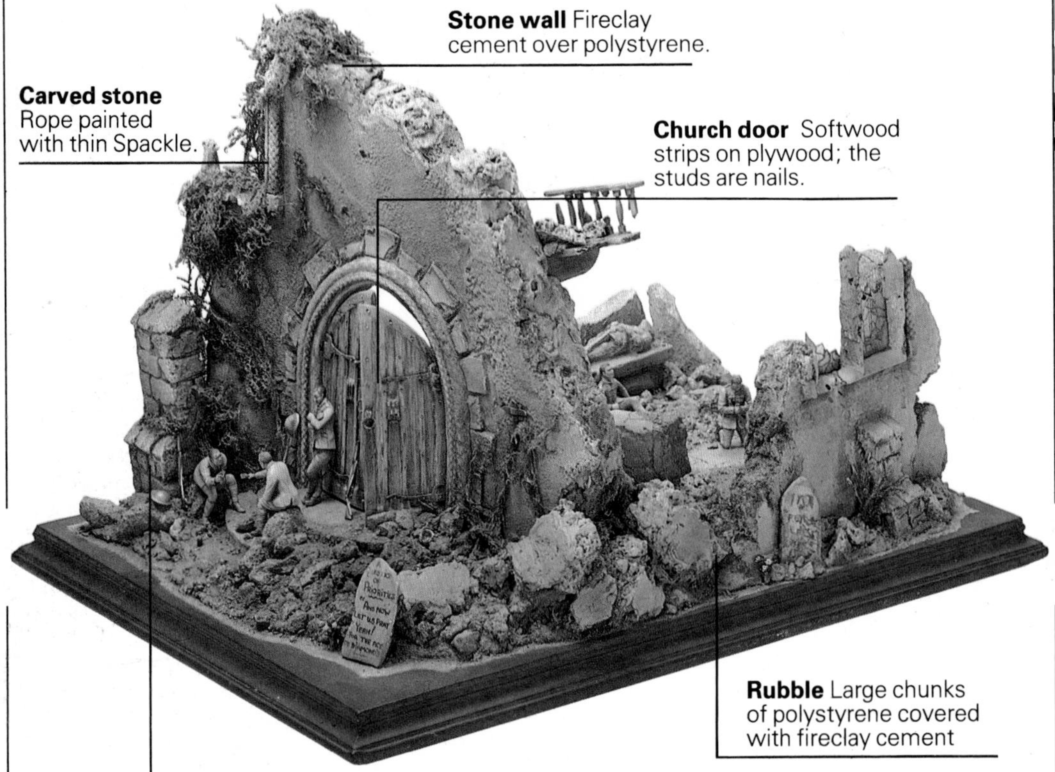
**Stone wall** Fireclay cement over polystyrene.
**Carved stone** Rope painted with thin Spackle.
**Church door** Softwood strips on plywood; the studs are nails.
**Rubble** Large chunks of polystyrene covered with fireclay cement
**Stone buttress** Fireclay cement on a wooden shape; let it dry until a skin forms; trace stones.

### Making a wall

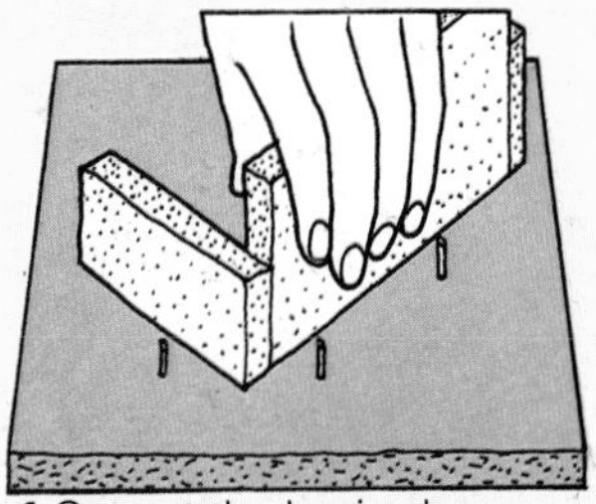

**1** Cut out the basic shape from polystyrene. Coat bottom with Spackle and push it onto nails in the base.

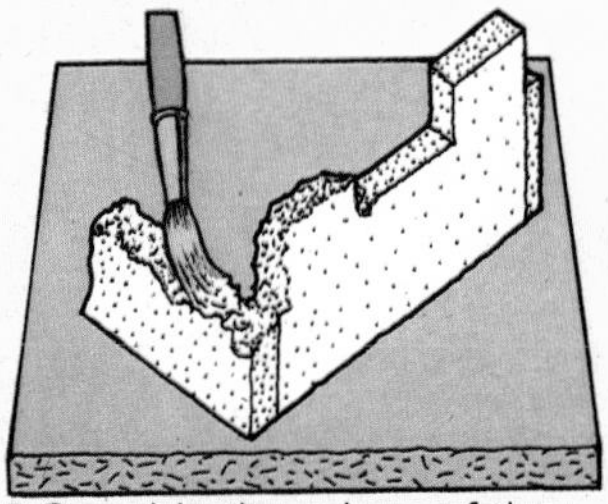

**2** Crumble the edges of the wall by applying paint stripper. The stripper will dissolve the polystyrene.

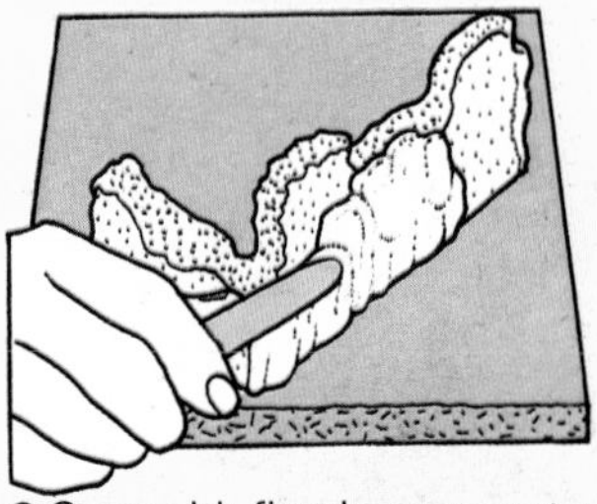

**3** Coat with fireclay cement to imitate stone, or Spackle for stucco or brick (for brick, see page 192). Paint wall.

**Charred rafters** Softwood strips charred with a match.

**Burnt wall** See below.

**Rubble** Pieces of real broken brick. See below.

**Stuccoed brick wall** Spackle over a polystyrene wall.

**Bullet holes** Punch holes in wall with awl; add a drop of paint stripper to break up the edge of the wall.

To make a burnt wall, blacken the surface by playing smoke from a piece of burning sprue over model. Do this outdoors.

Note how these pieces of broken brick have been positioned so as to appear random. Glue them in place with white glue.

## Brick wall

For a brick wall, build the wall described on page 190 and cover it with a thin, even layer of Spackle making a sharp edge at the corners. When dry, paint the surface a mottled brick color using almost pure oil paint so that the turpentine doesn't dissolve the polystyrene. Score the brick courses through the paint layer. Reduce the stark white of the Spackle below with washes of paint. Now create any other effect such as damaged or missing bricks (see below). Brick papers, although not as effective as this technique, are available in different scales from hobby and model stores.

**Cracked wall**
Form cracks by rocking wall just before the Spackle coat dries.

**Damaged and missing bricks** Make a damaged brick by scoring around the brick and pressing in; the center will crush leaving broken edges. To leave a hollow, cut $\frac{1}{8}$ inch (3 mm) deep around brick and flick out brick; darken hollow with paint.

**Stone-topped wall** Use copestones on top of a wall for an old-fashioned effect.

**Flaking stucco on a brick wall** For this effect, scrape and sand the Spackle until it begins to flake away. Paint the stucco on the Spackle and bricks on the polystyrene. Don't use turpentine on the bricks – it dissolves the polystyrene.

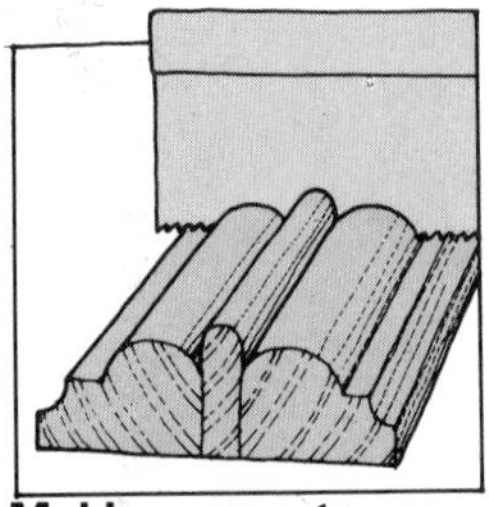

**Making copestones**
Glue a wooden molding to both sides of a flat wooden strip; to make the copestones, divide the strip into individual segments with a saw.

Glue segments to top of wall. Coat with fireclay cement using a brush and water to round edges. When dr recut joints and scrape the surface to make a stone texture.

# Railroads

SWIFT
Gulf Oil
Corporation
241
MW
BILLS
WOODSIDE UNION TERMINAL

# Planning a model railroad

Many modelers begin by acquiring a modest train set and gradually add extra track to accommodate more locomotives and rolling stock until they have amassed quite a substantial collection. Before you start, consider what type of railroad you wish to build so that you can work toward it from the beginning. With good planning, you will be able to expand and improve your layout, continuing to enjoy it as you become more experienced.

Think about the types of trains you want to run. If you are interested in passenger services, for instance, you will need a long track or a continuous loop so that the trains can build up to scale speed, or you can arrange the scenery to create the illusion of distance (see page 210). To run complex shunting exercises you will need several locomotives. If you like landscaping, make a layout which allows you to substitute one section of scenery for another without too much disruption to the train service.

Above all, choose a scale and plan which will suit the available space. With a minimum working area of only 1×6 feet (30×185 cm) you can run a railroad based on a single subject such as a small industrial line or a locomotive depot. One type of layout for a small space is called a "branch line-fiddle yard." The branch line might comprise a single-platform station and freight yard, an enginehouse and a pair of sidings, all modeled on a baseboard as small as 4×1½ feet (120×45 cm). The fiddle yard, which represents the other half of the system, is mounted out of sight on a similar-size baseboard. When a train arrives at the fiddle yard, the locomotive is lifted from the track and turned around, ready to go out on the branch line once again.

Another popular design is the modular railroad. It allows you to plan a large layout but build it in small, portable sections of about 2×4 feet (60×120 cm), which can be linked together later. One advantage is that you can enjoy all the facets of railroad modeling quickly in a small area, whereas on a large layout you may spend months just laying track. Some clubs specify dimensions for the sections so that one modelmaker can link his layout with those of others.

Larger layouts fall into two categories: end-to-end and continuous. An end-to-end layout can be straight or bend around into any shape, but it usually has a terminus at each end. To simulate the duration of a passenger service, an end-to-end layout needs a holding track where the train can wait out-of-sight until it is scheduled to arrive at its destination. On a continuous layout, the train runs around a loop for the necessary time. The simple oval is the most familiar form of continuous layout. You can position the station on a siding so that the train does not have to pass through it on each circuit, or incorporate a return loop which allows the train to enter the station from both directions and adds another route.

Branch line

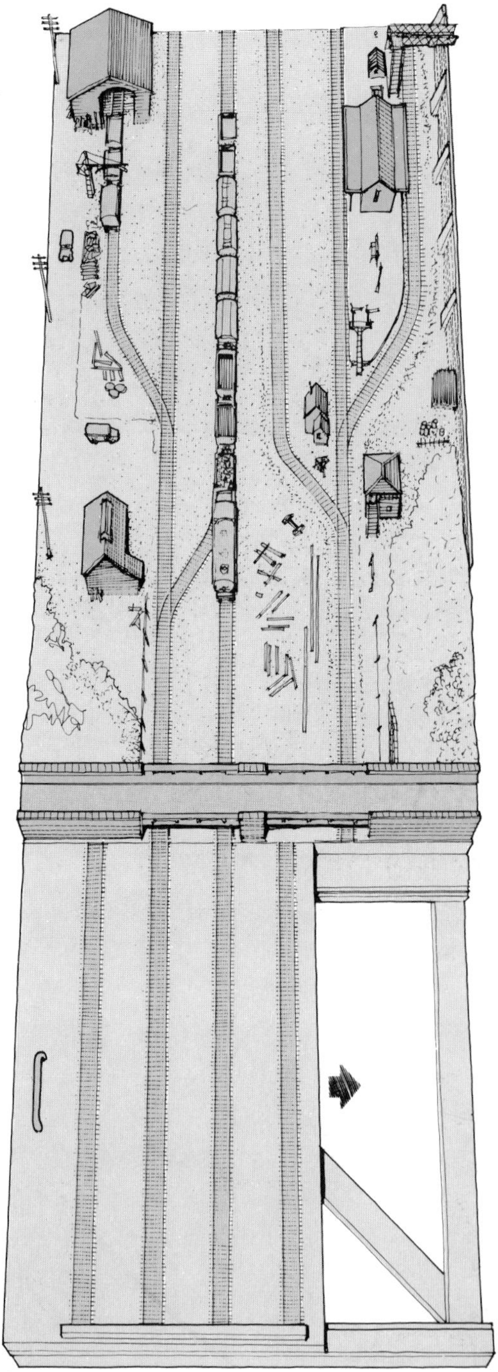

Fiddle yard

**The branch line-fiddle yard system** The locomotives are turned around at the fiddle yard. The yard may move to line up with two or more tracks at a time for inward and outward journeys.

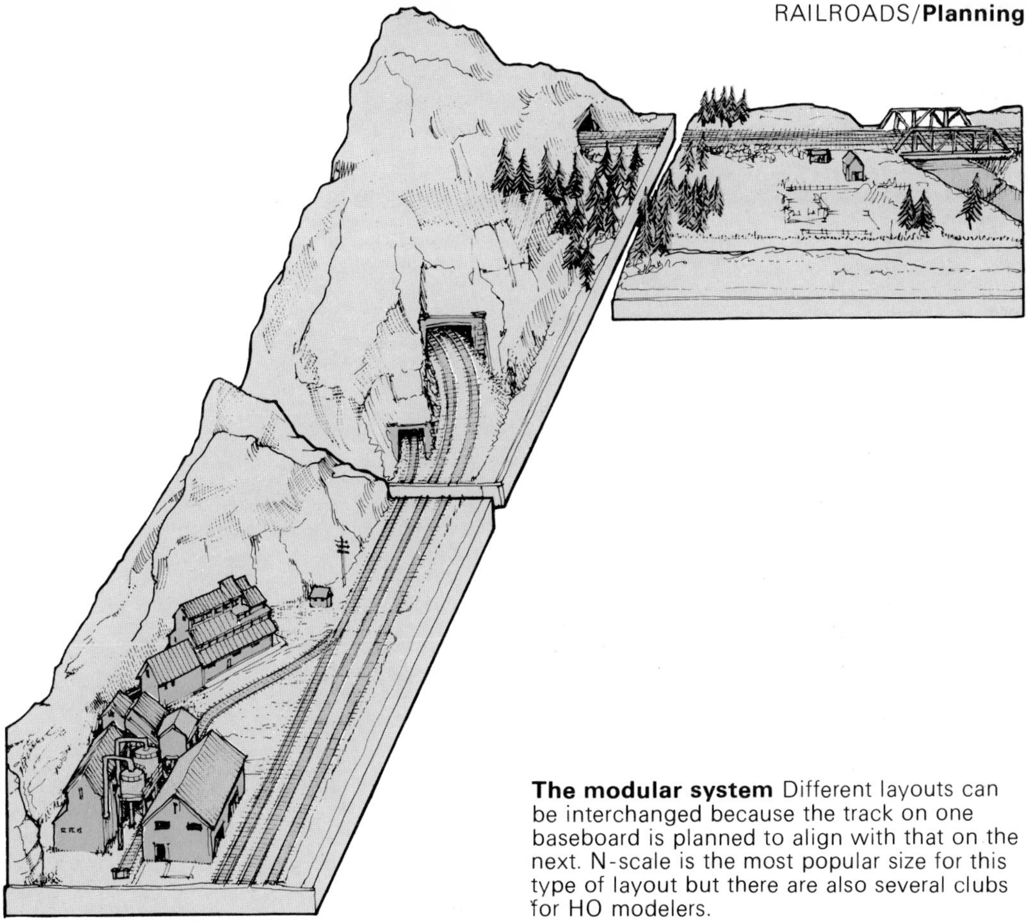

**The modular system** Different layouts can be interchanged because the track on one baseboard is planned to align with that on the next. N-scale is the most popular size for this type of layout but there are also several clubs for HO modelers.

## End-to-end layouts

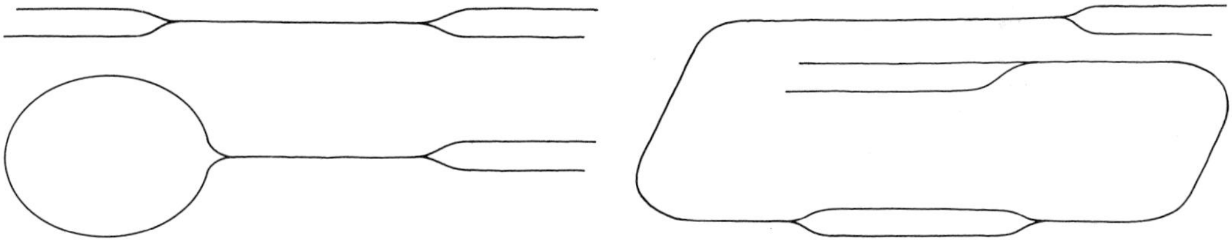

## Continuous layouts

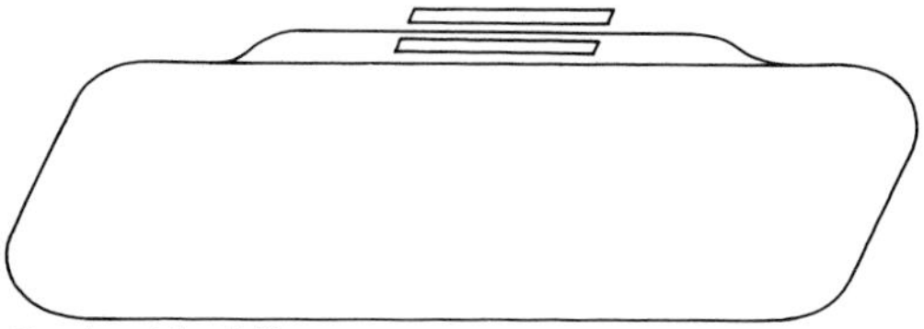

Oval with siding

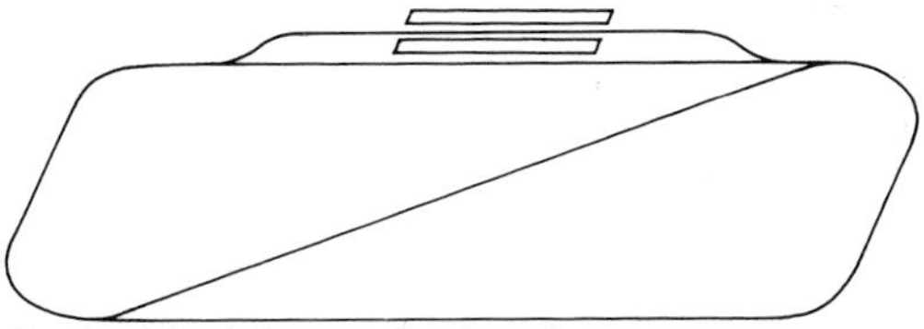

Oval with siding and return loop

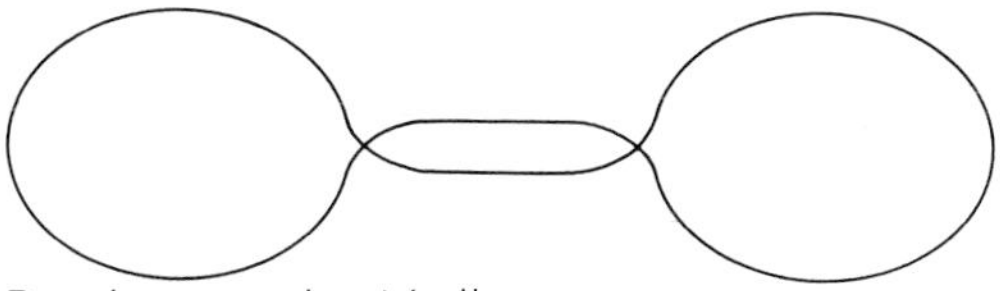

Dog bone or dumbbell

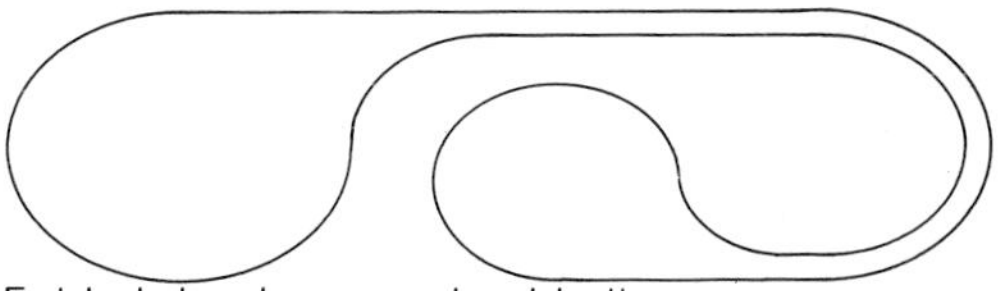

Folded dog bone or dumbbell

# Scale and gauge

The term "scale" refers to the relationship between the size of the model train and that of the full-size train. It is expressed as a ratio, for example 1:76 or 4 millimeters to 1 foot. "Gauge" is the distance between the inside faces of the heads of the rails and is given in millimeters or sometimes inches. In some cases, trains of different scales run on the same gauge track.

There are many scales for model railroads and each is specified by a letter or letters. The most popular ones for a home layout are OO in Great Britain (4 mm to 1 foot) and HO in the USA and the rest of Europe (3.5 mm to 1 foot). Both scales run on track with a gauge of 16.5 mm. Strictly speaking, HO is correct to scale while OO is "narrow gauge," although the difference is hardly noticeable. Since full-size continental and American trains are normally larger than British ones, the extra 0.5 mm to the foot makes British OO models about the same size as continental or American HO models. Both OO and HO models are large enough for customizing and lettering, yet quite a complex layout can be easily accommodated in the home.

N scale is also popular. Since it is a smaller scale and runs on narrower gauge track, you can fit four times as much track into the same space as for OO and HO scales, or take the same area and model the track and landscape truer to life. N scale is more expensive than OO and HO, and the track needs to be laid with more care to guarantee trouble-free running.

An even smaller size, Z scale, is available. Although more expensive and limited to continental-style trains, a complex layout can be literally modeled in a suitcase, making it easy to store and transport.

The only other widely available scale is O. Once the most popular scale, it is really only suitable for outdoor or club layouts.

Some specialists do not consider the common scales to be true-to-scale and they model in what are known as "fine scales."

Largely obsolete scales, such as S and TT, are still used by enthusiasts who deal in second-hand equipment or scratch-build.

| Scale | Ratio | Ratio in millimeters per foot | Gauge in millimeters |
|---|---|---|---|
| O | 1:43.5 | 7 | 32 |
| S* | 1:64 | $\frac{3}{16}$ inch per foot | $\frac{7}{8}$ inch |
| OO | 1:76 | 4 | 16.5 |
| HO | 1:87 | 3.5 | 16.5 |
| TT | 1:120 | 3 | 12 |
| N | 1:148 | 2 | 9 |
| Z | 1:220 | 1.4 | 6.5 |

*Measurements for this scale are never given in metric.

# Baseboards

Although many modelmakers begin with their train set running on the floor, this sytem has disadvantages: the layout has to be set up and dismantled every time the trains are operated; it is impossible to incorporate realistic scenery, and dust can cause bad electrical contact. Serious modelers fix the track permanently to a baseboard mounted above the floor.

There are two types of baseboard: the flat-topped table and the open frame. Easy to construct and very rigid, the tabletop type makes a strong, portable layout. It is ideal if you plan to incorporate large areas of industrial sidings or a fiddle yard. Rolling countryside with rivers and roads passing over and under the track is best supported on an open framework. On this type of baseboard, a narrow, plywood roadbed carries the track. You can combine both types of baseboard in a single layout if your scheme includes flat and hilly areas.

If you dismantle your baseboard, it is essential that you are able to realign the tracks accurately. To connect two sections of a flat-topped table, drill three holes in each end rail and screw them together. If the layout is to be moved regularly, drill two additional holes right through both end rails and insert bolts. To connect two sections of an open-frame baseboard, bolt metal plates to the inside face of the girders to brace the joint.

## Making a tabletop baseboard

You do not need to make complicated joints to hold the baseboard together as the sheet material over the top keeps the frame rigid. Begin by butt-jointing the corners of the frame, leaving a $\frac{1}{2}$-inch (10-mm) overhang on one side to prevent the wood splitting. Nail and glue the joint, then screw on metal corner brackets. Trim the overhang flush. Butt-joint cross members at 2-foot (600-mm) intervals along the frame.

To complete the baseboard, screw and glue a sheet of wood to the frame. Particle board is very strong but heavy; plywood is strong and sections can be cut and bent to form a sloping roadbed; wood-fiber insulation board is not quite as strong but it does not need extra sound-insulating material underneath the track.

## Making an open-frame baseboard

Build two L-girders by gluing one piece of well-seasoned softwood to another and screw them together at 12-inch (300-mm) intervals. For a frame up to 2 feet (600-mm) wide, screw and glue cross members every 18 inches (450 mm) along the length of the girders. For a wider frame, set the girders farther apart and let the cross members project. Attach diagonal softwood members to reinforce the frame, cutting off the ends at 45°. Fix additional cross members where needed for mounting roadbed. These extra pieces can be at any angle.

## Tabletop baseboard

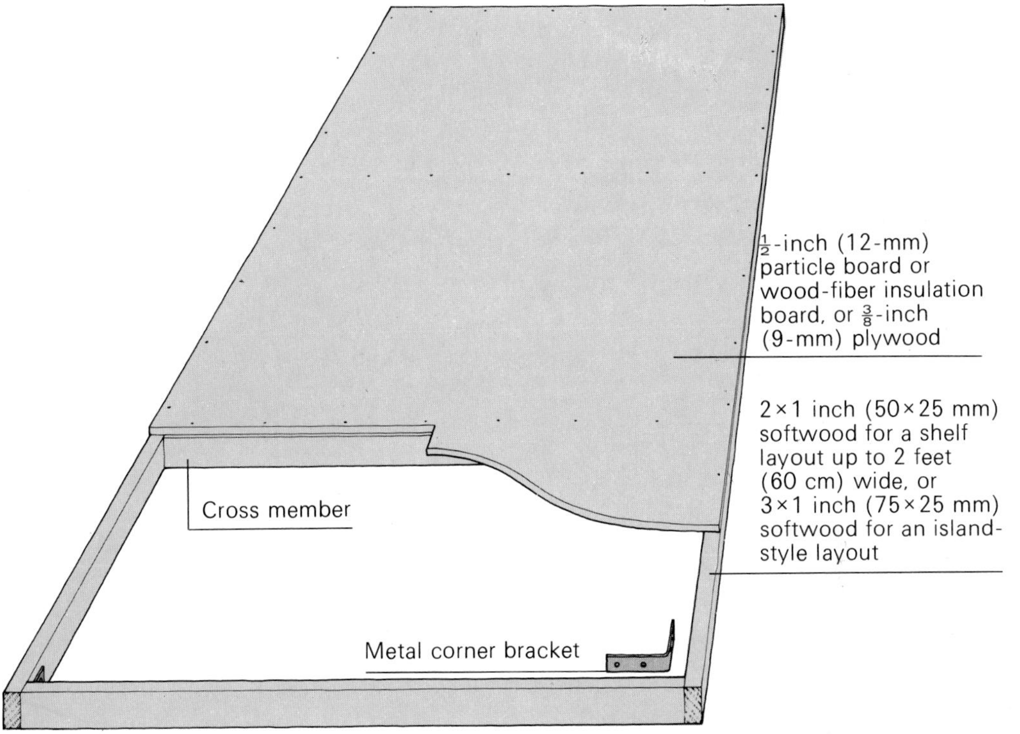
½-inch (12-mm) particle board or wood-fiber insulation board, or ⅜-inch (9-mm) plywood
2×1 inch (50×25 mm) softwood for a shelf layout up to 2 feet (60 cm) wide, or 3×1 inch (75×25 mm) softwood for an island-style layout
Cross member
Metal corner bracket

## Open-frame baseboard

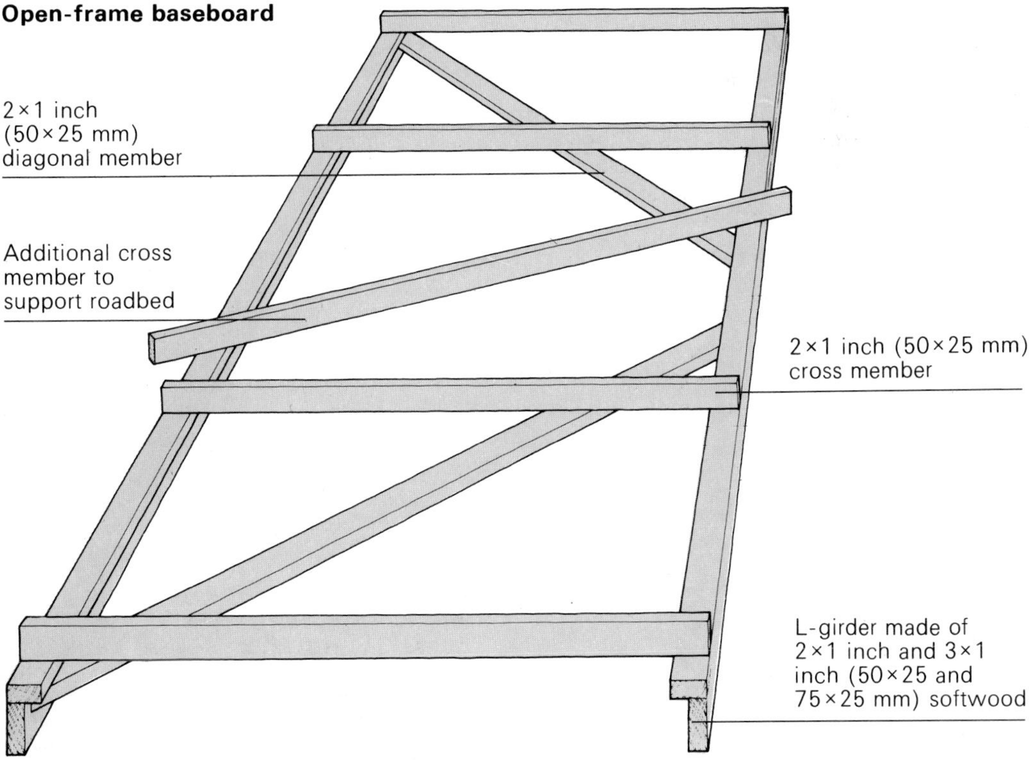
2×1 inch (50×25 mm) diagonal member
Additional cross member to support roadbed
2×1 inch (50×25 mm) cross member
L-girder made of 2×1 inch and 3×1 inch (50×25 and 75×25 mm) softwood

## Supporting baseboards

Baseboards can be mounted at any convenient level but bench height, which is 36 inches (900 mm) above the floor, is generally best. This is a comfortable position for working on the layout standing up. Moreover, when you sit down the layout is at eye level for maximum realism. The two methods for supporting a baseboard shown below and right can be used for both the flat-topped or open-frame type.

## Wall-mounted baseboards

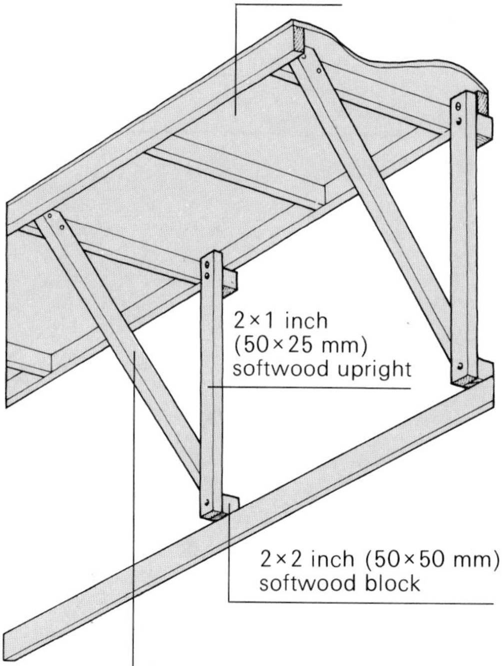


These do not have to be connected to the floor at all. This design provides good clearance below the layout and has a neat appearance. Always fix the structure to a sound masonry wall or directly to wooden wall studs.

Cut an upright to support every other cross member and both ends of the baseboard. Nail and glue blocks to each upright, one flush with the bottom end, another 1¾ inches (45 mm) from the top. Screw a piece of softwood to the wall for the uprights to rest on. Screw the uprights to the wall through the blocks, positioning each upright so that a diagonal member can be screwed to its side and to a cross member.

Hook the baseboard over the ends of the uprights. Rest the diagonal members next to the uprights on the horizontal rail. Screw them first to the cross member, then to the upright. Finally, screw through each of the uprights into the baseboard frame with the screw pointing slightly upward.

## Freestanding baseboards

To support a layout in the middle of a room, make up frames to fit between the long rails of the baseboard, screwing and gluing the joints together; then, screw a diagonal member to the frame and to the inside face of the baseboard. You will need to include a packing piece, the thickness of the diagonal member, between the vertical leg and the rail of the baseboard.

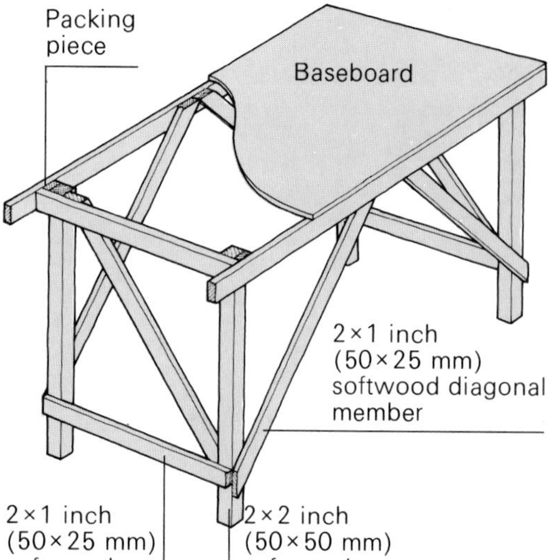


## Storing and transporting layouts

Not everyone has room to have a model railroad on permanent display and it can be an advantage to be able to store it out of sight. Likewise, you may want to be able to take your layout to a club meeting. Modular layouts, in particular, need to be portable so that sections can be interchanged or transported to another place. Tabletop baseboards are easy to carry and store because they are rigid and generally have low scenery. Open-frame baseboards are not normally designed to be moved.

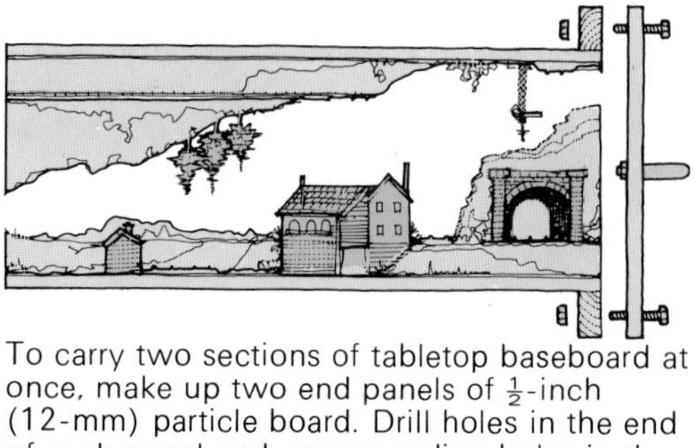

To carry two sections of tabletop baseboard at once, make up two end panels of ½-inch (12-mm) particle board. Drill holes in the end of each panel and corresponding holes in the baseboard to take bolts. Lay one section of the layout over the other and bolt them to the end panels. Allow enough space between the sections for the scenery. Attach a strong handle to the center of each end panel.

# Roadbed

Track can be laid over the underlay (see page 201) directly onto the surface of a tabletop baseboard. On an open-frame baseboard, however, you must build roadbed from $\frac{3}{8}$-inch (9-mm) plywood cut slightly wider than the track; allow extra for trackside equipment.

It is easiest to cut out plywood roadbed with a saber saw. Connect sections of roadbed with a butt joint, then screw and glue a piece of plywood underneath so that it overlaps the joint. Sand the surface of the joint smooth. To make a gradient, simply bend the plywood and support it at intervals with softwood scraps. Let the plywood follow a natural, gentle curve. Support long spans with a piece of softwood glued lengthwise underneath.

Gradients can be incorporated in a tabletop baseboard using the same techniques, as long as the top sheet is made of plywood. Sand any joints smooth.

Roadbed on an open-frame baseboard

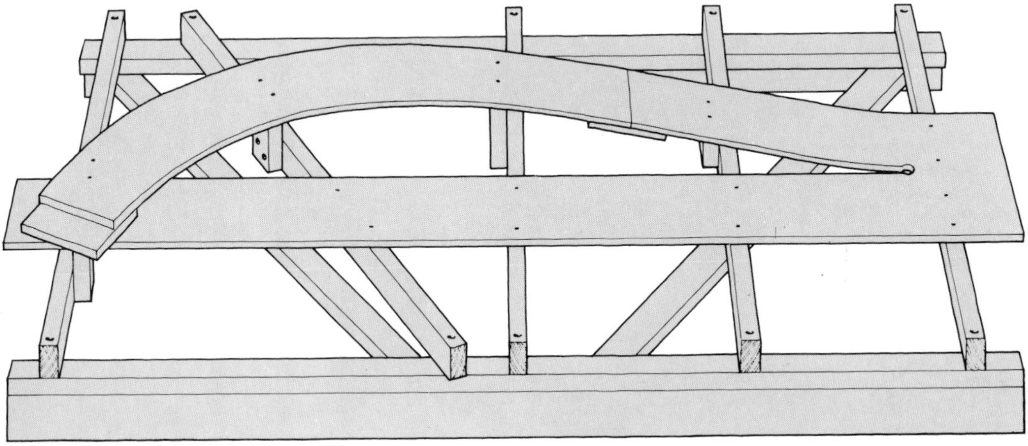

# Trackwork

Model track is made up of two rails, usually of nickel-silver or brass, joined by plastic or fiber ties. It carries the electricity from the power pack which is picked up by the wheels of the locomotive. Careful design and construction of the track is crucial to the smooth running of a train.

Sectional track is the most common type. It is the easiest to lay because the ties are linked in rigid lengths. As well as straight sections, there are curved pieces which are measured by their radius. Turnouts – often called switches – which form the junction between two diverging tracks, and crossings, come as separate pieces.

Flexible track is a kind of sectional track which can be cut to any length and bent to the required radius. It is particularly useful for forming the transition between straight and curved pieces of track.

Those modelmakers who really enjoy trackwork lay their own track, one tie at a time.

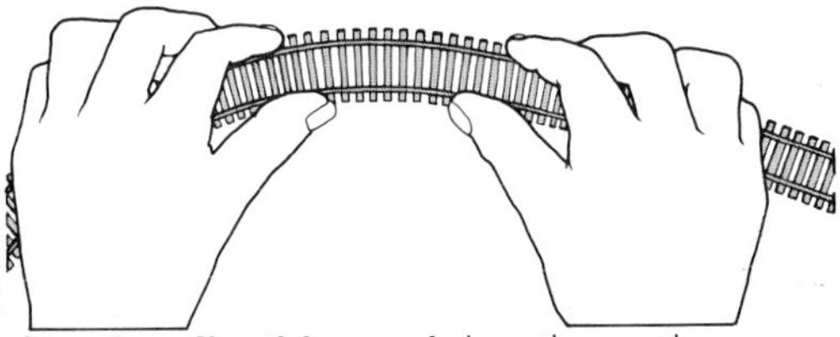

**Shaping flexible track** Lay the track on a flat surface and bend it gently by hand. Do not bend it in the air or you may twist it.

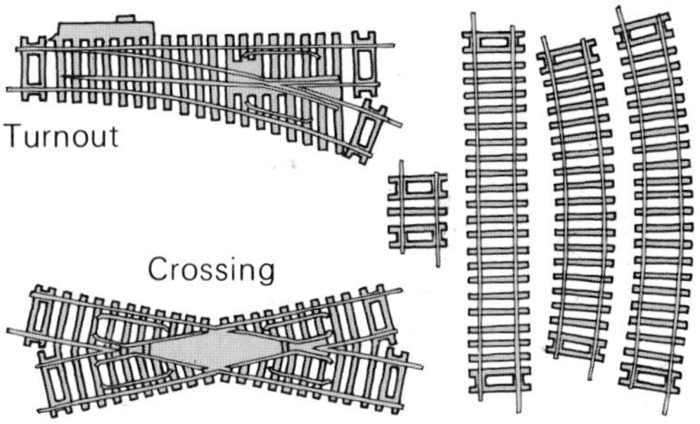


**Sectional track**

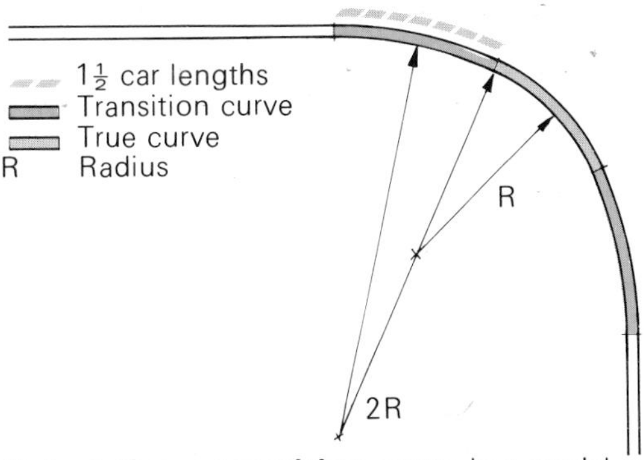


**Calculating a transition curve** In a model railroad, make the transition curve twice the radius of the true curve for about $1\frac{1}{2}$ car lengths. To mark the centerline see page 201.

## Joining track

Small metal joiners are used to connect one piece of track to another. The method is the same for joining both standard sectional and flexible track, and one type to the other.

Slip a joiner onto one rail of each piece of track – always the right-hand rail when the track is facing you so that sections can be linked either way around without repositioning the joiners. To connect the pieces of track, simply push the free rails into the joiners. Make sure that the rails align by sighting along them or by laying another piece of track with the same shape over the top. The tops of the rails should lie flush. Any slight unevenness can be filed flat, but if they are badly out-of-line, check the joiner and replace it if it is damaged. Different makes of sectional track can be joined although you may need to solder a wire connection between them or insert shims underneath one section of track to make a good junction.

Sometimes there is insufficient room to slide the tracks into the joiners in the normal way – for example, when a piece of new track has to fit into the space between two sections already fixed to the board. For these pieces of track, use the technique shown below right for filling in a gap.

When flexible track is bent into a curve, the inside rail, which has to cover a shorter distance than the outer one, becomes too long. Support the rail on a flat surface and against a piece of wood to prevent the rail from distorting, and cut the end off with a razor saw. Smooth the cut end.

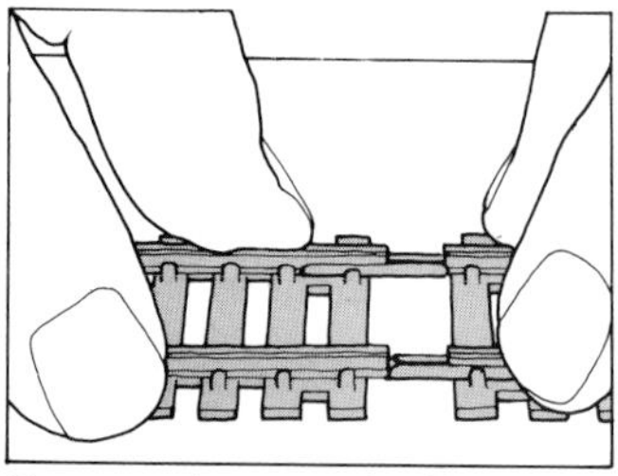

**Connecting tracks** Place the two pieces on a flat surface and push them together.

It is essential to align each piece of approaching track accurately with the turntable.

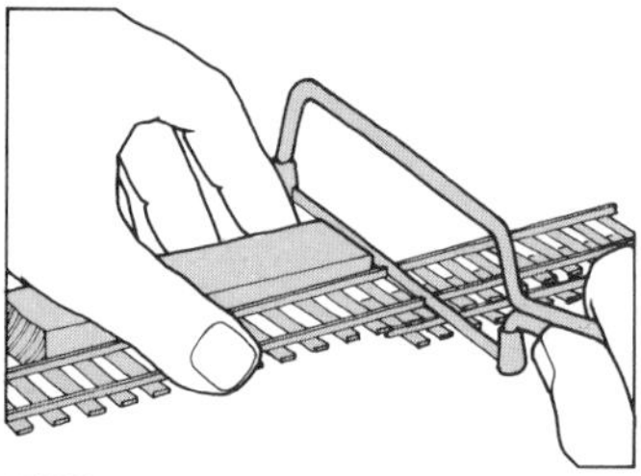

**Filling the gap between fixed tracks** Join one end of the filler piece in the normal way, then saw it to size. Support the track against a block of wood as you cut.

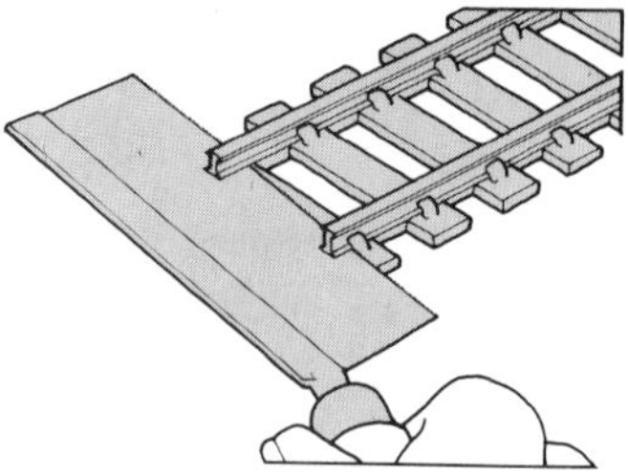

Disconnect the filler piece. Saw under each rail on both sides of the junction to separate it from the first tie and make room for the joiners.

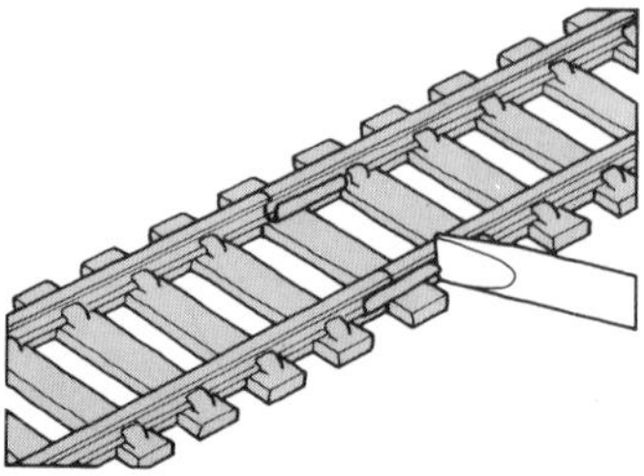

Cut two joiners to two-thirds of their normal length and slide them right onto the rails of one piece of track. Align the rails and slide the joiners over the junction.

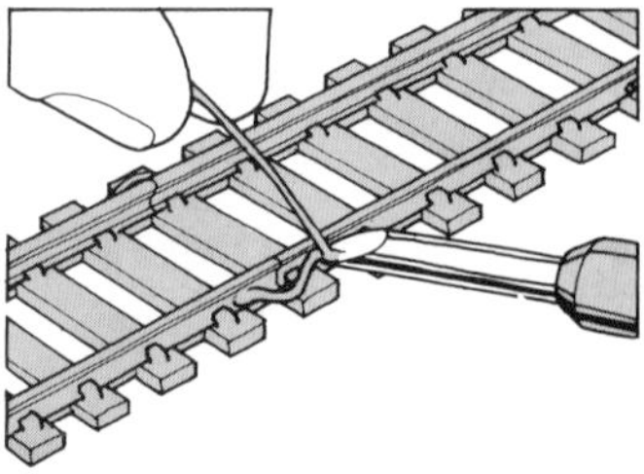

**Soldering tracks** If you have trouble maintaining good electrical contact, solder a wire between the outside faces of the two rails, instead of using joiners.

## Planning trackwork

Commercial track plans show the space required for a layout with each piece of track in position. If, however, you wish to plan your own layout, begin by making a rough sketch on graph paper. Then, using track stencils of standard lengths and radii, make a small-scale drawing of the layout. The stencils will help you establish the correct curves and angles of the turnouts as well as the amount of track you will need to buy.

Track can be purchased on the basis of the scale drawing, but if you are not sure that you will have enough space on the baseboard, and particularly if you are using flexible track, it is a wise precaution to draw the track layout full-size on paper. You can buy templates which make this job easier. Alternately, make your own from stiff cardboard, following the shape of track which you already possess. To gauge the position of flexible track, draw the centerline with an improvised compass as shown below.

Use standard curved sections as a rough guide to the minimum permissible radius. You will find that the radius of individual curves depends a great deal on the location of the track, its relationship to scenery and buildings and the type of stock which will run on the railroad. Generally speaking, for HO/OO scale a "branch-line" curve should have a minimum 15-inch (380-mm) radius while a "main-line" curve should be no less than 24 inches (610 mm). If in doubt, make the curve greater rather than smaller. Parallel track should be spaced a minimum of 2 inches (50 mm) apart, center to center. Experiment with the positions of buildings, and place stock on the rails to make sure that the relevant sections are able to accommodate the trains; a siding, for example, must be long enough to hold its quota of freight or passenger cars, and the length of the track between towns must look convincing. Transfer the final plan onto the baseboard. Mark the centerline of each piece of track and, where possible, mark where each section joins.

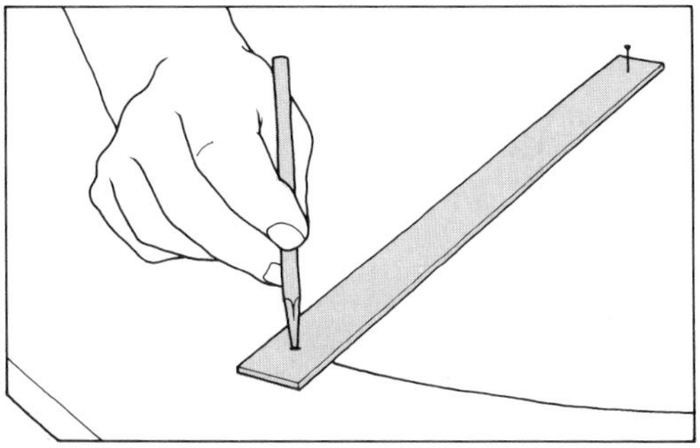

**Marking the centerline of a curve** Push a pin through one end of a straight piece of wooden lath or a strip of thick cardboard. Measure the required radius from the pin along the strip and make a small hole to take the point of a pencil. With the pin positioned in the center of the circle and the pencil set at the centerline of the track, draw the curve.

## Laying track

Track is usually attached to the baseboard over a layer of foamed plastic or cork to cut the noise level (only a wood-fiber base which is sound-insulating does not need an underlay.) Before fixing the track and underlay it is a good idea to connect up the track directly on the baseboard and check its alignment, looking carefully for any distortions and correcting the line where necessary. A little time and effort at this stage avoids trouble when you come to attach the track. Mark the position of the track on the board by drawing along the centerline between the ties and indicate the joins. On a small layout you can inspect all the track at once, but if your layout is large and you are using a lot of flexible track, you will have to check and lay sections of track at a time. Inevitably, modifications will have to be made but if the full-size plan is accurately drawn, these alterations to your original idea will be minor.

Attach the underlay to the baseboard, following the marked lines and adding the turnouts and crossings before the straight sections. Foamed plastic comes in rolls and specially shaped sections; secure it with glue. Precut rolls of cork with beveled edges are popular. To make the pieces follow a curve just bend them to shape. Some precut cork comes split in half lengthwise. Lay it as shown below. (The central join makes it easy to position the track accurately on top.) If you cut out your own underlay from sheet cork, be sure to leave a little extra material on each side of the track so that you can bevel the edges with a sharp knife after the track has been laid.

Attach the track following the same order as the underlay, starting with the turnouts and crossings, but join lengths of track to them to check the alignment before fixing them in place. Nail the track to the board through holes in the center of the ties.

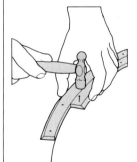

**Attaching cork underlay** For underlay which is split in half lengthwise, butt each half up to the centerline and stagger the joins. Nail the pieces to the board and lightly sand the joins smooth.

**Adding the track** Start the nails with a tack hammer and finish with a nail set. Do not drive them completely home or you may distort the shape of the track.

## Adding ballast

Fine granite chips are very realistic but many modelmakers prefer to use cork granules as they are less likely to damage the moving parts or finish of a locomotive.

Ballast looks more natural if it is laid after the trackside scenery has been built. Working on a small section of track at a time, sprinkle on the ballast and brush it level with the tops of the ties. Make sure that it is not up the inside of the rails and that turnouts can move freely. Fix the ballast to the base with a solution of one part white glue, ten parts water, plus a few drops of liquid detergent to make the solution flow (too much water warps fiber ties). Add the solution with a dropper, letting the liquid soak into the material. If you brush some along the sloping sides of the roadbed before adding the ballast, it will help the ballast adhere. Leave the ballast overnight to allow the glue to set hard. Remove any loose material.

Another method of application is to mix the ballast with a dry, powdered UF glue before brushing it onto the track. Spray the mixture with a solution of water and a little liquid detergent, then wipe the rails clean with a soft cloth.

## Cleaning track

Oxides and dirt on the rails cause poor electrical contact. To keep the trains running smoothly, the track needs to be cleaned periodically. One method is to apply track cleaning fluid in 2- to 3-inch (50- to 75-mm) sections spaced around the track, especially in likely trouble spots. Run a locomotive with several cars ahead of it over the whole track to distribute the fluid. This is a good way of cleaning track inside tunnels. Another method is to connect a special track cleaner between the power pack and track to ionize all the dirt particles; this cleans the rails, running wheels and locomotive motor. A simple way to clean the track is to rub a pencil eraser firmly over the tops of the rails.

# How the electrical system works

Most locomotives are powered by a 12-volt direct-current (DC) motor which runs on electricity fed to it through the rails. A power pack plugged into a wall socket supplies the electricity to the track. The system works by maintaining an electrical circuit between one terminal of the pack and the other via the motor of the locomotive. The electricity runs out on one rail and back on the other. If it finds its way back to the power pack without going through the motor, the system overloads and stops. This is called a short circuit. Insulated wires and rail joiners, and plastic ties keep the two sides of the circuit apart. In the locomotive, the wheels are insulated from their axles to prevent a short circuit. Brushes which connect to the motor touch the inside of the wheels and pick up the current. Some locomotives have uninsulated wheels on one side. In these cases, the motor is connected to the metal frame which is live, and to the brushes on the insulated wheels, to complete the circuit. Two locomotive designs, each with a different power route, are shown below.

**How the locomotive works** Electricity is transmitted through the wheels. The more wheels that are used for power transmission, the less effect poor contact will have on the performance of the locomotive.

### The microchip system

This new development in railroad modeling uses microchips to control the movement of the trains. The power pack feeds 21-volt AC to the track together with signals coded for each locomotive. A microchip in the locomotive converts the current into DC and feeds it to the motor as directed by the signal. A great advantage of the system is that several different locomotives can be run on the layout at one time, even on the same section of track. Two or more engines can pull a train, or one can pull and the other push. The wiring is extremely simple as only two wires are needed to operate the whole layout. Unfortunately, few sets are compatible with others and each set has a maximum number of trains that can be used, usually about sixteen. With the microchip attached, the locomotive cannot be run on a conventional layout.

## The power pack

This has a transformer and rectifier to convert the alternating current (AC) from the wall socket to 12-volt direct current (DC), and a rheostat which controls the speed of the locomotive. The pack also controls the direction of the train by switching the polarity of the power supplied to the track. Some can simulate the coasting and braking movement of a real train but your layout should have long, continuous runs to get the best out of this type.

On some power packs you will find an outlet for uncontrolled 12-volt DC. This is for an auxiliary throttle with the same controls as the main pack, but without a transformer and rectifier. These extra throttle units are used to operate different sections of track and, if they have a long extension cord, for walk-around control. The pack may also have an outlet for 16-volt AC to power turnout motors.

Every pack should come with a thermal circuit breaker to protect it against short circuits. Buy one if it is not included.

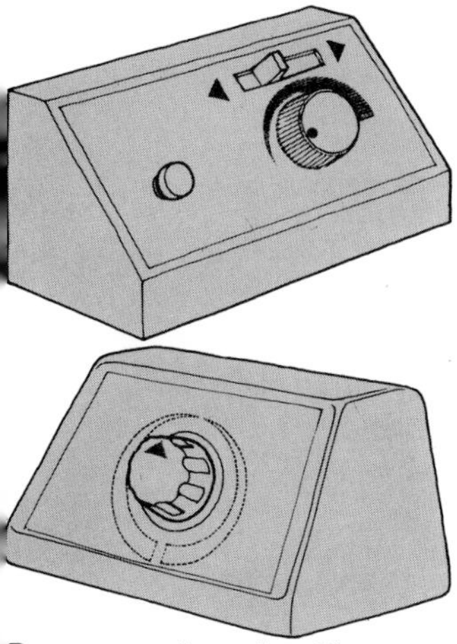

**Power pack styles** The top pack has a "reversing switch" for directional control and a knob for speed control. The lower pack combines both controls in one knob; the center position is "off," "reverse" is to the left, and "forward" to the right. Don't use both on the same layout: it is difficult to react quickly when you first change over.

# Wiring a simple oval for one locomotive

Attach two multistrand flexible wires to the 12-volt DC controlled outlet on the power pack, then connect each wire to a rail. If the track doesn't have terminals on which to secure the wires, solder them onto the rails. When the locomotive is on the nearest stretch of track it should run in the direction in which the reverse switch is thrown, or the control knob is turned. If it does not, change the wires over.

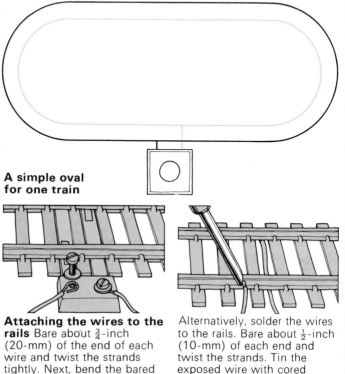

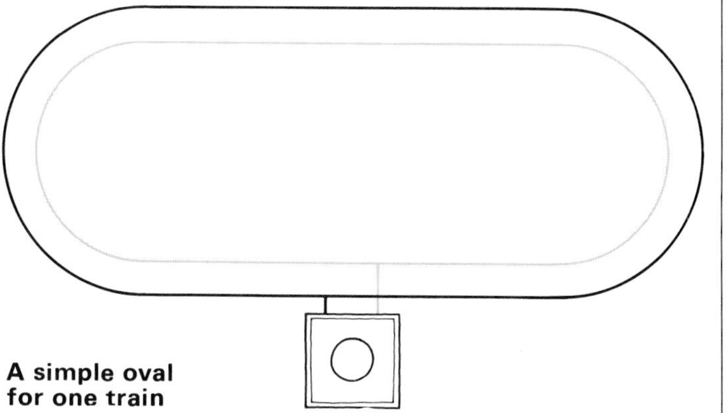

**A simple oval for one train**

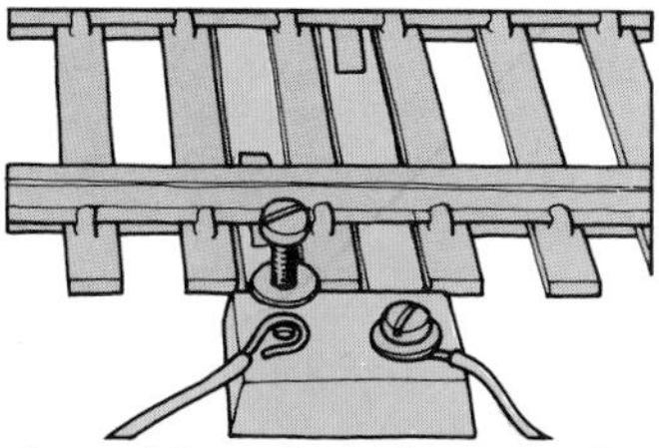

**Attaching the wires to the rails** Bare about $\frac{3}{4}$-inch (20-mm) of the end of each wire and twist the strands tightly. Next, bend the bared wire clockwise into a loop and hook it around the terminal screw; tighten the screw.

Alternatively, solder the wires to the rails. Bare about $\frac{1}{2}$-inch (10-mm) of each end and twist the strands. Tin the exposed wire with cored solder for electrical work. Don't leave the soldering iron on the rails too long.

# Wiring for more than one locomotive

As soon as more than one locomotive is placed on the layout it is essential to isolate one part of the track from another by cutting a gap in one or both rails, depending on the scheme. (It is best to incorporate an insulated rail joiner to prevent the gap from closing.) If the isolated part is at the end of a piece of track it is called a dead end. A separate piece of track which breaks up a section of through track is called a block.

Switches are used in many schemes to control the flow of the electricity. A single-pole, single-throw switch has a simple on/off toggle which controls current through one wire. A double-throw switch has two "on" positions to control two wires; the center position is normally "off." Double-pole switches control pairs of wires. These switches are essential for sophisticated wiring schemes, such as that for cab control. A rotary switch has several positions which are selected by turning a dial. The instructions for each wiring system will tell you which of these types to use.

## Dead ends

The plan on the right shows a simple layout with two dead ends – the minimum number necessary for the system to work. Each one should be long enough to take a complete train. There is a gap in one rail of each dead end where it meets the main line, and a single-pole, single-throw switch connects the gap.

One train remains stationary in a dead end while another runs around the live part of the track. To change over locomotives, direct the working locomotive into the vacant dead end and turn off the switch. Turn the other switch on to control the new locomotive.

## Blocks

These differ from dead ends in that they derive their power not from adjacent track but from a power pack, sometimes via switches. An accessory throttle unit can be used instead of a complete pack, but the latter provides more power to the layout. Although not always necessary, a gap is usually made in both rails to aid fault-finding.

The simplest arrangement uses one power pack to control two blocks; a single-pole, single-throw switch for each block turns the power on and off. This works rather like a layout with two dead ends: one locomotive remains stationary in one block while the pack runs the other. (If only one train is on the track, both switches can be on and it can run around the whole layout.) If each block is wired directly to its own power pack, it is possible to run both trains simultaneously. This system can be extended to include more blocks.

The return part of the circuit can be combined, by attaching the return wires to a common return wire, so that for most of the run only one wire is used, saving wire and simplifying the system. Moreover, a common return circuit only needs one connection at each baseboard joint and between baseboard and control panel. Both of the diagrams on the right show a common return circuit. Before wiring the system, decide which of the two rails is feed and which is return, as any confusion here will cause short circuits. On a straight piece of track the rail nearer the power pack should be feed, the other return. If the track is circular, the outer rail is feed and the inner, return. Run a stripped single-strand wire under the baseboard, clipping or stapling it in place, then solder the return wires to it. The feed wires, of course, must run separately to their respective blocks.

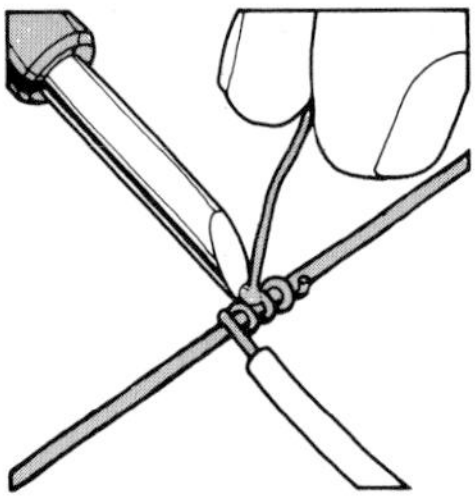

**Joining the return wires to the common return**
Strip the end of each return wire, wind it around the common return and solder it on.

**Layout with two dead ends**

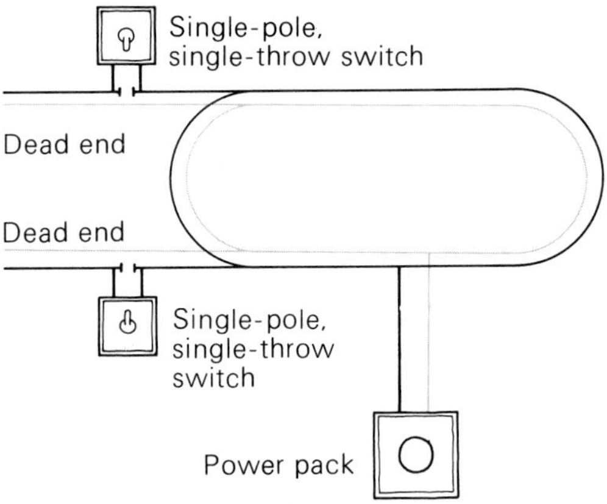


**Layout with two blocks and one pack**

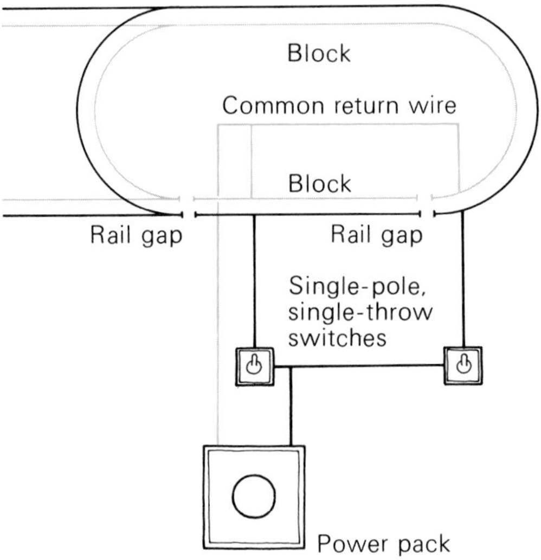


**Layout with two blocks and two packs**

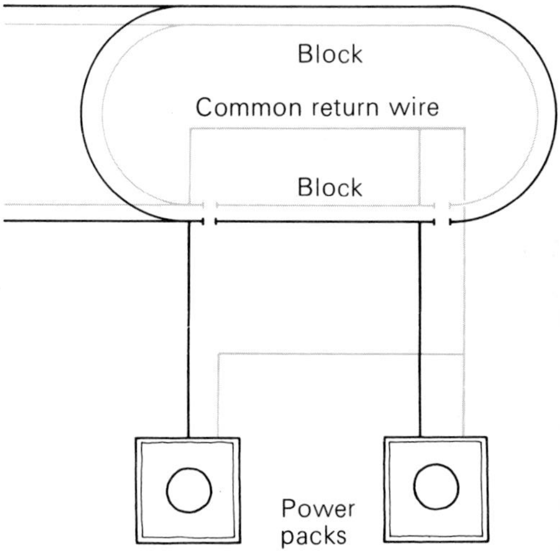

## Cab control

This system allows one operator using one power pack – his "cab" – to run a train anywhere on the layout without preventing other operators from using the remaining blocks. First decide how many trains you want to be able to run at one time (each train needs its own power pack and operator), and divide the layout into blocks, each capable of holding at least one complete train. Make up a wooden control panel with a diagram of the layout on it. Show each block in a different color to make identification easy.

For a two-cab system, mount a single-pole, double-throw switch on the control panel in the center of each block and connect it to the feed wire of each power pack. Place it so that the toggle points toward the pack which is on for that block. Any block can be rendered dead and a train held there by flicking the toggle to the center-off position. For one operator to take a train through the layout, the switches controlling the blocks through which the train must pass are thrown toward that operator, thus giving him control of the whole route. The switches can be banked together but it is more convenient to have them on the layout diagram in the appropriate positions. The power packs can be located at any convenient place around the layout, but for a small railroad it may be simpler to group them around the control panel.

If you wish to set up a system for three or more cabs, you will need to substitute rotary switches for the double-throw switches. Each rotary switch should have one input terminal per cab. Any spare terminals can be used for extra cabs in the future. There should be an "off" position between each terminal or, if there are plenty of spare terminals, an unwired terminal between each live one can serve as "off." Solder the feed wires from each power pack to the input terminals on the switches – each one should be in the same position on each switch. Solder the feed for each block to the output terminal on the appropriate switch.

**Two-cab control**

Single-pole, double-throw switch

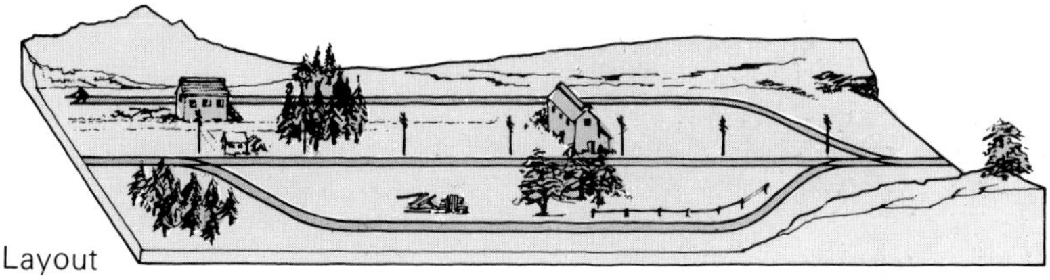

Layout

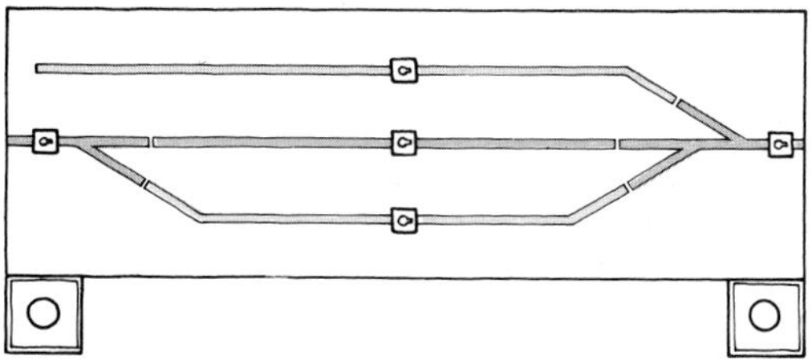

Control panel

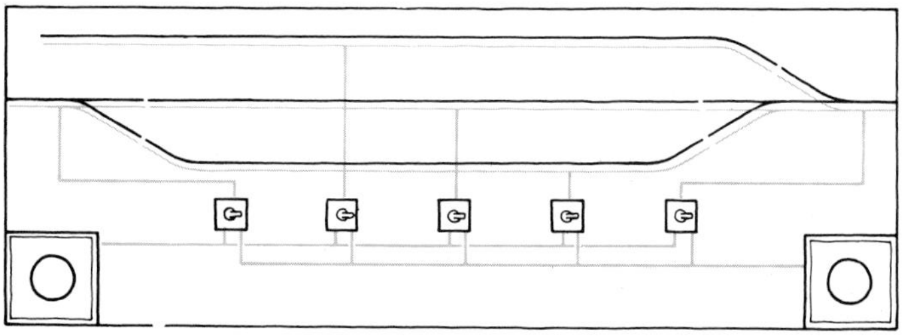

Wiring system (the common return wire is omitted for clarity)

**Three-cab control**

Rotary switch

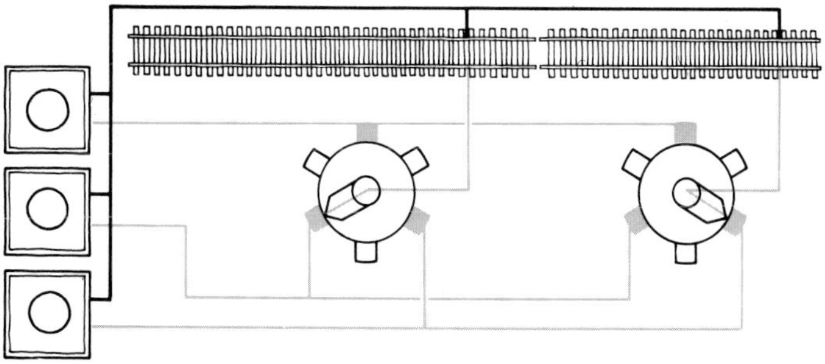

# Wiring a return loop

This type of loop is used to turn a train around. It can be just long enough to hold the longest train or it can be a larger feature of the general layout, but it must be isolated from the main track at both ends by rail gaps. (Although gaps at only one end of the loop would prevent a short circuit, the locomotive would stall as it tried to cross over them.) The loop can be controlled by the adjacent power pack or block via a reversing switch. This is simply a double-pole, double-throw switch wired so that when it is thrown, the polarity in the loop is changed. Another method is to provide it with a separate power pack or accessory throttle unit so that the train does not stop on its way through.

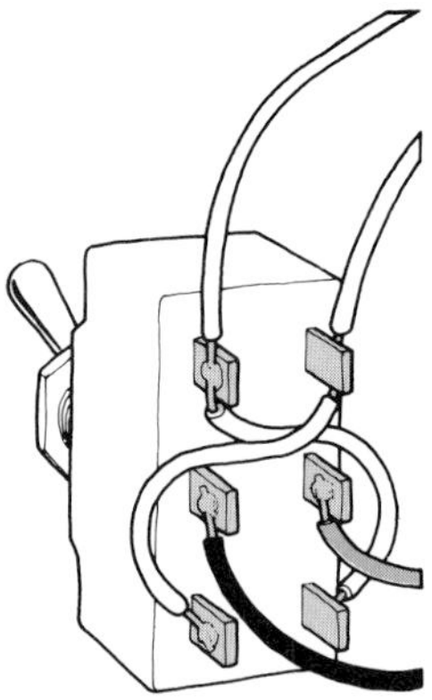

**Wiring a reversing switch** A double-pole, double-throw switch has one pair of input terminals and two pairs of output terminals. Connect the loop feed and return wires to one pair of outputs, then cross them over and connect them to the other pair of outputs. Connect the power pack wires to the input terminals.

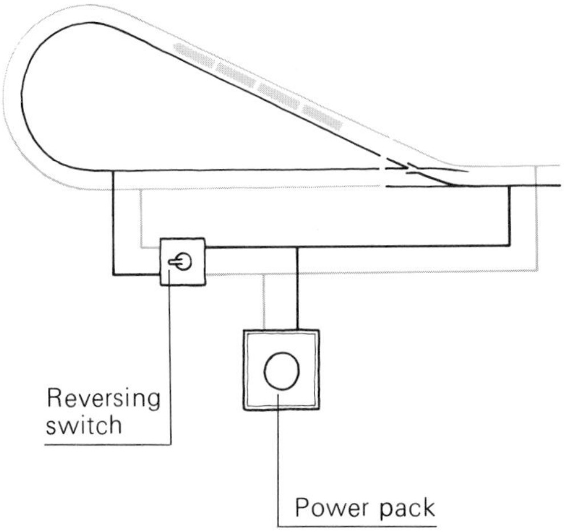


**Operating the loop with a reversing switch** Make sure that the turnout and reversing switch settings agree. Drive the train onto the loop and stop it.

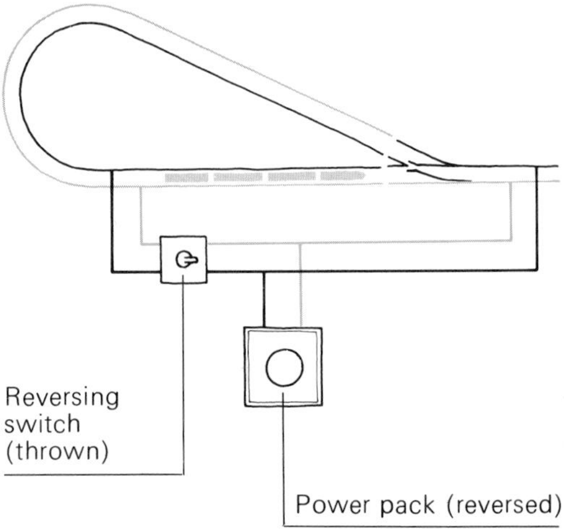


Throw the reversing switch and the power pack. Change the turnout and drive the train out of the loop.

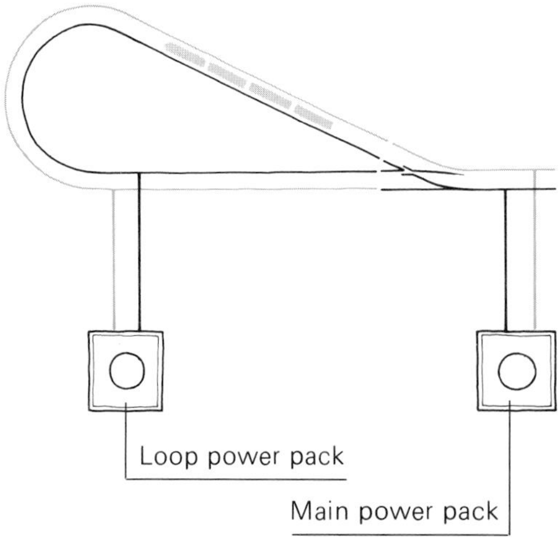


**Operating the loop with a separate power pack** Position the turnout. Set the two power packs to the same speed and polarity. Drive the train onto the loop.

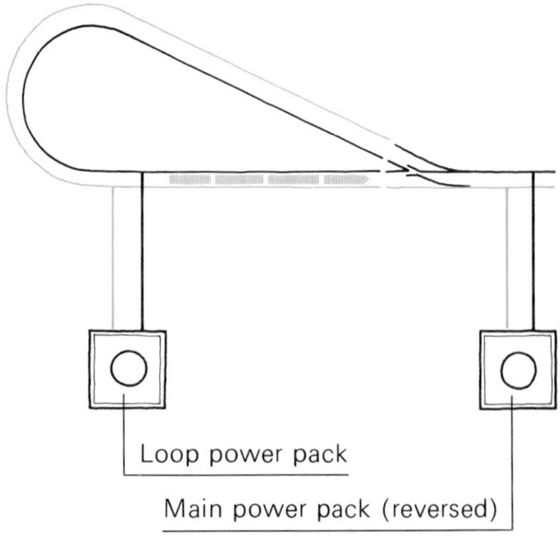


When the train is clear of the junction, throw the turnout and reverse the polarity of the main power pack. The train can now pass back onto the main line.

# Wiring a wye

Although electrically similar to a return loop, a wye is different in plan and operation. It has three turnouts instead of one and, when it is used to turn a train, the train is sent back to the main line travelling in the same direction as before, but facing the other way. A wye can also be used as a junction for diverging routes. As with a return loop, complete rail gaps are necessary to prevent a short circuit. The location of the gaps and the way in which the rails are wired depends on the wye's function.

## Reversing-only wye

This is used in conjunction with a reversing stub to turn a train. The reversing stub is isolated electrically from the main line by rail gaps and is connected to the power pack by a reversing switch. To turn a train that is on the main line, check that the stub is set to the same polarity as the main line, and position the turnouts to take the train onto the reversing stub; drive it onto the stub, clear of the turnout, and stop it (stage 1). Change the polarity of the stub using the reversing switch and throw the turnouts; the train can now be driven back onto the main line, facing in the opposite direction (stage 2). To make the train go back the way it came, set both turnouts for the main line and change the polarity of the rails.

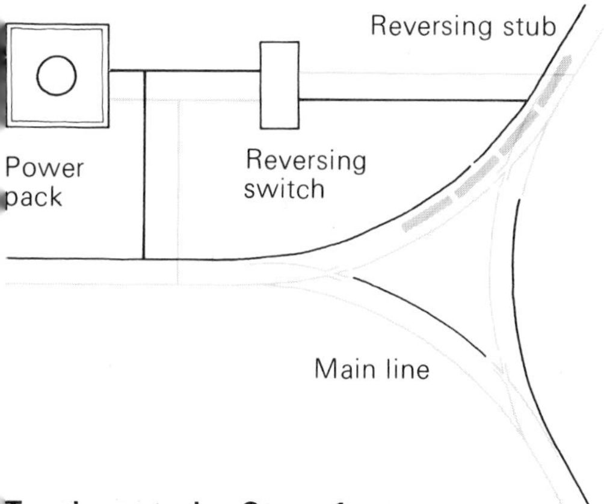


**Turning a train: Stage 1**

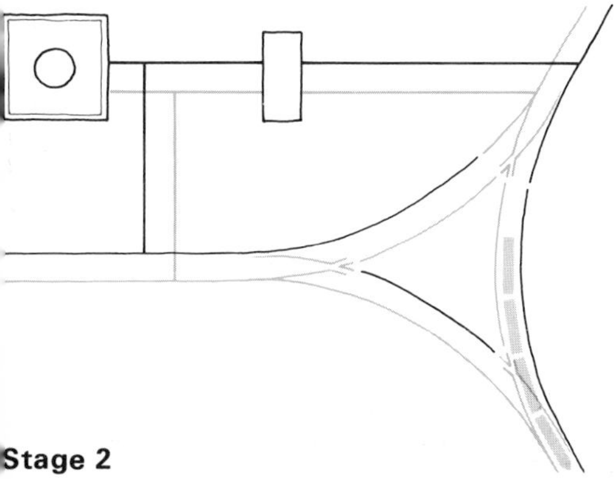

**Stage 2**

## Wye junction

It is best to wire a wye which serves as a junction between diverging routes in a different way from the reversing wye, so that two of the routes through the wye can be worked without changing the polarity. Choose the least-used route and make this side into a block by cutting gaps in the rails at both ends. This wye block should be long enough to hold a complete train. Wire it to a power pack through a reversing switch.

For a train to pass through the wye on the other two sides, it is only necessary to set the turnouts because the polarity on both lines is the same. For a train to pass through the wye block, position the turnouts and set the polarity of the wye block so that it is the same as the line on which the train is running; drive the whole train onto the block and stop it (stage 1). Reverse both the power pack and the reversing switch (this changes the polarity on the main line but keeps it the same on the wye block) and drive the train onto the main line (stage 2).

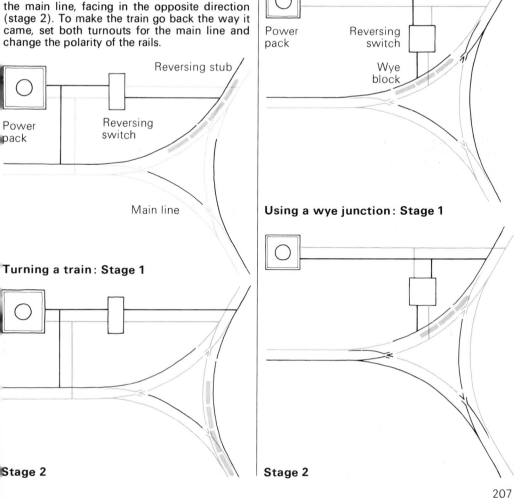

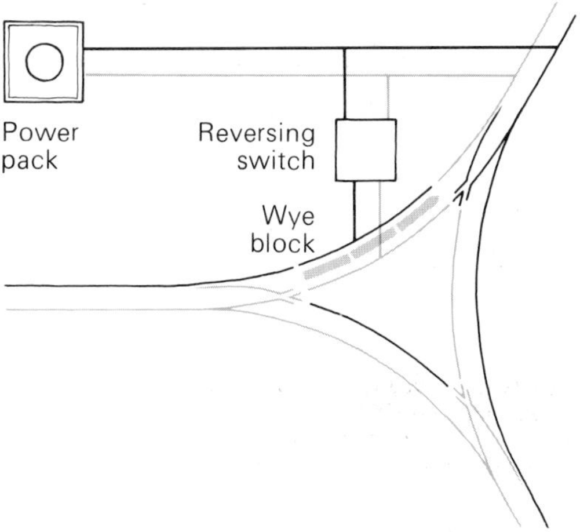


**Using a wye junction: Stage 1**

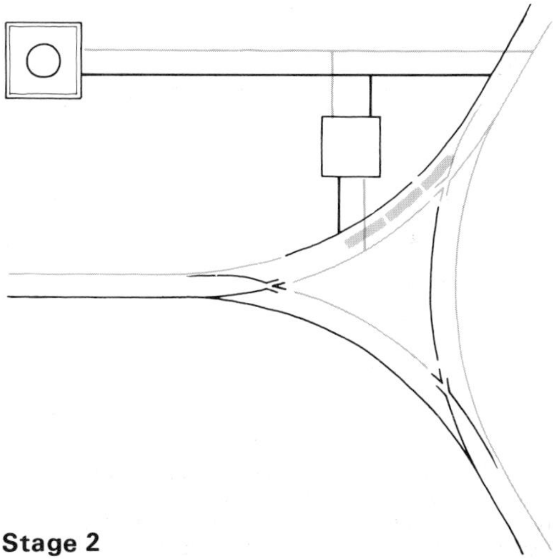

**Stage 2**

# Wiring a turnout

Like loops and wyes, a turnout must incorporate rail gaps to avoid a short circuit. The simplest way of making the rail gaps is to use a frog (the point where the closure rails join) of non-conducting material, and bridge the gaps with wire connections. A disadvantage of this system is that the locomotive may stall as it crosses the frog.

Another method of wiring a turnout is to use a live frog and make gaps in the rails beyond it. A live frog prevents the locomotive from stalling while crossing the turnout. Wire the closure rails and the frog together so that they are always of the same polarity, and use separate sprung contacts or a switch linked mechanically to the turnout to pick up power from the main live rails (power can be picked up from the rails directly by one of the closure rails but this can cause sparking and poor contact). An advantage of the live frog system is that a locomotive on the track against which the turnout is set would stall before it was derailed because it would be on rails of the same polarity. In our diagram, if the two right-hand tracks are sidings and the feed is from the left, there need be no rail gaps at the frog.

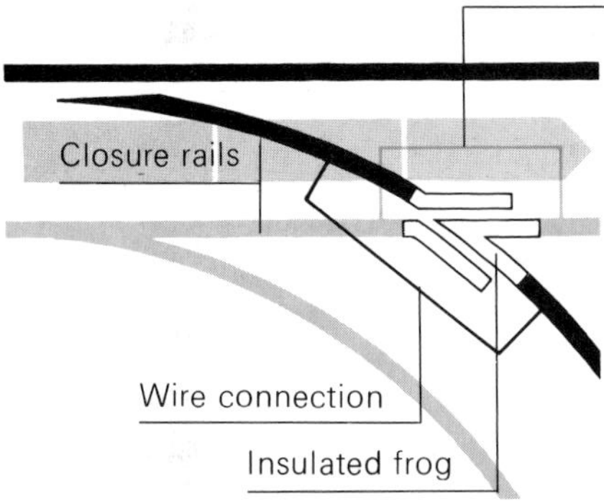


**Insulated-frog turnout**

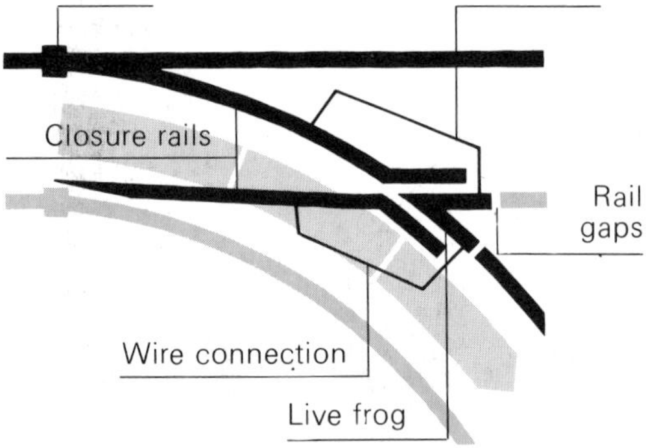


**Live-frog turnout**

## Moving a turnout

A turnout can be moved by a hand-operated lever or by an electric turnout machine. The turnout machine is a 16-volt motor which stands next to the turnout and is controlled by a pair of studs or push buttons which are usually placed on the control panel diagram on the appropriate route. Mount the studs or buttons in pairs, one on each of the diverging lines, as shown in the turnout-machine wiring diagram on the opposite page.

Most makes of turnout machine have three terminals: a common return and one for each direction of movement. Connect the return wires to the common return and the common return to the 16-volt AC return terminal on one of the power packs (a capacitor-discharge unit wired to the common return will help move the turnouts more positively and reduce wear on the motors); wire the other terminals to the appropriate stud or button. Connect the power pack's 16-volt AC feed to an electric pencil if you are using studs, or the input on the buttons. The pencil reduces the wiring on the control panel. To complete the circuit and move a turnout, just touch the stud with the pencil. Setting up a route using studs is easier if you make a groove in the control panel along the lines of the track and position the studs in the groove: the groove guides the pencil from one stud to the next. (If a turnout is already set correctly, nothing will happen when the stud is touched.)

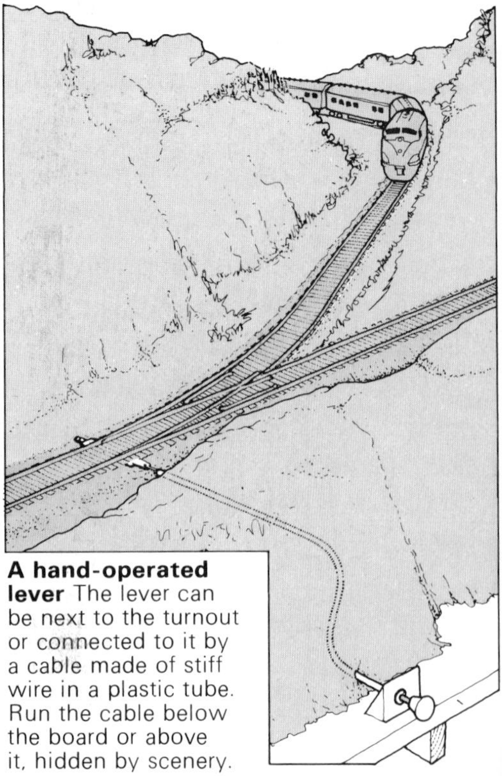

**A hand-operated lever** The lever can be next to the turnout or connected to it by a cable made of stiff wire in a plastic tube. Run the cable below the board or above it, hidden by scenery.

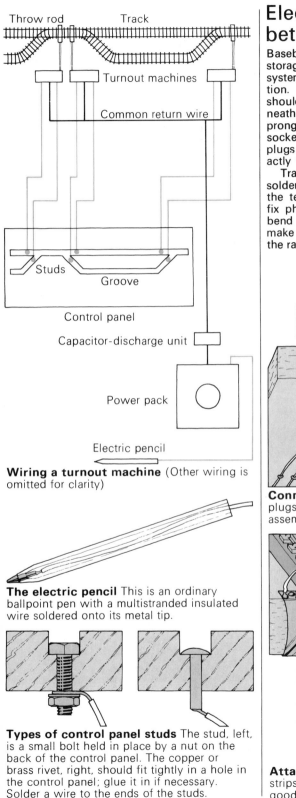

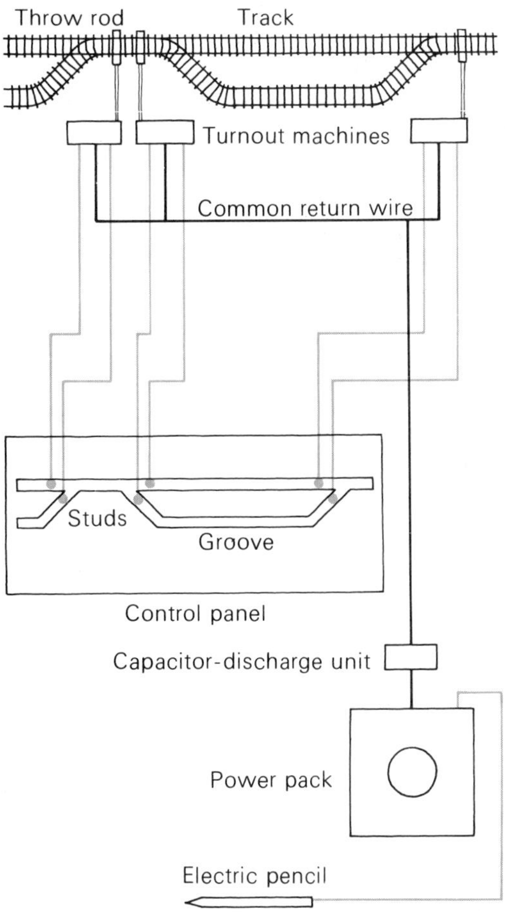


**Wiring a turnout machine** (Other wiring is omitted for clarity)

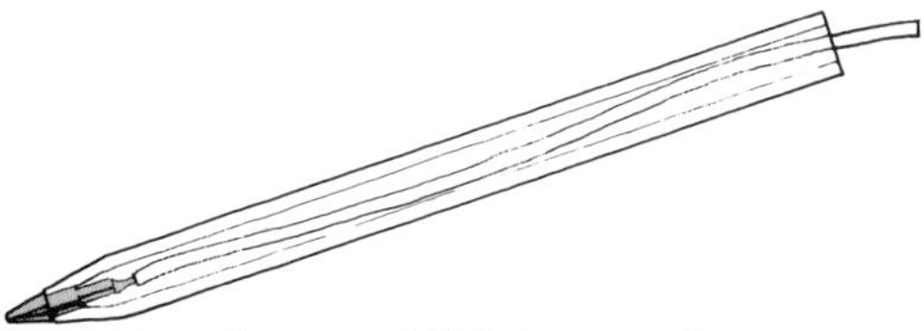

**The electric pencil** This is an ordinary ballpoint pen with a multistranded insulated wire soldered onto its metal tip.

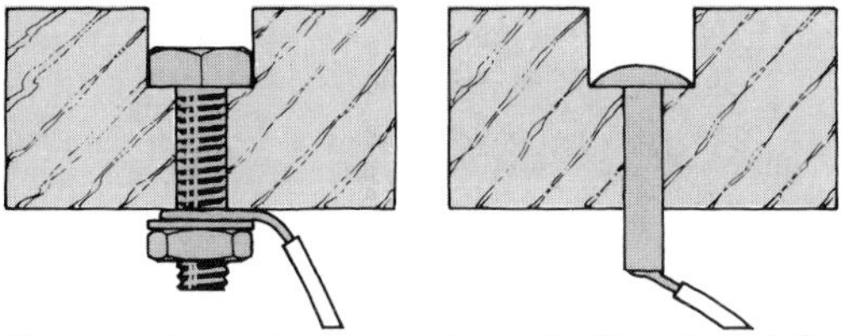

**Types of control panel studs** The stud, left, is a small bolt held in place by a nut on the back of the control panel. The copper or brass rivet, right, should fit tightly in a hole in the control panel; glue it in if necessary. Solder a wire to the ends of the studs.

# Electrical connections between baseboards

Baseboards which separate into sections for storage or transportation need an organized system of electrical connections at each junction. All the wires from the control panel should go to a numbered terminal strip underneath the panel and then to one or more multiprong plugs. Each plug should match up with a socket under one baseboard. Use multiprong plugs to connect one board to another in exactly the same way.

Track can also be joined via the plugs: simply solder the wires to the track, lead the wires to the terminal, then to the plug. You may also fix phosphor-bronze strips to each board and bend them over the edge so that the strips make contact when the boards are joined. Wire the rails to the strips to complete the circuit.

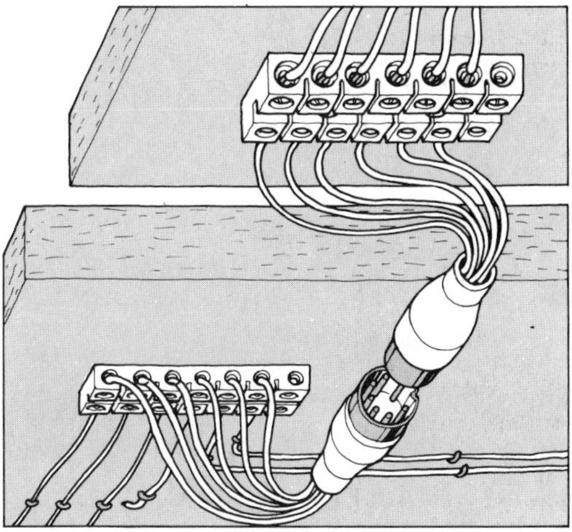

**Connecting baseboards** Use multiprong plugs between the baseboards to make assembly easier.

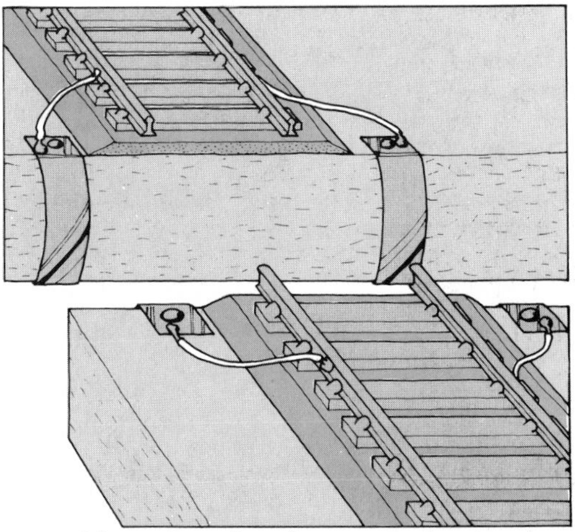

**Attaching phosphor-bronze strips** Let the strips project in a slight curve to guarantee good electrical contact with the next board.

# Planning the landscape

Although smooth curves and gradients and clearance of rolling stock must take precedence on a model layout, scenery and equipment should be developed together so that features such as roads, bridges, tunnels and rivers can be incorporated in the baseboard at an early stage. Avoid extreme changes in the character of the landscape so that the train does not pass unrealistically from lush farmland into desert scenery in a few moments.

The transition between town and country should be convincing. If you wish to incorporate both a large fiddle yard and open country in the layout you must create illusions. You could depict the suburbs of a large town or some outlying industrial center and model the countryside a few scale miles down the track. An alternative is to use the terrain to disguise the proximity of different sites. For example, place a range of hills in the center of an oval track so that one side can be modeled as a rural setting, the other as a townscape. Let the trains disappear into a tunnel before reappearing in another location, and heighten the illusion further by making the track emerge at a different level or at an unexpected angle.

Designing the track to run at different levels is a way of creating interesting scenic features as well as incorporating more track on a small site. Track can pass over and under roads and across streams, rivers and canals. One train can run along a hillside while another passes through it in a tunnel.

Consider the rise and fall of the landscape carefully. It is usually best to concentrate higher ground toward the back of the layout or, in the case of an island layout, roughly down the center. Very high terrain in the foreground not only obscures any track behind, but may also make it difficult to retrieve a derailed train. Rules of this kind can be broken for effect by, for instance, bringing part of a hill out to the front of the layout as a cliff face and passing a tunnel through it. A holding track can be situated out-of-sight behind the hill. High ground can also be used at the end or corner of a layout to disguise an obvious return loop or to soften the effect of a square corner.

Hills and mountains are usually modeled using the technique for making hollow-shell scenery (see page 161). If you wish to incorporate a rocky outcrop, build a wooden platform at the required height to support the rocks and secure them with Spackle. Attach chicken wire or cardboard strips to the roadbed and framework and run it up to the edge of the rocks. Before adding any Spackle, do test runs to make sure that there is clearance for the trains and protect the track with masking tape. Simple contours of Spackle or modeling clay and hills of polyurethane or polystyrene foam can also be included in a railroad layout.

Directions for modeling specific types of landscape, such as pastureland and desert, are in the dioramas and landscapes chapter.

## Cuts and retaining walls

Real railroad tracks do not follow the contours of the land. In order to keep a constant gradient they cut through scenery, forming banks on one or both sides of the track. Build banks out of plywood or cardboard and form a drainage ditch beside the track. A rock cut can have steep sides but an earth cut should slope at no more than 40°, unless you support it with a retaining wall. Model the earth or rock texture in Spackle or plaster spread on top. Small gullies can be made by running water carefully down the banks before the layer of Spackle or plaster sets.

Shape brick or concrete retaining walls in plywood or thick cardboard. Paint the surface or cover it with brick paper or embossed plastic sheet. For a stone retaining wall, half-bury real stones in Spackle or plaster. Two styles of wooden retaining wall are illustrated below.

**Plank wall** Glue thin planks of balsa or softwood together then add vertical posts. Set wall into bank.

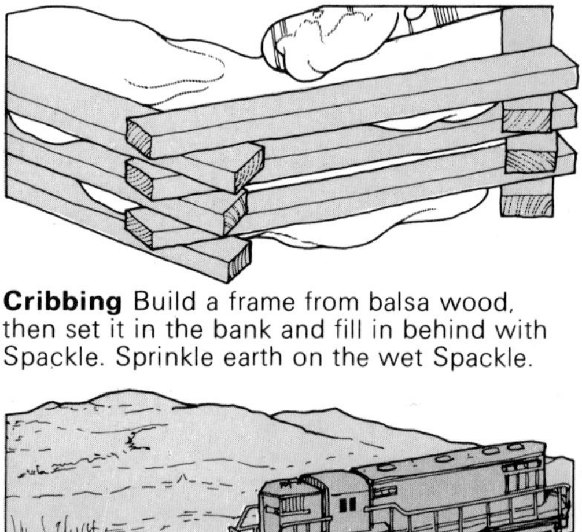

**Cribbing** Build a frame from balsa wood, then set it in the bank and fill in behind with Spackle. Sprinkle earth on the wet Spackle.

**Planning track on a mountain** To save space, raise one track above the other and build a retaining wall holding up an earth bank or a steep rock cut.

Every detail in this scene contributes to the realism. Note especially the weathering on the tunnel portal and the placement of the trees on the mountainside.

One way of separating the main line from a marshalling yard in a small area is to build the tracks on different levels.

# Tunnels

The hill through which a tunnel passes must appear large or difficult to negotiate so that the tunnel looks as though it was the only solution to the engineers who built the railroad. It is important to provide access to the tunnel so that you can rescue a derailed train. Leave the back of the hill open or cut out a section of baseboard from below. Another solution is to design the hillside in such a way that the train passes through several short tunnels behind the hill. Do not place turnouts or crossings in a tunnel and avoid joins in the track.

Tunnels always add a dramatic element to a scene. Here three tunnels emerge at different levels. The train in the foreground is about to pass under a bridge.

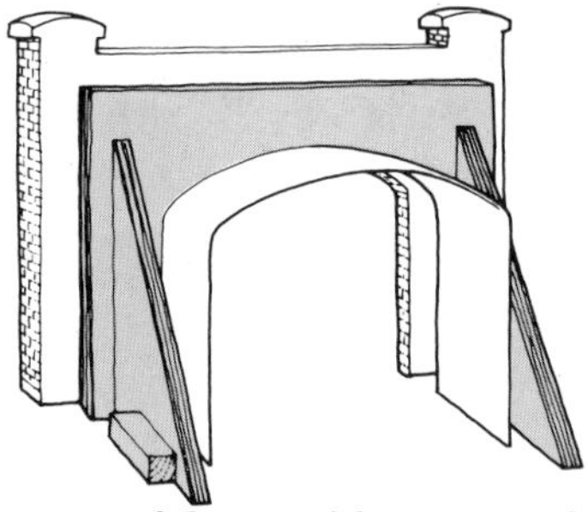

**Making a portal for a tabletop baseboard** Cut out a plywood shape to match the tunnel entrance but make the opening slightly larger. Glue triangular supports to the back. Glue the structure to the baseboard, supporting it with small blocks. Attach black paper to the edge of the opening. Glue the portal to the structure.

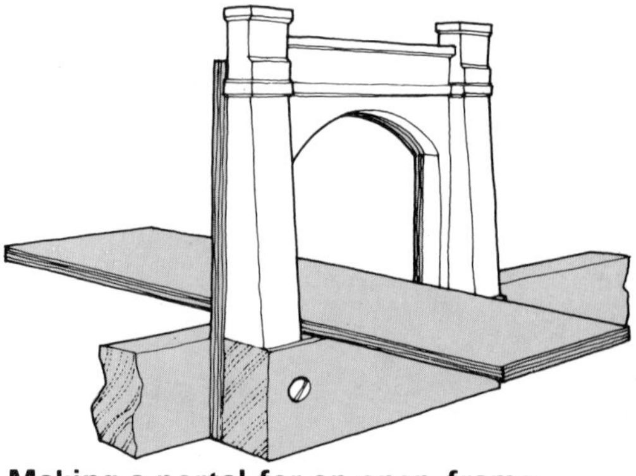

**Making a portal for an open-frame baseboard** Cut out a plywood shape, as left, but make the sides longer and screw them onto the frame. Screw a wooden strip under the roadbed to support the portal.

## Bridges

Railroad bridges passing over rivers and roads add interest to a scene. Although you will almost certainly have more bridges in your layout than in a real landscape, it will not be noticeable as long as you use the correct type each time. Always model the groundcover right up to the edge of the bridge so that the junction looks natural.

Plastic, cardboard or wood can all be used to model bridges. Companies such as Plastruct produce miniature steel beams and other bridge components in plastic. You can use the beams to make a long-span girder bridge: support them at intervals with columns.

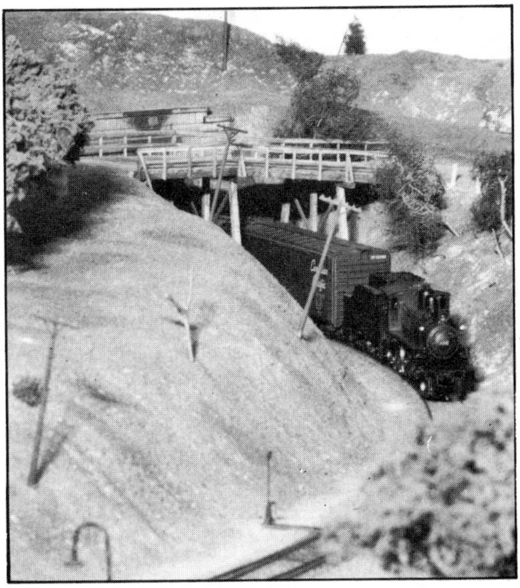

The simple wooden trestle bridge, right, is handmade. For more complex structures such as the metal girder bridge, below, you may wish to use a kit.

# Bridge styles

**Culvert** Use a metal or plastic tube to represent a culvert.

Alternatively, shore up the bank with balsa wood strips.

**Low bridge** Model wood or steel beams to carry the track over a stream and rest the beams on wood or concrete set into the bank.

**Through girder bridge** Model the lattice of steel girders from cardboard or plastic.

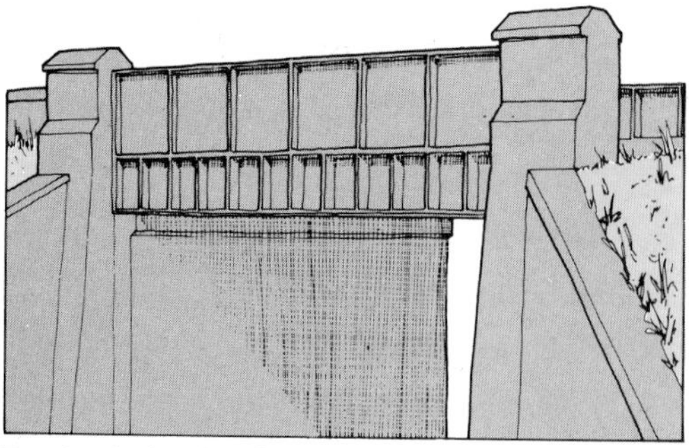

**Deck girder bridge** If the bottom can't be seen, make this bridge out of a solid piece of wood. Cover the outside with plastic and paint it to look like metal. Model the concrete or brick abutments in cardboard or wood, covered with the appropriate paper.

**Brick bridge** Cut the sides from thick cardboard or thin plywood. Bend and glue thin cardboard underneath. Cover the bridge with brick paper or embossed plastic sheet.

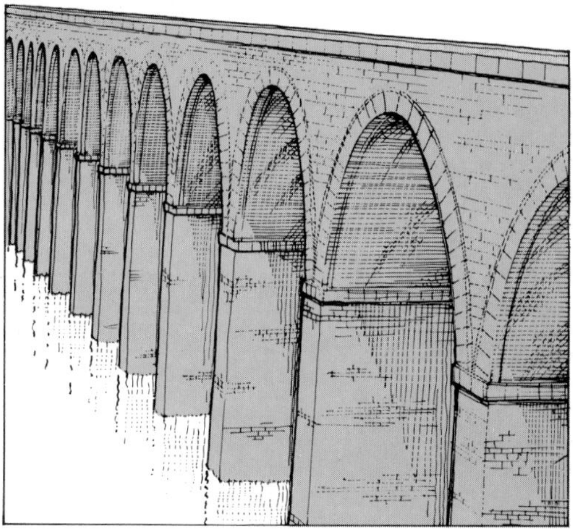

**Viaduct** Build a viaduct to cross a valley in the same way as a brick bridge. Roads, canals or more track can pass underneath.

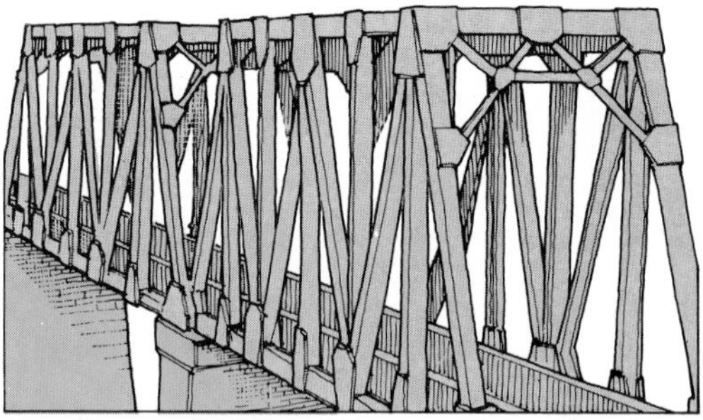

**Steel truss bridge** Although it is difficult to model this type of bridge to scale unless it is for a very large layout, it will look convincing with only one or two spans. Build it from scratch in plastic or assemble Plastruct components.

**Trestle bridge** Although this type of bridge looks complicated, it is easy to construct in balsa wood. Use this structure for long spans.

## Making the background

If a layout is positioned against a wall a painted backdrop will enhance the illusion of reality. Its landscape should be in character with the layout and it should recede smoothly into the distance. Objects not only appear smaller when they are far away, but less distinct, and the colors are softer, almost gray. A photograph can make a good background for a railroad, but choose one where the colors are not too bright and the foreground objects correspond in size to those on the layout.

Paint the landscape on paper or cardboard, then cut it out and paste it on the wall, hiding any joins with foreground detail. Use oil or watercolor washes and make bold strokes with a wide brush, suggesting shapes only, not small detail. The silhouette of a group of trees, for instance, will give the right effect when viewed from a distance and the washes will blend together to form subtle shades. Paint from the background forward, making the furthest colors pale and cool and the nearer ones darker. If you want a distinct edge between two colors, let the first color dry out a little before applying the next. For a soft, blended edge, apply the second color over a still-wet coat. Stipple on the paint to suggest the texture of leaves.

Consider using a cool gray color instead of a bright blue for the sky; it will be less obtrusive and merge with the background objects to unify the scene. If you want to paint a blue sky, make it darker at the top, gradually becoming lighter near the horizon. Use an airbrush and pale gray paint to suggest clouds and merge them with the lower section of sky. Avoid dramatic cloud scenes as they tend to distract the eye. The sky of a photographic background may not be high enough; cut it off along the horizon and paint a new one.

The transition between the three-dimensional detail and the images on the wall must be convincing. Avoid a noticeable line where the scenery meets the wall or flats by making the land dip just before the backdrop, or plant trees to disguise the junction. Trees and shrubs can be made progressively smaller toward the skyline to add to the illusion of depth. Make a river or road disappear behind a hill or building – don't let it run straight into the wall. Low-relief buildings are another effective way of bridging the gap between the foreground and backdrop, particularly in a cityscape. Unlike other types of scenery, they can be placed right up against the backdrop.

**Using flats** These are pieces of stiff cardboard with scenery painted on them. Use one or more flats to help make the transition between the three-dimensional landscape and the painted backdrop on the wall.

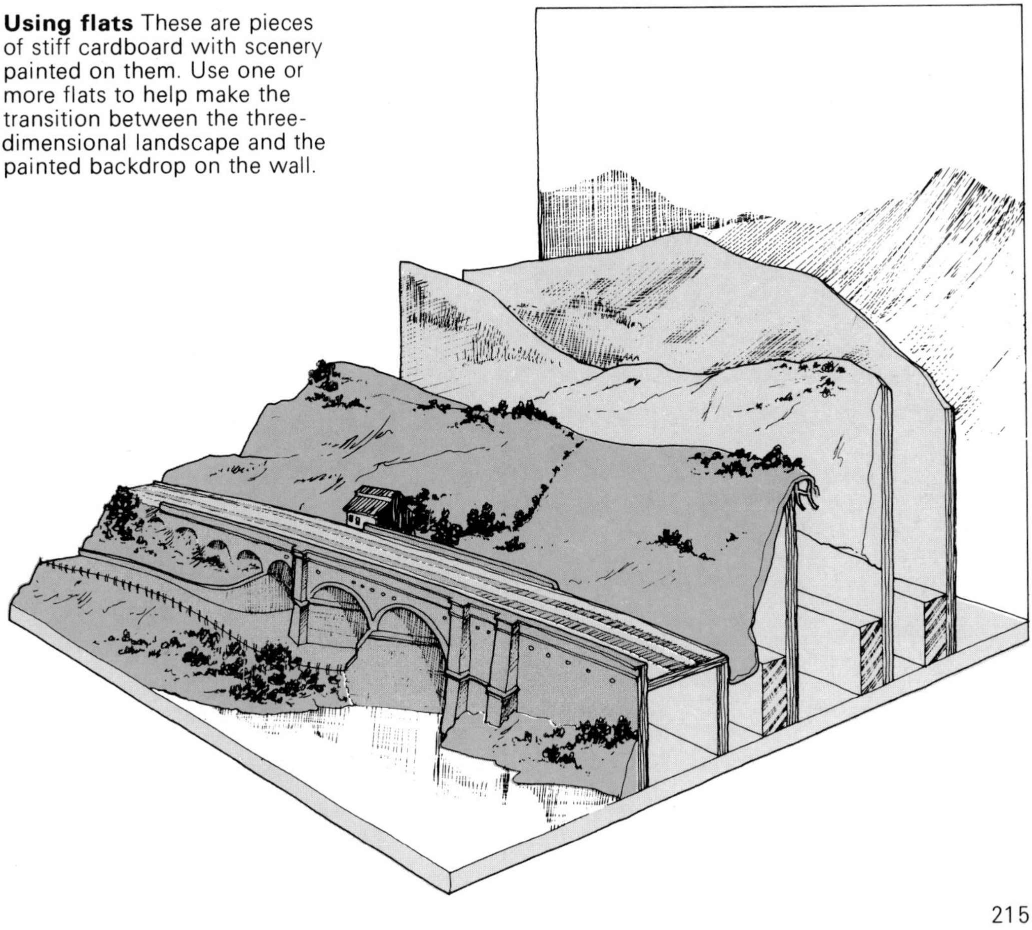

# Buildings

Kit or scratch-built structures are essential to add character to a railroad layout. Any type is possible, from stations and factories to barns and farmhouses, provided that it looks natural in the environment. Consider the state of the building, whether it is old and derelict or new, and weather it accordingly. You can even show a building under construction. If your layout stands against a wall you may want to model some of the buildings in low relief. In this case, only the front face and part of the side walls are constructed.

Kit buildings are easy to construct and available in many different styles. To improve a kit, add fine detail and textures, or replace overscale detail with a scratch-built item. Models can be altered to suit your layout by incorporating elements from other kits, as long as the styles are compatible. Kit windows and doors can also be used in a homemade structure. Plastic buildings need to be painted and weathered.

The techniques described on the following pages can also be used to make buildings for open-base or boxed dioramas.

Use a barn and silo to establish a rural scene. Paint the wood to look weathered.

For a half-constructed frame building, assemble strips of balsa wood in the same way as for a real one.

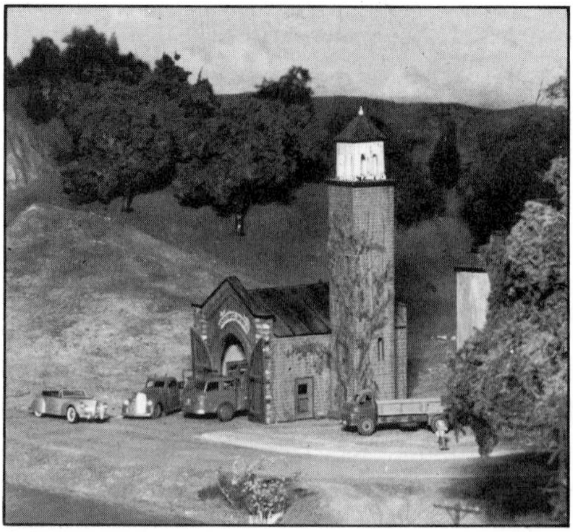

Add interest to your buildings by surrounding them with realistic detail, such as the trucks and cars around this firestation.

No yard is complete without an enginehouse. This one, a modified HO-kit roundhouse, is for trains of the Chesapeake and Ohio Railroad.

This building is modeled on a Canadian Pacific Railroad station in Ontario. Note the passengers waiting on the platform with their luggage.

# Building from scratch

The advantage of making a model from scratch is that you can build it to any scale and any design. Follow a store-bought plan or make your own on graph paper, after taking measurements of the original building or one similar to that you wish to model.

The simplest way to construct a building is to make a cardboard or plastic box using the method described below. A more complex building with extensions or sheds can be made by adding more boxes to the main structure.

Once you have made the box, judge the shape and proportion of the roof by eye. The easiest method is to fold a piece of cardboard in half, hold it on the model and trim it to size. Add the surface texture to the walls and roof before assembling the building. On pages 220 to 225 you will find techniques for modeling different textures, from bricks to corrugated iron.

Laminate strips of cardboard to form a chimney stack, or make one out of balsa wood. Add the surface texture, then cap the chimney with fireclay cement. Stick a chimney pot made from plastic or metal tube into the cement.

Make pipes from pieces of wire or heat-stretched sprue (see page 54). For a gutter, scratch a "V"-shaped notch along the edge of a piece of thick plastic and round off the bottom with a file and wet-and-dry paper. Cut the strip of gutter off the plastic, leaving extra on one side to glue it onto the roof.

The ruined buildings on pages 190 to 191, although intended for use on smaller dioramas, can be used equally well on a railroad layout.

For the best result, scratch-build industrial structures such as this O-scale grain elevator to suit your particular layout. Hand-paint miniature posters or cut out magazine advertisements.

## Making a building

**1** Cut out each wall then cut out the window and door openings. Add surface texture. Install windows and doors.

**2** Join the walls with rubber-based contact cement, then run white glue down the inside of each corner. Cut out a base and glue it in position.

**3** To brace the building, glue a piece of cardboard across the top edges of the walls or a vertical piece between the the walls. Attach a roof.

# Making roofs

This group of buildings shows an interesting combination of different roofing materials.

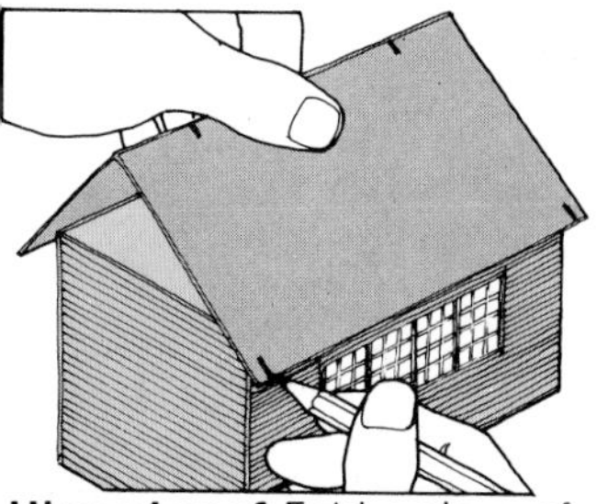

**Hipped roof** Fold a piece of cardboard in half. Hold it on the roof and mark the overhang and the tip of the roof at each end.

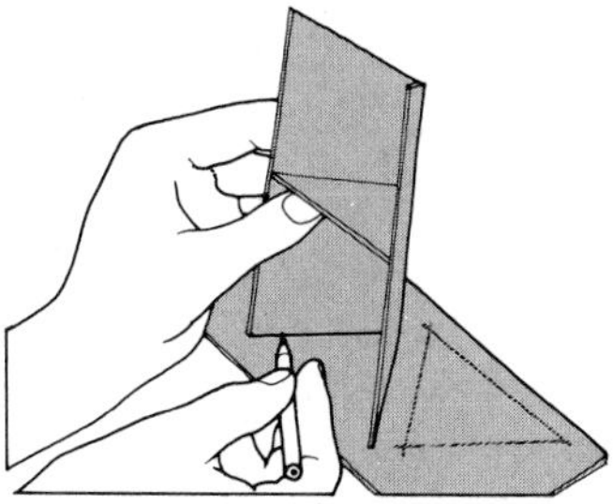

Glue a triangular piece of cardboard inside the roof as a brace. Lay the roof on a piece of cardboard and mark the end shapes.

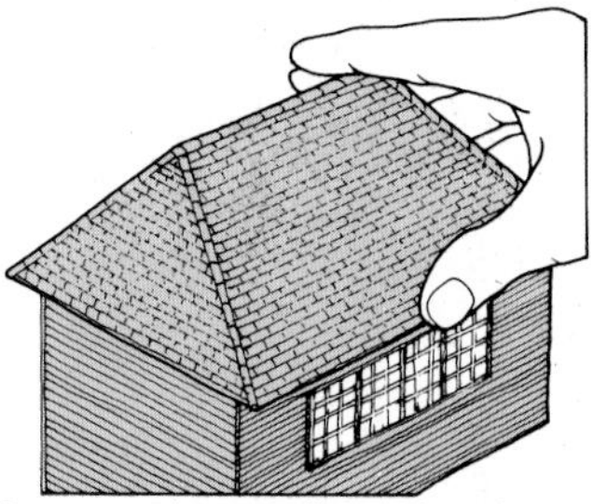

Cut out the cardboard ends and glue them onto the roof. Glue the hipped roof onto the building.

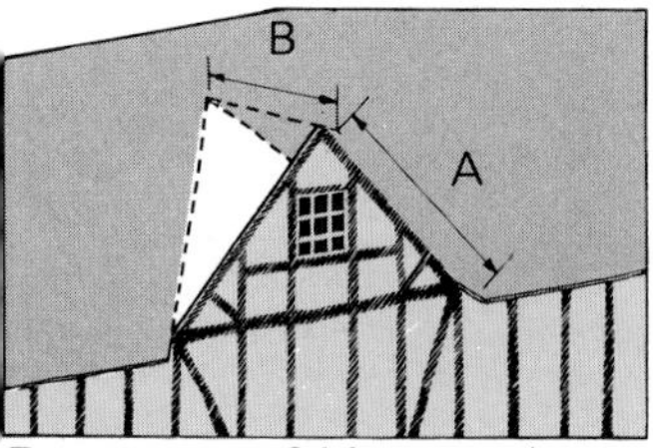


**Dormer roof** Measure the distances A and B in our diagram.

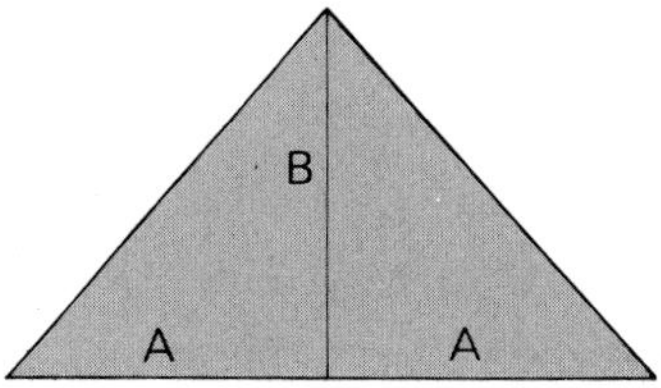


Draw a triangle on cardboard with a base twice the distance A and a height B. Cut it out.

Fold it in half and glue it onto the roof. Trim if necessary.

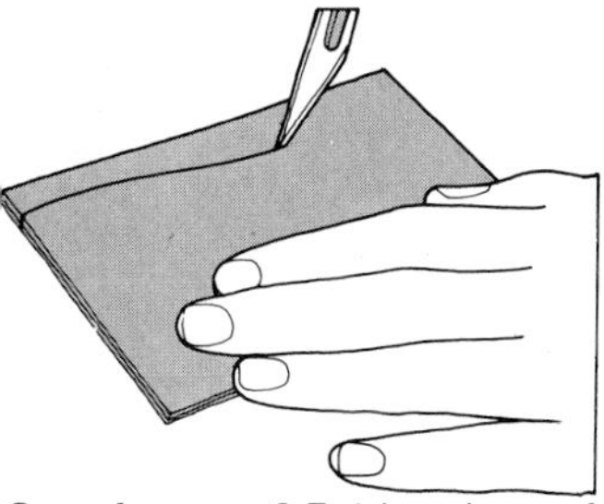

**Sagging roof** Fold a piece of cardboard in half and trim it to size. Cut a shallow curve along the ridge, leaving the roof in two sections.

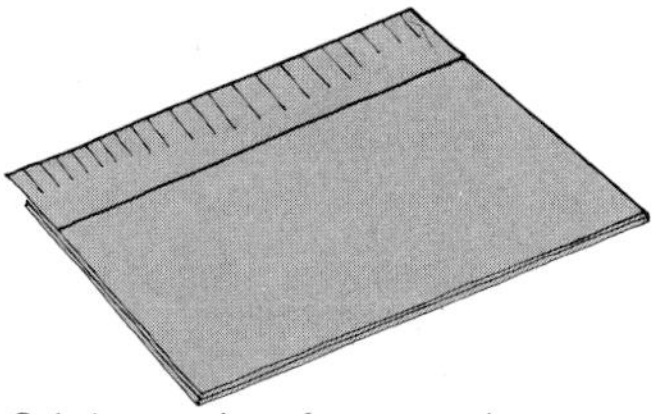

Stick a strip of paper along the curve of one section, letting it overlap the edge. Cut the projecting paper into tabs.

Apply glue to the tabs and fold them over onto the other half of the roof to rejoin the two sections.

# Wall surfaces

The most convenient way of imitating a brick or stone surface – particularly if you are working in a very small scale – is to cover the wall with printed paper or embossed plastic sheet. More realistic walls, however, are produced by hand using thin cardboard for bricks or wooden siding, or very thin layers of Spackle or fireclay cement for stucco. The instructions in this section use unlaminated cardboard as a base for the texture.

## Applying brick paper

**1** Lay the paper face up on coarse sand-paper; cover it with thin foam rubber. Run a roller over the layers to add texture.

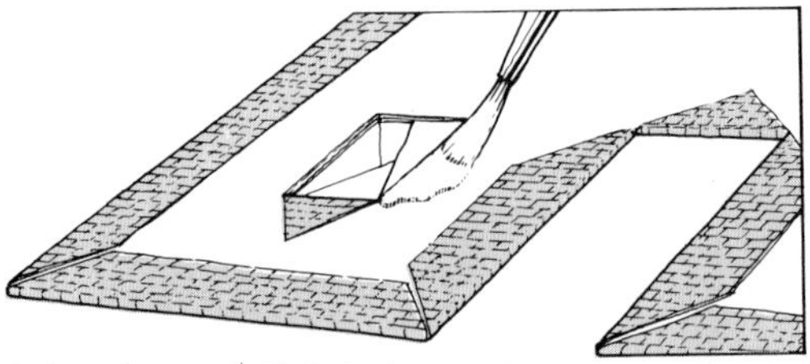

**2** Cut a panel slightly larger than the wall. Glue it to the wall, making sure that the brick courses align with those on the adjacent walls. Cut off the corners of the paper and cut diagonals across the windows and doors. Fold back the paper and glue it down.

**3** After assembling the walls, add a brick lintel over each of the windows.

## Applying plastic sheet

**1** If the texture is too round, define it by rubbing it lightly with very fine wet-and-dry paper.

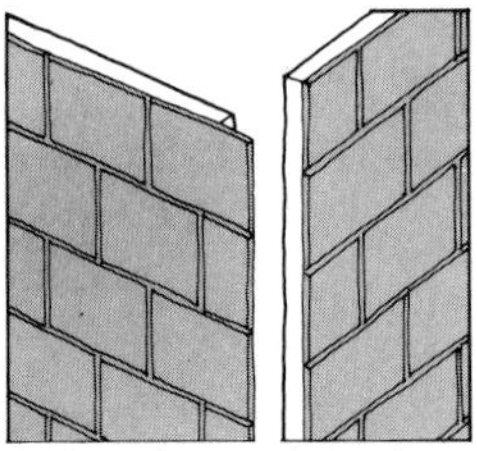

**2** Cut out a piece for each wall, leaving one side too long; glue them onto the walls. Assemble walls; trim.

**3** File stone shapes into each of the window openings.

**4** For a realistic texture, "grout" the stones with thin Spackle. Paint and weather the surface.

## Brick walls

The most effective way of reproducing the texture of a brick wall is to lay each brick individually. If possible, use computer punchings, known as "chads," or cut the bricks out of cardboard. The size of the bricks depends on the scale; for an HO/OO railroad, for example, cut out bricks $\frac{1}{8}$ by slightly less than $\frac{1}{16}$ inch (3×1 mm) in size. To keep the brick courses even, draw guidelines or glue graph paper onto a thin cardboard wall. Spread enough white glue on the wall to lay about 3 square inches (75 mm) of bricks at a time. Position each brick with the point of a knife.

Paint the wall with a wash of mahogany wood stain to simulate red bricks, or shellac for yellow bricks. Apply extra washes of black or brown for deeper colors. Run stains down the walls and pick out a few bricks, if you wish.

Add brick lintels or decorative stonework on top of the finished wall. The extra thickness of cardboard will not show.

## Stone walls

Make a press from casting resin to shape the texture in fireclay cement. This process produces a very realistic finish and you can adapt it to make other surfaces such as cobbles.

Cut out a thin cardboard wall and coat it with white glue. Spread a thin layer of fireclay cement onto the wall and sprinkle it with talcum powder; roll it flat with a can. Sprinkle more talcum powder over the wall, then rock the press into the cement, overlapping the edges of each impression. Flatten the texture slightly with your fingers and trim off any excess cement.

Before the cement dries, paint the wall with a thin wash of black oil paint then carefully dab on brown spirit-base wood stain. Bake the wall in a warm oven for about 5 minutes.

The wall will be distorted when it comes out of the oven. Flatten it; realistic cracks will form across the surface. Add any windows and doors, then back it with thicker cardboard.

Although made out of cardboard and fireclay cement, a model stone building will look convincing if, after attaching it to the baseboard, you build up the groundwork to hide the join.

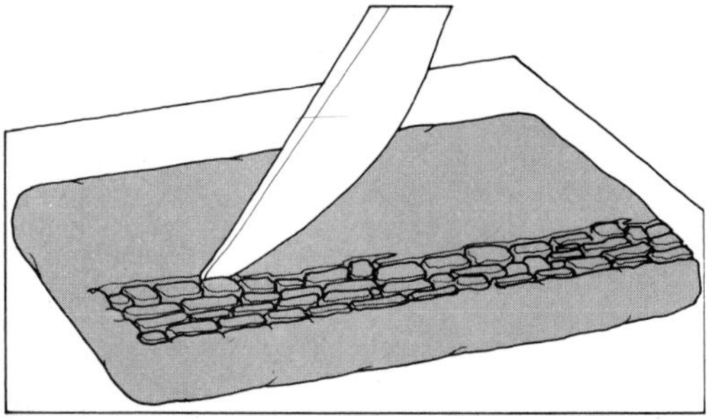

**Making a press** Roll out a slab of modeling clay to measure $4 \times 6 \times \frac{1}{2}$ inch ($100 \times 150 \times 12$ mm). Work the stone texture into the clay with a modeling tool.

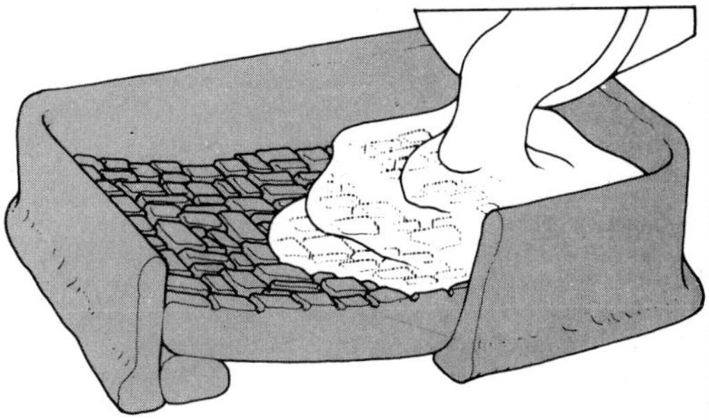

Support each end of the slab with rolls of clay and build a wall around it. Slowly pour in some casting resin. Let it set. Remove the modeling clay; wash press in hot soapy water.

## Stucco walls

To model stucco, brush water over a thin cardboard wall, and apply an even layer of white glue. Sprinkle the wall liberally with powdered Spackle. Tap off the excess powder and lay the wall face down on another piece of cardboard; rub the back to make a smooth surface. Turn the wall over and let the glue set.

Color stucco walls with spirit-base wood stains, shellac or paint. When the paint is dry, back the wall with a piece of thick cardboard, gluing windows and doors in between.

A concrete wall is made following the same method, but use powdered building cement and do not rub the back of the wall.

Weather stucco walls using different shades of paint. A uniform color looks unnatural.

## Wooden walls

Reproduce tongue-and-groove siding by scribing parallel lines in the cardboard wall with a pointed tool. For clapboard siding, glue on strips of very thin cardboard or balsa wood as shown below. Color the walls with oil paint washes or wood stain. The color collects realistically in the grooves.

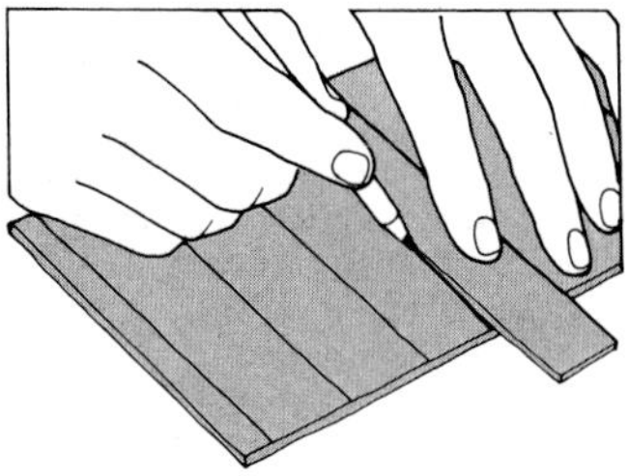

**Making a clapboard wall**
Mark wall studs on a cardboard wall. Cut out $\frac{1}{8}$-inch (3-mm) cardboard strips.

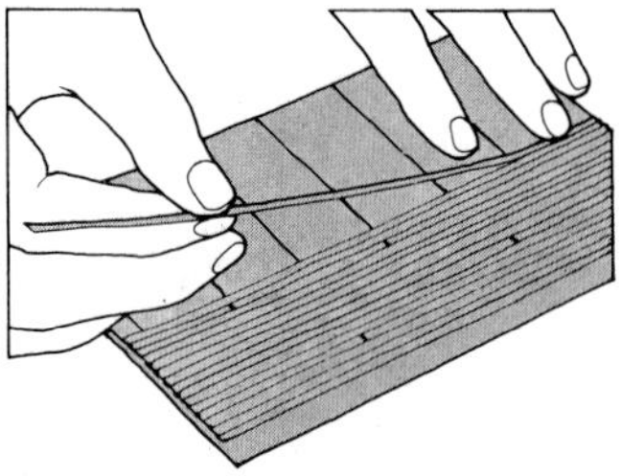

Glue them onto the wall, overlapping the previous strip each time. Lay some of the strips end-to-end with the join at a wall stud.

Fine detail, such as carved wooden posts and railings on a verandah and a white picket fence, adds character to a traditional clapboard house.

# Roof surfaces

You can buy many different textures, from paper printed with tiles or shingles to sheets of corrugated metal or plastic, or you can make your own. With the exception of thatch, it is easier to glue these textures onto the roof before attaching the roof to the walls. Tiles, shingles, corrugated iron and asphalt can be used equally well on walls.

## Tiles and shingles

Textured plastic sheet and paper printed with tiles or shingles can be applied directly to the roof. The paper can be cut into strips and overlapped for a three-dimensional effect, if you wish.

For a more realistic finish, cut individual tiles from very thin cardboard. For an HO/OO scale railroad, cut out $\frac{3}{16}$-inch (4-mm) squares. Mark guidelines on the roof and position the tiles with the point of a knife, overlapping and staggering each row. Color the roof with washes of mahogany wood stain. To bring out the texture, hold the roof almost flat and spray the lower edges of the tiles matt black. For roofing slates, color the cardboard with gray, blue and white washes before cutting the tiles.

Wooden shingles should be made from strips of paper masking tape and applied in the same way as cardboard tiles. Use wood stain to color the roof and to reduce the shine of the tape.

To make these ridge tiles, cut notches along the folded edge of a strip of paper, then cut the strip into individual tiles.

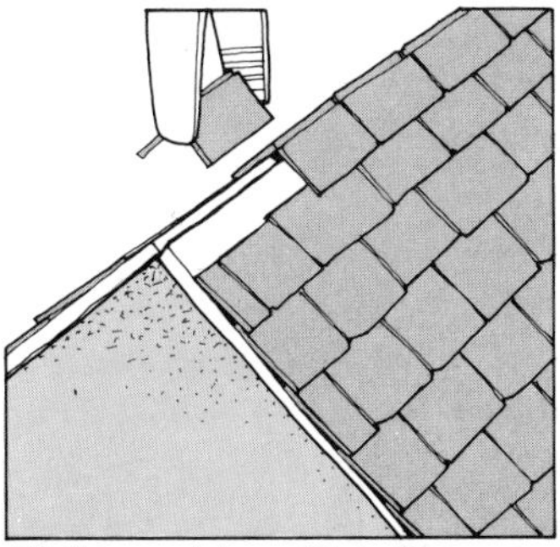

**Making ridge tiles** Cut out a narrow strip of thin cardboard. Score it down the center, then cut it into individual tiles. Fold each tile in half and glue it onto the roof.

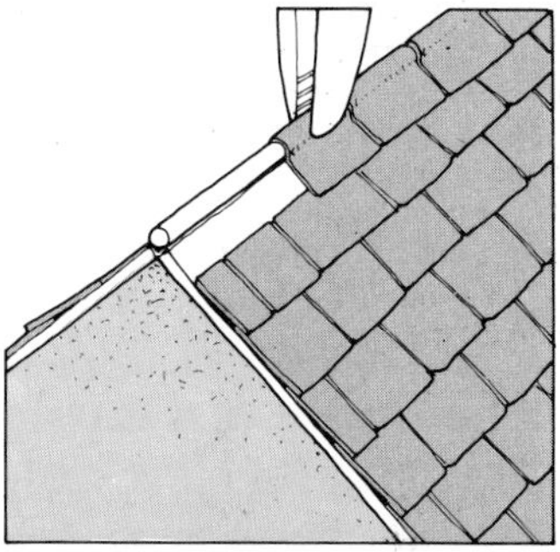

**Making decorative ridge tiles** Glue a thin rod along the top of the roof. Cut out paper tiles and glue them onto the rod. Pinch them so that they follow the rod's shape.

**Laying tile paper** Cut the paper into strips, two tiles deep. Cut between the tiles on the bottom row. If you wish, remove some tiles to simulate an old roof. Overlap the strips.

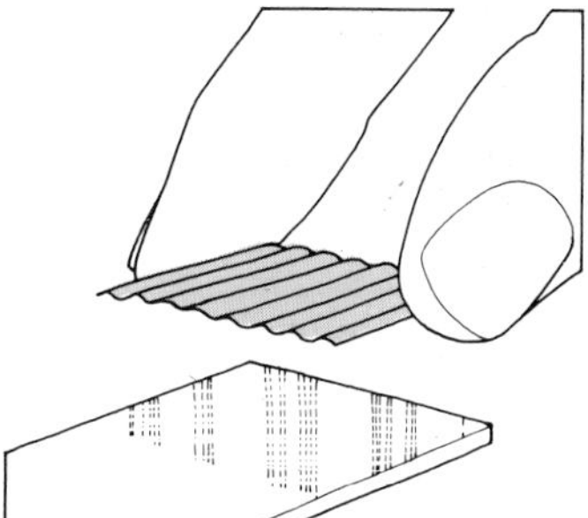

**Making Spanish tiles** Glue corrugated copper onto a piece of plastic for a press. Spread a thin layer of fireclay cement onto the roof as for the stone wall, page 221.

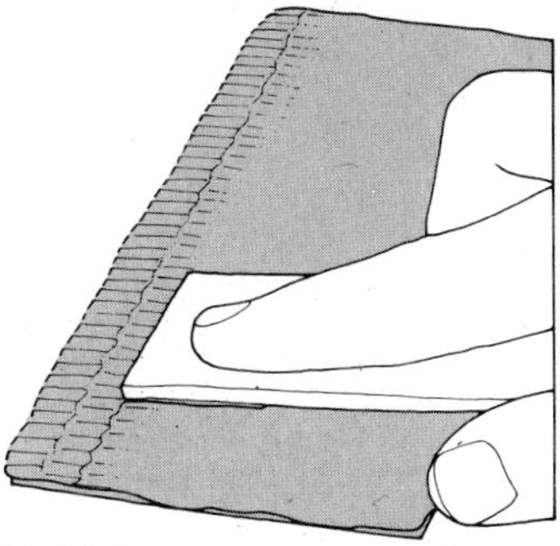

Hold the press at an angle to the roof and mark rows of tiles, working from the top down. Color the roof with mahogany wood stain and bake as for the stone wall.

## Thatched roofs

**Real thatch is made out of straw or reeds but you can reproduce the texture on a model successfully with thick wool. It is easiest to apply the pieces of wool after the cardboard roof has been attached to the building.**

Thatch is a traditional English roofing material for small cottages or farmhouses. Model the thatch right over the edges of the dormer windows.

**Making a thatched roof**
Soak the wool in water and liquid detergent. Cover the roof with white glue. Add the wool; apply more glue and sprinkle with grass powder.

Let the roof dry, then color it with wood stain. While the stain is still wet, sprinkle with powdered Spackle and brush in the direction of the wool. Leave to dry. Trim the ends.

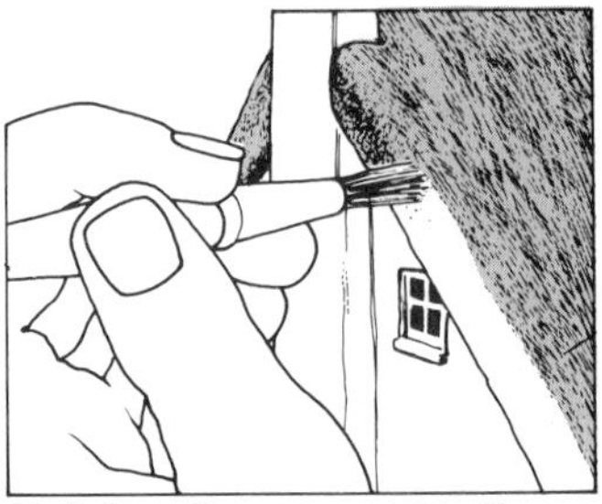

Build up the eaves with fire-clay cement. Stipple texture into the cement with a brush. Paint the thatch darker under the eaves.

## Corrugated iron roofs

**Use corrugated plastic or metal sheet for this type of roof, or make your own by shaping a strip of aluminum foil. Place the strip between two jar tops with ribbed sides and rotate them. Cut the strip into smaller panels. For a badly rusted surface, put the foil on a piece of coarse sandpaper and rub it lightly with your finger before corrugating it.**

**Paint the finished roof black or gray and streak on washes of rust-colored enamel paint.**

Model corrugated iron roofs on derelict buildings and sheds such as the one above.

## Asphalt and lead roofs

An asphalt roof is made from strips of masking tape or fine emery paper attached to the cardboard structure in vertical panels. Use thin cardboard or plastic strips to simulate the wooden strips that hold down the asphalt layer on a real roof. Color the masking tape with wood stain. If you wish the roof to look weathered, sprinkle on some talcum powder and lightly brush it off. Make a lead roof in a similar way.

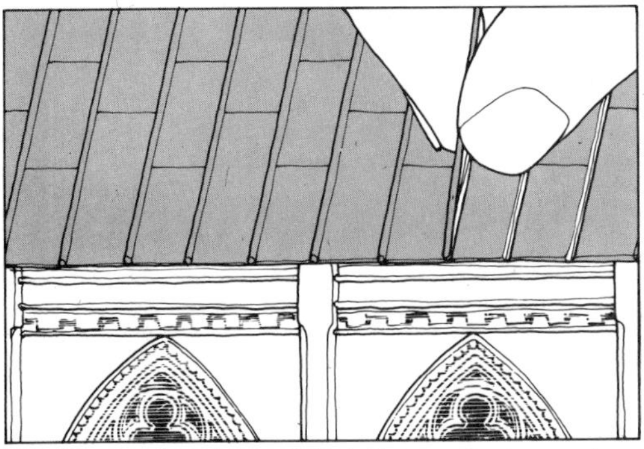

**Making a lead roof** Cut the vertical panels into pieces and lap them one over the other on the roof. Glue a thin plastic rod or a piece of heavy thread in between. Paint the roof with gray and green oil paint washes.

Asphalt is a roof covering often found on railroad buildings. Use it on structures such as the coal tower above and the water tower below.

# Windows

All model windows are made up of a cardboard frame with clear plastic for glass. Glue the frame onto the back of the window opening or the outside of the wall, depending on the style. For skylights, glue the frame over a hole cut in the roof before the roof is tiled. Clear plastic sheet comes with or without window bars. To make homemade window bars, scribe lines into the plastic as described right, or lay strips of painted self-adhesive tape or narrow drafting tape across the window. A soft plastic is the best one to use if you are scribing your own window bars.

Model some windows open to add life to the scene. Make an open sash window by cutting the plastic in half horizontally and gluing the top section to the frame in a lowered position before attaching the bottom section behind it. For an open casement window, cut the plastic to the exact size of the window, then cut it in half vertically. Glue the open section to the frame along the hinge line.

Windows do not have to be sparkling clean. If you are modeling a derelict building, simulate grimy glass by brushing a wash of dirty turpentine over the completed window. For cracked or broken glass, scratch or break the plastic before making the window. Frosted glass, in a factory window for example, is made by rubbing wet-and-dry paper over the back of the plastic or painting liquid polystyrene onto it (the polystyrene clouds the plastic).

Cardboard shutters make an interesting detail on a model building. Punch or cut out decorative shapes in each panel, if you wish. Glue colored tissue paper or fabric behind the window for curtains.

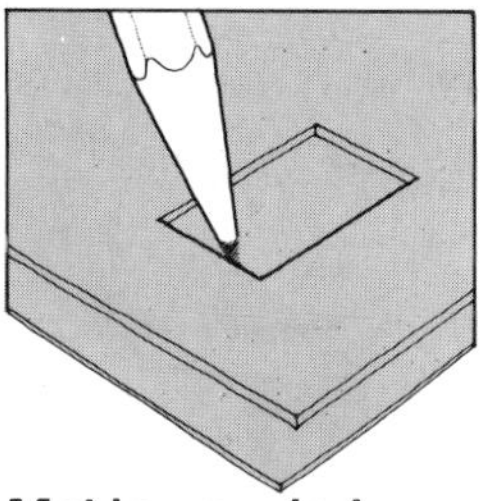

**Making a window** Lay the wall onto a piece of thin cardboard. Draw around the window opening with a pencil.

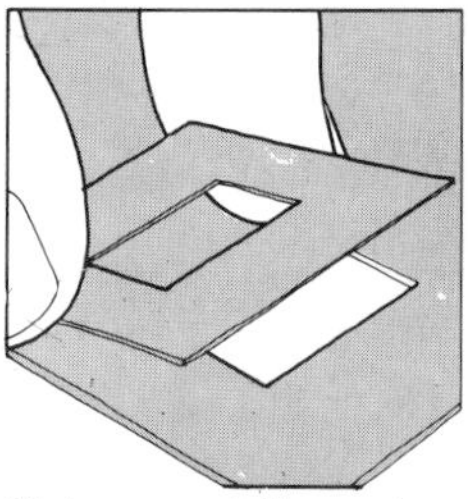

Cut around the outside of the mark, leaving enough cardboard to glue the window to the wall. Next, cut just inside the mark to form the opening. Glue it onto the wall.

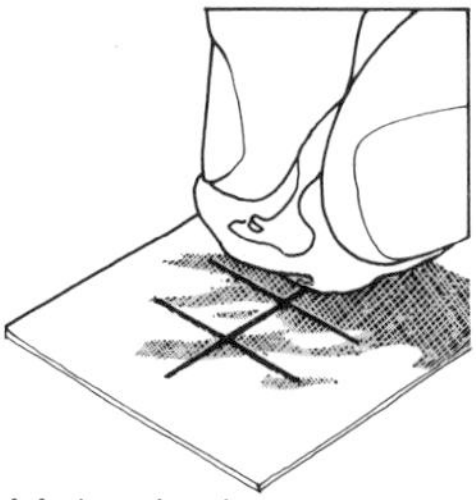

Make the bars: cut a piece of clear plastic slightly larger than the opening: scribe bars into it. Brush enamel paint over the glass and wipe it off immediately, leaving paint in the lines.

Glue the "glass" to the back of the frame with rubber-based contact cement. Lay transparent self-adhesive tape over the window to secure it. If you wish, add a cardboard windowsill.

# Doors

Like windows, doors are made from very thin cardboard. Make the door frame in the same way as the window frame in steps 1 and 2, first tracing around the opening in the wall, then cutting inside and outside the marked line. Glue a piece of cardboard behind the frame for the door. To model an open door, cut the cardboard to the exact size of the door but leave extra on one side for a hinge; score along the hinge line, bend it slightly then glue the hinged side to the back of the wall.

You can scribe parallel lines in the door to simulate tongue-and-groove construction, or make up a paneled door from two pieces of thin cardboard as shown below. If you want to make a door with glass panels, just substitute a single sheet of clear plastic for the plain piece of cardboard in step 2.

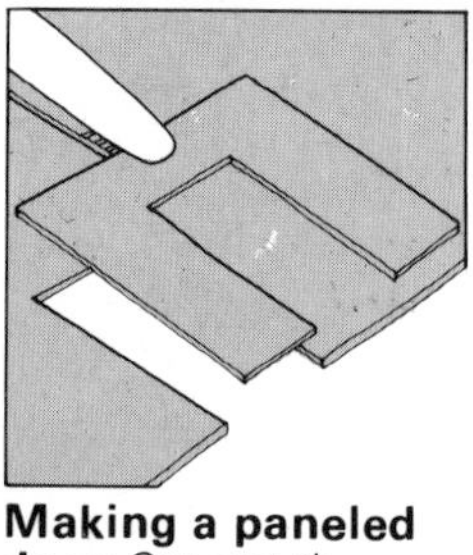

**Making a paneled door** Cut out the door frame, as for the window above, and glue it onto the wall.

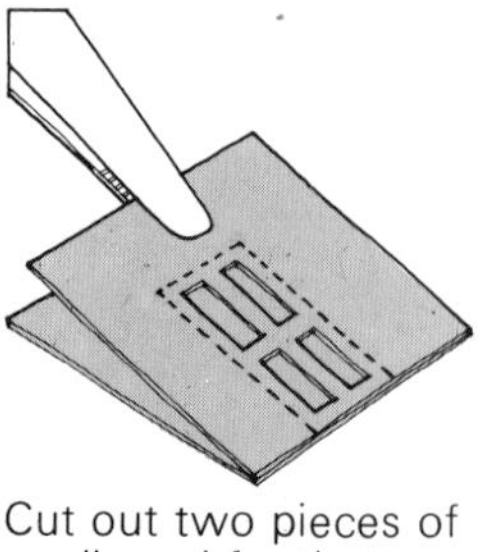

Cut out two pieces of cardboard for the door. Make holes in one for the panels. Glue them together.

Paint the door, if you wish, then glue it to the back of the wall, behind the door frame. Add a handle.

**Making a screen door** Spray a piece of nylon stocking black; stretch it across the back of the door.

# Motors and engines

# Types of engine

There are five different types of engine for working models. The simplest and cheapest of these is the rubber motor which is made from strips of rubber. It is used mainly by beginners on small airplanes.

The most flexible and popular engine is the internal combustion engine. It is powered by gasoline and is perfect for boats, airplanes and cars. There are two types: the glow plug and the diesel engine.

The $CO_2$ engine works in a similar way to the internal combustion engine but it uses compressed gas for fuel. Simple and quiet, it is used to power small airplanes.

An electric motor can provide power equivalent to a small internal combustion engine but it cannot sustain long runs. It is, however, quieter, easy to start and can be run indoors. It is used most effectively in powerboats, cars and some airplanes.

The steam engine, while having more of a specialist interest, is used mainly for boats. It can also be used in traction engines.

# Rubber motors

Rubber motors are used to drive lightweight airplanes and are normally supplied with the airplane in a kit. They consist of a rubber loop hooked to the propeller shaft and anchored at the back of the airplane by a dowel rod. To run the motor, you simply wind up the propeller with your finger and launch the airplane into the air as shown opposite.

This type of motor should be stored away from sunlight. It is not necessary to remove the lubricant before storing it. If the motor drops on the ground, wash, dry and relubricate it before using it again.

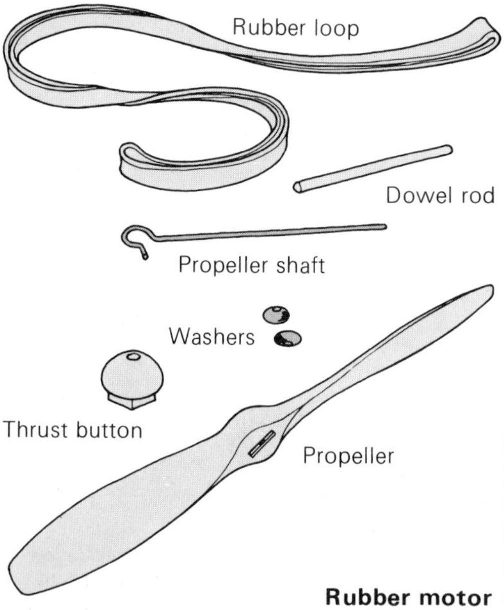


**Rubber motor**

## Assembling a rubber motor

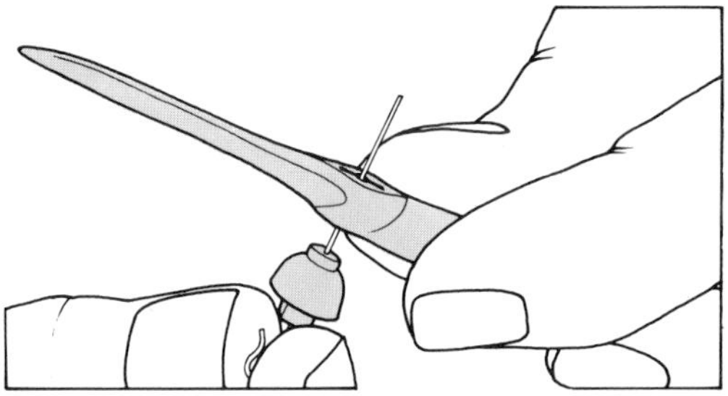

**1** Slip the thrust button, washers if supplied, and finally the propeller onto the propeller shaft. One end should be hooked but the shaft itself must be straight to work.

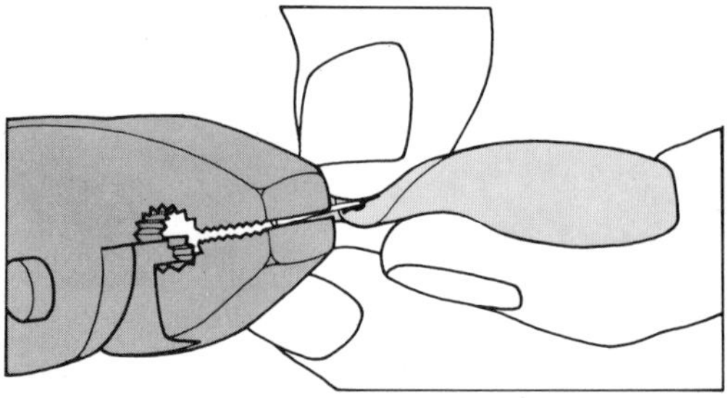

**2** Make a single right angle bend in the shaft at the other end so that it fits in the groove of the propeller boss. Wipe the lubricant supplied in the kit or pure castor oil over the rubber loop with your fingers.

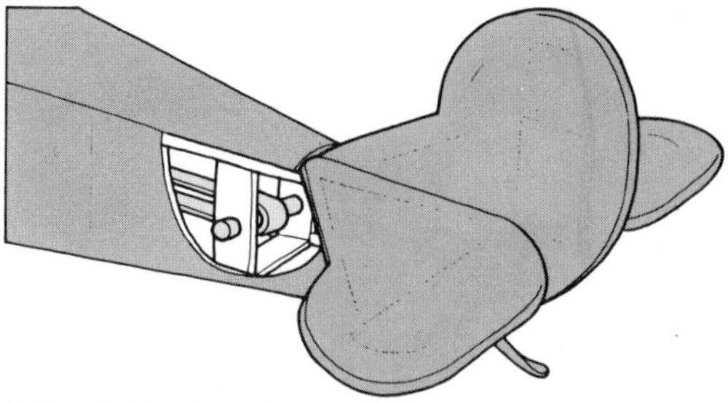

**3** Push the dowel rod through the holes in each side of the back of the fuselage, passing it through the rubber loop.

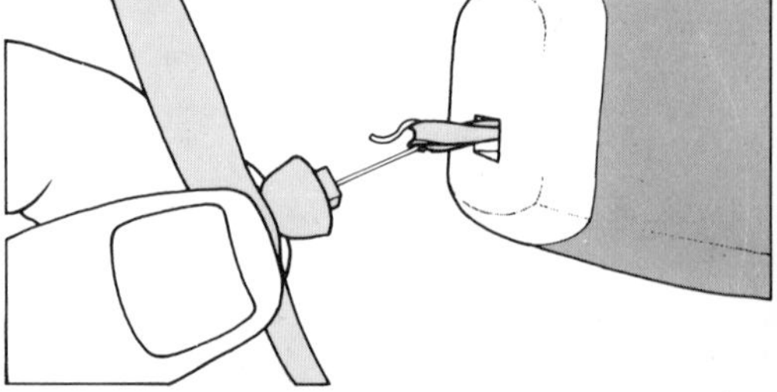

**4** The loop is usually slightly longer than the fuselage and will hang out at the front. Hook the propeller shaft to it and push the propeller assembly into place, leaving the slack motor lying in the fuselage.

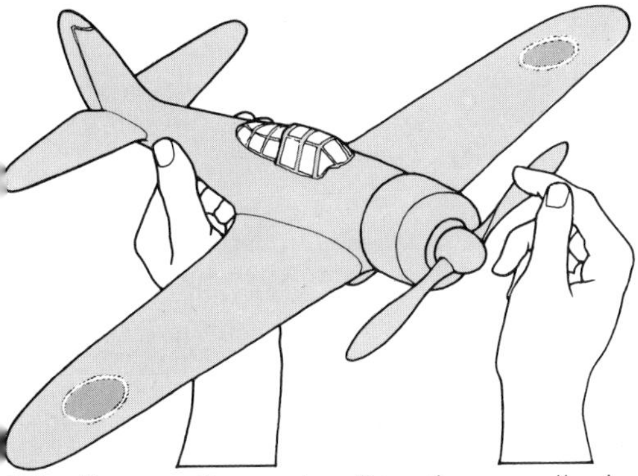

**Winding up the motor** Turn the propeller in a clockwise direction with your finger, until it feels tight. Keep hold of the propeller or the motor will unwind.

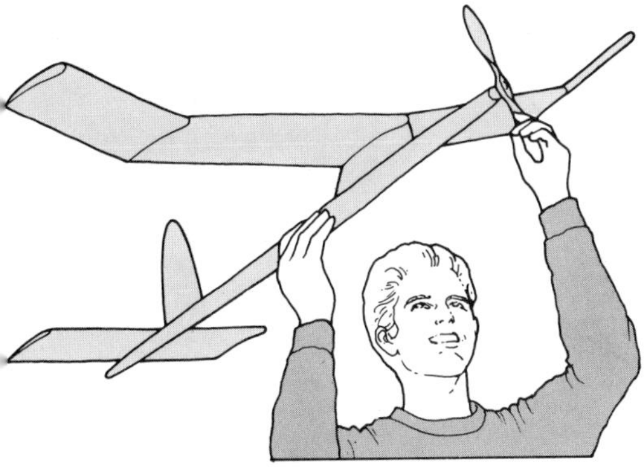

**Launching the model** Hold the model at head height facing into the wind, with one hand on the bottom tip of the propeller and the other under the fuselage. Release the propeller just before the fuselage.

## Multistranded rubber motors

More sophisticated motors to power larger airplanes can be made from a rubber strip. Cut a length of rubber strip weighing between a quarter and a third of the weight of the plane it is to power. Strips are available in widths of $\frac{1}{8}$, $\frac{3}{16}$ and $\frac{1}{4}$ inch (3, 5 and 6 mm). Tie the ends of the strip together, lubricate it, then make it into a multistranded loop of a suitable length as shown right.

This type of motor needs a specially shaped propeller shaft with a ring on the outside end for winding and an "S"-shaped hook on the inside end to prevent the motor from overriding the hook or jamming. Take a piece of wire for the shaft and form the "S"-shaped hook at one end, then cover it with a rubber or plastic sleeve. Slip on the nose block, a pair of washers and the propeller, then form the ring and drive arm at the end. Finally, drill a small hole in the propeller boss; insert the drive arm in the hole to lock it in position.

To assemble the motor, first anchor the knotted end of the rubber loop at the back of the plane with a dowel rod as described for the simple loop, opposite. Next, slip the loop onto the "S"-shaped hook and bind the ends of the hook together with wire so that the hook can't pull apart. Finally, push the propeller assembly into place.

You will need a hand drill and a friend to help you wind the motor. Make a piano-wire hook to fit in the drill and bend the end to hook behind the jaws of the drill. Place the hook in the ring of the propeller shaft. One person holds the model by the nose and rear anchor point, while the other walks backward turning the drill and stretching the motor to about three times the original length. Not more than two-thirds of the turns should be applied at full stretch. Make the remainder while walking back to the model.

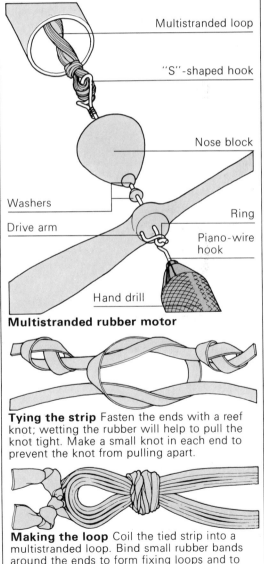

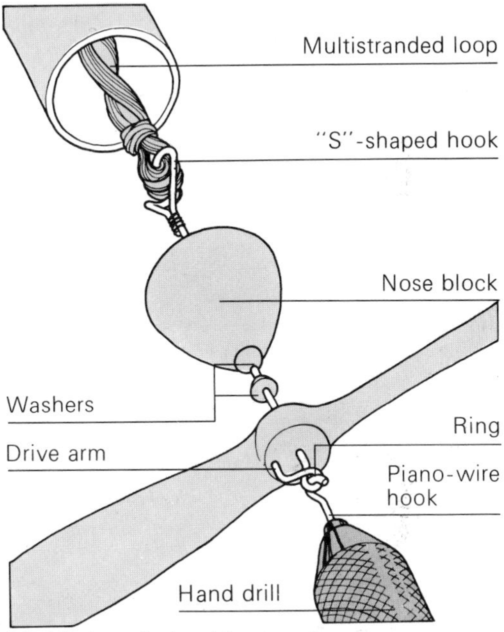


**Multistranded rubber motor**

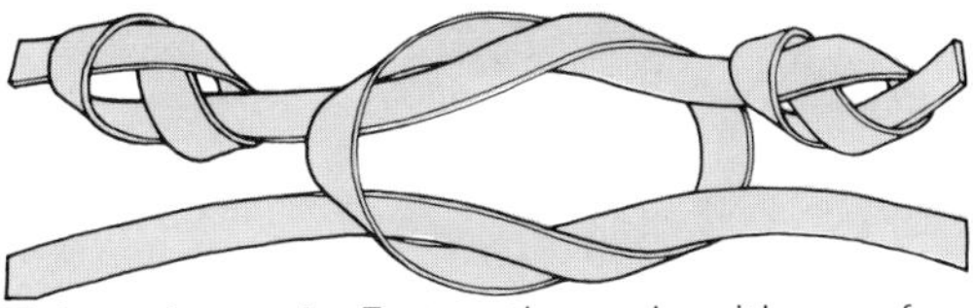

**Tying the strip** Fasten the ends with a reef knot; wetting the rubber will help to pull the knot tight. Make a small knot in each end to prevent the knot from pulling apart.

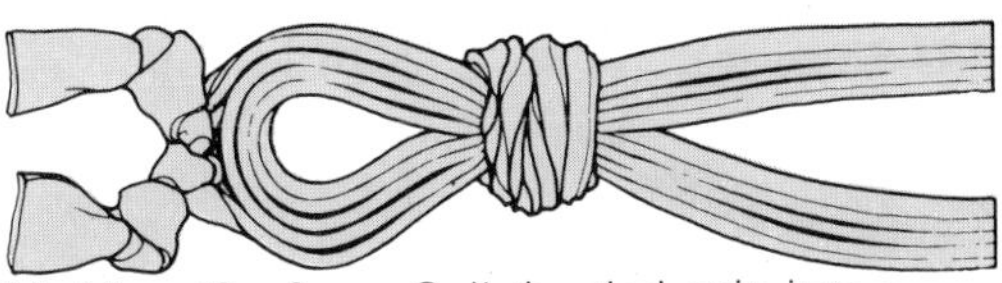

**Making the loop** Coil the tied strip into a multistranded loop. Bind small rubber bands around the ends to form fixing loops and to hold it in shape. The knot should be at one end.

# Internal combustion engines

The two types of model internal combustion engine, the glow plug engine and the diesel engine, both work on the same principle as full-size piston engines, but with a simplified carburetor.

The glow plug engine takes its name from the plug which fires it. Similar to a spark plug, the glow plug has a small wire element that is heated by an electric current. Once the engine has started, the electrical supply is removed and the engine keeps firing as the element continues to glow under pressure and chemical reaction with the fuel. Glow plug engines are light, run at high speed and can be throttle-controlled. They are the most popular type of model engine.

The diesel engine uses the heat generated by high pressure in the cylinder to ignite the fuel. The compression ratio is adjusted for starting and smooth running by a contra-piston. The diesel is a simple and efficient, slow-running engine. It is widely used, specially in Europe, although its popularity has declined because of its temperamental starting and greater vibration. Moreover, it does not usually come with a throttle. Nevertheless, free-flight and control-line fliers as well as boat modelers use diesels with great success.

The size of glow plug and diesel engines is specified by their displacement (the volume displaced by the piston in a single stroke). Glow plug engine sizes are given in cubic inches and diesel sizes in cubic centimeters. This system is worldwide. Generally speaking, the larger the displacement, the higher the power. The kit will recommend the size of engine to suit your model vehicle.

**Glow plug engine**

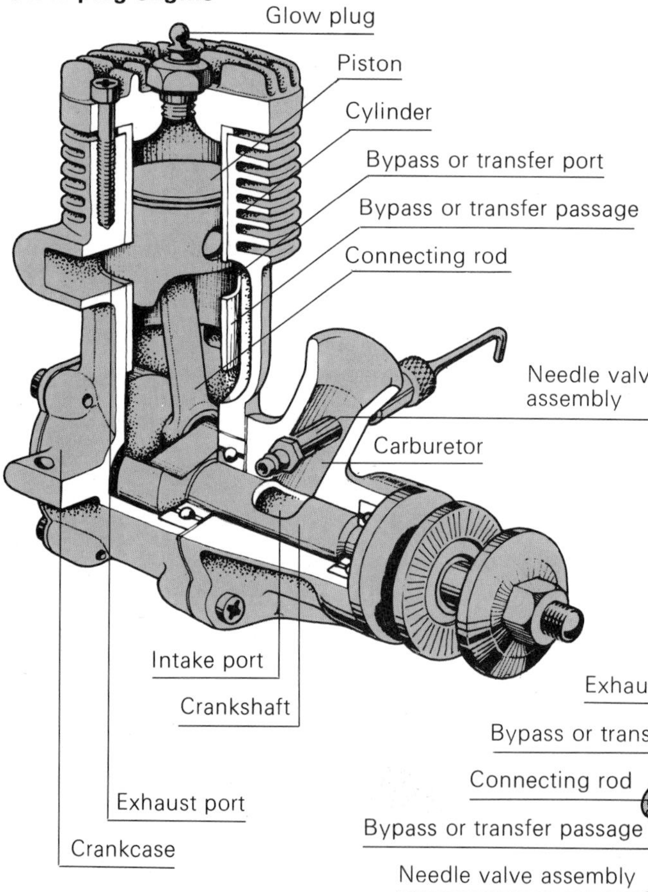


**Diesel engine**

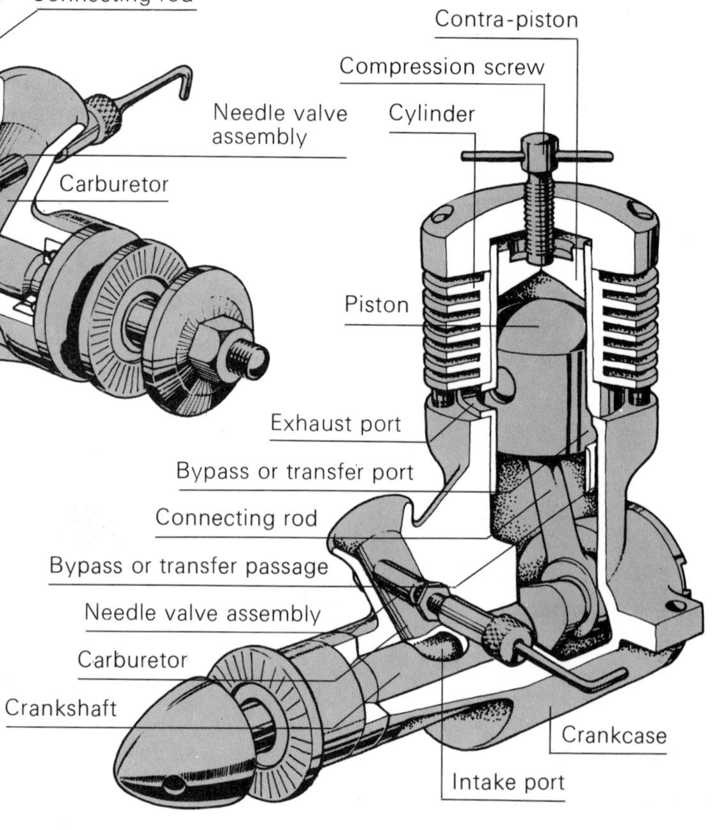

## Types of glow plug engine

Manufacturers produce engines of a particular displacement in different versions and glow plug engines offer the widest choice as illustrated below.

Engines are designed for either "sport" or "speed." A sport engine is best for non-competition models which are built and flown for fun. A speed engine is a high-performance engine designed to give the maximum output for competitions.

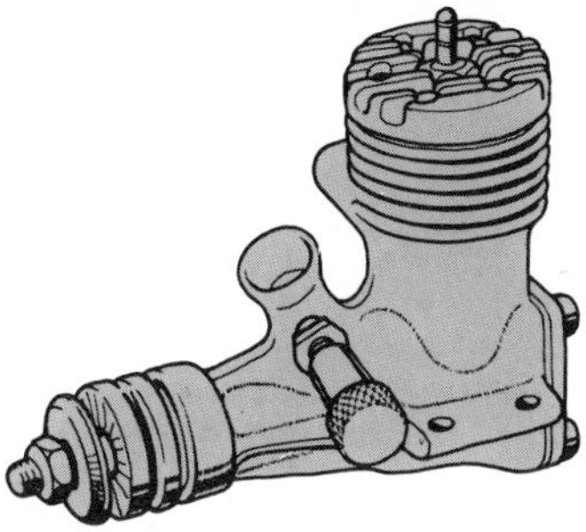

**Standard** A straightforward two-cycle, single-cylinder engine with a simple carburetor without a throttle. Air-cooled. Very reliable and easy to maintain. A sport engine. Cheaper than other types of engine.

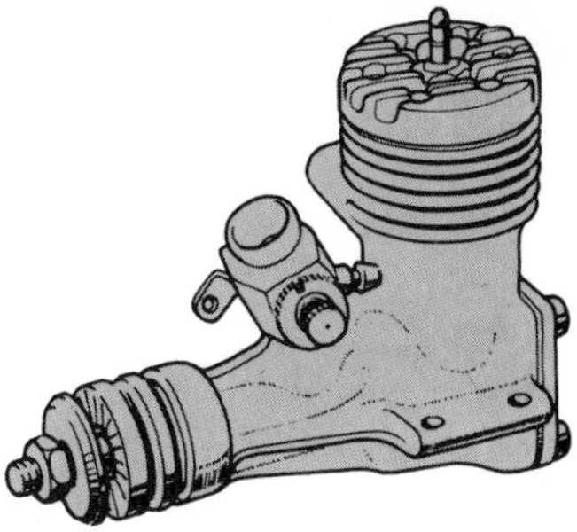

**Radio-control standard** A two-cycle, single-cylinder engine similar to the standard engine shown left, but with a throttle for use with radio-control models. Available air- or water-cooled in both sport and speed versions.

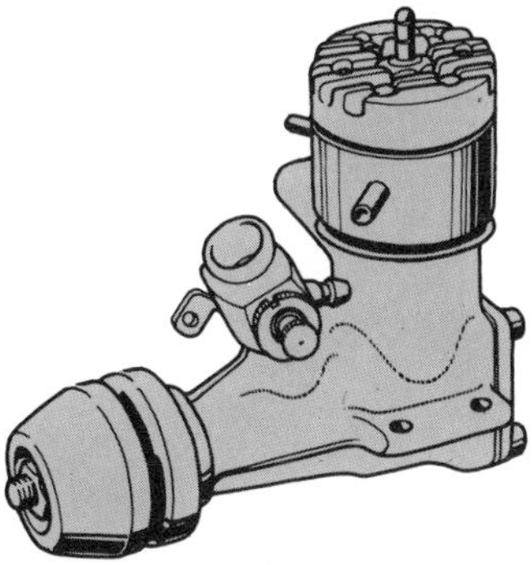

**Radio-control marine** A two-cycle engine with a water-cooled jacket for use in powerboats. The head may be air- or water-cooled. Has a flywheel to assist starting and running. Marine engines are also available in a standard version, without a throttle.

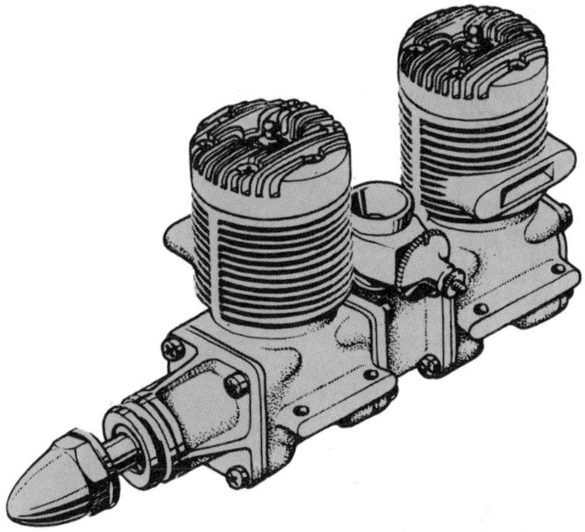

**In-line twin-cylinder** A sophisticated two-cycle engine which produces extra power and is very smooth-running. The two cylinders are arranged in a straight line and fire one after the other in succession. The engine has a throttle for use with radio-control models.

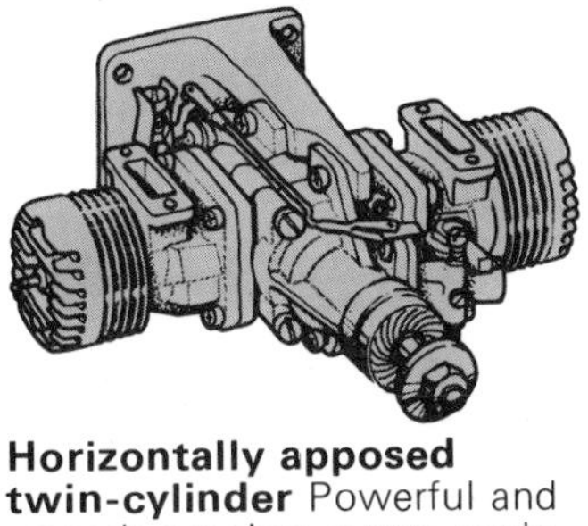

**Horizontally apposed twin-cylinder** Powerful and smooth-running, a two-cycle engine like the in-line twin-cylinder above, but the two cylinders face opposite each other and fire simultaneously. Comes with a throttle for use with radio-control models.

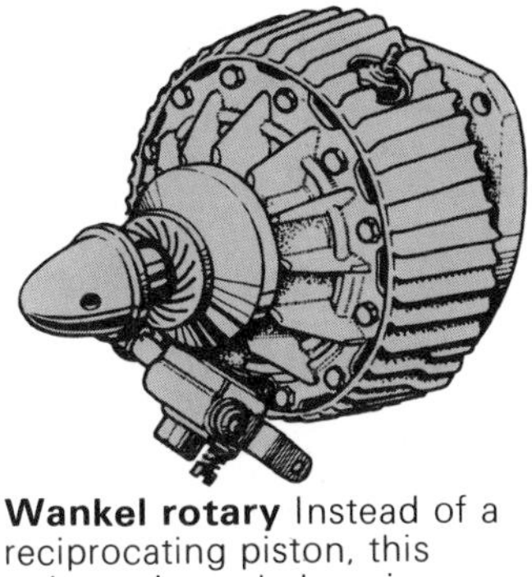

**Wankel rotary** Instead of a reciprocating piston, this unique air-cooled engine uses a rotor which runs in a specially shaped combustion chamber. One size only, with a throttle, it is extremely smooth-running and ideal for radio-control models.

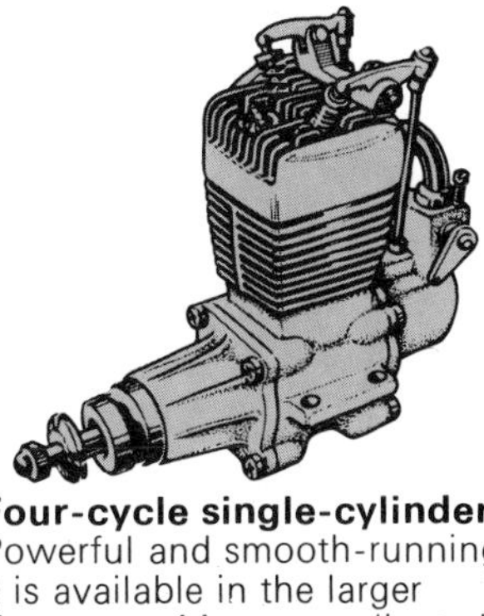

**Four-cycle single-cylinder** Powerful and smooth-running, it is available in the larger size range. More complicated than two-cycle engines, it has valves to control the fuel supply and exhaust cycle. Four-cycle engines are also available with twin cylinders.

## How an engine works

An engine is basically a cylinder with a piston moving up and down within it. When the piston moves upward it compresses a fuel and air mixture within the cylinder. When the mixture is ignited, expanding gases force the piston down. Once the engine is started, this action repeats itself in a regular cycle.

In a two-stroke cycle engine the piston makes two movements, one up and one down, for each firing of the mixture. In a four-stroke cycle engine the fuel is fired not on the second stroke but on the fourth stroke, after the piston goes through another cycle.

A two-cycle engine will four-cycle if there is more fuel than air. Although it is inefficient, a new two-cycle engine is often set to four-cycle initially to help break it in (see Breaking in an engine, pages 242 to 243).

## How a two-cycle engine works

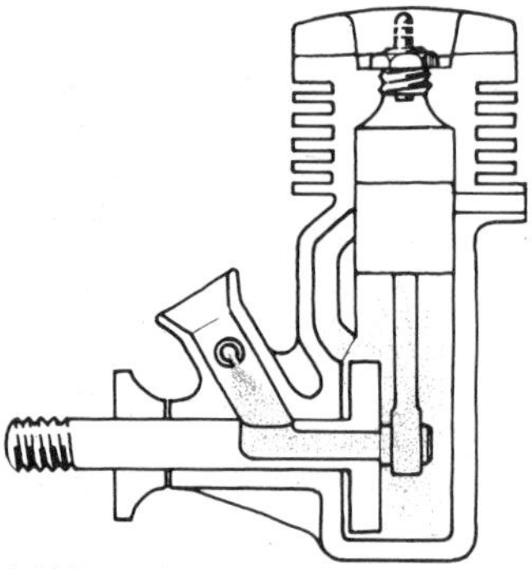

**1** When the propeller or flywheel is turned in an anticlockwise direction, the crankshaft rotates. This in turn drives the piston. As the piston rises to the top of the cylinder, known as "top dead center," the pressure inside the crankcase is reduced, causing a fuel and air mixture to be drawn in from the carburetor to fill up the crankcase.

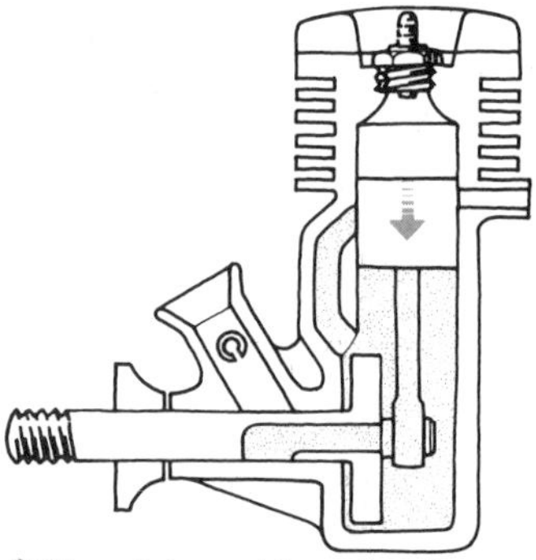

**2** The piston, driven by the momentum of the crankshaft, now begins its downward movement. The intake port closes at this point, trapping the fuel and air mixture in the crankcase. The mixture is compressed by the piston as it descends.

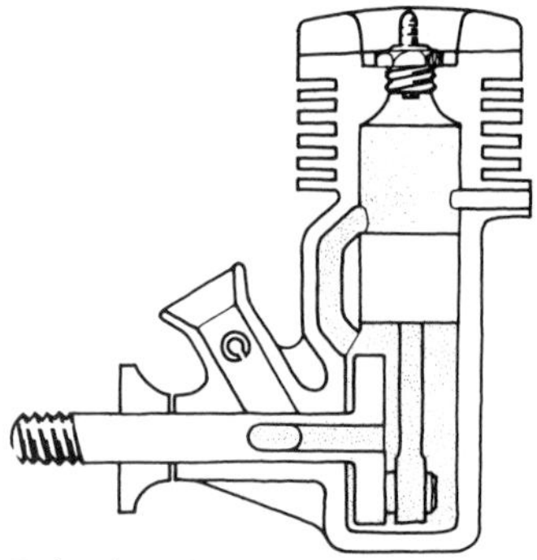

**3** As the piston approaches the bottom of the second stroke, known as "bottom dead center," it exposes the bypass port. The compressed fuel mixture now moves via the bypass passage and bypass port into the cylinder above the piston.

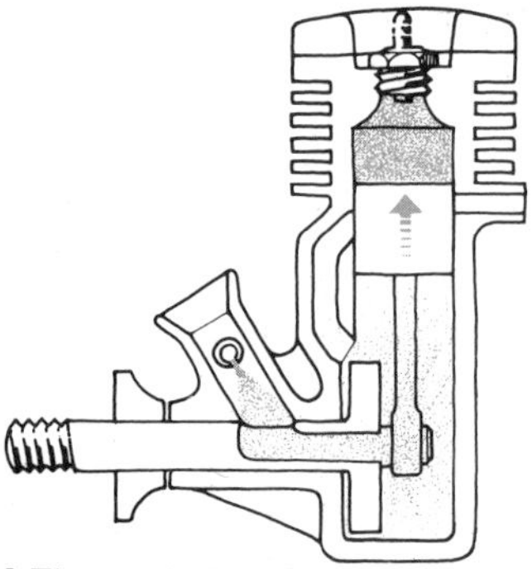

**4** The cycle is now repeated. The momentum of the crankshaft again causes the piston to rise, compressing the mixture against the cylinder head. At the same time, the intake port opens and a fresh amount of fuel and air mixture is sucked in from the carburetor to fill up the crankcase.

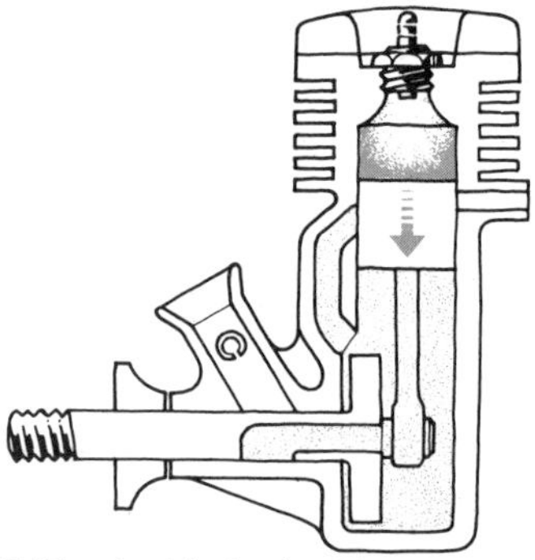

**5** The fuel is ignited just before the piston reaches top dead center, either by the heated element of the glow plug or the heat generated by the pressure on the mixture in the case of a diesel engine. The mixture explodes, producing rapidly expanding gases which force the piston down again.

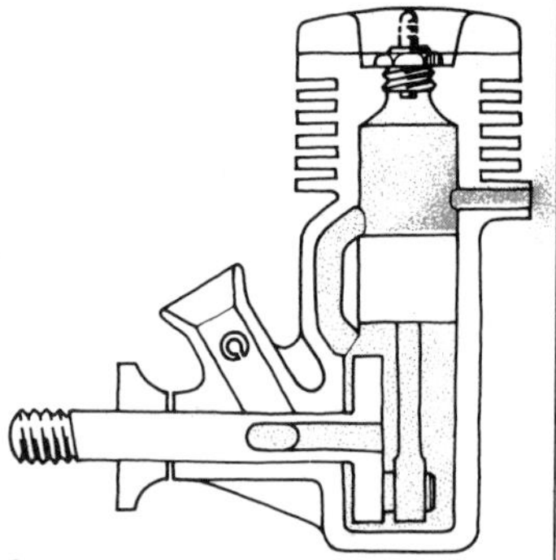

**6** As the piston descends, the exhaust port is exposed and the burned gases are exhausted. The piston then exposes the bypass port forcing fresh mixture into the top of the cylinder. The incoming mixture helps force out the remaining burned gases. The cycle 4 to 6 repeats continuously.

## Ports

The size of the ports and their position is important as they determine "when" and "how much" fuel and air mixture is delivered into the engine cylinder.

There are three different designs of intake port. The most popular is the front rotary type which consists of an opening in the side of the crankshaft connected to the crankcase by a passage in the shaft. Each time the crankshaft rotates, the opening passes the carburetor allowing fuel mixture to enter. The rear rotary intake port works in a similar way. It is an opening in a disk or drum which is connected to the rear of the crankshaft. The fuel mixture passes directly through the disk into the crank-case. A third type of intake port uses a reed valve. Here the intake of mixture is controlled by a thin metal flap which opens or closes according to the pressure in the engine. The reed valve intake port is found on smaller rear-induction glow plug engines.

Bypass and exhaust ports must work as efficiently as possible. Most modern engines have a single bypass port, although the larger ones sometimes have two or three. The exhaust port is usually opposite the bypass port and can be a single slot or, in larger engines, a series of "windows," but it is always larger and higher than the bypass port. The bypass port is shaped to direct the fresh mixture upward to help force out the burned gases. Some of the mixture, however, goes straight out the exhaust, which is wasteful and inefficient. In glow plug engines the top of the piston is sometimes shaped to deflect all of the mixture up and over, reducing waste. This shape is not suitable for diesel engines which have a domed or conical piston for the purpose.

Schnuerle porting is a system of bypass and exhaust ports designed to improve the gas flow without the use of a deflector on the piston head. A flat or domed piston is best because it gives a more even distribution of pressure. The system has three bypass ports, one either side of the exhaust port and one opposite. The side ports direct the fuel mixture toward the central "boost" bypass port. Because Schnuerle porting is more expensive to produce, it is normally only found in high-performance engines.

**Front rotary intake port**

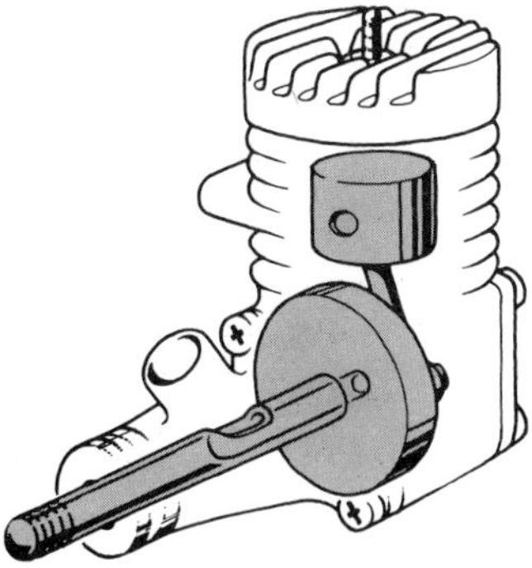

**Rear rotary intake port**

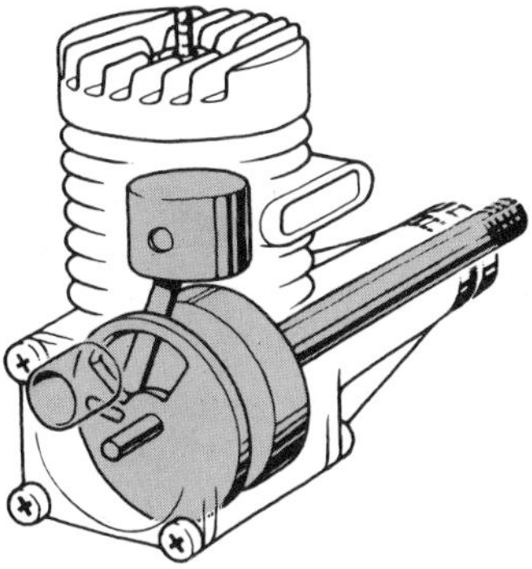

**Reed valve intake port**

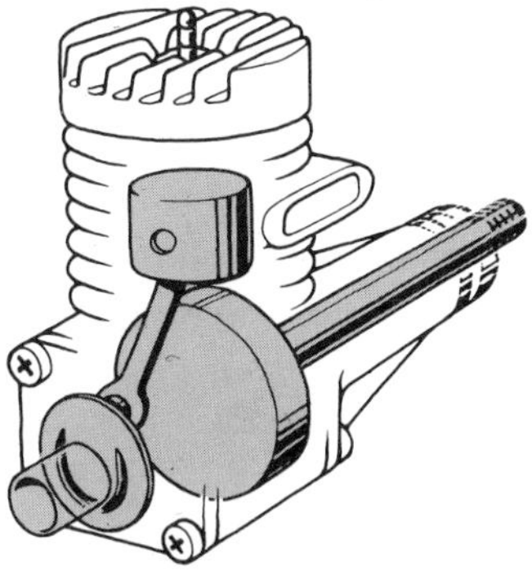

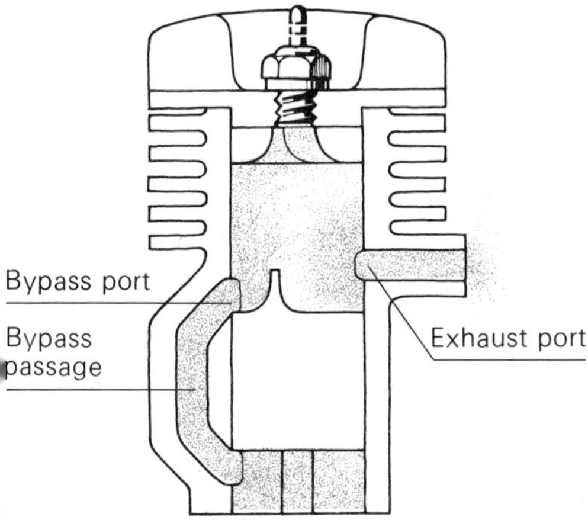


**Glow plug cylinder** Note how the bypass port and passage and the top of the piston are shaped to direct the fresh mixture upward to help expel all the burned gases.

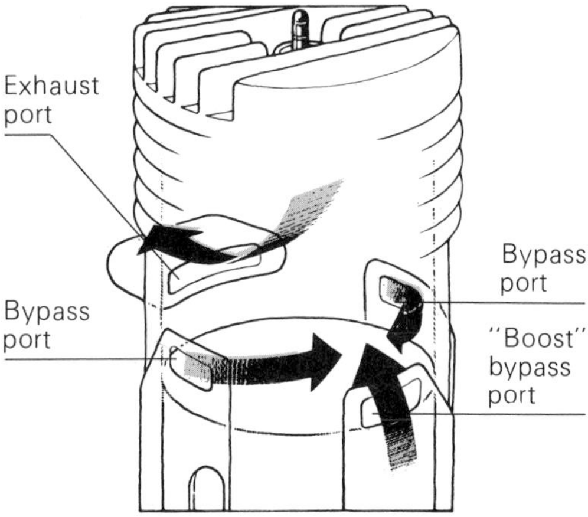


**Schnuerle porting** The position of the bypass ports causes the burned gases to be expelled efficiently and creates a more even distribution of pressure in the cylinder head.

## Simple carburetors

The carburetor controls the mixture of fuel and air, and when it has a throttle, the speed of the engine. Standard glow plug and diesel engines have a simple carburetor without a throttle which allows the model to run at a single speed only. It consists of a specially shaped air intake tube, called a venturi after an Italian scientist, with a narrow middle and flared ends so that the air speeds up as it passes through. Inside the venturi is a smaller tube called a spray bar. One end of the spray bar is attached to the fuel line; a needle valve screws into the other end. In the middle of the spray bar is a hole or "jet." The fuel is drawn from the jet by the low pressure created by the passing airstream. It is atomized into a fine spray and mixed with the air as it is drawn into the crankcase. (If you remove the spray bar for any reason, check the orientation of the jet first and make sure that you replace it in the same position. The nuts must be secure to prevent air from leaking.)

The needle valve controls the amount of fuel drawn in through the jet. By screwing it in or out the tapered point will decrease or increase the opening in the spray bar. Each engine has an optimum setting for the needle valve when the fuel and air supply are mixed in the right proportion. At this setting the engine gives its best performance. If more fuel than air is supplied, known as "running rich," the fuel is not burned efficiently and the engine revs drop. If too rich, the engine stops. You will recognize a rich setting by the increase in smoke from the exhaust and a distinct drop in pitch of the engine noise; the engine will begin to four-cycle. When more air than fuel is supplied, known as "running lean," the engine loses revs as it is starved of fuel. Too little fuel and the engine stops. An engine should not be run on a lean setting for long periods as it can overheat due to a lack of lubricant from the fuel, so damaging the engine.

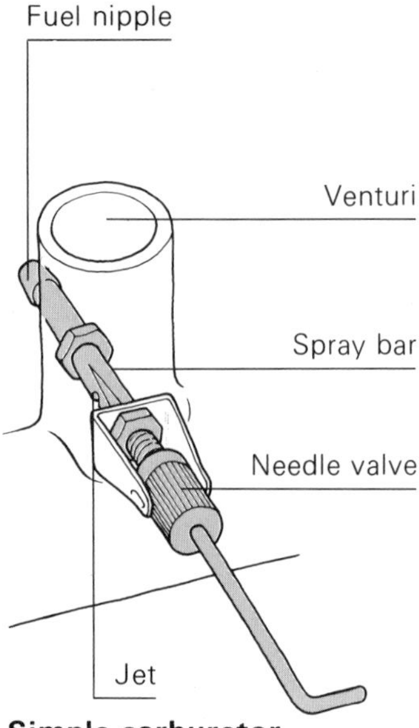


**Simple carburetor**

## Radio-control carburetors

Radio-control models which run at different speeds require carburetors with throttles. One version is the "butterfly" throttle. This is a disk which pivots in the venturi upstream of the spray bar to control the amount of air passing through. As the disk closes, the air flow drops so that less fuel is drawn from the jet. When the engine is idling, however, it tends to run very rich as the low pressure in the crankcase, unable to draw in air, pulls in more fuel; and if the throttle is closed completely, the engine floods and stops.

The barrel throttle, the most popular type in use today, is similar in principle to the butterfly throttle but it is more refined, providing full control at all engine speeds. In its simplest form, a "barrel" rotates around the spray bar or fuel jet. The barrel is linked to a throttle arm which is controlled by a servo. A large hole through the barrel matches the bore of the venturi and lines up with it when fully open. As the barrel rotates the size of the opening is reduced, so controlling the fuel and air mixture. An airbleed hole in the carburetor allows extra air into the engine when it is idling to prevent it from flooding. The size of the airbleed hole is adjusted by a screw.

More sophisticated barrel throttles are designed so that they reduce the amount of fuel automatically as the throttle closes. Three versions are illustrated opposite. There are other types of sophisticated throttle but they are less common and found only on high-performance engines.

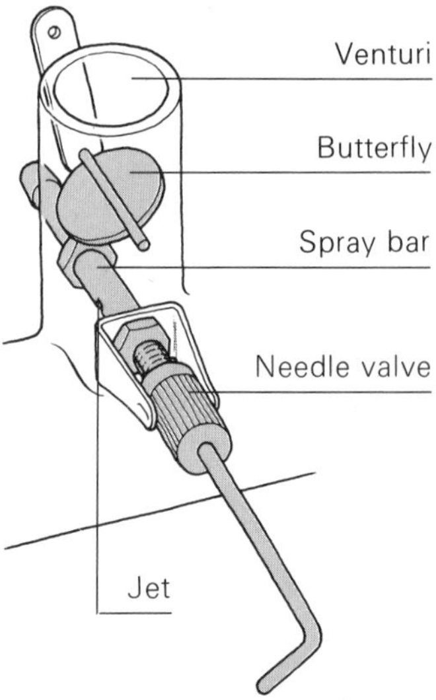


**Butterfly throttle** A disk pivots in the venturi.

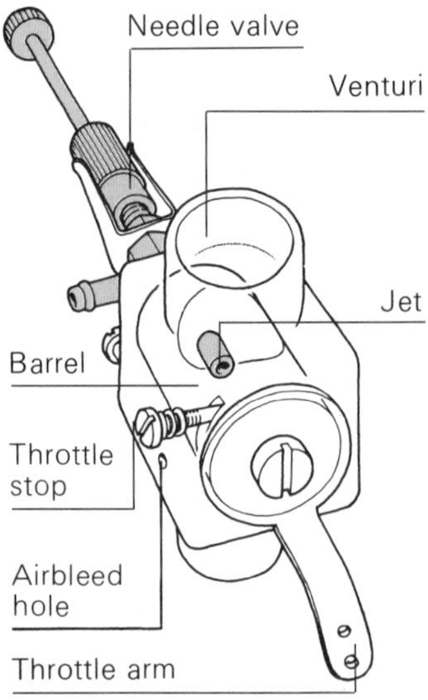


**Simple barrel throttle** A barrel rotates around the fuel jet to control the mixture.

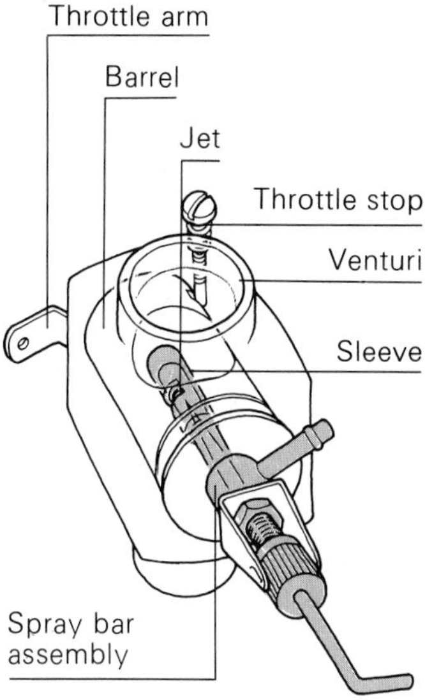


**Barrel throttle with rotating sleeve** Inside the barrel, a sleeve with a slot rotates around a modified spray bar with a slot for the jet. At full throttle the slots align.

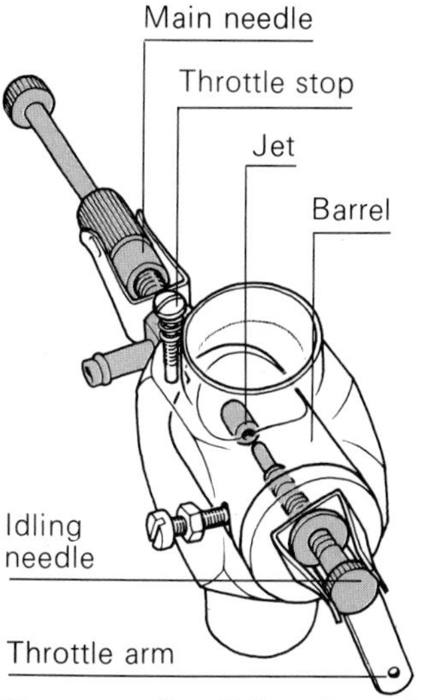


**Two-needle sliding-barrel throttle** This type has two needles: on one side a main needle valve connected to the fuel line and projecting into the venturi as an open-ended tube, on the other side a second "idling" needle. As the throttle closes, the barrel and idling needle slide toward the open tube and the needle enters the jet to reduce the flow of fuel to the engine.

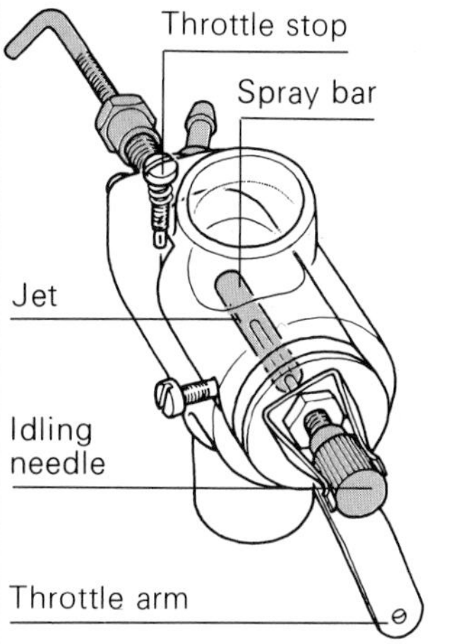


**Sliding-barrel throttle with rod-shaped idling needle** In this throttle the idling needle is a rod which passes down the center of a spray bar with a slot. As the barrel closes, the rod reduces the length of the slot.

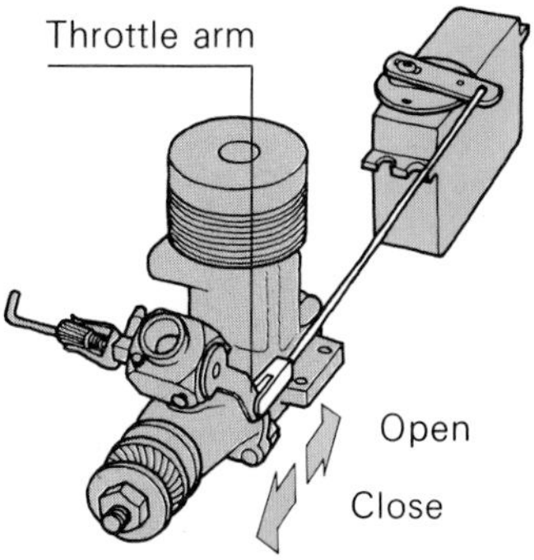


**Throttle linkage** An arm and pushrod link the throttle to the radio-control servo. The arm swings anticlockwise to open and clockwise to close.

## Setting a carburetor

The simple carburetor is easy to set because it only has one adjustment. First screw the needle valve in fully to close the jet, then unscrew it the number of turns recommended by the manufacturer.

The engine should run at this setting. If it bursts into life, revs quickly and stops, the mixture is too lean and the needle valve should be opened by half a turn. Start the engine again; if it reacts in the same way, open the valve a little more. If the engine runs roughly, spluttering fuel and oily exhaust smoke, then the setting is too rich. Screw in the valve to reduce the amount of fuel. Once the engine is running steadily, tune it finely by ear. At its most efficient it produces its maximum revs making a very smooth, continuous, high-pitched sound. If the needle is at the correct setting, the engine pitch will lower when the needle is turned to right or left. Remember that a new engine must be broken in before tuning it for maximum revs.

A radio-control carburetor has to be adjusted twice, once with the throttle open and a second time with the throttle closed. Make the first adjustment with the throttle open as described for a simple carburetor, setting the needle valve to give the maximum revs. You may wish to set an airplane carburetor slightly rich to compensate for the weaker mixture as the fuel tank empties or as the plane climbs steeply. Each time you launch the plane, test it to see if it needs to run slightly rich by pointing its nose upward.

The second adjustment sets the idling speed. At the correct setting the engine should run smoothly at low revs when the throttle is closed. For carburetors with a simple barrel throttle, close the throttle and set the throttle stop screw so that the engine continues to run. If it stops quickly, screw the throttle stop in to increase the idling speed. Open the throttle, start the engine and try again. If the engine runs erratically and stops, the mixture is probably too weak. Screw in the airbleed screw to reduce the amount of air. Restart the engine and adjust the airbleed screw slightly one way or the other as needed until the engine runs steadily. If the engine simply loses revs and stops, the setting is too rich. Turn the airbleed screw anticlockwise to let in more air.

To adjust the idling speed of carburetors with two needles, close the throttle and simply adjust the idling needle. Screwing in the needle weakens the fuel mixture; unscrewing the needle enriches it.

## Filters

Fuel and air filters prevent dirt from entering the engine and damaging it. Air filters are recommended for all types of model, especially boats and cars, and a substantial air filter is essential for cars despite the slight drop in engine performance it causes. Fuel filters should also be used on all engines, particularly radio-control engines with a throttle because of their fine fuel jets. Likewise, it is a good idea to filter the fuel from the storage can into the tank.

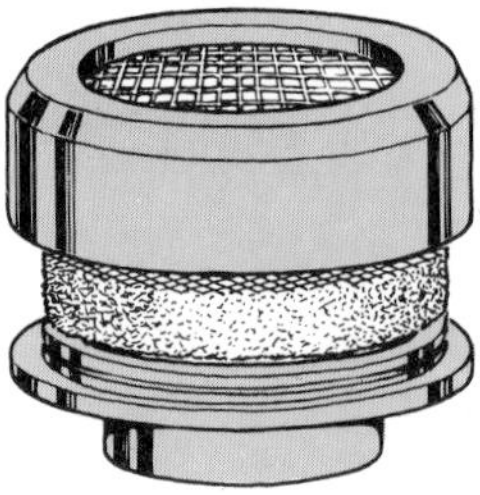

**Plug-on air filter** This air filter simply attaches over the mouth of the carburetor intake.

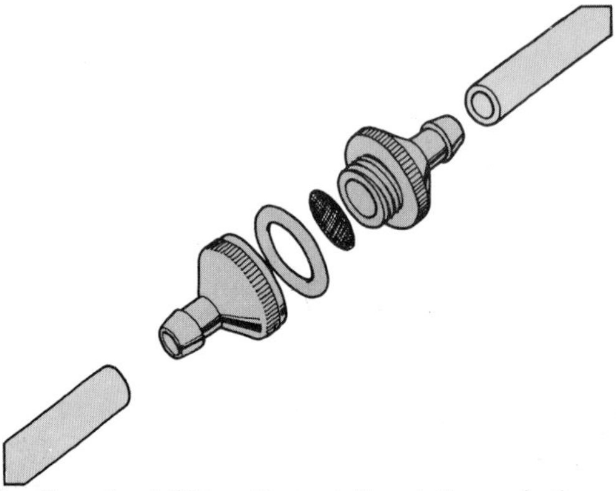

**In-line fuel filter** To install, cut through the fuel line and plug the cut ends into nipples on each side of the filter.

## Pressurized fuel supply

The efficiency and performance of an internal combustion engine is largely determined by the carburetor setting. The carburetor, however, is set when the model is stationary. When the model moves, not only can the relative positions of the carburetor and the fuel tank change but the engine can be affected by centrifugal and aerodynamic forces, all causing imbalances in the fuel and air supply. This is especially true of airplanes: when climbing, the fuel tank is below the engine making it difficult to draw in fuel, and when diving with the tank above, gravity makes the mixture richer.

A pressurized fuel system overcomes this problem. The simplest and most popular method of pressurizing the fuel supply is to tap the high pressure in the muffler. Another method is to tap the pressure in the crankcase. The effect on the engine is self-regulating: at high revs, the pressure increases as more fuel is demanded; at low revs, the pressure drops so lowering the fuel supply rate.

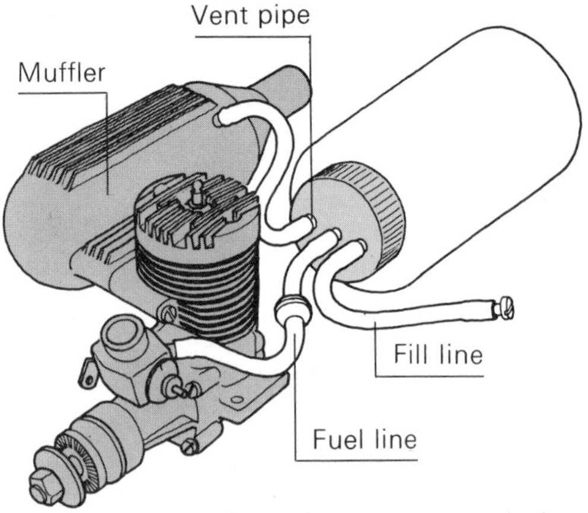


**Tapping the muffler** Connect one end of a flexible tube to a nipple on the muffler and the other end to the vent pipe on the fuel tank. Plug the end of the tank fill line with a bolt to seal the system.

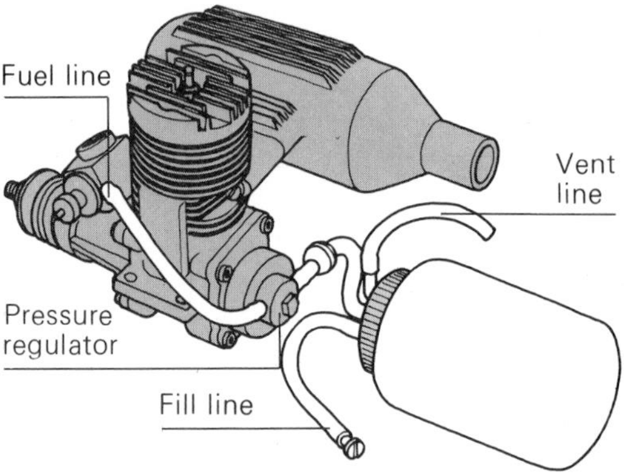


**Tapping the crankcase** The engine tends to run rich if you tap the crankcase using the simple arrangement of tubes described for tapping the muffler. Instead, attach a special pressure regulator or pump to the crankcase as shown above.

## Types of fuel tank

Many fuel tanks are available. They are usually made from tin plate or plastic and all have three pipes: the fill pipe, the vent pipe to equalize air pressure so that fuel can easily be added to or withdrawn from the tank, and the feed pipe which goes to the engine.

There are several designs to suit the different types of model. Control-line team racers, for instance, which are intended for level flight, usually take a rectangular metal tank. The feed pipe runs to the bottom of the tank and the fill and vent pipes jut through the top. In some cases the two pipes are bent forward into the slipstream of the airplane to provide simple pressurization.

Stunt control-line models use a tank with a modified wedge shape. The tank is symmetrical about its centerline which allows it to perform well either way up. The fill and vent pipes are on opposite sides so that they can swap roles depending on which way up the model is flying. Always install this tank on the "off side" of the model so that the centrifugal force will drive the fuel into the tapered side of the tank. Extra-large wedge-shaped tanks have an internal baffle to prevent the fuel sloshing during fast maneuvers.

Radio-control models often use round or square plastic bottles with the three pipes in a screw-on cap or stopper. Radio-control airplanes should use a variation of the bottle tank called a klunk tank. It has a flexible feed pipe to which is attached a brass nozzle known as the klunk weight. The weight keeps the pipe in the fuel as it moves in the tank. Free-flight airplanes can use either a rectangular tank or a plastic bottle without a klunk weight.

Special metal or plastic tanks are available for radio-control racing cars which have a flip-top cap on an extra-large fill pipe to speed up refueling. To keep the fuel from sloshing, they often have a chicken-hopper tank. This has two-tiers; the fuel is drawn from the bottom tank and the upper tank tops it up.

Tin plate or brass hull-shaped tanks are made for boats although you can also use plastic klunk tanks. These tanks are usually large and have a screw cap on top for filling. The feed pipe is at the bottom.

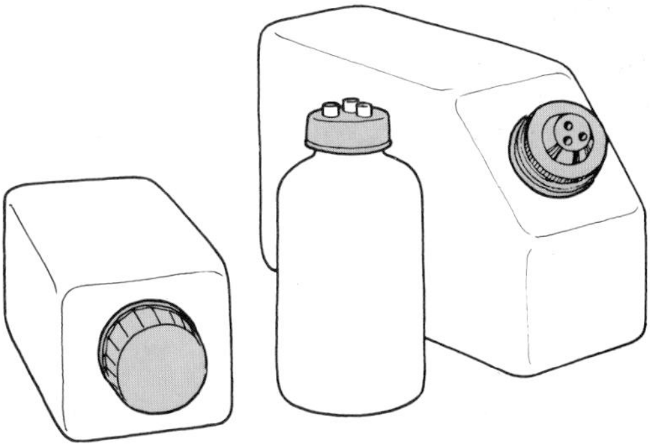

**Plastic bottles**

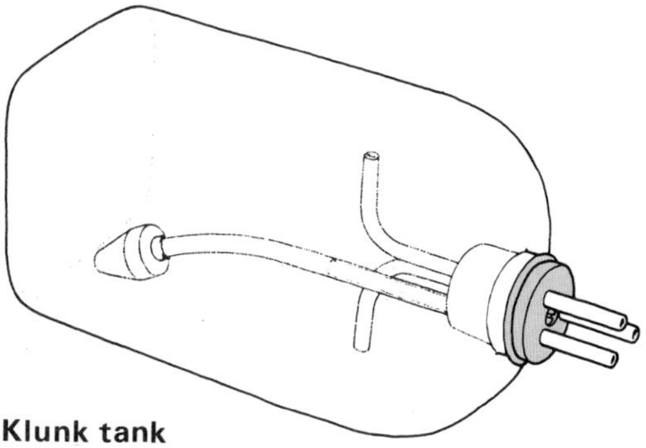

**Klunk tank**

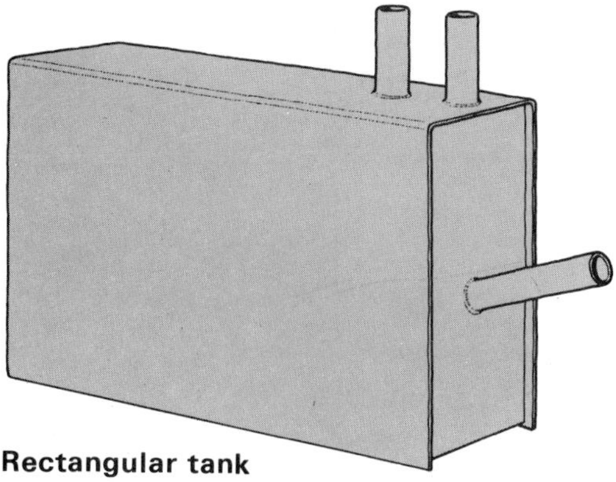

**Rectangular tank**

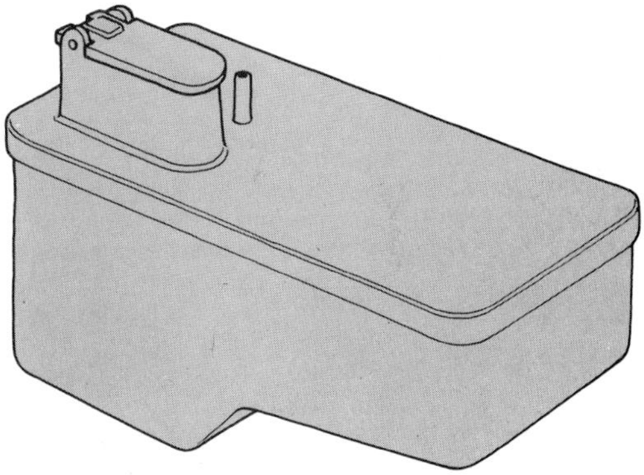

**Racing car tank**

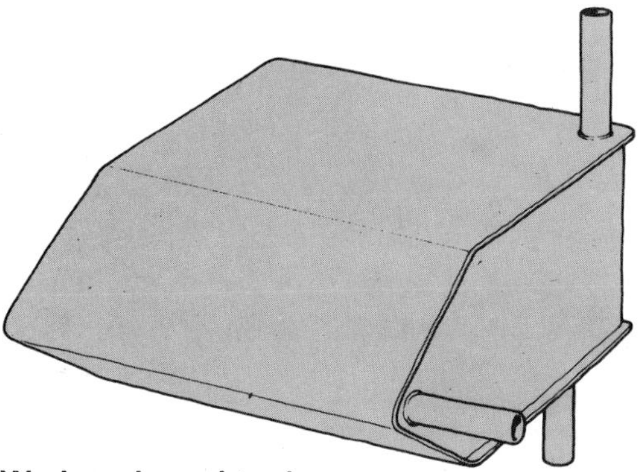

**Wedge-shaped tank**

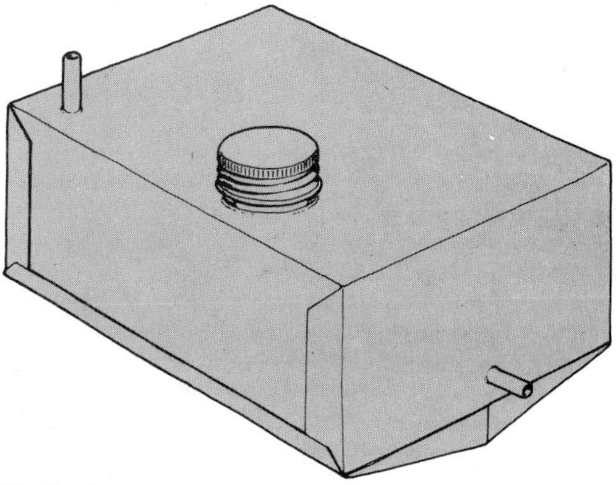

**Hull-shaped tank for boats**

## Mounting and filling fuel tanks

All fuel tanks should be positioned as close to the engine as possible to minimize fuel imbalances when the model moves (see Pressurized fuel supply, page 236). Likewise the center of the tank should be level with or below the carburetor jet or spray bar, never above it. Wedge-shaped tanks for control-line stunt planes should always be placed with their centers at the same level as the spray jet. If you cannot position the tank so that it provides a steady flow of fuel, you will need to pressurize the fuel supply by tapping the crankcase or muffler.

It is essential to fix the tank firmly. A loose tank may vibrate, causing the fuel to froth. Moreover, if the tank moves, the relationship of tank to carburetor can alter and affect the setting. To secure metal tanks, solder plates or straps to the tank then screw the tank to the model through them. For plastic tanks, the easiest method is to build a balsa wood bay to contain the tank. Fuelproof the balsa wood before adding the tank. Do not line the bay with soft foam packing material – the foam may become saturated with spilled fuel.

Models with an access hatch in the nose are easy to refuel through a short length of tube attached to the tank fill pipe, but if your model has an inaccessible tank, you will need to build a permanent extension tube that exits through the fuselage. To fill small tanks, use a plastic squeeze bottle. Simply place the nozzle in the fill line and squeeze. The tank is full when the fuel squirts from the vent line. For larger tanks such as those on radio-control models, the squeeze bottle is often too small. Transfer the fuel from the storage can to the model with a hand-operated or electric pump. These pumps can be operated in reverse so that unused fuel can be easily returned to the storage can. It is good practice not to leave extra fuel in the tank after running the model – it may spill during transport.

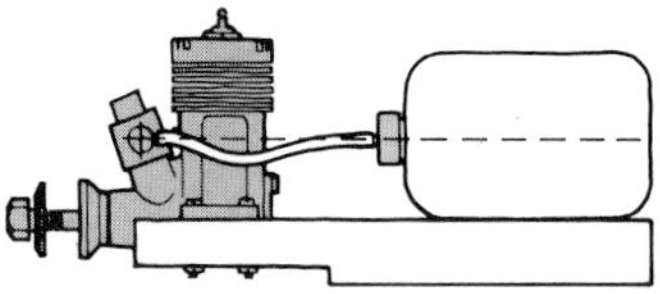

**Positioning the tank** The tank should be as close to the engine as possible, with its center level with or below the carburetor jet or spray bar.

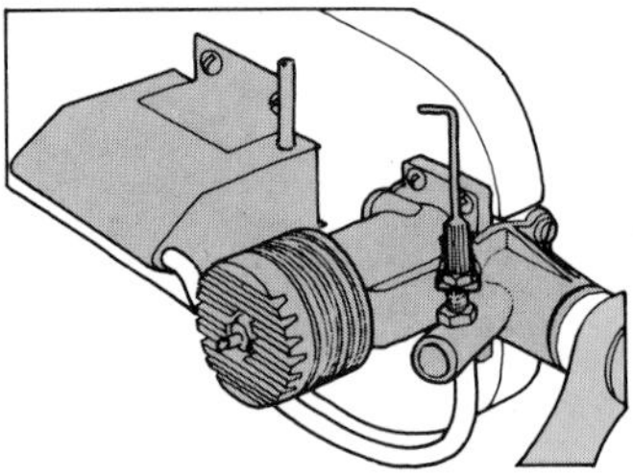

**Installing a metal tank**
Solder plates or straps to the tank; screw them to the model.

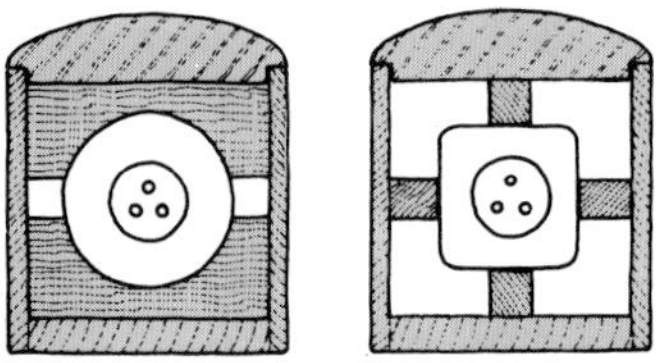

**Installing plastic bottles**
Build a balsa-wood tank bay. Make the wood grip the bottle.

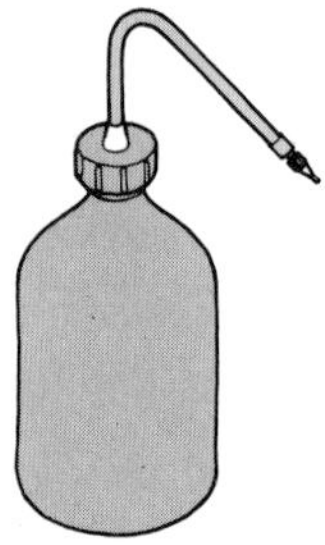

**Squeeze bottle**

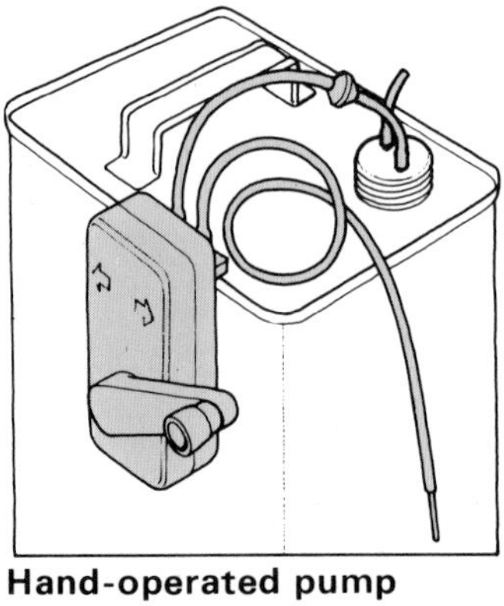

**Hand-operated pump**

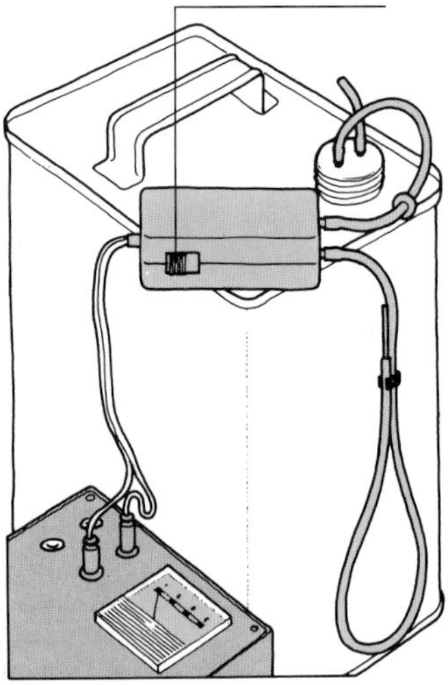


**Electric pump**

## Fuel

Special fuel is available in a range of mixes for glow plug engines. Some fuels have additives such as nitromethane for more power and smoother running. Although the more additive a fuel contains the more it will improve an engine's performance, it is still the design of the engine which governs its maximum speed. Always refer to the manufacturer's recommendations for the best mix for your engine.

Without an additive the fuel is known as straight fuel. It is a general-purpose fuel and good for breaking in an engine. Straight fuel with less lubricant is often used in high-performance engines in competition. With an additive it is known as "hot" fuel (although it is often referred to as "cool" when it contains a low percentage of additive [2 to 5%], or "cooking" when it contains a high percentage [16 to 25% plus]).

Diesel fuel comes in a more limited range of mixes as diesel engines are not very responsive to different mixtures. It has three ingredients: kerosene, ether and a lubricant. In equal parts the fuel is suitable for most engines. Racing engines use fuel with less lubricant.

Store fuel in a cool place. If it separates into white lumps, filter out the lumps, then shake the fuel to remix it.

## Glow plugs

A glow plug looks like a spark plug but, where the spark plug has a gap between the two electrodes across which a spark jumps, the glow plug has a platinum alloy element connection. When a current is passed through the glow plug, the element glows bright orange and ignites the fuel mixture. The element continues to glow when the electrical supply is disconnected, because of the reaction between the platinum element and the glow fuel mixture, and keeps the engine firing.

Glow plugs are classified according to the heat generated by the element. The three most common are hot, standard and cool, and are usually color-coded red, yellow and blue respectively. The hot plug generates a lot of heat quickly and is used when the weather is cold or with a straight fuel, particularly in engines with low compression. Starting is usually easier with this type. A cool plug used in a low-compression engine on straight fuel may be difficult to start. The standard plug is a general-purpose plug for use with all types of engine and in all conditions. The cool plug is used in engines running on hot (high nitromethane content) fuel such as high-compression racing engines. A hot plug used with hot fuel can cause pre-ignition and shorten the life of the plug by overheating it. Most manufacturers specify plugs for their engines; some supply their own. Experiment to find the best combination of plug and fuel for your particular engine and always keep a selection of plugs on hand when you operate the model.

Glow plugs are made with two lengths of thread, either short reach or long reach. Check to see which length is recommended for your engine as a long reach plug can hit the piston at top dead center on some engines. The reach of the plug also has an effect on engine performance because of the position of the element in the cylinder. The short plug may be cooler if shielded from the fuel mixture by the cylinder head, whereas the long reach plug which projects into the main flow of fuel and air may be hotter and, therefore, more responsive.

The design of the element also varies. Some have a vertical spiral inside the center of the body while others have a flat coil over the end. Radio-control glow plugs made for engines with a throttle, have a special idle bar bridging the end to protect the element from becoming wet and less efficient when the engine is idling on a rich fuel mixture. Another type of plug which works well for both simple carburetors and those with a throttle, has a soft iron heat-sink core around which the element is wound. Whatever the design, the element in a well used plug can become clogged with fuel residue and affect the engine's performance. It should be replaced.

A glow plug is connected to the battery for starting by a glow clip or connector and two cables, a red one linking the central electrode and the positive side of the battery, and a black one linking the plug body and the negative side of the battery. Glow plugs are designed to be used with a 1.5-volt battery or a 2-volt storage battery. Some can be used with both. Although no harm can be done by using a 1.5-volt battery with a 2-volt plug (the engine will simply not fire), you can overload a 1.5-volt plug with a 2-volt supply unless you install a resistor in the electrical circuit.

To check that the glow plug and battery are working properly, remove the plug with a plug wrench. Connect the glow clip to the plug and observe the element. The element should turn orange. If it turns dull red, the plug may be worn or the battery run down. If it is yellow, you are using a battery with too high a voltage. Some glow plugs have a glass insulator which allows you to check the element without removing it from the engine.

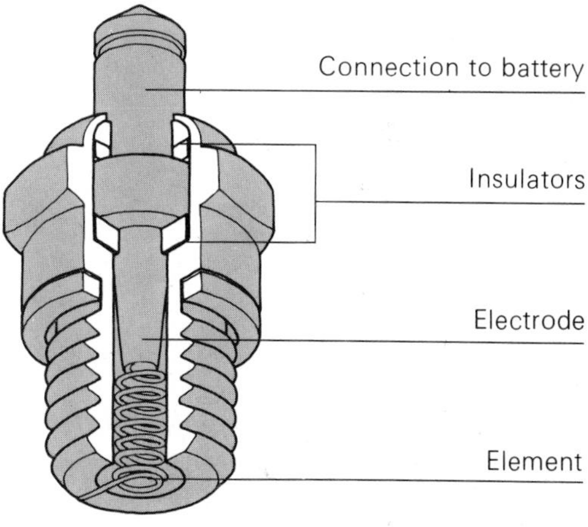


**Glow plug**

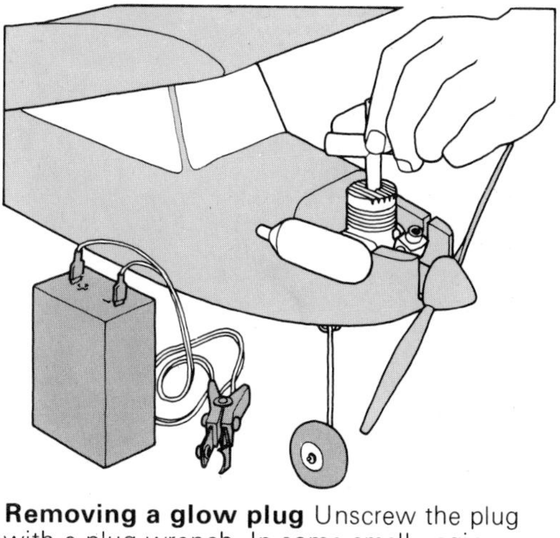

**Removing a glow plug** Unscrew the plug with a plug wrench. In some small engines the plug and cylinder head must be removed together with a special wrench. When you replace the plug, always make sure that the copper gasket sits properly and avoid overtightening it.

## Mufflers

An internal combustion engine should have a muffler on the exhaust port duct to reduce its high-pitched noise. Competition rules in particular limit the noise level to a specific number of decibels.

Mufflers work by allowing the exhaust gases to expand in a chamber which slows them down and results in a drop in noise level. They are always carefully designed to match specific engine sizes to minimize any back pressure caused by the expanding gases. Back pressure affects an engine's performance; therefore, any change from the recommended muffler may result in a loss of power or cause overheating.

Most mufflers are the standard torpedo shape with or without an internal baffle. You can also buy an after muffler to attach to a standard muffler to reduce engine noise even more. One type of muffler designed for scale airplanes is compact but less effective. High-performance engines will often have a tuned pipe, a long muffler which will only match the engine for which it is designed. Boats can use standard mufflers but special tube-shaped mufflers are also available. Cars usually have pot mufflers. Always follow the manufacturer's instructions for attaching the muffler; the method varies according to its construction.

A muffler needs little maintenance. Check the joint between the engine and manifold occasionally and tighten the bolts if they have worked loose. After operating the engine always tip up the model to drain any fuel residue from the exhaust expansion chamber to prevent it running back into the engine. This is particularly important if the model has a tuned pipe. Water vapor is a by-product of the fuel used in a glow plug engine and it can condense, run into the engine and corrode the ferrous metal parts. Periodically wipe out the inside of mufflers with removable ends. Those mufflers with a fiberglass filter can have the filter replaced.

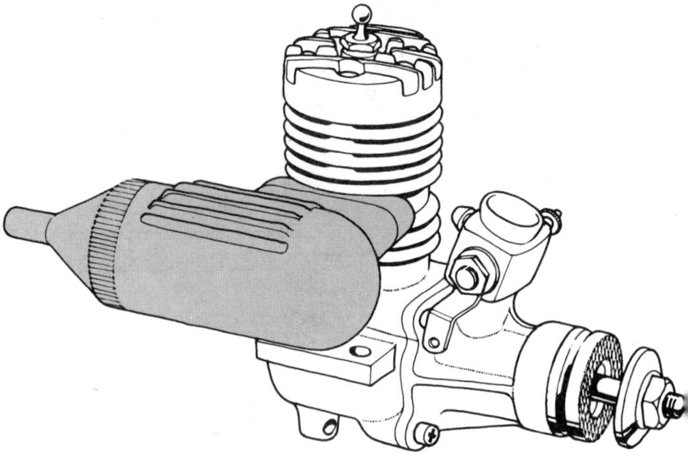

**Standard muffler**

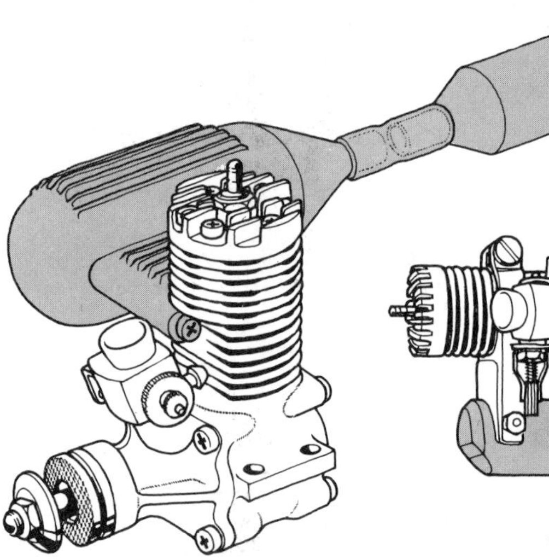

**Standard muffler and after muffler**

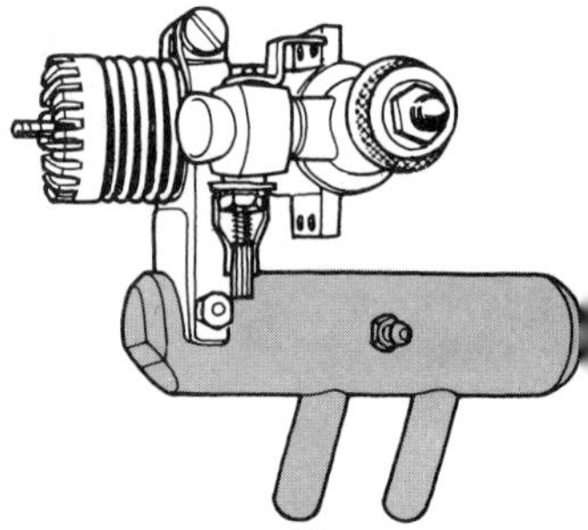

**Compact muffler for airplanes**

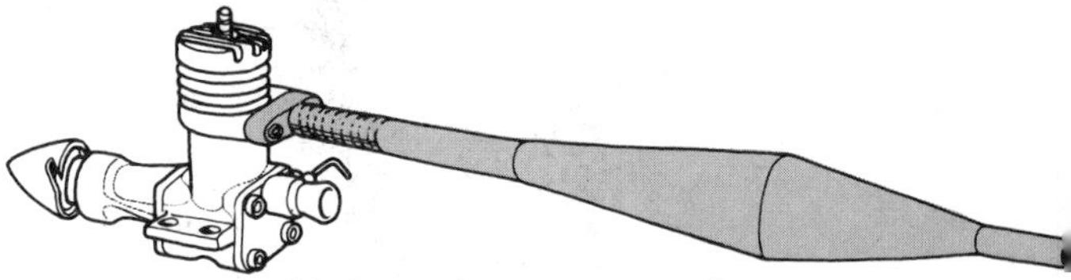

**Tuned pipe on high-performance engine**

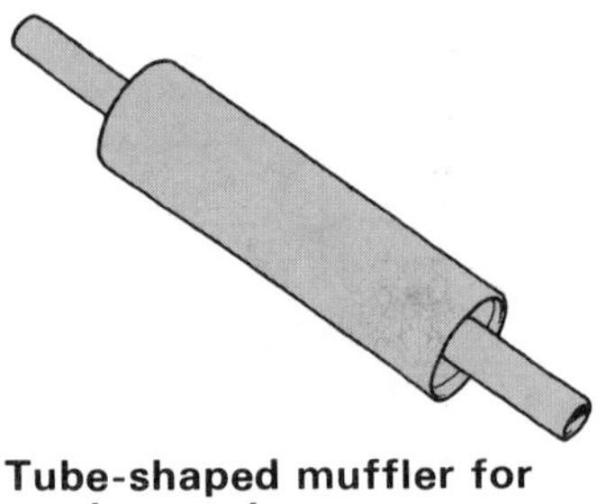

**Tube-shaped muffler for marine engines**

**Pot muffler for cars**

## Starting an engine

Make sure that the engine is securely mounted in the model or on a workbench. Fill the tank with the correct fuel and in the case of a glow plug engine, use a suitable plug. For airplanes, also check that the propeller is the right size and at the correct angle for starting. Remember that an engine must always be broken in before it can be run at full speed for any length of time (see Breaking in an engine, pages 242 to 243).

Glow plug and diesel engines have slightly different procedures for starting. However, each requires a starting force which is nearly always in an anticlockwise direction. There are four ways of applying the starting force to an engine. Flick starting is the traditional method of starting an airplane engine. Some small engines come with a spring starter, a spring around the crankcase which connects to the propeller or propeller cam. Hand-held electric starters are used to start airplanes, boats or cars, particularly those with larger engines. They run off a 12-volt storage battery and have interchangeable drive wheels for different models. There are two types of drive wheel for airplanes, one which is used on the spinner, the other on the propeller boss. Drive wheels have a groove for turning the belt on marine engines. Marine engines can also be whip started with a leather cord.

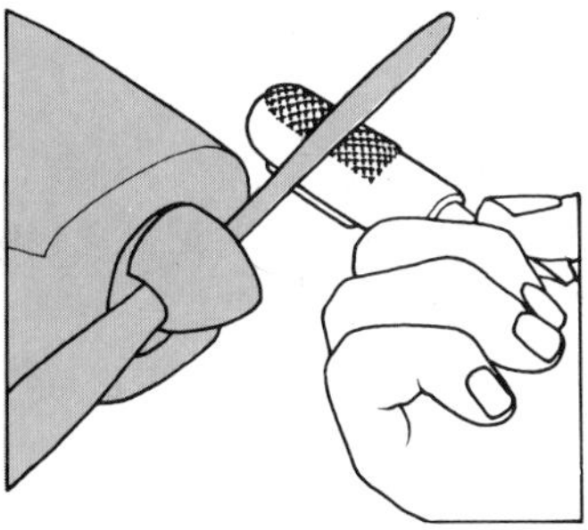

**Flick starting an airplane engine** Place your finger midway along the propeller blade and, with a flick of the wrist, spin the propeller anticlockwise. You can protect your finger with a rubber sleeve.

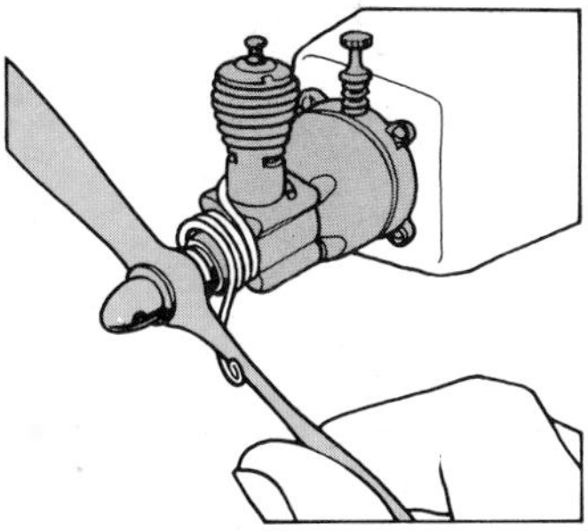

**Spring starting an airplane engine** Connect the spring to the propeller or propeller cam. Pull propeller back and clockwise about half a turn, then release it. The spring will pull the propeller back and detach itself automatically.

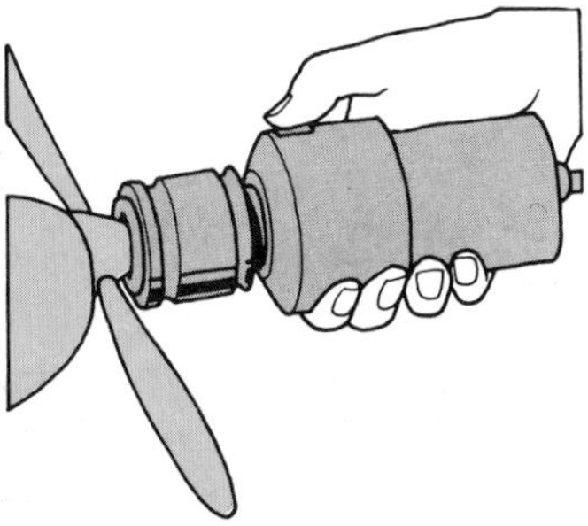

**Starting an airplane with an electric starter** Hold the model steady and push the driver against the spinner or propeller boss. Press switch to start. As the engine fires and picks up speed, remove the electric starter.

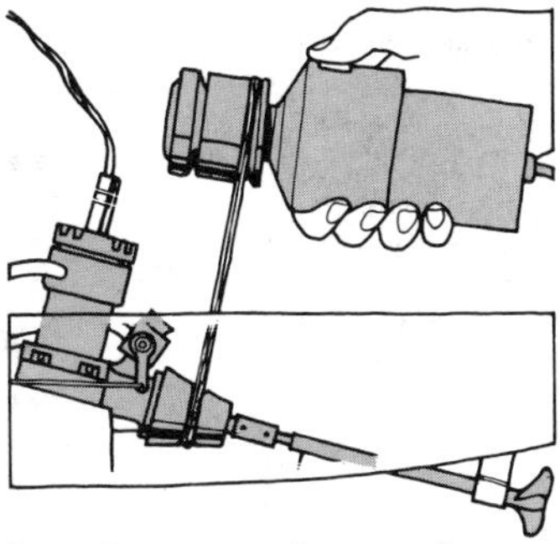

**Starting a marine engine with an electric starter** Place belt in grooves of flywheel and starter. The starter must face the front of the engine for belt to rotate in correct direction. Lift starter to hold belt under tension; press switch. When engine is running, let belt go slack and leave in boat, clear of flywheel.

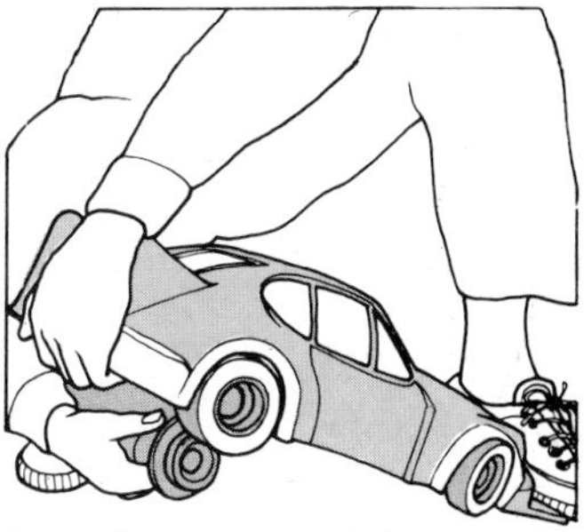

**Starting a car with an electric starter** Hold the back of the car up, with the front against your foot or a stable object. Hold the drive wheel against the flywheel and press switch to start.

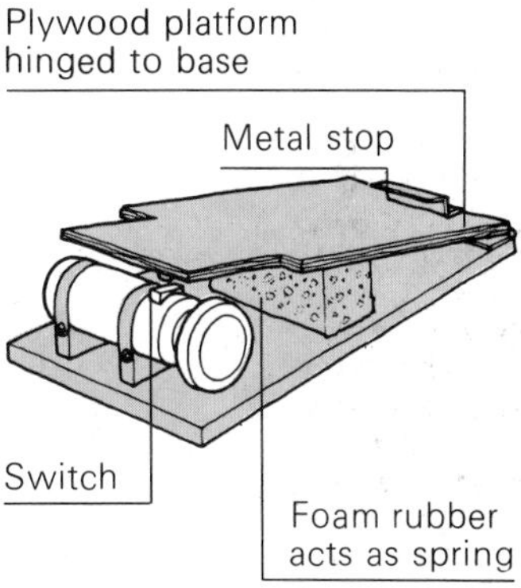


**Starting platform for cars** Build a stand to make it easier to start the car.

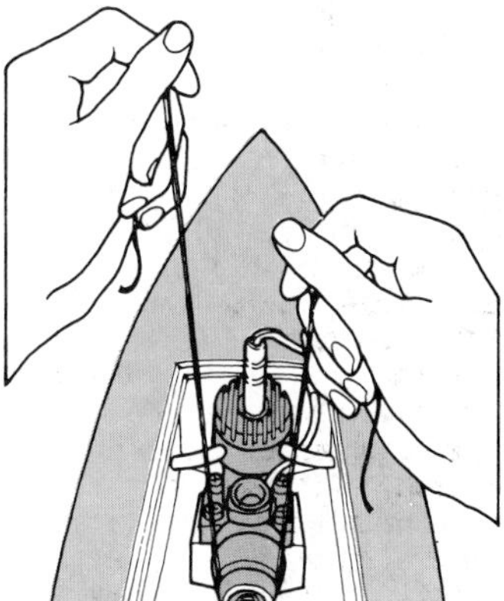

**Whip starting a marine engine** Pass a leather cord under the flywheel and hold it under tension. Make the flywheel turn by pulling the cord sharply with one hand and releasing it moments later from the other.

## Starting a glow plug engine

Begin by screwing the needle valve lightly to close the jet – do not overtighten. Next, unscrew it the recommended number of turns to open the jet. Set the throttle if the engine has one, in between fully closed and half open; you will find the best position with practice.

It helps the engine to start if you add some fuel to it. To prime an engine, cover the carburetor intake with one finger (or, in the case of an engine with a pressurized fuel system or an inaccessible intake, the exhaust outlet); at the same time, turn the engine over by turning the propeller of a plane or the flywheel of a boat or car. You will know that the fuel has reached the engine when you hear a change in the sucking noise. Another method of priming the engine is to inject a little fuel from a bottle into the carburetor intake or exhaust port, but don't inject too much or the engine will flood.

Next, attach the glow plug clip to the engine and apply the appropriate starting force (see page 241). The engine should start promptly and continue to run. Detach the clips (do not leave them on with the engine running; you may shorten the battery's life or overload the plug). Finally, fine tune the carburetor to produce the maximum revs (see Setting a carburetor, page 235).

## Starting a diesel engine

Diesel engines are usually used only in airplanes and boats, not cars. They have two controls to set, the needle valve and compression screw. To start a diesel engine, open up the needle valve by the recommended number of turns and reduce the compression by turning the compression screw anticlockwise. Prime the engine as described for a glow plug engine and try starting it by applying the appropriate starting force. The engine should be reasonably easy to turn over when the compression is low.

If the engine does not start, turn the compression screw clockwise by a quarter of a turn to raise the compression and try again. Repeat until the engine runs. Do not set the compression so high that the engine becomes difficult to turn over as this strains the engine and too much force can permanently damage the connecting rod.

Once the engine continues to run, close the needle valve by about a quarter of a turn to weaken the mixture, then screw in the compression screw slightly until the engine runs smoothly. As the engine warms up you may need to adjust both settings slightly for the engine to give its best performance.

## Stopping an engine

To stop an engine, shut off either the fuel or air supply by pinching the fuel line or covering the carburetor intake respectively. You can also stop an engine by completely closing the throttle or needle valve, but you will have to reset the carburetor when you restart it.

## Breaking in an engine

Model engines are made to very fine tolerances. When the working surfaces are new they are not perfectly matched, and as the parts move against each other they can create friction and cause the engine to overheat. Nearly all new engines need to be broken in so that they can run safely at full speed. Only a few small glow plug engines do not need to be broken in as their size makes them much less susceptible to overheating.

It is easier and less risky to break in airplane and car engines out of the model and secured on a workbench where you can take corrective measures instantly. This is known as bench running. A boat engine can be broken in either in the model or on a bench, but in either case, you must keep it water-cooled.

Special test stands are available to hold the engine, or you can make your own mounting board. Screw the stand or mounting board firmly to the workbench. Never grip the engine in a vise as it can damage the crankcase.

When you bench run a boat or car engine, temporarily attach a well-balanced wooden airplane propeller (a nylon propeller may disintegrate at high revs) instead of a flywheel. Airplane engines should use a propeller with a finer than normal pitch but with the same or slightly smaller diameter, to reduce strain on the moving parts of the engine.

The manufacturer will recommend how an engine should be broken in, but most engines should be run for 30 minutes at full throttle on a rich mixture, with stops at 5-minute intervals. The excess oil from the rich mixture reduces the friction and heat, and the stops allow the engine to cool down.

Begin by filling the tank with the recommended fuel for breaking in, usually a straight fuel or one with a low nitromethane content for glow plug engines, and a fuel with a high percentage of lubricant for diesels. Hold the throttle on radio-control engines fully open with a pushrod. Start the engine and adjust the needle valve to a rich setting so that the engine is four-cycling. Run the engine for about 5 minutes, then stop it and allow it to cool for a short while. Restart the engine and repeat the process at least six times. Engines with a throttle can be set to idle for a minute between bursts at full throttle instead of stopping.

The engine still needs careful attention after this basic breaking in. Adjust the mixture to a leaner, although still rich, setting so that the engine is two-cycling, and replace the normal propeller on an airplane engine. If the engine begins to slow down and overheat, open the needle valve to a rich setting immediately, and in the case of an airplane engine, replace the smaller propeller – the engine needs more breaking in. When the engine runs continuously at top speed without slowing down or overheating, it is broken in. Install it in the model and run it on a slightly rich setting to begin with, keeping a close check on it.

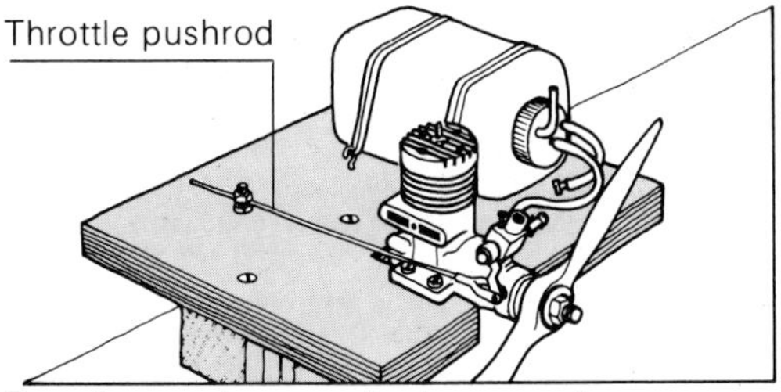


**Bench running an airplane engine**

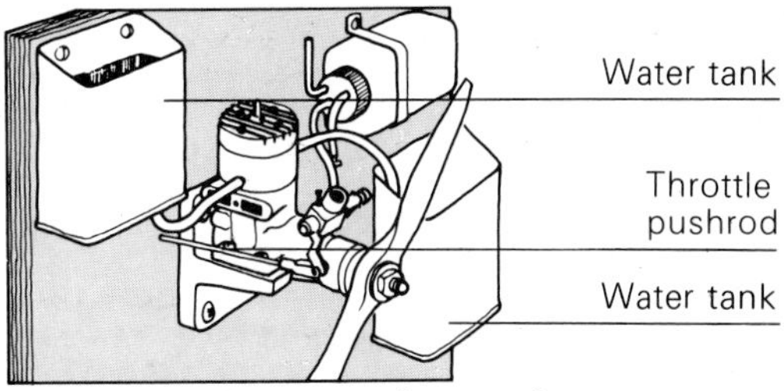


**Bench running a marine engine**

## Fault finding: glow plug engine

| Will not start | Runs roughly | Stops |
|---|---|---|
| Spin the engine faster. | Fuel mixture too rich: screw in needle valve. | Run out of fuel: fill tank. |
| Wrong fuel: check type. | Partially blocked jet: remove needle and blow through jet. | Fuel mixture is too weak: unscrew needle valve. |
| Needle valve closed: open as recommended. | Overheating: increase ventilation or check water-cooling system on a boat. Check fuel type and needle-valve setting. | Blocked jet: remove needle and blow through jet. |
| Blocked jet: remove needle and blow through jet. | Propeller size wrong: check recommended size. | Blocked fuel filter: clean and replace. |
| Engine flooded: remove plug and blow dry. Turn engine over with fuel supply disconnected. | Glow plug worn: replace. | Check boat propeller for weeds. |
| Battery low: recharge. | Wrong plug: change type. | Plug burned out: replace. |
| Plug worn or broken: replace. | | |

## Fault finding: diesel engine

| Will not start | Runs roughly | Stops |
|---|---|---|
| Spin the engine faster. | Fuel mixture too rich: screw in needle valve. | Run out of fuel: fill tank. |
| No fuel: fill tank | Overheating: increase ventilation or check water-cooling system on a boat; check fuel type and needle-valve setting. | Fuel mixture too weak: unscrew needle valve. |
| Needle valve closed: open as recommended. | Propeller size wrong: check recommended size. | Blocked jet: remove needle and blow through jet. |
| Blocked jet: remove needle and blow through jet. | Engine misfires or slows down: adjust the compression screw. | Blocked fuel filter: clean filter and replace. |
| Engine flooded: unscrew compression screw and turn the engine over with fuel supply disconnected, or blow through exhaust port. | | Check boat propeller for weeds. |
| No compression: screw in compression screw. | | |

# $CO_2$ engines

The $CO_2$ engine is a clean, silent, two-cycle engine powered by compressed carbon dioxide gas. It is very small and light and intended for use in light, free-flight airplanes. Most $CO_2$ engines are single-cylinder engines although there is a horizontally apposed twin-cylinder and a multi-cylinder version available. The engine comes with a gas tank and a propeller. One special design has the gas tank built into the engine body.

A $CO_2$ engine works like a two-cycle internal combustion engine except that the piston is driven by $CO_2$ gas which enters the cylinder head directly through a ball valve. To start the engine, simply flick the propeller in an anticlockwise direction. The only maintenance the engine needs is a regular injection of thin oil through the exhaust port.

Because of the low temperature of the gas, it is often an advantage to mount the engine and the fuel line so that they are partially exposed to the air flow. The air prevents the engine from icing up. The design with the built-in tank can be completely enclosed inside the fuselage because its particular construction keeps the gas from freezing.

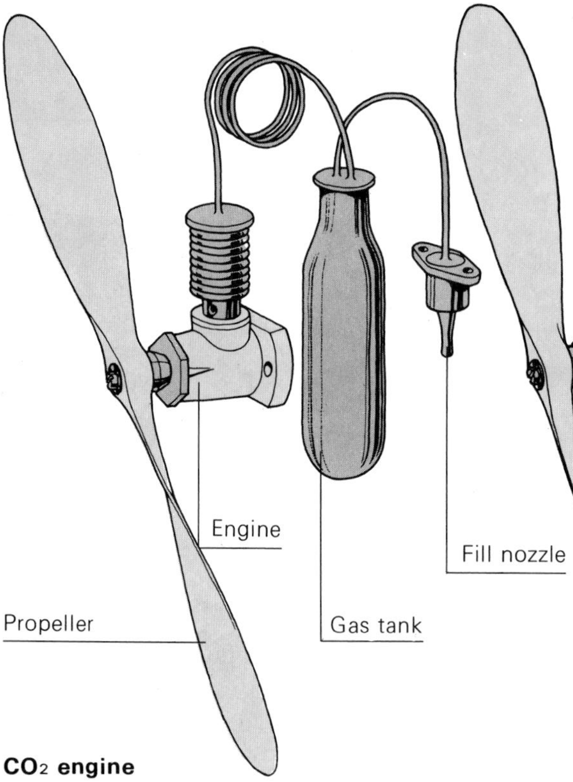


**$CO_2$ engine**

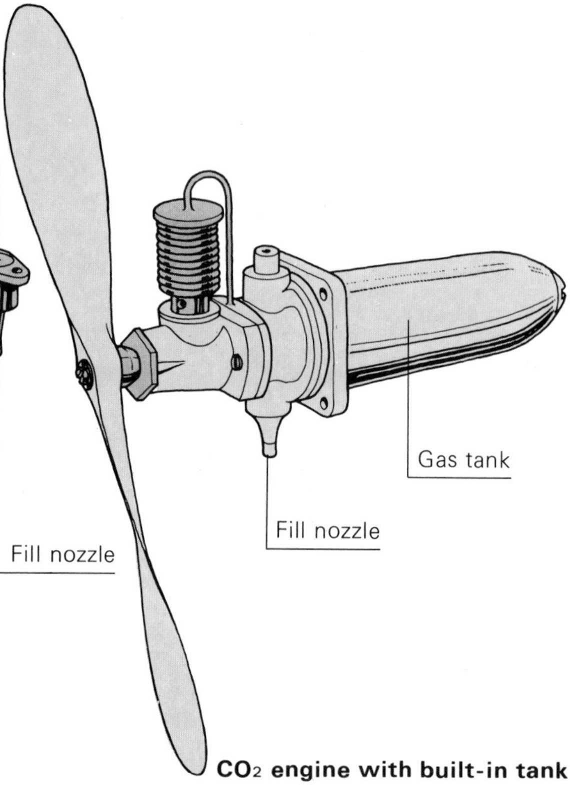


**$CO_2$ engine with built-in tank**

## How a $CO_2$ engine works

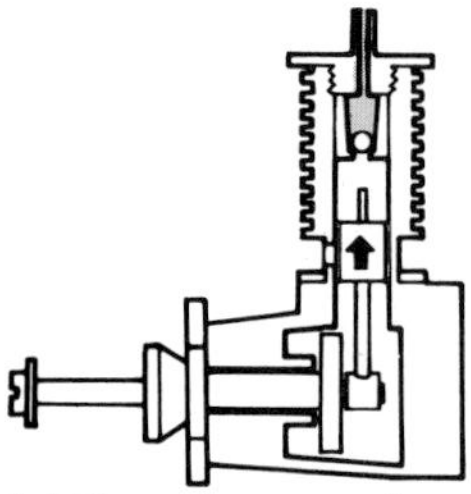

**1** When the propeller is turned anticlockwise, the shaft which is attached to it rotates. This in turn drives the piston up.

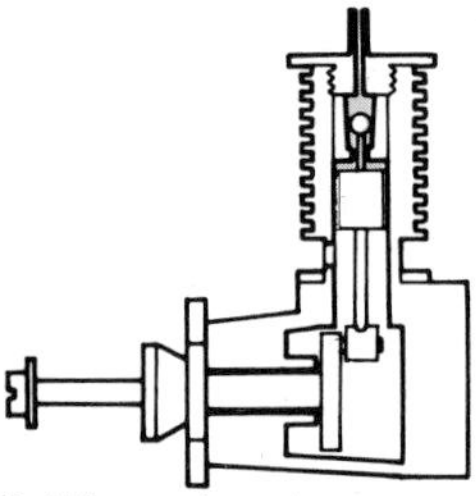

**2** When the piston reaches the top, the spigot on its crown opens a small ball valve, letting in compressed gas.

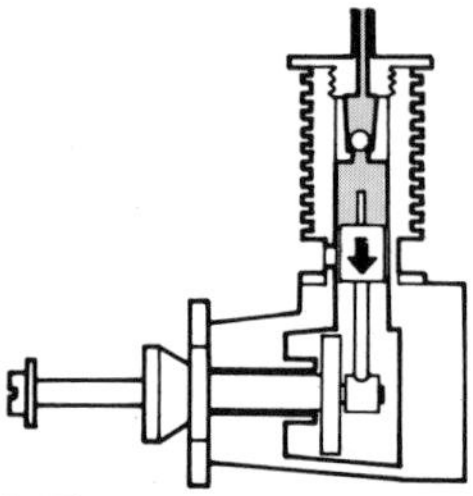

**3** The gas expands rapidly so forcing the piston down. As the piston descends, the ball valve automatically closes.

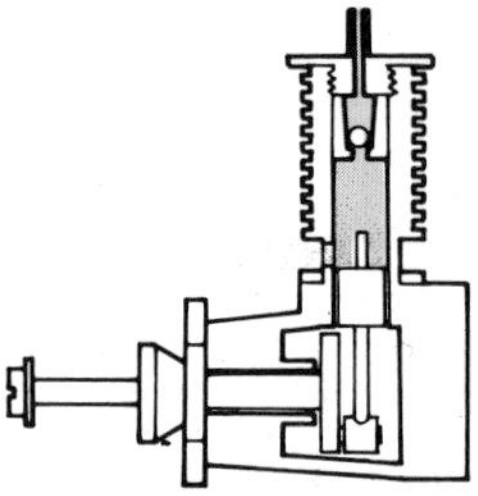

**4** When the piston reaches the bottom, the spent gas escapes. The momentum of the propeller drives the piston up again.

## Tuning the engine

The $CO_2$ engine is designed to run at a single speed. Tune your engine so that it gives its best performance by increasing or decreasing the distance between the ball valve and the piston spigot. The closer the spigot is to the ball valve, the more gas is let in and the faster the engine will run. The distance can be altered by turning either the top of the cylinder or a nut behind the prop driver, as shown below. If too much gas is delivered, however, the propeller will feel difficult to flick and the engine will backfire making a popping sound. Moreover, because of the nature of the gas, if too much is injected at once, the engine may ice up and stop. If too little gas is delivered, there will be insufficient pressure to run the engine.

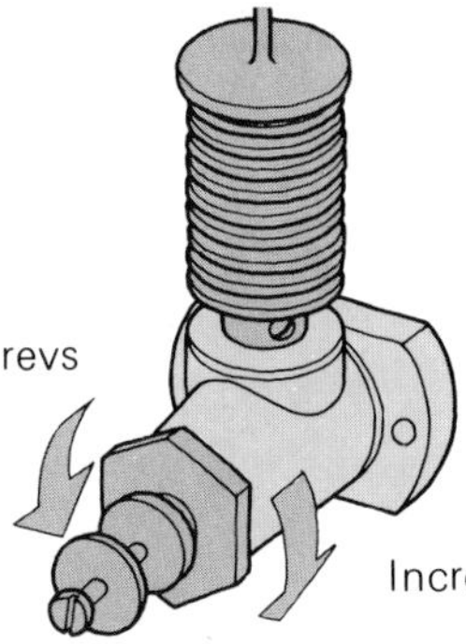


**Adjusting the engine** Turn the nut behind the prop driver clockwise to increase the revs or anticlockwise to decrease them. On some engines the adjustment is made by turning the top of the cylinder.

## Mounting and filling the tank

Although the cylinder itself can be mounted in any direction, up, down or sideways, if it is to work best the gas tank should be mounted vertically with the copper fuel line at the top. If the tank is taller than the fuselage, let it project through the bottom. Take care to position it so that the plane balances correctly (see page 294). Roll any extra line into a coil – do not cut it. The coil is usually formed above the cylinder head so that it is in the airstream, but it can be anywhere along the pipe. Secure the fill nozzle with screws or epoxy glue in a convenient and well-supported position in the fuselage. You may need to reinforce the side of the fuselage with balsa wood pieces to take the pressure when you fill the tank.

Use a charger to fill the tank. The charger takes a disposable bulb of $CO_2$ gas, such as a Sparklet bulb. Put the bulb in the charger, nozzle up, and screw the cap down tightly. Push the charger nozzle firmly onto the engine fill nozzle as shown right. Never unscrew the charger cap to replace a $CO_2$ bulb without first opening the valve by unscrewing the charger nozzle a few turns to make sure it is completely empty. Retighten the nozzle before you insert the new bulb.

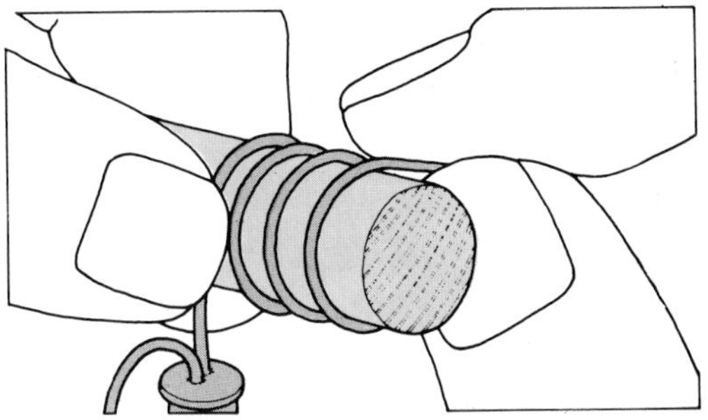

**Coiling the line** Roll any extra line around a dowel rod not less than $\frac{3}{8}$ inch (10 mm) in diameter. Avoid sharp bends.

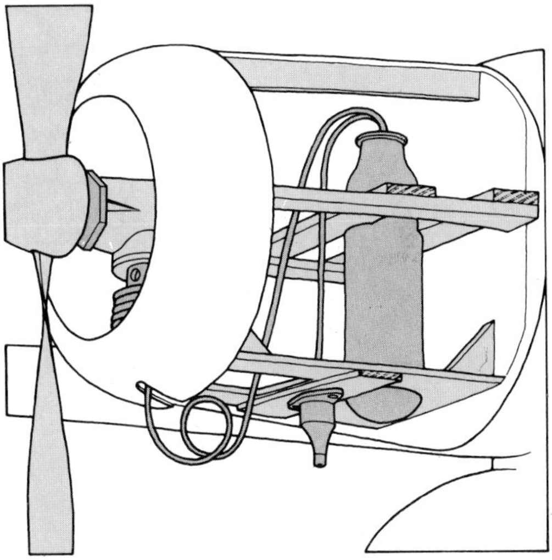

**Mounting the tank** Support the tank vertically with balsa strips or blocks but do not enclose it; air must circulate around it.

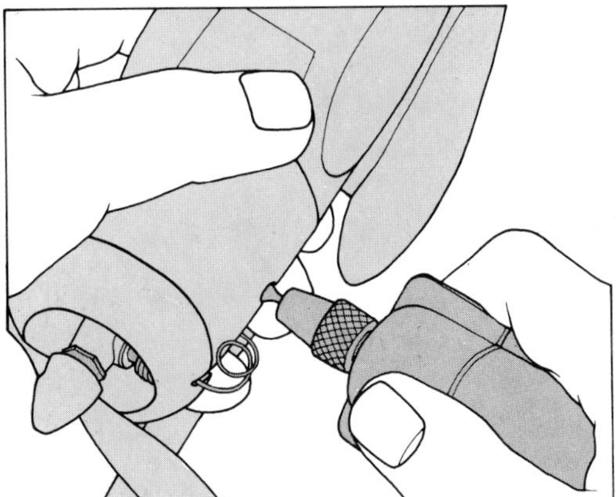

**Filling the tank** Push the charger nozzle onto the fill nozzle for about 5 seconds. If the charger is nozzle up, it fills the tank with what is known as a "gas" charge which gives a short run; if it is nozzle down, it produces a "liquid" charge giving a longer run.

# Steam engines

A steam engine uses steam under pressure to drive a piston in a cylinder. The steam is generated by a burner heating water in the boiler. The appeal of steam power is in the simplicity of the system and the smell of oil and steam which give the model a character akin to the real thing. Until the introduction of reliable internal combustion engines and electric motors, steam engines were the only power source for model boats and trains. As these other engines developed, the use of steam declined, and it now is a specialized area of modeling reserved for the skilled engineer who builds most, if not all, parts of the model and engine from scratch. Simple engines are available, however, which are easy to install and allow the general modeler to power a vehicle with steam.

Broad-beam boats such as tugs and fishing vessels are the usual steam-powered models; their proportion and character suit steam well. Although steam engines are heavy and bulky, their weight adds essential ballast and the hull is able to accommodate all the components. The engine must, however, be easily accessible for preparation and maintenance, so most steam-powered boats have removable superstructures and decks. The hull should also be well ventilated to allow the burner to function properly and the heat to escape. The inner surfaces of the engine compartment should be sealed with heatproof paint.

## Types of steam engine

The most popular designs are the oscillating, slide-valve and piston-valve engines. The single-cylinder oscillating engine is the simplest. The cylinder is mounted on a metal stand and pivots on a pin against the face of the stand. When the crankshaft rotates, the cylinder rocks from side to side and a port in the cylinder aligns alternately with an intake and exhaust port in the stand. Once the steam is built up, you simply spin the flywheel to start the engine. If you want to run the engine in reverse, swap the intake and exhaust connections. A small bore, single-cylinder oscillating engine will power a 20- to 30-inch (50- to 75-cm) hull. A multi-cylinder engine gives more power.

The slide-valve engine is more efficient and can power larger boats. It has a conventional fixed cylinder and the steam is fed into it above and below the piston in turn, through a valve chest. The valve in the chest is synchronized with the movement of the piston. Once the steam has built up, the slide-valve engine will start on its own, as long as the piston is not at the very top or bottom. A twin-cylinder slide-valve engine set so that one of the pistons is not at the top or bottom when the engine stops, will always start on its own; this is the best arrangement for radio-control models. A piston-valve engine works on the same principle, but it has a piston valve instead of a slide valve.

To control the speed of a steam engine, you need to attach a special valve.

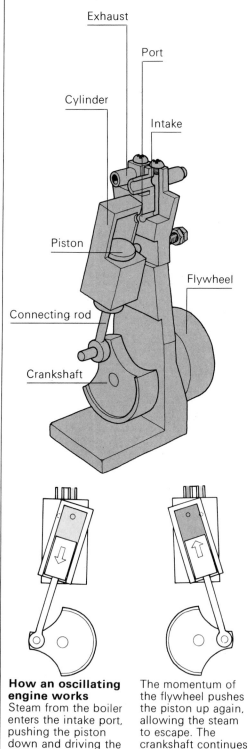

**Oscillating engine**

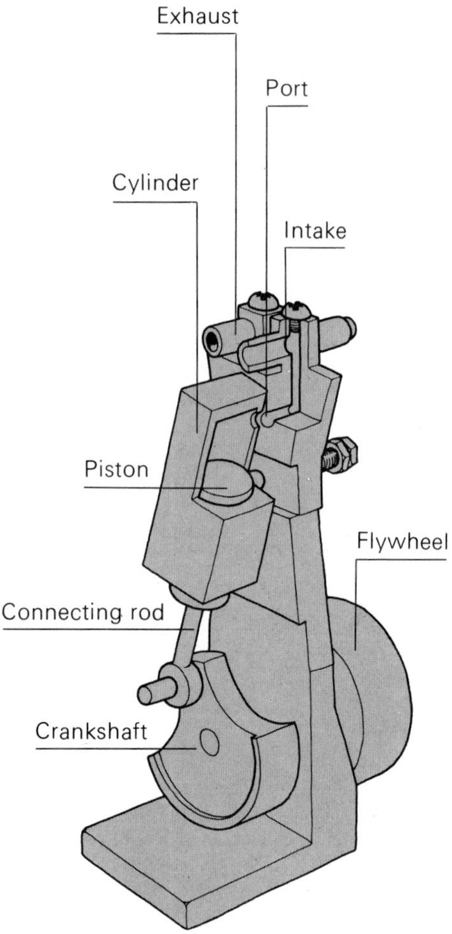


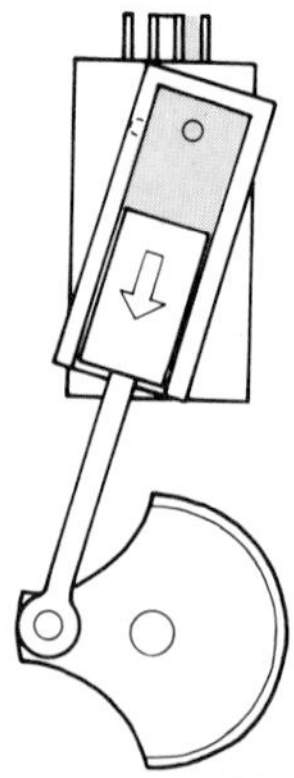

**How an oscillating engine works**
Steam from the boiler enters the intake port, pushing the piston down and driving the crankshaft and the flywheel around.

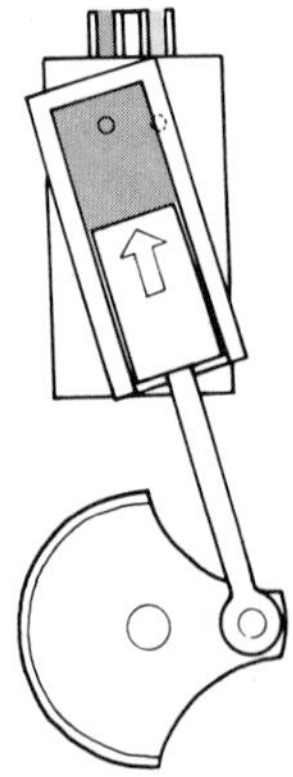

The momentum of the flywheel pushes the piston up again, allowing the steam to escape. The crankshaft continues to rotate and the cycle is repeated.

## Slide-valve engine

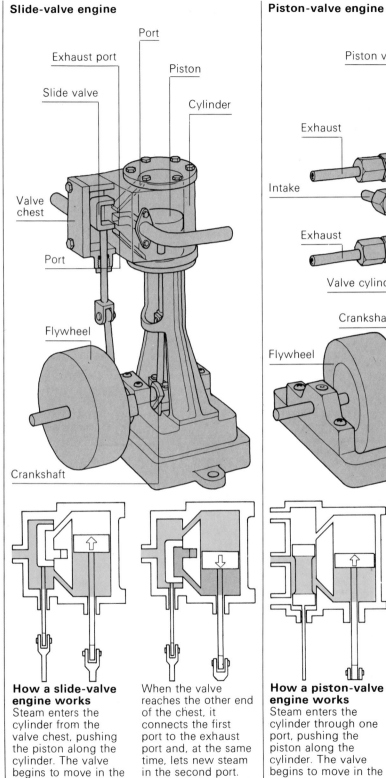

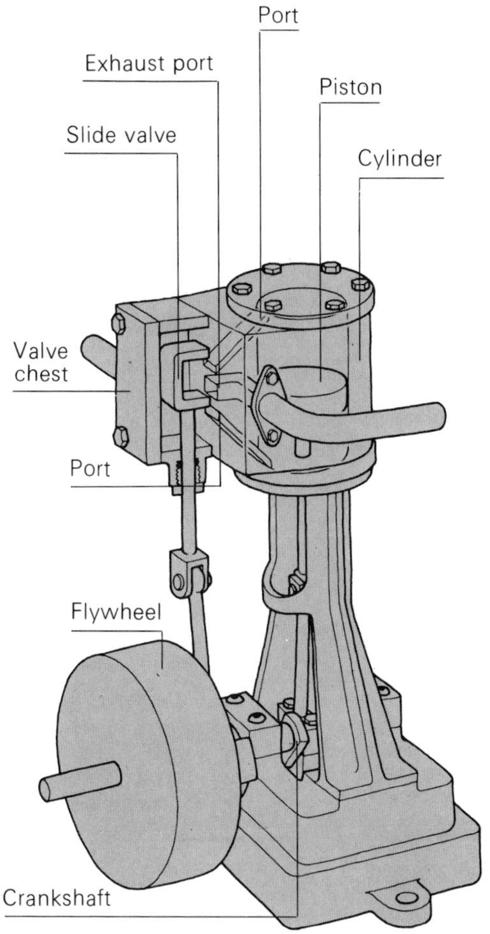


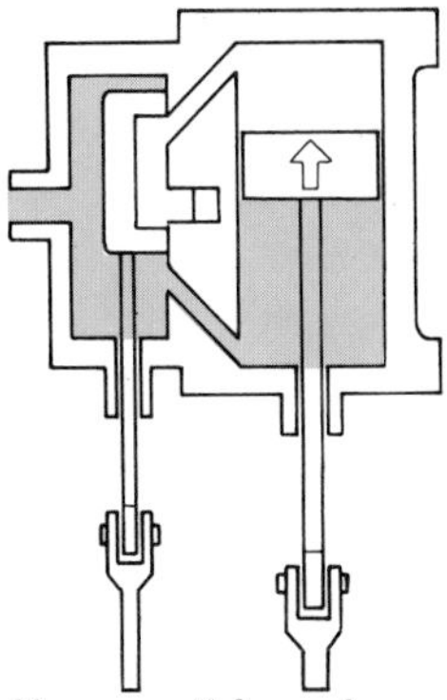

**How a slide-valve engine works**
Steam enters the cylinder from the valve chest, pushing the piston along the cylinder. The valve begins to move in the opposite direction.

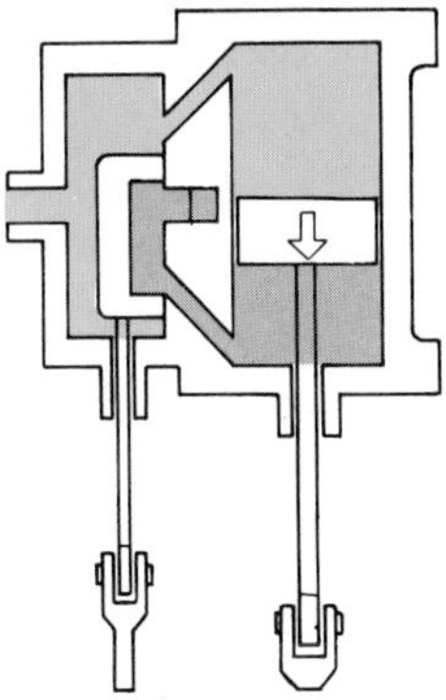

When the valve reaches the other end of the chest, it connects the first port to the exhaust port and, at the same time, lets new steam in the second port. The cycle is repeated.

## Piston-valve engine

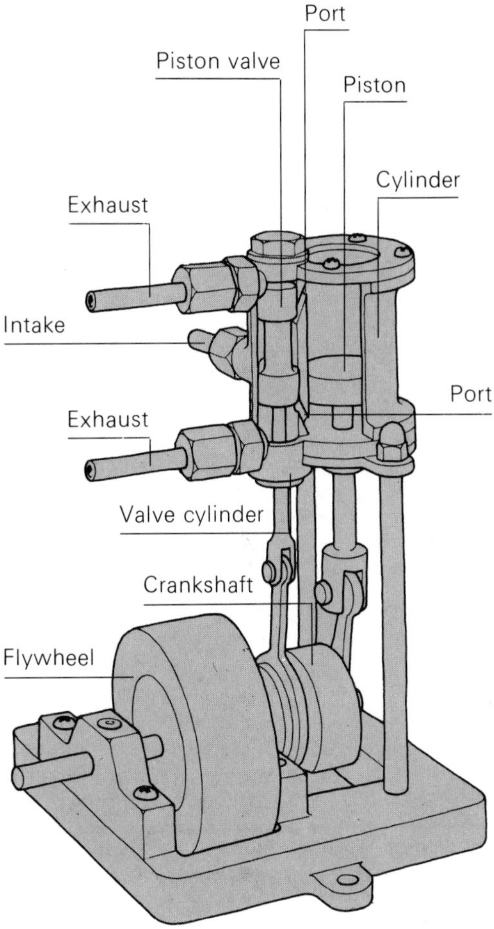


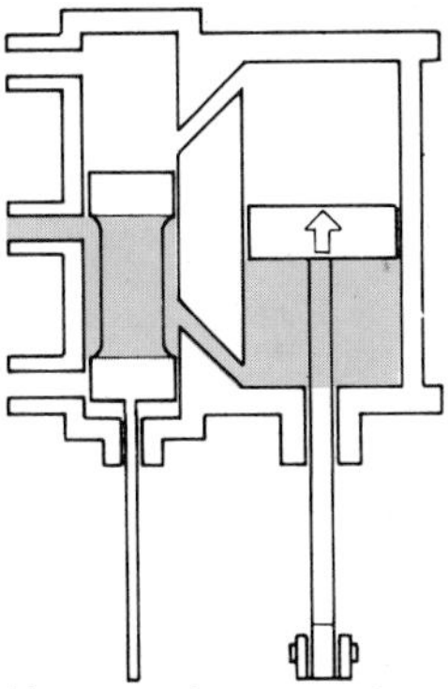

**How a piston-valve engine works**
Steam enters the cylinder through one port, pushing the piston along the cylinder. The valve begins to move in the opposite direction.

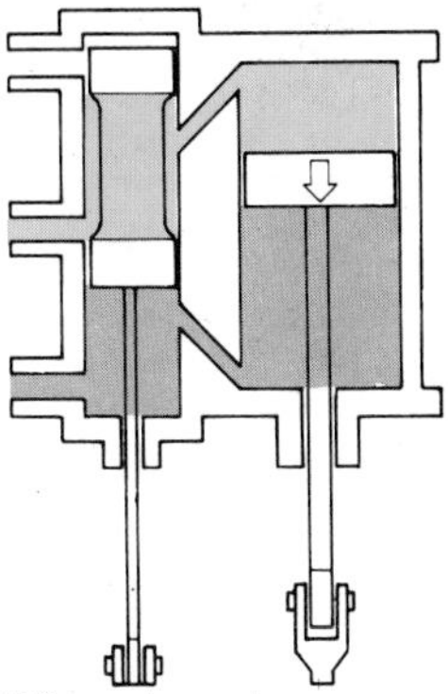

When the valve reaches the other end, it connects the first port to the exhaust port and lets new steam in the second port, in the same way as the slide-valve engine.

## Boilers

An engine needs a boiler which can provide sufficient steam pressure. Oscillating and small slide-valve engines normally use a potboiler which produces steam at a pressure of about 30 psi (2 bars). The potboiler is a simple cylinder supported over a spirit burner or a solid tablet fuel burner.

A center-flue boiler can produce about twice the steam pressure of a potboiler. It is heated by a blow-torch-like burner running on liquified gas, kerosene or gasoline. A fire tube directs the flame through the center of the boiler, increasing the heating area. There are several variations of the center-flue boiler available, each with a different arrangement of fire tubes. This type of boiler improves the boat's stability because of its low center of gravity.

The most powerful engines run on boilers which produce superheated steam, "dry" steam without water droplets. The steam from the boiler is superheated by carrying it in a pipe which passes directly through a flame.

Boilers should always be filled up to the recommended level, usually three-quarters full, and never allowed to run dry with the burner functioning. Some boilers have a glass end for checking the water level.

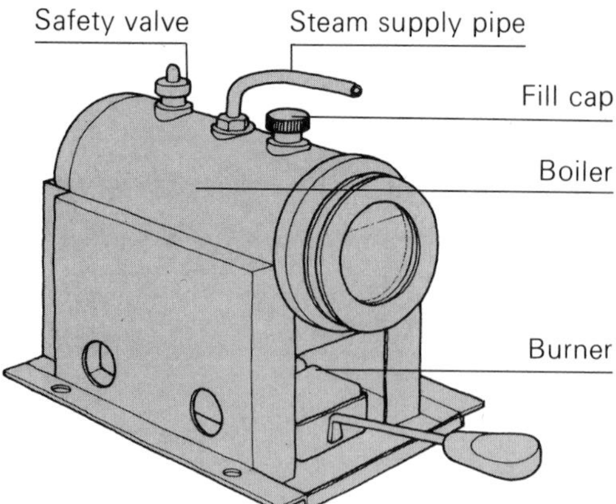


**Potboiler**

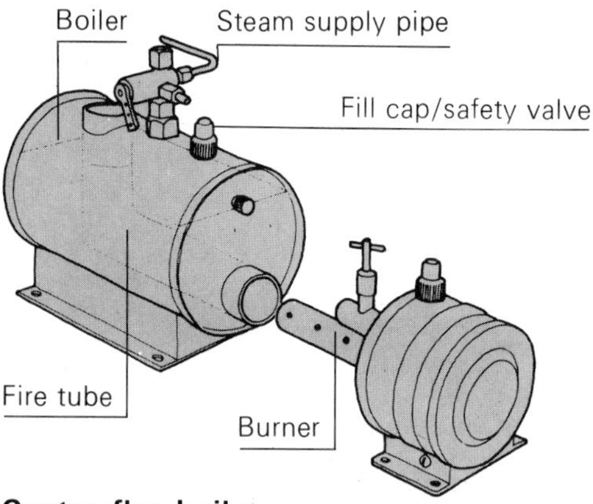


**Center-flue boiler**

## Lubricating the engine

A steam engine needs to be well lubricated to run smoothly and to reduce wear on the sliding faces. The faces of an oscillating engine must be oiled liberally before you run it each time. Use standard car oil and apply it when the engine is warm.

A displacement lubricator is often used to oil slide-valve and piston-valve engines automatically. It is a vertical tube installed in the steam pipe near the engine. As steam from the boiler passes over the oil-filled tube, water droplets or "condensate" gradually fall to the bottom of the tube and displace the oil. The oil is then carried into the cylinder by the steam. A plug allows the water to be drained off.

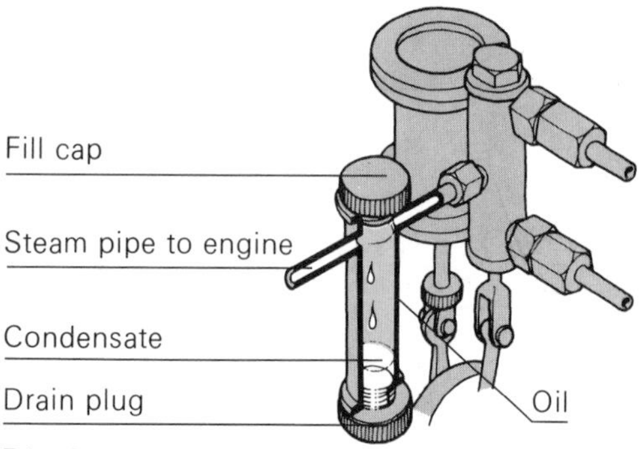


**Displacement lubricator**

## Breaking in a steam engine

A steam engine, like an internal combustion engine, should be broken in gradually. Mount it on a workbench so that it doesn't have to drive the weight of the model, and apply plenty of oil to all the moving parts. Bench run the engine until it will spin freely with the flick of a finger when the engine is cold, before installing it in the boat. Some manufacturers recommend that you connect the engine to a low pressure compressor (the type used for spray-painting, see page 73) and run it on compressed air instead of steam. This method is clean and convenient.

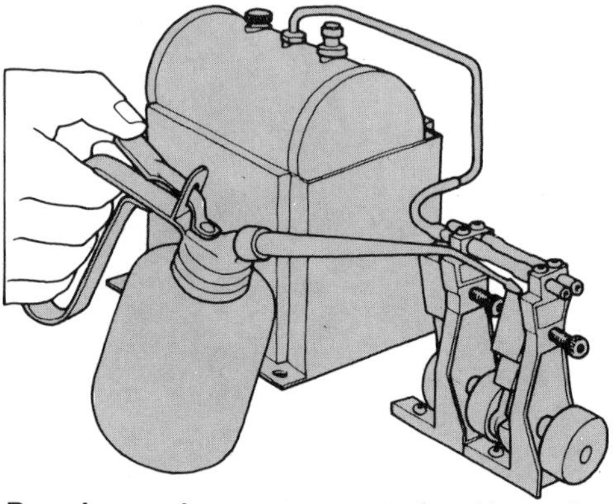

**Bench running a steam engine** Keep all the moving parts of the engine well-oiled.

# Electric motors

In the past electric motors were restricted to boats and cars because of the weight of the battery. Modern motors, however, are much lighter and powerful enough to be used successfully in airplanes.

Although an electric motor has a shorter run than an internal combustion engine, lasting approximately 3 to 10 minutes, it does have many advantages. Not only is it quiet and clean running, but it is virtually maintenance-free. Recharging is the only regular servicing it requires. Because it does not use gas, it is much cheaper to run than an internal combustion engine. Moreover, an electric motor needs no special tuning and is ready to go with a flick of the switch.

Motors are made in sizes from .020 to .40, the size indicating that they have a power output equivalent to a glow plug motor of that displacement. The motor, battery and accessories can be bought separately or wired and ready for installation. A twin-motor system is also available. It uses a single battery of twice the normal capacity so that both motors run down together. For a three-motor system, simply wire a third motor into a twin system; for a four-motor system, use two twins. Electric motors are ideal for multi-engine models because all the motors can be controlled by a single switch, unlike internal combustion engines which require a complicated throttle linkage to make them work in unison.

**Single-motor system**

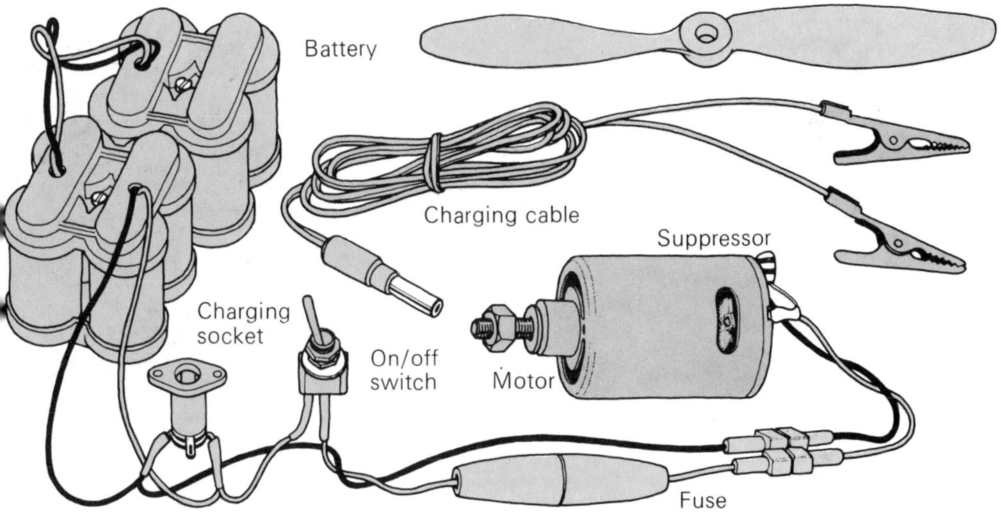


**Twin-motor system**

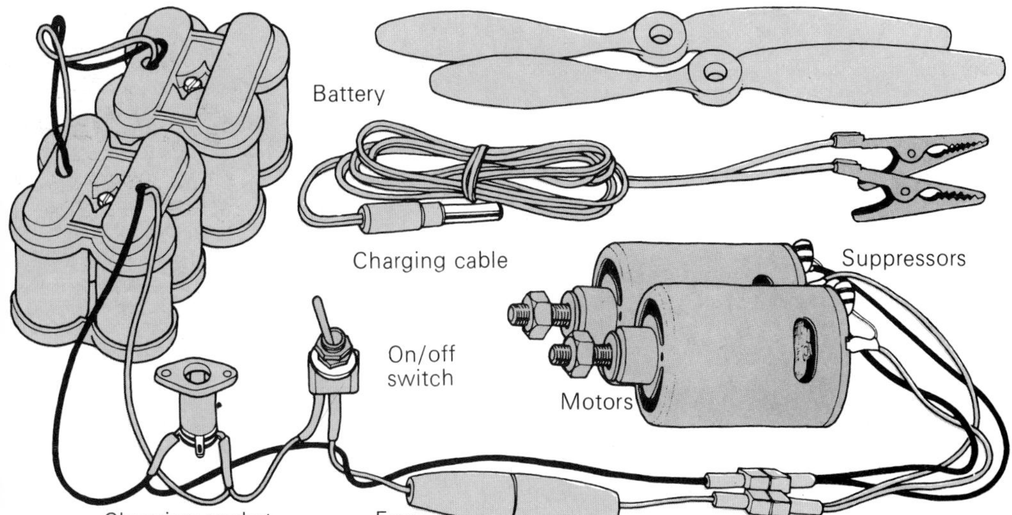

## How an electric motor works

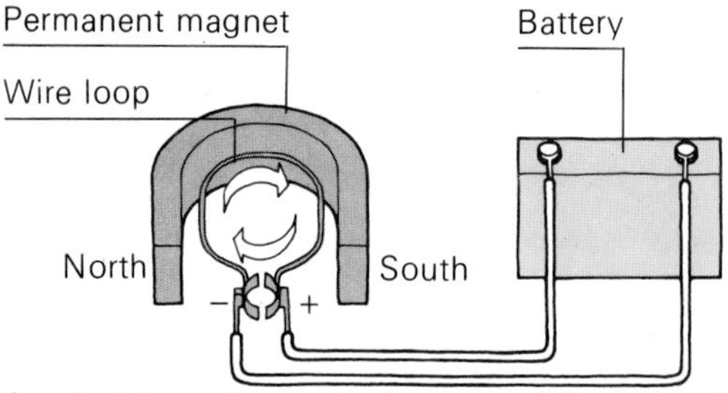


An electric motor works because of the natural attraction and repulsion of magnets. When an electric current passes through a wire a magnetic field is created, and if the wire is made into a loop and placed between the north and south poles of a permanent magnet, it will move. The wire is called an electro-magnet. This simple arrangement of magnets is the basis of an electric motor.

In a model electric motor, the permanent magnets, called field magnets, are fixed to the inside of a cylinder. At the center of the cylinder are three or more electro-magnets mounted on a shaft which is free to rotate. Each electro-magnet consists of a coil of copper wire around an iron core which concentrates the magnetic field. The electro-magnets are known collectively as the armature.

Model electric motors always use direct electric current (DC) rather than alternating current (AC). It is fed to the armature through brushes. The brushes are contacts fixed to the cylinder casing which rub against other contacts mounted on the motor shaft, each of which is wired to one electro-magnet in the armature. These inner contacts are grouped together and called the commutator. When the motor is switched on, electricity is fed to one electro-magnet. It becomes magnetized and is deflected sideways by the field magnets, making the shaft turn and bringing new contacts on the commutator to meet the brushes. The process repeats itself to keep the shaft turning continuously. The direction in which the shaft turns can be reversed by simply swapping the positive and negative cords from the battery.

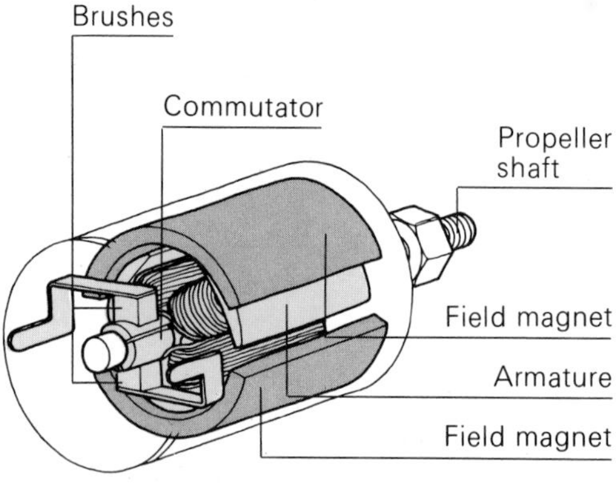


## Batteries

Electric motors use nicad (nickel-cadmium) batteries which take only 15 to 30 minutes to charge. The batteries come as packs of 3, 4, 6 or 8 cells, each cell with an output of 0.6 or 1.2 amps. The more powerful the motor, the larger the battery it requires. You may need to use more than one battery pack for very powerful motors.

To charge a battery, plug the charging cord into the charging socket in the battery and connect the two terminals on the other end of the cord to a 12-volt storage battery or to the cigarette lighter of a car if it has the same type of connection (the car engine must not be running). The cord is a specific length to suit the battery and should never be shortened. Leave the battery to charge for the time recommended by the manufacturer. A charging monitor or rapid charger will help you to judge when the battery is fully charged; the latter shortens the charging time. Some of these devices shut off the supply automatically when the battery is charged.

A nicad battery becomes warm as the current is drawn from it. Always allow air to circulate around the battery in the model to keep it from becoming hot, and let the battery cool before recharging it. A hot battery gives a shorter run and will not charge fully. If the motor runs for progressively shorter lengths of time, you may not be letting the battery cool sufficiently before recharging it.

The propeller or gears on a vehicle also affect the life of the battery as the more load put on the motor, the faster the power drains from the battery. A fine-pitched propeller or low gear, for instance, allows the motor to reach its running speed with less effort. Follow the manufacturer's recommendation – a propeller that is too large or a gear that is too high will overload the battery and damage it.

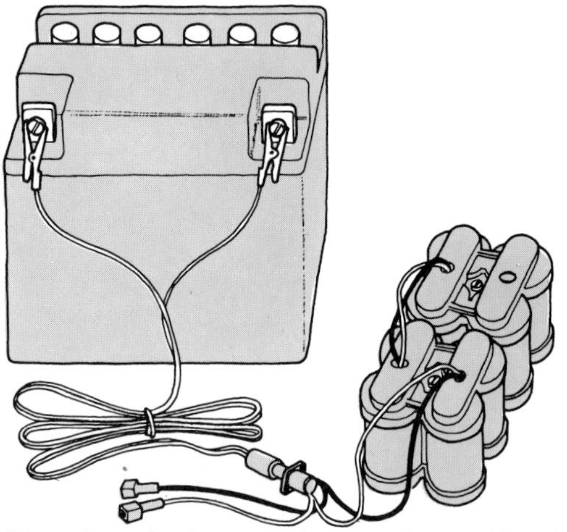

**Charging the battery** Connect it to a 12-volt storage battery with the charging cord and leave to charge for the recommended time. Only charge a cool battery.

## Controlling the speed

To control the speed of an electric motor, you need either a resistor or an electronic speed controller to regulate the current supplied to the motor. The simplest resistor has a switch with three positions, high, low and off. Another has an arm which rotates around a circuit board; it gives more speeds, including reverse, and a smoother transition between them. A third type has an arm which slides across the resistor. Because the arm is in constant contact with the resistor, you can adjust the motor from full speed through to stop without any breaks. All these devices are controlled by a servo (see Servos, pages 259 to 260). Resistors heat up, particularly when the motor is running at low speed, so be sure to allow air to circulate around them.

Electronic speed controllers plug directly into the radio receiver and do away with the need for a servo. Like the resistor with the sliding arm, they give control over the motor's entire speed range. They are, however, more efficient than resistors as they do not cause any loss of power.

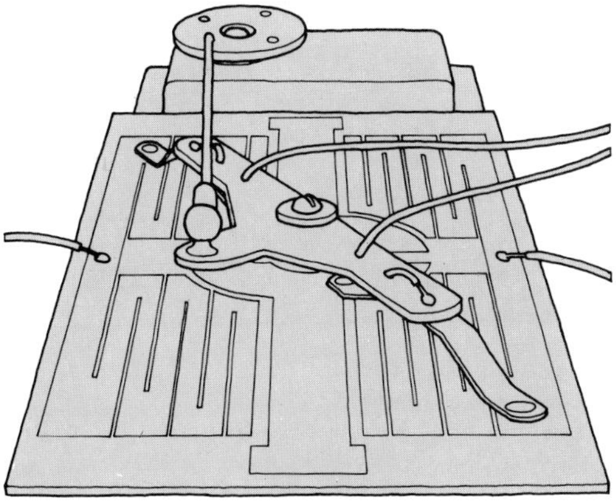

**Resistor with circuit board**

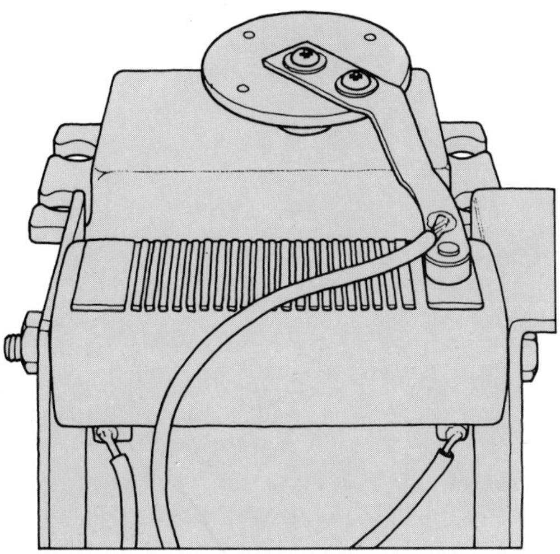

**Resistor with sliding arm**

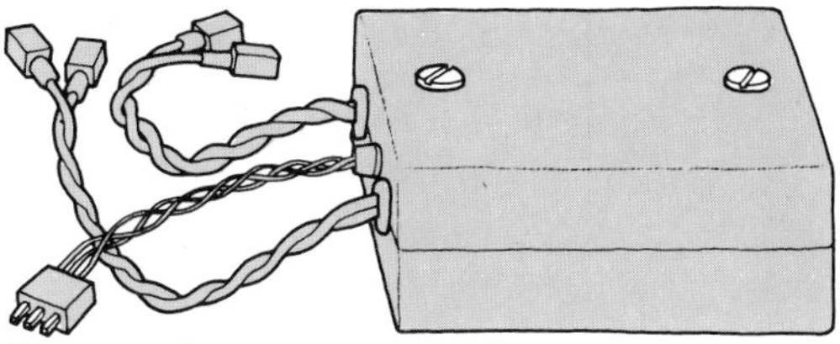

**Electronic speed controller**

## Avoiding interference

Electric systems in radio-control models need to be installed carefully to avoid interference with the radio receiver, which can affect control. All electrical connections should be secure and soldered. If possible, the battery and motor should be positioned near each other to reduce the length of the cords, and both should be sited away from the radio receiver, particularly its antenna, and the servos.

Electric current can jump (arc) between the brushes and commutator, and motors almost always come with a suppressor attached to the terminals to reduce any effect this may have on the radio signals. If your motor does not have a suppressor, solder one on. A motor with carbon brushes and inside a metal casing is less likely to cause radio interference.

**Positioning an electric motor**

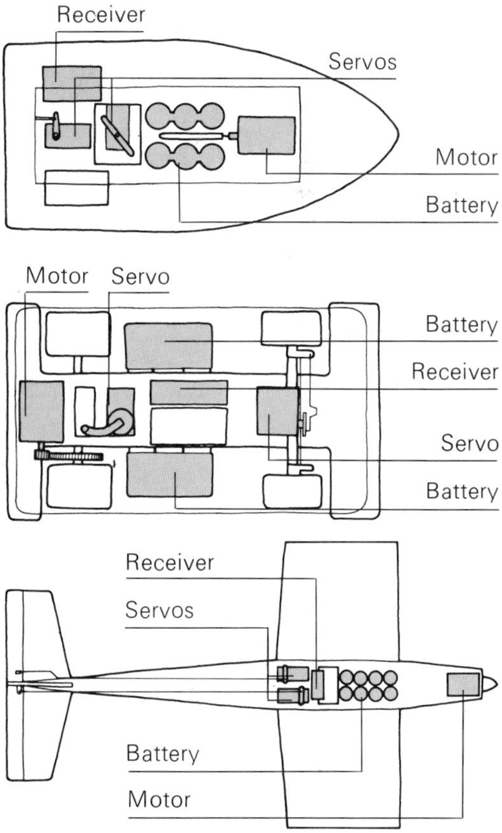

## Casings for electric motors

Some motors have lugs on the outside for fixing the motor to the model; others do not. You can buy special casings for those that do not have lugs. If the motor fits loosely in the casing, wrap masking tape around the sides of the motor to increase its diameter.

Airplane modelers usually make their own casing from wood or cardboard.

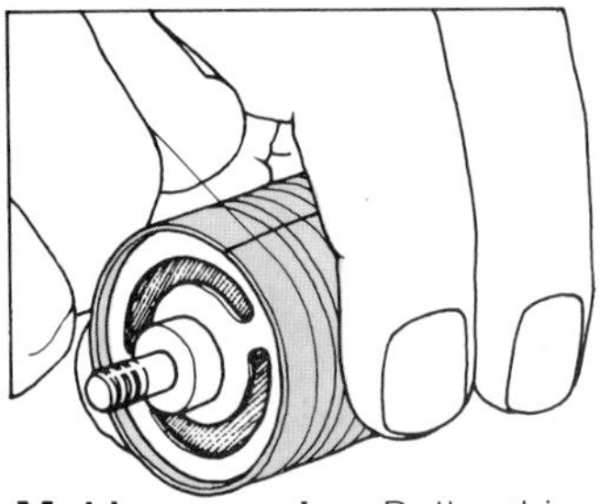

**Making a casing** Roll a thin piece of plywood, balsa wood or cardboard around the motor. Glue it lightly and bind with thread or tape.

# Propellers

These are measured by their diameter and pitch (the distance the propeller would travel in one revolution if turned in a solid medium). A large pitch is known as coarse or high; a small pitch as fine or low.

The coarser the pitch, the faster the model will move, providing the engine has the power to take the extra load. Kits and plans usually specify an engine capacity, and engine manufacturers often recommend prop sizes. Experiment with a higher or lower size to find the best prop for your model.

Aircraft propellers are made of wood or nylon. Wooden and reinforced-nylon props suit all engine sizes; plain nylon props cannot be used with high-speed engines as they may break up. Wooden props are more easily damaged in a crash than nylon ones.

Boat propellers are nylon or metal. Nylon ones have the advantage that they shear if badly fouled. A metal prop lasts longer but it can transfer strain to other components.

# Gears

Model motors generally operate at high speed and produce a low torque (turning force). Some models can use the motor's power directly to drive a propeller; however, all cars, many boats and some planes use gears to translate the motor's power into different ratios of speed and torque.

The simplest gear system consists of a drive gear wheel fixed to the motor's drive shaft, engaging a second gear wheel. To change the speed and the torque, you simply alter the relative sizes of the two wheels.

The speed and torque of the two gears is inversely proportional to their circumference (see below). The circumference is measured by counting the number of teeth.

Most gear systems in models involve a step down from a high speed motor to a slower output with more torque: a small gear wheel on the motor's shaft drives a larger one on a shaft which drives the wheels or propeller. You can make fine adjustments in performance by changing the size of the gear wheels slightly.

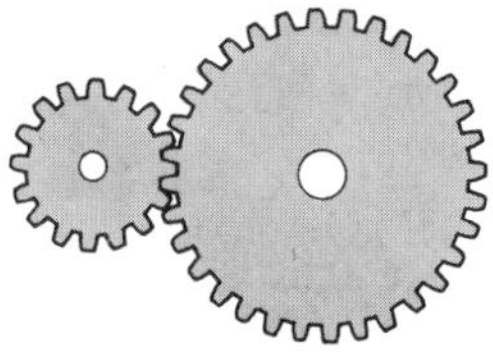

**Gear speed** If the circumference of the driving gear A is half that of the driven gear B, then B will turn at half the speed of A but with twice the torque.

**Changing the direction of rotation** Add a third gear wheel to change the direction of the propeller.

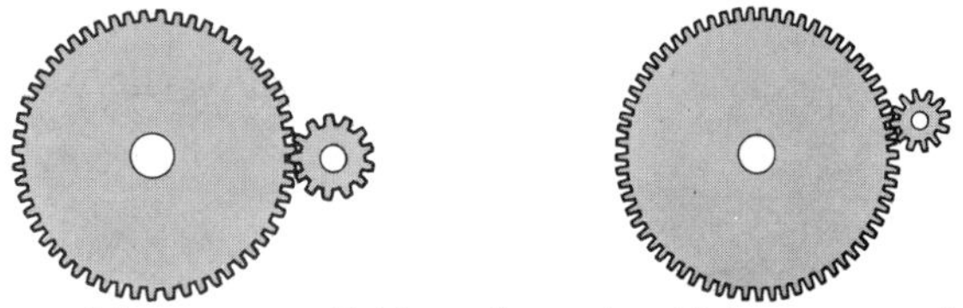

**High and low gears** If 13 teeth on the driving gear and 56 on the driven gear give a moderate reduction in gear speed, 12 and 65 will give a lower speed with more power.

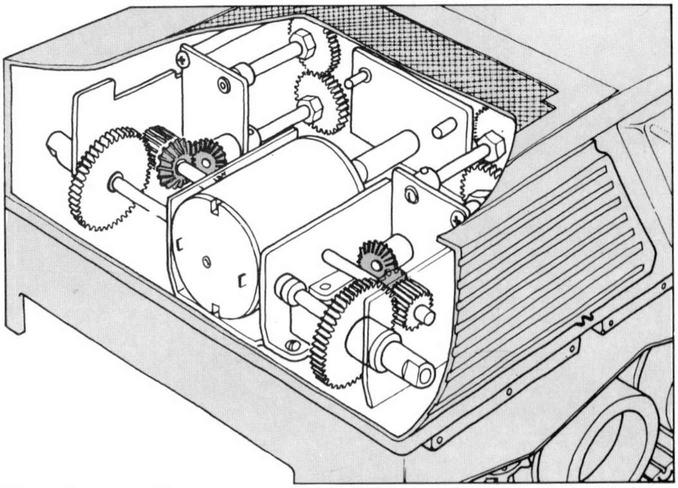

**Bevel gears** These gears are used to change the angle of the shaft, as well as alter the ratio of speed to torque.

# Radio control

# Radio-control models

The most rewarding and entertaining aspect of modelmaking is often to control a model remotely. While newcomers may find the array of equipment, the intricacy of installation and the techniques for maneuvering intimidating, all that is needed is a knowledge of the way the controls work and the proper way to install the equipment; any early anxieties will soon be overcome, especially if you begin with a simple model. Airplanes, boats and cars are the most popular models built for radio control but you will find that the systems they employ can be applied to any vehicle.

In very simple terms, a radio-control system works when a transmitter, held by the operator, sends out a coded radio signal. The signal is picked up by a receiver in the model which decodes it and directs it to the appropriate servo. A servo is an electro-mechanical unit which converts the signal into mechanical movement to operate the moving part or parts of the vehicle. The movement of the servo is directly in proportion to that of the transmitter control stick. Usually, one servo operates one control surface. For each servo there is a separate radio signal and this is referred to as a channel. Radio sets are described by the number of separate signals they can send. A four-channel transmitter, for example, can operate up to four servos.

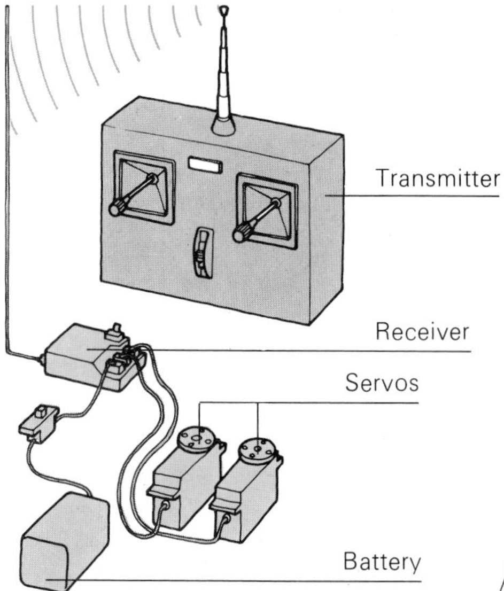


**How a radio-control system works** The receiver picks up and decodes the signal from the transmitter. It sends the signal to the servo which translates the signal into action.

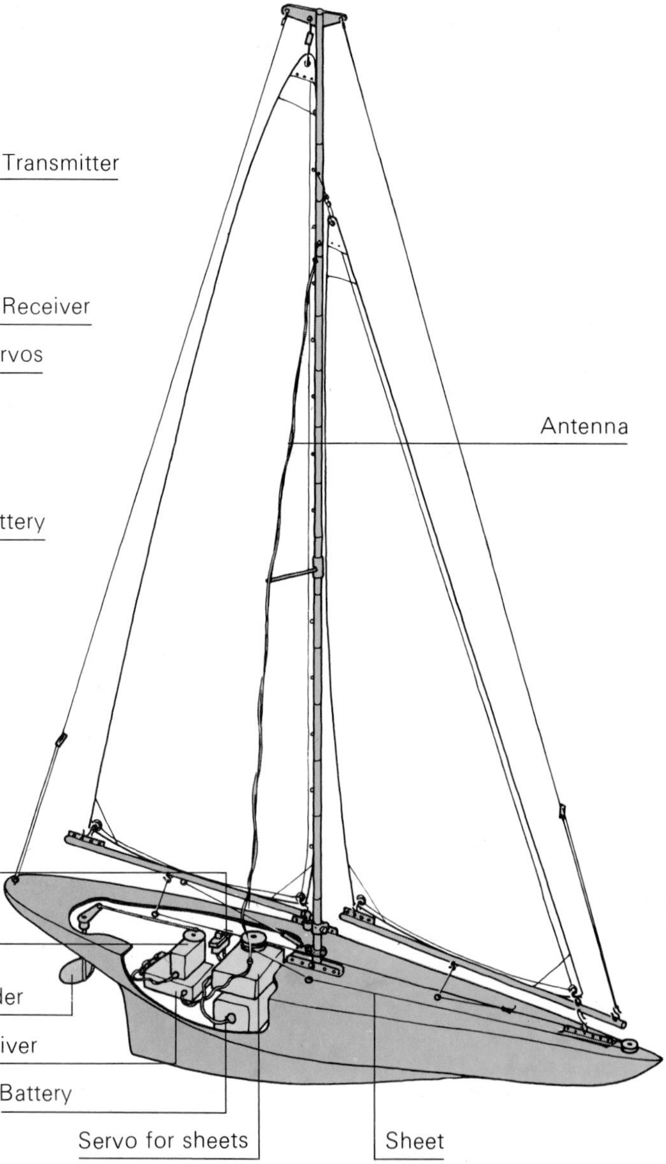


**Sailboat** The rudder and sheets are operated by remote control.

**Racing car** Two servos, one for the throttle and one for the steering, control this car.

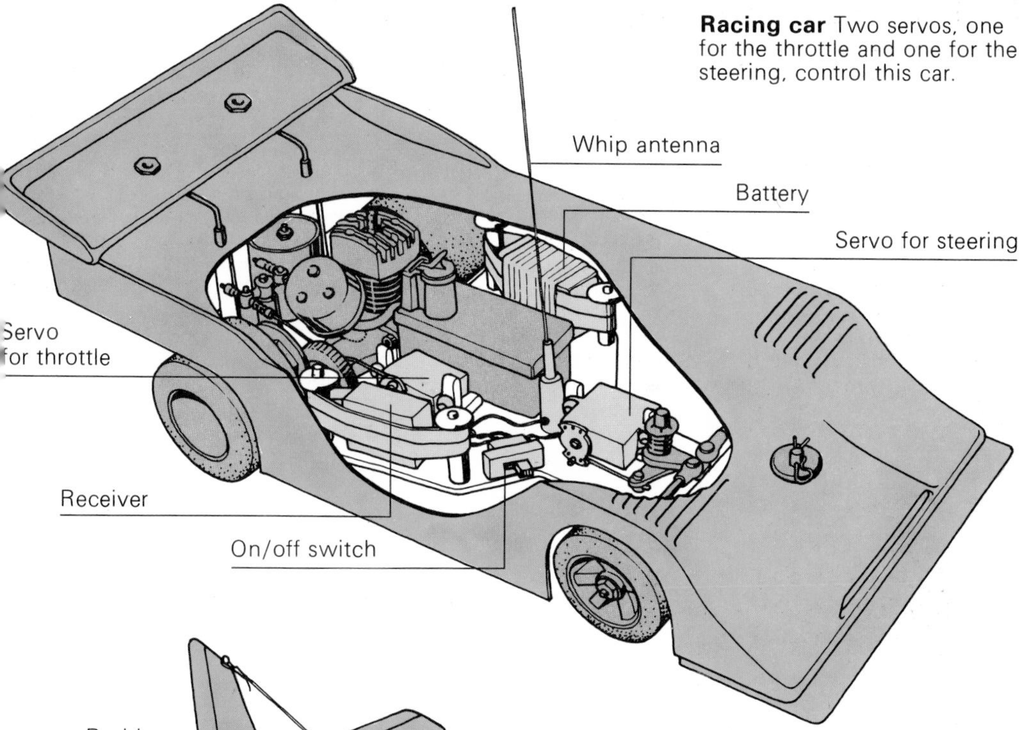


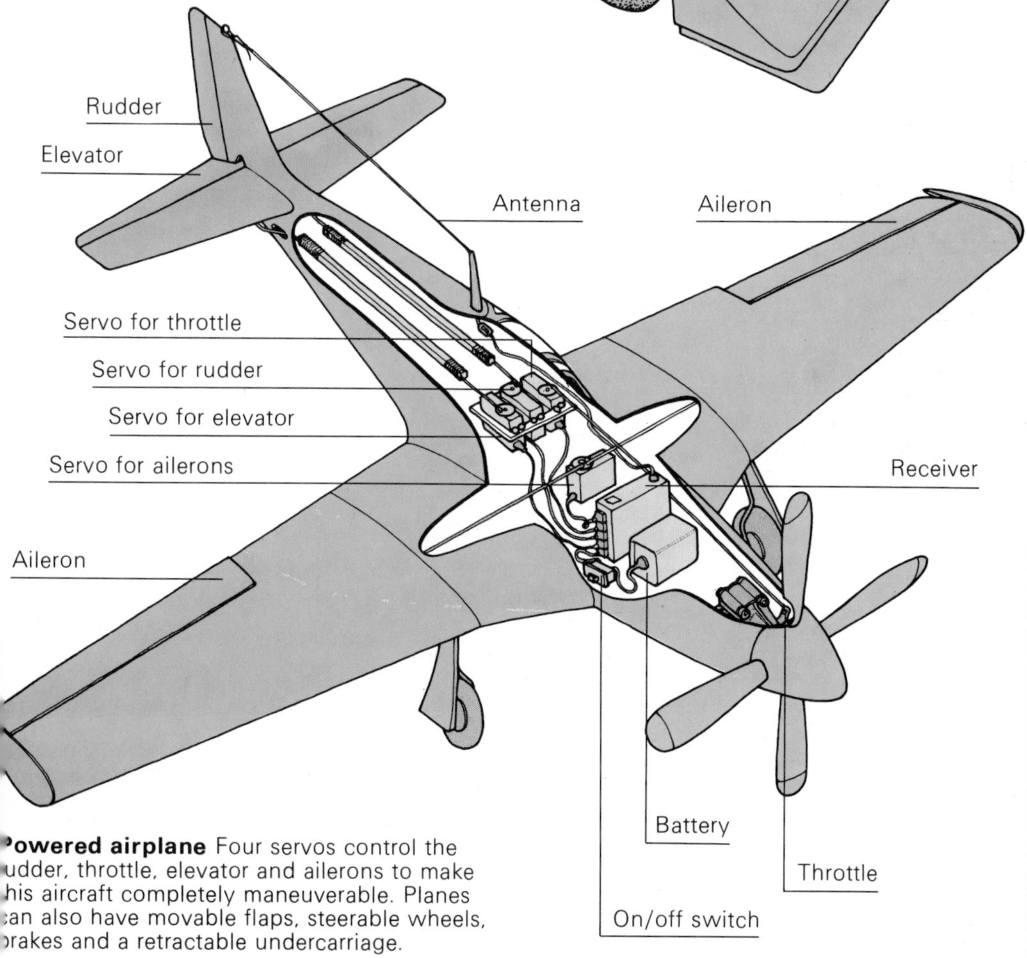


**Powered airplane** Four servos control the rudder, throttle, elevator and ailerons to make this aircraft completely maneuverable. Planes can also have movable flaps, steerable wheels, brakes and a retractable undercarriage.

# The transmitter

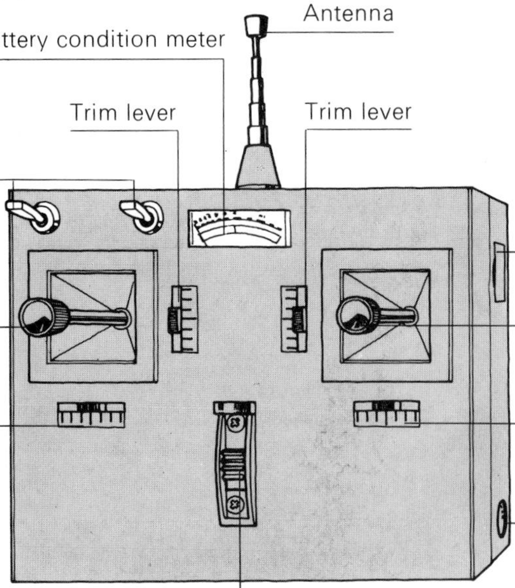


This is your control panel. It is a light, rectangular case which can be held comfortably with one or both hands. The number of control sticks and levers and the directions in which they move vary according to the number of channels and the design. A transmitter with two sticks, one moving right and left for the steering and one up and down for the throttle, gives complete control of a powerboat or car. This is called a full-house system. A wheel replaces the steering stick on some transmitters. A transmitter with full-house control for a powered airplane must have four channels for the rudder, elevator, ailerons and throttle. The most popular four-channel set has two sticks; each stick moves both horizontally and vertically and to any angle through 360° to give control of two servos simultaneously. The sticks for directional control are self-centering – when you release the stick it returns to neutral where the vehicle runs straight. The throttle stick is usually ratchet-controlled so that it will stay in position without finger pressure.

Next to the control sticks are their respective ratchet-operated trim levers. They are used when the stick is at neutral to make small corrections to the path of the model so that it runs straight and level. Trim levers should never be used constantly. If you find that you are using them continually, adjust the linkage between the servo and control surface. A trim lever can also be used with the throttle stick to cut the engine.

Some radio transmitters have adjustable rate switches to limit the movement of a control surface by reducing the servo's throw over the full range of the control stick. Usually, there are two rate switches used for either the ailerons and elevator or the rudder and elevator of an airplane. Although rate switches are normally used with high-performance aircraft in competition or when weather conditions make the model oversensitive for normal control, a beginner can employ them to desensitize the controls while he learns to fly. They are also helpful for aerobatic maneuvers such as a string of slow rolls where you can preset the ailerons, eliminating the need to balance several controls.

Transmitters come in different modes. The term "mode" refers to the arrangement of the primary controls. These are the controls which operate the direction of the model. With boats and cars, only steering is primary, whereas with airplanes, the elevator and rudder or elevator and ailerons are primary (in some models the ailerons supersede the rudder for direction control). When two primary controls are operated by two sticks, the transmitter is in mode I; when one stick operates two primary controls, the transmitter is in mode II. Transmitters with only one primary control are considered to be in mode I.

The different modes require different handling so choose a transmitter that feels right and suits your natural co-ordination. If you belong to a club, it is a good idea to choose the mode most used by other members so that an experienced person can quickly take over your transmitter in an emergency and prevent a crash. Some transmitters include a flight-training or "buddy" box connection for extra safety. It allows an instructor using the same make of equipment to plug into the beginner's set and take control when necessary.

## Transmitter designs

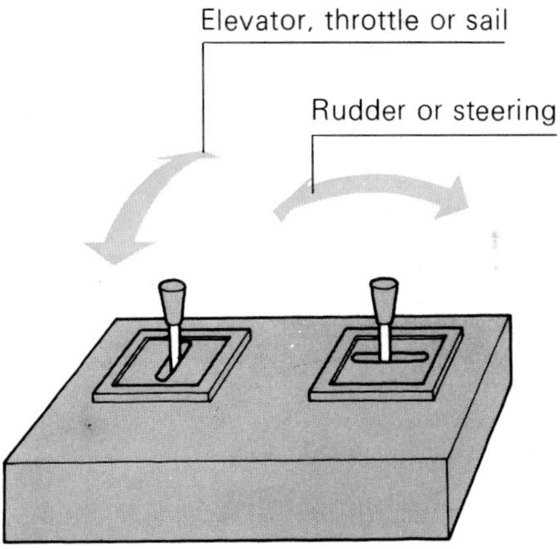


**Two-channel, two-stick transmitter in mode I**

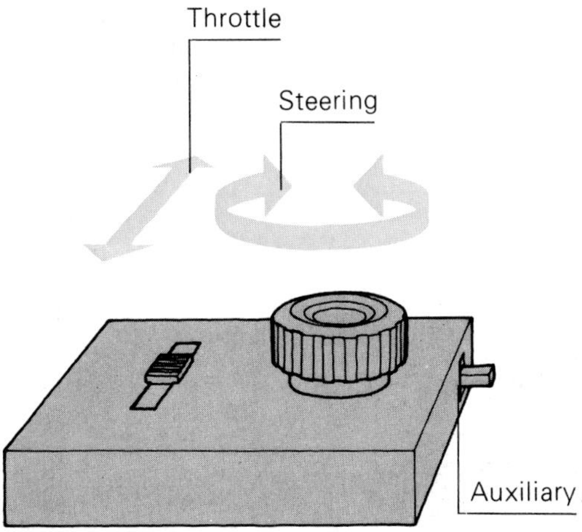


**Three-channel transmitter for car or boat in mode I**

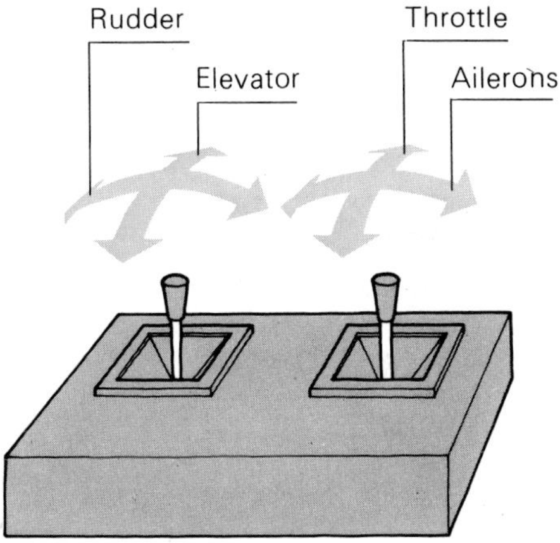


**Four-channel, two-stick transmitter in mode I**

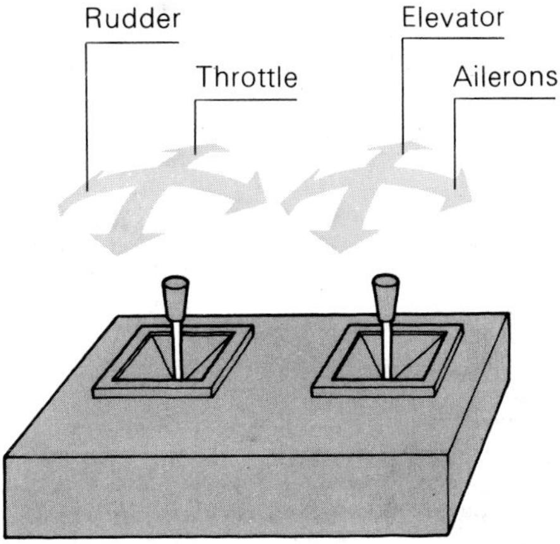


**Four-channel, two-stick transmitter in mode II**

## Frequency

Most transmitters operate on the 72 MHz (4-meter) band although there are some which use the 50 to 54 MHz (6-meter) and 27 MHz (11-meter) band. The 27 MHz band used to be very popular but it is now subject to interference by people using citizens band radios. Each band has several frequencies and the frequencies are color-coded. Only one model can use a specific frequency at any one time in an area. Two models using the same frequency will interfere with each other's signals and may crash, so never operate your transmitter without first making sure the frequency is free. Most clubs insist that a member flies a small, appropriately colored flag on the antenna of his transmitter to indicate which frequency he is using. A pair of color-coded crystals, one for the transmitter and one for the receiver (don't interchange them), determines the transmitter's frequency and you can buy extra crystals for changing frequency in the field.

### Transmitter frequencies

| MHz | | Color code |
|---|---|---|
| 26.995 | | Brown |
| 27.045 | | Red |
| 27.095 | | Orange |
| 27.145 | | Yellow |
| 27.195 | | Green |
| 53.10 | | Black and brown |
| 53.20 | | Black and red |
| 53.30 | | Black and orange |
| 53.40 | | Black and yellow |
| 53.50 | | Black and green |
| 72.08 | aircraft only | White and brown |
| 72.16 | | White and blue |
| 72.24 | aircraft only | White and red |
| 72.32 | | White and violet |
| 72.40 | aircraft only | White and orange |
| 72.96 | | White and yellow |
| 75.64 | aircraft only | White and green |

# Installing the equipment

Equipment should be positioned so that it is accessible and so that the vehicle balances properly. Most assembly plans allow for this, but if yours does not, follow these guidelines. Place the battery, the heaviest item, ahead of the other components so that if it is thrown forward in a crash, it will not damage them. Put the receiver behind the battery, and the servos behind the receiver. (Cars have less space to accommodate the radio equipment and there is usually only one possible arrangement; see page 255 for a typical layout.) To keep the equipment dry in a boat, place it all in a plastic box, including the servos.

Check the vehicle's balance before fixing any of the equipment in place (see pages 294, 306 and 330 for balancing). In an airplane, make sure that you include the linkage, temporarily assembled with tape. Adjust the distribution of weight by moving the battery or servos slightly forward or backward.

# The receiver

This is a very sensitive piece of equipment which needs to be protected from vibration or damage, especially during a crash or heavy landing. Never leave it unsupported. While you shouldn't attach it permanently to the body of the vehicle, as you may need to remove it to change the crystal, it should be surrounded on all sides with at least $\frac{3}{4}$ inch (20 mm) of firm foam packing material.

Position the receiver's on/off switch inside the vehicle where it can't be touched accidentally when you handle the model, and fix it to a servo tray or former. If access is difficult, attach a switch extension and let it project through a small hole in the side of the vehicle, away from the exhaust.

Do not let the receiver antenna touch any metal parts and keep it clear of the battery and servos to avoid interference. In an airplane, the antenna should be fully extended and exit directly from the fuselage. Never cut it short or roll it up inside, as this reduces the receiver's range. To avoid straining the connection between the antenna and the receiver, leave a little slack in the antenna and attach a plastic toggle to it just inside the fuselage. Make a loop near the end of the antenna and attach it to a pin in the tail fin with a rubber band. The band should hold the antenna under light tension.

Use a whip antenna when a long antenna is impractical such as for boats and cars with a shorter operating range. To install it, cut a piece off the receiver antenna equal to the length of the whip antenna, then solder the receiver antenna to the base of the whip antenna. Coil the flexible section to a minimum of $1\frac{1}{2}$ inches (40 mm) in diameter and leave it inside the model vehicle.

Boats with tall masts do not need a whip antenna. Just run the receiver antenna up the mast, attaching it securely at the top.

# Batteries

A radio-control set has two batteries, one for the transmitter and another for the receiver and servos. Some sets run on dry-cell batteries; others use nicad (nickel-cadmium) batteries. Dry-cell batteries are cheaper but you must buy replacements when they run down. Nicad batteries are rechargeable and a good choice for modelers who use their set constantly.

A dry-cell battery is a 1.5-volt barrel type which clips into small pockets in a plastic box. Standard dry cells can be used for both the transmitter and receiver but the receiver battery will run down faster because the receiver uses more power. If, for convenience, you want the batteries to have the same life, use high-power alkaline-manganese cells for the receiver.

Nicad batteries come in a range of sizes from 225 to 500 mah (milliampere-hour). The size refers to the battery's output. Most radio-control systems come with the appropriate battery and charger. Follow the manufacturer's instructions for recharging the battery. As a rule, a standard nicad battery should be charged at one-tenth of its power output. Thus, a 225 mah battery needs a charger which delivers 22.5 milliamperes and, if it is completely flat, it will take 10 to 14 hours to charge (it does not harm a standard battery to be left charging beyond the specified time). If it is not completely drained, recharge it for about eight times the period it has been used; or, use a charger-discharger to drain the battery, then recharge for the recommended time. Fast-charge nicad batteries which take only 10 minutes to recharge are preferred by some modelers. Unless charged at the recommended rate, they may overheat and explode.

All batteries must be mounted securely. Use rubber bands or servo tape (see opposite) to hold car batteries; airplane batteries should be wrapped in foam rubber and packed into the storage compartment. Boat batteries must be waterproof: keep them in a plastic bag in the waterproof box which contains the rest of the equipment (see page 327).

**Charging nicad batteries** Plug the charger into the battery socket in the transmitter case and into the socket in the receiver battery. Connect the charger to your house current or a car battery for the recommended time.

# Servos

There are two basic types of servo. The rotary servo has a disk or arm which rotates backward and forward through approximately 75°. The linear servo has two arms which move backward and forward in opposite directions. (See page 327 for winch servos for sailboats.)

The rotary servo, which is widely used in airplanes, is more flexible. Both the disk and arm have more than one position for the linkage: the outer holes give more movement, the inner ones less. In addition, the rotary servo case can be placed at different angles to the line of the linkage. As the disk or arm rotates, however, the linkage moves from side to side and you must leave room in the model for this travel. The linear servo, which does not cause any sideways movement, is often used where space is limited but it can only be positioned parallel to the linkage and its throw is not adjustable. To modify the amount the linkage moves, you must incorporate a bellcrank or change the position of the linkage on the control surface horn (see pages 262 to 263).

Both rotary and linear servos come in two versions: a rotary servo will turn either clockwise or anticlockwise for a given movement of the transmitter control stick; one arm of a linear servo will move forward while the other moves backward or vice versa. These versions allow you to arrange the connection between servo, linkage and control surface in different ways (see Planning the linkage, pages 263 to 264).

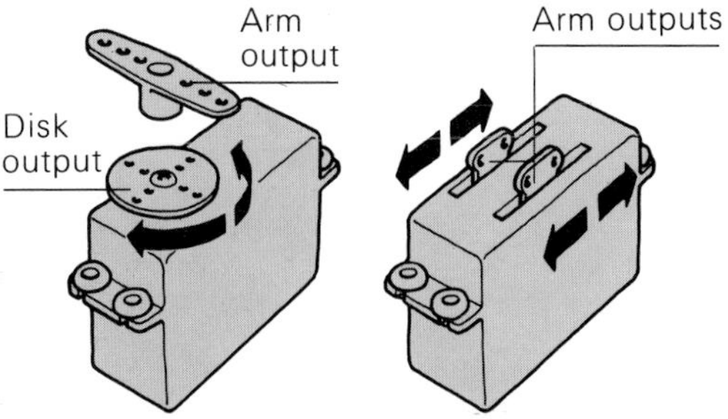


**Rotary servo** **Linear servo**

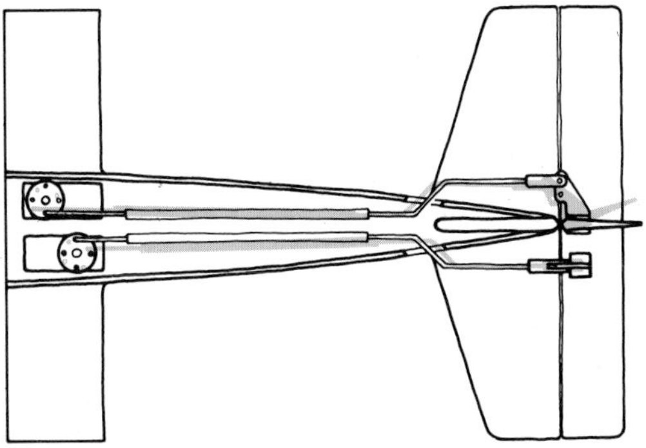

**Positioning a rotary servo** To make sure that you have enough room for the sideways movement of the linkage, you may need to cut a slot in the side of an airplane's fuselage.

## Mounting servos

The most convenient way to install servos is to place them in a servo tray, then screw the tray to hardwood bearers on each side of the vehicle. The tray comes with its own rubber grommets to prevent vibration being transmitted to the servos, and these should not be overtightened.

If a tray will not fit in your model, screw the servos individually to wooden bearers or to mounting brackets on the vehicle. Use rubber grommets to absorb vibration and do not let the servo touch the structure at any other point. Servo tape, a foam strip with adhesive on both sides, can be used to attach the servo if screws are impractical, but the surface must be clean and smooth.

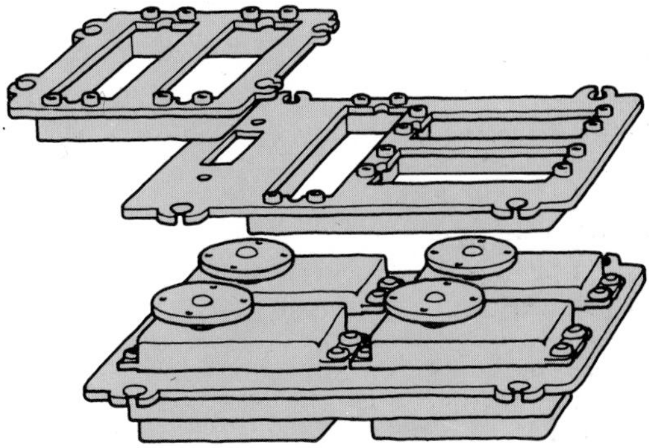

**Servo trays** You can buy plastic trays for two, three or four servos.

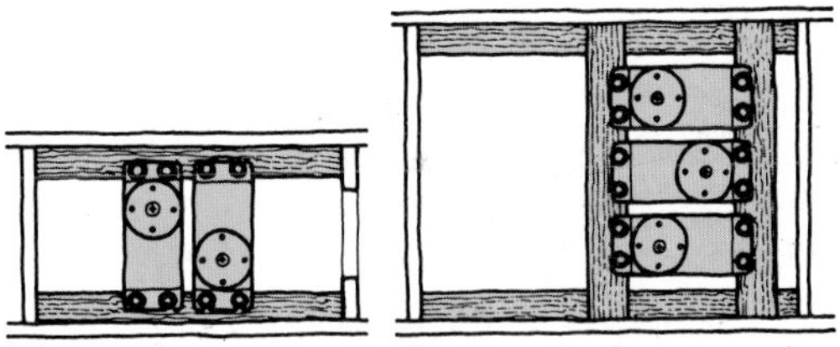

**Mounting servos individually** Screw each servo to wooden bearers. In a wide-bodied vehicle, screw them to cross bearers.

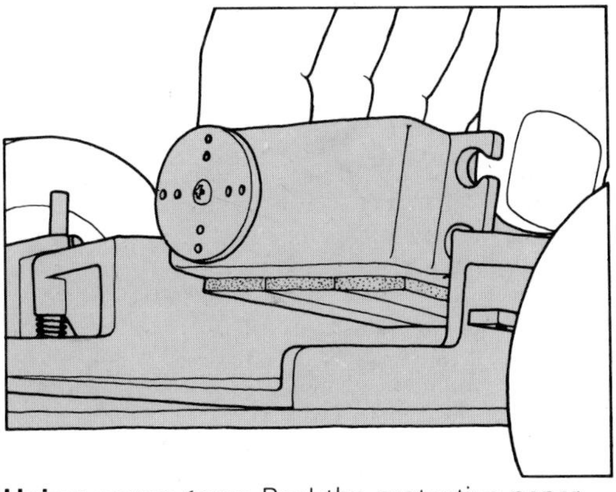

**Using servo tape** Peel the protective paper from one side and stick the tape to the servo. Peel off the remaining paper and press the servo into position.

## Mounting aileron servos

Model airplane wings are usually a single piece which fits on top or below the fuselage. The servo for the ailerons is mounted in the center of the wing panel. For inset ailerons, place the servo on its side to keep the pushrods in a straight line; for strip ailerons which have a shorter linkage, position it upright. You will need to cut out a space for the servo in a foam wing, but never cut away the spars to make room in a built-up wing.

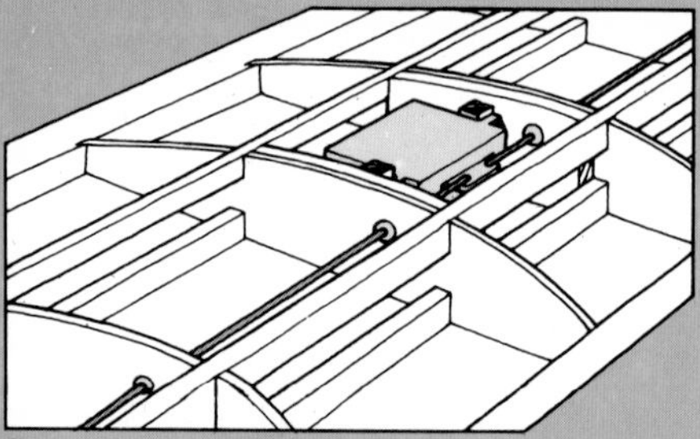

Servo for inset ailerons

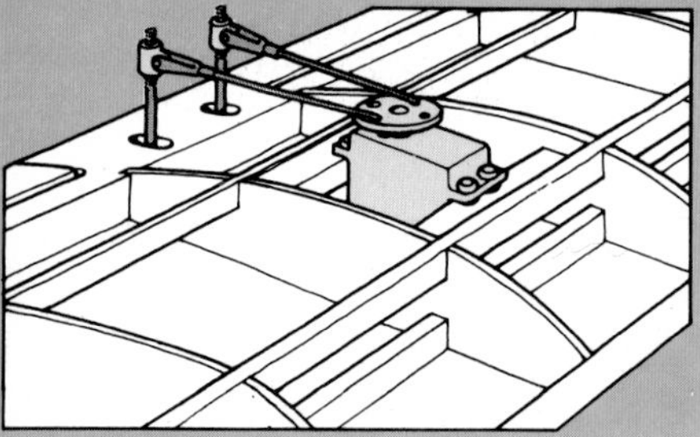

Servo for strip ailerons

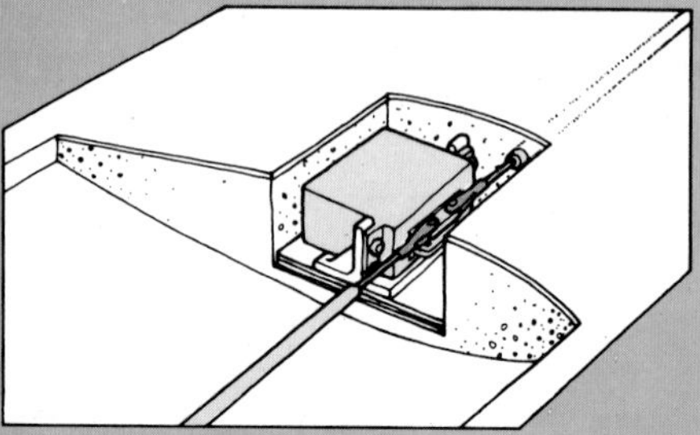

Servo for inset ailerons in a foam wing

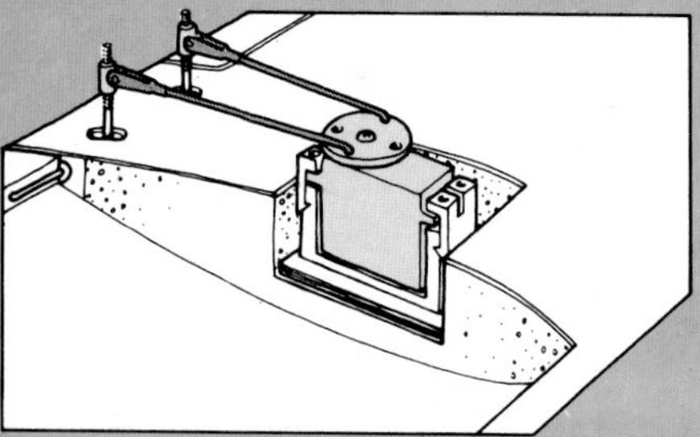

Servo for strip ailerons in a foam wing

# Linkages

Not all plans show the linkages between servo and control surface and you may need to choose which types to use and calculate their position and length. The information below will help you arrange the linkages. (See pages 327 to 328 for sailboat linkages.)

There are two kinds of linkage: rigid pushrods and flexible cables. Pushrods should be used for straight runs; cables are best for controlling the throttle, a boat rudder or the nosewheel steering in an airplane, where the runs are short. Balsa pushrods are the most popular of all linkages. They are light but stiff and will break in a crash, preventing serious damage to the servo. All-wire pushrods are often used for short runs but they can also be used to link inset ailerons in a built-up wing if you pass the wire through the ribs. Thin metal-tube pushrods are suitable for long runs in boats.

You can hook a pushrod directly onto the servo or horn on the control surface as shown below or use one of the connections opposite. Cables require a clevis or a brass connector on the servo end and a clevis at the other.

## Calculating the length of the linkage

Roughly estimate the linkage length when you balance the vehicle (see page 258) by taping the parts together (they should be longer than needed). Once the servos are installed, you can calculate the size of each linkage exactly. Begin by setting the control surface and servo at neutral. Connect the linkage to the control surface horn, then cut the other end to size.

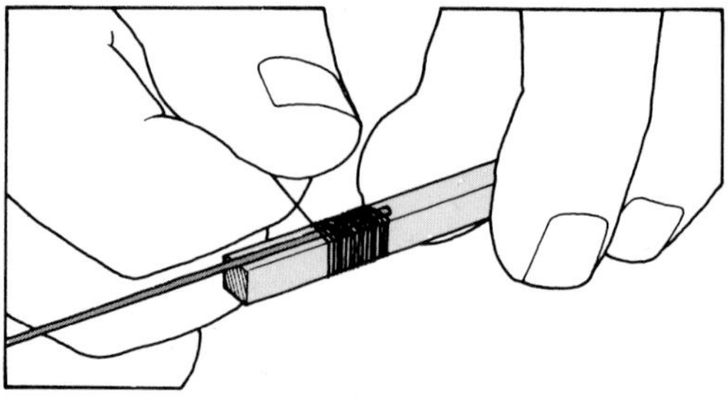

**Assembling a balsa pushrod** Drill a hole 1 inch (25 mm) from each end of rod. Bend the end of one piece of wire and insert it in a hole. Bind it with thread. Attach another piece of wire in the second hole in the same way. Coat the thread with balsa cement.

**Hooking the rod onto the servo**
Make a right-angle bend in the wire and slip it on the servo output from above or below. If necessary, make a second bend to prevent the wire falling out.

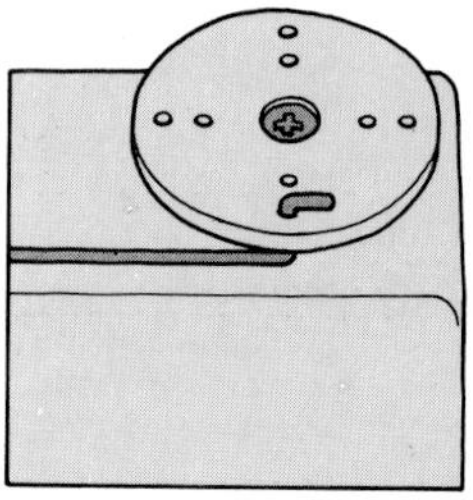

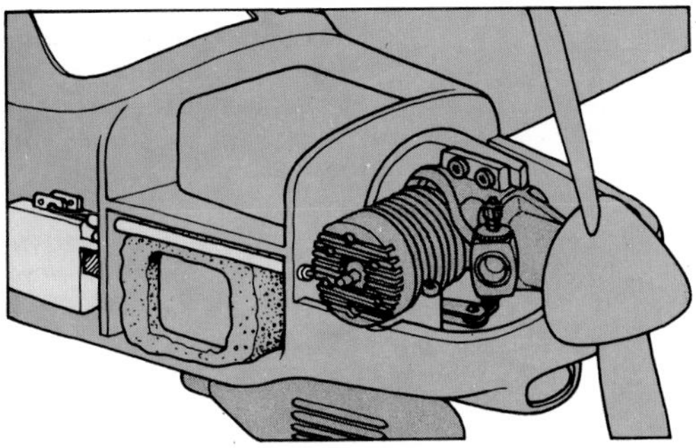

**Wire pushrod** To prevent the rod sticking where movement is restricted, guide it through a nylon tube fixed to the vehicle.

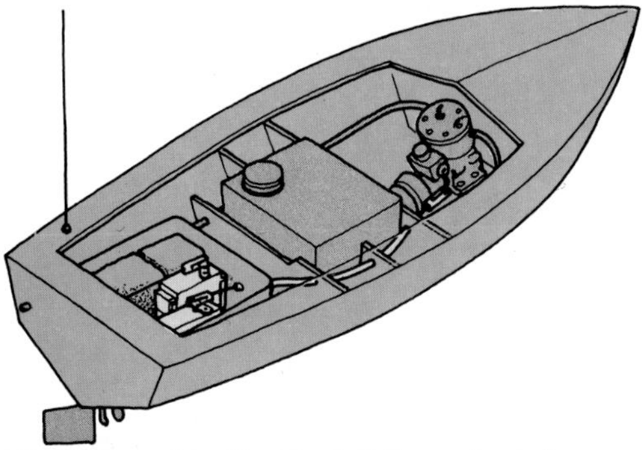

**Flexible cable** First install the outer tube, then insert the cable. If the cable is too long, it will distort; if it is too short, the outer tube will touch the clevis when the servo is at full throw.

## Protecting the throttle servo from damage

**The servo arm usually travels more than the throttle arm. To absorb the extra movement, use a wire pushrod bent into a zigzag or attach an override.**

Wire pushrod

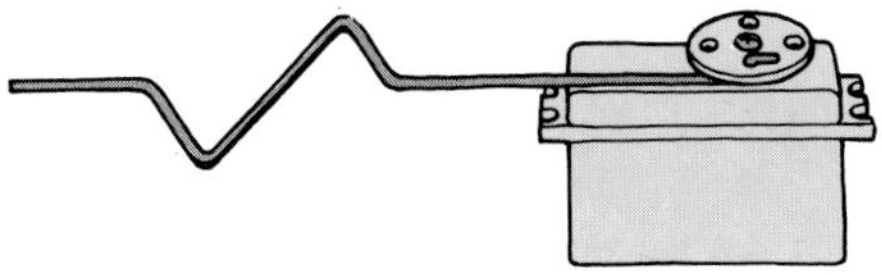

Override

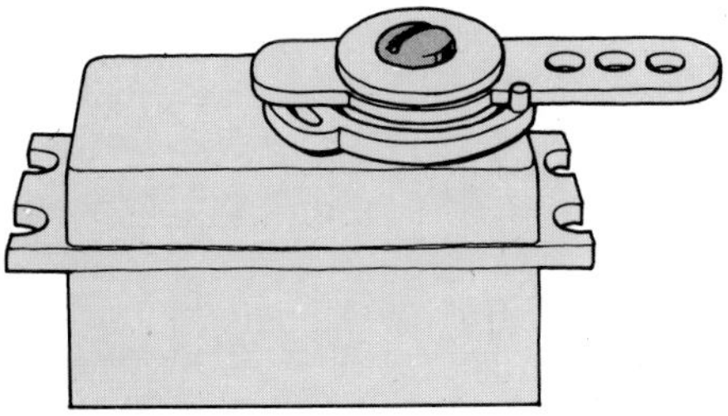

### Connections for pushrods and cables

Plastic keeper: Snap the keeper onto the end of the pushrod wire to prevent it from slipping off the servo, bellcrank or horn.

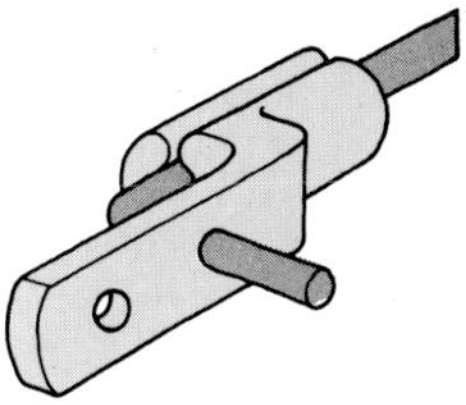

Threaded metal clevis: Screw it in or out to adjust the length of the linkage.

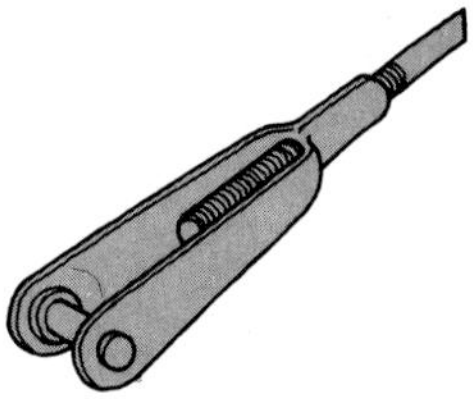

Unthreaded metal clevis: Solder this clevis onto the pushrod or cable.

Nylon clevis: Screw it onto a threaded metal pushrod or a cable with a coupler. Use it on the throttle arm to avoid metal-to-metal contact which causes radio interference.

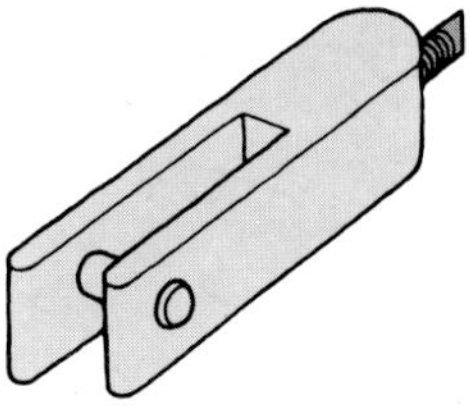

Coupler: Use this device to join unthreaded wire or cable to a threaded clevis at the control surface end.

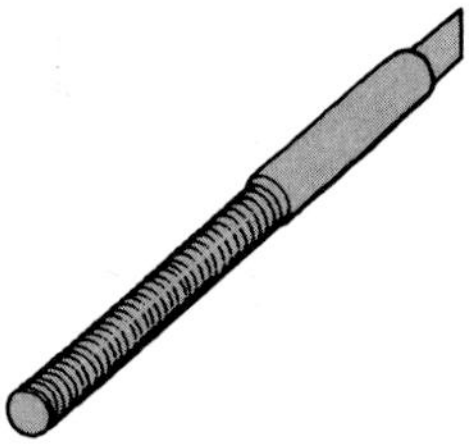

Ball link: Attach the ball to the servo output or horn and screw the socket onto the pushrod. Snap socket on ball to connect rod. Ball links reduce vibration.

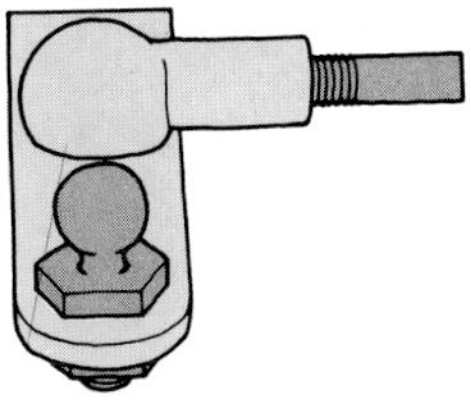

Brass connector: Insert the rod or cable in the connector and secure it with a bolt. Hook the connector on the servo output and snap on retainer.

## Bellcranks

These are pivoting levers which often form part of a pushrod linkage; they are used to change the pushrod's path. You will find them in an airplane with inset ailerons such as the one on page 255, where they allow the pushrod to run out along the wing then make a right-angle turn to connect with the aileron. Bellcranks are also used to alter the direction in which the control surface moves for a given movement of the transmitter control stick (see page 264). Most have more than one position for the linkage so that you can adjust the amount of movement – the outer holes give the most movement. Single-arm bellcranks are used exclusively for this purpose.

Bolt bellcranks to pieces of thin plywood in the model but make sure that they are free-moving. Hook the pushrod onto the bellcrank in the same way as for hooking it to a servo. Pushrods are rarely connected to bellcranks by clevises because of the lack of clearance. For the optimum mechanical leverage, place the rod at a right angle to the bellcrank arm.

### Types of bellcrank

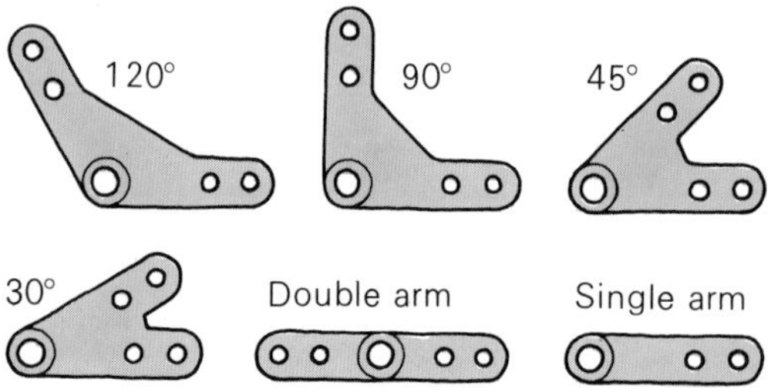


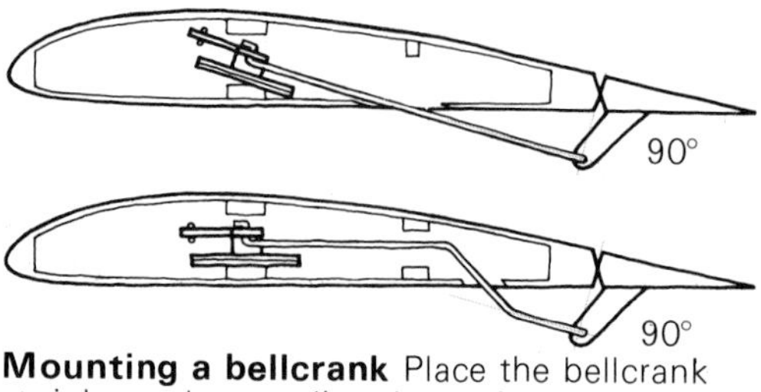


**Mounting a bellcrank** Place the bellcrank at right angles to a line drawn from the hinge to the horn-pushrod connection when the control surface is at neutral; or, bend the pushrod.

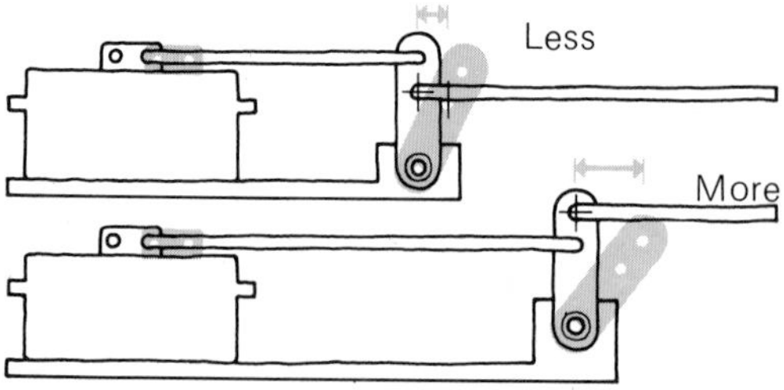


**Using a single-arm bellcrank to increase the amount of movement** Move the pushrod which connects with the control surface to the hole farthest from the pivot point.

## Horns

Pushrods and cables connect to a lever on the control surface called a horn. Horns take a lot of stress and you should always bolt them on for strength – don't use glue alone. Sometimes they come with a backing plate which fits on the opposite side to spread the load of the bolts. To prevent a soft-balsa control surface being crushed by the bolts, set a piece of hard balsa into the surface.

### Types of horn

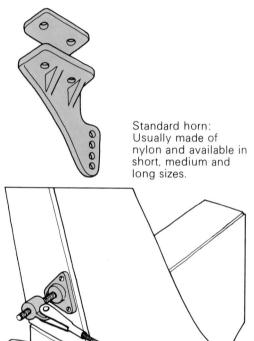

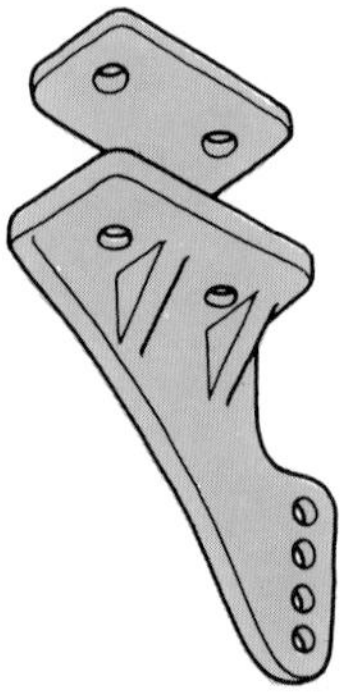

Standard horn: Usually made of nylon and available in short, medium and long sizes.

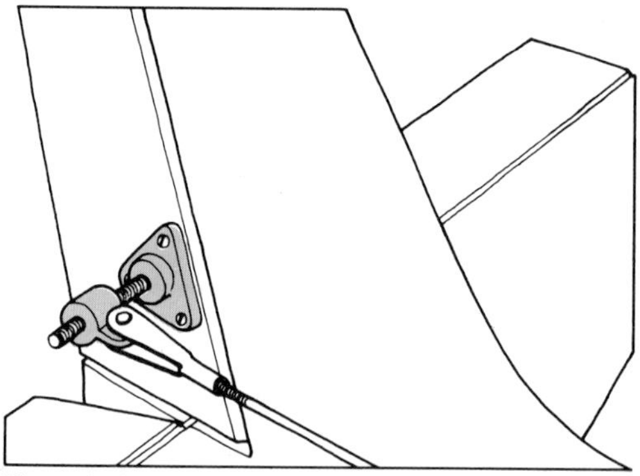

Threaded horn: Use on swept-back control surfaces such as this rudder where the angled hinge line affects the movement of the horn and can make the linkage stick.

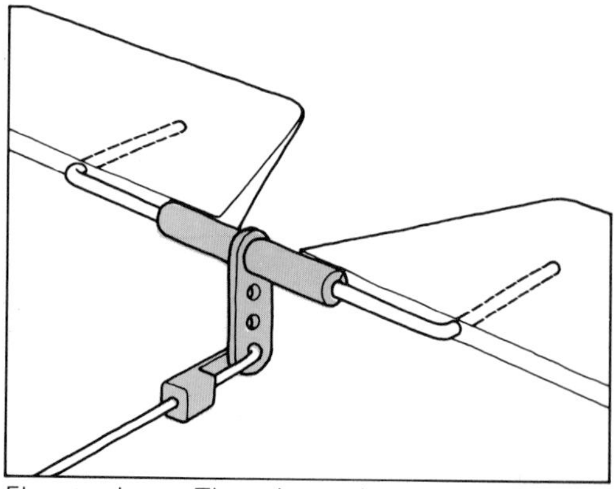

Elevator horn: The wire ends connect the two halves of the elevator to a single pushrod.

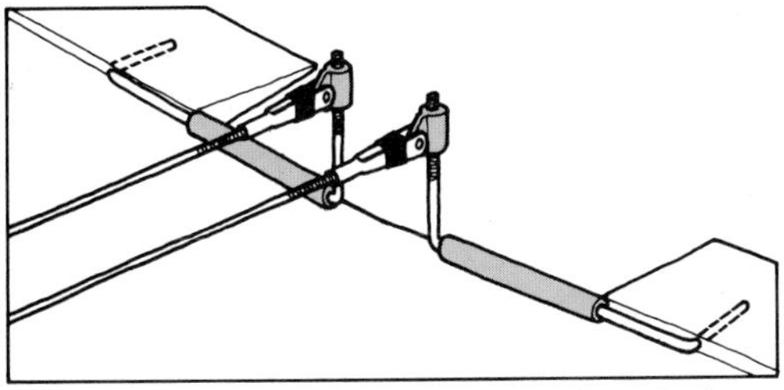

Torque rod: Use for strip ailerons. Attach the tube to the wing and one arm to the aileron. The threaded arm is the horn.

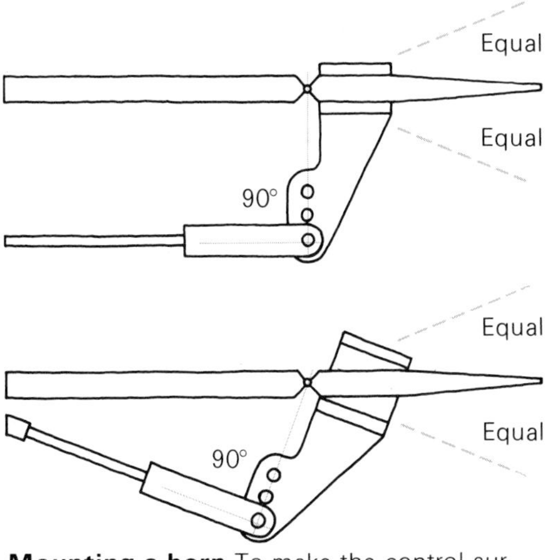


**Mounting a horn** To make the control surface move an equal amount in both directions, set the horn at a right angle to the pushrod or cable. If necessary, adjust the angle of the horn with balsa wedges. Check the angle by eye or use a small piece of cardboard as a guide.

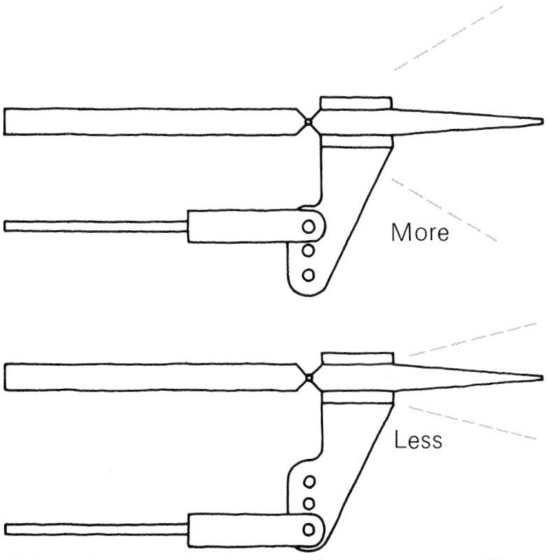


**Adjusting the amount of movement** The nearer the pushrod is to the control surface, the more the surface moves.

## Planning the linkage

Always arrange the linkages so that they are as straight as possible and make sure that there is a minimum of friction but no slack between all the connections. In this way the linkage will provide the most positive transfer of movement to the control surface. Remember, too, that a good linkage is one which makes the most economical use of the available space.

There are several factors which affect the direction in which the control surface moves: the direction of the servo (clockwise or anti-clockwise and forward or backward, see page 259), the side of the servo to which the linkage is connected, the position of the bellcrank, and the position of the horn on a rudder. Linkages can thus be set up in different ways, and several variations are shown on the following page.

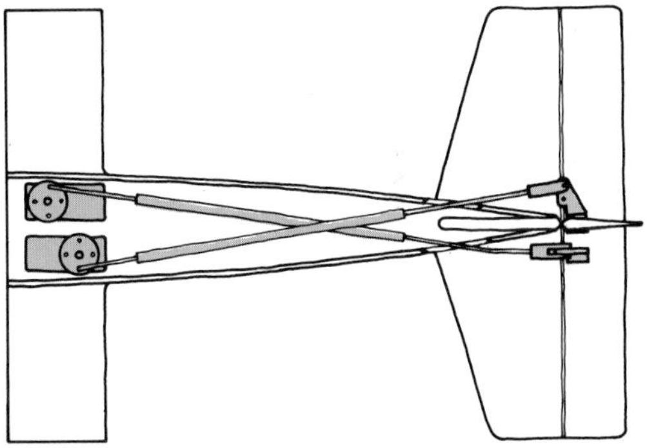

**Making a direct linkage** In a restricted space, cross one pushrod above the other so that you make as straight a path as possible.

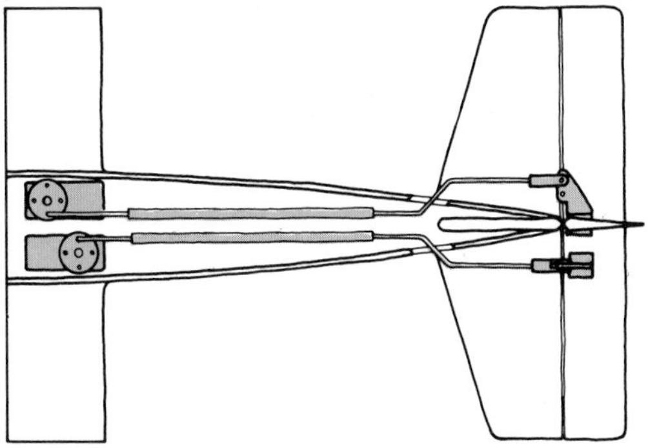

Alternately, bend each wire at the end.

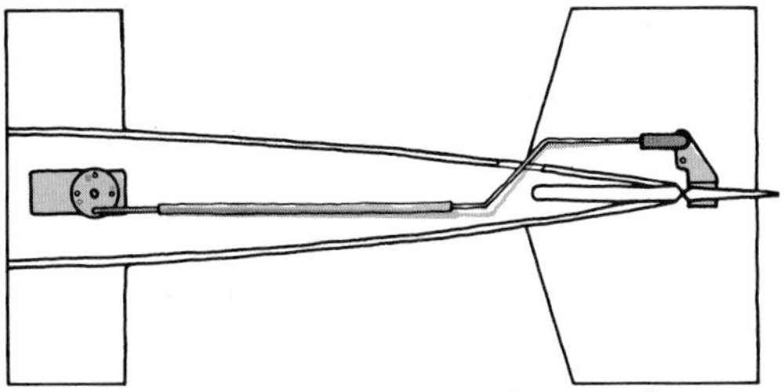

Do not bend the wire too much on a slim pushrod as the rod may bow when it pushes and pulls the horn.

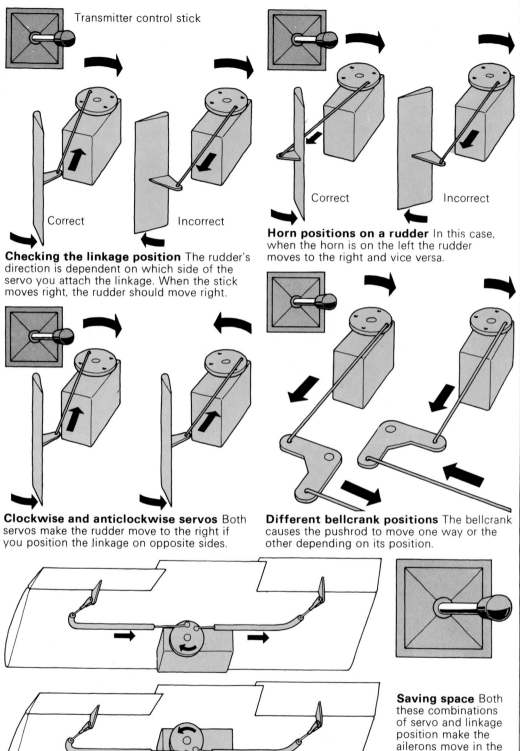

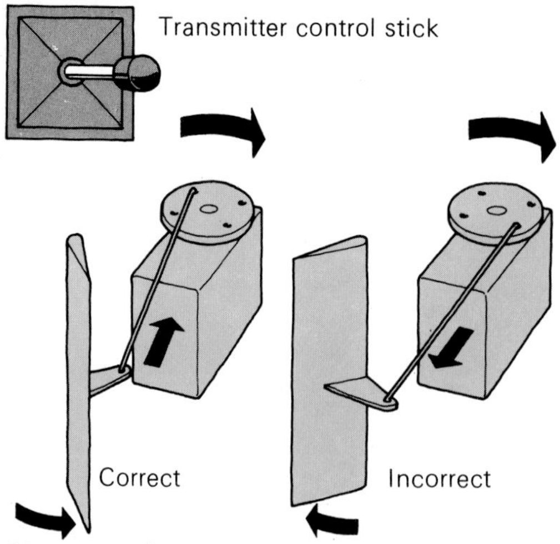


**Checking the linkage position** The rudder's direction is dependent on which side of the servo you attach the linkage. When the stick moves right, the rudder should move right.

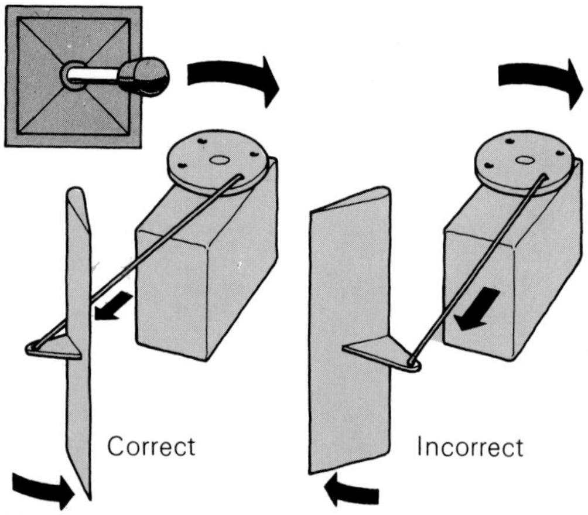


**Horn positions on a rudder** In this case, when the horn is on the left the rudder moves to the right and vice versa.

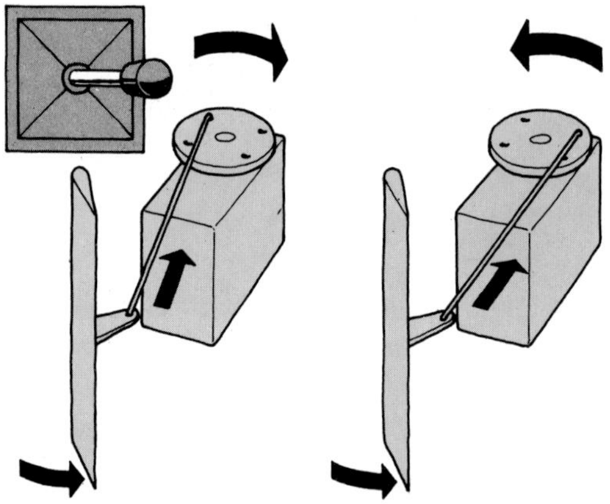

**Clockwise and anticlockwise servos** Both servos make the rudder move to the right if you position the linkage on opposite sides.

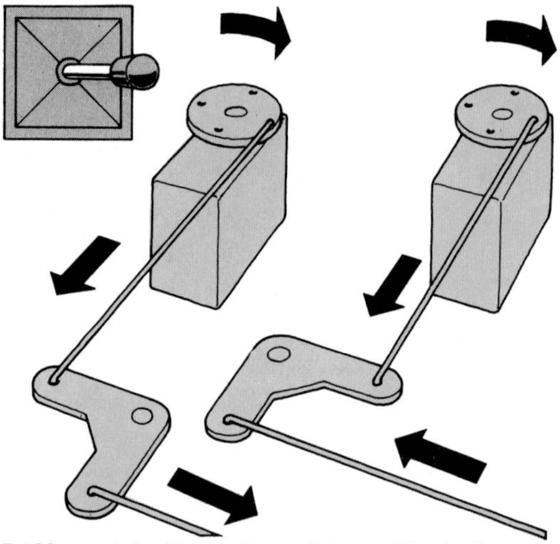

**Different bellcrank positions** The bellcrank causes the pushrod to move one way or the other depending on its position.

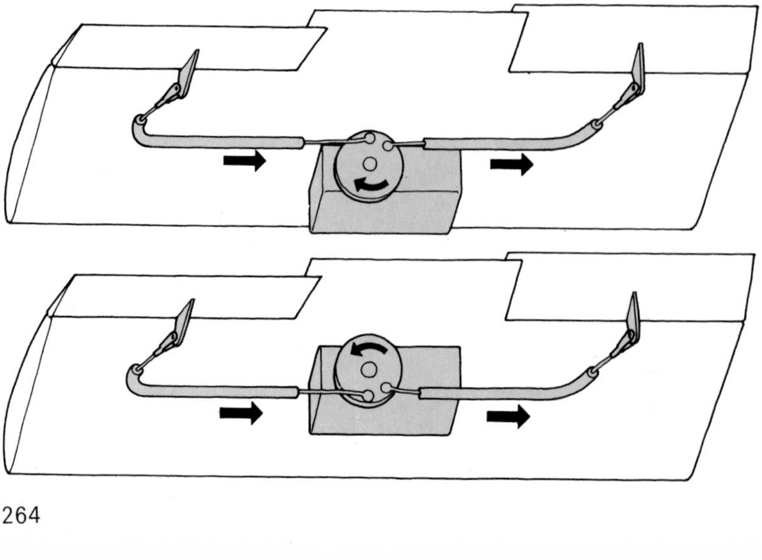

**Saving space** Both these combinations of servo and linkage position make the ailerons move in the same way. Choose the arrangement which fits your model vehicle best.

# Airplanes

# Choosing a model

This model is called a Slo Fli because its large wing area allows it to fly at scale speed.

Airplanes are the most difficult models to build as they must be able to fly. The risks of failure are higher than with other working models. If you've never tried aeromodeling, start by building a simple airplane and progress to more complex and usually more expensive ones later. Choose a kit that is easy to construct. It should be robust as the first flights will probably involve some heavy landings and a model that is wrecked on its first outing is unlikely to give much encouragement to a new hobby.

If your main interest is flying an aircraft rather than making it, then an ARTF (almost-ready-to-fly) kit is a good type to start with. This has ready-made components which may or may not need finishing before final assembly. Although simple to build, it is usually more expensive than kits which require more work.

If you enjoy making a model, then buy a kit airplane with built-up construction. There are many airplane styles which use the traditional balsa-frame technique.

The cheapest models to buy and run are those with the simplest power source, usually gliders or small rubber-powered airplanes. Aircraft which are designed to be powered by a glow plug or diesel engine, or an electric or $CO_2$ motor, are more expensive. Electric and $CO_2$ motors are quiet and easy to run and maintain, but glow plug and diesel engines are found in a wider variety of models. Whichever type you choose, the motor or engine should not be too powerful – .15 cubic inches or 2.5 cubic centimeters at most.

A control-line airplane makes a good first step toward powered flight. Such a model is controlled by two lines held by the operator, and flies in circles around him. It usually has a simple profile fuselage and is powered by a glow plug or diesel engine.

Radio-control models can be tackled with confidence once you have gained some experience in building and flying free-flight airplanes. The construction techniques are similar to other aircraft but flying has to be learned. Although some radio-control airplanes are self-stabilizing, others, particularly the scale type, need to be controlled all the time. Modelers who are new to radio control should start with a trainer model which is inherently stable. Although some high-winged, slow-flying scale models can be used for training purposes, a lot of work goes into making them, and one crash can spoil all the effort.

Whatever stage of aeromodeling you have reached, it is an advantage to join a club. Much can be learned from fellow members and the club will give you access to a flying field and other activities. Most hobby shops will give advice on local clubs, or you can find addresses in specialist magazines.

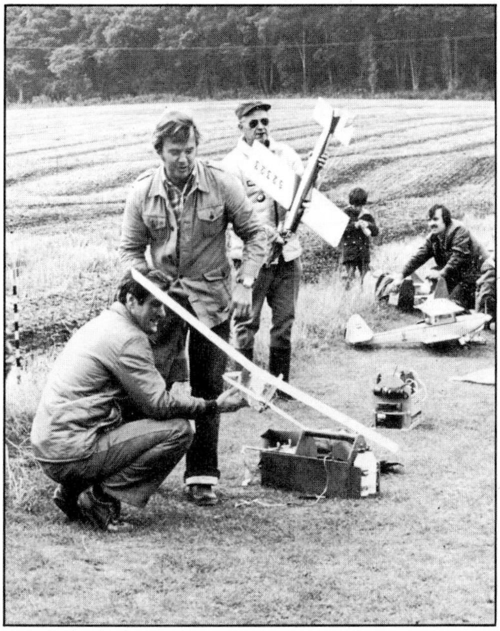

Some club members prepare their radio-control models, above, while another member makes his handsome sport biplane do a banked turn, below.

The control-line model, left, makes a high circuit around its operator.

# How an airplane flies

The propeller provides the thrust to move the aircraft forward. Air flowing over the wings as the aircraft moves forward produces an upward force called lift. The two forces of thrust and lift must overcome air resistance (drag) and the aircraft's weight in order to make it fly.

An airplane wing is specially shaped to improve lift. The upper surface is raised in a smooth curve, with the highest point about one-third back from the leading edge. This shape makes the air flowing over the wing travel further and, therefore, faster than that flowing underneath. The resulting pressure drop on the upper surface combined with the pressure rise on the bottom surface of the wing produces an upward force.

The leading edge of the wing is blunt to improve stability, and the trailing edge is sharp to make the air flow smoothly. To improve lift, the trailing edge is often curved down, forming a hollow underside which makes the airstream accelerate downward. This wing is not suitable for aerobatics as it doesn't fly well upside down. A more symmetrical wing provides better inverted flight, if less lift.

The larger the area of the wing's surface, the more lift it provides. A glider, for example, has long wings with a large lifting surface to compensate for its lack of thrust.

The angle at which the wings meet the airflow, known as the angle of incidence, also affects lift. It is set for the most efficient flight by the angle at which the wings are attached to the fuselage.

The position of the wings relative to the center of gravity influences the airplane's lateral stability. A high-winged aircraft is inherently more stable than a low-winged one. An aircraft with dihedral wings – wings which tilt up from root to tip – is even more stable.

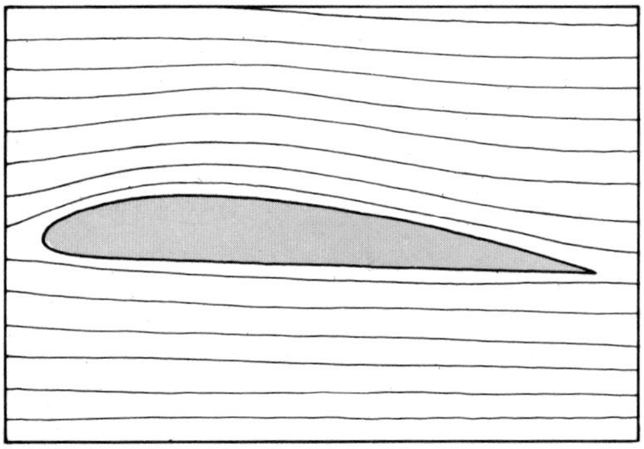

Flat-bottomed airfoil

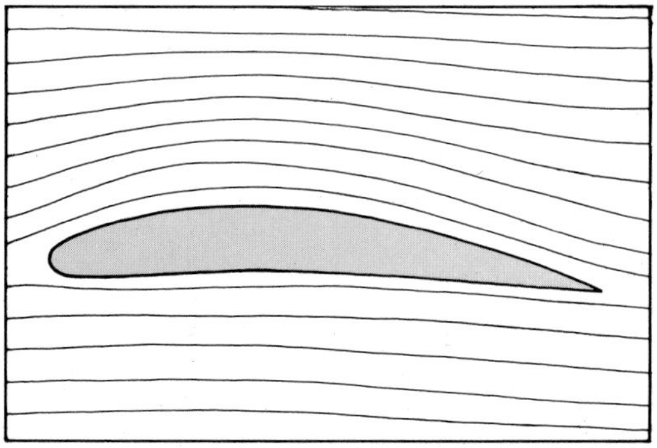

Undercambered airfoil

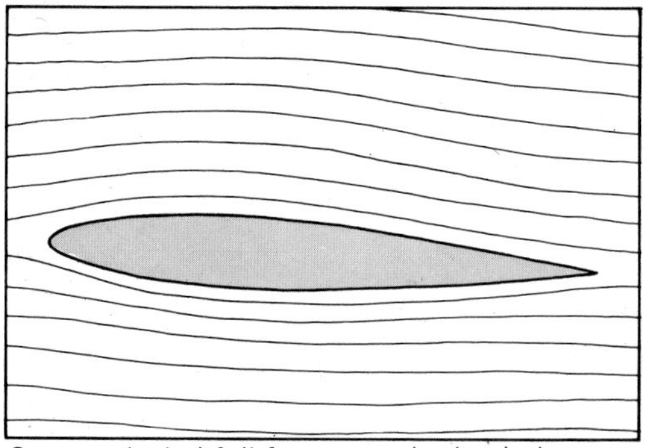

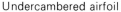

Symmetrical airfoil for an aerobatic airplane

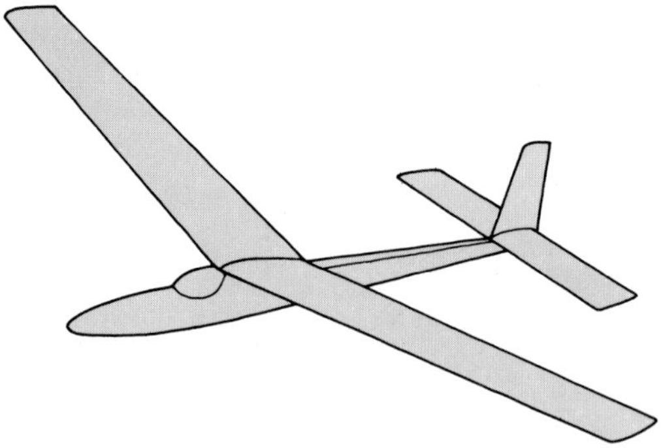

An aircraft with dihedral wings is very stable.

## How a glider flies

A glider produces forward motion by adopting a nose-down attitude. In this position the lift is not diametrically opposite to the weight and this produces a small forward force sufficient to overcome drag. A glider can stay airborne as long as the air is rising faster than the glider is falling through it. The rising air can take the form of a thermal (a body of air rising because it has been heated by the ground) or an updraft (wind which is deflected upward by features such as ridges, hills or cliffs).

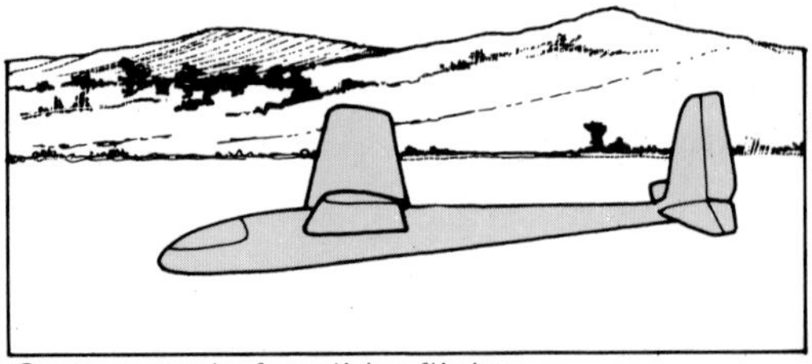

Correct angle for glider flight

## How the control surfaces work

Attitude on fixed-wing aircraft is controlled by hinged flaps – the control surfaces. They form part of the trailing edges of wings, tail plane and fin and are known as the ailerons, elevator and rudder, respectively. A control surface works by deflecting the airstream passing over it, producing a force on the aircraft in the opposite direction to the deflection. Control surfaces are always located as far as possible from the center of the airplane in order to provide the maximum leverage.

Ailerons are linked to move in opposite directions so that, when operated, one wing lifts and the other drops, making the aircraft bank. They are often arranged to move up more than down so that in a banked turn, the drag increases more on the inside (low) wing than on the outside one. This slows down the inside wing and speeds up the outside one, helping the aircraft around the turn.

The rudder makes the aircraft turn right or left. At the same time it makes the airplane slip sideways, called yawing. When used on its own, it tends to push the nose down.

The elevator gives fore-and-aft control by raising and lowering the tail.

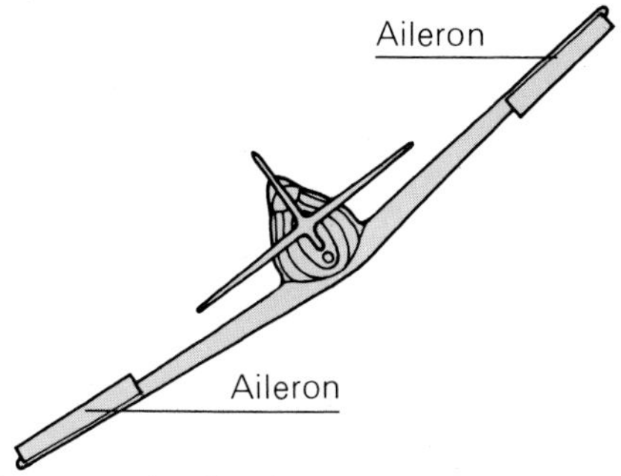


Ailerons make the airplane bank.

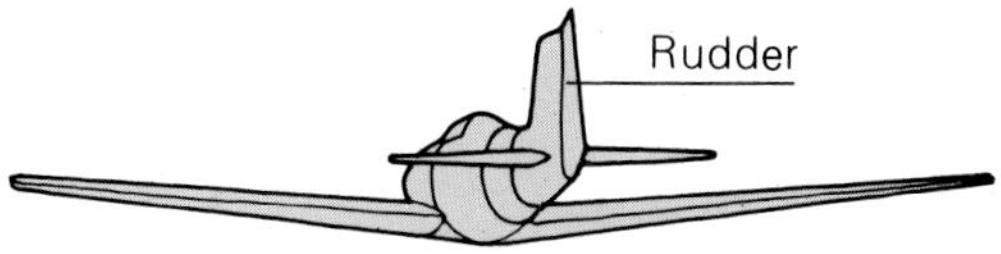


The rudder makes the airplane turn.

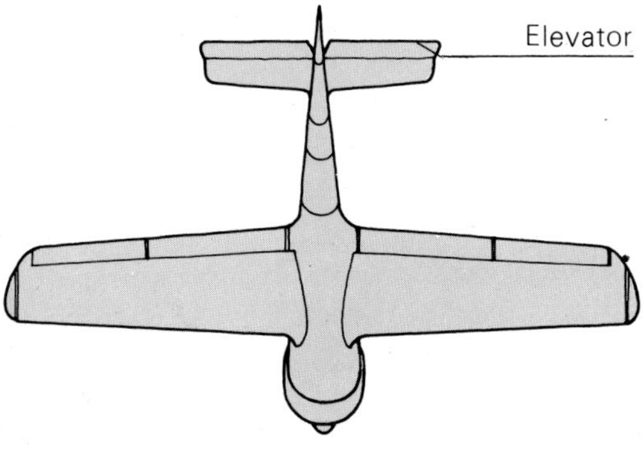


The elevator makes the nose rise or drop.

# Building an airplane

Construction varies according to the design of the airplane and the materials used to make it but you will find on the following pages methods of building the most common types of model. The information is divided into two sections: the fuselage and the wings; the latter includes tail-plane construction because it is closely related.

See pages 28 to 31 for reading and preparing plans and setting up a work station.

# The fuselage

It is important that the fuselage be well constructed as its function is to position and hold the wings and tail plane accurately and firmly. It must be strong enough to resist the twisting and bending forces of the flying surfaces and the pull of the motor if it is a powered model; it must also be able to absorb landing shocks and, when required in some instances, to carry radio equipment.

The shape of the fuselage adds more to the style of the aircraft than any other element, but it is not necessary for a model fuselage to be an exact copy of a real one. Few competition aircraft, whether powered or not, resemble full-size aircraft. They are simply designed to perform well. Some modelers use the same set of wings on more than one fuselage to create a "new" model. Scale models, on the other hand, are meant to be replicas of the full-size aircraft.

Built-up construction is appropriate for early aircraft. Carved balsa sheets and blocks are often used to imitate airplanes with curved metal panels. These two forms of construction can also be combined. A small model which must be light would almost certainly have to be of built-up construction. The same aircraft in a larger scale may require the heavier and stronger balsa-sheet method.

## Materials

Balsa wood, because of its lightness and versatility, is the most widely used material for building fuselages, but plastics are becoming increasingly popular. Kit manufacturers now produce fuselages molded in foamed plastic or fiberglass, or vacuum-formed from sheet plastic, for those who do not want to spend too much time making one. The weight of a fiberglass fuselage limits its use to large, powered aircraft or gliders which need a strong material at the expense of overall weight. Metal is not often used for structural work, although aluminum tube is sometimes found in competition models. Thin aluminum sheet can be employed for engine cowlings or for covering a scale model. See Basic techniques for cutting and shaping wood and metal.

Open-frame fuselages have to be covered to make a smooth, airtight surface. Covering materials include tissue paper, fabric and plastic film. Instructions for applying them are on pages 288 to 291.

## Simple fuselages

The simplest of all is that for a rubber-driven stick model. It is a rectangular strip of hard balsa to which all the components are attached.

The hand-launched glider has a profile fuselage. Like that for the stick model, it is a hard-balsa strip, but it is shaped to help the aircraft glide. The nose is rounded, often in an elliptical curve, and the curve tapers to the tail to reduce the weight at the back of the aircraft. The edges are rounded to prevent them being damaged and to make the model more comfortable to handle. A lead weight in the nose counterbalances the weight of the tail. To make the weight, glue a strip of lead over the nose or glue a disk-shaped pellet into a hole in the side. Be sure to check the balance of the model before fixing the weight in place. Balsa-wood "cheeks" can be glued to either side of the nose to cover the weight or give more form to the fuselage.

A profile fuselage is sometimes used for control-line trainers because it is sturdy and because the model is always seen from its best angle as it circles the operator. Control-line fuselages are sometimes shaped to follow the contour of a real aircraft, giving a simple scale appearance. The engine is mounted sidewinder fashion to hardwood bearers which are glued into the balsa fuselage (see Mounting motors and engines, page 277). The nose may be reinforced with plywood glued to each side.

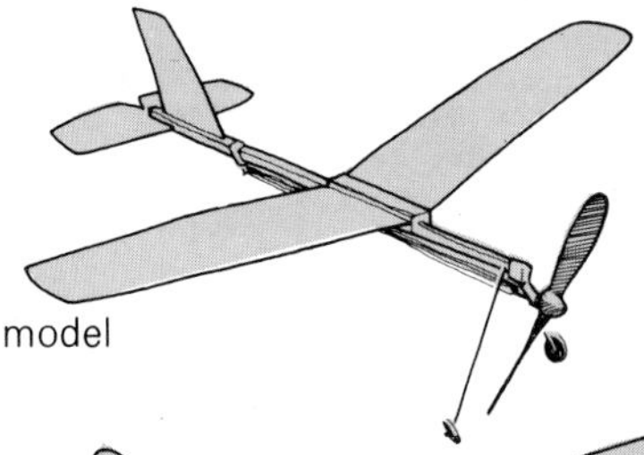

Stick model

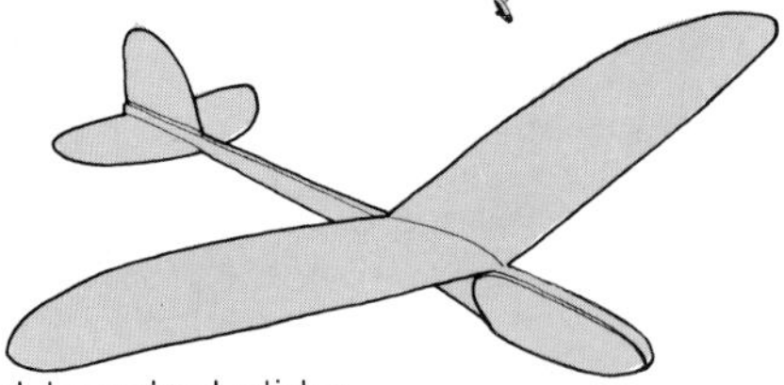

Hand-launched glider

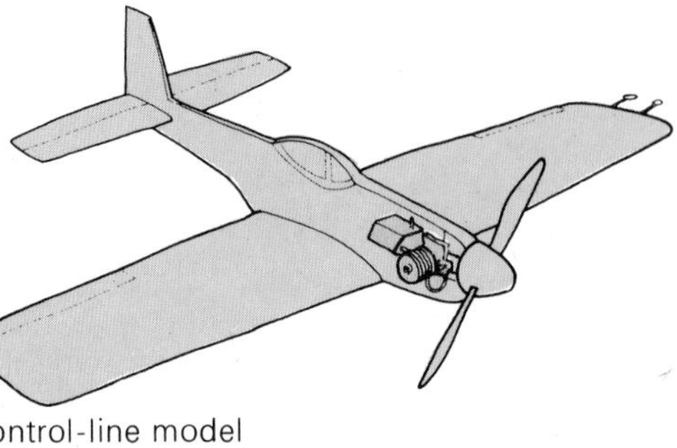

Control-line model

## Built-up construction

This technique makes a lightweight, fully three-dimensional fuselage which is shaped like a long, tapering box. A rigid, wooden frame is made up, then covered with a thin, airtight membrane. This method can be used for both beginner's models or more sophisticated aircraft. Assemble it with care because even the simplest model can inadvertently be made with a built-in warp.

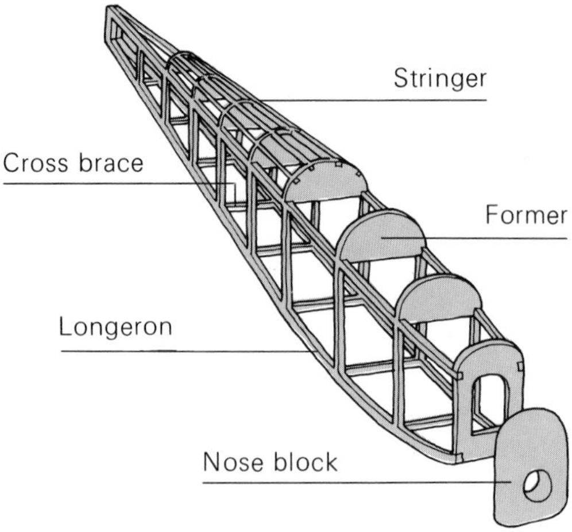


**The parts of a built-up fuselage**

**Stage 1: Making the sides**

Pin the plan to a board and prepare its surface as described on page 31. Carefully select the balsa strips for the longerons, checking to see that they have the same amount of stiffness by bending them – they must be as closely matched as possible. Although kit manufacturers select their balsa for quality, one or two may differ in stiffness. Buy extra longerons to match the good ones if necessary.

Both side frames must be identical so build them together, one on top of the other, on the plan. Begin by pinning the longerons in position, placing the pins either side of the strips. If the plan shows the longerons tapering toward the back, bend them into a shallow curve. Light sections bend easily but stiffer sections need to be dampened with water or steamed to make bending easier (see Bending balsa wood, page 46). Allow the wood to dry before gluing it.

Next, cut out and glue the vertical strips in position, one pair at a time. In this way any discrepancy can be accommodated as the work progresses. To calculate the length of a strip and the angle of the cut, hold an overlong strip in place so that it bridges both the top and bottom longerons. Sighting straight down, mark the cut lines with a knife, then cut the strip to length on a cutting board with a razor saw. Use the strip as a guide to cut an identical upright. Balsa cement tends to squeeze out as the strips are pushed into place. To guarantee a good bond, apply a thin film of cement to both halves of the joint and allow it to set, then apply a fresh layer of cement and assemble the parts.

Remove the completed side frames from the board when the cement has set hard. If they are stuck together, carefully cut them apart with a single-edged razor blade, cutting from both ends toward the center.

Stage 1

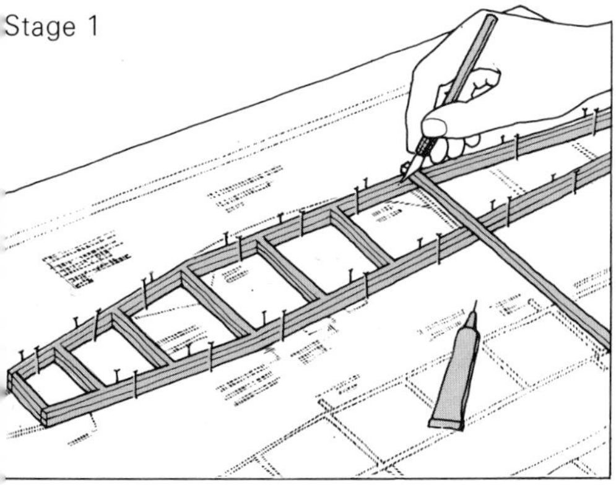

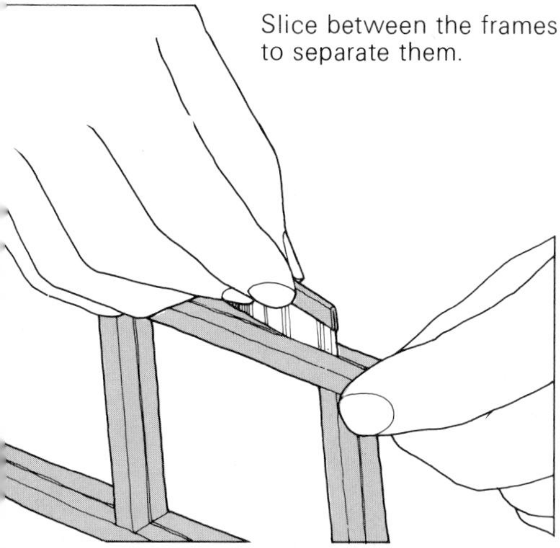

Slice between the frames to separate them.

**Stage 2: Joining the side frames**

Correct alignment is essential at this stage. The cross braces and formers must be at a right angle to the centerline of the plan view. Fuselages with parallel sides at the front are the simplest to build and can be assembled starting from the nose end. Those which taper toward both the nose and tail should have the formers attached to the widest part first.

Working from the plan view, cut each pair of cross braces to size. Pin the longest cross brace or braces in position on the plan. Apply cement to the ends and place the side frames against them. Push pins into the board against the frames to press them together. Glue on the matching top brace or braces. To apply pressure to the top joints while they set, push a pin into the board a short distance from each side of the fuselage, hook a light rubber band onto the pins and stretch it over the frame. As you work, check that all the angles between the various parts are symmetrical. It is a good idea to make balsa wood or cardboard templates based on the plan before assembly. Hold them in place to check the angle or temporarily fix them to the model with cyanoacrylate glue to hold the frame steady (cut them off later when the fuselage is complete). Check right angles with a small try square or triangle. If necessary, adjust the tension on either side of the rubber band to pull the frames upright. Continue attaching the cross braces, working toward the nose or tail to the point where the sides begin to taper. Allow the joints to set.

Before joining the tail ends, you may need to trim their inside faces to give a wider gluing area and a thinner edge. One technique is to sand or file both faces at once with a double-sided sanding board or a file placed between the frames. You may also sand a bevel on each face before joining the side frames together, taking the angle from the plan view.

Glue the ends together, making sure that they are accurately aligned and exactly level. Hold the joint with pins, clothespins or a clamp until set. A balsa fillet glued into the angle at the tail helps to reinforce the joint. Glue in the remaining cross braces, working toward the ends.

Some fuselages have curved longerons that prevent the sides touching the board along their full length. These fuselages require a slightly different method of assembly. If only the bottom longerons are curved, build the fuselage upside down on the plan. If the longerons on both the top and bottom surfaces are curved, attach one pair of cross braces at a time. When one pair is set, remove the rubber band and reposition the structure so that the next joint is brought into contact with the plan. Repeat this process along the length of the fuselage. In some cases it may be more convenient to assemble the sides off the plan, placing rubber bands around the components to hold them together. Glue the tail ends and the nose cross braces together first to help keep the frame true, then glue the intermediate cross braces between the side frames. Keep a constant check on the angles as assembly progresses.

Stage 2

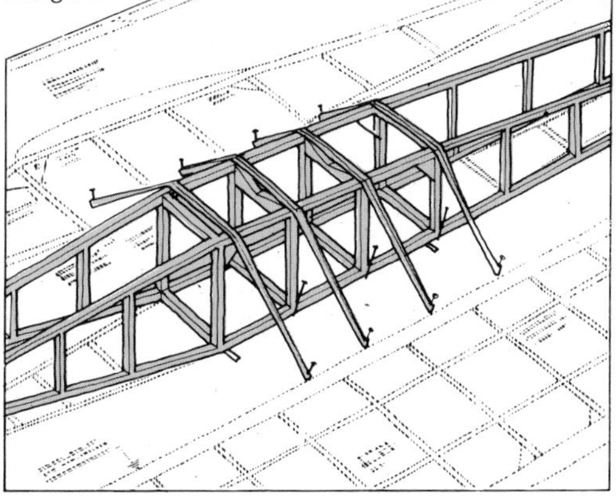

## Half-keel built-up construction

Stringers glued to formers make the shape of this fuselage which is often used for small, scale models. The covering material bridges the stringers, creating a faceted surface. The stringers must be as closely matched as possible so, before you begin to build, it is advisable to ascertain that they have the same amount of stiffness by bending them.

To make assembly easier, the formers are split horizontally or vertically in two. The stringers can be glued into notches in the edges of the formers, although they should never be set in flush because the formers will show through the covering material. More care is needed if the formers are unnotched because the positions of the joints have to be marked and the stringers held accurately in place while the glue dries.

The method described below involves completing one half of the fuselage on the board before removing it to build the other half. Some modelers prefer to remove the half-fuselage from the board once the main side stringer is attached. Then, they add the remaining half-formers and main stringer, followed by the rest of the stringers, attached in diagonally opposite pairs to balance each other. This method needs more care to avoid warps.

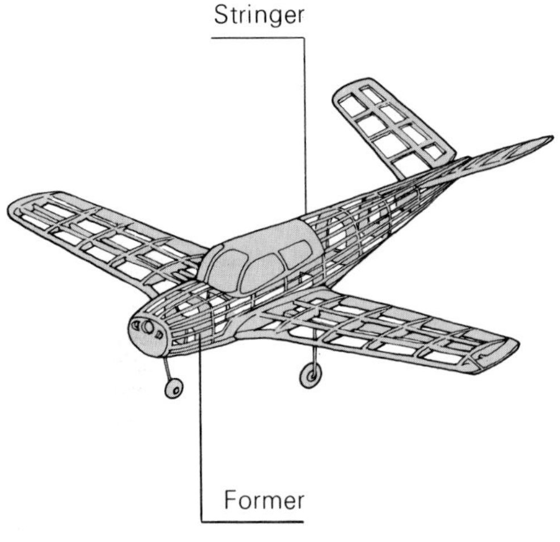


### Stage 1: Making one half-fuselage

Pin the two keel strips, usually cut from sheet balsa, onto the side view of the plan if the formers are split vertically, or onto the top view if the formers are split horizontally. Glue the half-formers across the keel strips, working backward from the nose. Make sure that each one is at a right angle to the keel strips with a try square and allow the glue to set.

Next, glue the main side stringer to each of the formers and to the keel strips at the tail end. Glue the rest of the stringers in place, working on alternate sides of the main stringer. Always start by gluing one end of the stringer to the nose former, as this end of the fuselage usually has the most curve; allow some extra to overhang. Let the glue set, then bend the stringer into place along its full length without any glue to check its curve. If necessary, mark the stringer where it meets the formers so that you can repeat the curve when you glue it. Finally, glue each joint in turn, working toward the tail.

The stringers, which are usually bent dry, need to be held in place while the glue sets. Thicker strips can be pinned and glued with a slow-setting adhesive such as balsa cement or white glue. Thin stringers, which may be split by pins, can be secured with rubber bands looped over pins in the board, but make sure that the band tension is correct or the stringers will be distorted. You may also use a cyanoacrylate glue to fix the stringers in place.

When all the stringers are attached and the glue is set, carefully remove the half-fuselage from the board.

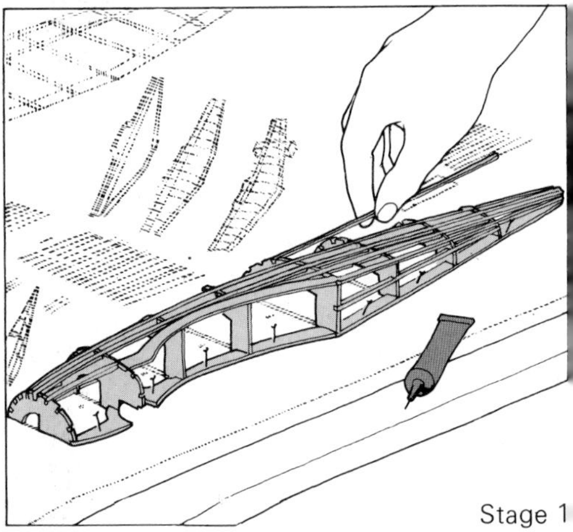

Stage 1

### Stage 2: Completing the fuselage

Glue the remaining former pieces to the half-completed fuselage, then add the rest of the stringers. Be sure to match the curves on the first side so that the fuselage is symmetrical.

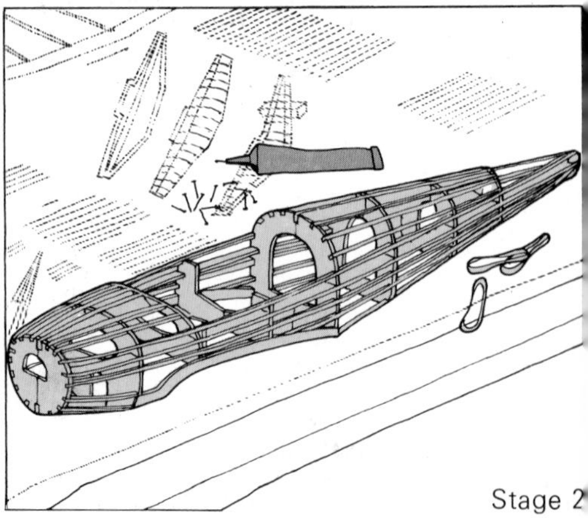

Stage 2

## Tube-jig built-up construction

This is similar to half-keel construction but each former is a single piece of wood, with a hole cut in the center, which slides onto a tube running down the center of the fuselage. The tube keeps the formers in line during construction and may be removed when the structure is completed. It can be made of any stiff, straight material. A square-sectioned strip of hardwood or a narrow aluminum tube suit longer fuselages.

Some small rubber-powered kit models have a cardboard tube which remains inside. The rubber motor passes down the center. If the motor breaks it is contained within the tube and does not damage the balsa structure.

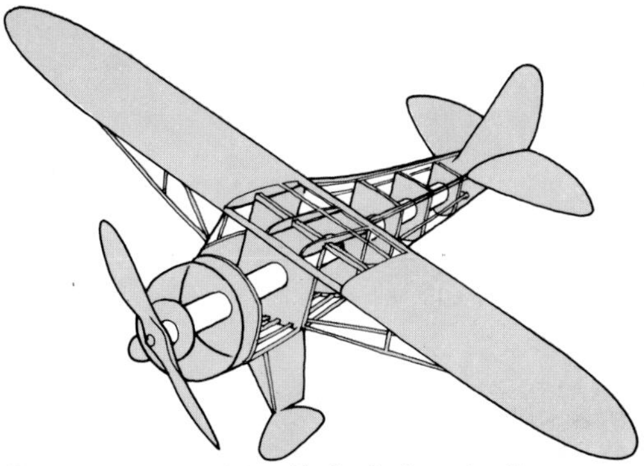

Small-scale model with built-in tube jig

## Slab-sided construction

Although a slab-sided fuselage is heavier than the open-frame type, it is usually stronger and more straightforward to make. Many radio-control trainers are made using this technique.

Usually, formers are used to hold the sides together and keep them square, making assembly easier. Sheet balsa is ideal for making formers, but only cut small holes for the linkage runs as large ones leave short, weak grain. You may also lap joint four balsa strips to make a strong former with a large opening. Plywood formers are tougher and you can cut larger holes in them which makes them lighter.

Make straight-sided fuselages as described in stages 1 and 2 below. Fuselages which have rounded surfaces must be built from carved or bent sheet, or planks (see page 274).

**Stage 1: Joining the sides**

Like the open-frame systems on pages 270 to 272, the balsa sides must be identical in shape and quality. Cut out both sides together: pin two pieces of sheet balsa together, mark up the top one, then cut through both at once. Prefabricated sides should be pinned together, then trimmed to match, using the wing and tail plane position to align them (never alter the wing and tail plane reference points or you may affect the angles of incidence).

Mark each side piece right and left, for reference. Next, transfer the position of the formers from the plan's side elevation to the inside face of each side. The sides cover their position when laid over the plan, so first extend the lines on the plan beyond the top and bottom edge. Position one side on the plan and transfer the exposed marks. Join up the marks with a ruler across the inside face. Place the second side on the first and transfer the edge marks onto it; join them up.

If your plan incorporates longerons, glue them to each side before assembling the sides. Likewise, thin-plywood reinforcements, known as doublers, should be glued onto the front section while the sides are flat.

The sides of the front section of the fuselage, from the nose to the trailing edge of the wing, are usually parallel. The formers at this point meet the sides at a right angle. Attach them to one side first, making sure they are vertical with a try square. When the glue has set, stand the structure over the plan view and attach the other side piece. Use pins or rubber bands to hold the parts together. Finally, glue the tail end together and attach the remaining formers or cross braces. Keep checking the fuselage for symmetry as the work progresses.

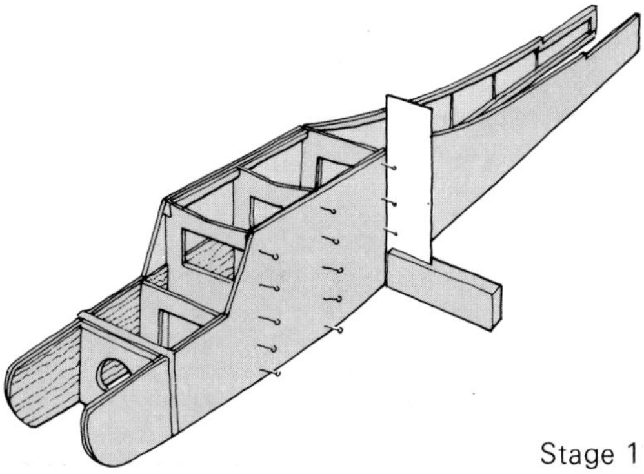

Stage 1

**Stage 2: Covering top and bottom**

Cut the top and bottom balsa sheet with the grain running from side to side as this gives a stiffer structure and easily follows a curve from front to back. Cut the sheets oversize and trim them after gluing.

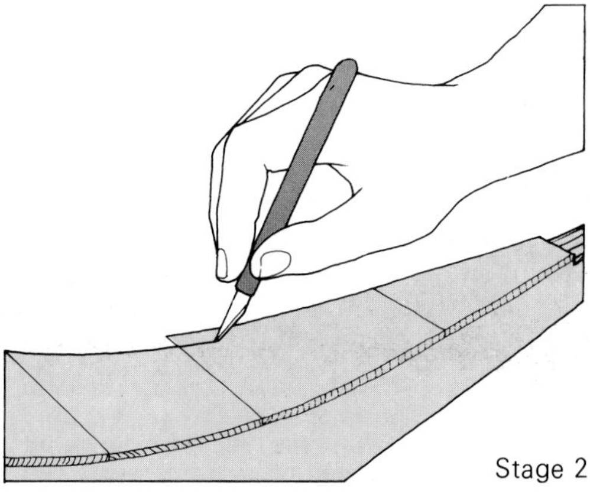

Stage 2

**Carved sheet balsa**
This method can be used to produce any rounded shape, including compound curves. Roughly form the fuselage with pieces of thick balsa sheet, then shape it accurately with a modeling knife, razor plane and sanding block.

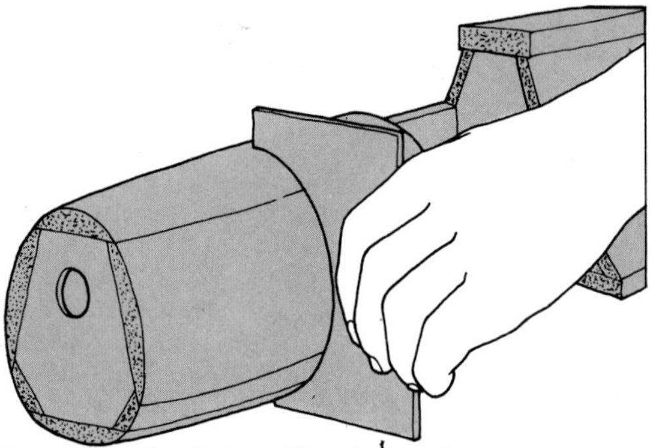

**Carving the balsa** Check the shape as you work with templates of half of each sectional view, traced from the plan. The sectional view is usually shown at each former, a convenient reference point for checking the shape on the model.

**Bent sheet balsa**
Use soft-balsa sheet to cover a single curve only, wrapping it over the formers. The thickness of the sheet depends on the size of the model. Tighter curves need thinner sheet. Two or more thin layers can be applied if you need a stronger structure.

Cut the sheet slightly longer than the area to be covered (the grain should run from front to back) and dampen the outside face to help it bend without splitting. Center the panel on the apex of the curve and pin it in place. Mark the panel where it touches the fuselage all around its outer edge. Remove the panel and cut it to shape, or carefully cut it in situ. Check it for fit and glue it in place. You will probably need to butt joint the edges of two or three pieces to cover the fuselage.

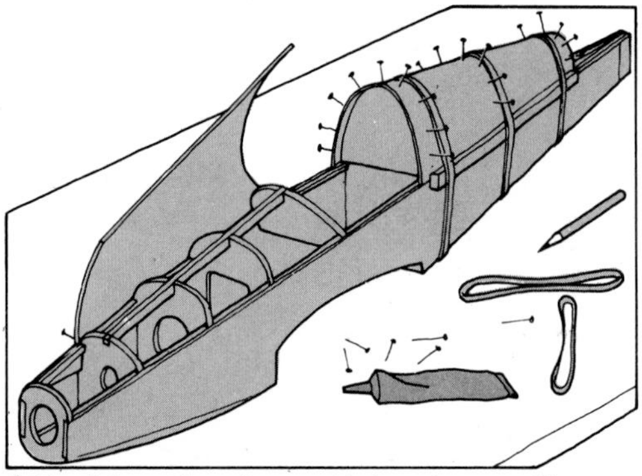

**Attaching the sheets** If the pieces will not stay pinned in place while the glue sets, loop rubber bands over the fuselage. Use a piece of scrap wood to apply extra pressure.

**Balsa planks**
These are used to create a simple curve. Glue soft-balsa strips of the same thickness side-by-side over the curve of the formers, then sand the surface smooth. Bevel the edges of the strips slightly to make a close fit. The thicker the strips, the more critical this becomes. It is not a good idea to leave the strips square in section and fill in the grooves with Spackle because any slight movement in the wood may cause the joint to show through the finish. Moreover, the filler adds weight to the model.

Each strip needs to be tapered to fit the narrower part of the fuselage. To do this, pin the first and second strip in place, with the second overlapping the first at the tail end. Mark a line on the first strip, following the bottom edge of the second. Remove the strips and cut along the marked line. Glue the cut strip in place. Pin the second strip to butt up against the fixed strip, then pin a third one, overlapping the second; repeat the process. Work from each side of the fuselage toward the top and bottom. When all the strips are in place, sand the completed shape smooth.

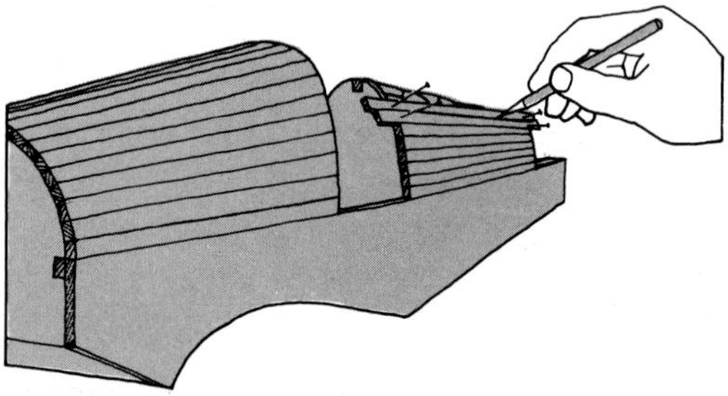

## Slab-sided glider fuselage

Some model gliders have a very slim fuselage constructed from strip and sheet balsa. The strip balsa components which make up the top, bottom and formers, are assembled over the plan. A nose block cut from thick balsa sheet is added to this frame, then the frame is removed from the building board. An oversize piece of sheet balsa glued to each side and trimmed flush with the frame completes the fuselage.

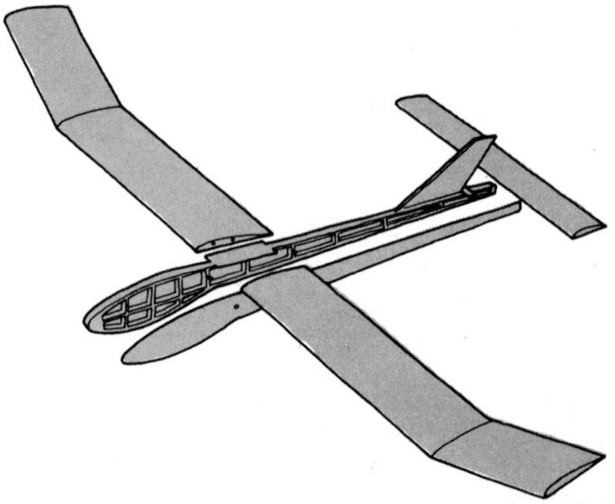

# Cowls and nose blocks

Powered models have a hollow cowl covering the engine. It can be part of the fuselage or a separate unit that is screwed on. Built-in cowls are normally made of carved balsa; the other type are often plastic or aluminum shapes sold as kit accessories. Some experienced scale modelers beat their own metal cowls from thin aluminum or zinc sheet. Complex shapes are usually molded from plastic. Metal cowls are generally circular for use on models with radial engines. Unlike powered models, gliders have a permanently fixed, solid-balsa nose block.

## Built-in balsa cowls

To make the engine easily accessible, radio-control trainer models do not have a true cowl. Instead, the engine is usually mounted vertically in an open-topped nose section. Balsa side "cheeks," which follow the line of the fuselage, are added to give the nose its shape. The portion under the engine is filled in with a piece of balsa and carved to the correct profile. Sometimes the engine compartment has a lid or hatch for a more realistic appearance. The cover can be shaped from thick sheet balsa to give a flat top, or built up with formers and thin sheet when a deeper shape is required. Using self-tapping screws, fix the cover to hardwood blocks glued to the formers or, if preferred, attach the cover with snap fasteners.

Semiscale models – ones which represent a full-size aircraft but are not exact replicas – often have the engine and muffler mounted sideways or upside down to make them less obvious. The engine is usually not fully enclosed as in the case of a true scale model. Balsa cowls for this type of airplane vary in construction. The method shown, right, suits a World War Two fighter. If you wish, instead of attaching the former and spacer to the spinner as in step 1, you can support the former on balsa spacers glued to the first fuselage former, known as the firewall, then add the thick balsa pieces. You will have to make careful calculations from the plan so that the former is at the correct angle and distance from the firewall for your engine.

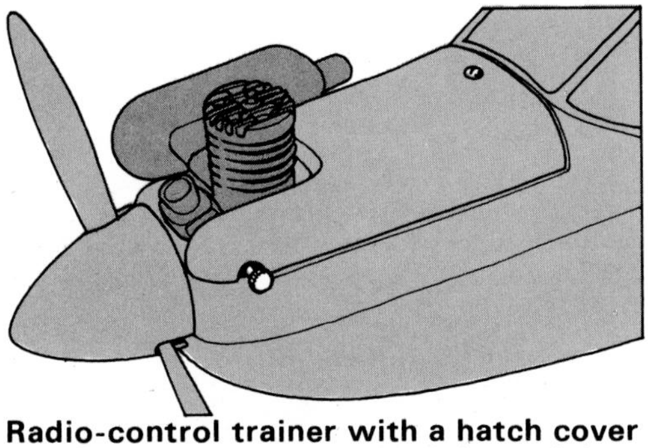

**Radio-control trainer with a hatch cover**
On this model the cover extends beyond the engine firewall to give access to the fuel tank. This allows the filler tubes to be tucked neatly out of sight.

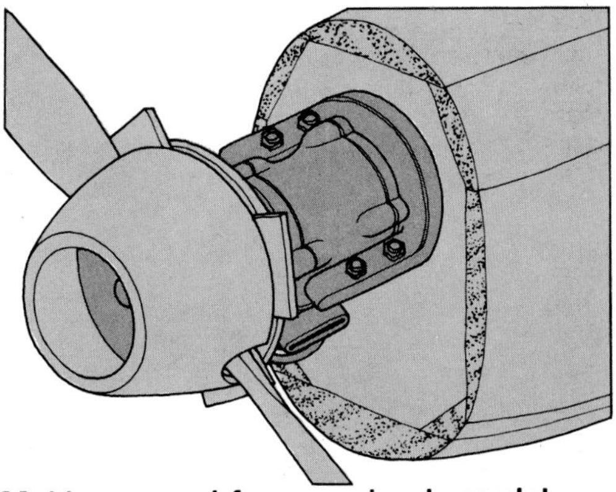

**Making a cowl for a semiscale model**
Temporarily attach the engine, including the propeller and spinner, to the fuselage. Tack-glue a former to the back of the spinner, inserting shims in between.

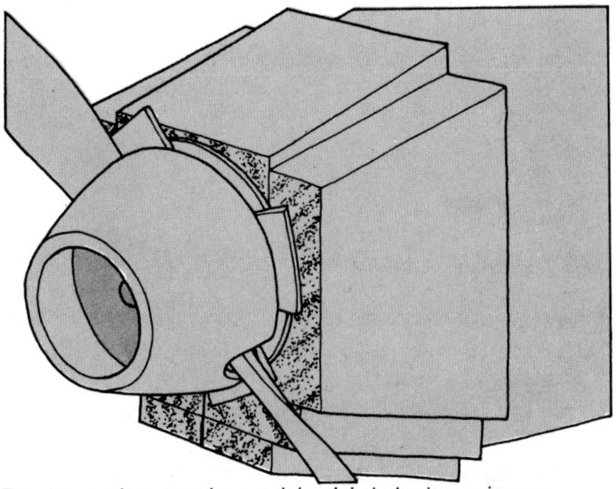

Enclose the engine with thick balsa pieces, leaving an opening for the cylinder and muffler. The section over the opening must be detachable for maintenance so glue the pieces that make up the section together, but only temporarily glue the section to the fuselage.

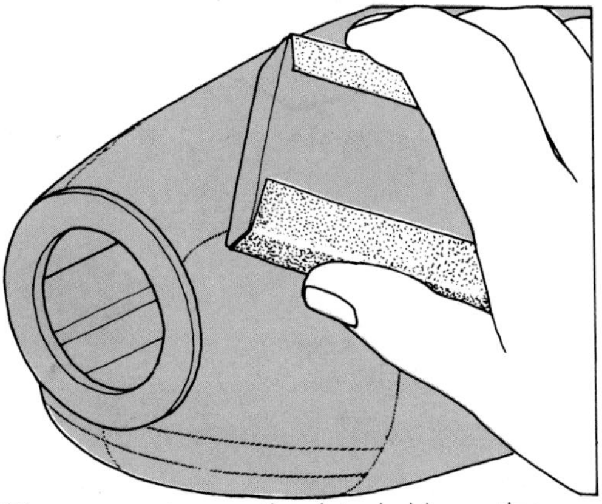

When set, cut away the detachable section and remove the engine. Carve and sand the nose piece to shape. Make a drain hole in the bottom and fuelproof the inside surfaces.

## Plastic cowls

Although not as strong as balsa cowls, vacuum-formed plastic cowls are simple to install. Before fixing a plastic cowl in place, it is usually necessary to cut holes for the engine, muffler and propeller.

First, cut the cowl to length with a razor saw, then cut a hole in the front to clear the engine prop drive. Mount the engine so that there is clearance between the spinner and the front of the cowl. Try the cowl on the fuselage. If it fouls the cylinder head and/or the muffler, cut holes in the side for them. Mark their position and approximate size on the outside surface, then drill a small hole in the center and pare away the plastic with a modeling knife. A round needle file or an electric grinding tool can also be used to make the holes. Finally, make a small access hole for the needle valve.

The plastic tends to split when the model makes a bad landing so, after cutting the holes, reinforce the cowl with cloth tape. Thoroughly clean off all the grease and roughen the inside surface, then apply a thin layer of contact adhesive. Wrap the cloth tape around the inside of the cowl.

Plastic cowls are usually screwed to the fuselage through the back edge. This, of course, means that the cowl can be easily removed to allow for cleaning and regular servicing of the engine.

**Mounting a plastic cowl** Set the cowl in a rabbet as shown or slide it onto a shaped fuselage. Fix it to the fuselage with small screws.

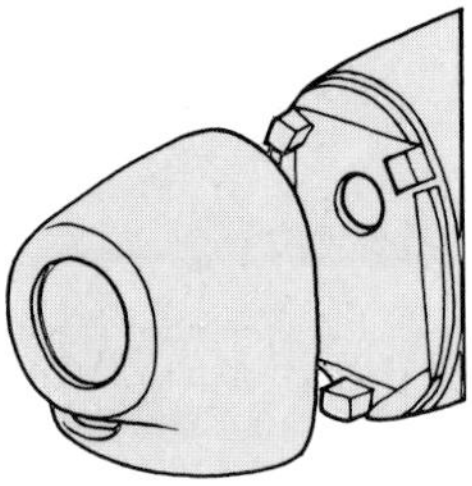

## Nose blocks

These are made of solid balsa and are tough enough to withstand a heavy landing. Use a single balsa block if the size is available. Glue a tracing of the plan view and a tracing of the side view on the top and side surfaces of the block, respectively. Cut around the outline on one side with a fret or coping saw then, with the nose piece cradled in the waste piece, cut around the other outline. Glue the nose piece to the front former and, when set, carve and sand the corners to produce the exact contour, following the line of the fuselage.

If you cannot find a balsa block of the correct size, laminate thick sheets of balsa. Cut the pieces from the same sheet to guarantee a constant density and glue them together with the grain running in the same direction to make carving easier. You can assemble the pieces to form a rectangle and shape the rectangle as described above, or you can cut the pieces so that they approximate the shape of the nose when glued together, as shown right.

## Metal cowls

A true-to-scale metal cowl often completely encloses a model engine so that, unlike some plastic cowls, there is no need to cut a large hole for the cylinder head. You must, however, drill a small access hole for the needle valve and one for the glow plug clip of a glow plug engine or compression screw of a diesel engine.

Metal cowls are usually screwed to the front former through metal brackets glued to their inside face. Three brackets evenly spaced around the cowl should be sufficient. Cut the brackets from aluminum angle strip or bend small aluminum strips. Drill a hole in each bracket. If the edge of the cowl butts up against the former, then align the brackets with the edge. If the cowl overlaps the fuselage, you need to set the brackets back from the edge. To calculate the distance from the edge, see below. Use epoxy adhesive to attach the brackets, first roughening the inside surface of the cowl with coarse abrasive paper to provide a key. If necessary, reinforce the joint after the glue has set with fiberglass tape and resin. Finally, drill holes in the former and screw the cowl in place, working through the front opening.

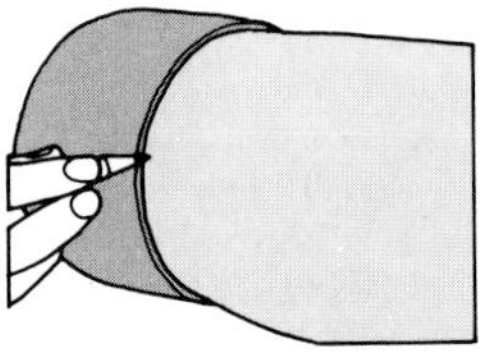

**Calculating the position of inset brackets** Hold the cowl in place and mark its end on the fuselage. Remove the cowl.

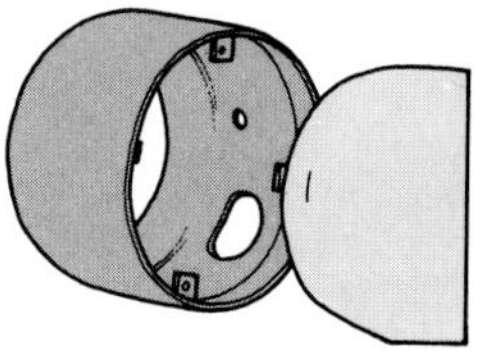

Measure the distance from the mark to the front former. Transfer this measurement to the inside of the cowl and scribe a line all around. Place the brackets on this line.

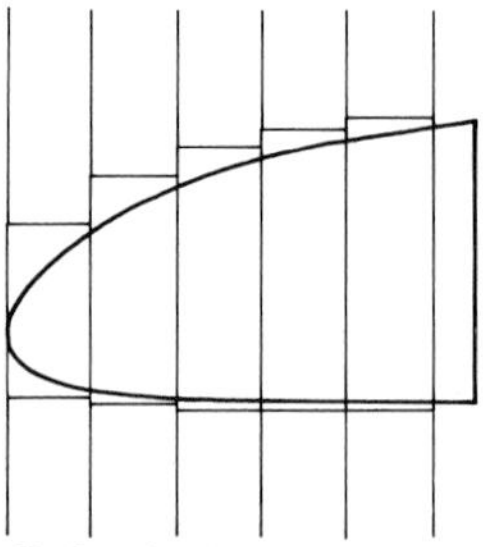

**Calculating the size of the laminations** Draw vertical lines on the plan and side view of the nose block. Space the lines apart by the thickness of the sheet balsa. Draw horizontal lines in between.

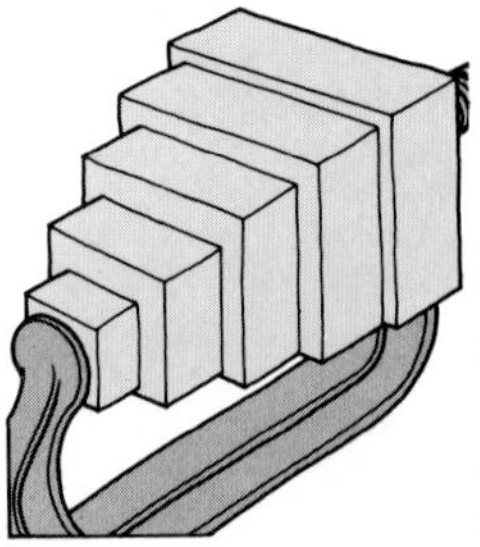

**Making the block** Cut out the balsa pieces and glue them together. Measure in from the edges to check that they are positioned as shown on your drawing. Clamp the block until set. Carve to make the shape.

# Mounting motors and engines

Below are instructions for mounting an internal combustion engine, a $CO_2$ engine and an electric motor. Methods for installing rubber motors are on pages 228 to 229. Turn to the Motors and engines chapter for information on running all types.

## Internal combustion engine

This type of engine can be mounted upright, inverted, sideways (known as "sidewinder") or at any angle in between. A sidewinder-mounted engine is usually positioned with the cylinder head on the starboard side so that the needle valve is at the top for easy access and the muffler is neatly tucked away below. This is also a good position for a control-line model as the bulk of the engine's weight is on the outside of the flying circle. Scale aircraft often have inverted engines placed at a 45° angle to keep the glow plug above the engine's lowest point and thus prevent flooding when starting up.

Internal combustion engines are bolted in place through lugs. Usually, the lugs are on the side for mounting onto horizontal bearers ("beam" mounting). Sometimes, the lugs are situated around the back edge for mounting onto the front former or firewall ("radial" mounting).

Some engines are set at an angle to the centerline of the fuselage. This is known as "downthrust" when it is angled down, or "sidethrust" when it is angled sideways. Downthrust is used to compensate for the power of the engine pulling the nose up. Sidethrust is used to compensate for the model turning left because of the torque effect of the engine. Sidewinder engines are always angled to the starboard side when sidethrust is needed. The amount of downthrust and sidethrust needed will be shown on the plan.

The direction of the thrust can be built in as the fuselage is assembled by setting the engine bearers or the firewall former at the correct angle. For a slight angle, build the bearers or firewall square and pack out the engine with washers or plastic wedges molded especially for the purpose. This packing method does not work to give sidethrust for a beam-mounted engine. Instead, bolt the engine at the correct angle to a $\frac{1}{8}$-inch (3-mm) sheet-alloy bearer plate, cutting part of it away to clear the crankcase, and screw the plate to the bearers. For slight sidethrust on a beam-mounted engine, enlarge the holes in the bearers to adjust the position of the engine (care must be taken not to overdo this).

Traditionally, beam-mounted engines are bolted to hardwood bearers, not less than $\frac{3}{8}$ inch (9 mm) square in section. The bearers extend back into the fuselage and are jointed into the model. Radial-mounted engines are bolted directly to the firewall. Commercial engine mountings, made from diecast alloy or molded nylon, are available, and they can be used for both types. Fasten the engine in place with Allen-head machine screws. Do not use flathead screws as these concentrate the load. Use spring-lock washers and apply special locking adhesive or use self-locking nuts to prevent the screws from working loose. If the construction of the model makes it impossible to reach behind the firewall to install a radial-mounted engine, attach blind nuts to the back of the wall as you build the fuselage; screw the engine to them from the front of the compartment later.

This beam-mounted internal combustion engine is packed with a wedge to give some degree of downthrust.

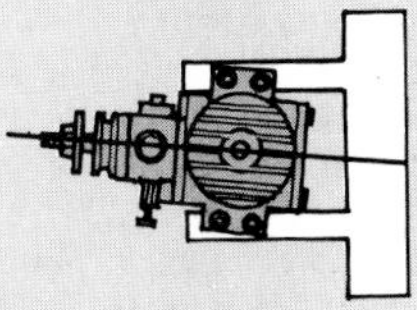

This engine is on bearers with enlarged holes to give some degree of sidethrust.

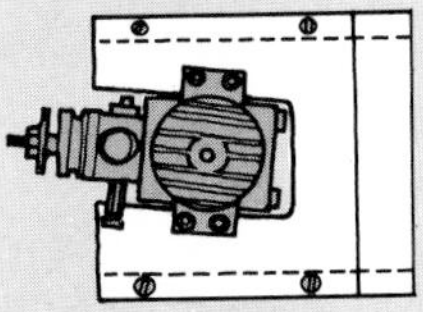

For a greater amount of sidethrust it is usually best to mount the engine on a plate bearer.

## $CO_2$ engine

This engine usually has radial mounting lugs. Bolt it to a thin plywood former in any radial position.

Like the internal combustion engine, some degree of downthrust and sidethrust is usually needed and the amount will be specified on the plan. If you have converted a model from rubber power, experiment to find the correct angle. As a rough guide, use 2 to 6° of downthrust and 2 to 4° of sidethrust. Set the plywood former at an angle or pack the engine with small washers.

## Electric motor

The cylindrical motor may already have side lugs or you can buy a casing with side lugs and beam mount the motor, but a plain motor without lugs is more common for aircraft. Usually, the motor is inserted in a homemade balsa tube (see page 252), and the tube bonded with resin into the nose or under the wing, as required.

# Wings

These must be strong and generally they are straight, although advanced modelers sometimes build in a carefully calculated twist to make a particular model more stable. Wings can be made in one piece, or in separate panels which join together at the top or bottom of the fuselage, or plug into the side.

Gliders usually have long wings with a short chord (the distance from the leading to the trailing edge), while powered airplanes have shorter wings with a longer chord. These are known as high-aspect ratio and low-aspect ratio wings, respectively.

## Solid-balsa wings

Used for small hand- or catapult-launched gliders, solid-balsa wings are the simplest to make. They are usually the flat-bottomed type. The wings in a kit may or may not be cut out. If they are not, or if you are scratch-building from a plan, cut around the outline, then shape the wing as described below. Stages 2 and 3 describe the method for joining dihedral wings.

Sand the tail plane to shape as for the wings. If it is made of thin material, just round off the edges carefully.

**Stage 1: Shaping the airfoil section**

This is the most critical aspect of wing construction. Make a paper template of the airfoil and temporarily glue it to the root end of each wing. Mark parallel lines about ½ inch (12 mm) apart along the top surfaces. For asymmetrical wings be sure to mark each correctly: one as the left and the other as the right.

With a razor plane, carefully plane the top surface to the airfoil contour using the lines as a guide and leaving a faceted surface. Work from the root end of the wing to the tip, and from the leading and trailing edges toward the thickest part of the wing.

Next, shape the surface with a sanding block. Hold the wing next to the edge of the building board so that you can use the sanding block at the correct angle. Work across the grain with a slight rocking motion, constantly checking the shape against the template. When you have shaped the wing section, turn the wing and let the tip project. Sand about one quarter of the wing length at the tip, to produce a shallow taper. The leading edge should blend into the trailing edge. Finally, smooth the whole surface working with the grain. Remove the templates.

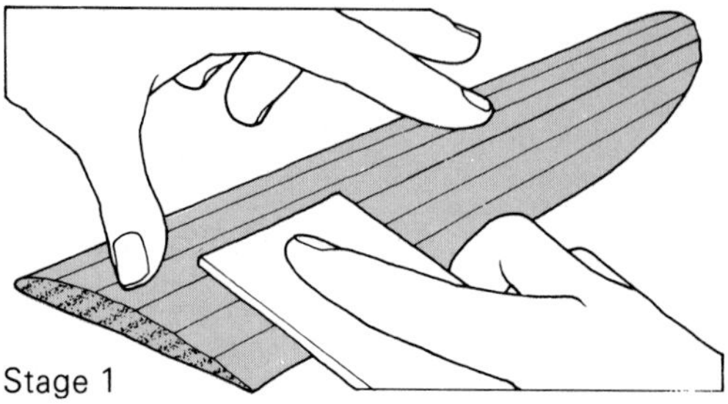

Stage 1

**Stage 2: Beveling the wing roots**

The wing roots need to be beveled so that, when joined, they form the correct dihedral angle. Working with one wing at a time, position the root flush with and parallel to the edge of the building board. Support the other end with a block at the required angle. Holding a sanding block upright and using the building board as a guide, bevel the edge. Be sure to remove the same amount from each wing.

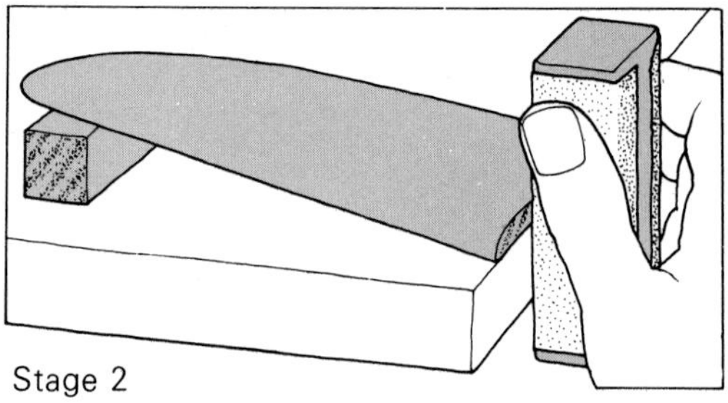

Stage 2

**Stage 3: Joining dihedral wings**

Glue the wings together. If you wish to make a stronger joint, brace it with a plywood strip cut to the dihedral angle. Cut a slot for the strip in each wing with a file before gluing them.

The wings can be supported in two ways while the glue sets. One method is to hold one wing flat on the board and support the other under the wing tip so that the angle formed between wing and board is equal to twice the dihedral angle. Strap down the flat wing with rubber bands hooked over pins, or push thumbtacks into the building board, letting the heads overlap the wing. The second method is to rest the joint on the board and support both wing tips at the correct dihedral angle.

## Built-up wings

This method is used primarily to save weight. The open framework consists of shaped ribs and some form of wing tip, joined by spars and a leading and a trailing edge. The shape of the rib determines the section of the wing. The structure is covered with a thin, airtight membrane to provide a strong and lightweight lifting surface.

**Parts of a built-up wing**

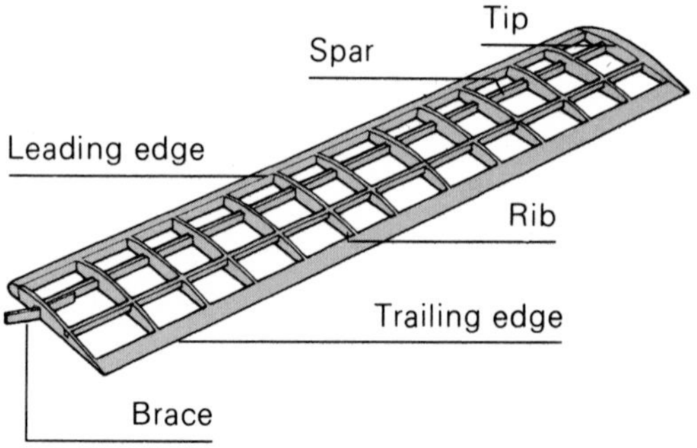

## The ribs

Die-cut kit ribs require little or no work. Ribs printed on sheet balsa need to be cut out. If the ribs are conveniently printed one above the other, first cut them from the sheet in a block, using a ruler to guide the knife along the ends. This method guarantees that the ribs are all the same length. Cut out the curves freehand. If the shapes are interlocking, you will have to cut the ribs out one by one.

Next, cut the notches for the spars. Use a razor saw or a knife to cut the sides of a large notch, and a chisel blade in a modeling knife or a woodworking chisel to chop out the waste. Small notches can be cut with a small flat file which has one toothed and one smooth side. If the width of the file is less than the width of the notch, cut down to the bottom of the notch using the toothed edge, then turn the file so that the smooth edge is on the bottom and file away the remaining waste on the side.

When all the ribs are cut, place them together and push them onto a short length of spar material to align them. Any differences in shape will be clearly visible. Sand all the ribs together to make them identical.

## Making scratch-built ribs

Cut the ribs from quarter-grain balsa with the grain running lengthwise. Ribs can be marked individually but, if you need a lot of ribs, make a pair of rib templates from thin plywood or aluminum sheet. Mark out one template, then cut them together to make sure that they are identical. While they are still together, drill two holes to take a threaded metal rod for clamping the ribs together later.

To cut out a single rib, hold one template on the balsa sheet and cut around it with a modeling knife. Score the position of the spar notch and cut it away after cutting out the rib. Alternatively, clamp several rib-size pieces of balsa together between the templates. Shape the block with a razor plane and sanding block, using the templates as a guide. Cut notches with a file while the ribs are clamped.

Ribs for a tapered wing can be made using the clamping method as long as the main spar is at a right angle to the ribs. However, because the ribs at the root are larger than those at the tip, care must be taken when lining up the templates. Align the template spar notches. Also, align the bottom edges of a flat-bottomed wing, and the centerline of a wing which has two convex surfaces.

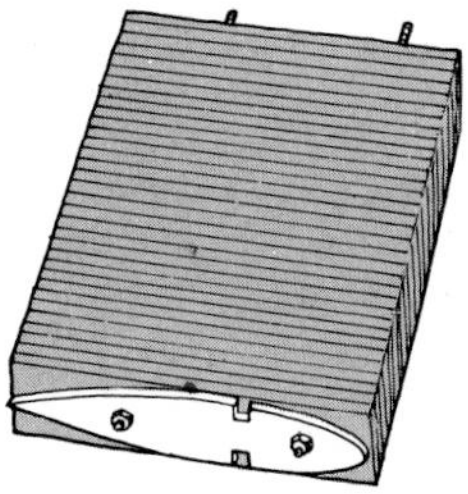

**Clamping the pieces together** Using the holes in the templates as a guide, drill through the balsa pieces. Pass a threaded metal rod through the holes to clamp the pieces together.

## The leading edge

Kit leading edges may or may not be shaped. You can buy ready-shaped edges separately or you can make your own from balsa strips. Leading edges must be strong but not too heavy, so select the grade of balsa for scratch-built edges carefully. Small sections can be made of hard, quarter-grain balsa or even doweling; average sections can be medium-grade, and large sections, soft or light balsa.

Small sections are often set into the ribs on a diagonal so that there is more area for gluing, then sanded to shape after assembly. Larger sections are usually roughly planed to shape before assembly as shown below.

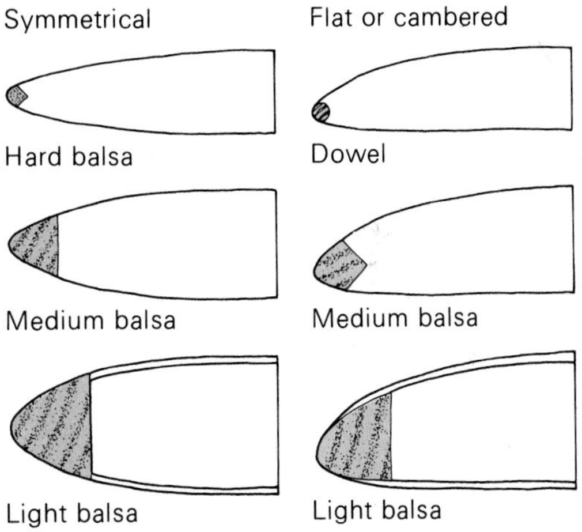


**Leading edge shapes** Leading edges are made in two sections: symmetrical and flat or cambered. The weight of the balsa and the method of attachment depends on their size.

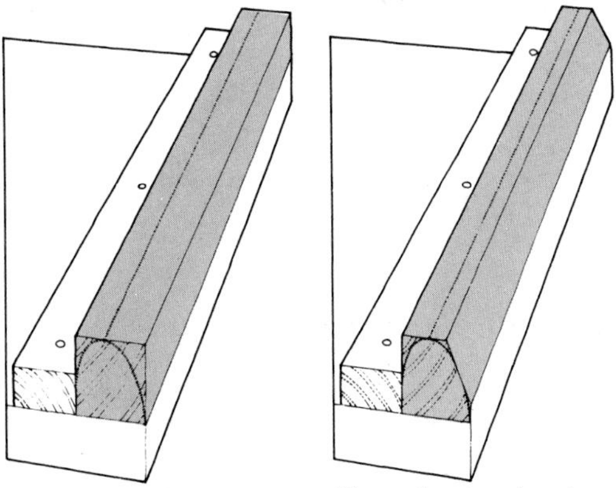

**Shaping a large-section leading edge** Set the edge in a rabbet formed by the building board and a balsa strip. Mark the curve on the ends and the apex of the curve on the top.

Plane the top front corner off the strip. Turn the edge around and remove the other corner. After assembly, carefully shape the faceted edge to the exact airfoil contour with a sanding board.

### The trailing edge

Made of solid or sheet balsa, the edge should be as thin as possible. It is usually left slightly square as a feathered edge is easily damaged.

Solid balsa edges are the most common. If you are building from scratch, choose rectangular sections of lightweight quarter-grain stock; larger sections can be made of medium-grade balsa. Plane it to shape as described for large-section leading edges on page 279, but be sure to plane and sand both surfaces.

The ribs can be butt-jointed to the trailing edge if a gusset is glued into the corner to reinforce the joint but, usually, the ribs fit into notches along the edge. Pin the trailing edge in place on the plan and mark the rib positions, then remove it and cut the notches with a thin file (don't use a knife – it may cut too deep and weaken the edge). Sometimes the ribs are cut to fit over the edge. This makes a strong joint, because of the larger gluing area, and a very narrow trailing edge as can be seen above right.

Sheet-balsa trailing edges may be strips set into the edge of the ribs, or an extension of the wing covering. In either case, first attach one side, trimming the overlap with a razor plane so that it matches the angle of the ribs. Then glue on the second piece and trim it flush with a razor plane.

## Spars

Their function is to stiffen the wings. Their number and shape varies according to the wing design. Usually, there is a main spar which is larger in section than the others.

Always use a straight-grained wood for spars. Balsa is the most common material but spruce is used where extra stiffness or a slim section is required at the cost of a little extra weight. Make sure that the spars in each wing are evenly matched.

Never cut the spars where they meet the ribs. Notch the ribs or cut through each rib completely and glue both sides of the rib to the spar.

**Methods of joining a solid-balsa trailing edge**

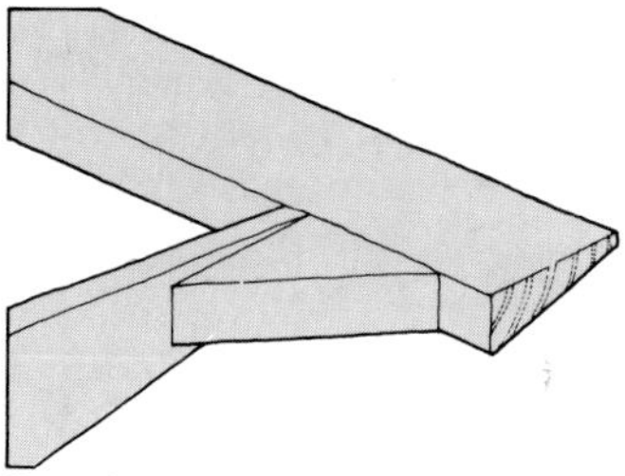
Butt joint

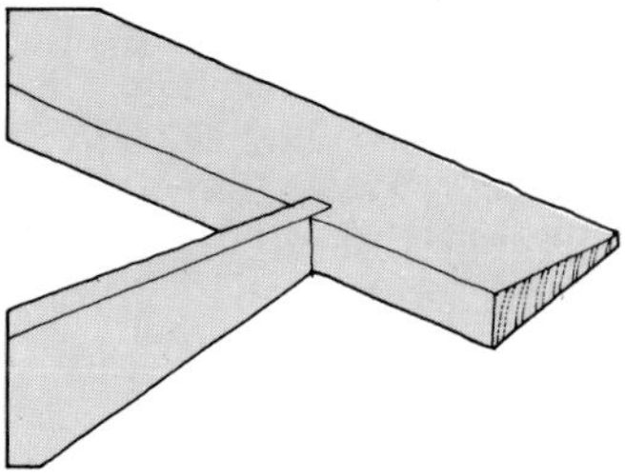
Notched joint

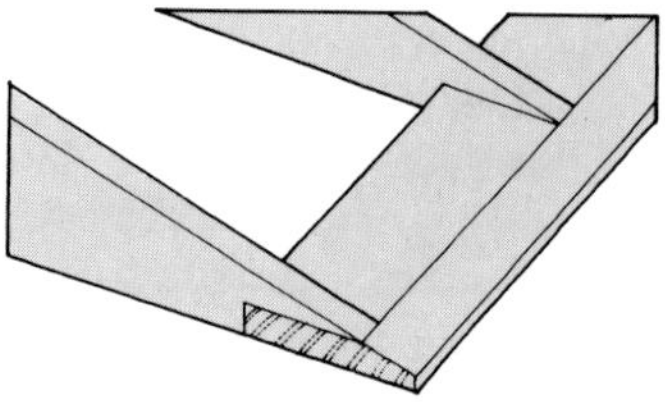
Ribs cut to fit over the edge of a flat-bottomed wing

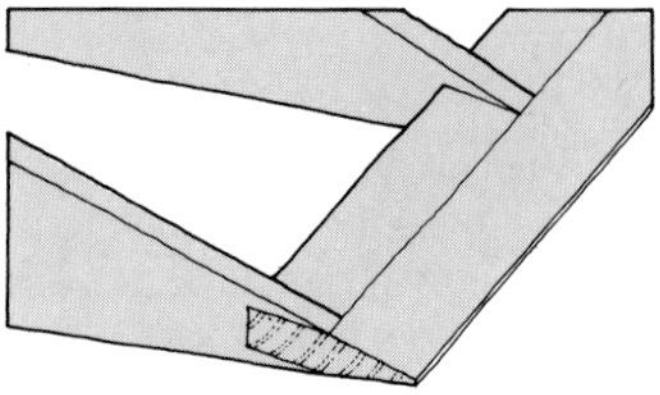
Ribs cut to fit over the edge of a symmetrical wing

**Two types of sheet-balsa trailing edges**

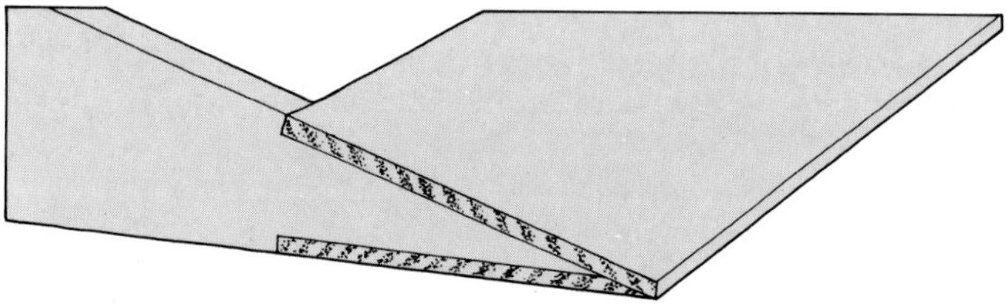

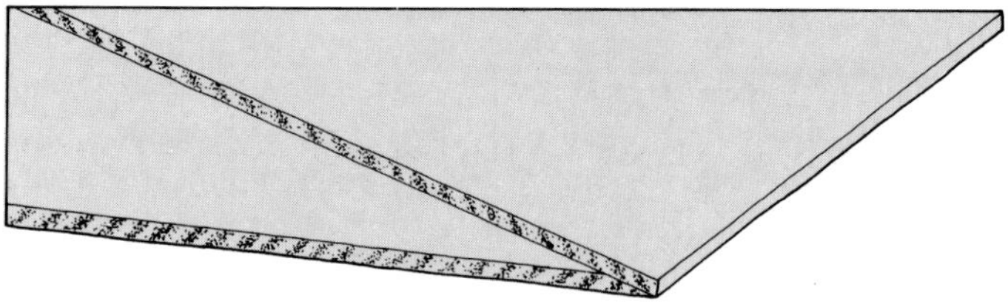

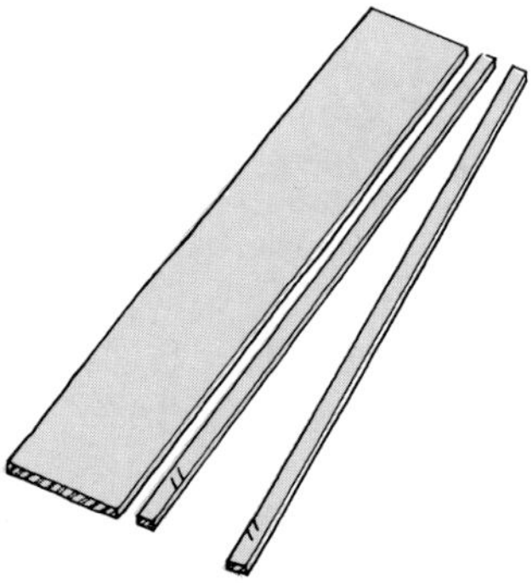
**Cutting sheet-balsa spars** To guarantee an evenly-matched pair of spars, cut them out side-by-side on the sheet. Mark the root end before cutting.

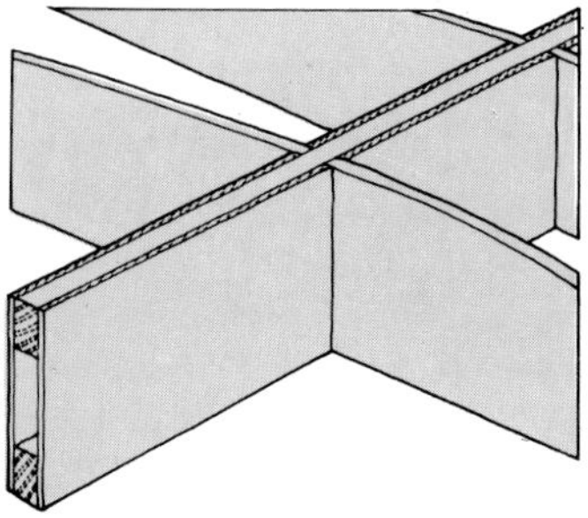
**Making a box spar** Use box spars in a large model to save weight. Run one spar through the top edges of the ribs and another through the bottom edges. Glue pieces of sheet balsa to the spars in between the ribs, with the grain vertical.

## Wing tips

The most functional and robust wing tip is a carved balsa block. If you wish to reduce the weight of the tip, drill a series of shallow holes in the inside face before you cut out the shape. Rounded tips are usually made of scarf-jointed balsa pieces. Use laminated balsa or hardwood strips to form a very thin wing tip.

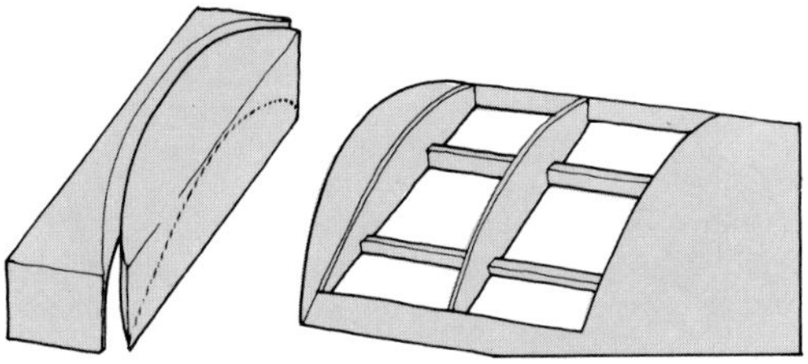

**Making a balsa-block wing tip** Mark the airfoil section and plan view on the block. With a fret saw, cut out the plan view, keeping to the waste side. Then, using the waste to cradle the shape, cut out the airfoil section. If the block moves in the waste, pin them together. Trim the remaining corners with a knife, glue in position and sand to shape.

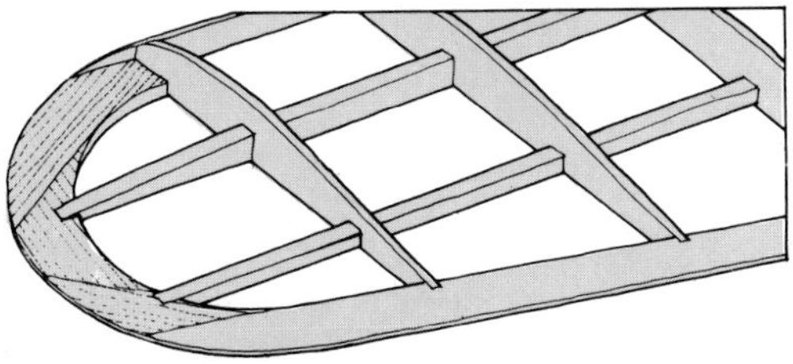

**Making a scarf-jointed wing tip** Use lightweight quarter-grain balsa for the pieces, making sure that the grain runs lengthwise in each piece. Make notches in the tip for the spars. The main spar may need to be trimmed to an angle and any top spars cracked at the last rib and bent to meet the tip. Remove the wing from the plan and sand the tip to merge with the leading and trailing edges.

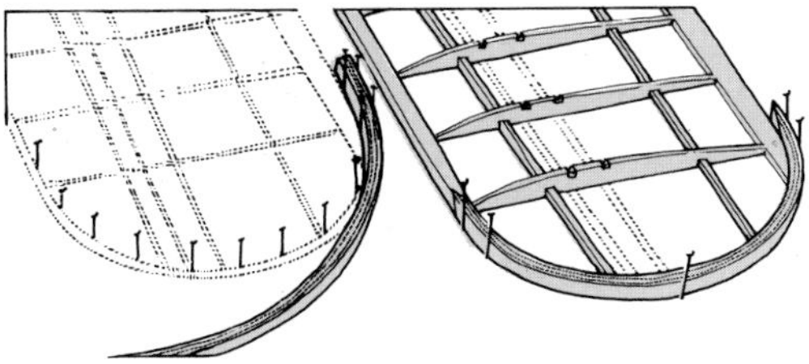

**Making a laminated wing tip** Push pins into the board along the inside curve of the plan, keeping the pins vertical. Glue thin, overlong, strips of balsa or hardwood veneer together. Place the glued strip against a pin at one end, letting the strip overshoot; push a pin firmly into the board so that it holds the strip in position. Work the strip around the curve and leave to set. Remove the pins and join the tip to the leading and trailing edges. Trim and sand it to shape.

## Assembling a built-up wing

Begin by pinning the leading edge, trailing edge and main spar or bottom spars in position on the plan. Use three or four ribs evenly spaced along the wing to judge the exact position of the edges and spars before pinning, taking account of any slight discrepancy in rib size. The components of a flat-bottomed wing can be pinned directly to the board. Under-cambered or symmetrical wings are not as easy to set out because only part of the shape comes into contact with the board. In these cases, therefore, use wood scraps to keep the raised parts at the correct angle and height.

Apply balsa cement or white glue to the contact areas of each rib and the pinned-down components. Place each rib in position, making sure it is vertical with the aid of a small try square. Set the root ribs at the correct dihedral angle, using an angle template. Wipe away excess glue from the joints. A small web of glue left in the corners helps to reinforce the joint, but it must be on both sides of the joint or the wood will distort. Keep the glue off the top and bottom surfaces as much as possible because it can soak into soft wood such as balsa and harden it locally. This makes sanding more difficult as the softer areas will wear down faster, leaving an uneven surface. Finally, add any top spars. Do not remove the wing panel from the board until the glue is set.

Sometimes it is more convenient to assemble most of the wing on the plan and add the leading edge after the wing has been removed from the board. In this case, use light rubber bands to hold the leading edge in place while the glue sets. Likewise, the bottom spar of an under-cambered wing can be added later to avoid having to use wood scraps for support.

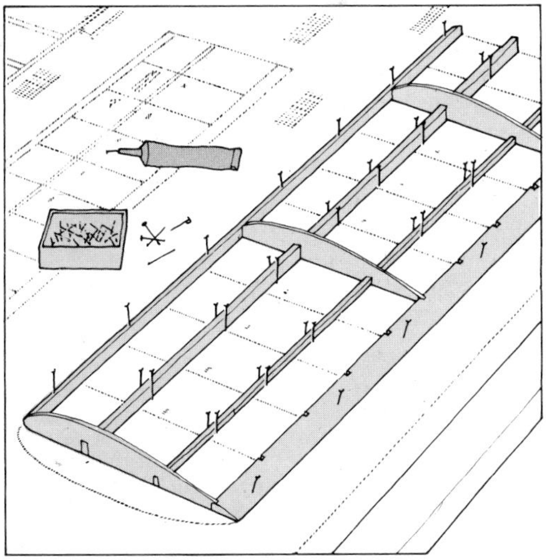

**Setting out the parts** Push the pins right through the leading and trailing edges. Hold spars in place by trapping them between two pins. Do not pin through the spars because it can weaken them.

**Joining horizontal built-up wings**
Horizontal wings are often made as separate sections which plug together. This makes them easy to transport and less liable to damage.

A common method is to join the wings with a pair of dowels. The dowels plug into paper tubes glued through the first two or three ribs. Make the tubes from gummed paper strips. Begin by waxing a dowel to prevent the paper from sticking to it. Wet a strip and wrap it around the dowel, gummed side out. Start at a slight angle so that the strip forms a spiral around the dowel. Work back the other way with another strip, but with the gummed side in so that it sticks to the first strip. Repeat to build up a stiff tube. When dry, remove the dowel.

Cut or drill holes in the wing ribs to take the tubes; glue the tubes in place with the wings held together. Place a strip of polyethylene sheet between the wings to prevent them from sticking. When set, cut through the tubes with a razor saw to separate the two wings. Glue the dowels into one pair of holes.

Aluminum tube with matching heavy-gauge wire in place of the dowels can also be used. First, bind the tube to balsa bearers with thick wire, and then glue.

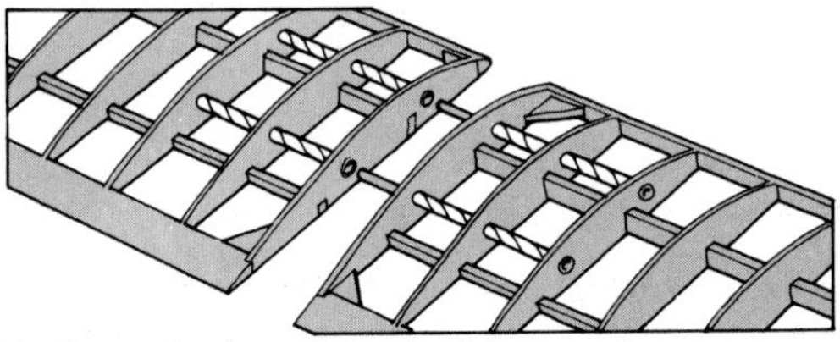

Horizontal wings joined with dowels

**Joining dihedral built-up wings**
First bevel the ends of the panels as described for solid-balsa wings on page 278 and attach the root ribs, then glue the root ribs together as shown below. Reinforce the joint with plywood braces glued to the sides of the main spars. The braces should be cut with the grain of the outside veneers running lengthwise.

Dihedral wings do not have to be permanently joined. You can, if you wish, make them plug together like horizontal wings, using the aluminum tube and wire method described above. Just bend the wire to the dihedral angle.

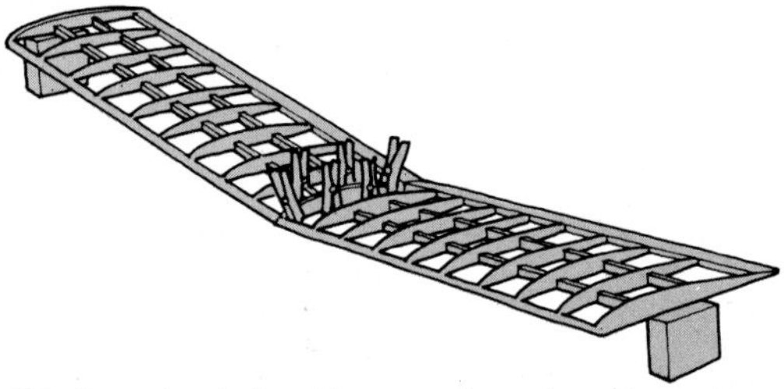

**Gluing the joint** Support the wing tips with blocks. Check the angles and the fit of the braces, then glue the joint. Use clothespins to hold the pieces together.

**Adding sheet-balsa covering**
To increase the rigidity of the wing on larger models, cover the front, between the leading edge and the main spar, with $\frac{1}{32}$- or $\frac{1}{16}$-inch (1- or 1.5-mm) sheet balsa. Pin and glue it to the ribs, spars and leading edge with the grain running along the span. It is also usual to cover the bay between the root rib and the adjacent rib, especially if the wings are to be fixed to the fuselage with rubber bands. Glue sheet-balsa strips to the uncovered rib edges to compensate for the thickness of the sheet.

For some power models, where strength is needed at the expense of weight, the wings are completely covered. These models need fewer ribs and spars because of the stiffness of the sheet. The top and bottom sheet meet in a point so a separate trailing edge is often omitted.

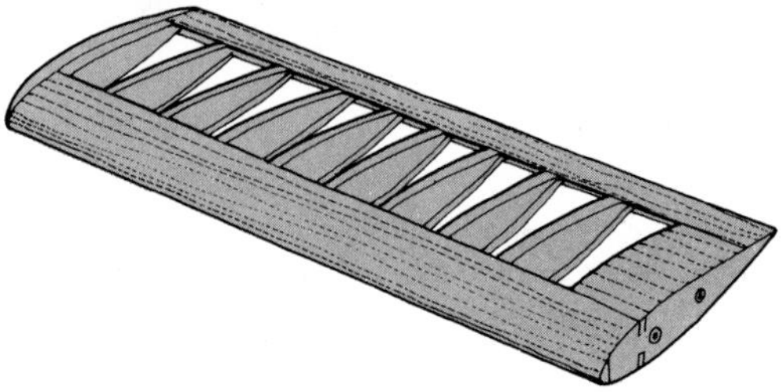

Sheet-balsa covered wing

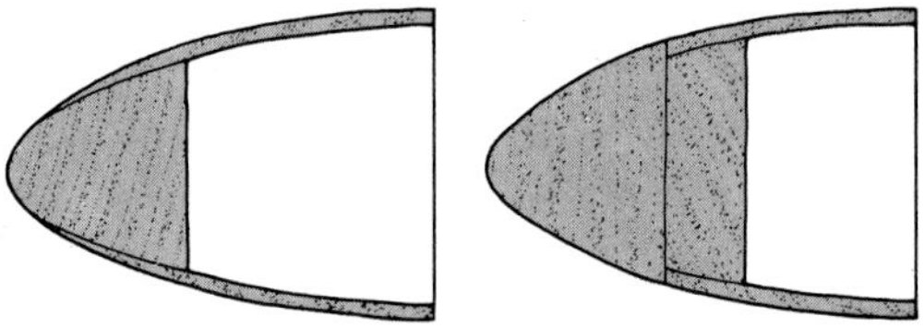

**Forming the leading edge** If the sheet laps the leading edge strip, sand it to follow the contour. For a thick edge, glue the sheet to a false leading edge, then attach the shaped leading edge strip to the front face.

## Foam wings

Polystyrene foam, a rigid but lightweight plastic, is a popular material for airplanes. Some models, mainly those with $CO_2$ motors and small-scale powered aircraft, have all the major components made from expanded polystyrene; many larger kit models include foam wings.

Cut from blocks of foam with a hot-wire tool, foam wings are covered with a thin veneer to make them stiffer and to create a hard, smooth surface. They are usually supplied in two panels which simply need gluing together, although some have separate leading and trailing edges which have to be attached. Not only are they easy and quick to assemble, but a smooth, straight surface is almost guaranteed. Radio-control models often come with the landing gear blocks and the radio control linkages – usually the flexible-cable type – already installed. To locate the parts beneath the veneer, feel the surface. Trim away the veneer to expose the opening.

### Assembling kit foam wings

This method is for a typical wing for a radio-control model with ailerons and with the linkages already installed.

Begin by gluing the two wings together at the root, making sure that they are properly aligned at the front and back and that they are at the correct dihedral angle. Use white or epoxy glue – never use balsa cement, cyanoacrylate glue or fiberglass resin; they attack the plastic. Hold the parts together with self-adhesive tape until the glue sets. Reinforce the joint with fiberglass cloth and resin, but leave the cut-out for the aileron servo clear.

Next, glue on the leading and trailing edges, using tape or pins to hold them in place until set. Make sure that the joints are close-fitting and completely sealed, or the finish applied later might penetrate the foam and dissolve it.

When foam wings have ailerons, it is necessary to glue a false trailing edge piece in the aileron recess to carry the hinges. The side of the recess must also be lined with a thin strip of balsa. Sand the applied strips to shape after gluing them on.

Glue on the wing tip blocks and carve and sand them to shape, then hinge the ailerons to the wings (see Hinging the control surfaces, pages 285 to 288).

Finally, line the cut-out for the aileron servo with sheet balsa for added strength, and cut the holes for the aileron linkage tubes.

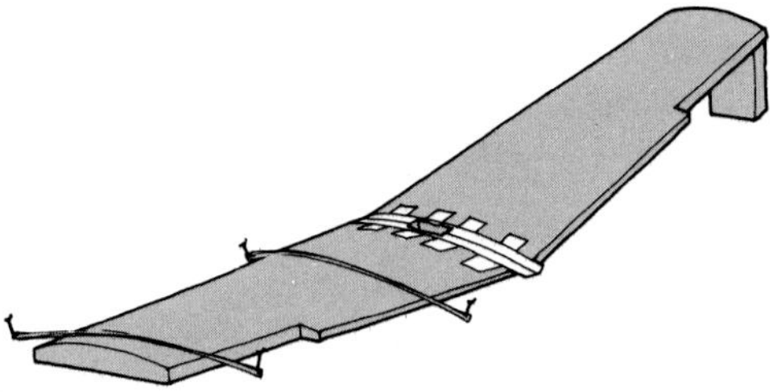

Joining the wings

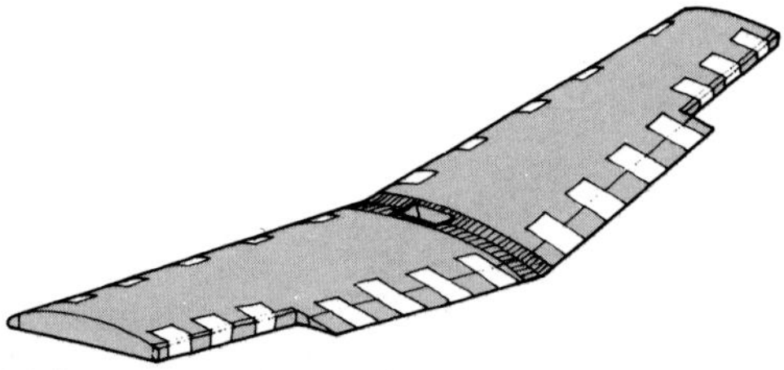

Adding the leading and trailing edges

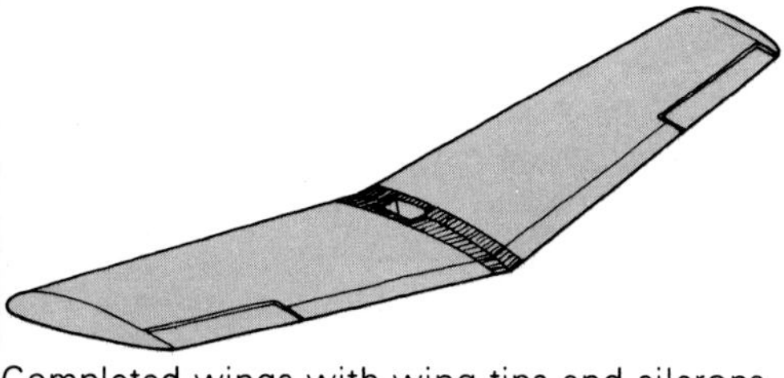

Completed wings with wing tips and ailerons

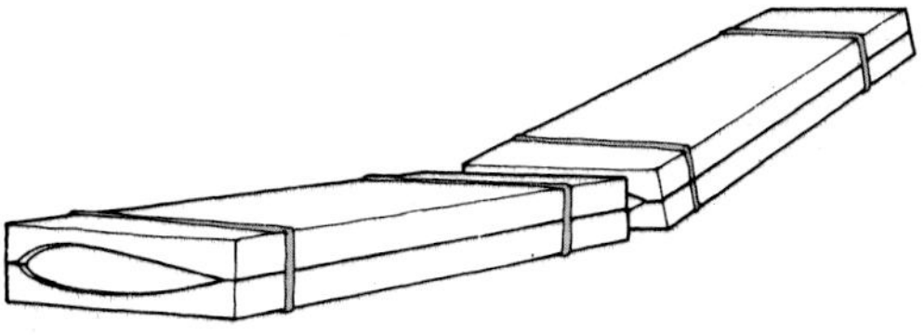

**Kit foam wing** The wing panels are packed in the waste pieces left after cutting the shape from the block. Keep these pieces as they make a good protective packing for storing and transporting the completed wing. Hold the packing in place with rubber bands.

### Making cut-outs

It is sometimes necessary to make cut-outs in foam wings to take support blocks or linkage runs. If the cut-out is for a support block, make a rectangular cut-out; if it is for a linkage run, make a wedge-shaped one. First, mark the cut-out on the veneered surface, then follow the directions below.

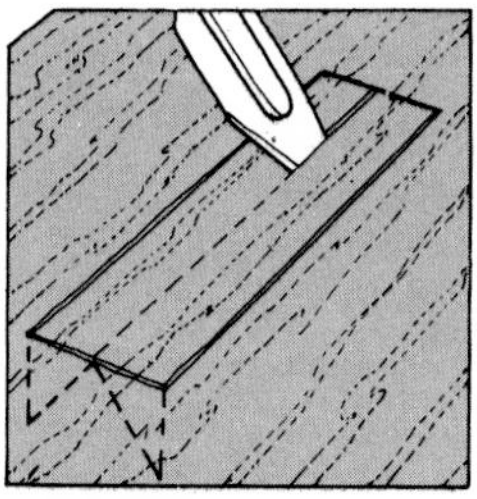

**Making a rectangular cut-out** Holding a knife vertically, cut around the shape, keeping a check on the depth of the cut. Then, cut away the surface and some of the foam by making two angled cuts which slant away from the center.

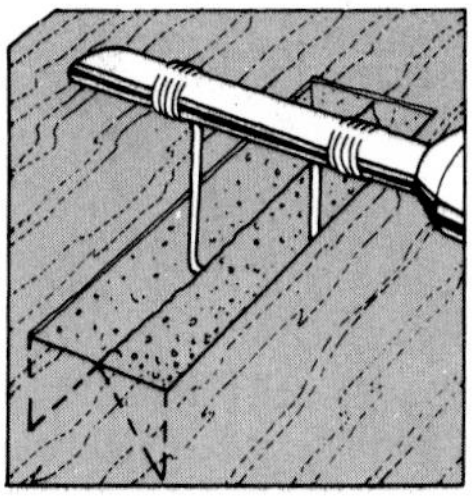

To remove the remaining ridge of foam, make a heated cutting tool: bend stiff copper wire to fit the width of the cut-out and bind it to the tip of a soldering iron with wire. Cut away the foam ridge, leaving a flat-bottomed hole.

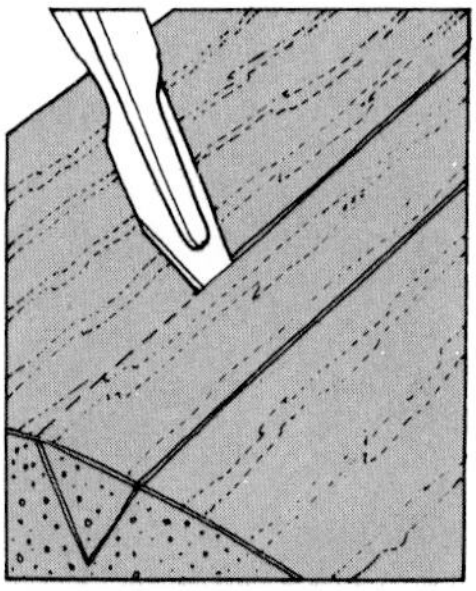

**Making a wedge-shaped cut-out** Angle two cuts to meet at the required depth to form a wedge-shaped strip. Lift out the strip and insert the linkage.

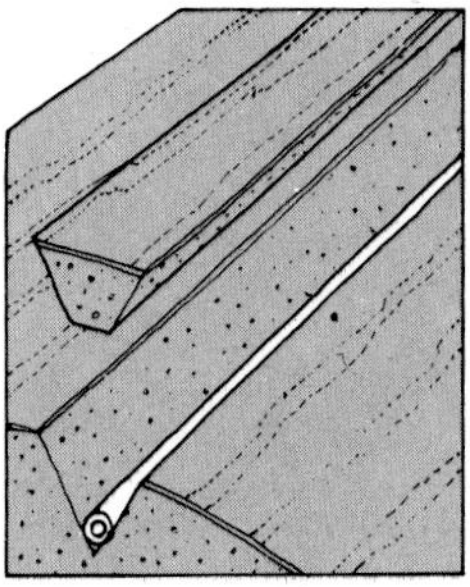

Cut away the tip of the strip to make space for the cable. Check that the strip is flush with the surface when the rod is in position; glue the strip back in place.

### Making wings from foam blanks

The blanks (you will need one for each wing) and the hot-wire tool are available from specialist suppliers. The tool is a nickel-chrome wire stretched across a frame.

Begin by cutting out two plywood airfoil templates, one for each end of the wing, and mark each one with an equal number of vertical lines. The lines are to help you keep the tool at a right angle to the wing chord as you cut. For a wing with a parallel chord, both templates will be the same size and the lines the same distance apart. For a tapered wing, the tip template will be smaller and the lines proportionally closer together. Mark the chord on each template.

Next, mark the foam blank so that you can position the templates in the correct relationship. First, draw a horizontal line across each end of the block, then draw a vertical line on one end to correspond with the one on, or nearest to, the widest part of the root template: transfer the vertical line across the top of the blank and down the other end. Pin the templates in place, matching up the marks. Place weights on the wing to hold it on the work surface. To cut out the wing, just trace around the templates with the hot-wire tool. Work steadily, using the vertical lines to regulate the speed of the cutting action. Working too fast causes the wire to bow, giving a distorted cut; working too slowly allows the wire to melt the foam and creates shallow ridges. (Practice on scrap material until you feel confident of producing a smooth cut.) Cut out the second wing to match.

The trailing edges are likely to be slightly wavy and they are easily damaged so, after cutting out the shapes, trim each one and glue on a balsa edge. The leading edges can also be replaced with balsa, if you wish, but it is not always necessary.

Stiffen long, thin wings by setting a balsa spar into the surface of the foam. Use a short spar to increase the wing's strength at the root end, or a long spar which will prevent the wing from bending.

Finally, veneer the wings as shown below. Sand the dihedral angle at the root end of each wing and assemble the wings as described for kit wings on page 283.

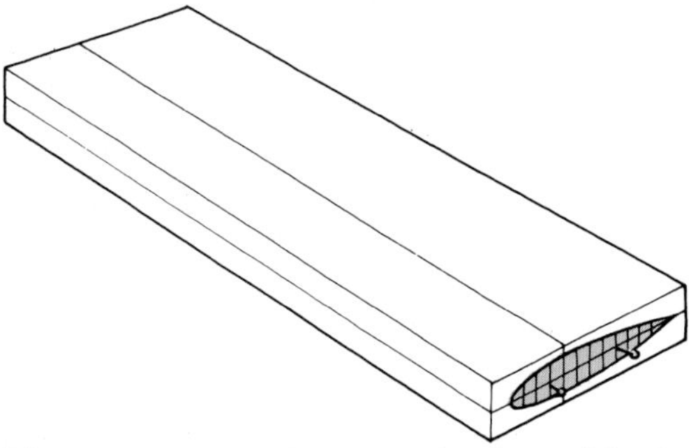

**Pinning the templates to the foam blank** Align the chord line on each template with the horizontal lines on the blank, and the vertical line at the widest part of each template with the vertical lines on the blank.

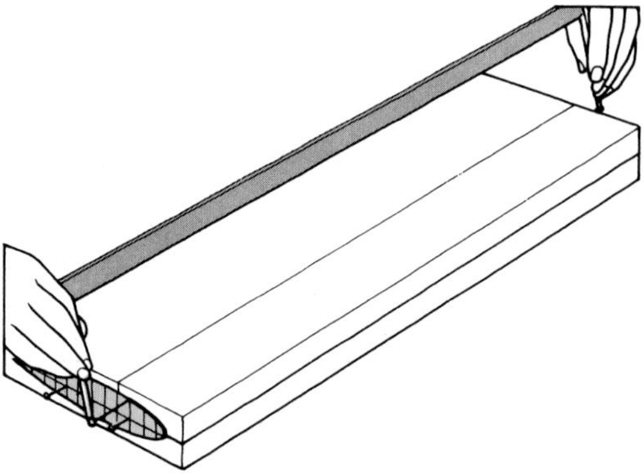

**Cutting out a wing** A small wing can be managed by one person, but a large wing needs two people.

### Veneering a foam wing

Thin, close-grained, hardwood veneer or medium-grade balsa can be used to cover the shape. The grain should run lengthwise on the wing. Veneer comes in wide sheets so that the shape can be covered in one piece. Sheets of balsa need to be butt-jointed, either with tape before applying them to the wing or as they are applied to the wing. In the latter case, wrap the first piece around the leading edge. If it will not form the correct contour, attach a separate solid-balsa leading edge and glue separate sheets top and bottom, as shown for covering a built-up wing on page 282.

Use a latex-based contact adhesive to bond the veneer, not a petroleum-based one. Apply the glue to one side of, the veneer and both sides of the foam shape, and allow the glue to dry for the recommended time. Then, cover the wing as shown right. Bevel the ends of dihedral wings after covering.

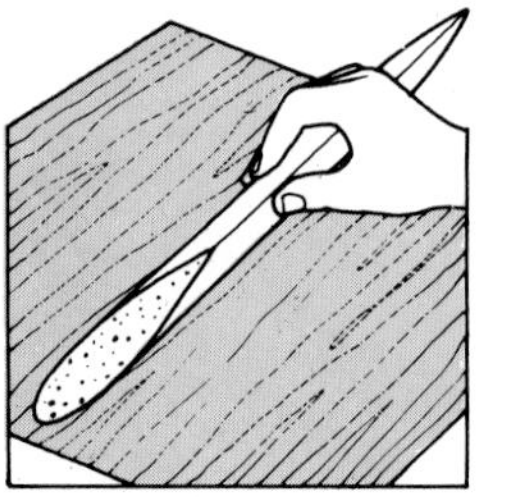

**Covering the wing** Press a flat-bottomed wing straight down, positioning the leading edge in the center of the veneer. For a symmetrical wing, let the leading edge touch first, then roll it onto the veneer.

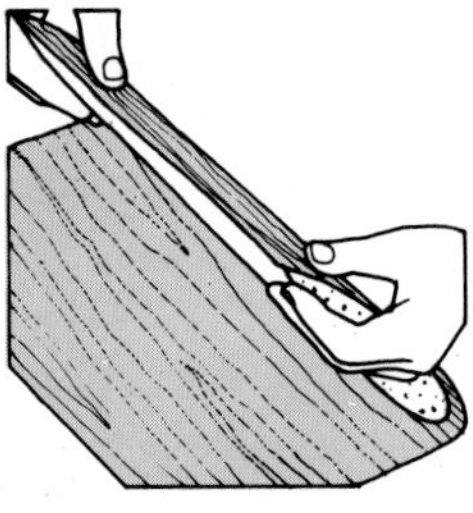

Maintaining a firm downward pressure, roll the half-covered wing onto its leading edge, then onto its other face. Rub both surfaces with a cloth pad to press the veneer in place. Trim the edges flush.

# Attaching wings to the fuselage

Traditionally, the wings and tail plane are attached to the fuselage by rubber bands looped over dowels. The rubber bands allow the wings and tail plane to dislocate or spring off in a crash, thus absorbing some of the shock and, in some cases, preventing the wing from breaking. It is a simple but rather crude-looking technique, and not at all appropriate if you are constructing genuine scale models.

Nylon bolts provide a neat and unobtrusive fixing that is very secure. The bolts screw into plastic brackets or wooden blocks glued inside the fuselage. Usually, two bolts are used through the back of the wing and the leading edge is held in place by a dowel. The alignment of the components is critical so the bolts and blocks or brackets should be installed as one unit.

First, attach the front dowel and make sure the wing is seated correctly. Calculate the position of the bolts in the wing and drill holes for them. Push the bolts through the holes and screw on the blocks or brackets. Apply epoxy adhesive to the blocks and position the wing on the model. Bond the blocks to a fuselage former or another bearing surface. When set, unscrew the bolts and remove the wing. The blocks can be reinforced with adhesive or screws. The fixing should be strong enough to hold the wing firmly in place while, ideally, still allowing the fitting to break away if ever the airplane crashes.

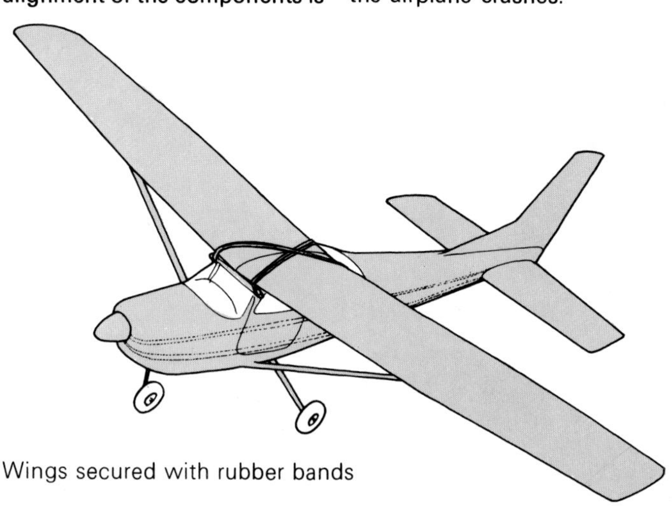

Wings secured with rubber bands

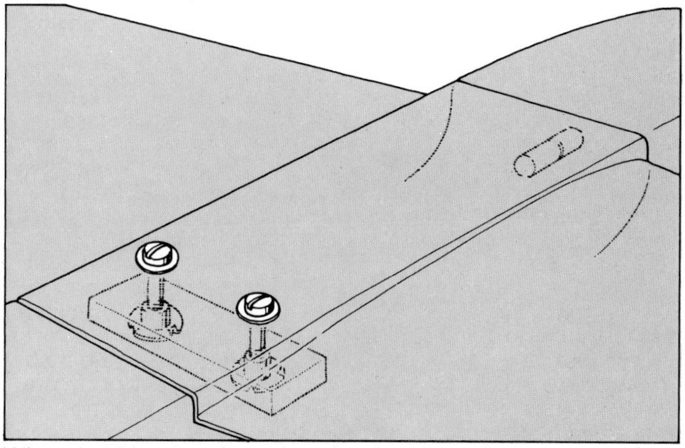

Wings held in place by a dowel rod and two bolts

# Hinging the control surfaces

Hinges fall into two categories: top and center types. A top hinge can be used for ailerons and the elevator, while the more common center hinge can link all surfaces.

You will need to cut away some of the material along the hinge line to allow the control surface to move. A top hinge usually has only the control-surface edge beveled. The center hinge has both meeting edges beveled or rounded which can cause air turbulence. A plastic fairing strip can be used on larger models to avoid this problem. It works best with the pin hinge illustrated on page 287. Glue the concave part of the fairing to the model and the convex part to the control surface.

Hinges must be installed accurately. Each hinge point must be perfectly aligned or the movement of the joint will be restricted. The pivot must operate smoothly but without slack. Cloth tape and thread hinges, in particular, should not span too large a gap or the control surface will misalign or flutter.

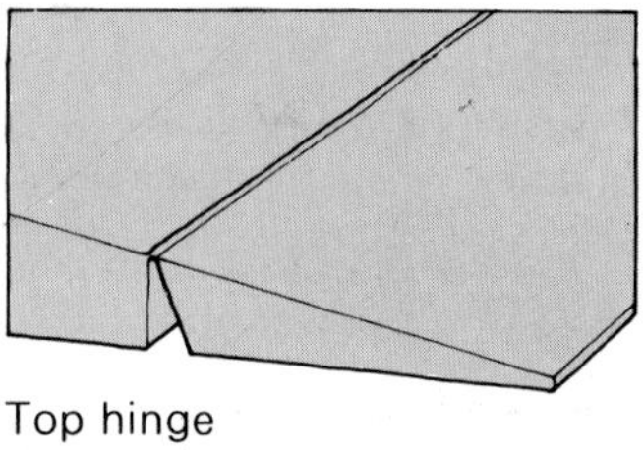

Top hinge

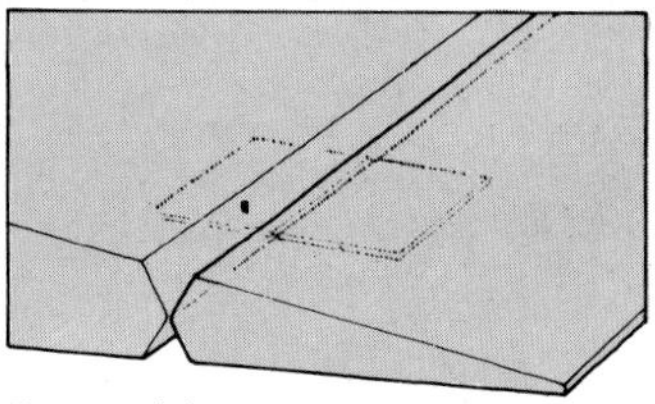

Center hinge

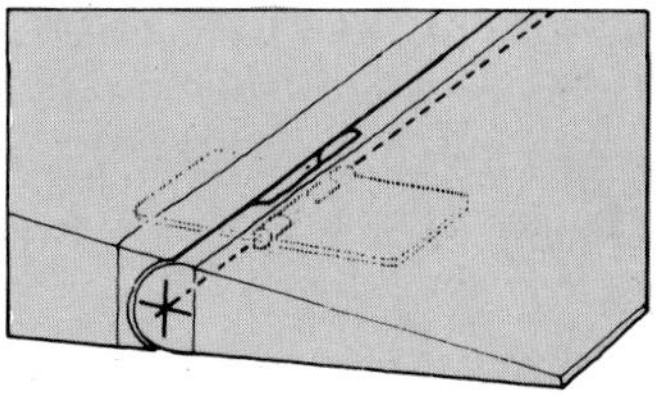

Center hinge with fairing

## Stitched hinge

This is a simple, effective center hinge, made by passing a thread under and over the fixed and moving surfaces in a zig-zag path. Use multi-strand fishing line – it is tougher than sewing thread – and drill the holes before decorating and finishing the model.

Begin by marking a line on the top surface of each part, about $\frac{3}{8}$ inch (10 mm) from the hinge line. Mark the holes about $\frac{1}{4}$ inch (6 mm) apart along the lines, positioning the holes in one row opposite the spaces in the other row. The number of holes depends on the surface being hinged. A typical arrangement for a tail plane is three or four, equally spaced, eight-holed hinges. A typical rudder has one full-length hinge. Drill the holes with a fine twist bit.

After decorating the model, temporarily tape both parts together, leaving a fine gap. Thread a needle and tie a knot in one end of the thread. Starting at one end, push the needle through a hole from underneath. Pass the needle and thread down through the gap and up through the first hole on the opposite side. Continue in this way, keeping the tension even. When you reach the end, pass the thread back through the gap and work back to the beginning. Secure the thread by passing it through the last hole a few times. Cut it off close to the end and seal it with a dab of balsa cement. Seal each hole with a drop of dope.

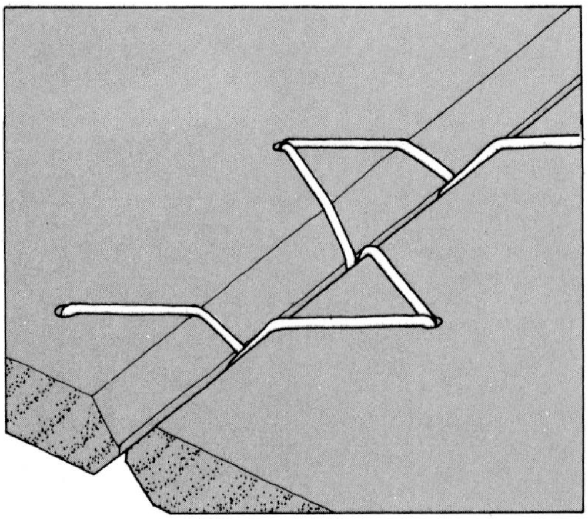

## Tape hinge

This hinge, often used on control-line airplanes, is usually made before the model is finished. Use $\frac{1}{2}$-inch-wide (12-mm) cotton or silk tape cut into $1\frac{1}{2}$-inch (40-mm) strips. The strips can be applied along the entire hinge line or in 3-inch-long (75-mm) groups. Leave a little space between the strips in each group; $\frac{1}{16}$ inch (2 mm) is sufficient.

Bond the ends of the strips to the model with balsa cement but do not put glue on the part of the tape that will flex. Cover and paint the model in the normal way but take care not to impregnate the fabric along the joint as paint stiffens the fibers.

## Making a tape hinge

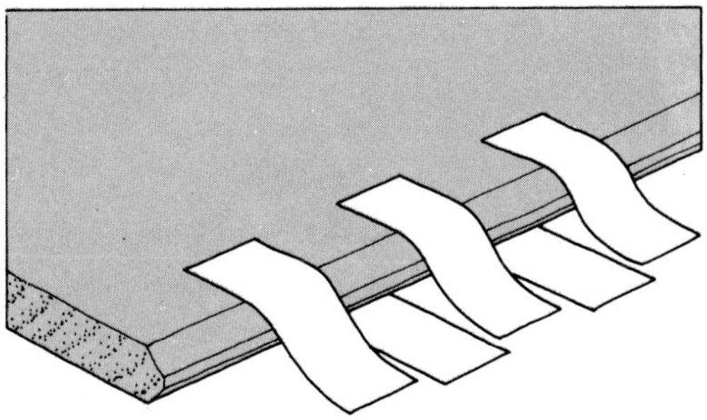

**1** Bond the strips to alternate faces of the fixed panel. Pin the panel or weight it down on a flat board.

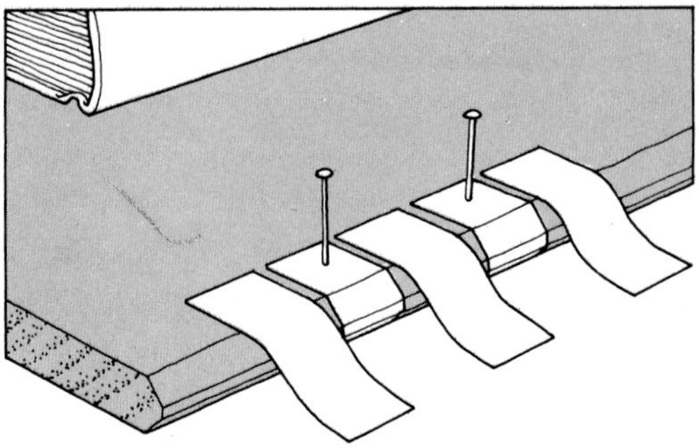

**2** Temporarily pin the bottom tabs to the top surface. Apply glue to the loose tabs.

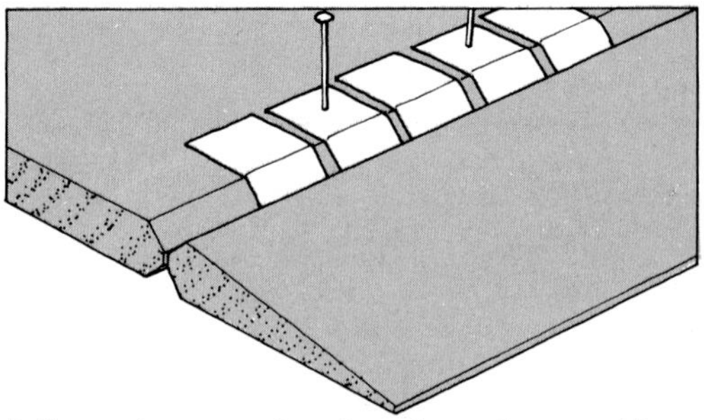

**3** Press the control surface into place, making sure that it fits closely along the hinge line.

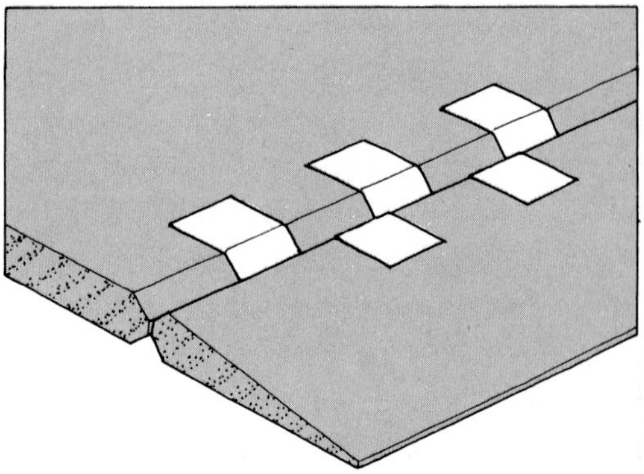

**4** Unpin the remaining tabs and bond them to the top face of the control surface.

## Plastic hinges

A number of plastic hinges are available, the simplest being thin, flat tongues, with or without a crease across the middle. These are glued into slots in the edges of the wing and control surface with contact adhesive.

The slots must be perfectly aligned to work smoothly. It is easier to mark their position if the edges are square so cut the clearance bevels after the slots have been made. Tape the bottoms of the two components together, making absolutely sure that the edges which are to be hinged are flush. Mark the slots then take the components apart.

Use a modeling knife with a normal cutting blade or a special slotting blade to produce an even cut. To guarantee that the slots are at the same level, support the blade on a strip of scrap material, as shown right.

When you have completed the slot bevel the edges and glue the hinges in place with contact adhesive, quick-set epoxy or cyanoacrylate glue. Some glue will wipe off the hinge as it is inserted so, to prevent the two parts being hinged from sticking together, place a piece of polyethylene sheet cut to fit over the hinge, between them. Pull the sheet away after the glue has set.

To reinforce the glue fixing, peg the tabs by sticking toothpicks through them. Drill two holes, slightly smaller than the diameter of the toothpick, on a diagonal through each flap. Apply glue to the hole and push the stick through. Cut off the ends of the stick flush with the surface. An alternative to pegging the tabs is to drill the holes three quarters of the way through the control surface and fill them with quick-set epoxy glue. A third method of reinforcing the fixing is to drill down to the hinge, apply cyanoacrylate glue to the surrounding wood, then plug the holes with balsa.

Another type of plastic hinge is the pin hinge. The two halves are joined by a conventional knuckle joint with a metal pin passing through the center. The pin is usually removable. The flaps are made with holes to reinforce the glued joint, or ridged to grip in the slot. Although freer moving than the tongue type, this hinge is thicker and needs a wider slot. Drill a hole at each end of the cut line with a fine drill bit then make two parallel cuts with a modeling knife to join the two holes, using a wood shim as described right. If necessary, use a nail file with the end ground to an angle to help pick out the waste or open up the slot. Glue the flaps into the slots as described above for the simple tongue hinge. Hinges with removable pins should be separated and attached individually. This prevents the parts from sticking together and allows the fixed and moving parts of the model to be finished before they are assembled.

Another design of this type is the dowel hinge. Some have a molded-in horn. Dowel hinges are the easiest to install: just insert each end in a drilled hole.

**Cutting a slot**
As you cut, rest the knife on a scrap strip just under half the thickness of the edge.

Use a hooked blade to remove waste material.

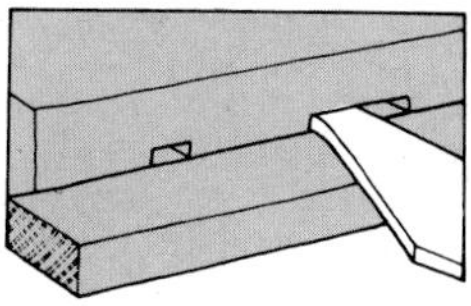

**Pegging a tongue hinge**

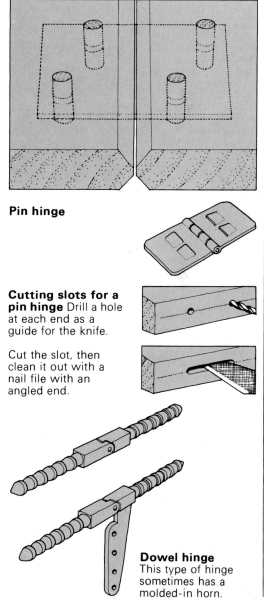

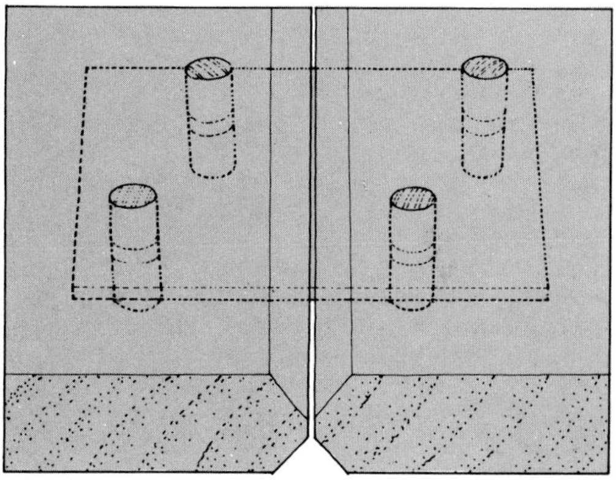

**Pin hinge**

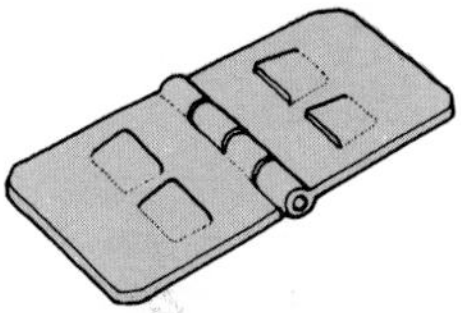

**Cutting slots for a pin hinge** Drill a hole at each end as a guide for the knife.

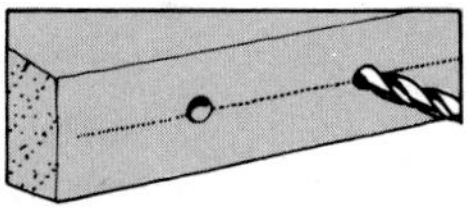

Cut the slot, then clean it out with a nail file with an angled end.

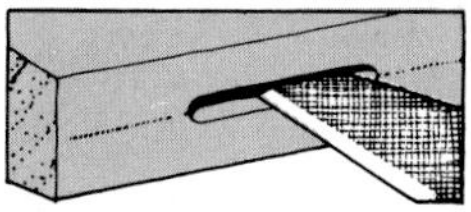

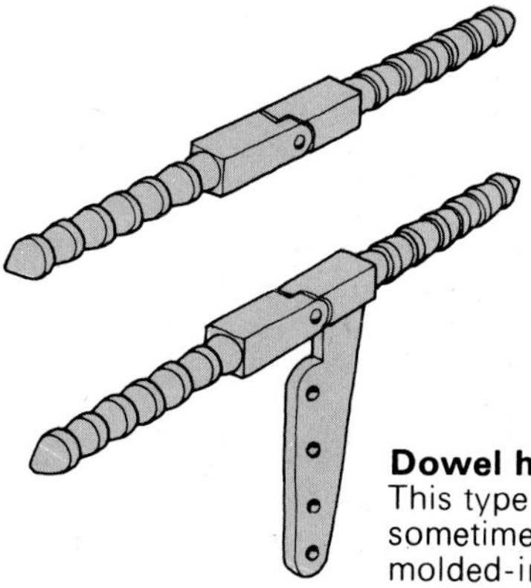

**Dowel hinge**
This type of hinge sometimes has a molded-in horn.

## Plastic-film hinge

Self-adhesive heat-shrink covering material, such as Coverite, Monokote or Solarfilm, makes an aerodynamically "clean" top hinge which is easy to apply and to operate. After forming the hinges, cover the model with the same material for an attractive finish, as described on pages 290 to 291.

## Making a film hinge

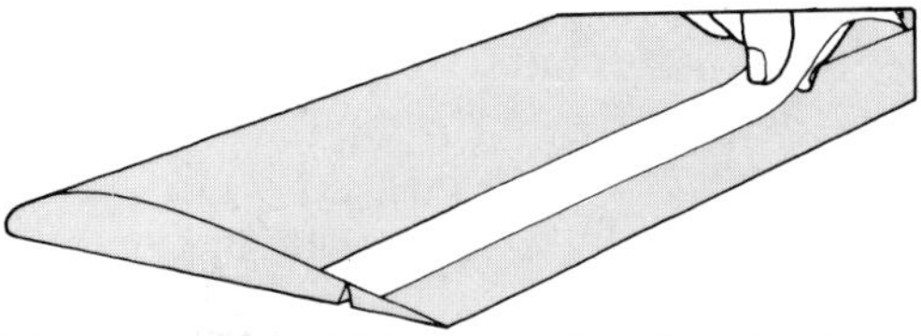

**1** Temporarily hold the control surface in place with a 1-inch-wide (25-mm) strip of masking tape applied to the top surface.

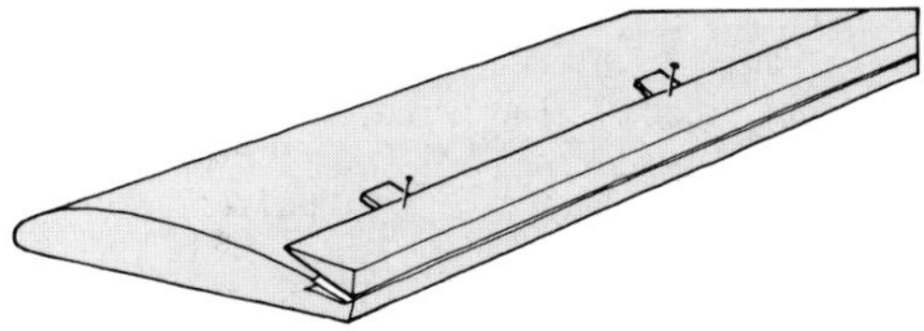

**2** Pin the control surface back, making sure that the edges are flush. Cut a strip of film the same length as the control surface and $\frac{1}{2}$ inch (12 mm) wider than the two edges together.

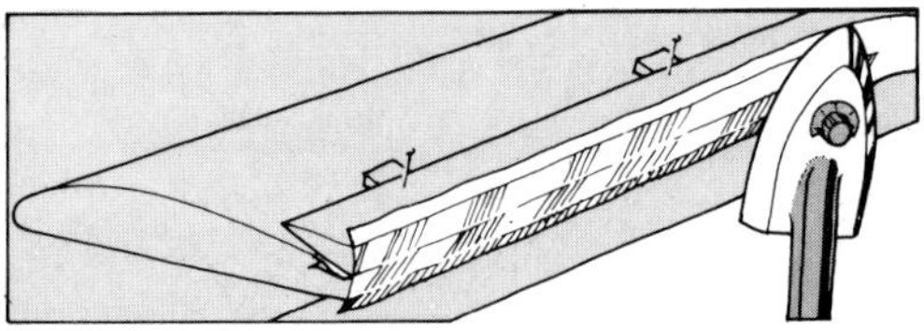

**3** With the panel overlapping the table edge, tack the strip to the edges with an iron, letting $\frac{1}{4}$ inch (6 mm) of film overlap top and bottom.

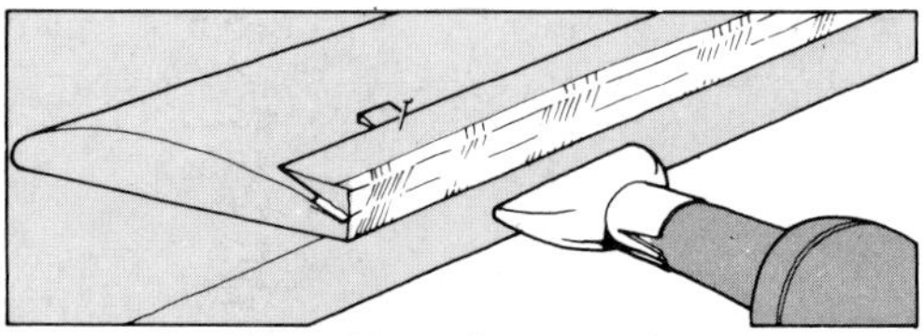

**4** Heat the film with an iron or a heat gun to shrink it in place. Remove the pins; fold the control surface back.

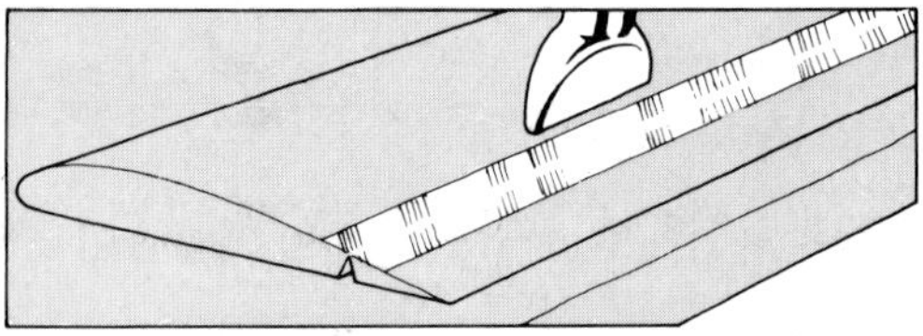

**5** Remove the masking tape and replace it with a 1-inch-wide (25-mm) strip of film tacking it in place and shrinking it as described.

# Coverings

The framework of a model with built-up construction must be covered to provide a continuous, contoured surface. Tissue paper, fabric and plastic film are common materials. Shrinking dope, or heat in the case of plastic film, is applied to pull the material taut and produce an airtight skin. Water is also used as a shrinking agent for tissue paper and fabric. A few coats of dope are needed after the material dries to seal the surface and shrink it further.

Always choose the weight or thickness of the covering to match the model as the wrong covering may distort the frame when it shrinks. This is especially true of coverings that are sealed with dope. As a guide, use lightweight tissue for a lightly built model, mediumweight for a model of average construction, heavyweight for models built with large-sectioned material. Use the same rule of thumb for fabric covering, but take the lightest fabric as equal to the heaviest tissue.

Models with sheet-balsa or veneer surfaces can be painted without a covering material, but you will find that the application of tissue paper or fabric before painting improves the strength of the model and provides a better surface on which to apply the paint.

Tissue paper is available in a range of weights. The lightest is used for small rubber- or engine-powered models. It is usually applied dry in a single layer, then shrunk with water and finished with dope. Two layers are sometimes applied for strength, with the grain of the sheets running in opposite directions. A stronger, laminated tissue is used on larger models. This can be applied wet or dry. Although tissue is lightweight, relatively easy to apply and adds stiffness to the frame, it is prone to puncture and does not easily mold around compound curves.

Compound curves are easier to cover with fabric than with tissue. Silk and nylon coverings are particularly suited to scale models of fabric-covered aircraft. They are applied wet and, when dry, they are sealed with dope. Silk is available in both light- and heavy-duty grades for use on medium and large models. It shrinks well and is stronger than tissue, but it is also heavier because of the extra coats of dope needed to seal the surface. Nylon is tough and is used on larger models where strength is required at the expense of weight. It must be applied as smoothly as possible with a minimum of wrinkles because it does not shrink as much as a silk covering.

Plastic film is the quickest means of finishing a model as no dope or paint is needed. It comes in opaque, translucent and metallic colors, with a glossy finish. The woven type is fabric-textured. Film has a heat-sensitive adhesive backing and will shrink when heat is applied. Fuelproof, lightweight, yet resilient, plastic film can be successfully worked around compound curves; however, it does not stiffen the structure as much as doped coverings or cover large sheeted areas easily.

## Preparing the surface

Inspect the structure for bad joints, rough grain, dents or squeezed-out glue. Smooth any rough areas and high spots with a sanding block. Apply water to remove dents – the water swells the grain. Fill any remaining gaps or depressions with a fine filler such as Spackle. Sand the surface after the filler has dried and wipe it with a damp rag. The airplane can now be covered with plastic film, but for tissue- or fabric-covered models, apply two coats of thinned dope to all surfaces that will be covered with the material. Rub the surface down after each coat of dope to make sure that any raised grain is removed.

## Applying tissue and fabric

The procedure for applying these materials is the same. Cut out a piece to cover a section of the model, leaving a 1-inch (25-mm) overlap all around. If you are applying the material wet, spray it all over with water, then carefully blot off any excess water.

Stick the piece on the framework, bonding it around the wing's outer edges only (the piece underneath a concave-bottomed wing must also be bonded to each rib). Dope can be used as an adhesive. Apply it on top of the material with a narrow brush so that it penetrates. Use thinned dope for light tissue; full strength for heavier coverings. Work it in with your finger to make it penetrate, if necessary.

A thin paste is available for bonding dry tissue. It is easier for the beginner to use because it does not dry as quickly. Apply the paste to the frame, spreading it in a thin layer with your finger, then add the material. Trim the piece, then repeat the process until the model is covered.

If you have used dry tissue, spray or brush the model with water to shrink the covering; leave it to dry.

Finally, coat the model with shrinking dope to seal and strengthen the surface.

### Covering the wings

Do not attempt to cover the wings in one piece. Cover the top and bottom separately, and start a new piece each time there is a change in angle or contour. Cut each piece so that the grain of the material runs along the span of the wing. If you cannot see the grain on a piece of tissue, tear it: the grain follows the direction in which the tissue tears easiest. On fabric, it follows the selvage.

Apply one bottom piece first. Lay it in position and bond it to the center of the root end. Lightly pull the material along its length and glue it at the center of the wing tip. Glue the material to the center of the leading and trailing edges, again lightly pulling it into place. Finally, working from the center of the panel toward the ends and pulling diagonally on the covering, bond it all around the edges of the frame. When set, trim off the excess material along the leading edge and the top of the trailing edge. Glue down any loose edges.

Attach the top piece following the same procedure. If the wing tip is rounded, cover the wing up to the last rib and treat the tip separately. Trim around the top piece, leaving about $\frac{1}{8}$ to $\frac{1}{4}$ inch (3 to 6 mm) to overlap the bottom piece; glue it down. If you are covering dihedral wings with tissue, cover the top and bottom of the other panel in the same way, letting the material overlap slightly at the joint. If you are using fabric, cover the other panel only after the first has dried.

A fabric or tissue cover applied wet will have begun to dry out and the wing needs to be pinned down, as shown below, to prevent it from warping as the material shrinks. A tissue cover applied dry should now be dampened and pinned down in the same way (treat each wing separately). Although a rigid wing built with thick-sectioned wood is not generally likely to warp, pinning it down in this way guarantees a straight surface.

**Adding the material** Stick it to the middle of the four sides before bonding it all around the edge.

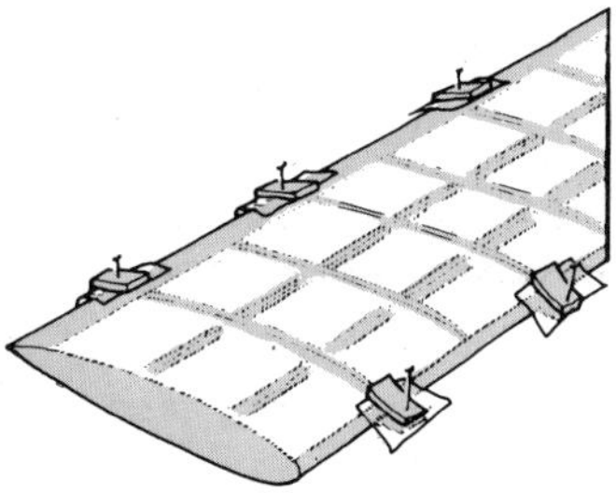

**Pinning the wing** Support the wing above the board with balsa pieces of even thickness. Place the pieces under the edges with polyethylene in between. Hold the panel down with short lengths of balsa pinned to the board and positioned over the supporting pieces. Never pin through the frame.

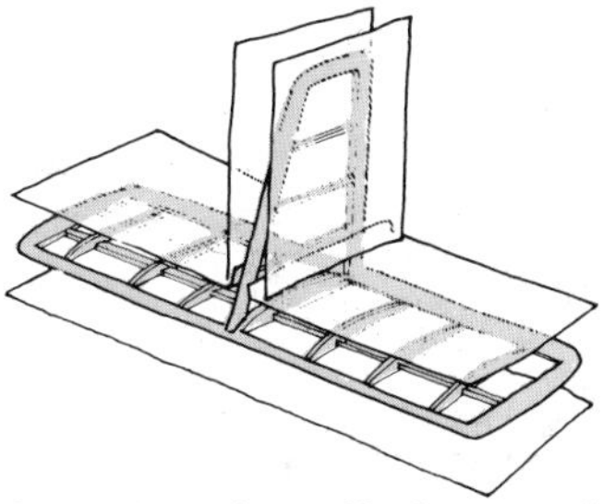

**Covering the tail plane and fin** Apply the material as for a wing, using separate pieces for each side. If they are constructed as one unit, cover the bottom of the tail plane first, followed by the top surfaces, and finally both sides of the fin.

**Covering the fuselage**
Use the same technique to cover the fuselage with tissue or fabric. A simple box-shaped fuselage can be covered with four pieces: cover the sides first, followed by the bottom and top. A round fuselage takes more skill because of the taper toward the nose and tail. Cover it with long strips.

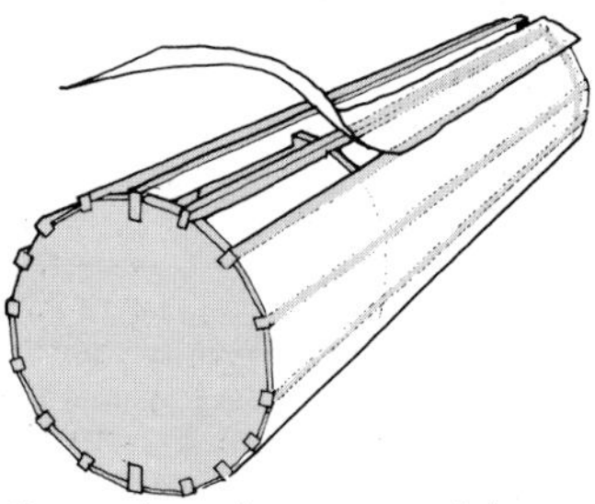

**Covering the nose with tissue** Cover the fuselage with oversized strips, bonding and trimming each in turn. Always overlap the edge of the previous strip.

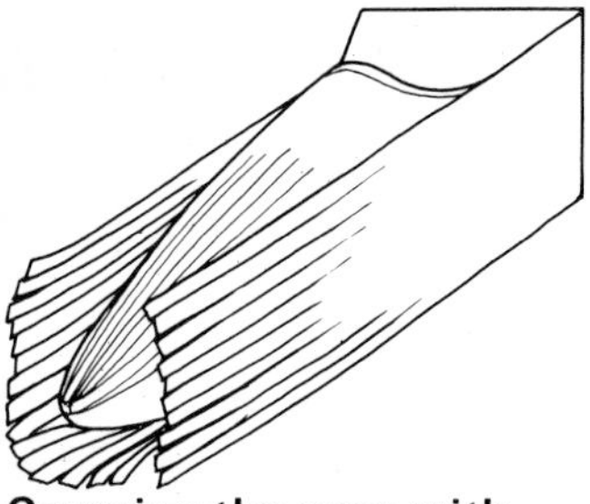

**Covering the nose with tissue** Cover the fuselage but leave the end free. Cut the material back to where it has adhered. Starting from the middle of each panel, bond the strips to the nose. Sand smooth after doping.

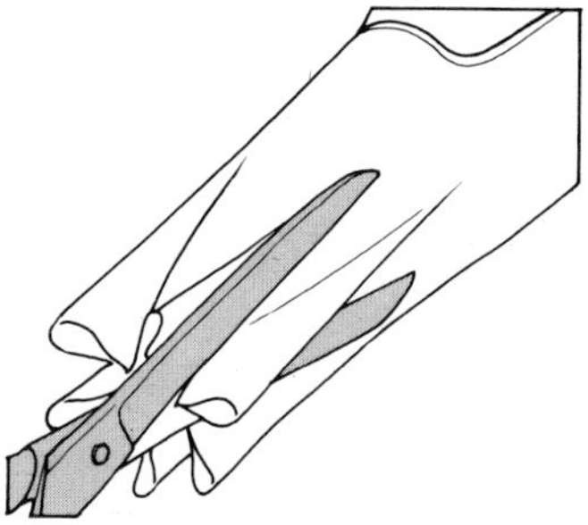

To cover a nose with fabric, pinch the material into tucks and cut away the excess. Butt up the edges.

**Doping**
Apply two or three coats of clear shrinking dope with a soft, flat brush to the tissue or fabric-covered frame. Use half-strength dope for tissue coverings and full-strength dope for fabric. Spread it evenly and do not apply too much at one time or blobs will form on the inside. Treat each wing in turn, pinning it down as described on page 289. Allow each coat to dry thoroughly and lightly rub it down with fine wet-and-dry paper before adding the next. Take care not to wear through the material over the ribs and edges of the framework. The model may need more coats to build up a fine finish but remember that each coat adds more weight.

Colored dope, used purely for its finish and not for shrinking, is available. Enamel, epoxy or polyurethane paint can be used over clear dope to add color, if you wish, but apply it lightly. The paint should be just thick enough to give the required color. Doped and enamel paint finishes on a glow-plug-powered model should always be given a final coat of clear fuelproofer.

## Applying plastic film

You will need a heat-sealing iron and a heat gun (a domestic iron and hair drier can be used but these tools make the job easier), a cutting tool, plus a soft cloth or a tissue pad for pressing the film into place.

Plastic film attracts dust which may show through the finished covering so, after preparing the surfaces to which the film will adhere, wipe over the entire framework with a damp rag. A vacuum cleaner can be used to extract dust from the inside corners.

Apply the film in separate pieces following the same sequence as for tissue and fabric covers. Overlap the pieces to allow for shrinkage. Some curves can be covered in one piece because of the film's flexibility. If a piece is badly applied, just reheat it and it will peel off. The strip should then be discarded (do not attempt to reuse it).

**Covering a wing**
Lay the film, right side down, on a flat surface. Place the framework on the sheet and cut the film to shape, approximately 1 inch (25 mm) wider all around. Peel off the film's backing paper and lay the film, adhesive side down, on top of the balsa framework.

With the heat-sealing iron, tack the film to the edge at the root and tip. If the tip is shaped, tack it to the last rib; work on the tip end after the main panel is in place.

Next, carefully tack the film to the center of the leading and trailing edges. Working toward the root and tip and lightly pulling the covering diagonally to ease out the wrinkles, tack down the edges. Pull the film around the edge of the wing tip and tack it in place. (The heat softens the film and allows it to stretch around the curve without wrinkling.) Run the iron all around the edge of the frame, bonding the film in place. Trim the overhanging film to within $\frac{1}{4}$ inch (6 mm) of the frame, then press down all the loose edges with the heat-sealing iron.

The easiest method of shrinking the film is to blow hot air over it with a heat gun. Work on two bays at a time, starting at the wing root, and hold the gun about 3 to 4 inches (75 to 100 mm) away from the surface (holding it too close can burn holes in the film). If you use a domestic iron, pass it about $\frac{1}{8}$ inch (3 mm) above the surface of the film; however, the iron will mask the surface, making it difficult to judge the condition of the film.

When all the wrinkles are removed and the film is still hot, press the film onto the framework with a soft cloth or tissue-paper pad. To remove air bubbles on sheet-balsa parts, prick them with a pin, then reheat the film and press it down. Repeat to cover the rest of the wing.

Follow the same procedure for covering the fuselage, tail plane and fin, first tacking, then shrinking and pressing the material in place.

### Sealing the joints

Wipe off any adhesive that squeezes out of the joints with a cloth dampened with cellulose thinner, but do not allow the thinner to seep under the edges of the film.

Although plastic film is fuelproof, the adhesive backing is not, so you must seal the joints on a model powered by an internal combustion engine with fuelproofer.

Use colored trim – either a brand-name tape or strips cut from film – to hide the seams or for decoration. Iron the trim onto the base color and smooth it with a cloth. To prevent bubbles forming under the trim, make a series of pin holes through the covering where the trim will be positioned to allow the trapped air to escape.

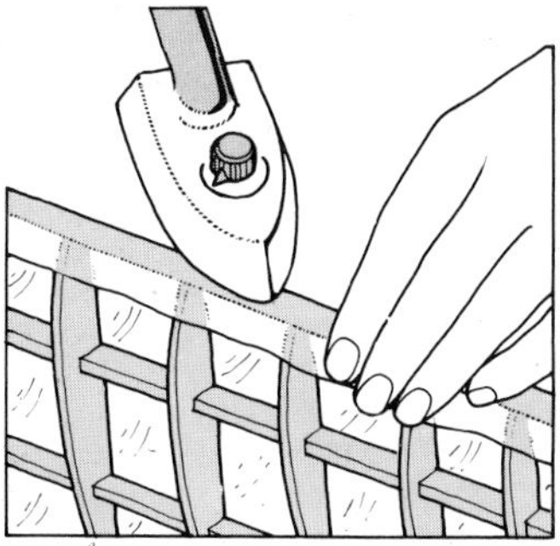

Tacking the film in position

Shrinking the film

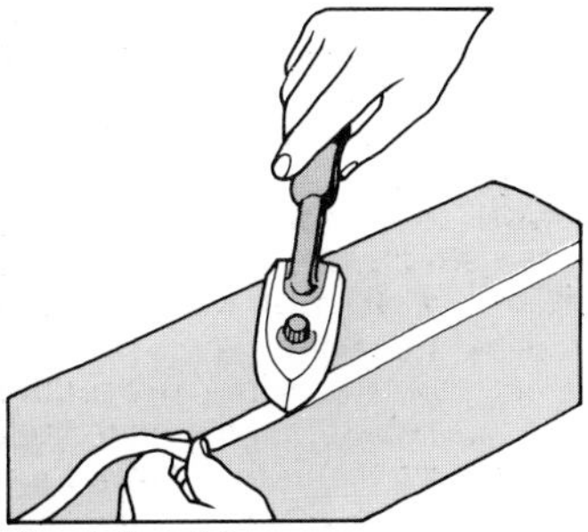

Applying trim

# Landing gear

There are two types of landing gear, excluding floatplanes: tricycle and two-wheel. The latter touches at a third point with a tail skid or wheel. Their primary function is to support the model during takeoff and landing. Although many gears are very often homemade from wire or, in the case of some larger models, sheet alloy, several manufactured legs are available. The kit or plan will give the size and position of the parts but it helps to understand some of the factors governing their design, especially if you wish to experiment.

The position of the gear in relation to the model's center of gravity, for example, affects the balance. If the two-wheel type is very close to, but forward of, the center of gravity, it can cause the airplane to tip over on landing. On the other hand, if it is well forward, it adds weight to the nose, saving ballast. Generally, the most suitable position is about a quarter of the way between the nose and the center of gravity. A tricycle landing gear is more stable. Its back two legs should be just behind the airplane's center of gravity.

The length of a tricycle nose leg affects the angle of incidence. If it is too short the wings will tilt down, making it difficult for the model to take off. Usually, the leg is set so that the wings are at zero incidence or angled slightly up. The leg must also be long enough to allow the propeller to clear the ground, especially as the model comes in to land.

Make sure that your materials are of the proper size. Wire that is too thin will not take the strain, while overthick legs can add unwanted weight. The simplest landing gear and the one least likely to twist is that bent from a single piece of wire. The spring in the wire provides the suspension – the longer the leg and the thinner the wire, the more spring the landing gear will have. For a heavy model, tie the legs together with a thin wire to stop them spreading; bend the wire up slightly in the middle to give the legs some spring.

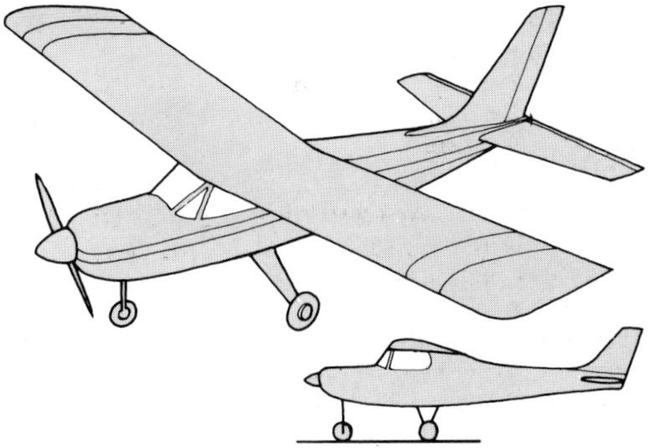

Tricycle landing gear

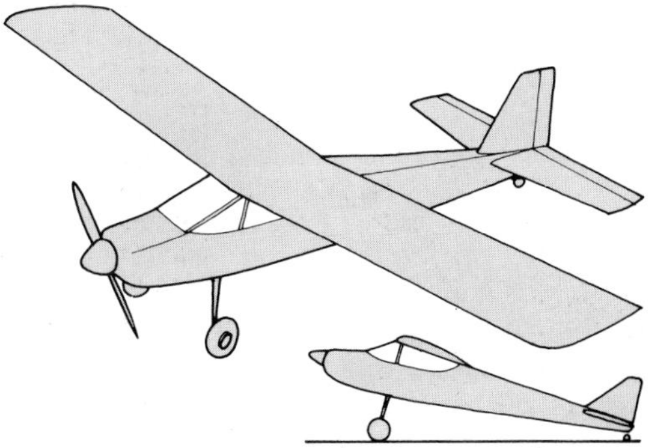

Two-wheel landing gear

## Attaching two-wheel landing gear

Most wire landing gear are attached to one of the formers. However, those for rubber-powered motors, where the interior space must be kept clear, are often bent back and secured to the bottom of the fuselage.

There are several methods of attaching the wire. One is to bind it to the former of a light model with fine wire or thread. Drill small holes, not more than $\frac{1}{4}$ inch (6 mm) apart, to take the wire or thread. Reinforce the fixing with an epoxy adhesive, if you wish. For triangulated scale-type landing gear it may be necessary to bind the wire to a hard-balsa strip with thread, then glue the strip to the former. Nylon clamps are useful for larger models. Screw or bolt them on, locking the bolts with a touch of adhesive or lock nuts. Yet another method is to sandwich the wire and a wooden shim in between the plywood former and another piece of plywood. Bolt all the layers together and strengthen the assembly by adding touches of epoxy adhesive.

A sheet-alloy landing gear can be bolted to a built-in plywood plate in the bottom of the fuselage, but modelers often design them to fall off in a rough landing by attaching them with rubber bands. The bands loop over a pair of dowels glued to the formers or a plywood plate. A wire landing gear can also be fastened with rubber bands.

Low-wing airplanes often have the legs attached to the wings. For light aircraft, just make a double bend at the top of each leg and bind it to the main spar. For heavier aircraft, use a commercial landing gear set. This has preshaped wire parts and hardwood mounting blocks. The legs twist in the blocks to absorb landing shocks.

The tail wheel is linked to the fuselage by a wire which is attached in much the same way as the main landing gear. Bend the end into a loop to spread the load.

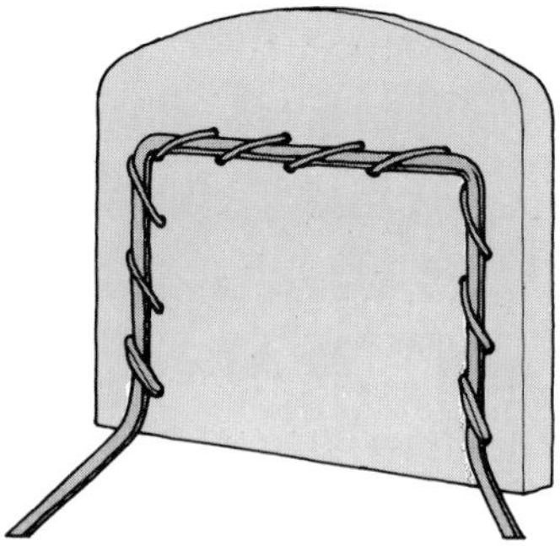

Wire landing gear attached to former with fine wire

Wire landing gear bound to balsa strips

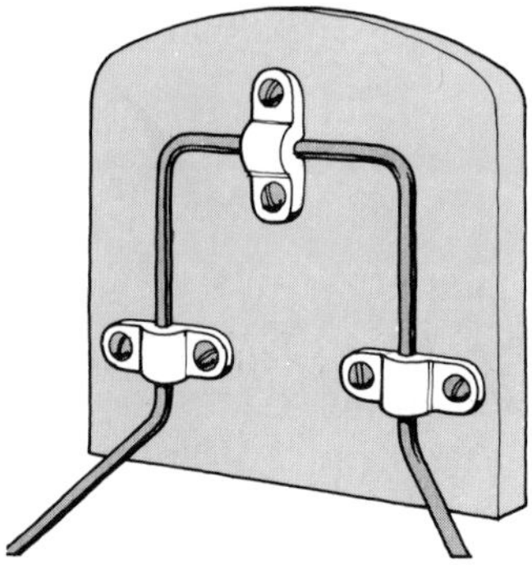

Wire landing gear held by nylon clamps

Wire landing gear and plywood sandwiched in between a former and more plywood

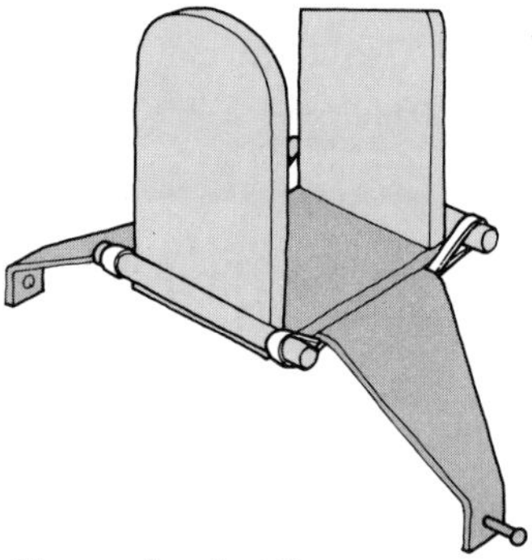

Sheet-alloy landing gear held by rubber bands

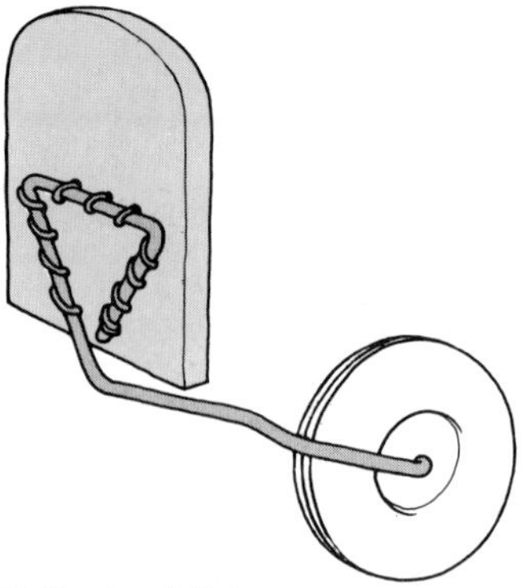

Tail wheel fixing

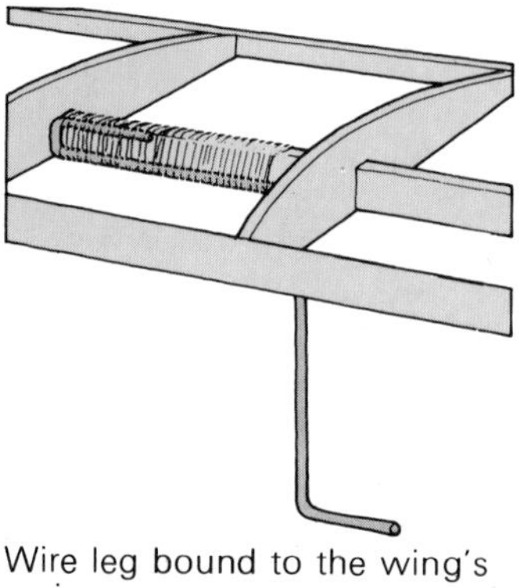

Wire leg bound to the wing's main spar

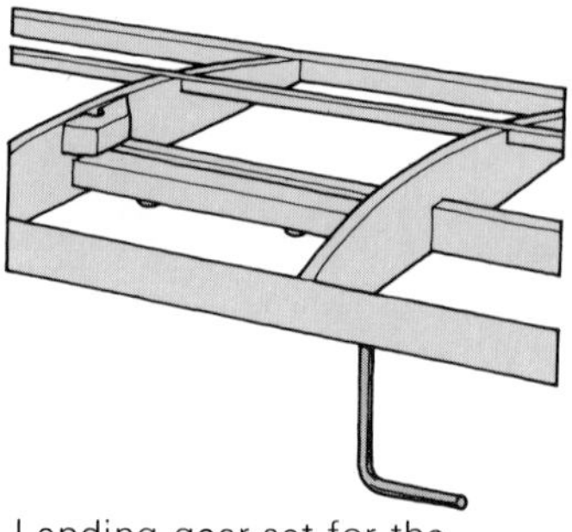

Landing gear set for the wings of heavier models

## Attaching tricycle landing gear

Attach the main legs to the model as described for two-wheel landing gear. Fix the nose wheel to the firewall. Molded mounts are available for clamping it in place. For heavier aircraft, use a nose leg with a shock-absorbing spring near the top.

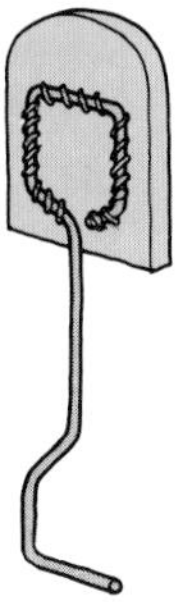

Simple wire nose leg bound to firewall

Sprung nose leg for heavier airplanes

## Steerable nose wheel

This is connected to the rudder linkage of a radio-control airplane so that when the rudder is operated the wheel automatically responds. Usually, it is set to move half the distance of the rudder. To adjust its movement, reposition the linkage in the servo output or the bellcrank.

The leg pivots in a nylon mounting block. The tiller linkage can be double- or single-armed and above or below the mounting block. Most units bolt to the firewall but a belly-mounted type is also available.

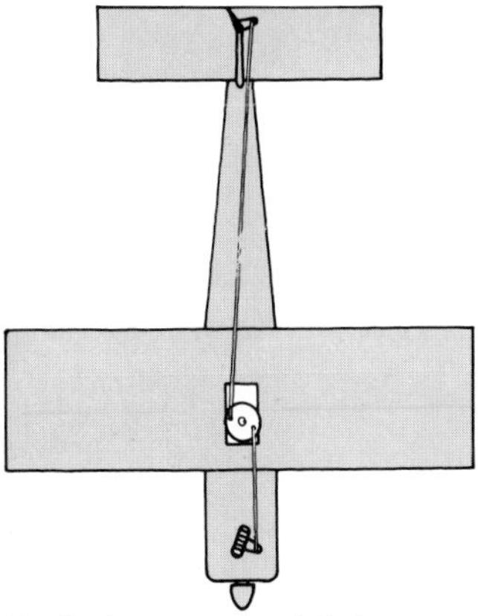

Typical nose-wheel linkage

## Steerable tail wheel

For two-wheeled aircraft, steering is via the tail wheel. The wheel leg can be linked to the moving rudder but, for heavier models, a direct link to the rudder pushrod is better as it avoids strain and loss of motion through the rudder hinges.

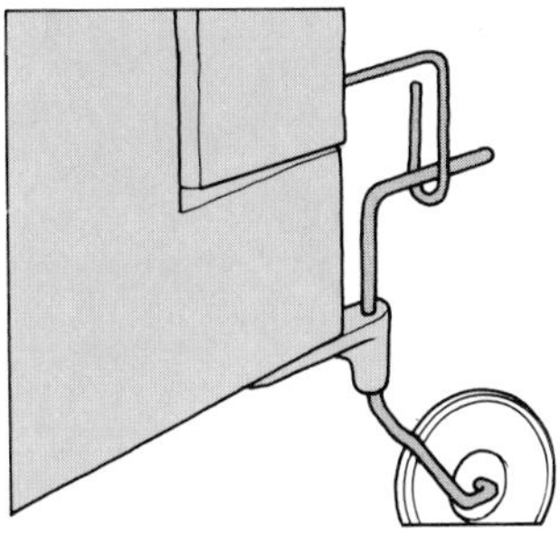

**Linking the wheel to the rudder** Pass the leg through a nylon tail-wheel mount or a brass tube on the fuselage, then bend it to make a lever arm. Bind or epoxy-glue a wire loop to the rudder and slip it over the arm.

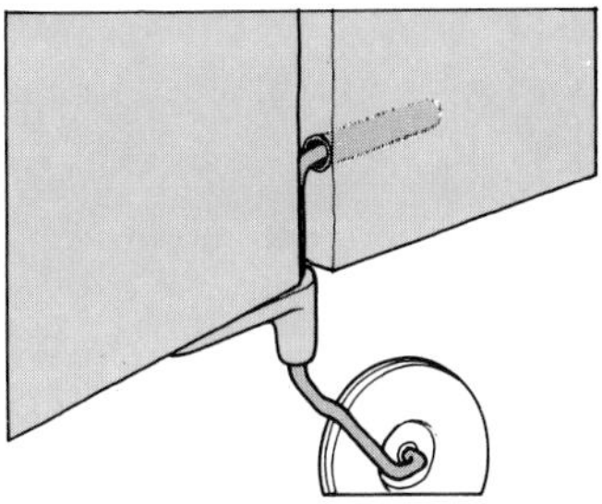

As an alternative, install a brass tube in the rudder to take the lever arm.

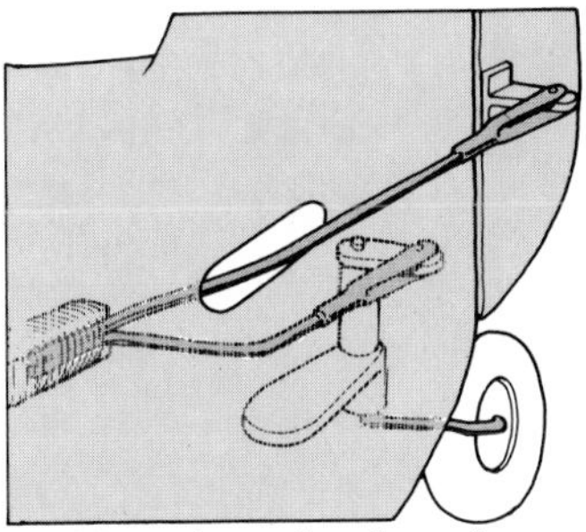

**Linking the wheel to the rudder pushrod** Attach a horn to the wire leg then connect it to the rudder pushrod. For scale models with sufficient space, the horn linkage can be arranged inside the fuselage.

## Retractable landing gear

These are manufactured as complete units for the more sophisticated remote-control model. Most are operated by a mechanical linkage although some run on compressed gas. Special "retract" servos with low gearing to take the heavy load are available and the landing gear mechanism itself usually has a spring to ease the strain on the servo. Each landing gear unit is designed as a neat nylon plate or housing which can be bolted or screwed into the wing or nose.

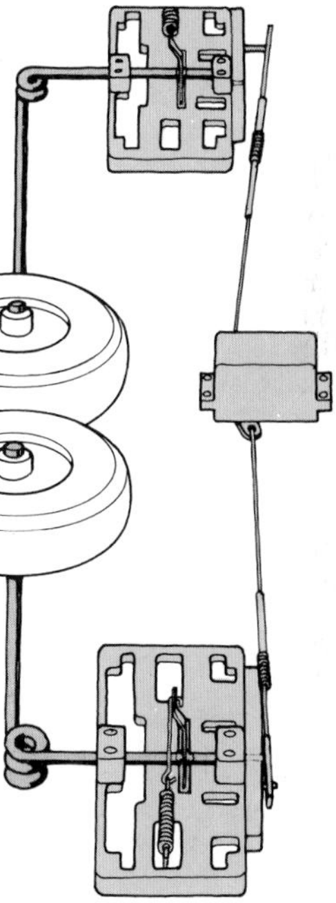

Typical retractable landing gear installation

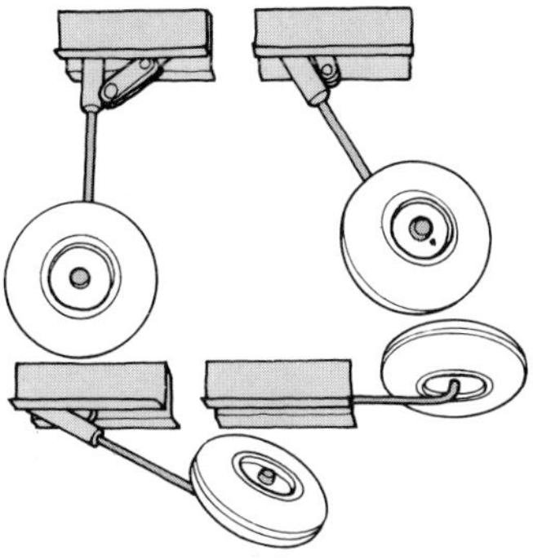

For greater realism some landing gears revolve through 90° as they close.

## Attaching wheels

Wheels should spin freely on their axles but without too much sideways movement which causes them to rub against the legs. Most are made with center holes to suit standard wire gauges. If you need to enlarge the hole, bore it with a twist drill. Use a vertical drill stand to keep the bit straight. For a soft, balloon tire, support the hub rather than the tire (a bottle cap makes a simple jig). For a smaller hole, insert a brass tube of the appropriate bore, fixing it in place with epoxy adhesive. If the hub is nylon, solder the tube to the landing-gear wire axle to make a better bearing.

For vertical legs with a sharp right-angle bend at the axle, use packing washers or a collar to prevent the wheel from touching the leg, and a collet to keep the wheel on the axle. Tighten the screw on the collet or attach it permanently with epoxy or cyanoacrylate glue between collet and axle. As a precaution, smear a little grease on the axle where the wheel runs to prevent it from sticking.

For aircraft with splayed legs it is necessary to fix the packing washer in place as it tends to slide around the bend. The most satisfactory method is to solder it. Use a jig to keep the washer at a right angle to the axle as you solder (see below). A collet can be used to keep the wheel on the leg but another soldered-on washer is better as it weighs less. This time the hub holds the washer square. Place a thin piece of cardboard between wheel and washer as a spacer and to prevent the hot soldering iron from damaging a plastic hub. Tear away the cardboard after the joint has set.

**Soldering a washer on a splayed leg** Make a jig: drill a hole, the diameter of the axle wire, through a block of wood. Slide the washer onto the axle, followed by the block. Sit the block on the work surface and solder on the washer.

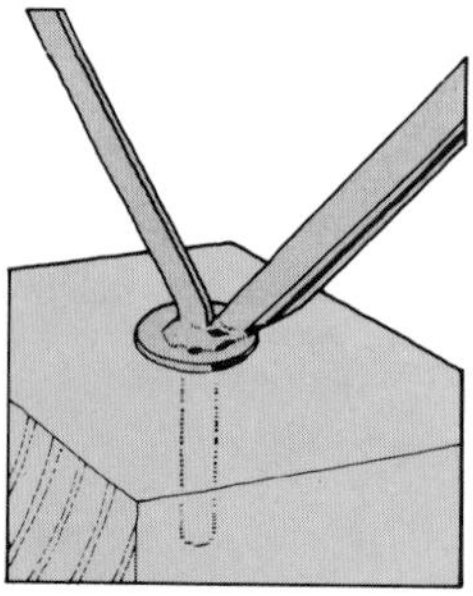

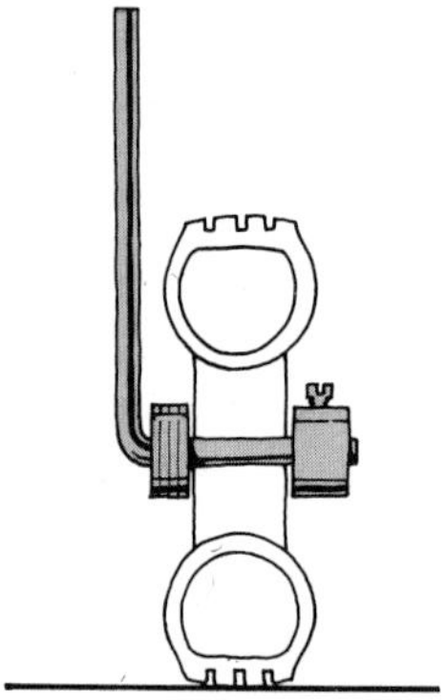

Wheel on a vertical leg

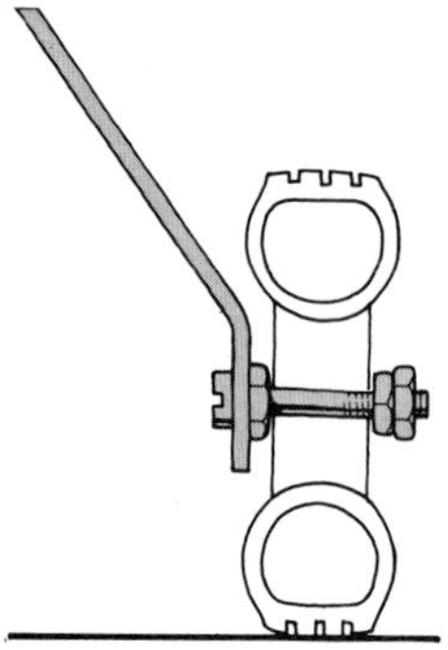

Wheel on sheet-alloy legs

# Trimming and flying your airplane

Careful building does not guarantee that your airplane can be launched into perfect flight. Most models, whether free-flight or radio-control, need to be trimmed. Begin by checking the balance and the alignment.

The balance point, usually marked with a symbol and the letters C.G. (center of gravity) is shown on the plan. Support the model with the tip of a finger under each wing and in line with this point. A slight nose-down attitude is acceptable, but the tail should never drop below level. Move some weight fore or aft until the balance point corresponds with that on the plan. For radio-control models, adjust the balance by repositioning the battery or servos before fixing them in place. The fuel tank should be empty when you test the balance of a powered aircraft.

Make sure the wings and tail plane are correctly positioned by looking at the airplane from in front and above. The model should be perfectly symmetrical; misalignment will upset any adjustments made later. If your model is designed to be taken apart for transport, as most are, make sure that the rubber bands or bolts holding the wings are tight, and check the alignment each time you assemble your model and after a rough landing.

**Checking the balance** Symbols for center of gravity or balance point

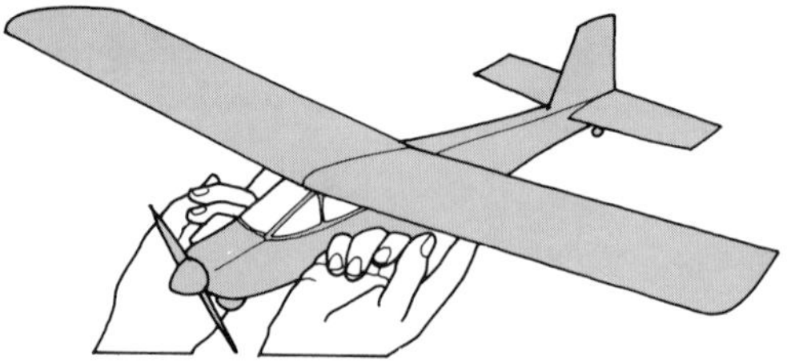

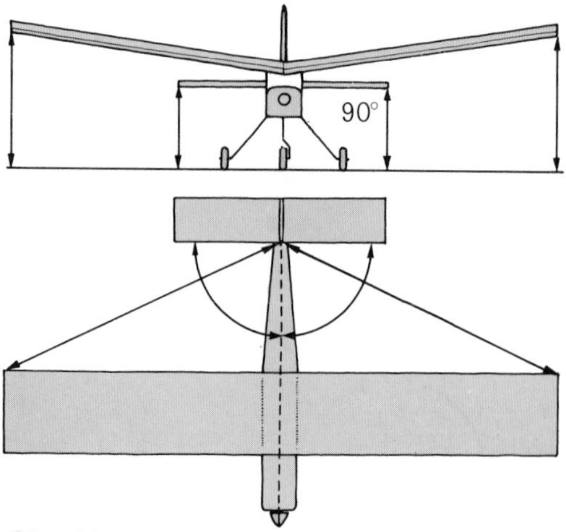


**Checking alignment** The measurements and angles should be symmetrical.

## Trimming a free-flight airplane

A free-flight airplane is not ready to fly until you have test-glided it. Always test-glide over level, grassy ground on a calm day. Launch your model from shoulder height, with the nose slightly down and into the wind. It should make a long, straight, gentle glide. If the model glides down at a steep angle or brings its nose up and stalls, you may have launched it at the wrong speed. Try increasing or decreasing the speed to check and if the airplane still does not follow the correct angle, trim it as described below. (Some powered airplanes may need to fly under power for a short run in order to gain height for testing.)

### Test-gliding a free-flight airplane

Correct glide angle

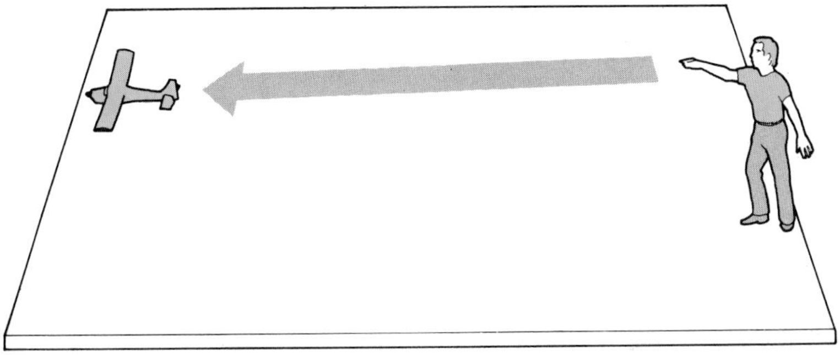

If the model glides down at a steep angle, shim up the trailing edge of the tail plane or the leading edge of the wing with a thin strip of balsa.

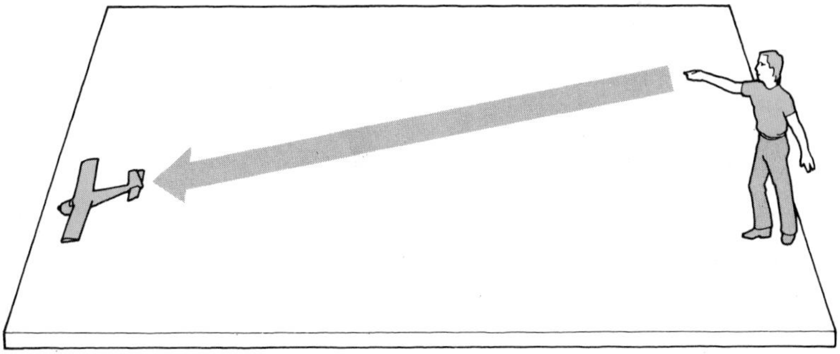

If the model brings its nose up and stalls, shim up the leading edge of the tail plane or the trailing edge of the wing. If a powered model stalls with the engine running, also try more downthrust on the engine.

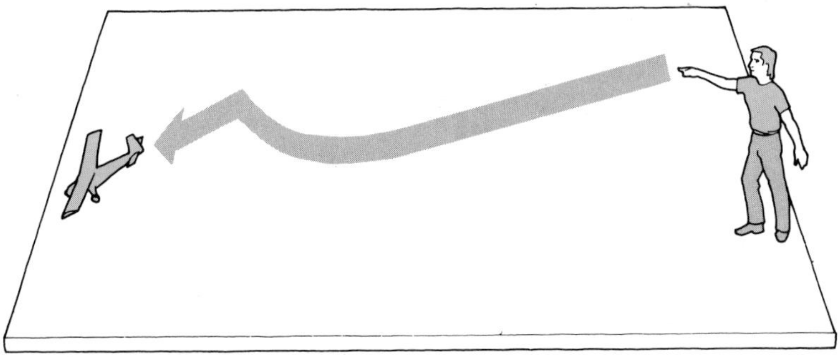

A model that turns to the left under power, may need more sidethrust to counteract the torque effect of the engine. If you wish, you can use this tendency to turn to make the model fly in circles.

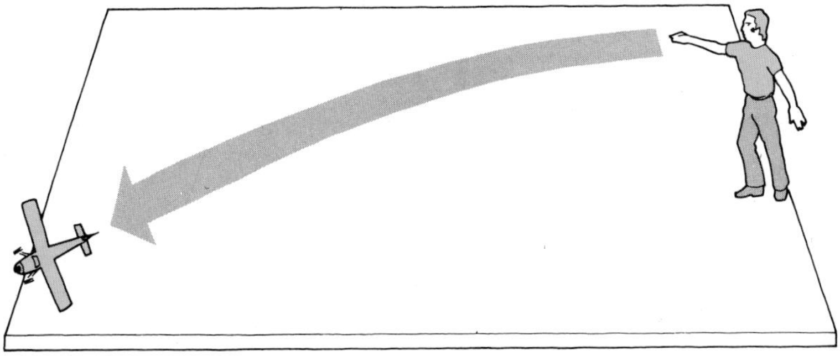

## Trimming a radio-control airplane

Make sure the batteries are fully charged before leaving for the field. Before you launch the model, turn the radio system on, transmitter first, and see that the control surfaces move freely over their full reach. It is also a good idea to test the range of the system so that you know how far you can let the model fly. This is particularly important if you are trying out a new model. Follow the method recommended by the manufacturer. Usually, the test takes two people. One person holds the transmitter; the other walks away holding the model above his head until control is lost (at this point the model should be too small to be seen properly). Establish a simple order of control movements beforehand so that you can make sure all is working well at a distance. The range in the air should be twice the distance of the ground range. A powered model should be range-tested with the engine running.

Trimming is often done in two stages. Both stages are needed for light, powered aircraft, while the first is also used for gliders and the second for heavier, powered aircraft.

The first stage test-glides the model. If you are a beginner, it is best to let an experienced flier operate the controls so that any instability can be attributed to the model, not pilot error. Launch the airplane into the wind with all controls at neutral. If the airplane descends steeply, zooms up and stalls, or wanders right or left, balance the elevator and rudder trim controls until it glides straight and level. Transfer any trim settings to the linkage by adjusting the clevises at the control horns so that the trim controls can return to neutral.

The second stage is to try a short, powered flight. Set the engine to run just below peak performance and hand-launch the airplane with a straight push. Fly the model to a safe height using the control sticks, then set the trim controls. After the flight, reset the linkage and neutralize the transmitter controls. If a lot of trimming proves necessary, adjust the engine side- or downthrust and run another trial flight. A trimmed model should fly straight and level under power and follow a gentle glide when the engine stops, without transmitter control.

## Flying a radio-control airplane

Control-stick positions

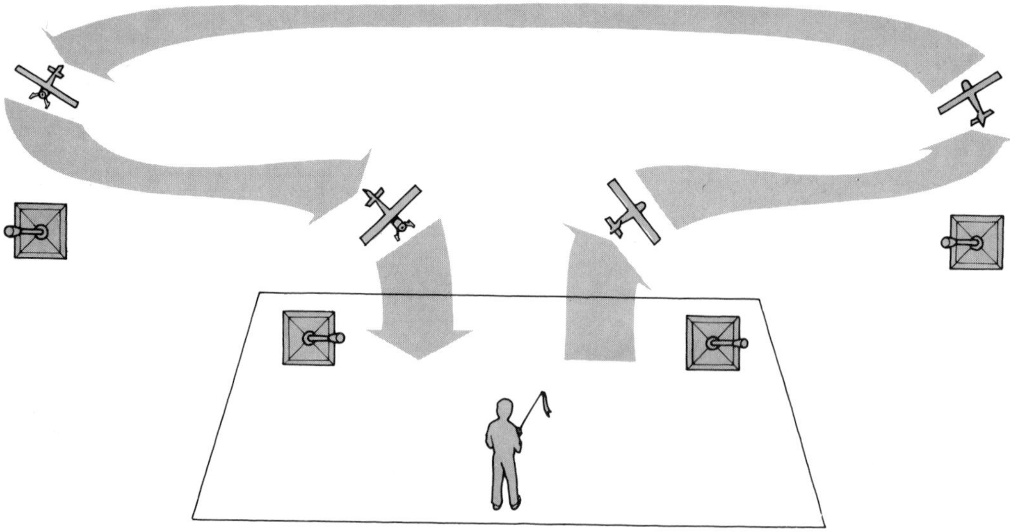

The functions of the control surfaces are described on page 269, but only experience will tell you "when" and "how much" control to apply. Start with a trainer airplane. It is designed to be stable and it will correct itself when the sticks are released, if the operator loses control.

An airplane, like the trainer, can be controlled by the rudder alone but for smoother, banked turns you need to learn to operate the rudder and elevator together, or the elevator and ailerons without the rudder. The most sophisticated models use all three controls in a turn and need a three-function radio.

Start with a dry run at home to get the feel of the control sticks. Set the model in front of you and switch on the radio system. Operate the sticks, watching the amount of movement on the control surfaces, and imagine the model's responses. First operate the transmitter from behind the model as if it were flying away from you, then turn the model around to represent it coming toward you. The latter operation generally takes more practice because, to make the model airplane turn to your right, the rudder or aileron control stick is moved to the left and vice versa.

### Your first flight

Ask an experienced aeromodeler, such as a flying club instructor, to accompany you. Let him control the model to a safe height, then you can take over the transmitter. A "buddy" box connection which allows the instructor to plug into the learner's set and take control when necessary is a convenient teaching aid. The sets must be the same make.

Launch the airplane into the wind and let it climb gradually in square circuits to an altitude of about 200 to 300 feet (60 to 100 m). At this height any errors can be corrected. Keep the airplane upwind of you as it will tend to drift downwind; if you lose control, the wind will carry the model back to you. Use the square circuits to practice 90° turns and straight, level flying. When you feel comfortable with this maneuver, fly in the opposite direction, then try figures-of-eight.

Anticipate the model's responses to each command to make it fly smoothly. Move the control stick a little and, as soon as the model responds, release it to return to neutral. Do not use full stick movements or you will overcontrol and have to correct with an opposite signal. Make your first flight short so that you don't lose concentration.

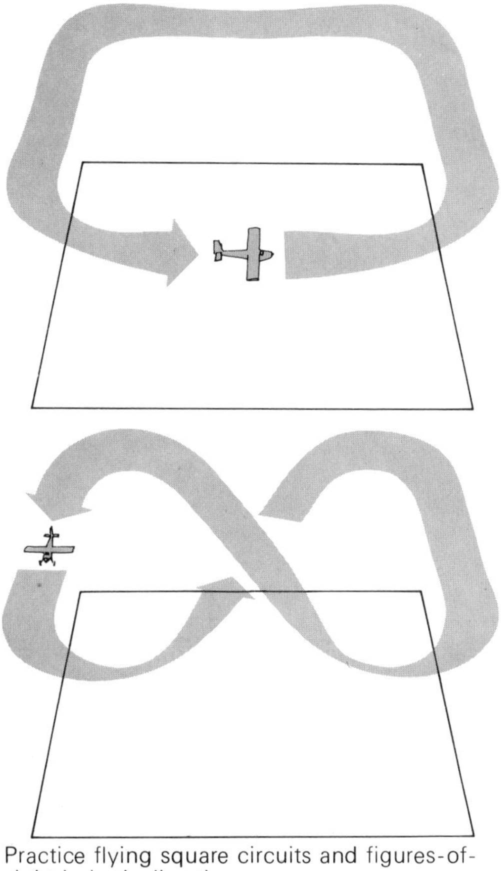

Practice flying square circuits and figures-of-eight in both directions.

### Landing

High-speed landings are risky, therefore, unless your airplane has a throttled engine, bring it in when the engine runs out of fuel. It is a good idea to let the instructor carry out the first landing so that you can observe.

Following the pattern below, allow the model to lose height in an upwind leg, then fly it downwind in a gentle glide (cut back the throttle, if there is one). Note the height as the model passes in front of you so that you can judge when to turn the model across the wind. Still losing height, turn it across the wind, then make the last turn into the wind. The model should settle into a shallow descent and gently come into land. If you misjudge the approach angle and the model begins to under or overshoot the landing area, do not try to correct it. It is better to land short or long than to take measures which may cause the model to crash. With practice, you will be able to refine the landing by feeding in a little up elevator to make the model glide in level or slightly tail down.

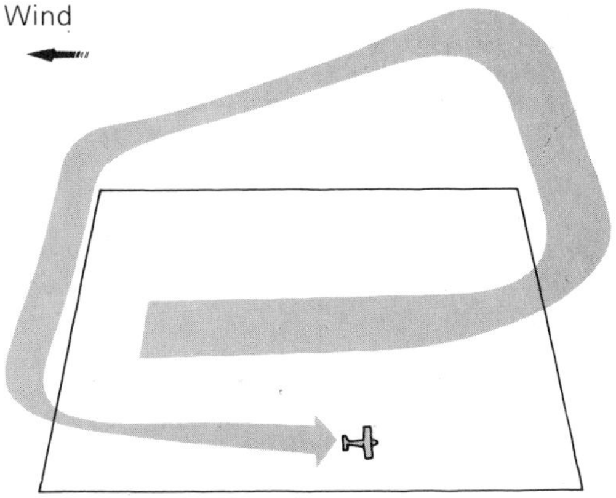


Starting with an upwind leg, make the airplane lose altitude gradually until it comes in to land on another upwind leg.

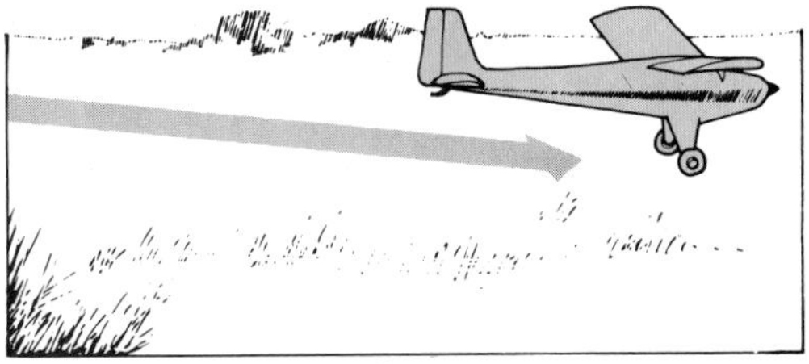

Basic glide-angle landing

Tail-down landing

## Launching a glider by towline

Slope soarers are designed to be hand-launched from a cliff or steep hillside but thermal soarers need to be pulled into the air by a towline made from nylon monofilament fishing line. A ring on the end of the line slips over a hook on the bottom of the glider. One person holds the glider at an angle facing into the wind; another runs with the line to pull it into the air. The glider rises rapidly like a kite until the line is more or less vertical. The line is then pulled from the hook under the glider by a small parachute and drifts back to the ground.

A glider can be launched by one person if a length of elastic cord, called a hi-start, is added to the towline. Fix the elastic cord to a stake in the ground (a corkscrew-shaped stake sold especially for the purpose will hold it securely). Stretch the line downwind and attach it to the glider. Release the model and the line, allowing the cord to pull the glider into the air.

High-speed winches are available to launch the model and to wind in the line as it falls to the ground. Another way of launching is to tug the glider into the air with a radio-control powered aircraft. Only advanced fliers should use powered models.

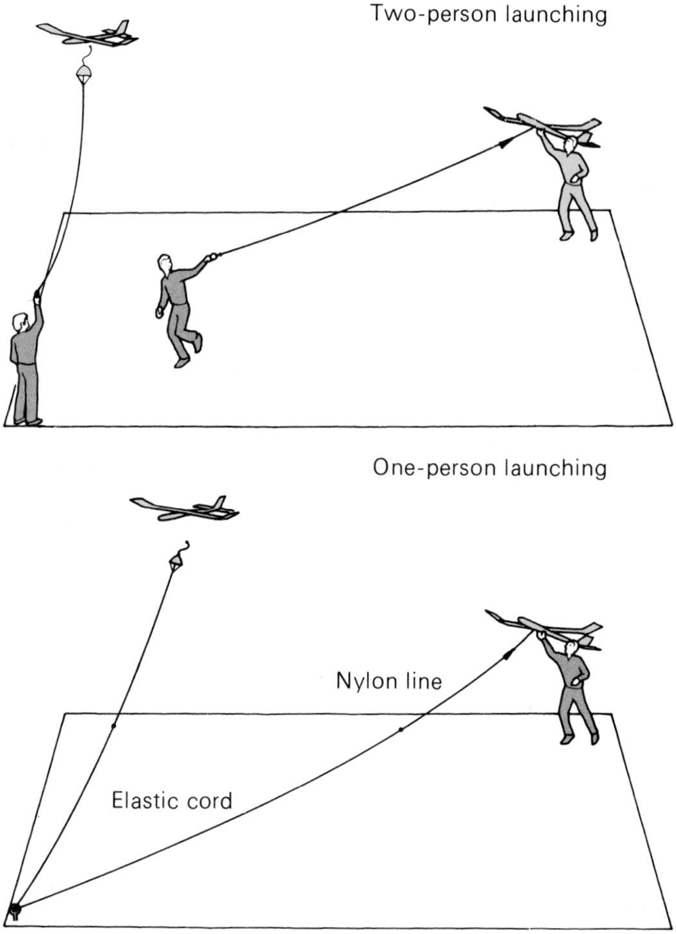


### The autorudder

This is used for free-flight thermal soarers which are easily lost if flown on a straight course. The autorudder remains straight for takeoff but makes the glider fly in circles when the towline detaches.

To make an autorudder, build a rudder with a horn on each side and hinge it to the fin in the normal way. Push a pin into the fuselage on each side of the rudder to act as a stop. One pin – usually the left one – stops the rudder in the center; the other stops it at an angle. Calculate the position of the latter pin according to how tight a turn you wish the glider to make. Loop a rubber band onto the right horn and then onto another pin so that the band pulls the rudder against the stop. To hold the rudder straight during the launch, run a thread forward from the left horn. Attach a ring to the thread and slip it over a pin in a vertical brass tube fixed to the side of the fuselage. The pin should be loose in the tube, held in place only by the tension on the line. Tie an extension of the towline to the bottom of the pin.

With the ring in position on the hook the extension is slack but, when the towline detaches from the glider, its weight pulls the pin from the tube, freeing the line which holds the rudder straight. The rudder is then pulled over by the rubber band. Fix a staple in the side of the fuselage to prevent the thread from hanging down.

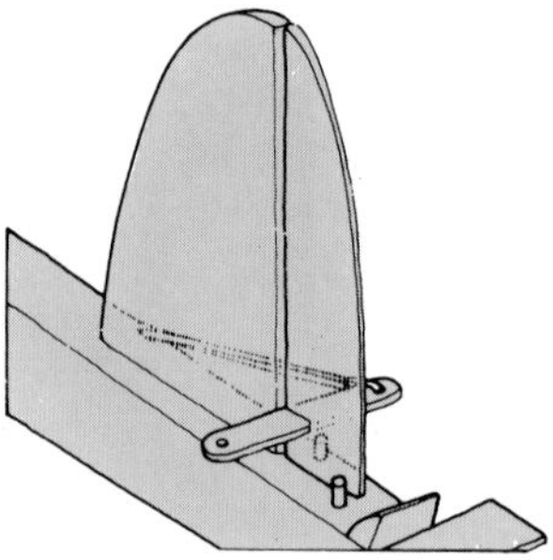
Autorudder installation

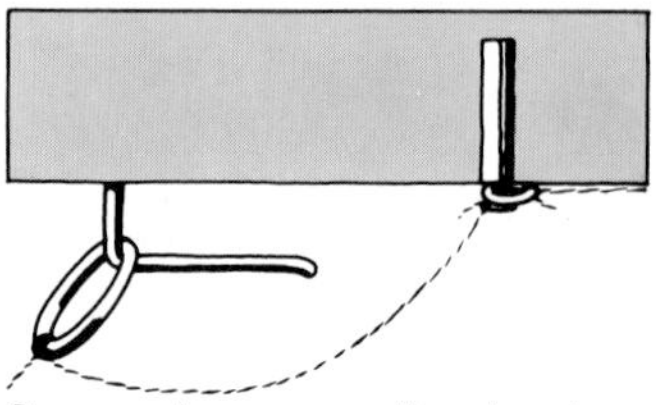
Connection to towline hook

## Dethermalizers

Even a circling free-flight glider will be lost if it gets trapped in a thermal and keeps rising. Build in a dethermalizer so that the glider descends after a predetermined time.

A dethermalizer device is composed of a timer – either a fuse or clockwork type – and a tail plane which is designed to tip up to an angle of about 60° when released by the timer. When the tail plane tips up, the glider sinks.

Mount a one-piece tail plane on top of the fuselage with its leading edge against a block. Pass a rubber band over a horn on the top of the tail plane, over the leading edge and under the fuselage, so that the band pulls the tail plane up. Pull the tail plane down into the flying position and secure it. The method of securing it and the way it releases depend on the type of timer that you select. See below and right.

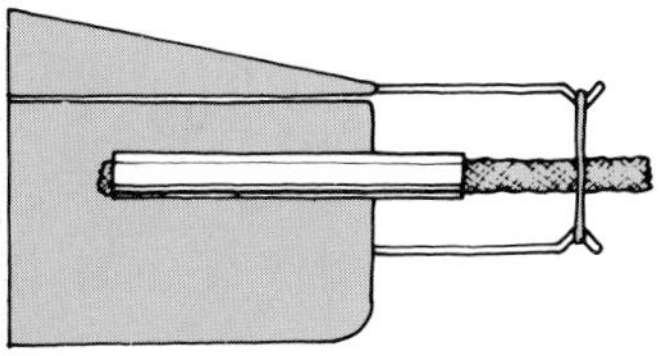

**How a fuse timer works** One wire projects from the center of the trailing edge of the tail plane and another from the back of the fuselage. A thread or a rubber band looped over the wires holds the tail plane down. Positioned in the loop is a slow match fuse held in a metal tube attached to the side of the fuselage.

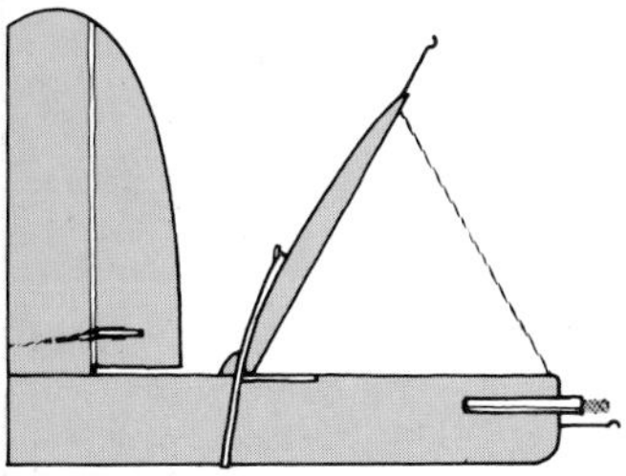

When the fuse burns through the loop, it releases the tail plane. The duration of the flight is thereby determined by the amount of fuse allowed to project through the loop.

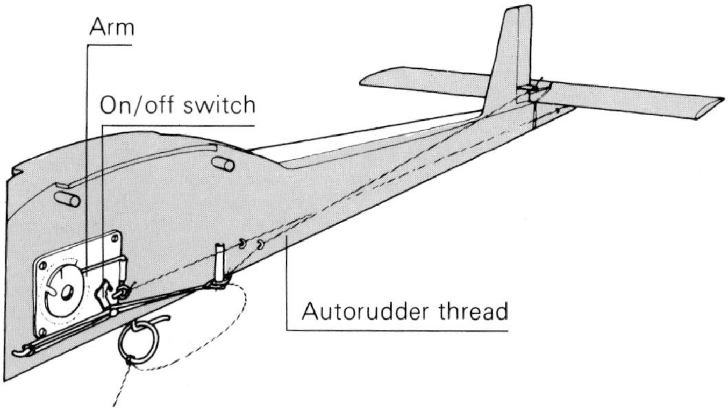


**How a clockwork timer works** The timer is mounted on the side of the fuselage. It has an on/off switch, a rotating disk and an arm. When one end of the arm is trapped under the disk, the other projects from the fuselage and traps a ring on a thread which holds the tail plane down. The switch is held "off" by a rubber band held by the pin which keeps the autorudder straight. Another rubber band, weaker than that holding it "off," tries to pull the switch "on."

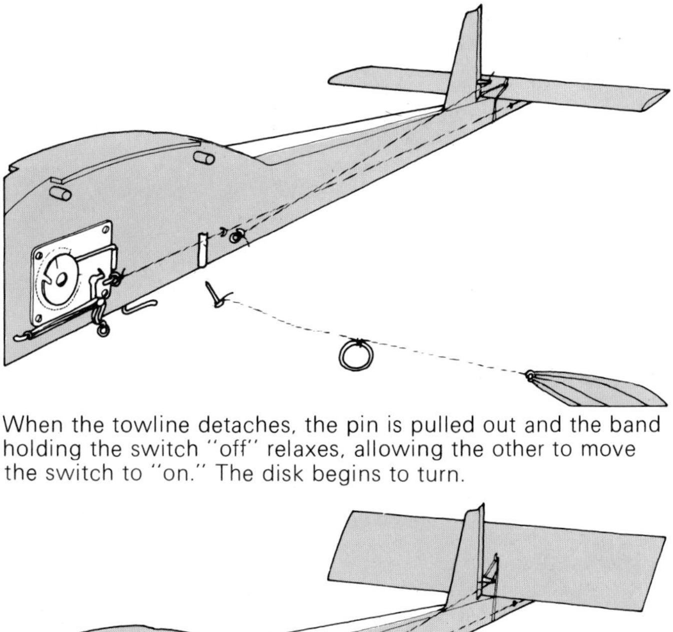

When the towline detaches, the pin is pulled out and the band holding the switch "off" relaxes, allowing the other to move the switch to "on." The disk begins to turn.

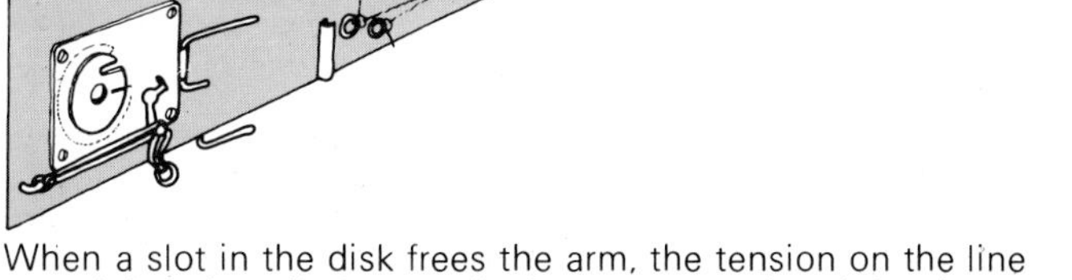

When a slot in the disk frees the arm, the tension on the line restraining the tail plane pulls the arm around and the ring slips off, allowing the tail plane to pop up. A staple on the side of the fuselage is positioned to stop the ring on the tail plane thread when the tail plane is at 60°.

# Control-line airplanes

This type of model flies in a circle around its pilot. He controls its movements with a handle attached to two lines from the airplane. Pioneered in America around 1940, control-line flying is cheaper than radio control and is often the first step in controlled flying for the beginner. Although the airplane is restricted to circular flights, the variety of maneuvers – climbing, diving, loops and inverted flight – offers a great deal of enjoyment. Moreover, it covers a range of interests. As well as sport and scale flying, there are several competition categories, including combat, stunt or aerobatic, speed and team racing.

The combat airplane is basically a flying wing to which is attached a paper streamer. In competition, two airplanes fly simultaneously in the same circle with the aim of cutting the opponent's streamer. Points are given for each cut made within a set time.

Competing stunt airplanes fly solo and have to follow a sequence of maneuvers, winning points for their execution. Both combat and stunt flying require skillful control.

In speed flying, the plane is designed to fly as fast as possible against the clock. In this case, aerodynamic efficiency and engine performance are all extremely important.

Team racing requires a pilot and one or two mechanics to service the model for each race. One mechanic, starting and refuelling the model, is usually sufficient. Airplanes with a glow plug engine often need a second mechanic to hold the plug cables. A team racer has to cover a specified number of laps as quickly as possible, racing against one or more aircraft. The length of the race, which can be from $1\frac{1}{2}$ to 10 miles (2 to 16 km), determines the tactics employed. The model can be set to run fast and use more fuel, or slower to save a refueling stop. An average pit stop takes about twenty seconds.

## The linkage

Only the rise and fall of this type of aircraft can be controlled and this is by the elevator alone, or for stunt models, elevator and wing flaps.

A wire pushrod links a horn on the elevator (see Pushrods and Horns, pages 260 and 263) with a control-line bellcrank. Two lead-out wires run from the bellcrank to the control lines. The handle completes the system at the other end of the lines. The lines must be the same length so that the elevator is horizontal when the handle is vertical for neutral.

Two ways of linking stunt-plane wing flaps are shown. In both cases the flap is set to move less than the elevator.

When the aircraft is flying the lines must be under tension. Otherwise, the pilot loses control. To keep tension on the lines, the center of balance is forward of the bellcrank pivot point, making the nose point out from the flying circle. In addition, a weight on the outer wing tip compensates for the weight of the lines dragging the airplane inward. The rudder is permanently set a few degrees to the right so that the model is always pulling out.

**Typical linkage**

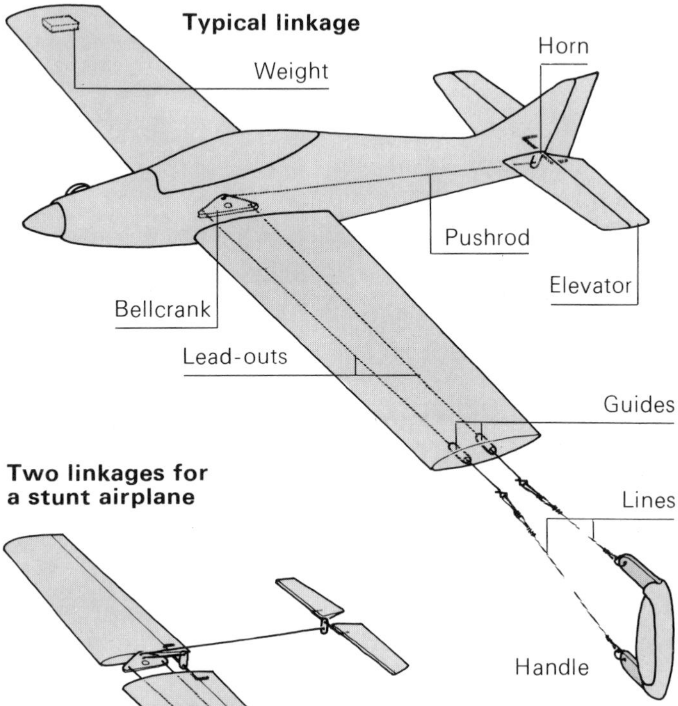


**Two linkages for a stunt airplane**

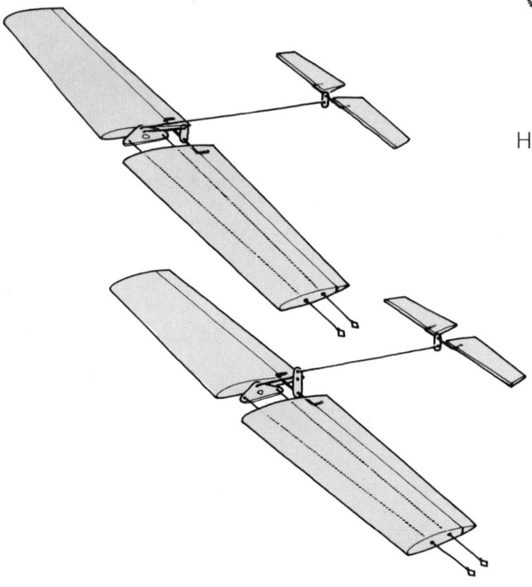

## Controlling the airplane

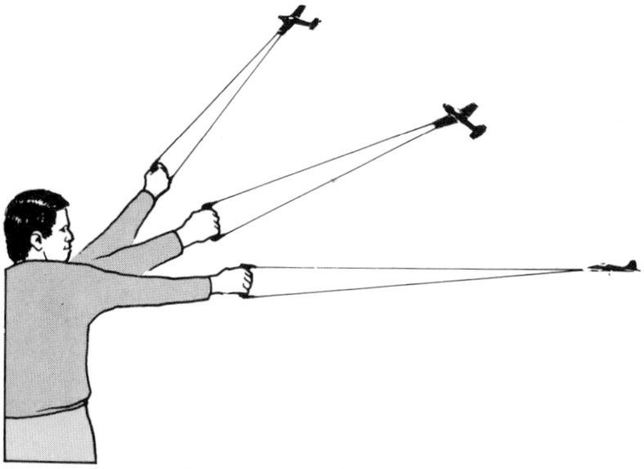

Hold the handle at arm's length and control the model by lifting or lowering your arm (tilting the handle from the wrist requires sensitive control). Hold the handle upright for level flight, tilt it up to climb, and down to dive. When the model is flying upside down in aerobatic maneuvers, it gives the opposite responses. If the model turns inside the circle and the lines slacken, step backward and reestablish the tension.

## Handles and lines

The handles are designed to be held comfortably in one hand. Some come with a line-length adjuster; others have different positions for the lines to alter the sensitivity.

The lines are made from nylon or single- or multistrand wire, and come in different thicknesses to suit the weight and power of the model. They can be bought cut to length with loops, ready for use. To get the best performance, use the weight of line specified for your model. Lines for sport flying should be about 50 feet (15 m) long.

Nylon lines are easy to use and maintain, and are best suited to beginners with small lightweight aircraft. They do not often kink and can, therefore, be wound around the handle for storage. They are, however, rather elastic, which gives the controls a spongy feel.

Single-strand, lightweight piano wire is stronger than nylon, causes less drag and readily slides over itself when twisted after a loop maneuver. However, it is difficult to use and maintain and is not recommended for the beginner. The end loops are difficult to form because of the nature of the wire, and the lines tend to kink. A kink causes the wire to snap at that point under load, so never use a line with a kink or one that has been straightened. A line that has been twisted tends to loop when slack. Always avoid pulling the line or the loop will tighten and kink.

Multistrand lines are less likely to curl up when released from the reel. This type, although slightly more expensive, is the most popular with beginners and experienced fliers alike. It is more flexible than single-strand wire, which allows it to absorb a certain amount of rough treatment without kinking. Moreover, if a kink occurs and goes unnoticed, the line shouldn't break because it is unlikely that all the strands will go at once. Any broken strands can be detected by running the lines through your hand as you walk from the model to the handle; this should be done prior to every flight. Like the single-strand type, it doesn't stick when twisted about itself during a loop maneuver. The end loops are tricky to make, particularly with heavyweight line.

Lines must be carefully looked after. Always check their condition and remove any grass or leaves before taking them in, and store them on a reel or drum. Nylon lines can take a tight curve but a reel for a wire line should have a diameter of not less than 3 inches (75 mm). To transfer the lines to the reel, first detach them from the handle and hook them onto the reel, then take in the lines, rolling the reel toward the model. Do not wind the lines around the reel as this can twist them. When the lines are unhooked from the lead-outs they can be secured on the reel with a rubber band.

### Handles

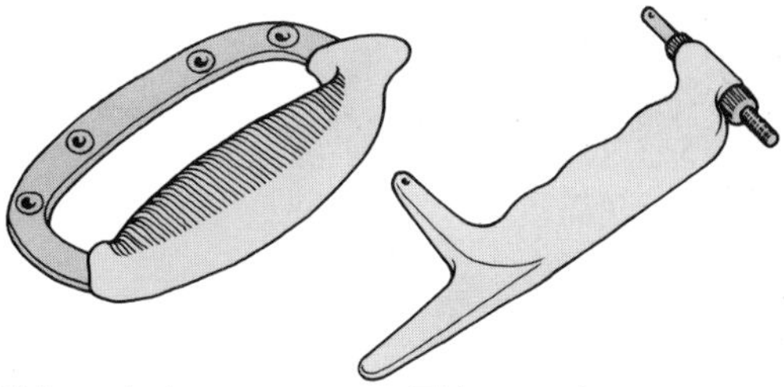

This style has two positions for the lines. The inner holes produce less elevator movement than the outer ones, for a given movement of the handle, and are used by the beginner to prevent overcontrol.

This type has a screw to correct any slight difference in the length of the lines. The spiked end can be stuck in the ground to keep the lines untangled and it helps to distinguish top from bottom.

### Attaching the line to the handle

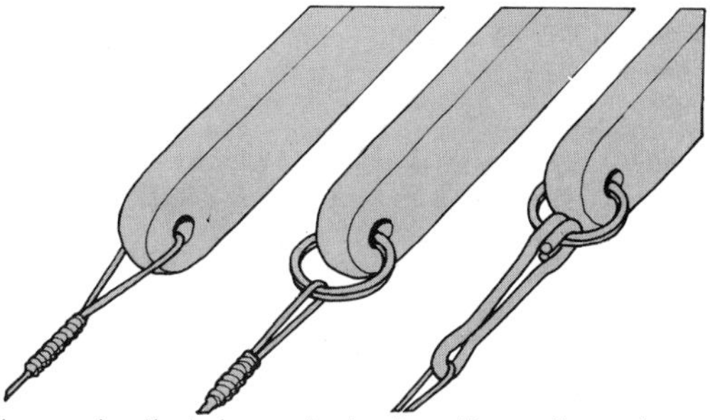

Loop the line through the handle or through a split ring. A line connector works best as one handle can be used for different lines.

### Making a loop

Just tie the end of a nylon line to form a loop. Single- or multistrand wire should be bound with fine single-strand wire or clamped in a metal tube. Some manufacturers supply an eyelet for use with the tube method; this is trapped by the line which is pulled taut around it.

**Making a loop in a nylon line** Make a loop at the end with a bowline knot. Pull the knot tight and trim the end. Test the loop for strength by slipping it over a convenient fixture and pulling on the line.

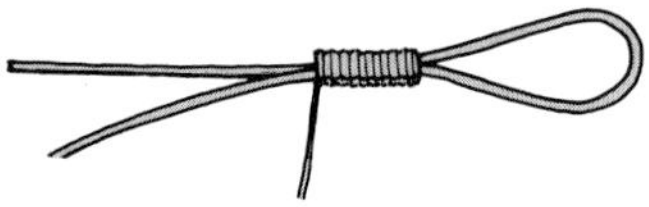

**Binding method for a wire line** Make a loop in the line about 4 inches (100 mm) from the end. Bind a wire around the line working backward from the loop for 1 inch (25 mm).

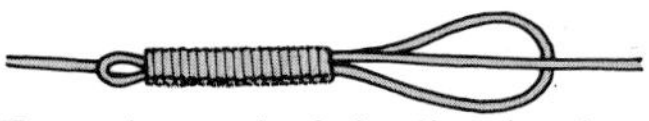

Turn the end of the line back along the bound section and continue binding up to the loop. You may need to flatten the part at the bend with pliers. Tie off the binding wire and trim the ends.

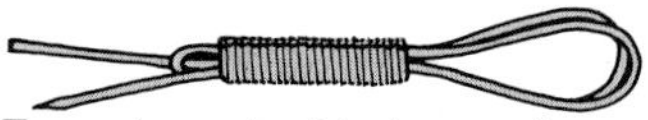

To make a double loop, allow extra line at the end initially, and follow the method described, forming the second loop beside the first.

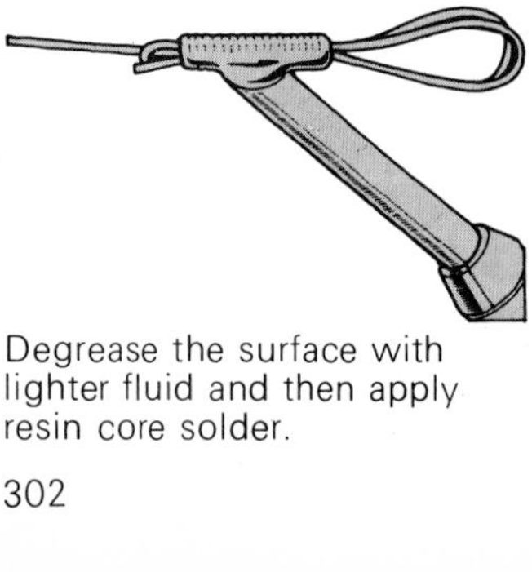

Degrease the surface with lighter fluid and then apply resin core solder.

**Tube method for a wire line** Slip a $\frac{3}{4}$-inch-long (20-mm) piece of brass or copper tube over the end. Bend the line over and back through the tube to make a $\frac{1}{2}$-inch-long (12-mm) loop.

Push the end of the line back through the tube and pull it with pliers to draw the loop into the tube.

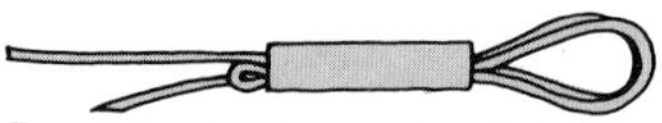

For a double loop, feed the end back through the tube and pull it through to make a loop to match the first one.

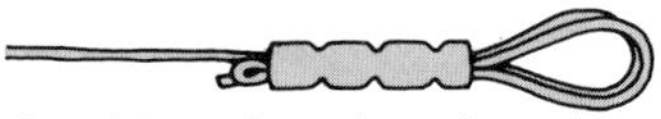

Carefully crimp the tube with the cutting jaws of a pair of pliers. Trim the wire ends, then apply a resin core solder to the ends of the tube to reinforce the joint.

## Control-line bellcranks

These have the same function as radio-control bellcranks: to change the path of the pushrod so that it turns a corner. The size of the bellcrank, measured across the longest side, will probably be specified on your plan if it is not supplied with the kit. The size is important as the distance between the pivot point and lead-out holes affects the sensitivity of the control. The more the elevator moves for a given movement of the handle, the more sensitive the control. A small bellcrank has the lead-out holes close together and is more sensitive than a large one. Similarly, the distance between the pushrod hole and the bellcrank pivot alters the sensitivity: the inner hole gives less elevator throw and the outer hole more.

The amount of movement is also affected by the pushrod's position on the horn (see Horns, pages 262 to 263). Like radio-control bellcranks, the pivot must operate smoothly and without slack. The nylon type are supplied with a bush for easy installation. For the flat metal-plate type, it is advisable to make a bush cut from brass tube the same diameter as the bolt. The bush should be slightly longer than the thickness of the bellcrank. Bolt the bellcrank to a plywood plate attached to the fuselage.

## Wire connections

Typical pushrod and lead-out connections are shown below, but for more information on linkage connections turn to pages 260 to 263. Control-line pushrods are the wire type. Use thick wire or heavy-duty multistranded cable for the lead-out wires.

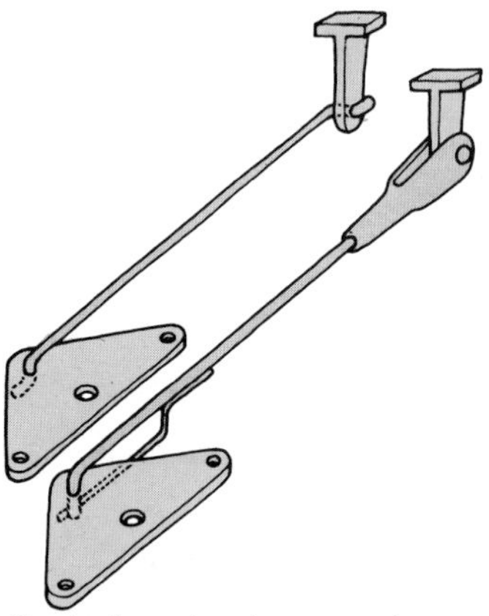

Typical pushrod connections

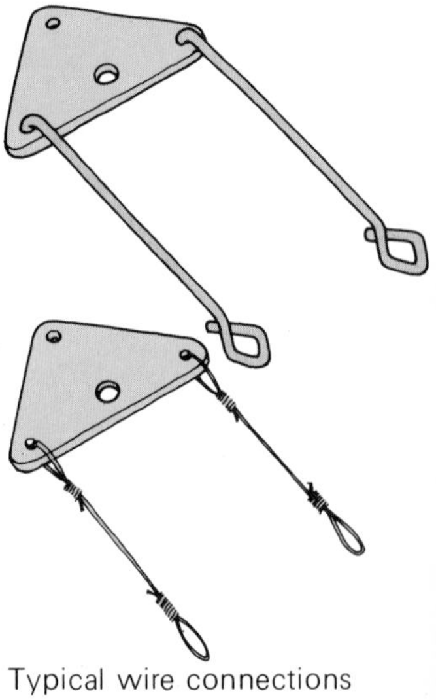

Typical wire connections

# Boats

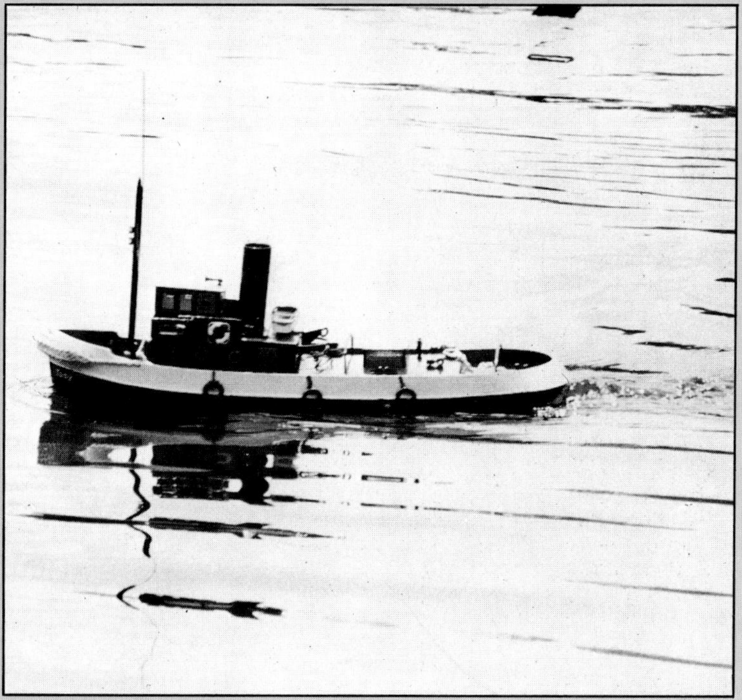

# Modeling boats

Boats fall into two categories: sail and power. Within these categories there is a range of models to suit everyone's interest and skill. There are superb craft for the more advanced modelmaker such as large-scale sailboats with automatic steering or radio-control sails and helm which perform as well as full-size yachts. Powerboats also enjoy a vast following. Racing boats achieve fantastic scale speeds and there are true-scale replicas of real vessels which, when underway, look every bit as detailed as the best static model. Beginners, however, should tackle a fairly simple design at first, perhaps a free-running sailboat or an electric powerboat with a hard-chine hull. This chapter explains the many types of construction and methods of control and propulsion to help you build from a kit or plan.

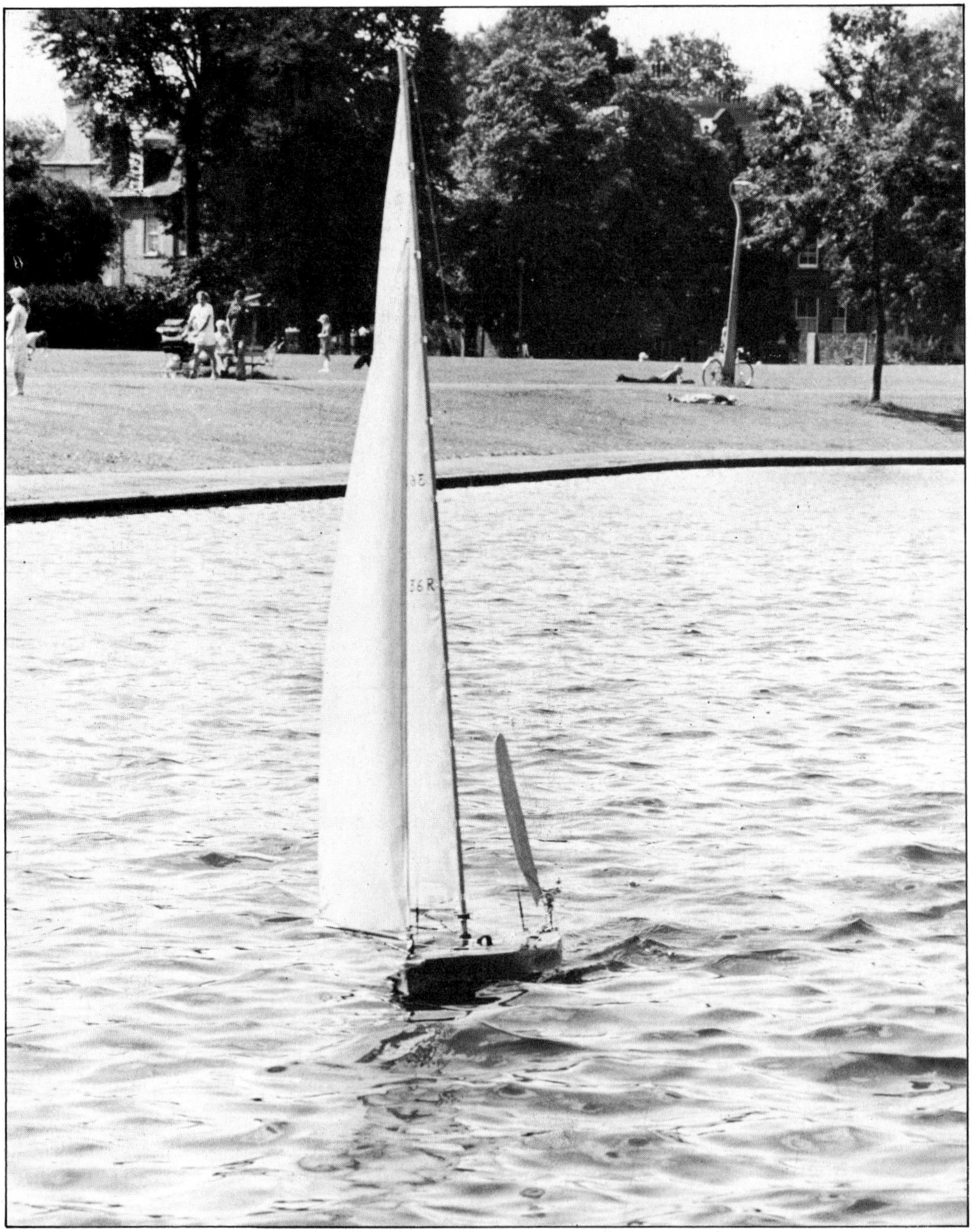


This sailboat has vane steering gear which keeps it at a constant angle to the wind.

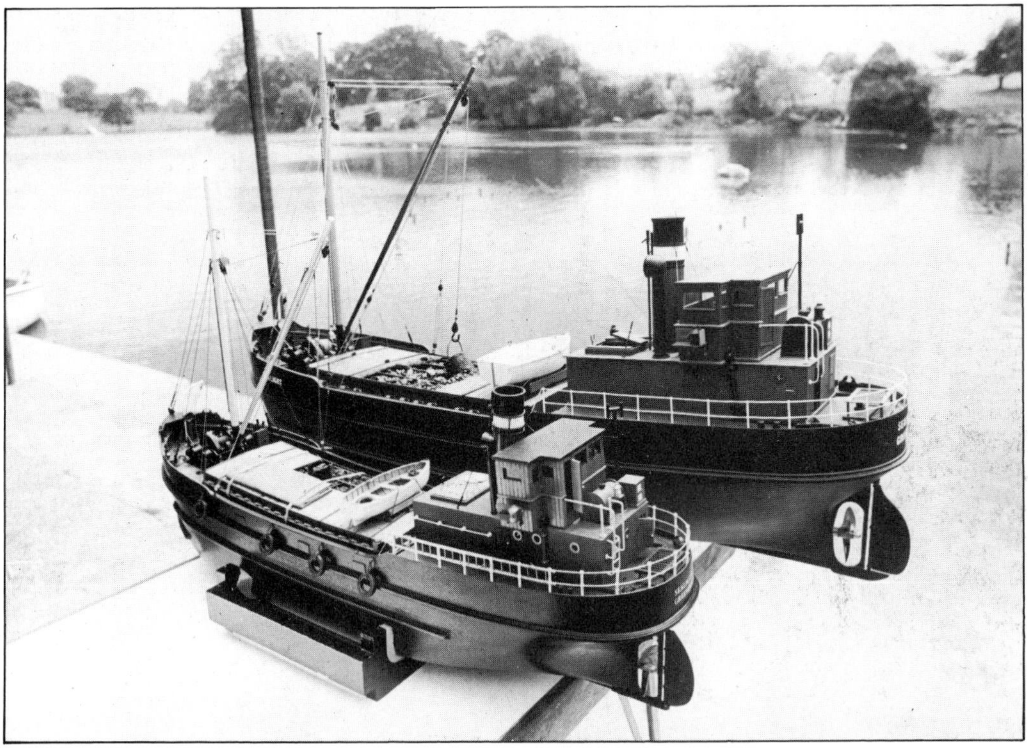

These are true-scale replicas of a collier, built to different scales.

This racer is planing at top speed. The radio equipment is in a watertight box at the rear.

# How a boat floats

A boat floats because it displaces more than its own weight in water. Unlike an airplane, a boat can be quite heavy or carry a lot of weight as long as the weight is distributed so that the boat is stable.

The lower the center of gravity, the more stable the boat is. The mast of a sailboat adds weight and tends to make the vessel tip, so a sailboat has a deep keel with a weight at the bottom to counterbalance the mast and wind pressure on the sails. The weight must also be distributed correctly between stern and bow. There is always more weight near the stern so that the bow is slightly up and offers less resistance to forward movement. Moreover, if there is too much weight at the bow, the boat is difficult to steer and may plow under the surface of the water. Check your model's balance by placing it in the water: the water should come just to the waterline specified on the plan or indicated on the kit hull. If it does not, shift some equipment or add ballast (small weights) until it sits properly in the water. The ballast should always be placed as low as possible in the boat.

The shape of the hull also affects the boat's stability. The wider the hull, the steadier it is. A broad-beamed tug, for example, is very stable, whereas a canoe tips easily. A catamaran has two separate hulls, which makes it an extremely stable craft. However, when it does capsize, it turns completely upside down and is difficult to right. To make a catamaran easier to recover and to prevent its mast from being damaged on the pond bottom, attach a masthead float to keep the mast horizontal.

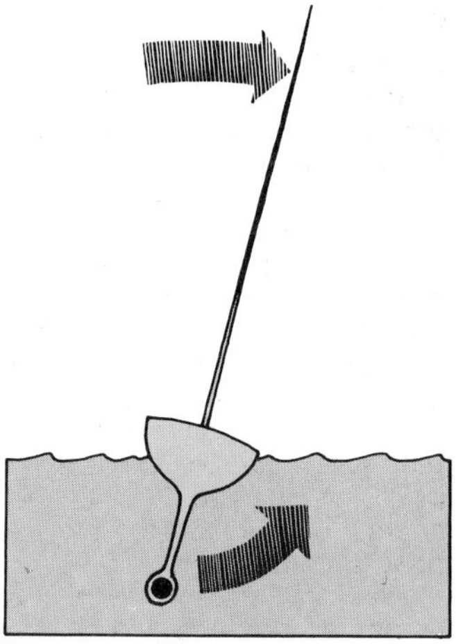

**How a sailboat stays upright** A weight at the bottom of the keel counterbalances the weight of the mast and wind pressure on the sails. When the boat heels over, or tilts, in a gust of wind, the keel acts to keep it upright by resisting the water.

# How a boat sails

The wind on the sail creates the driving force. When the boat goes in the same direction as the wind, it is simply pushed along. When it turns at an angle to the wind, it continues to go downwind but will move sideways not forward – called making leeway – unless it has some form of keel or centerboard to provide resistance to the sideways movement. All sailboats make some leeway but they are designed to have as high a resistance to sideways movement as possible while keeping the resistance to forward movement as low as is possible.

The angle of the sail has to be adjusted for maximum thrust according to the boat's position in the wind. See the diagram right for the correct sail position in the wind.

The different courses the boat takes relative to the wind are known as running, reaching and sailing close hauled. When the boat turns into the wind, called tacking, it momentarily loses the wind in its sails, then the boom swings over and the boat continues on its new course.

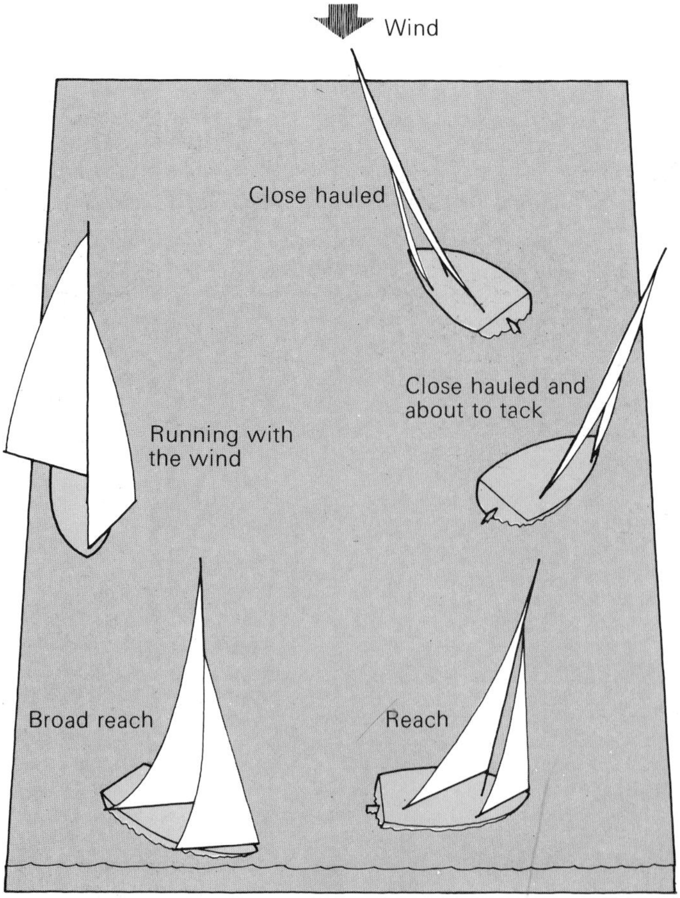

# Hulls

Boat hulls fall into two groups: those which move through the water, called displacement hulls, and those which ride over it, planing hulls.

Displacement hulls are designed to offer as little resistance as possible to the water flowing around them. There is little or no up thrust generated by the flow, and the draft (the vertical distance measured from the waterline to the lowest point of the hull) does not change significantly when the boat is underway.

Planing hulls present an angled surface to the water, producing lift which raises the hull in the water. This reduces drag and allows the hull to move very fast. All parts of a hydrofoil lift right out of the water except for its planing surfaces.

Model hulls can be made of wood, fiberglass and vacuum-formed plastic. Solid-wood hulls are simple to build and make a good sailing hull, but they are not suitable for racing powerboats because of their weight. Hard-chine hulls are another easily constructed type of wooden hull. They are light, can plane and suit high-performance speedboats as well as sailing vessels. Planked wooden hulls, used most often for sailboats, take skill to build but look very authentic. Fiberglass hulls are not difficult to make but take time. The finished hull is smooth and used for both high-performance speedboats and sailboats. Vacuum-formed plastic makes a smooth, light shape for power- and sailboats. Most modelers prefer to buy rather than build them.

**Displacement hull**

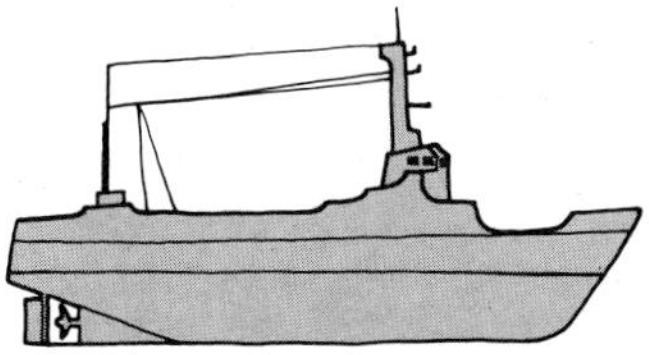

**Planing hulls**

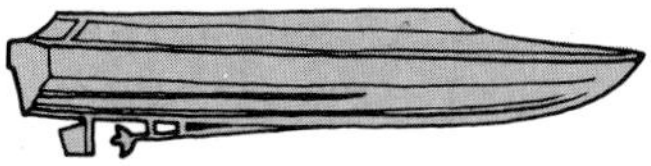

Deep vee

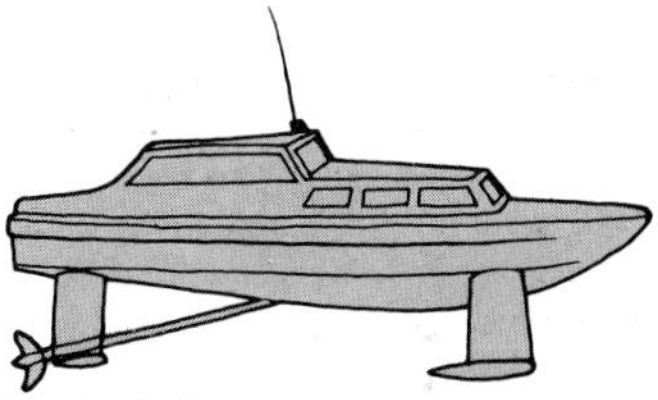

Hydrofoil

**The parts of a hull**

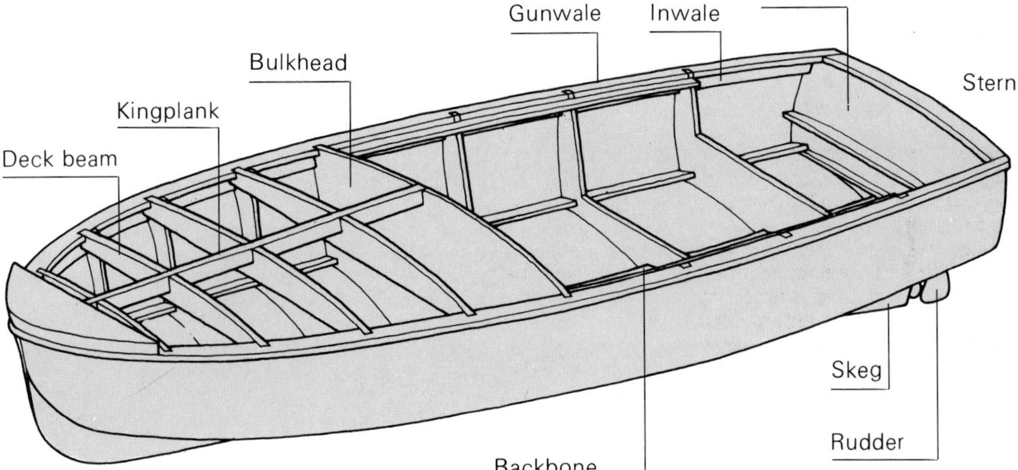


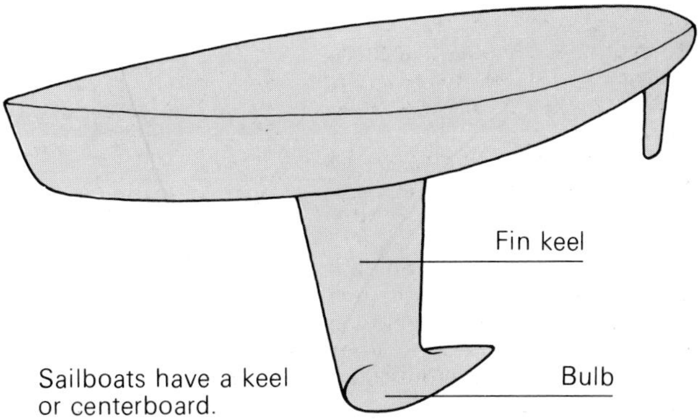


Sailboats have a keel or centerboard.

## Solid-wood hulls

Generally, only smaller boats can be made out of a single block of wood as it is difficult to find suitable wood in large sizes. Choose soft, easily worked wood, such as pine, obeche, balsa or jelutong, for the hull.

**Stage 1: Cutting and marking the block**
Cut a rectangular block to the overall dimensions of the hull and plane it square (if a keel is to be faired into the hull, include its base with the hull to avoid a feathered edge or gap). Referring to the plans, mark the block with the centerline, stations, plan and side view, and hull cavities.

Stage 1

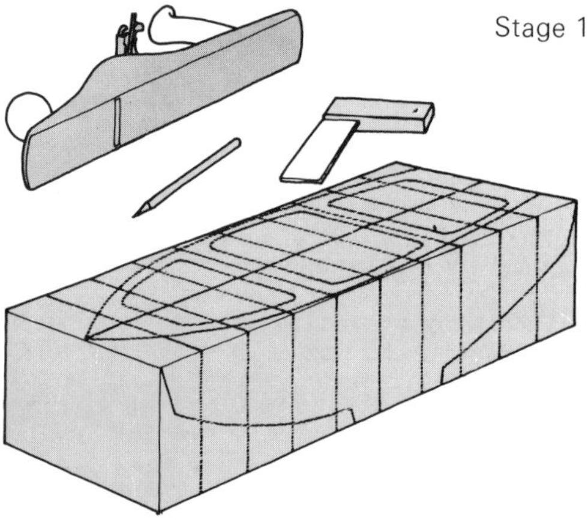

**Stage 2: Hollowing out the hull**
Using a drill stand and power wood bits, drill out the hull cavities. Calculate the depth and position of the holes carefully to avoid cutting too deep. Also, be sure to leave sufficient material in between each cavity so that you can attach a wood strip in stage 4 for holding the hull in a vise. Hollowing out the hull reduces weight and allows you to redistribute it to improve the boat's stability or sailing characteristics (see How a boat floats, page 306). It also provides space for equipment.

Stage 2

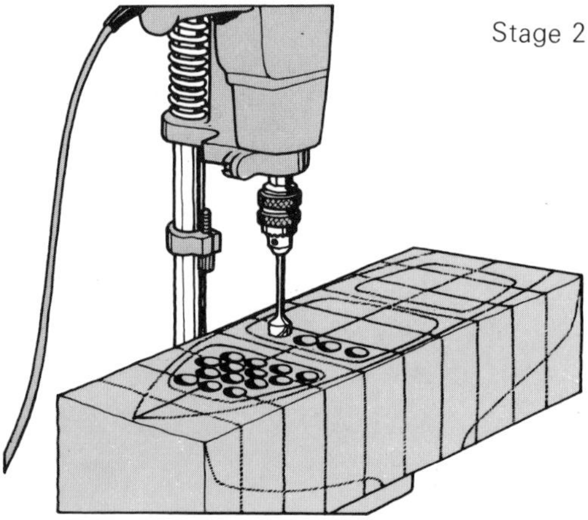

**Stage 3: Cutting out the hull**
Cut around the side profile with a frame or band saw; cut around the plan view on the top of the block. If you use a band saw, replace the side profile pieces holding them with tape for a flat base for sawing around the plan view.

Stage 3

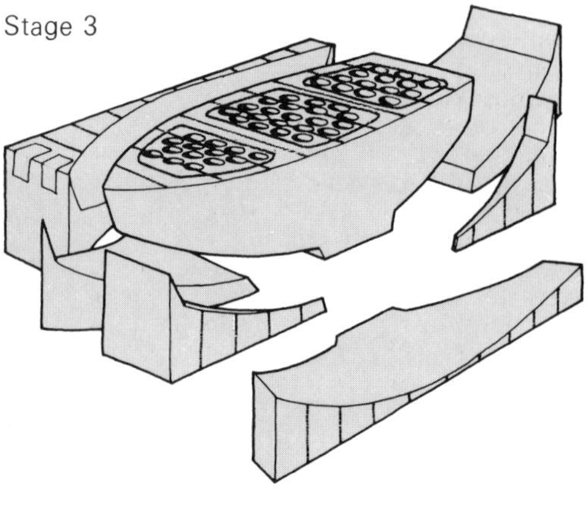

**Stage 4: Shaping the hull**
Mark the station lines down the sides with a try square. Invert the hull and mark the lines across the bottom; mark the centerline. Using the sectional view, cut a full template from thick cardboard or plywood for each station. Number the stations on the hull and the templates. Screw a wood strip to the top side.

Hold the hull upside down in a vise by the wood strip and remove surplus material with a wood chisel, rasp or spokeshave, working with the grain, toward bow and stern. Check the shape periodically with the templates and renew the station lines before they disappear. While the hull is still upside down, drill any holes for mounting a keel, skeg, rudder or propeller shaft. Where the keel is mortised in, drill a row of holes and clean up with a chisel.

Smooth the inside of the hull with a large, curved gouge or, for narrower, deeper recesses, a spoon bit gouge. Work with the grain in diagonal sweeps from the ends inward.

Shape the top surface of the hull to receive the deck (see Decks, page 321).

Stage 4

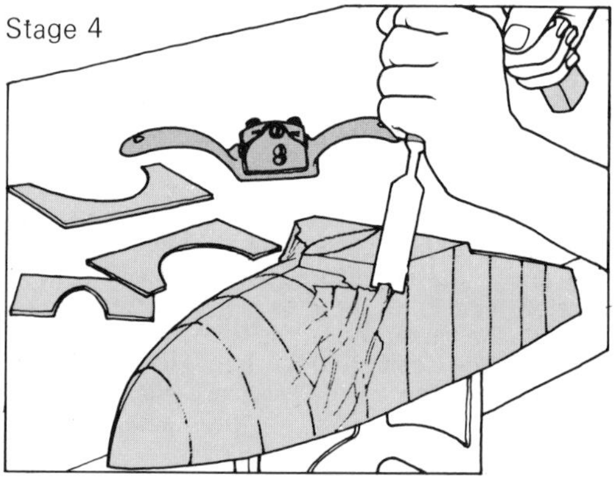

## Bread-and-butter hulls

These are assembled from wood laminations which are preshaped from planed boards, glued together, then gouged and sanded to the final shape. The wood is the "bread" and the glue, the "butter." The joints may be horizontal and parallel to the waterlines, or vertical and parallel to the buttock lines (the lines which define the shape of the hull in vertical, lengthwise slices). In the former case, there is normally a vertical joint on the centerline to make it easier to cut out the laminations. Any lack of lateral symmetry during shaping can be seen by checking the relative positions of the joints.

The method described below is for waterline laminations. If you are modeling a boat with buttock line laminations, mark at least one waterline in stage 2 to aid alignment during assembly. Also, if you intend to use a plug-in fin keel or a propeller shaft, cut slots for them in the center lamination before assembly. To prevent buttock line laminations from spreading when they are clamped in stage 3, leave a piece connecting bow and stern at the top of the center lamination; cut it away later or use it as a king-plank. An alternative is to use a plywood lamination for the center, shaped to the complete profile of the boat, including keel and skeg.

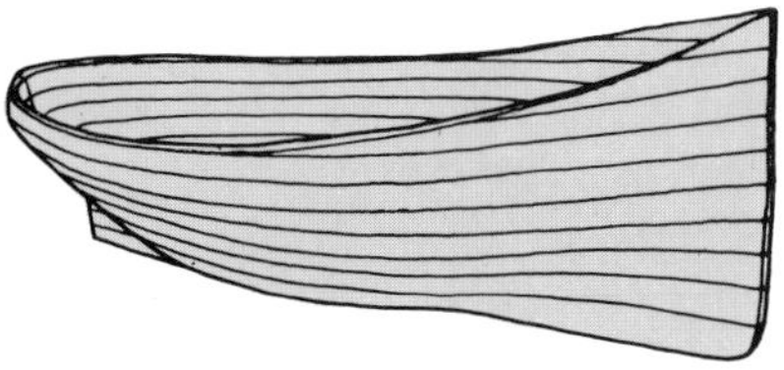

Waterline laminations

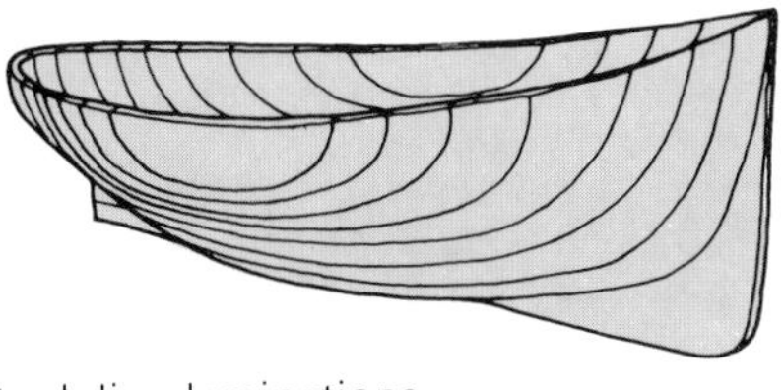

Buttock line laminations

### Stage 1: Plotting the laminations

Place a piece of tracing paper over the sectional plans and trace one of the station lines, the centerline and the waterlines. Draw the hull thickness inside the station line. The distance between the waterlines is the thickness of each lamination. The outer and inner edges of any lamination at any station are where the outer line of the hull cuts the top of the lamination (A) and the inner line of the hull cuts the bottom of the lamination (B). Repeat to make tracings for all stations. If the distance between the waterlines doesn't match the thickness of your wood boards, you can replot them to make the best use of the existing wood. Plotting buttock line laminations is the same process turned through 90°.

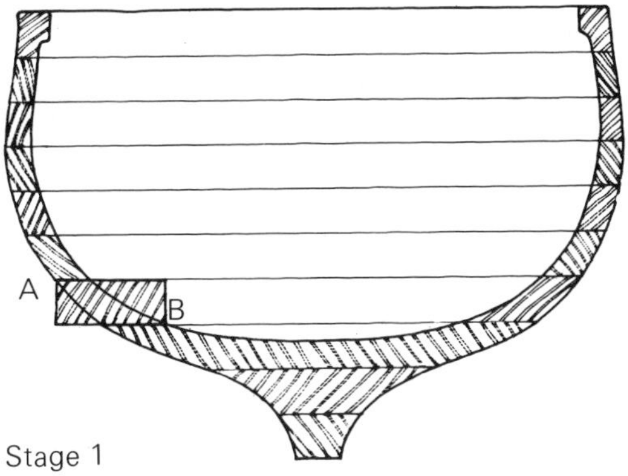


Stage 1

### Stage 2: Cutting out the laminations

Make each lamination in two halves. Begin by planing the boards to the correct thickness. It is important that they are flat when assembled so first clamp the edges of the boards together and plane across them before cutting out the shapes; any error in squareness will cancel out so long as either board is not turned end-for-end. This method guarantees a perfect fit.

Working on one half-lamination at a time, mark the stations on the edge of a board, square them across and number them. Using dividers, transfer the dimensions from the tracings to the wood; make the edge of the wood correspond to the centerline of the drawing. The need for partial laminations and the thickness of the hull at bow and stern can be determined by checking the plan side view. Join up the marks with a flexible ruler or join with French curves.

Cut out the laminations, leaving extra material at the ends for clamping lugs. (An alternative method is to cut the inner curves, glue and clamp the boards together, then cut the outer shape.) Mark the station lines all around one set of half-pieces and use them as templates to mark the other set.

Another method of marking out the boards is to make a set of cardboard templates. The templates can be positioned to make the best use of the wood and can be used again for building another hull.

Stage 2

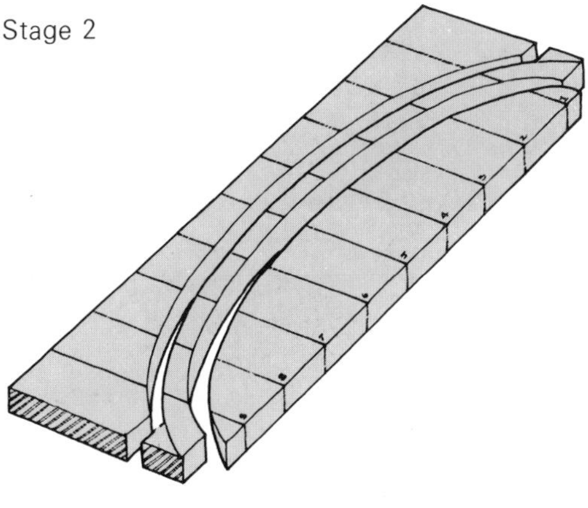

**Stage 3: Assembling the hull**
Screw or clamp each pair of half-laminations together with waterproof glue and let them dry before assembling them. Begin by laying the complete lamination for the top of the hull on a flat, rigid board covered with polyethylene sheet or wax paper. If this first lamination does not extend the length of the hull, fill in the space with a spare piece of board of the same thickness (wax it so that it isn't accidentally glued). Apply glue to the lamination and position the next one on top of it. Slide it about to squeeze out air and excess glue, and align the centerlines and station lines. Repeat this process with the next lamination. Clamp these three together and let them dry before adding the rest of the laminations in groups of three.

Take care when clamping the hull as it may distort if you overtighten the clamp or if the pressure is uneven. Always make sure that the marks align after clamping. Small hulls can be clamped using a "workmate" bench. Place a second flat, rigid board on top of the assembly and grip both between the jaws of the bench. Apply equal pressure with both handles. It may be easier if the "workmate" is laid on its side. Bolts passing through both boards or "C" clamps may be used instead of the "workmate." Individual clamps can be made from 1×2 inch (25×50 mm) softwood with the 2-inch (50-mm) side in line with the bolts. If necessary, cut away the ends to reduce the length of the bolts. Steel or aluminum channel can also be used as a clamp. Another method of applying pressure is to place weights such as books, bricks or water-filled cans on the top board. Take care to get the pressure even. Less force is applied to the assembly than with clamps but it is controllable.

Stage 3

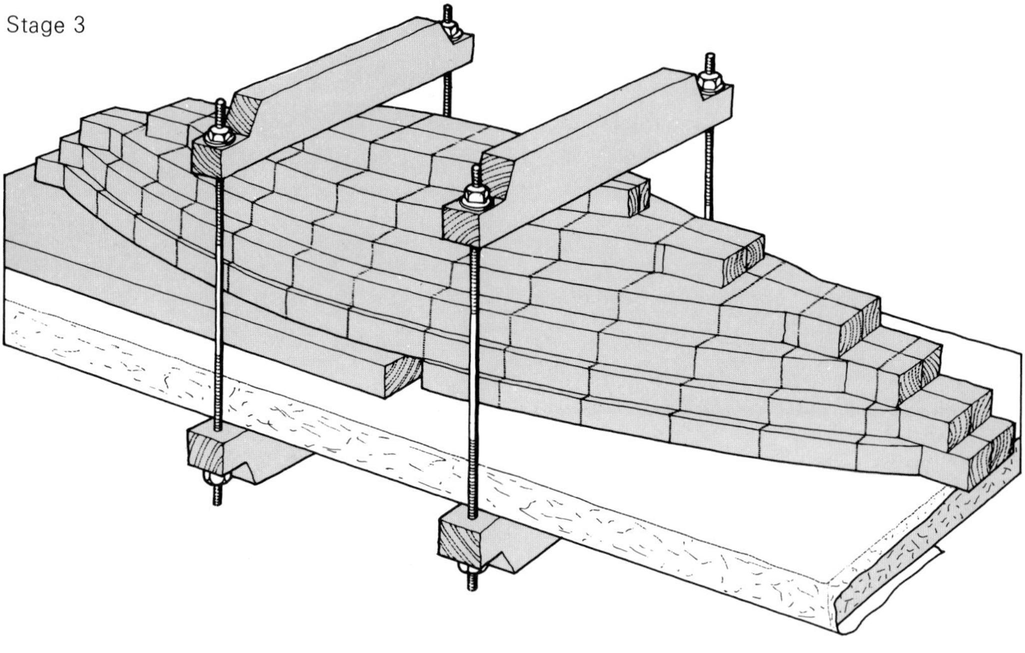

**Stage 4: Shaping the hull**
When the glue has set, remove the clamps. If your original calculations were accurate the joint lines between boards will be on the intended surface and only the protruding material in between will have to be removed.

First, place the hull right way up on the bench. Support the bow and stern with spare wood. Screw the hull to the bench through the bottom with at least two screws as far apart as possible. Clean up the inside with gouges as described for a solid-wood hull, stage 4, on page 308.

Finally, invert the hull and fix it to the bench using long bolts or a bench holdfast. Smooth the outside as for a solid-wood hull. Working the bow and stern will be easier if they overhang the edge of the bench.

Stage 4a

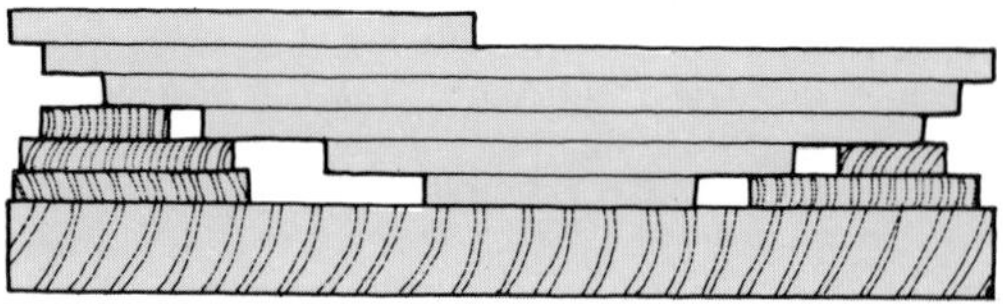

Stage 4b

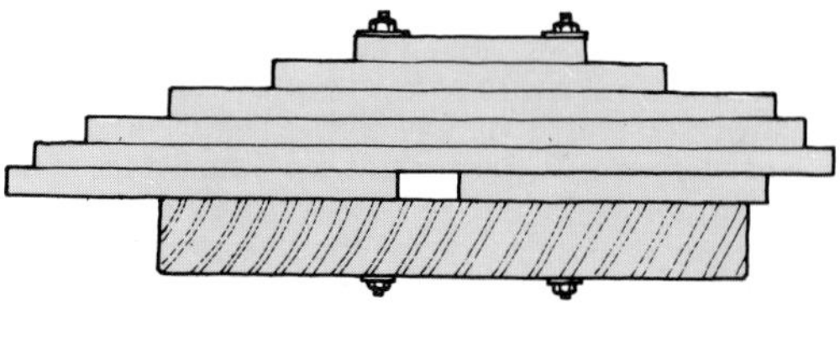

## Planked hulls

These are light, strong and constructed in a way which closely resembles the method of building full-size planked hulls. The planks are shaped over transverse wooden frames, temporarily fixed to a building board. When the frames are permanently built in to the hull, they are called bulkheads. Bulkhead construction is the easiest method for beginners. When they are temporary, they are called shadows or formers. In this case, they are used to position the backbone, inwales and ribs, and are removed after laying the planks. Ribbed structures are lighter than bulkhead ones and lack interior obstructions.

### Bulkhead construction

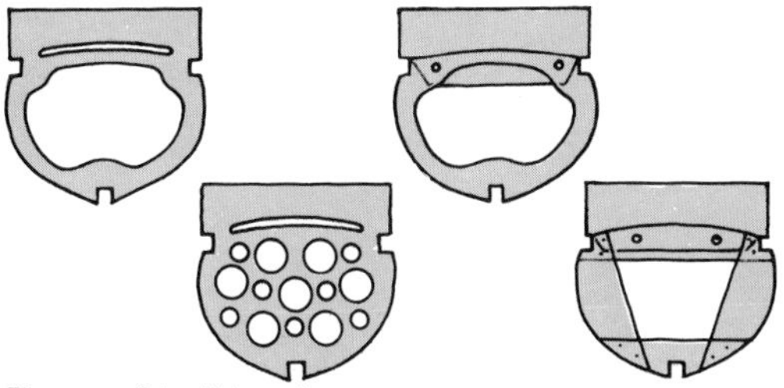

Types of bulkhead

On the sectional plans draw a line $\frac{3}{4}$ to $1\frac{1}{4}$ inches (20 to 30 mm) above the highest point of the hull to represent the building board. Make a tracing of each station line on a separate piece of paper, including the deck and building-board lines. Draw vertical lines from the deck edge to the building line. Inside the station line, draw a line representing the thickness of the hull, deck, inwales and backbone. This line plus the extension to the building line is the shape of the bulkhead.

Make the bulkheads out of resin-bonded plywood. The extensions may be partially severed to be cut off later or temporarily attached by screws. Cut out or drill through their centers to reduce their weight. Another method of construction is to join strips of plywood or solid wood. Mark the centerlines. One face of each bulkhead should sit on the station line. Bevel the edges of each bulkhead to match the taper of the hull for this position. Cut notches for the inwales and backbone, making the cuts at the same angle as the edges. Cut away the corners of the backbone notches to allow water to run to where it can be removed.

Next, fix the bulkheads to the building board. Screw a square-section wood strip at a right angle and flush with the end of each extension. Mark the station lines and centerline on the board. Screw the bulkheads to it from the back and through the wood strips, making sure that the station face of each bulkhead is positioned on the station line. A wood strip screwed to the back of the board will make it easier to hold the board in a vise. To form the bow (and stern of a double-ended hull), add a stempiece running forward from the first bulkhead. It should have a notch for the inwales and align with the bottom of the notch for the backbone. Let the last bulkhead form a transom stern.

The final stage before laying the planks is to glue the inwales and backbone into the notches. They can be made of solid lumber or plywood, or laminated from veneers which will follow the curve more easily. Choose a tough, straight-grained wood such as ash, pine or beech. If you use veneers, apply them one at a time, letting the glue dry before adding the next, and hold them in place with pins and clothespins. Fair the backbone into the stempiece, draw a centerline on both, then plane them to follow the contour of the bulkheads. Reinforce the bow and stern.

An alternative method of bulkhead construction includes a complete or partial plywood hull profile, sometimes with keel and skeg, running down the center of the hull. The bulkheads may need to be split.

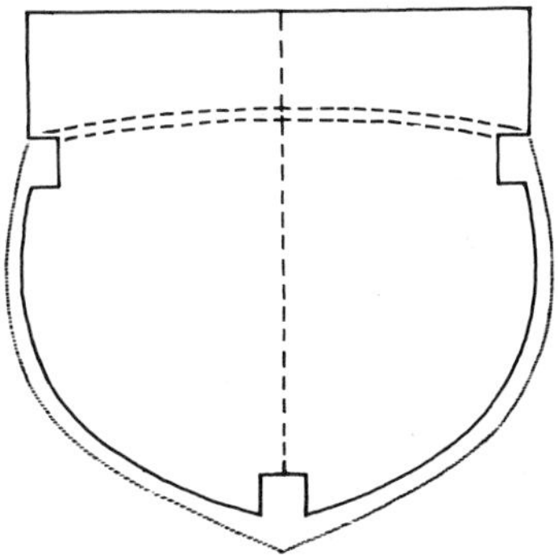

Drawing for a bulkhead

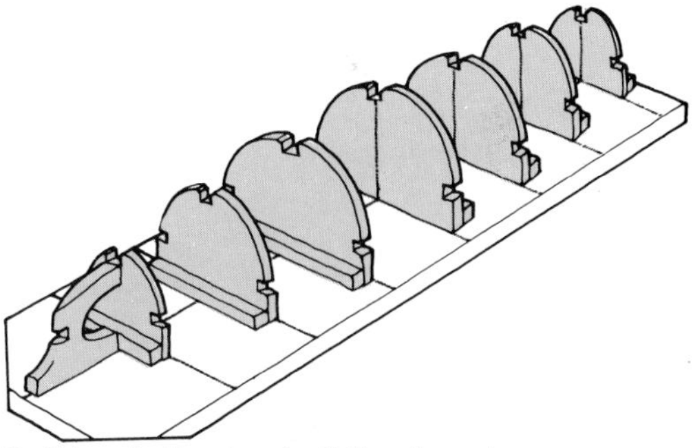

Bulkheads fixed to building board

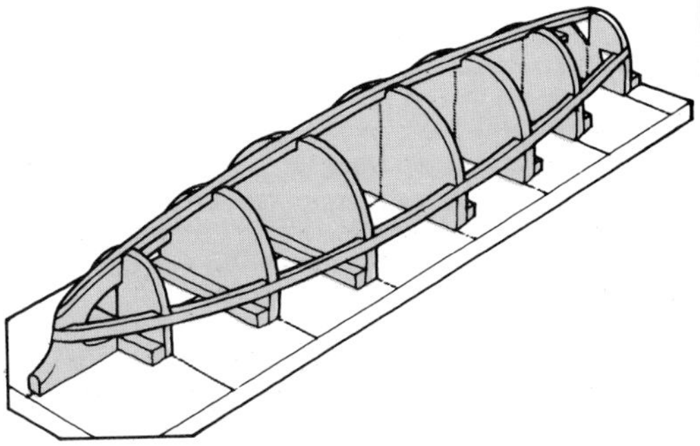

Inwales and backbone added

### Ribbed construction

Usually, ribs are cut from $\frac{1}{32}$ to $\frac{1}{16}$ inch (0.8 to 1.5 mm) plywood and are $\frac{1}{4}$ to $\frac{1}{2}$ inch (8 to 13 mm) wide, depending on the size of the boat. They can be a single piece or in two halves if the sides of the hull meet at a sharp angle at the keel. Ideally, ribs near the bow should be slightly curved if they are to follow the contour exactly, but this is not vital.

To build a ribbed hull, proceed as described for bulkhead construction but make shadows instead of bulkheads. These are smaller than bulkheads by the thickness of the ribs which are laid over them. As with bulkheads, the shadows should be beveled to allow for the taper of the hull. Attach them to the building board in the same way, screwing through from the back. Wax the shadows to prevent hull members from adhering to them in later stages.

Add the backbone and inwales and file a notch in them, flush with the shadows, to accept the ribs. Glue the ribs in place, holding them with pins until dry. The hull is now ready for planking. After planking remove the shadows by twisting them out, one by one.

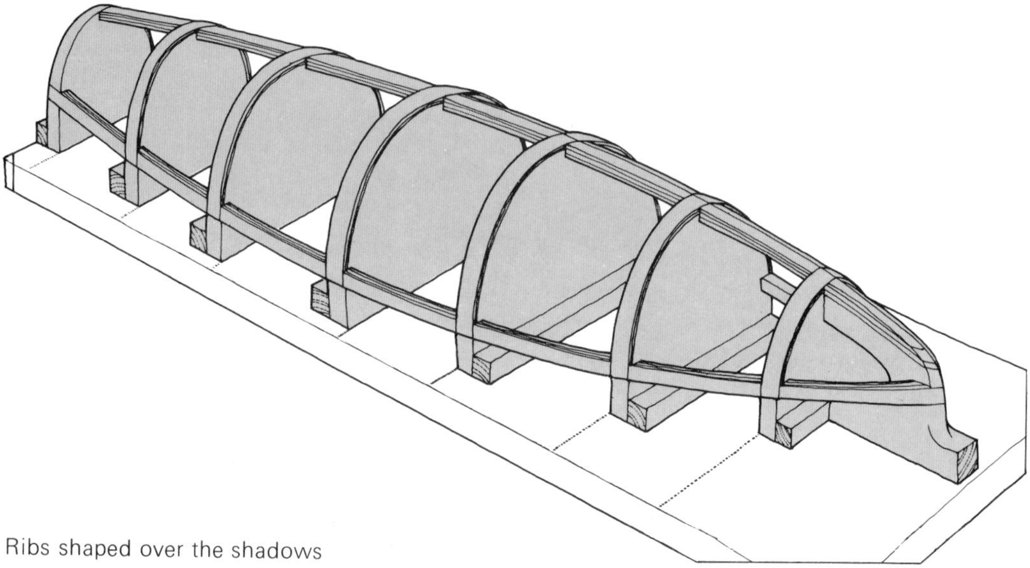

Ribs shaped over the shadows

### Carvel planking

This is a type of flush, butt-jointed planking. Veneers or plywood can be used, with the thickness varying from $\frac{1}{8}$ inch (2 mm) for hardwood on a small boat to $\frac{1}{4}$ inch (5 mm) for softwood on a big boat. The planks should be, as far as possible, of equal width. To calculate the width, measure the length around half a bulkhead at or near the center of the hull and divide this length into equal units, usually between $\frac{1}{2}$ to $\frac{3}{4}$ inch (12 to 20 mm). Bear in mind that the planks should not be reduced to less than half their original width to taper at bow and stern.

To attach a plank, apply glue to the bulkheads or ribs, transom, stem and the edge of the plank already in place; position the plank and secure it with pins until the glue is dry. Work from the gunwales to the keel. Where the planks on one side meet those on the other at the bow, chisel the ends of alternate planks flush so that the corresponding plank on the other side can lap it.

An alternative to planking right up to the bow is to stop inwales, backbone and planks on the last bulkhead and complete the hull with bread-and-butter laminations. If the laminations are shaped before planking, the planks can be carried over them to make a stronger bow.

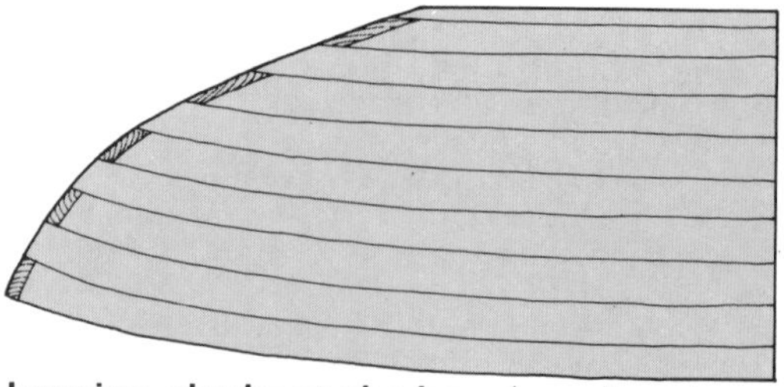

**Lapping planks at the bow** Lap alternate planks so that the ends interlock for strength.

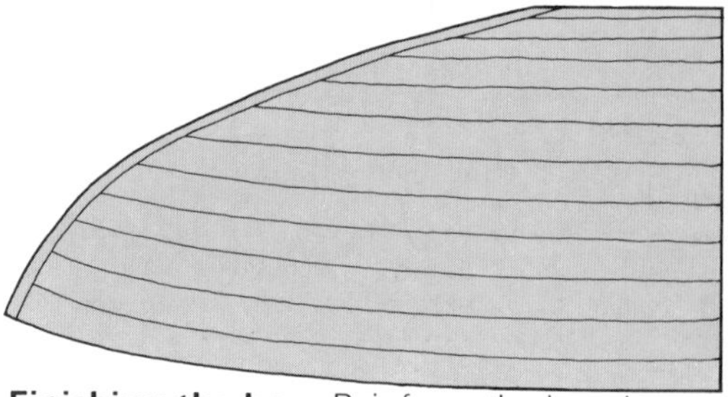

**Finishing the bow** Reinforce the bow by sanding it flat and gluing on a fillet. Sand the fillet flush with the planking.

### Clinker planking

This differs from carvel planking in that the planks lap one another like weather boarding rather than butting together. It is usual to pin as well as glue the planks together. In full-size boats the planks are riveted, adding considerable strength to the hull. Plywood is better than solid wood which tends to split when pinned near the edge. Use soft brass pins and drill holes for them with a slightly smaller diameter. Hammer the pins right through the hull and, once they have emerged, cut them off inside and clinch them.

### Diagonal planking

Instead of the conventional fore-and-aft method of planking, round-bilge hulls can be made very strong by laying short planks on the diagonal in two or more layers which cross each other at a right angle. This produces what amounts to a molded ply hull. Longitudinal stringers notched into the bulkheads or shadows are substituted for the ribs of the conventional method. The stringers need not form part of the finished hull as the planking imparts ample strength and stiffness.

The best material for the planks is veneer, but you can also use plywood or cardboard. The planks can be cut overlength and trimmed in situ when the glue is dry. Start laying the planks in the middle and work toward the ends. Glue the first layer to the backbone, inwales and stringers, if they are to remain, and the second layer to the first one. A good fit between planks is not essential for strength, but it improves the appearance, especially if you are finishing the surface with clear varnish.

### Skinned hulls

These are carvel or diagonal planked hulls covered with fiberglass cloth or a fabric. Substitute thicker planks of balsa for hardwood planks to speed up the planking process (accuracy is less important than with normal planked hulls). Keep the joints in the fabric to a minimum to reduce the amount of finishing which will be needed later on.

Apply one or more layers of material and, when set, rub the surface down with wet-and-dry paper. Fill any depressions with resin filler. In the final finishing stages it is easier to see irregularities if the hull is painted one overall color. Use a resin-base paint. The paint will also help fill small holes and rebond fibers that may have been exposed by the rubbing down. Running a hand over the hull will also detect irregularities, but beware of injuring yourself with fiberglass splinters which may have been produced during bonding.

The inside of the hull can be treated in a similar way to increase its strength and to waterproof the balsa. Local reinforcement can be added using other materials such as papier mâché or terylene and glue. The inside does not need to be rubbed down but splinters should be removed.

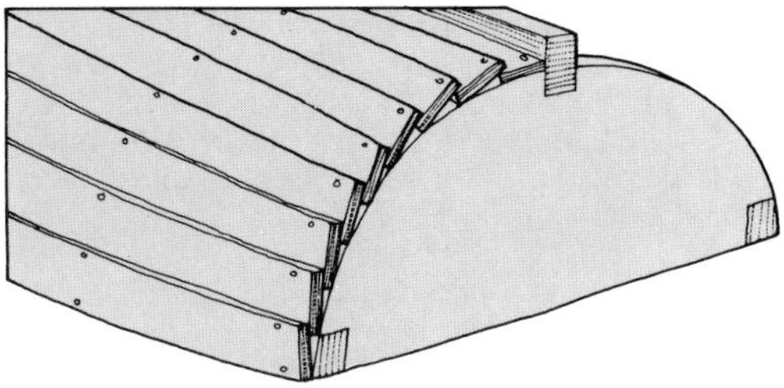

**Laying clinker planks** Fix the first plank next to the backbone and overlap each preceding plank as you work up the hull's side.

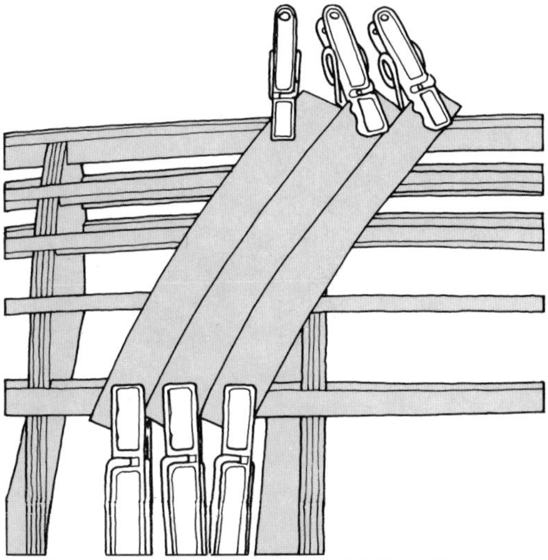

**Laying diagonal planks** Hold them in position with clothespins while the glue dries.

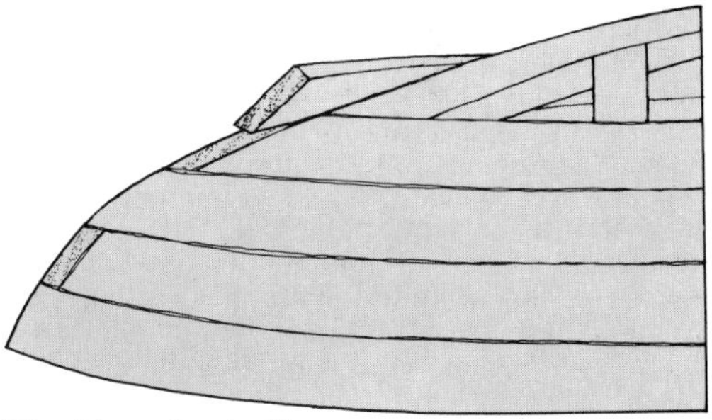

**Planking the hull**

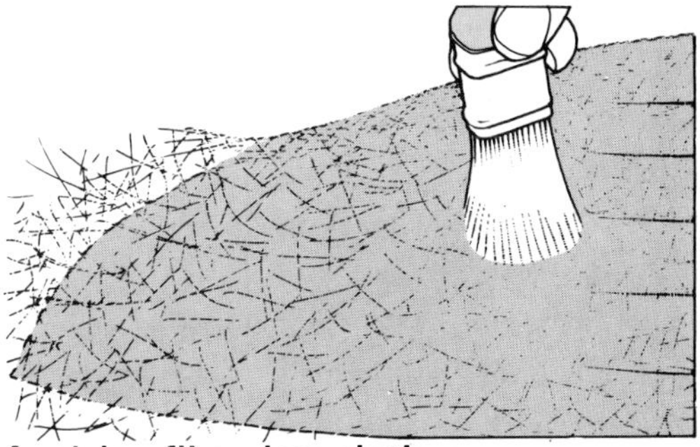

**Applying fiberglass cloth**

## Hard-chine hulls

These hulls have curved or flat surfaces which meet to form edges running longitudinally. Hard-chine hulls are less efficient than round-bilge designs when sailing across the wind because of turbulence created by the chines moving at an angle through the water. However, in other respects they are equal to round-bilge hulls and are superior at high speeds because they plane.

Hard-chine hulls are potentially lighter and quicker to build than round-bilge designs. Mold them in fiberglass as shown below, or shape them over bulkheads or shadows as described for a planked hull on pages 311 to 312. In addition to the backbone and inwales of a planked hull, a hard-chine hull usually has longitudinal chine members to carry the edges of the panels, although neither inwales, backbone nor chine members are essential. Panels can be cut oversize, attached, then trimmed in situ. Suitable materials for the panels include plywood, cardboard or sheet metal. Brass or tinplate panels are easy to solder together at the meeting joints.

Diagonal planking can be used with a hard-chine design for a decorative finish, but it is only necessary for covering double curves.

## Fiberglass hulls

These are molded from layers of fiberglass mat impregnated with resin. See pages 56 to 58 for working with fiberglass. The advantages of this hull are a high strength-to-weight ratio, easy repair and a good finish without the need to paint; the disadvantage is the time needed to make the mold.

In the case of a hard-chine design, it may be easiest to build a plywood or hardboard mold from scratch, rather like building a hull inside out. Treat the mold with wax and a release agent.

With more complex shapes it is easier to make a fiberglass mold from a pattern. This pattern may take the form of an existing hull or it can be carved from solid wood, made of bread-and-butter construction or shaped in plaster, wax, clay or modeling clay. If you are carving a pattern from solid wood, make templates from the plans to check the shape as you carve. Whatever type of pattern you use, always prepare it carefully as the surface finish affects the performance of a boat. By adding extra pieces to the mold pattern as shown opposite, it is possible to form inwales. Molded inwales add strength to the hull and provide a convenient surface for attaching the deck.

Mold the hull with care, first adding a gel coat, then applying several layers of mat for rigidity. Leave to cure. Bulkheads, engine mounts and mast steps should be glued in position while the hull is still in the mold. Glued-on inwales, in place of molded-in ones, can be added now, too.

Decks can be molded separately in fiberglass. The method allows you to make turtleback and detailed designs.

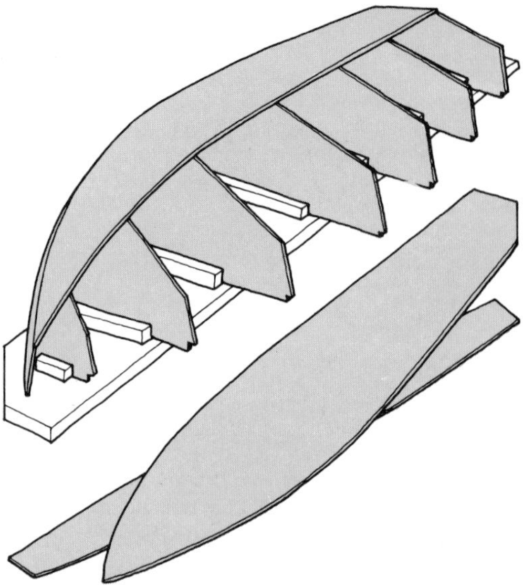

**Building without longitudinal members** Glue the panels together over the bulkheads or shadows, then reinforce the joints with fiberglass strips. Add the inwales after removing the hull from the building board.

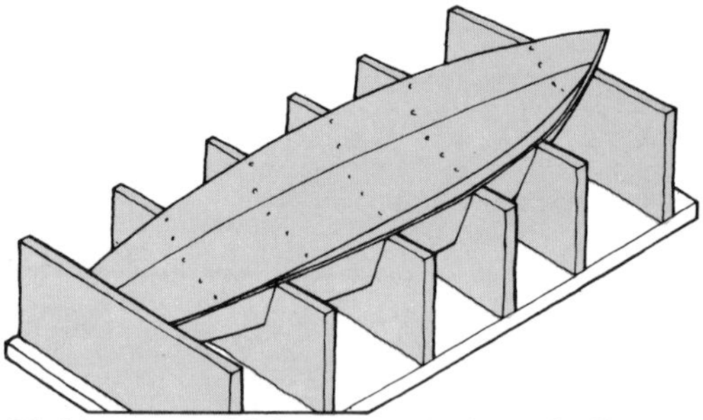

**Making a mold for a hard-chine hull** Working from the plans, cut transverse formers to carry the panels, allowing for the thickness of the panels. Nail and glue the panels in position, smooth side inside, and fill all holes and cracks.

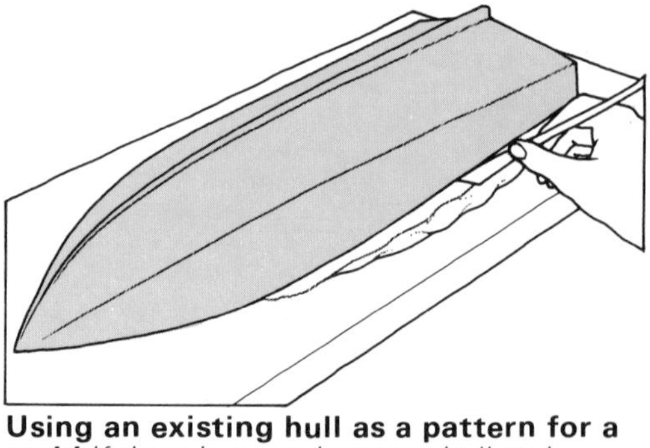

**Using an existing hull as a pattern for a mold** If there is a gap between hull and baseboard, fill it in to avoid trapping the hull in the mold and to control the shape of the edge.

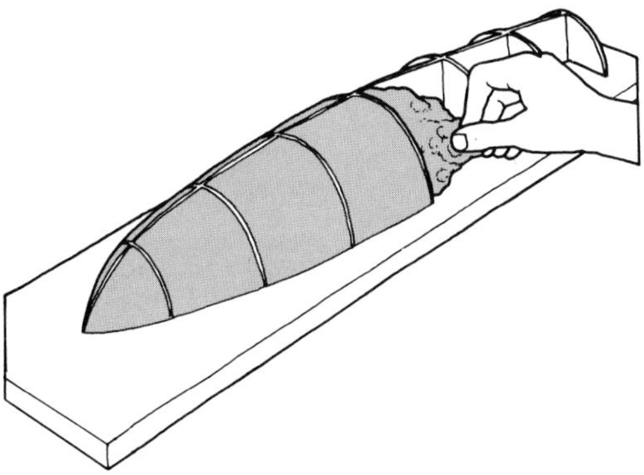

**Making a mold pattern from modeling clay** Trace profiles from the plans onto cardboard or plywood, mount them on a baseboard, then fill in the spaces with clay.

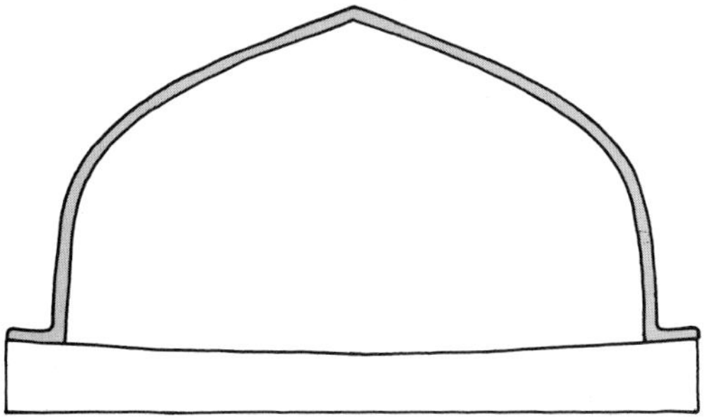

**Molding inwales** Add extra pieces to the mold pattern to form an external flange. Make sure that the flange follows the camber of the deck, if there is one.

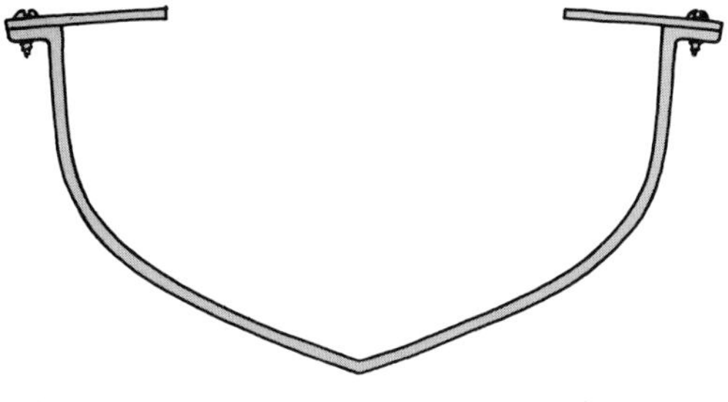

When the mold has cured, screw a strip of plastic laminate to the edge, letting it overhang inside.

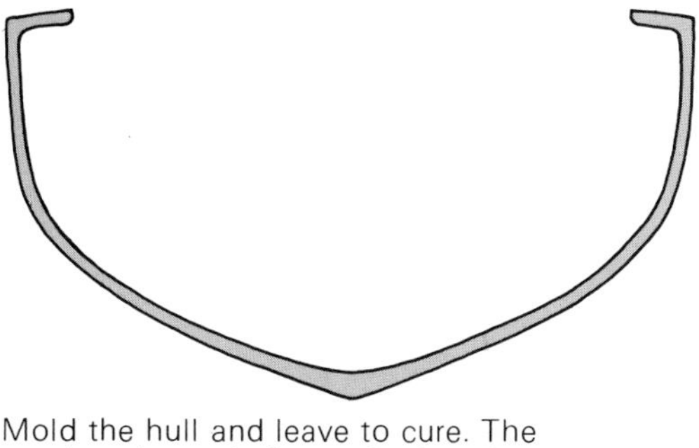

Mold the hull and leave to cure. The overhanging strip forms the inwales.

## Vacuum-formed hulls

A wide variety of ready-made vacuum-formed hulls are available, including turtleback designs, which only require fitting out. Although they can be made at home, an expensive machine is needed for the shaping process.

Take care when adding internal reinforcements, such as bulkheads or mast steps, as gluing to polystyrene or acrylobutyl styrene (the usual materials used for the hull) is not easy. There are specific adhesives for gluing each of these materials to itself. To bond other materials to the hull, use epoxy or contact adhesives and roughen the surface before gluing. (See Adhesives, pages 39 to 42.)

### Buoyancy for racing powerboats

As powerboat racing inevitably involves high-speed impacts between boats, it is essential to build buoyancy into the hull to avoid the loss of expensive equipment. A convenient method is to mold polyurethane foam, which comes as a ready-to-mix liquid in two parts, directly into the hull. The foam also adds considerable strength and reduces the noise made by the hull as it rides over the water.

The access hatch to the compartment to be filled should be about 2 inches (50 mm) in diameter. Following the manufacturer's instructions, estimate the volume of the compartment and thoroughly mix slightly more liquid than needed. (If it is difficult to estimate the volume because the hull has a complex shape, mix too little to fill the compartment and repeat as necessary.) Pour the mixture into the compartment immediately after mixing. When the foam begins to emerge from the opening, temporarily restrict its exit to force it to fill the whole space by holding a piece of wood across the opening. Remove the wood after a few seconds to allow the foam to complete its expansion. When set, saw off the projecting part with a hacksaw blade and cover the exposed surface with a thin layer of fiberglass to protect it from abrasion.

Where weight is critical, as with electric racing boats, or where a thin vacuum-formed hull might be distorted by the expanding foam, add buoyancy by packing the hull with expanded polystyrene in the form of broken ceiling tiles or loose beads, or polyethylene "bubble sheet" packing material.

Another method of adding buoyancy is to insert inflatable plastic bags into the hull cavities, then blow them up.

# Keels

The keel, sometimes called a fin, is the vertical member which projects below the bottom of the hull.

A shallow keel can be built integral with the hull as a keel cum backbone, with the lead weight at the tip. It may be a simple plywood shape or part of bread-and-butter construction. Include the base of a bread-and-butter keel with the last hull lamination to avoid a weak joint where hull meets keel.

A bread-and-butter keel can be held on by bolts, screws or dowels passing through the hull. To make it removable for easier transport and to relieve any stress caused by the weight, just extend the bolts and enclose them in a tube or a block of wood; secure the bolts with wing nuts. The tops of the tubes or blocks should be above the waterline to prevent water from entering the boat, and attached to the bulkheads or cross beams to spread the load. The keel will be stronger if you carry the bolts or lengths of threaded rod right through the keel; cast the bolts into the lead weight or fix them to the weight with counterbored nuts.

It is best to make deep keels separately from the hull and hold them in a plywood, fiberglass or plastic laminate box built inside the hull, or in a mortise built into a bread-and-butter hull. Deep keels produce a lot of leverage when the boat heels so attach the box or mortise to deck beams or bulkheads to spread the load. Also, extend the box or mortise above water level to prevent water from entering. Fix the keel in place by pushing a wedge into a slot in the keel and the edge of the box or mortise, or screw a wing nut onto a bolt built into the keel. The keel can be permanently attached to the hull, if you wish, but be sure to bring it through to deck level and brace it to spread the load.

Deep keels can be cut from marine plywood or solid wood with the grain running lengthwise. They can also be molded from fiberglass in two halves, then glued together with the retaining bolts trapped in between. Another method of construction is to bend two skins of thin plywood around a metal girder and carry the girder into the hull; glue the plywood along the meeting edges. A similar type can be made from tinplate or sheet aluminum. Solder the edges of the tinplate; epoxy-glue the aluminum. Hollow keels can be filled with foamed plastic to add stiffness and exclude water (see Buoyancy for racing powerboats, page 315). Use a single strip of aluminum to make a thin, blade-like fin; round off the leading and trailing edges with a file to make it more streamlined.

Deep keels can also be built in as part of a complete hull profile cut from plywood.

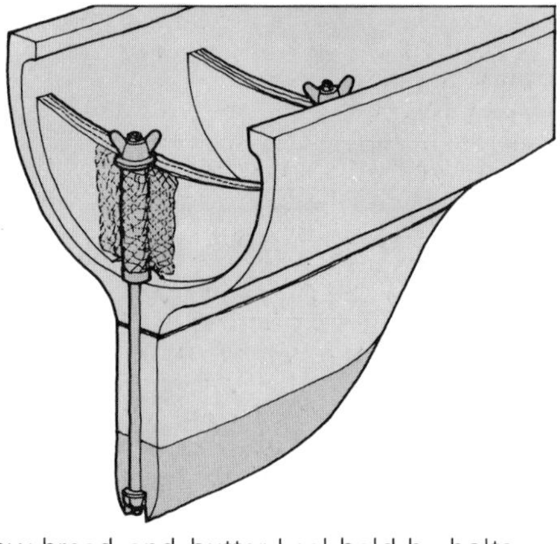

Shallow bread-and-butter keel held by bolts

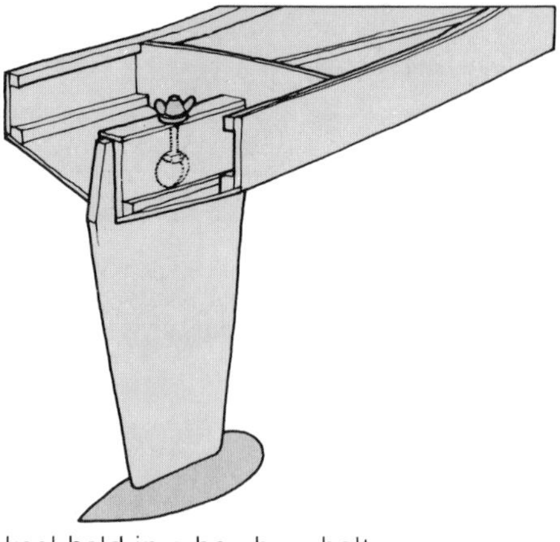

Deep keel held in a box by a bolt

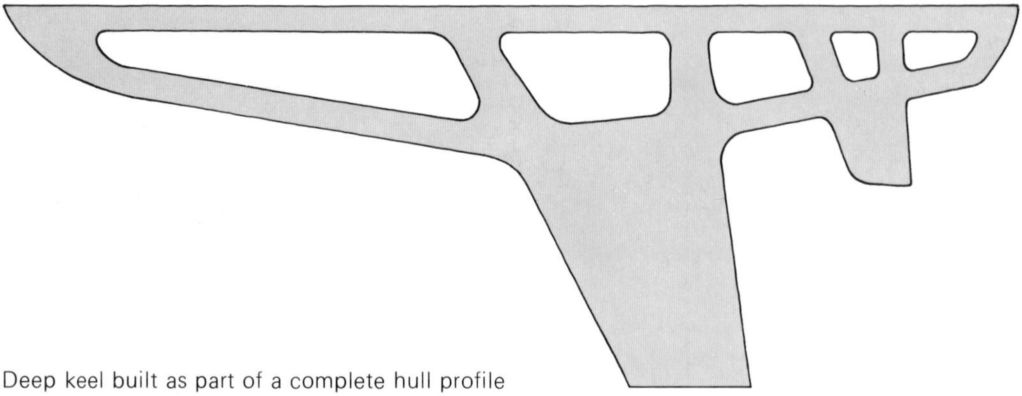

Deep keel built as part of a complete hull profile

## Keel weights

Lead ballast should be at the tip of the keel to balance wind pressure on the sails. Bread-and-butter keels may have this weight forming the tip. Hollow fiberglass keels can contain lead shot inside. Narrow-bladed keels need a teardrop-shaped metal bulb at the tip to minimize drag.

**Keel weight construction**

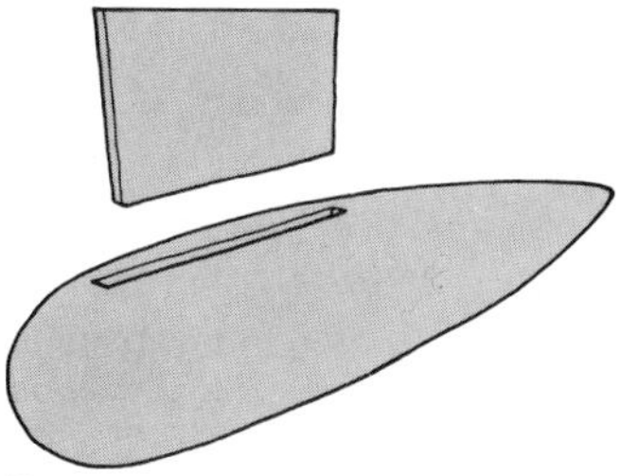

Keel epoxy-glued into a mortise in a lead bulb

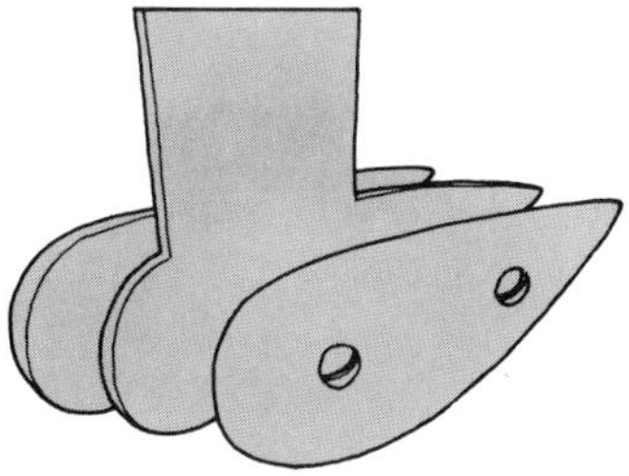

Bulb cast in two parts then screwed and glued to keel

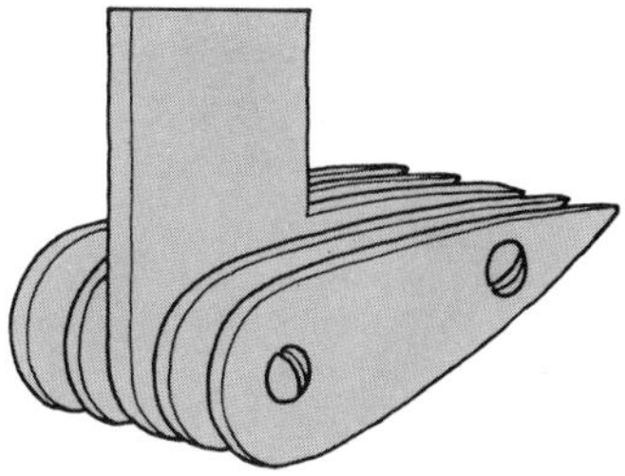

Bulb made of lead-sheet laminations, glued and screwed through keel

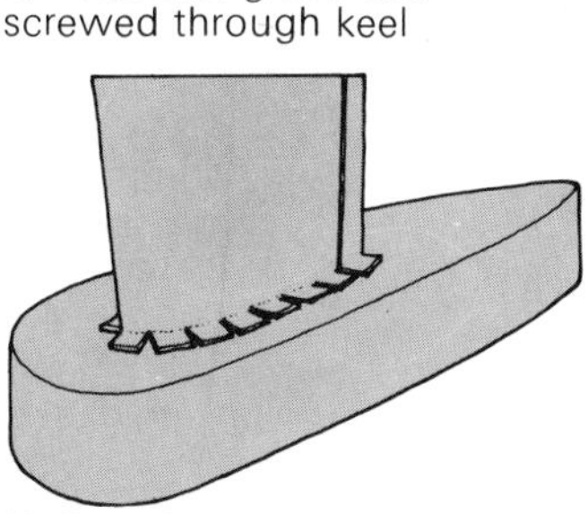

Hollow tinplate keel soldered to a lead bulb

# Rudders

The direction of the hull is controlled by the rudder. It produces sidethrust when placed at an angle to the stream of water passing over it, making the hull turn. When the rudder moves to the right, the boat turns to the right and to the left when the rudder is turned to the left.

Rudders are placed at the back of the hull where they produce the most turning force. They are designed to pivot at a point between their leading edge and center because a rudder which pivots at its leading edge tends to be pushed back to a straight course by the water and forces a sailboat making leeway to windward. If the areas behind and in front of the pivot were equal, a rudder would not tend to be turned by the water at all; however, in practice, some self-centering is usually desirable.

There are three types of rudder in general use: those used with radio-control power- and sailboats which are called "spade" rudders because of their shape, those used with self-steering gear in sailboats, and ratchet-operated rudders for free-running power- and sailboats. Both radio-control and ratchet-operated rudders can be used in pairs, linked together by a pushrod.

## Radio-control rudders

These can be installed in the hull or outside on the transom. The bearing for an in-hull rudder is formed by the close fit of the rudder shaft in the rudder tube or by a bush at each end of the tube. The tube is often filled with grease or oil to keep out the water. The shaft may pass through the deck or end inside the hull, but the tube should end above the waterline to prevent water entering the hull. Fix the top end of a tube which ends below deck level to a bulkhead or a cross beam. The joint between the tube and hull bottom must be made absolutely watertight.

Transom-mounted rudders for powerboats are held in a bracket which attaches to the transom. Sometimes the bracket carries one or two propeller-shaft struts and engine-cooling water scoops. Some incorporate a shear pin which breaks on impact with an obstruction, allowing the rudder blade to pivot upward rather than damage the hull. Others have a replaceable blade which bends or breaks on impact, or a flexible tiller arm to protect the servo gears.

Radio-control rudders are controlled by a tiller arm, usually sold with the rudder, which is attached to the top of the rudder shaft by a built-in clamp. The clamp allows the tiller to be fixed at any angle for convenient linking to the servo, via a pushrod. The pushrod is inserted into one of the holes in the tiller arm – the nearer to the rudder pivot that the pushrod is placed, the more the rudder will move for a given movement of the servo. (See Linkages, pages 260 to 264.)

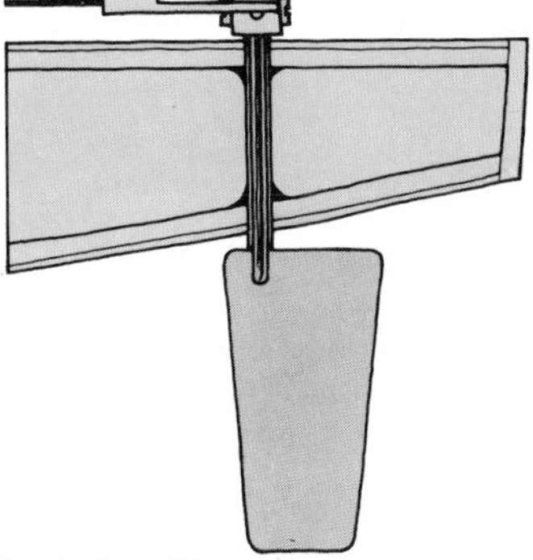

In-hull rudder

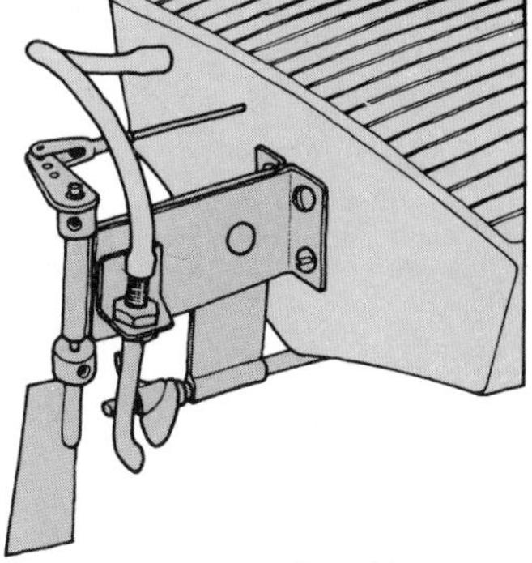

Transom-mounted rudder

## Self-steering gear for sailboats

This allows a sailboat to steer a straight course at a predetermined angle to the wind, without radio control. The wind provides both the power to move the rudder and the directional reference.

Most self-steering systems are the vane type. The vane, a wing-like structure, is mounted nearly vertical on a pivot so that it tends to align itself with the wind. It is connected to the rudder in such a way that when the boat is deflected from its preset course, the rudder automatically moves in the opposite direction to bring the boat back on course. The vane has to be reset for any change in course, including when tacking.

The Draper system, a variation of vane steering, uses two gear wheels, one fixed to the top of the rudder shaft and one on the pivot to which the vane is attached. To set the course, you just lift the vane gear wheel out of mesh, turn it to the desired angle and remesh it. Another simple type uses a pin in a slot and a friction clamp to set the angle of the vane.

Braine steering gear employs a self-centering spring and the pressure of the wind on the mainsail via sheets hooked to the tiller, to control the working of the rudder.

Tacking systems are essential for racing yachts. They allow the vane to switch from one tack to another when the boat is turned by hand at the bank. If the steering system has an adjustable spring, called a gye, the boat will tack on its own in mid water. Set the gye to pull the vane across when the wind slackens momentarily.

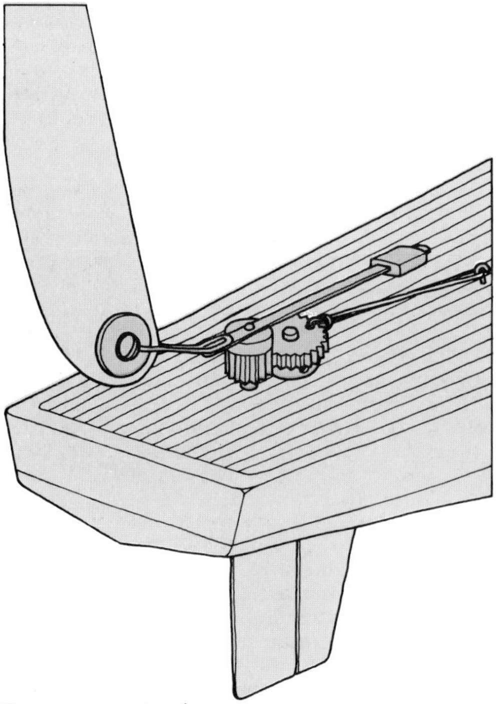

Draper vane steering

### Mounting rudders for self-steering gear

Pass the rudder shaft through the hull in a tube, leaving clearance between shaft and tube. The tube should be sealed into the hull. Rudder friction must be kept to a minimum so use a pin bearing at the bottom of the rudder shaft and a pin or knife-edge bearing at the top. The bottom bearing can be cantilevered from the skeg or keel.

The successful operation of a vane steering system depends on a delicate balance between the forces of wind and water; therefore, it is desirable to neutralize the weight of the vane and the buoyancy of the rudder when the boat heels by adding counterweights to the steering gear. (Rudder buoyancy is usually sufficiently countered by the weight of the tiller arm.) Adjust the weights by trial and error with the boat in the water.

## Ratchet-operated rudder

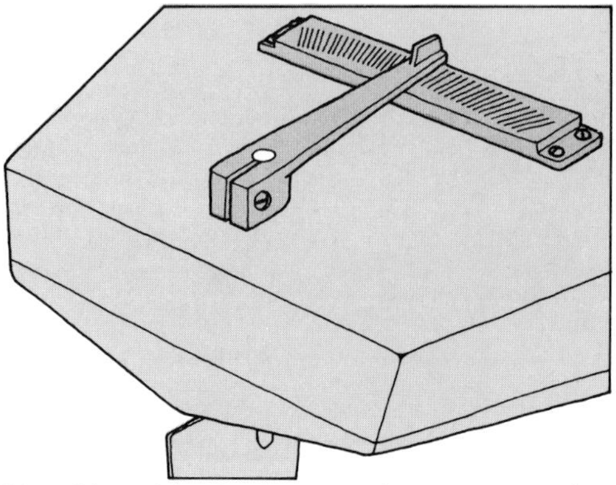

Use this rudder for free-running power- and sailboats. A lug on the tip of the tiller arm presses against a serrated plate. The tiller can be set for any position.

# Trim tabs

The attitude of a planing powerboat is controlled by trim tabs, either preset or radio control, mounted on the bottom edge of the transom. They can be used individually to resist roll caused by propeller torque, or together to adjust fore and aft trim – with the tabs raised, the bow rides high; lowered, the bow rides low.

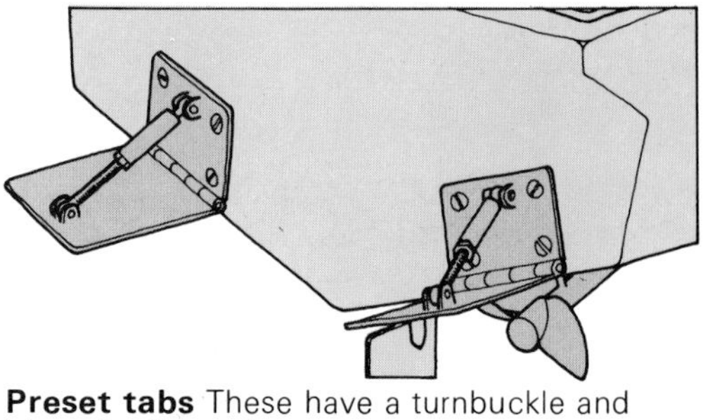

**Preset tabs** These have a turnbuckle and hinge for fine adjustment.

# Mounting motors and engines

A marine engine, whether internal combustion, electric or steam, is mounted backward so that it pushes the model through the water. It can be inboard with the propeller projecting through the hull, or outboard with motor and propeller swiveling together, dispensing with the need for a rudder. Inboard-outboard and jet drives are variations of these two types.

Turn to the motors and engines chapter for information on running and breaking in.

## Inboard motors and engines

These are the most common. Both internal combustion engines and electric motors can be mounted inboard; steam engines can only be mounted inboard.

In each case, the position of the engine is critical. Its center should align exactly with the centerline of the hull or the boat will tend to turn, although high-powered craft may need some sidethrust to compensate for the torque effect of the engine. Likewise, the angle of the engine and propeller-shaft assembly to the hull affects the boat's performance. Bad alignment may cause vibration which damages the components. The recommended dimensions are usually given on the plan or come with a preformed plastic hull.

Internal combustion engines and electric motors are beam-mounted through side lugs in the motor casing. The lugs can be bolted to wooden bearers or bolted to one of a range of commercial mounting plates. One popular aluminum-alloy plate can be screwed to a wooden block shaped to follow the contour of the hull and bonded in place with fiberglass resin, or fixed to posts bonded to the hull. Steam engines have to be base-mounted onto a wooden platform.

The standard propeller shaft runs in a tube with a bearing at each end to reduce friction. It is connected to the engine by a coupling which, in turn, reduces friction on the bearings. The tube forms a waterproof seal at the bottom of the hull. The shaft itself should be lubricated with oil or grease to restrict the entry of water. Use a special flexible shaft or a universal coupling between shaft and prop for boats which need the propeller positioned horizontally with the engine at an angle. For vertically mounted steam engines where the shaft is at an angle, use a flexible shaft or a universal coupling between engine and shaft.

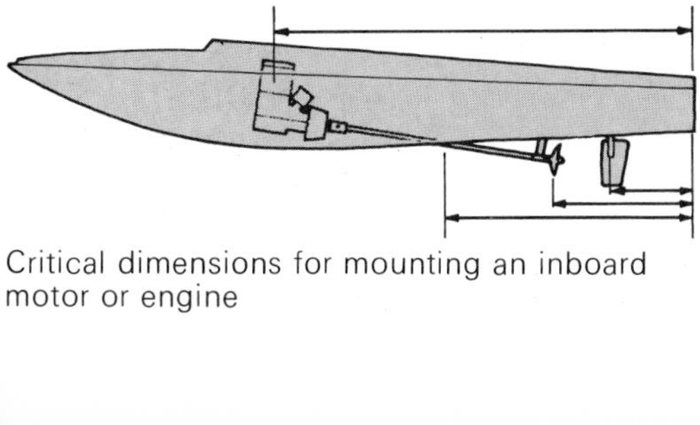

Critical dimensions for mounting an inboard motor or engine

### Mounting procedure

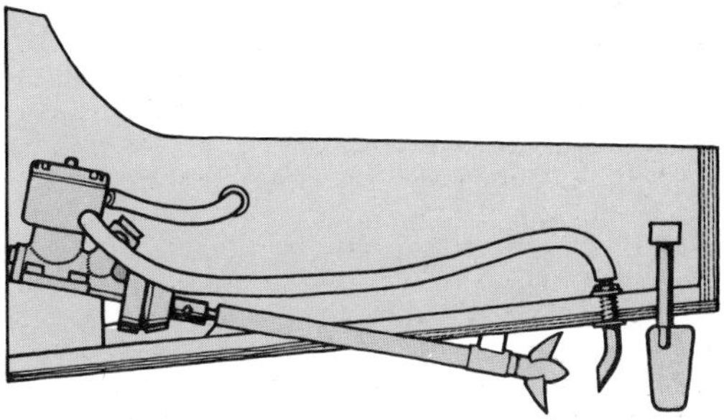

Standard propeller-shaft installation

If you have not made provision for the propeller shaft when constructing the hull, cut a slot for it through the hull. Begin by marking the shaft tube's entry and exit points, working from the plan. Next, drill a vertical hole, the diameter of the tube, right through the hull at each point. (It may be necessary to reinforce both sides of the keel.) Cut a slot between the holes using a miniature keyhole saw.

Temporarily assemble the engine and the propeller shaft (the shaft should be in its tube and with the strut if one is to be used) and position the assembly in the hull with the engine mount, to test for fit. It is easier to align the assembly accurately if it is rigidly joined so clamp a split tube over the coupling, if you are using a ball and socket or universal coupling, to lock it. Replace other types of coupling with a piece of threaded tube. Adjust the engine mount or reposition the engine assembly until engine and prop shaft are at the correct angle. If you are using the type of mounting plate which screws to a wooden block, cut the block to the approximate angle, then attach the plate to the block. Test and trim the block until the mount is at the exact angle. Bolt the engine to the plate for the last few checks.

When you are satisfied that the assembly fits correctly, tack the mount, propeller shaft tube and strut to the hull with fiberglass resin. Recheck all the dimensions before the resin cures. Remove the engine and shaft after the resin sets and apply self-adhesive tape or modeling clay to the bottom of the hull around the tube to close the slot. Reinforce the mounting and propeller tube joints with fiberglass tape and resin. When set, peel away the tape or clay and fill any depressions in the surface with color-matching resin filler. Replace the engine and shaft, this time with the flexible coupling. Attach the propeller afterward.

Marine internal combustion engines have water-cooled heads which need to be supplied with water. Install a water scoop behind the propeller. Use a plastic tube to connect the scoop to the bottom input of the engine jacket. Attach another plastic tube to the output; this tube should exit through the hull above the waterline. Seal the joints between tubes and hull with fiberglass resin.

## Couplings

It is impossible to align the propeller shaft and engine perfectly. Flexible couplings are used at the joint to absorb any movement caused by misalignment and reduce friction and strain on the bearings. Four types are shown below.

If there is too much slack between the inboard end of the shaft and the coupling, the coupling may disconnect when the engine is put into reverse. Pack out the inboard end of the shaft with a distance piece, allowing a small amount of play, so that the propeller thrust is taken by the outboard shaft-tube bearing.

Ball and pin coupling: This type allows for axial misalignment.

Universal coupling: This should be used in cases where there is designed-in misalignment.

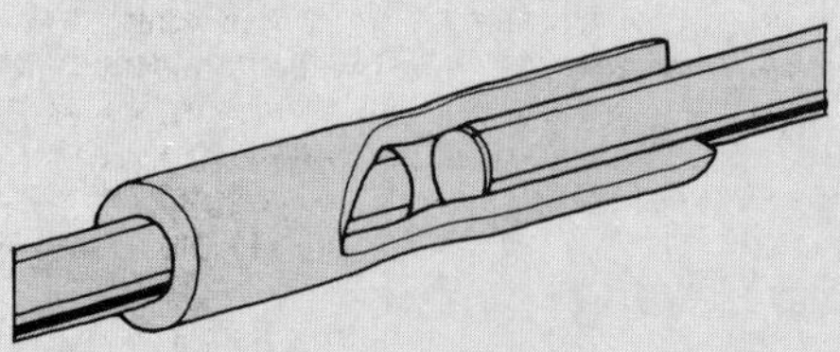

Soft coupling: A flexible plastic tube, this accommodates radial and axial misalignment but very little longitudinal movement.

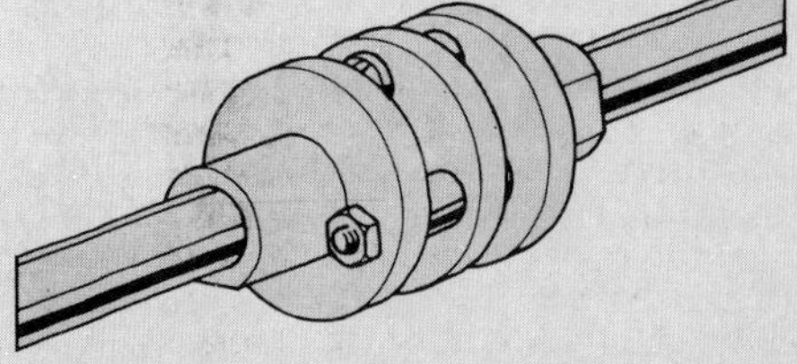

Soft coupling: In this case, a thin rubber disk is attached to the components by metal strips. It absorbs a small amount of longitudinal and axial misalignment but no radial.

## Inboard-outboard motors

These consist of a motor (usually electric), transmission and steerable propeller, and are either transom- or bottom-mounted. A rudder is not needed, simplifying installation and making maneuverability good.

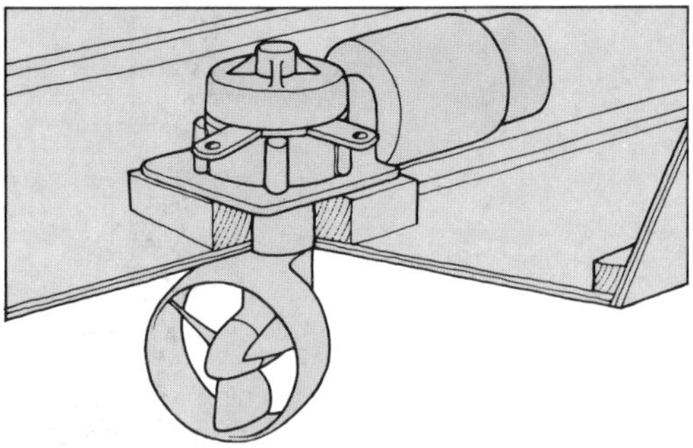

## Outboard motors and engines

Outboards are usually electric but may be internal combustion. The transmission and propeller, which form a single unit, are mounted on the outside of the transom. No rudder is needed. Like inboard-outboard motors, maneuverability is good; installation is even simpler as it is not necessary to pierce the hull.

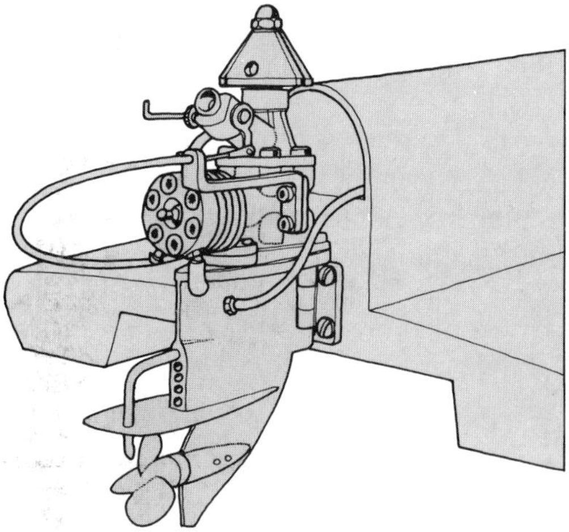

## Jet drives

These systems have an inboard motor, either electric or gas-powered, driving a propeller in a duct. Water enters the duct from below the hull and is driven out through a nozzle at the back, propelling the boat forward. The nozzle swivels to steer the boat. Sometimes the system includes a reversing nozzle.

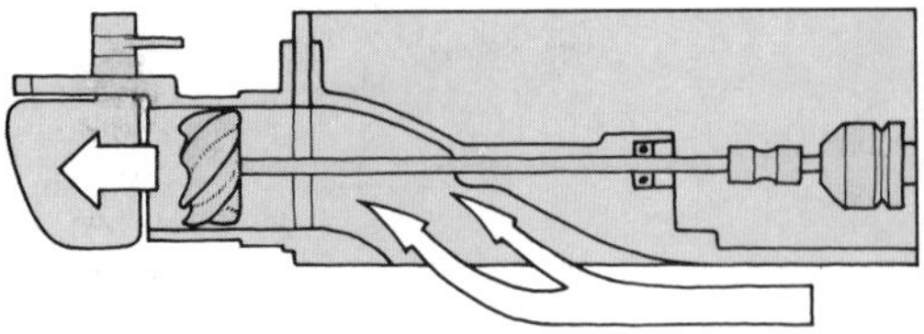

# Decks

Most decks require some form of internal support, particularly flat decks. If it is not provided by the hull structure, for example by the bulkheads of a planked hull, you will need to install deck beams and a kingplank. Cut beams from plywood or solid wood. Work from the plan, or plot their shape from the hull by measuring the height of the deck centerline above the gunwales and the distance between the inwales at each deck beam location.

Decks can be made from structural veneer, marine plywood, plastic laminate, molded or flat fiberglass, acrylobutyl styrene, polystyrene or aluminum. If the deck centerline is straight or has the same curve as the sheer line, cut the deck from one piece of flat sheet material. To mark the cut line, first cut out an oversized blank of the material and fix it temporarily to the hull with two widely spaced screws. Invert the hull and mark around the edge, bending the deck into contact with the gunwale if necessary. Remove the deck before cutting along the line. If the deck has compound curves, it will have to be molded or made up of several pieces of sheet material.

Plot the outline of any openings in the deck, then cut them out. Internal details in contact with the deck can be made to print their image on the bottom of the deck: just apply paint to the details, then press the deck onto them. Cut a hole in the transom or deck for draining off water. (Keep it sealed when the boat is in the water with a rubber stopper. The end of a car tire valve and cap, or a plastic, tablet tube and cap, glued in the hole is also effective for keeping any water out.)

Before gluing on the deck, mount any deck fittings which are not supported by deck beams and require reinforcement. Fittings near a hatch can be installed after decking by putting a hand through the opening. Any nut or reinforcement on the deck underside should be attached so that it is not lost if the fitting is later removed and replaced. Begin by plotting the positions of the fittings, then glue pieces of $\frac{1}{8}$ inch (3 mm) plywood to the bottom of the deck to spread the load and to provide a good material to screw into. Another method is to glue on large washers or metal plates. Nuts can be glued or soldered to them, or holes pierced in them to take self-tapping screws to reduce strain on the deck when rigging (run the screw in and out of the hole before attaching the plate).

Glue the deck in place using waterproof woodworking adhesive for wooden decks and hulls, and epoxy or contact adhesive for the others. (Test the compatibility of the adhesive beforehand on scrap material.) It may also be necessary to screw down thermoplastic material. Roughen the meeting surfaces well, particularly with plastic materials. Screw in the two screws and hold the deck down tight all around with adhesive tape. The tape gives a light, even pressure and reduces the risk of distorting the hull.

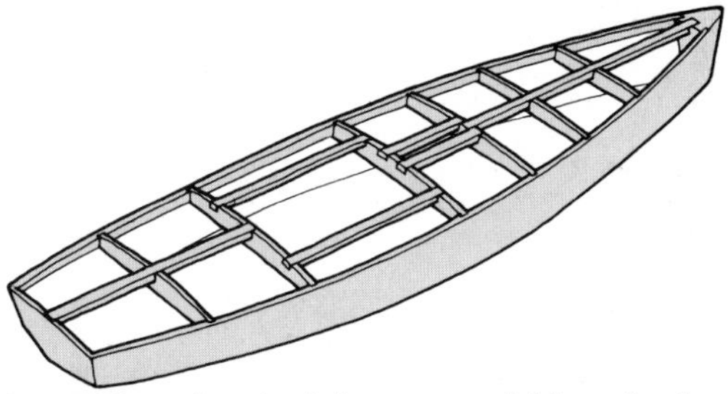

**Installing the deck beams and kingplank**
Glue the beams into the inwales, then glue the kingplank into the beams. You can allow for through masts or hatches by stopping the kingplank and then using carlings (short longitudinal members) to support the deck.

Another method is to butt joint short lengths of kingplank between the deck beams then reinforce the joints with wooden corner blocks.

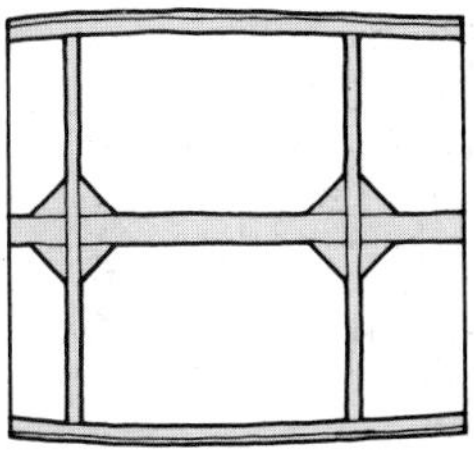

## Hatches

You will need access to the hull to maintain the engine, to adjust radio-control linkages or simply to remove water. The entire superstructure or a large part of the deck of many electric- and steam-powered boats is removable. Often, one side is hooked in position and the other held by rubber bands or ball or magnetic catches. A simple magnetic catch can be formed by two strips of magnetic rubber, one on the main structure, the other on the cover. Many powerboats rely on friction and a good fit to hold the cover on. The best method of making the superstructure or cover watertight is to run a self-adhesive, foam-rubber strip around the edge.

For smaller hatch covers, just screw a piece of sheet material over the opening in the deck or flush with the deck, onto a rubber seal – a clear plastic cover will allow you to make visual inspections of the equipment without removing the cover. If you need frequent access to the hull, let a container, such as a sandwich box, tobacco tin, storage jar or resealable coffee tin, with the bottom cut off, into the deck and seal the raised edge of the hatch (the coaming) to the deck with mastic. You can also scratch-build a hatch and cover from plywood, solid wood or plastic. Run a self-adhesive, foam-rubber strip around this type of cover to make the hatch watertight. A simple and light way of holding on the cover is to fix one end of a rubber band or spring to the cover and the other end to the hull bottom. The tops of both the container or scratch-built types should be easy to remove. A range of commercial hatch coamings and covers is also available.

# Masts, booms and rigging

These fittings hold the sails in the correct position. There is a wide variety of designs and, although most can be bought, many modelers build their own from scratch. The illustration below shows one of the most common types of rigging. For other types, see page 326.

**Typical rigging for a free-running Bermuda-rig sailboat**

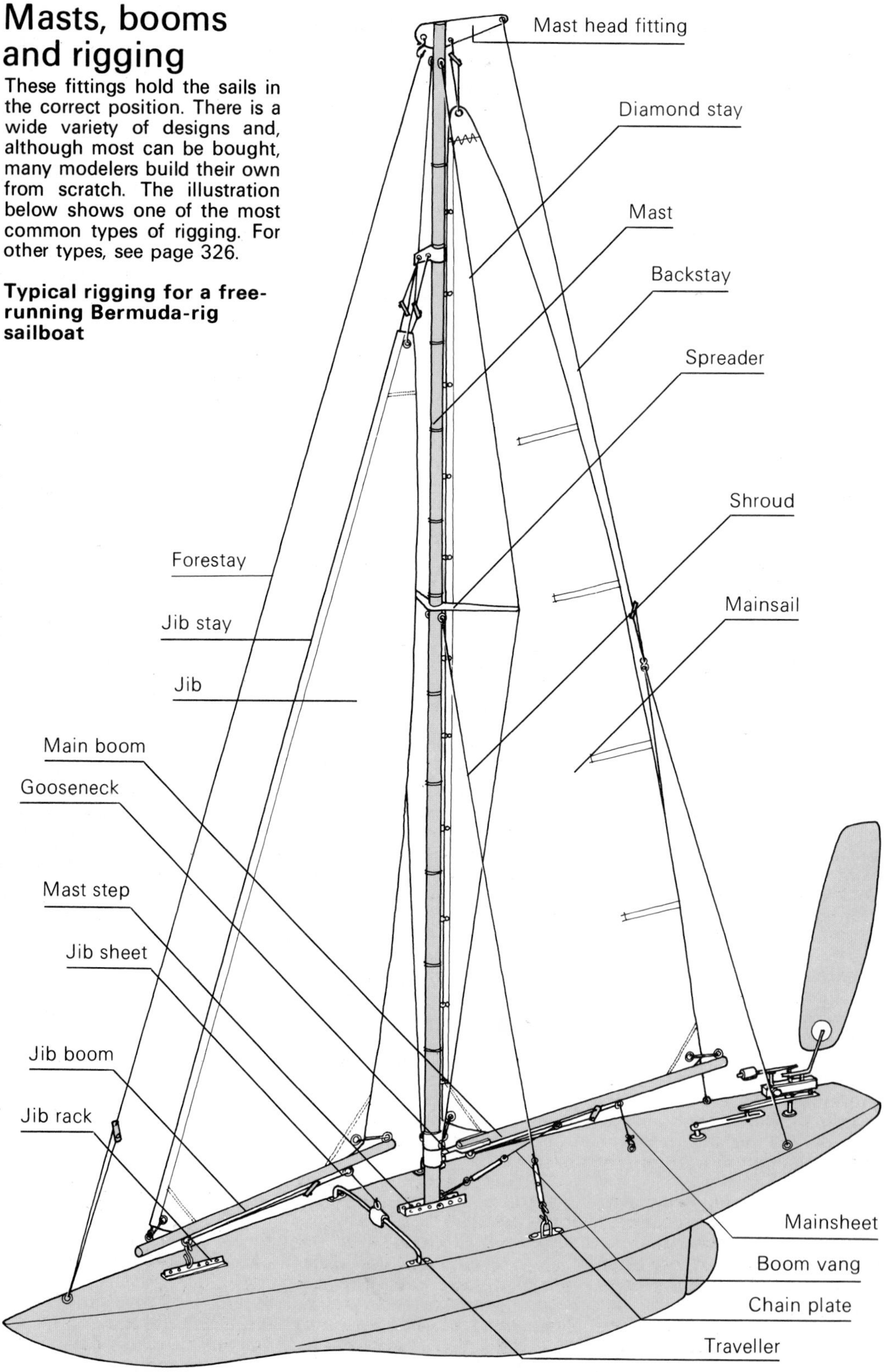

## Masts and booms

Masts must be light, rigid and strong to resist the pressure and pull of shrouds, stays and sails. Too heavy a mast may make your model tend to tip over. Spruce, light alloy tubing, fiberglass or carbon fiber are all suitable materials for mast construction.

Masts may be rectangular, square, round or streamlined in cross section. The streamlined type has a groove down the trailing edge for holding the vertical edge (the luff) of the sail; its shape improves the air flow over mast and sail, especially when the mast has a pivot at top and bottom so that it swivels to align with the wind direction.

Masts may be fixed (stepped) on the deck or inside the hull. They are attached to a metal fixing (the mast step) which usually allows their position to be adjusted fore and aft. The mast step may be an inverted "T" or "U" shape in section with slots or holes to engage a pin or bolt passed through the foot of the mast, or a flat plate with holes into which a peg on the end of the mast fits. The former type should be confined to deck use because of the difficulty of inserting the pin inside the hull; the latter type can form the bottom pivot of a pivoting mast. Brace the deck under a deck-mounted step to carry the force from the mast down to the backbone or a block on the hull bottom. Fix the step for a through-deck mast firmly to the backbone or a reinforcing member on the hull bottom. The slot where the mast passes through the deck should be closed with a mast slide to prevent water from entering (the slide also gives lateral support to the mast and, if locked, fore-and-aft support in addition).

The main boom extends aft from the mast and pivots on a gooseneck. It must be both strong and light, and may be of wood, light alloy tubing, fiberglass or carbon fiber. The boom tends to be pulled up by wind pressure on the sail and a boom vang or a traveller is needed to hold it down, just like on real boats.

Unlike full-size sailboats, the jib on a model sailboat is usually also equipped with a boom. If the mast can be adjusted fore and aft, the jib boom must attach to a jib rack – a fitting similar to a mast step – or to a pivot on a fore-and-aft sliding post. Jib booms, like main booms, may need a boom vang or traveller. If the jib boom is too low for a boom vang or traveller, hold it down with a wire hook just aft of the tack of the sail. Slip the hook through an eye on the boom, then into the jib rack.

The spinnaker (the sail used for sailing downwind, see page 326), also needs a boom. It attaches to the gooseneck fitting on the mast.

## Shrouds and stays

Wire or cable shrouds and stays support the mast.

Shrouds extend from the gunwales just aft of the mast to below the top of the mast. They are fixed in place with chain plates and usually tightened with turnbuckles.

The forestay runs from the bow, and the backstay from the stern, to the mast head or a mast head fitting. A mast head fitting should be strong, rigid and light – light alloy sheet or "T"-section are good materials. (A pivoting mast needs a bearing between the mast head and fitting.) A jib stay holds the luff of the jib. A bowsie (see page 324) is usually sufficient for tensioning fore-, back- and jib stays.

Diamond stays are used to control the flexing of the center part of the mast and produce a good aerodynamic curve in the sail. They are held away from the mast by wooden or metal spreaders and are tensioned by turnbuckles.

A jackstay is sometimes used to attach the luff of the sail to the mast. It is a taut wire or cord run up the back of the mast, bound to the mast every few inches and made fast to a wire ring at top and bottom. Stainless steel wire clips sewn onto the luff are used to fasten the sail to the stay.

## Sheets

These are lines of flexible, braided synthetic fiber which control the swing of the boom. Unlike full-size boats, there is little advantage to operating mainsail and jib independently so the sheets for both are often linked and controlled together. On free-running boats, their length is adjusted by one or more bowsies. The sheets on radio-control boats run to a servo winch via eyes and/or pulleys (see Radio-control boats, pages 327 to 328). To make a loop in the end of a sheet, tie a bowline knot.

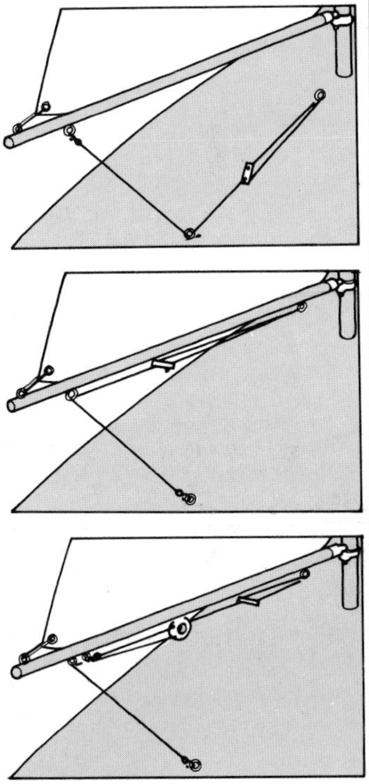

Mainsheet rigging for free-running sailboats

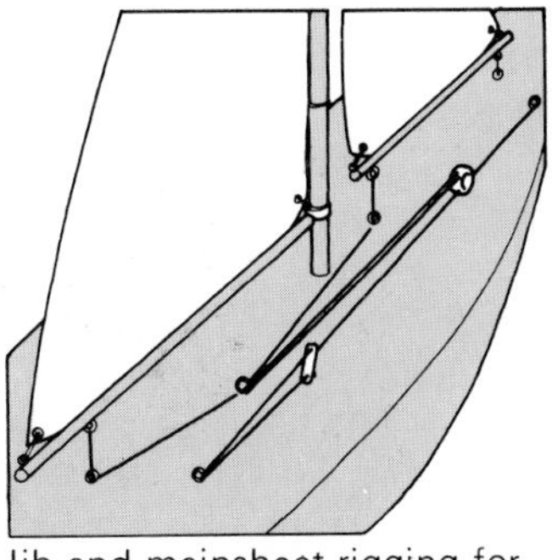

Jib and mainsheet rigging for a free-running boat

## Mast and boom fittings

Wire eyes and eye bolts can be passed through holes in a metal-tube mast. Hooks can be slipped into holes in the mast. A mast band can be fixed around tube or wooden masts, and booms attached to it via eyes. Booms can also be connected to the mast by a gooseneck. Cleats are used to attach lines temporarily.

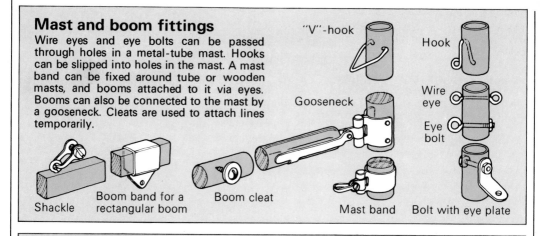

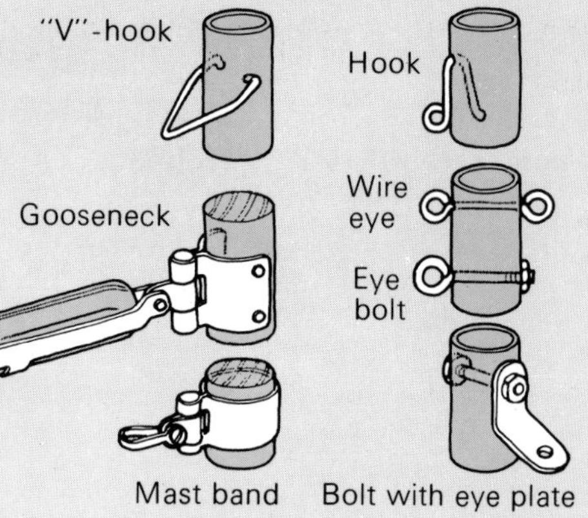


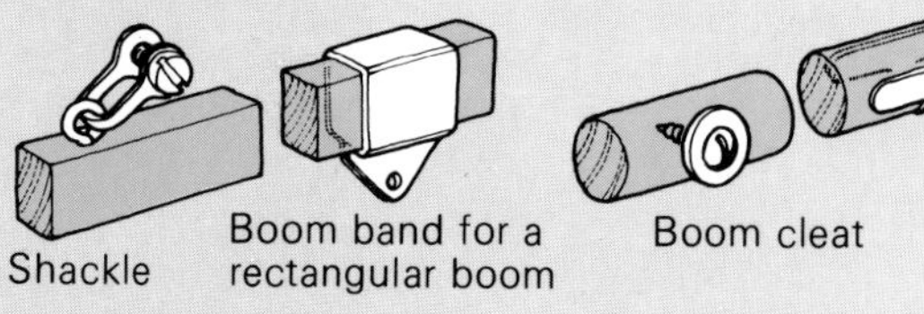


## Other fittings

Use hooks and eyes to attach lines to a deck. The simplest type screws into a reinforcing block or deck beam. Eye bolts screw into a nut or threaded plate under the deck. Sheet-metal, wire and pad eyes can be held down with screws or bolts. Pad eyes are the strongest because they have more than one fixing. Wire eyes can be strengthened by brazing the ends. Chain plates are stronger than eyes and are used to hold shrouds which are highly stressed. Several different designs are available, two of which are shown below. Fasten them with screws or bolts.

Use shackles, line connectors or double hooks to join lines together or to attach them to eyes. Tension lines by tying them off to an eye or a cleat, or by using a turnbuckle or bowsie. Turnbuckles are used for boom vangs and shrouds. They take in a limited amount of line only, but hold it under considerable tension. Adjust them by rotating their body. Bowsies are quicker to adjust and take in more line, but they hold it under less tension. Use bowsies for stays, sheets, uphauls, downhauls and outhauls.

A traveller can be used in place of a boom vang to hold down a boom (see page 323). You can scratch build a traveller from certain types of curtain track.

Pulleys are used to change the direction of a sheet or halyard and make it easier to pull in. Radio-control sail linkages, for example, often incorporate pulleys to reduce strain on the servo. Pulleys can be mounted on the deck or attached to a shackle on an eye or ring bolt.

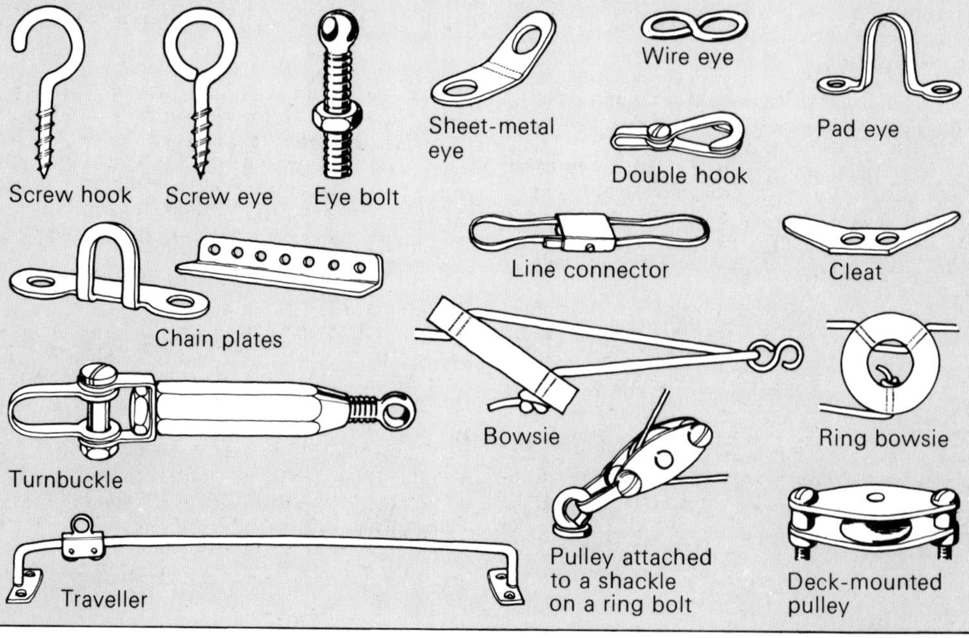

# Sails

There are many different ways of rigging a sailing vessel. Some of the basic types are shown below and on the following page.

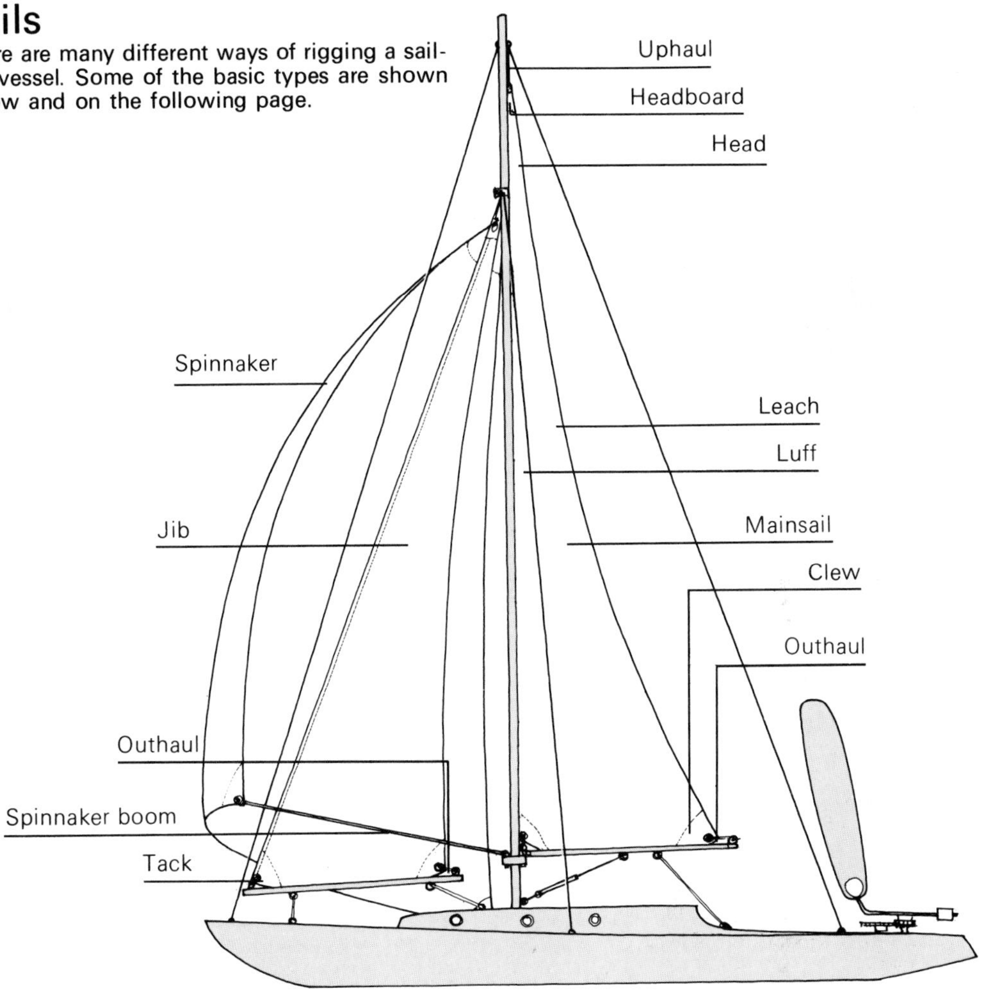


## Bermuda rig

This simple and efficient rig is almost universally used on both model and full-size racing yachts. Make model sails from light nylon or terylene sailcloth, with the exception of spinnakers, which should be made from lightweight polyethylene. Always use thread of the same fiber as the sailcloth so that thread and sails do not shrink at different rates, causing the sails to pucker unattractively.

Cut out the sails following full-size paper patterns and allow for any hems or pockets. Patterns can be made by enlarging scale drawings. Usually, the luff of the sail is hemmed or taped with the same material as the sail, and the foot and leach are left plain. Unhemmed edges should be sealed by applying heat or a water-resistant adhesive. You may wish to reinforce the clew and tack with triangular patches of fabric. The head can be reinforced with a triangular piece of plastic, called a headboard. The leach is often stiffened by inserting small pieces of wood, called battens, into pockets along its entire length.

Ways of attaching the luff to the mast or the jib stay are described below and on page 326 but, whatever method you choose, it must be held taut. Lines attached to the corners of the sail – the uphaul, downhaul and outhaul – are used to tension the sail. The outhaul controls its curve which should be greatest when running with the wind.

### Pocket sail

This sail has a hem at the luff which tapers from top to bottom and fits over the mast. It is aerodynamically superior to other types because of its clean profile; however, any mast fittings above boom level must be easy to remove and replace to allow the sail to be changed. If your model has a spreader, you will need to cut a hole in the luff for it and, if the spreader is the type which slides over the mast, it must be able to slide on and off with the sail.

Jibs can also be the pocket type. One is illustrated on page 322. They function by sliding over the stay.

### Luff groove sail
This type of mainsail, illustrated on page 325, has a length of cord sewn tightly into the luff hem. The cord slides down a groove in the mast; the thickness of the cord prevents the sail from pulling away. Although not as aerodynamically clean as the pocket sail, it is better than lashed- or clipped-on ones, particularly if it is used on a swiveling mast.

### Lashed- and clipped-on sails
The mainsail can be lashed to the mast through a row of eyelets along the luff, or clipped to a jackstay with stainless steel wire clips sewn to the luff. Jibs can also be attached to the jib stay by wire clips.

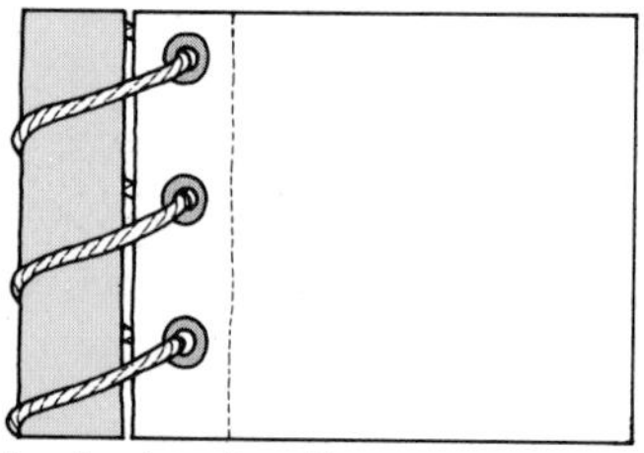

Lashed mainsail

### Spinnaker
This is a flat or part-spherical, symmetrical, polyethylene triangle used when sailing downwind and may be set with or without a jib. It is suspended from the mast and held out by a boom rigged from the gooseneck fitting located opposite the main boom.

Rounded spinnakers must be made from several pieces welded together or joined by single- or double-sided adhesive tape or contact adhesive. Tape can also be used for reinforcing.

### Wing sails
Wing sails are completely rigid and resemble an airplane wing in construction and shape. Their airfoil is symmetrical because they must work equally well on both tacks and, therefore, they lose the advantage of being able to flex to suit the angle of the wind. The angle of the sail to the wind can be controlled in the conventional way by the use of a sheet.

## Square rig
Square or rectangular sails hang from horizontal spars called yards. This rig does not sail to windward well because the sails and yards do not turn under wind pressure like the Bermuda rig; they have to be pulled to the correct angle.

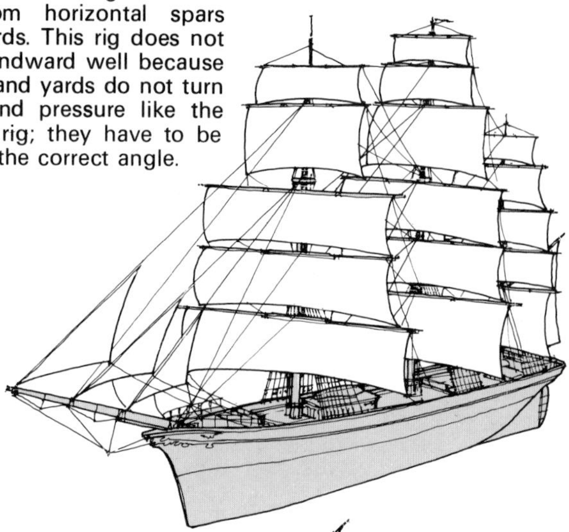

## Lateen rig
This combines features of both square and Bermuda rigs and sails well to windward.

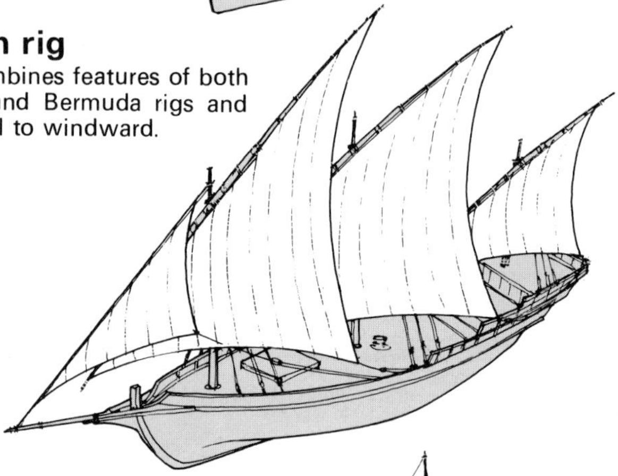

## Gaff rig
This is like the lateen sail except that the luff is attached to the mast. The upper spar is called the gaff. The space between gaff and mast may be filled with sail, the result resembling a Bermuda rig.

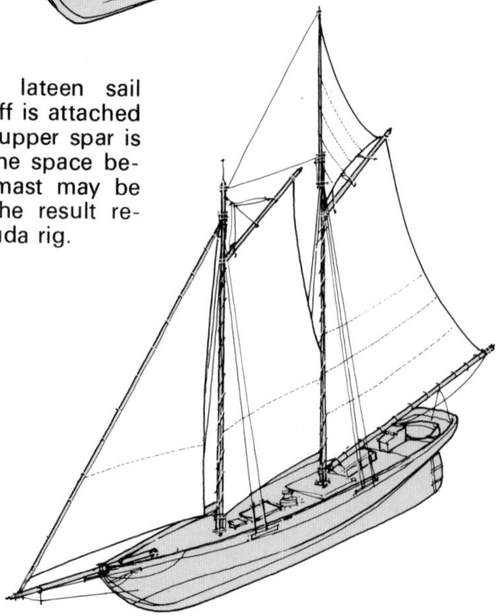

# Radio-control boats

You will learn about how a radio-control system works and find general information about installing equipment and linkages in the chapter on radio control.

Powerboats and yachts usually use a two-channel radio. Powerboats use one channel for rudder and one for throttle. Scale powerboats may use more channels for "extras" such as swiveling gun turrets, lifeboats or an anchor. Yachts have one channel for the rudder and the other for operating both sails together. Three channels are sometimes used for separate control of the main and jib sheets; however, this arrangement is difficult to control as the relative position of each sail is often very difficult to read at a distance.

No special linkages are needed for powerboats but sailboats use a special winch servo for taking in the sheets (see Sail linkages, page 328). Linear servos are best for boats – the rotary type move the linkage from side to side, making it difficult to seal the waterproof box which holds the equipment. (If you do install a rotary servo, place it well back from the exit and use a flexible-cable linkage; the cable will absorb some of the sideways movement inside the box.) Pushrods should be made of wire or aluminum tube with wire ends. Flexible linkages should be all-plastic, if possible, as steel cables can corrode. To protect steel cables, apply some heavy oil then twist the cable in the tube with the aid of a hand drill to push the lubricant through.

Like in other radio-control vehicles, the linkage runs should be as straight and direct as possible. Where the linkage is forced to make a detour, for example where a rudder linkage has to bypass a fuel tank, use a flexible cable or install a bellcrank to change the direction of the pushrod. Another method is to solder a copper tube through the tank to allow the linkage to pass directly to the rudder.

The equipment should be installed as low as possible for stability, particularly in yachts. Before fixing it in place, test the boat's balance (see How a boat floats, page 306).

## Waterproofing the radio equipment

All the equipment must be protected from water if it is to remain in working order. It is best to keep the receiver, batteries, on/off switch and servos in a watertight box. (Although waterproof servos can be mounted outside the box, access and maintenance is easier if they are inside.) A purpose-made plastic box with a transparent top is available but a plastic sandwich box works just as well.

Arrange the components in the box to give the most convenient linkage runs. The servos should be securely mounted on rubber grommets in servo clips or in a servo tray. Protect the equipment from vibration by packing it in some foam rubber.

Make all the exits watertight. Seal the holes for the rudder and throttle pushrods with a rubber bellows or grommet. A smear of grease will prevent the pushrod from sticking and keep moisture out. A short length of nylon or brass tube bonded to the box with silicone rubber sealant can also be used; slip a close-fitting rubber tube over the pushrod and stretch it onto the brass tube to make a good seal. This method can also be employed at the end of a length of flexible cable.

Seal the hole through which the antenna passes with a spot of silicone sealant. Remember to loop the antenna through a short plastic tube where it meets the top of the box. This guarantees that any pull on the antenna will not strain the receiver.

If a receiver plug has to run from the box to a waterproof servo elsewhere in the hull, you will need to cut a large hole. Buy a blanking grommet to suit the size of the plug and cut a hole in the box to match. Make a cut in the grommet and pass the receiver plug through it. Seal the cord in the cut with silicone rubber sealant. If the grommet does not form a watertight seal in the hole in the box, apply sealant between the box and the grommet. The plug connection outside the box should be sealed with waterproof tape or a light, rubber tube slipped over the connection.

Keep a small bag of silica gel crystals in the box to soak up any moisture (the bag can be dried out in the oven when necessary), and open the box to give it an airing when the boat is not in use. It can remain open if stored in a dry room, but if you are keeping the boat in a damp garage, reseal it with the silica gel bag inside and inspect it often.

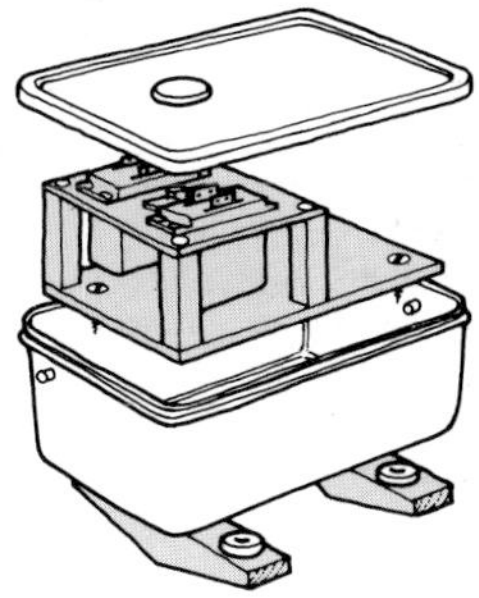

**Mounting servos in the box** Attach the tray to a marine plywood base cut to fit the box. Screw the base to bearers in the hull, through the box bottom, with brass wood screws. Use rubber washers between box and bearers.

**Sealing exits**

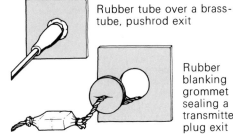

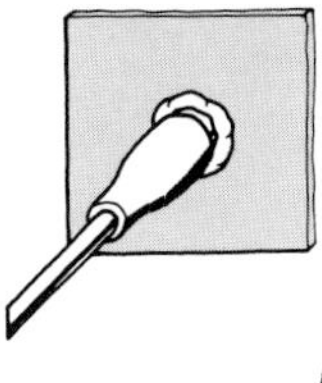

Rubber tube over a brass-tube, pushrod exit

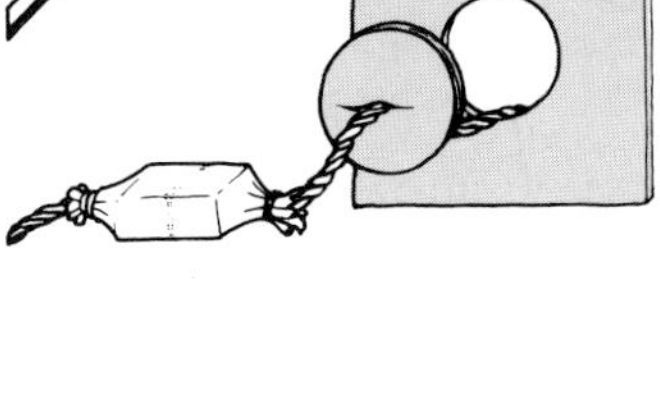

Rubber blanking grommet sealing a transmitter-plug exit

## Sail linkages

A winch servo is the simplest means of taking in the sheets. It has a reel output to take in a cord, with a travel of up to 21 inches (53 cm). The reel can be mounted on the surface of the deck or stowed below in the watertight box. A deck-mounted linkage is simpler to trim and maintain and allows the parts to be easily disconnected for transfer to another model. This type of servo sometimes needs a separate battery pack to power it.

When the jib and mainsail are controlled together, the linkage must be set up so that the sheets move the sails equally. Two ways of arranging the linkage are illustrated below. In each case, the sheets from the jib and mainsail run to their own pulley or eyelet on the centerline of the deck, then their ends are tied to a main sheet line which runs to the servo. The distance between the pulley or eyelet and the fixed point of the jib or mainsail must be the same, and both sheets must attach to the main line either fore or aft of the deck eyelets. Otherwise, the sails will not move together or by the same amount.

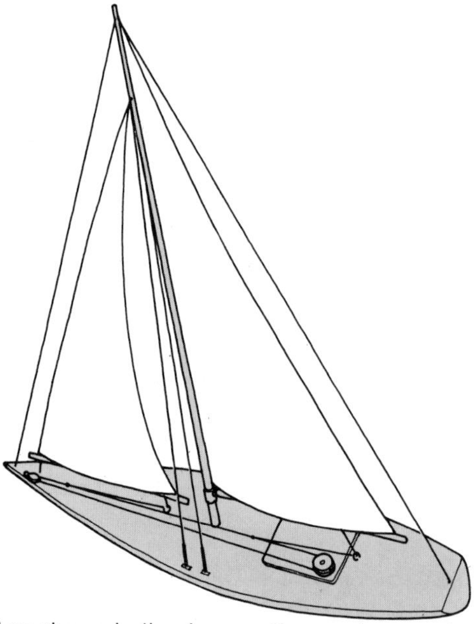

Here the main line is a continuous loop and attaches to a double-track winch. As one end is played out, the other is reeled in. The winch can be at one end of the loop or anywhere in between, to suit the position of the radio gear in the hull. In the former case, the line is wound on to each track from opposite sides and in the latter, from the same side.

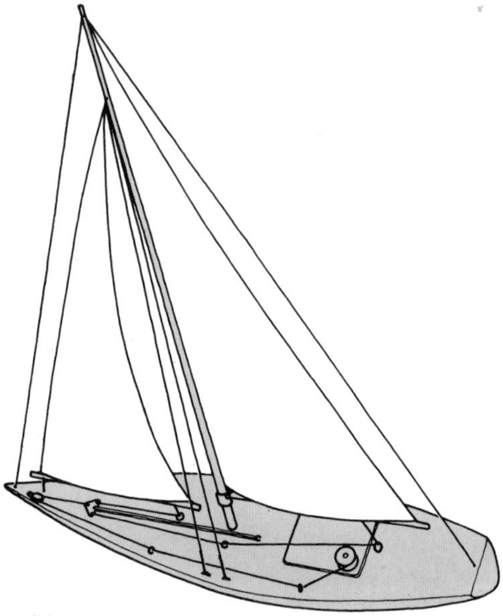

In this case, the main line from the winch servo runs around a pulley at the bow and attaches to one corner of a triangular plate. The jib and mainsheet are one continuous length of line which passes through the other two corners of the plate. A light rubber band fixed to plate and deck keeps the lines taut and prevents them from tangling.

### Leads for below-deck servos

If you install the servo below the deck you will need to make a frictionless lead for the main line. The ceramic liner and hardwood bead shown right make good leads or you can use a brass tube bent to follow the path of the line. A vertical, flared copper tube will prevent water from entering the hull if you position its mouth above the deck. In this case, elevate the deck eyelets to keep the sheets in one plane.

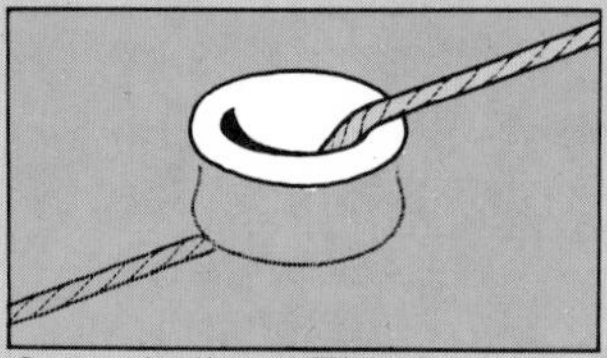

Ceramic liner: This is a fishing line guide. Bond it in a vertical hole drilled in the deck. The smooth, curved edge allows the line to run at almost any angle.

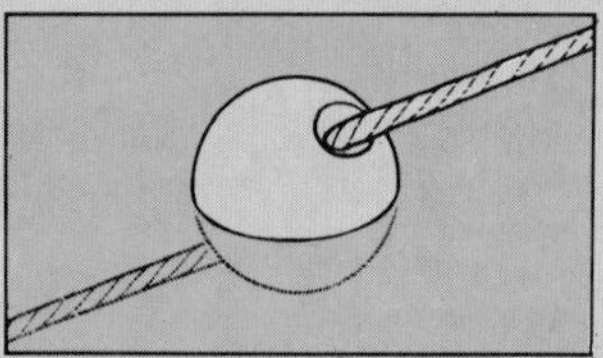

Hardwood bead: Countersink the hole at each end, then bond the bead in place at the required angle. To make a smooth surface, pull a waxed piece of string back and forth in the hole.

# Cars

# Radio-control cars

Number 3 makes a fast getaway at the start of this outdoor race for 1:12 scale electric cars.

This is the fastest growing area of working models; racing extremely fast cars is an exhilarating pastime. It is a hobby that can be enjoyed not only individually at home but at club level where cars can be run on special tracks, in parking lots, school grounds, or halls. Car racing is also followed at international level with all the activities of a highly competitive sport. IFMAR, the international organization for model car racing, sets down the rules and arranges race meetings throughout the world to promote the sport and establish world champion drivers.

There are two main types of car: 1:8 scale internal combustion models and 1:12 scale electric ones. Formula and sports cars have the largest following, although stock cars and roughrider types are also popular. The roughrider is designed to move over uneven ground and is ideal for running in the yard at home or for cross-country racing. All use two-channel radio equipment: one channel for the steering, the other for the throttle and brakes.

Car models are made from kits which usually contain all the components, machined and finished, ready for assembly. Some drilling and finishing may be needed but, by and large, little construction. More expensive, ready-assembled cars are also available. There is a wide range of accessories to complement the kits, from extra parts to items for special tuning.

Car bodies are made in molded plastic and usually held on with clips. There are a number of styles to represent the various classes in 1:8 and 1:12 scales. To make a car eligible for a race in a different category, just change the body. Most body shells come in plain white or clear plastic for you to finish as you wish. You can paint the body to represent a real racing team car or invent your own design – see painting custom cars, stripes and lines, and decals (pages 82 to 83, 84, and 88 to 89).

Success in racing depends on the performance of the car and the driver's skill. The car must be tuned and racing strategy adjusted to suit specific conditions. Always set up the engine and linkages to give smooth-running, maximum output and, above all, reliability, and choose a chassis and the type and size of tires for good traction. Balance is an essential element in making the car handle correctly so distribute the radio components evenly, with more weight over the rear axle to improve road holding. The aerodynamics of the body shape and the wing setting also influence the driving characteristics. This chapter explains a model car's basic components and their functions, and includes a section on driving. Information about breaking in and running motors and engines is in the Motors and engines chapter. The radio-control chapter describes how this system works.

## Assembly procedure

Gas-powered and electric cars are different in detail and come in various stages of completion, but the basic components remain the same. Use this assembly procedure as a guide.

1 Assemble the chassis and bumpers.

2 Mount the axles, including the stub axles, steering arms, wheels, bellcrank and trackrods, on chassis.

3 Connect clutch assembly of gas-powered car to engine crankshaft.

4 Install the motor or engine.

5 Add the receiver, batteries and servos; connect the linkages.

6 Paint the body; clip it onto the car.

# Gas-powered cars

Cars powered by an internal combustion engine are generally made in 1:8 scale, although in America the 1:12 scale is also popular. According to IFMAR regulations, the 1:8 scale cars can measure up to $25\frac{1}{2}$ inches (648 mm) long and $10\frac{1}{2}$ inches (267 mm) wide, depending on class type. Their engines should not exceed 3.5 cubic centimeters.

A gas-powered model car has many of the characteristics of a full-size vehicle, including similar sound effects and smell. The drive is transmitted to the back axle via a clutch, and braking is mechanical, often by a disk brake. The best gas-powered cars run at speeds of up to 60 miles per hour (100 kilometers per hour) and, just like real cars, require quick reactions and good judgment to control them.

Cars are normally raced outdoors because of exhaust from the engines. Indoor events can only be staged in large, well-ventilated halls where the cars are limited as to the amount of nitromethane added to the fuel. This restriction affects performance.

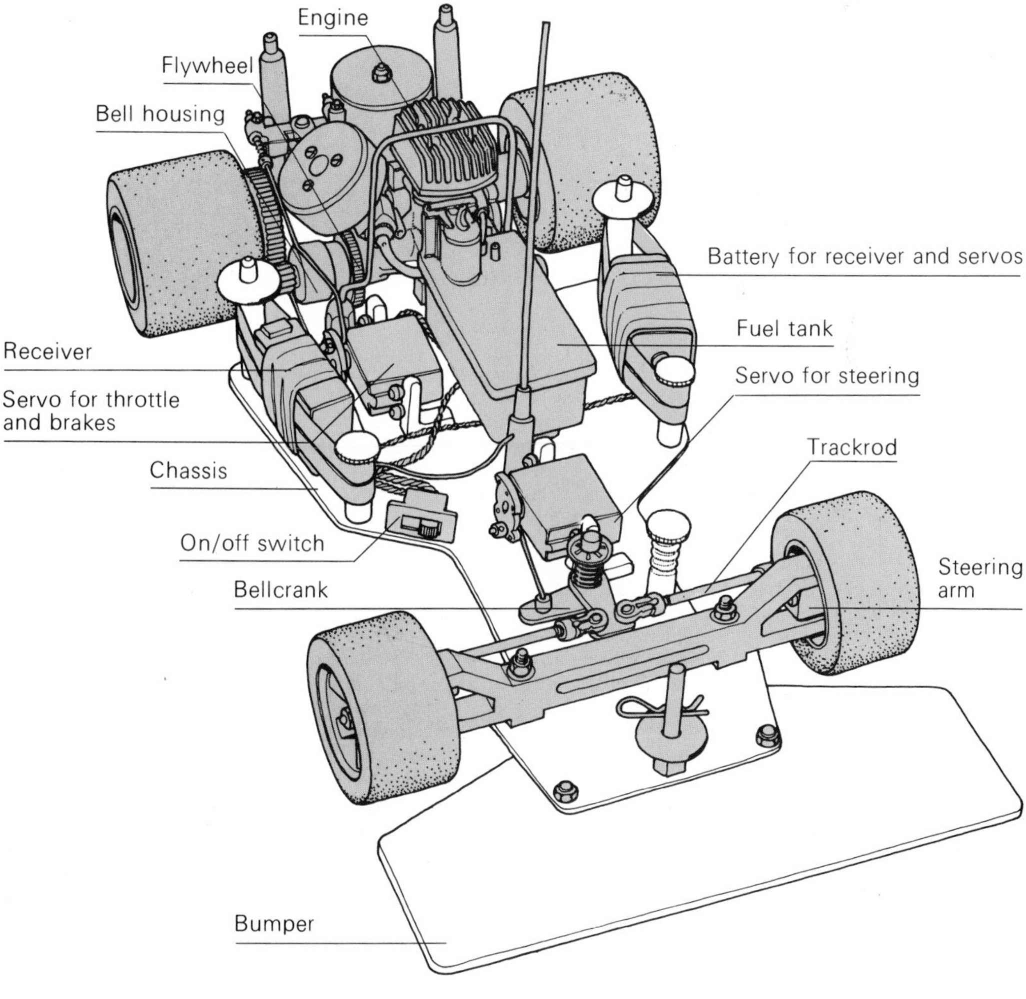

## The chassis

Gas-powered model cars have a two-part chassis: the back section, or power pod, is a rigid alloy plate which carries the engine and transmission; the front section is a semi-flexible plate made from metal alloy or fiberglass which carries the radio gear and steering. The front plate is designed to provide simple suspension for the front axle (independent suspension systems are currently being developed by manufacturers). Differently shaped front plates are available offering degrees of flexibility; metal alloy plates are more rigid than fiberglass ones. Use a stiffer chassis for smooth tracks and a flexible one for rough tracks. Some specialists trim their own chassis plates to suit particular track conditions. Be certain to round off any sharp edges with a piece of abrasive paper.

The chassis must be straight and true for the car to run properly. A fiberglass chassis is able to absorb hard knocks; with a metal chassis there is always the risk that it will twist, seriously altering the fine setting. If after a crash your car seems to handle differently, check the steering linkage and then the chassis to see if it is twisted. To inspect the chassis, empty the fuel tank and wipe the car down to remove any oil residue. Turn the car upside down and sight along the chassis from front to back. If the front and back edges do not look parallel, the chassis is probably twisted. To make certain, strip off its fittings and stand it on a flat surface, such as a piece of glass. Slight misalignment can be corrected by twisting the plate in the opposite direction in a vise. A badly twisted chassis should always be replaced.

### Bumpers

These are flat plastic plates which bolt to the front and back of the chassis assembly. Usually, they are not predrilled so that you can make them fit any body style. They should not project beyond the limit set by class rules.

## The clutch

This connects to the flywheel on the side opposite the engine, and transmits the engine drive to the back axle. It is made up of two, three or four plastic, hard-fiber or metal shoes inside a cylindrical case called a bell housing. One end of each shoe pivots on a pin on the flywheel. When the engine runs at high speed, centrifugal force makes the shoes swing outward and press against the bell housing, causing the housing and the gear wheel on the end of it to turn. When the engine speed drops, springs on the shoes pull them in, thereby disengaging the clutch.

You can adjust the clutch by modifying the tension of the springs or by trimming off some of the shoes with a junior hacksaw to make them shorter and lighter. The shorter the shoe, the lighter the grip, so do not reduce the length by more than 50%. A clutch with more slip is used when racing in wet conditions because it takes up smoothly and makes driving easier. A clutch with more "bite" is preferable in dry conditions. Experiment to see which clutch setting best suits your style of driving and the track conditions. Test shoes can be kept for other occasions.

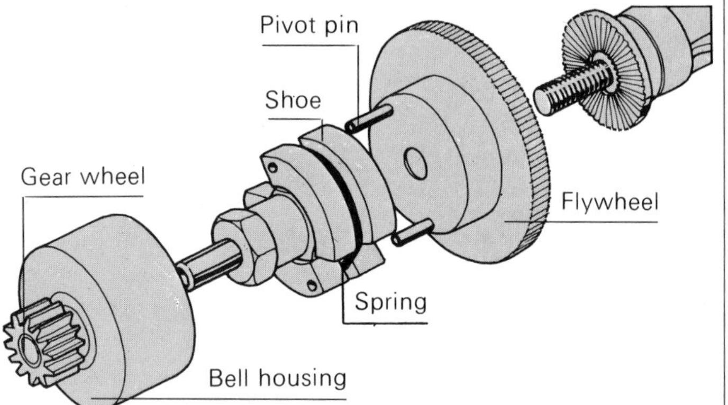


## Mounting engines

Engines are mounted on metal blocks which are ready for bolting to the chassis. The holes for the engine lugs, however, are not usually drilled so that the blocks can be used with any make of engine. To mount an engine, first bolt the blocks to the power pod through the slots, spacing them to accommodate the engine crankcase. Place the engine, complete with flywheel and clutch, on the blocks with the small gear wheel of the clutch meshing correctly with the ring gear on the rear hub. Mark the position of the engine fixing holes through the lugs. Remove the engine and blocks, and drill and tap the blocks. Replace the engine assembly, check the gear mesh and alignment, then tighten up the bolts.

Every engine needs a muffler to comply with radio-control car rules. Kit mufflers should meet with international standards. Some mufflers bolt or clamp directly to the engine. Others, such as the popular pot muffler illustrated on page 240, attach to a manifold bolted to the engine. A short length of flexible silicone tube should be used between muffler and manifold to prevent metal-to-metal contact.

If the engine does not have a special modified head with large fins to aid cooling, attach a heat sink head to dissipate the heat generated by the engine. There are several different designs of heat sink and all function equally well. Choose one to suit the car's body shape. An air filter is essential for a car engine so be sure to install one. Check its condition and clean it regularly. A fuel filter is also recommended. For more information, see Filters on page 236.

## Brakes

The brakes in gas-powered cars share the same servo and transmitter control stick as the throttle. It is an integral system, timed to work in sequence. When the engine is throttled back, the clutch disengages and the engine ticks over without driving the axle. When the transmitter control stick is pulled back further, the brake is applied, bringing the car to a standstill.

The settings must be perfect if the car is to reach its full potential. The diagram below shows a typical brake and throttle linkage. Light override springs can be included to prevent strain on the servo. Collets are ideal for adjusting the springs to your liking.

There are two types of brake: band and disk. A band brake is a lined metal band which works by applying pressure on the clutch bell housing. This method is satisfactory but it can generate a lot of heat, particularly on a twisting race circuit which requires a lot of braking to be done.

The disk brake has proved more effective. It is a disk fixed on the rear axle and sandwiched between two brake linings in a caliper assembly. When the servo is operated, one lining pushes against the other and clamps the disk. Some disks are drilled with a series of holes to reduce heat.

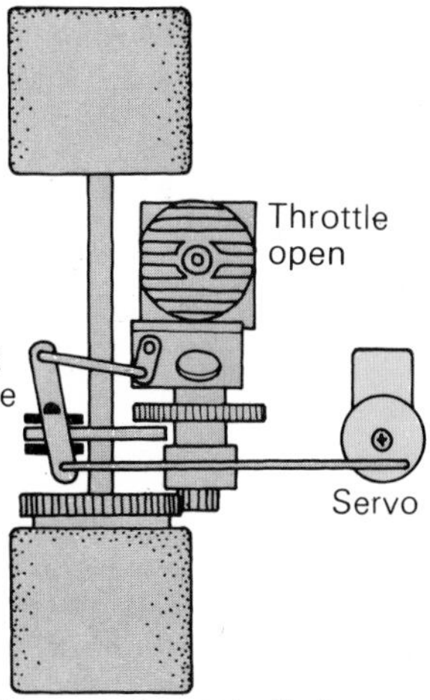


**Brake and throttle linkage**
When the throttle is open the brakes are off and vice versa.

# Electric cars

Electric-powered cars are built in 1:12 scale and measure up to 17¾ inches (450 mm) long and 6¾ inches (172 mm) wide. Although they can reach only 30 miles per hour (50 kilometers per hour) – about half the speed of the fastest gas-powered car – they can reverse, so they are very maneuverable. Moreover, they are clean to run and not excessively noisy, and, therefore, suitable for indoor driving. Electric cars are less expensive to buy and simpler to maintain and run than internal-combustion cars. Braking is electrical via the motor; they do not have a clutch. There is no need for fuel containers, a large battery for an electric starter or a battery for a glow-plug ignition. All that is required for the motor is a charging pack to regenerate the batteries. Their main limitation is a short race time of about ten minutes before the battery runs down. Recharging, however, takes only ten to twenty minutes so that the cars are soon operational again.

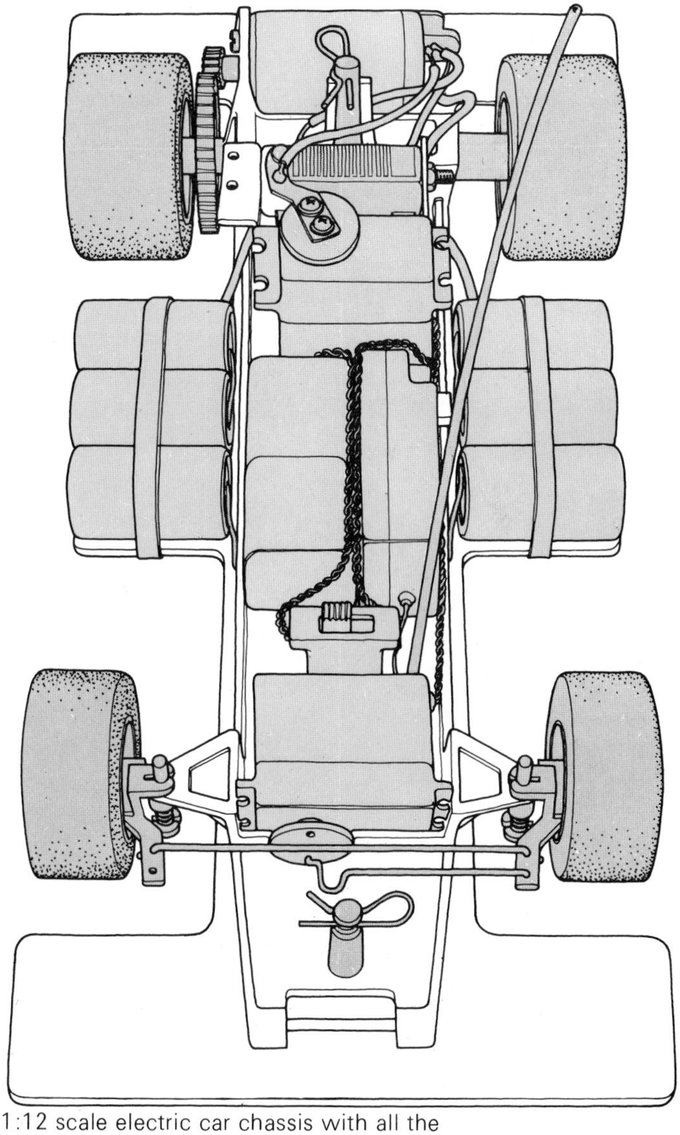

1:12 scale electric car chassis with all the equipment in place.

## The chassis

Electric cars usually have a metal or plastic one-piece chassis. It does not need to be as robust as that for a gas-powered car because electric cars are lighter, run on smooth indoor tracks and are not subjected to such rough conditions. However, if a metal chassis is twisted in a crash, straighten it as described for the two-piece type on page 332, or replace it.

## Mounting motors

Car motors are normally plain cylinders without lugs. Sometimes the front face of the motor is screwed to a molded-in stand on one side of the chassis. In other designs, the motor is clamped between end plates. Some kits come with the motor already in place.

## Braking

Unlike a gas-powered car which has mechanical brakes, an electric car is braked by a resistor or an electronic speed controller (see Controlling the speed, page 251). One system, known as electrodynamic braking, makes the car stop quickly by shorting out the motor.

# Gearing

A car motor, whether internal combustion or electric, runs much faster than needed for the road wheels. Gear wheels are used to reduce the speed. (Turn to page 252 for an explanation of how gears work.)

Car ratios range approximately between a high of 4:1 and a low of 6:1. Kit cars are usually supplied with intermediate gearing but you can adjust them to suit a particular circuit or race conditions. A high gear gives more speed for a simple oval track; a low gear is a good choice for a twisting track with many corners and short straights, because it gives a lower top speed with more acceleration. To alter the gear ratios, change the large ring gear, the small gear on electric cars or the clutch bell housing carrying the small gear on gas-powered cars. Extra gears are sold as accessories. The diameter of the rear tires will also affect the gear ratio: the greater the circumference the higher the gear. In a long race over rough track, for example, tire wear reduces the wheels' circumference, and thus lowers the ratio.

Generally, the small gear is metal and the large one, plastic. The meshing between the two is critical so follow the recommended tolerance specified in the kit. It must not be too tight or slack. You should be able to make fine adjustments without remounting the motor or the engine.

Inspect the gear wheels regularly and clean away any built-up dirt with an old toothbrush. Large pieces of grit can distort or damage the teeth of the softer plastic gear ring. Some reshaping can be done with a modeling knife or needle file but if the teeth are really worn down, replace the gear wheel rather than risk impaired performance.

## How a differential axle works

Most model cars have a one-piece back axle, but it is often desirable to install a differential gear in between two half-shafts so that the wheels can turn at different speeds when the vehicle rounds a corner. There are two types of differential gear in common use.

One design has a pair of bevel gears on the inboard ends of the two half-shafts. These engage with two idler bevel gears mounted in a carrier surrounding the gears. The carrier is driven by the engine. When the car runs straight, the whole thing rotates as a unit. When the vehicle turns, the inner shaft slows and the idler gears turn, transmitting more drive to the outer shaft.

Pairs of spur gears produce the same effect. Each half-shaft has a spur gear on its inboard end. Engaging with these are two or three small spur gears. The small spur gears are mounted on a carrier which, like the bevel gear type, is driven by the engine.

**Types of differential gear**

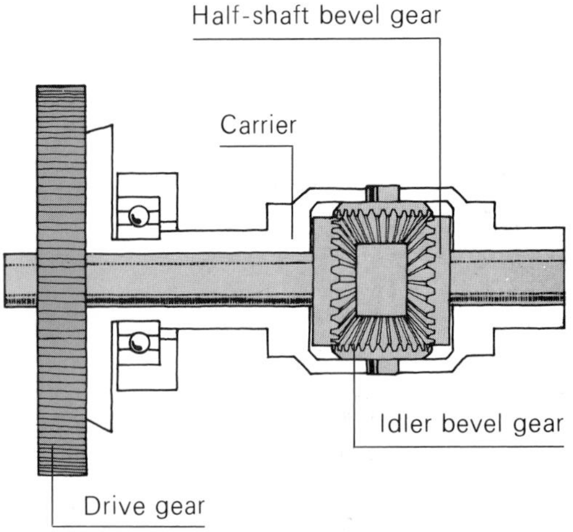


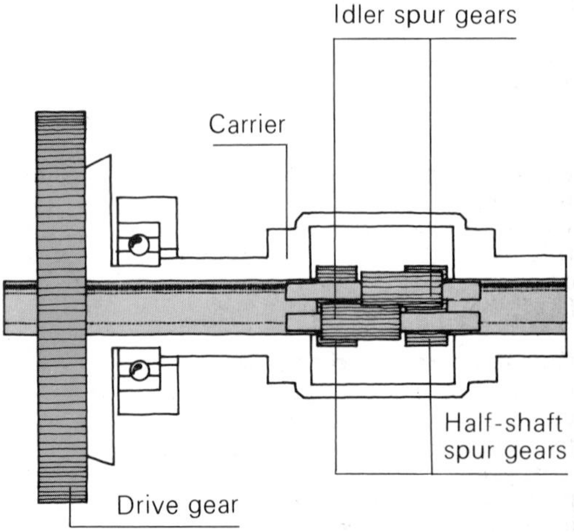

# How steering works

The steering wheels must be set up to roll around the same center to prevent them from skidding sideways in a turn. The simplest arrangement is cart steering where the whole axle pivots about its center. However, this system takes up a lot of space and can exert a great deal of force on the steering mechanism.

Full-size cars work on the Ackerman principle. Each front wheel pivots individually on a stub axle connected by a steering arm to a trackrod. When the wheels are set for straight running, a line through the steering and trackrod pivots passes through the center of the back axle. When the car turns, lines through the pivots of the front axle converge at the same center as a line through the back axle (see the diagram below).

Model manufacturers have found that a variation of Ackerman steering improves the performance of model cars. They place the center point slightly ahead of the back axle, when the car is running straight.

**Ackerman steering**

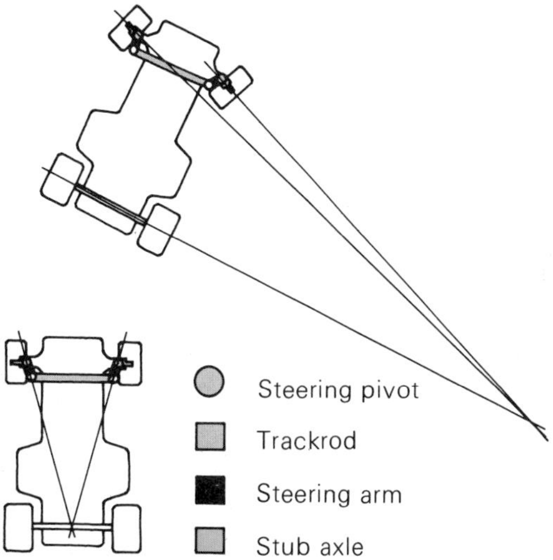


### Spindle trail and castor angle

To make the wheel run straight, manufacturers often set the steering pivot forward of the stub axle (spindle trail), or angle it backward (castor angle). Castor angle makes the shape of the tire's road-contact patch change when the wheels turn a corner. Some manufacturers use this angle in conjunction with spindle trail to compensate for roll caused by too much flexibility in the chassis.

### Camber angle and toe-in

Camber angle is the degree the wheel tilts from the vertical. It makes the wheel tend to turn in the direction it is leaning.

Toe-in is the amount that a pair of wheels point inward when viewed from above. A small amount improves stability.

## Connecting the steering linkage

Assemble and set the steering carefully: both axles must be mounted at exactly 90° to the axis of the chassis. Any misalignment will make the car wander.

Connect the servo linkage, bellcrank and trackrods so that all the components and their movements are symmetrical. The neutral position of the servo output and the bellcrank must be at 90° to the pushrod's line of movement and the trackrods should be the same length. The wheels must not be biased to one side or the other when the servo is at neutral. If they are, change the length of the pushrod or move the servo forward or backward.

If the neutral position on the servo is incorrect, the wheels will turn more to one side than the other. In this case, reset the output on the servo spindle to the center position and change the pushrod length, or move the servo backward.

The position of the pushrod on the servo output and bellcrank determines the amount the wheels move. For the least movement, most suitable for beginners, place the pushrod in the inner holes of the output and the outer holes of the bellcrank. For the most movement and greater maneuverability, place it in the outer holes of the output and into the inner holes of the bellcrank.

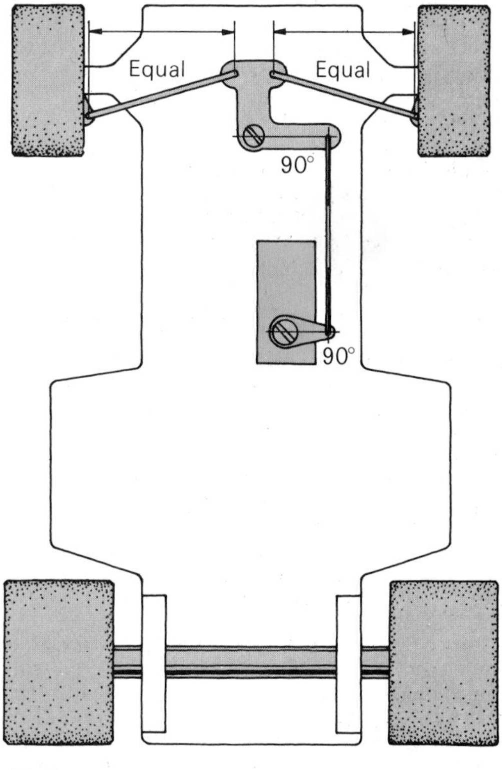


All the parts of the linkage and their movements must be symmetrical.

# Wheels

These must be balanced in size and shape for the car to run straight when accelerating. A good wheel is concentric and has a flat tread and slightly rounded edges. You can buy complete wheels or separate tires and hubs, or bond your own tires from laminated rubber rings and center them on store-bought hubs. Manufactured wheels should be bought in matching pairs.

Tires are made in a range of densities and in various sizes. You can experiment with density and size to find the best combination for the car and track. Usually, the rear tires are larger in diameter and wider than the front ones to improve traction, and the smoother the track, the softer the tires should be. If your car tends to oversteer, try firmer, smaller diameter, or narrower tires on the front to reduce front-wheel grip. If it tends to understeer, change to softer, larger diameter, or wide tires to increase front-wheel grip. Race rules specify a minimum width and diameter. The maximum diameter is self-limiting as larger tires tend to bounce more. Hubs are made to a standard diameter.

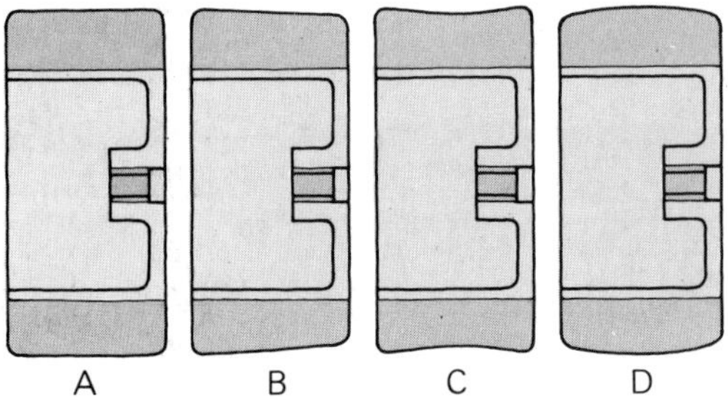

Wheel profiles: A's shape is correct. B, C and D are incorrect.

## Attaching a tire to a hub

Good adhesion is very important to withstand the high forces put on the tires when cornering. If the hub is smooth, roughen it with an abrasive paper to provide a textured surface for the glue. Apply a contact adhesive around the hub and inside the tire. While the glue is still wet, press the hub into the tire. Wipe away any that squeezes out, then allow the wheel to dry (this can take some time).

Do not wait until the glue is touch-dry before joining tire and hub as normally recommended for this type of adhesive or the tire will stick instantly before it is in place. If this does occur, try applying adhesive solvent around the joint to wet the glue.

To remove and replace a tire previously bonded with a contact adhesive, cut and peel away the old tire. Remove any remaining rubber and adhesive with an adhesive solvent before installing a new tire.

If an edge begins to peel during a racing session, apply a small amount of cyanoacrylate glue around the rim. Failure to spot a weak edge could lead to pieces of rubber breaking away, unbalancing the tire.

## Shaping tires

Homemade tires are likely to be uneven and in need of balancing, and commercial tires often have square edges which can make the car skip sideways when cornering. Tires can be trued and the edges rounded with a sanding block and a bench-mounted power drill.

First make a jig, as shown below. To use the jig, slip a long bolt through the wheel hub and clamp it with a nut and washer, then place the projecting end of the bolt in the drill chuck. Run the drill and feed the block into the wheel. When you have removed sufficient rubber, mark the position of the back edge of the block on the baseboard so that an identical wheel can be produced by stopping the block on the same line. This method creates a lot of dust so wear protective clothing. To round off the edges, use the sanding block held in your hand.

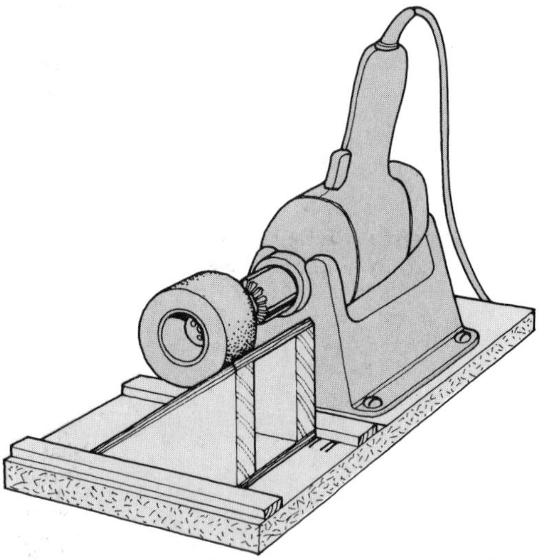

**Making a jig** Hold the drill in a horizontal stand mounted on a baseboard. Build a sanding block and slide it between two wooden strips nailed and glued to the base (the strips must hold the block at a right angle to the stand). Bond a medium-grade abrasive paper to the top face of the block.

## Improving tire traction

In some conditions, particularly indoor races on smooth floors, standard tires do not have enough grip. To improve traction, coat the tread with a silicone sealant.

Begin by mounting a pair of wheels on a length of doweling or a metal rod. Squeeze the sealant onto a piece of cardboard. Roll the wheels through the sealant to coat them evenly. The coarseness of the texture depends on the quantity of sealant applied to the cardboard and how much it is rolled out. Experiment to determine which texture gives the best result. After coating the wheels, support them on the spindle, clear of the surface, and allow the sealant to cure thoroughly.

# Driving practice

Practice in a wide, flat, open space, such as a parking lot or a playground. The car must be set up to run straight before maneuvers can be accomplished easily. A car that is unstable is difficult to drive and will not take corners well.

Begin with the throttle control only, leaving the steering control set at neutral. Make the car accelerate, decelerate, and brake in various degrees to assess the car's reactions across the whole speed range. When you have mastered this control, practice steering.

Mark each end of a simple oval circuit with a tin can or another convenient object. Practice driving the car around the circuit at low speed to familiarize yourself with the steering control. Try to follow a consistent path. Run the car around the course both in a clockwise and anti-clockwise direction.

Next, try combining left and right steering in one circuit by following a figure-of-eight pattern. With practice, you will be able to control the speed accurately on approaches to all corners.

To simulate a race course where the track width is limited, chalk a line around the end markers, about 10 feet (3 meters) away, and try keeping the car inside the line. Finally, practice racing against a competitor.

**Practice courses**

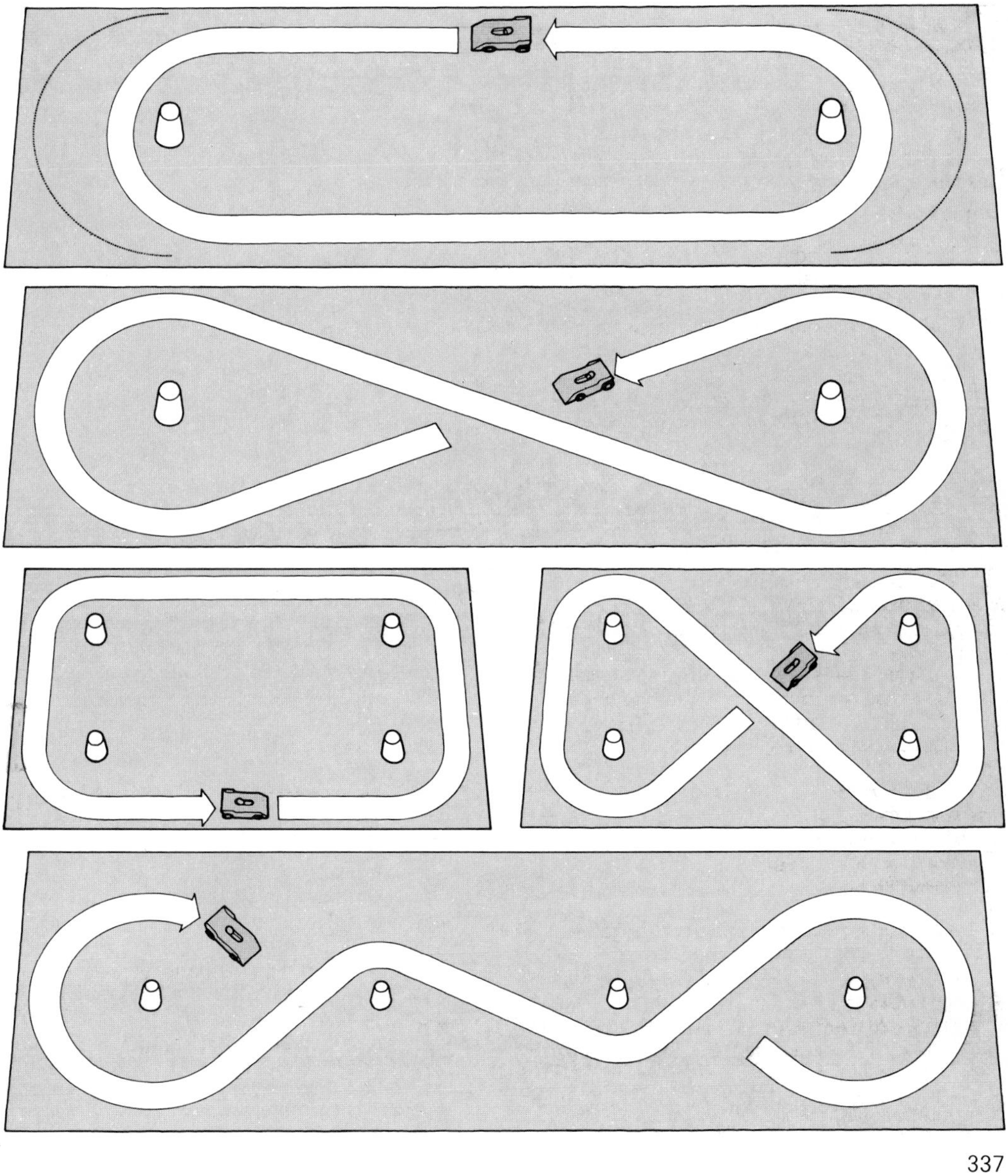

## Taking corners when racing

There are three ways a model car can take a corner. Each demands skilful handling of the controls along with good judgment and timing to drive the car around corners on the correct line, at speed.

One technique, which is also used by full-size racing cars, is to throttle back or brake on the approach to the bend, drive into the bend, then accelerate out, while following the widest curve possible within the confines of the track. This allows the car to be held at the safest maximum speed.

The second method is to keep to the inside line which is the shortest distance around the bend. This may require dropping the speed more, but model cars accelerate at a tremendous rate so any lost time is easily regained. Moreover, by taking the inside line, a competitor can be prevented from getting ahead. When two cars are approaching a corner side by side, the car on the inside has the right of way. If the outside car has a better line and is slightly ahead of the inner car, then he should be given the right of way to avoid a potential collision.

A third way of taking a corner is to use a skidding technique more akin to rally driving than Formula One racing. The corner is approached at speed, then the brake is applied, causing the rear wheels to skid outward; at the same time, the front wheels are turned into the direction of the skid to regain traction and control. By the time the car is under control, it has travelled well into the bend and is heading in the correct line for a fast exit.

This model car is taking the corner like a full-size racing car.

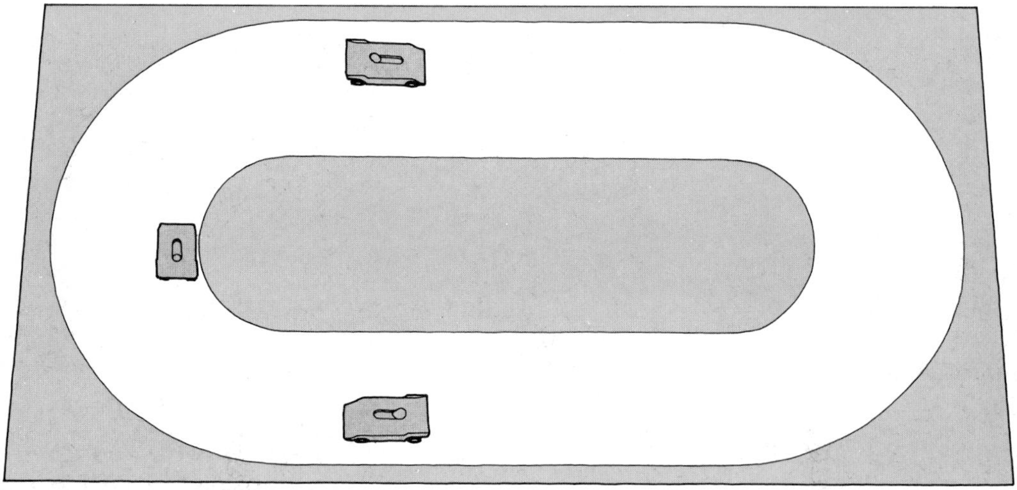

By following the inside line this car is preventing a competitor from passing.

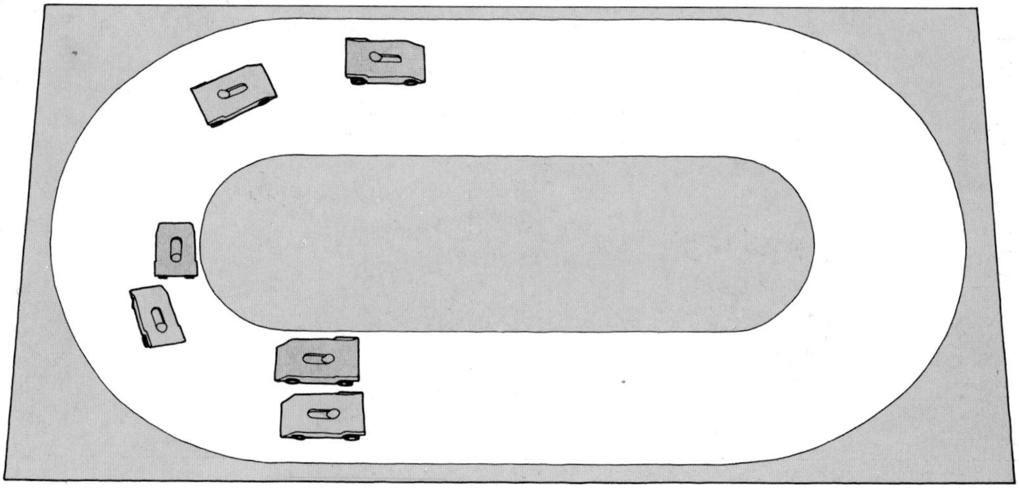

This car is using the skidding technique.

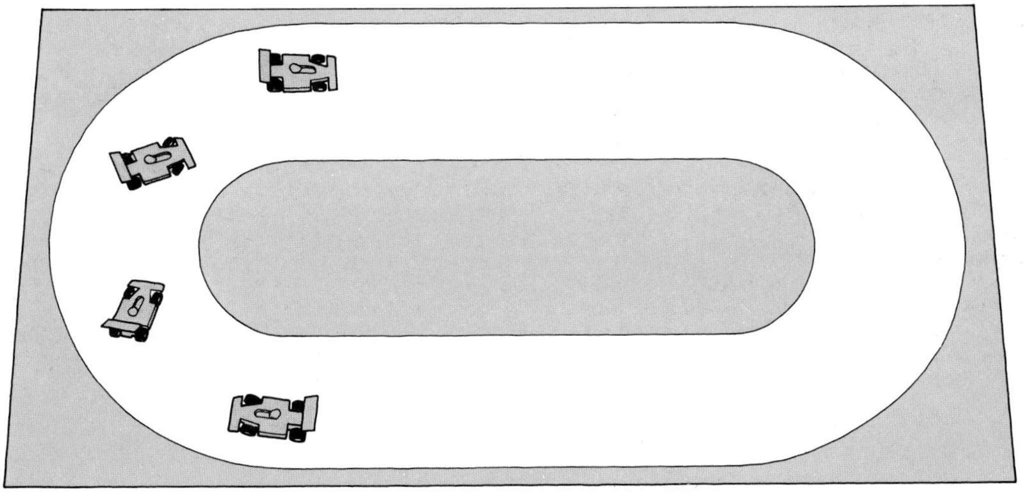

Stand on a chair or a wooden platform to get a good view of the circuit.

# Useful addresses

## Societies

| | |
|---|---|
| International Plastic Modeler's Society<br>Box 2555, Long Beach<br>California 90801 | Kit and scratch-built plastic models of all types |
| National Model Railroad Association<br>2191 Bunts Road<br>Lakewood, Ohio 44107 | Railroads |
| NTRAK<br>Jim Fitzgerald<br>2424 Alturas Road<br>Atascadero<br>California 93422 | N scale modular railroads |
| The Southern California Modular Railroad Club<br>PO Box 121<br>Tustin, California 92680 | HO scale modular railroads |
| AMA (Academy of Model Aeronautics)<br>815 Fifteenth Street, NW<br>Washington DC 20005 | All types of flying models |
| AMYA (American Model Yachting Association)<br>Executive Secretary:<br>Barbara Maire<br>2716 Briarwood Drive West<br>Arlington Heights<br>Illinois 60005 | Radio-control sailboats |
| International Model Power Boat Association<br>24310 Prairie Lane<br>Warren, Michigan 48089 | Powerboats |
| NAMBA International (North American Model Boat Association Int)<br>Exec.: Mrs Myrtle B Coad<br>6073 Sunrise Drive<br>Lower Lake<br>California 95457 | Powerboats and sailboats |
| IFMAR (International Federation of Model Auto Racing)<br>President: Ted Longshaw<br>Beech Tree House<br>West Hill, Downe<br>Orpington, Kent<br>England BR6 7JJ | Racing cars |
| ROAR (Radio Operated Automobile Racing)<br>7822 Eby Lane<br>Overland Park<br>Kansas 66204 | Racing cars |

## Manufacturers and suppliers

| | |
|---|---|
| Tower Hobbies<br>PO Box 778<br>Campaign<br>Illinois 61820 | General model supplies |
| Valley Plaza Hobbies<br>12160 Hamlin Street<br>North Hollywood<br>California 91606 | General model supplies |
| Patty's Corner Inc<br>PO Box 565<br>West Paterson<br>New Jersey 07424 | Tools |
| Dremel<br>Division of Emerson Electric Company<br>4915 21st Street<br>Racine<br>Wisconsin 53406 | Miniature power tools |
| Badger Air Brush Company<br>9128 W Belmont Avenue<br>Franklin Park<br>Illinois 60131 | Badger airbrushes |
| Floquil-Polly S Color Corporation<br>Rt 30 North<br>Amsterdam<br>New York 12010 | Model paints |
| Krasel Industries Inc<br>1821E Newport Circle<br>Santa Ana<br>California 92705 | Micro scale decal products |
| Bare-Metal Foil & Hobby Co<br>19419 Ingram<br>Livonia<br>Michigan 48152 | Bare-metal foil and decal sheets |
| Top Flite Models Inc<br>1901 N Nawagansett Avenue<br>Chicago, Illinois 60639 | Monokote covering kits |
| Woodland Scenics<br>PO Box 266<br>Shawnee Mission<br>Kansas 66201 | Scenic modeling supplies |
| Plastruct Engineering Model Associates<br>1161 Monterey Pass Road<br>Monterey Park<br>California 91754 | Miniature plastic girders and other structural parts |
| The Black Watch<br>PO Box 666<br>Van Nuys<br>California 91408 | Figures |

| | |
|---|---|
| Cameo<br>PO Box 3035<br>Glendale<br>California 91201 | Figures |
| The Soldier Shop<br>1013 Madison Avenue<br>New York<br>New York 10021 | Figures |
| Coulter-Bennett Inc<br>12158 Hamlin Street<br>North Hollywood<br>California 91606 | Historex figures and accessories plus other ranges of figures |
| The Squadron Shop<br>23500 John R Hazel Park<br>Michigan 48030 | Military figures |
| Series 77 Miniatures<br>7861 Alabama Avenue 14<br>Canoga Park<br>California 91304 | Series 77 figures |
| Wm K Walthers Inc<br>5601 W Florist Avenue<br>Milwaukee<br>Wisconsin 53218 | Model railroad mail order company |
| Aurora Plastics Corp<br>West Hampstead<br>New York | Aurora static-vehicle kits |
| Monogram Models Inc<br>Morton Grove<br>Illinois | Monogram static-vehicle kits |
| Revell Inc<br>4223 Glencoe Avenue<br>Venice<br>California 90291 | Revell static-vehicle kits |
| Carl Goldberg Models Inc<br>4734 W Chicago Avenue<br>Chicago<br>Illinois 60651 | Airplane kits and accessories |
| Hobby Lobby International<br>Rt 3, Franklin Pike Circle<br>Brentwood<br>Tennessee 37027 | Airplane kits and accessories; general modeling supplies |
| Midwest Products Co Inc<br>400 South Indiana Street<br>Hobart<br>Indiana 46342 | Airplane kits and general modeling materials |
| Sig Manufacturing Co Inc<br>Route 1, Box 1<br>Montezuma<br>Iowa 50171 | Airplane kits and accessories |
| Sterling Models<br>3620 "G" Street<br>Philadelphia<br>Pennsylvania 19134 | Airplane and boat kits |
| Astro Flight Inc<br>13377 Beach Avenue<br>Venice<br>California 90291 | Airplane, boat and car kits; electric power systems |
| Cox Hobbies<br>Division of Leisure Dynamics Inc<br>4400 West 78th Street<br>Minneapolis<br>Minnesota 55435 | Airplane, boat and car kits; internal combustion engines |
| Dumas Products Inc<br>909-G E 17th Street<br>Tucson, Arizona 85719 | Boat kits and accessories |
| Associated Electrics Inc<br>1928 East Edinger<br>Santa Ana<br>California 92705 | Radio-control car kits |
| Bolink Industries<br>PO Box 89653<br>Atlanta<br>Georgia 30366 | Radio-control car kits and accessories |
| Team Associated<br>Associated Electric<br>1928 East Edinger<br>Santa Ana<br>California 92705 | Radio-control car kits |
| Model Rectifier Corp<br>2500 Woodbridge Avenue<br>Edison<br>New Jersey 08817 | Radio-control model kits and equipment |
| World Engines<br>8960 Rossash Avenue<br>Cincinnati, Ohio 45236 | Engines |
| Fox Manufacturing Co<br>5305 Towson Avenue<br>Fort Smith<br>Arkansas 72901 | Internal combustion engines and fuel |
| Futaba Corporation of America<br>555 West Victoria<br>Compton<br>California 90220 | Radio-control electronic equipment |
| Kraft Systems Inc<br>450 W California Avenue<br>PO Box 1268<br>Vista, California 92083 | Radio-control equipment and accessories |
| Du-Bro Products Inc<br>480 Bonner Road<br>Wauconda<br>Illinois 60084 | Radio-control linkages and accessories |

# Glossary

## A

**AC (alternating current)** Electric current supplied to households which reverses its direction at regular intervals.

**Aft** Toward, near or at the rear of a boat or aircraft.

**Airfoil** Wing, tail plane or fin of an aircraft.

**Airscrew** Aircraft propeller.

**Amidships** In or toward the middle section of a boat.

**Amp (ampere)** Unit of measurement of the flow of electric current in a conductor.

**Animate** To change the pose of a figure or alter the "moving" components of a static vehicle.

**Aspect ratio** The ratio of wingspan to chord of an aircraft.

## B

**Ballast** Weight added to a vehicle to stabilize it. Also, material distributed along railroad tracks to form a bed between rails and ties.

**Beam** The width of a boat at its widest point.

**Bevel** Sloping edge of a workpiece. Also, tool used to mark out a bevel.

**Built-up construction** Open-frame construction for the wings and fuselage of model aircraft; usually balsa.

**Bulkhead** Solid partition dividing the interior of a boat.

**Burr** Edge raised on metal by cutting or filing.

## C

**Center of gravity** The center about which the model is at rest.

**Chamfer** A 45° bevel.

**Chord** Width of an aircraft wing or tail plane measured from leading to trailing edge.

**Control surface** A movable flap used to change a model's attitude or its direction of movement.

**Convert** To change the identity or character of a model figure or vehicle.

## D

**Datum** A point, line or plane used as a basis for taking measurements.

**DC (direct current)** Electric current which flows continuously in one direction. Batteries produce DC.

**Differential movement** Where one part functions at a different rate from another.

**Displacement** Weight or volume of water displaced by a floating boat.

**Downthrust** The downward misalignment of the main axis of an engine.

**Drag** Resistance produced by moving a vehicle through air or water.

**Dry brushing** The application of very small amounts of color with a brush from which most of the paint has been removed.

## E

**Elevation** True projection of an object viewed from the side, front or back.

## F

**Fillet** Narrow strip of material used to round off the inside junction of surfaces. Also, narrow strip added to outside edge to reinforce or shape.

**Fish plates** Sometimes used to describe the joiners connecting pieces of model railroad track.

**Fixed-wing airplane** Aircraft with conventional wing construction instead of the rotating "wings" of a helicopter.

**Flange** A raised edge or rim, such as the part of a train wheel which locates on the inside of the rails.

**Flaps** Aircraft-wing control surfaces which increase both lift and drag for slow-speed flying.

**Flash line** The thin film of metal or plastic produced along the seam of a badly fitting mold.

**Fore** Toward the front of a boat or aircraft.

**Former** Member used for shaping, especially a cross-sectional member in an airplane fuselage.

**Free-flight airplane** An aircraft which is not under any form of remote control.

**Full-house control** When a radio transmitter has channels for the steering and throttle of a car or boat, or the ailerons, rudder, elevator and throttle of an aircraft.

## G

**Grass powder** Powdered foam sprinkled onto glue to simulate grass in dioramas and railroad landscapes.

**Grommet** A rubber insert.

**Groundwork** Scenic effects such as sand, earth and grass.

**Grout** To fill the spaces between bricks or stones with plaster or cement.

## H

**Highlight** To lighten the surface of a model with paint.

**Horn** Projection from a model's control surface to which the linkage is attached.

## I

**Incidence** Angle at which a wing or tail plane is presented to the airflow.

## J

**Jig** Apparatus for holding a workpiece while assembling or shaping it.

## L

**Lamination** Thin layers of material glued together.

## M

**Mask** To cover a model to produce decorative effects or to protect it from being inadvertently painted.

## N

**Narrow gauge** Railroad with rails spaced closer together than those of standard gauge.

## P

**Plan view** True projection of an object viewed from above.

**Points** British term for a turnout or switch.

**Port** Lefthand side of either a boat or aircraft when facing forward.

**Pyrogravure** Electric needle for engraving plastic.

## R

**Rabbet or rebate** A recess cut out of the edge of a workpiece.

**Ratchet** In model boating, a toothed strip used to preset the tiller.

## S

**Scale model** A replica of a full-size object built to scale.

**Scratch-built model** One built with raw materials which does not incorporate ready-made components.

**Shadow** Removable former used to shape a boat hull.

**Sidethrust** Sideways misalignment of the main axis of an engine to counteract torque.

**Spinner** Boss which fits over the hub of a propeller.

**Stall** Sudden loss of lift by an airfoil due to insufficient air speed. Also, to stop an engine by slowing it down below the level at which it will operate.

**Standard gauge** Accepted measurement of the distance between the rails of a railroad.

**Starboard** The righthand side of a boat or airplane when facing forward.

**Station** A datum line representing a section through an object.

**Stipple** To paint short touches with the tip of a paintbrush.

## T

**Template** Pattern made from thin sheet material to guide a marker or cutter.

**Thinner** Solvent used to thin paint and clean brushes.

**Topsides** The sides of a boat hull which extend above the waterline.

**Torque** Turning force.

**Transparency** Any transparent model component, such as a cockpit canopy or a car windshield.

**Trim** Setting of control surfaces to produce the required flight or sailing characteristics.

## V

**Volts** Unit of measurement of the force of electricity flowing in a conductor.

## W

**Wash** Very thin paint applied to produce a light stain.

**Wash-in** More incidence at the wing tip than at the root.

**Wash-out** Less incidence at the wing tip than at the root.

**Watt** Unit of power, normally referring to electricity.

**Weathering** The process of simulating age or wear on a model, usually with paint.

# Index

# C

# Authors' acknowledgments

We are especially grateful to those individuals who permitted us to photograph their models for inclusion in the book and a list of their work is found below. We apologize for not including every model that was photographed, but no model was excluded for any reason other than lack of space.

**Gary Allum** 18 to 19; 20 top left; 111 bottom; 117 top; 125 bottom

**Gary Allum** and **Terry Wills** 140 top

**A Arnold** 106 bottom

**P Attlee** 305 bottom

**George Baker** 25 bottom

**Charles Bard** and **Frank Dubery** 211 top; 213 top; 216 top, bottom left and bottom right; 217 bottom; 218

**Bare Metal Foil & Hobby Co** 79 top and bottom

**Bexley Model Boat Club** 305 bottom

**Paul Bridgwater** 25 top

**G Brown** 156 center

**Dennis Bryant** 16 bottom

**John G Campbell** 222 bottom

**G Craddock** 102 top left and bottom right; 108 center; 133

**J Crowley** 7 top right; 137 center left 144 left; 150; 151 left and right; 152 center

**Lionel Currie** 219

**Cygnets Model Power Boat Club** 24

**David Day** 16 top; 26 bottom

**Bob Denness** 103 top; 137 center right

**Allan Downes** 12 top left; 182 bottom right; 184 center right; 188; 220; 221; 222 top; 223 top; 224 top and bottom

**Arthur Freeland** 265

**Dennis Green** 6 bottom left; 90 to 91; 92; 94 bottom right and details left; 95 top; 96 bottom left; 98 top; 99 bottom; 101; 102 top right; 103 bottom left, bottom center and bottom right; 107; 108 top left; 127; 136 center; 144 right; 145 top, center and bottom; 147 left; 149 top; 156 bottom; 162 to 163; 165; 166 to 167; 169; 170 to 171; 173; 174 to 175; 177; 178 to 179 center and details; 180; 181; 182 top and center; 183 top, center left, center right and bottom; 189; 190; 191 all; 192 top, center left, center right and bottom

**Ray Habgood** 82 top, bottom and details; 83

**J P Hearn** 140 bottom left

**Historex** 102 bottom left; 108 top right and bottom

**A Jackson** 5 top; 7 bottom right; 98 center and bottom; 99 top, second from top and second from bottom; 117 center; 138; 147 right; 182 bottom left; 184 center left and bottom; 185 bottom left; 186 top and bottom; 187 top left, top right, center right, center left and box

**D Johns** 143

**A W Lane** 2; 5 bottom; 193; 212; 213 bottom; 217 top; 225 bottom

**K Lewis** 159

**Alan Locks** 304 top (near boat)

**D Maskell** 10 bottom left; 93; 125 top

**Preston Monahan** 10 top left and center left; 88; 95 center right; 124 bottom

**K Northop** 153 right

**P B Racing Products Ltd** 26 top, center

**Richard Philpott** 142; 149 bottom

**Edward Pollard** 141

**K Rawlinson** 20 to 21 top right and bottom

**Peter Roake** 17 bottom

**B Ruffy** 137 bottom

**Les Shearn** 104; 106 top; 137 top; 140 center left; 152 bottom center and bottom right; 153 left; 154 center

**Jeremy Stratton** 136 bottom

**Brian Thomas** 14 top and bottom; 15 top and bottom; 85 bottom; 86 top and bottom; 87 center left; 96 right, top to bottom; 105; 113; 114 left and right; 118; 121 top and bottom; 123 center and bottom; 128; 131

**Ray Vine** 304 top (far boat)

**Terry Wills** 8 top left, center right and bottom; 87 bottom; 94 top; 95 center left; 123 top; 124 top; 126

**Cliff Young** 12 bottom left and bottom right; 200; 211 bottom; 225 top

**In addition, we would like to mention certain individuals who gave generously of their time and experience to furnish us with much of the material contained herein.**

**Gary Allum** for explaining how to detail military vehicles.

**Chris Baker** of Model Flight Accessories for information on electrical power systems and their application in working models.

**Eric Bennett** and **Ian Skilling** of Eltham Models for their expertise in the fields of marine and aeromodeling, the loan of reference material and for their goodwill and patience in answering questions.

**David Brand** of MacGregor Industries for helping to simplify the complexities of radio-control equipment.

**Frank Cribbens** of Morris and Ingram for his advice on the use of Badger airbrushes.

**John Dean** of Micro-Mold for not only supplying reference material, but also for his keen interest in the project.

**Allan Downes** for demonstrating his techniques for making miniature buildings for which he is justly famous.

**Dennis Green** for his sustained advice and assistance, plus a mass of information, much of which has never been published before. In addition to methods for building and painting figures and vehicles, he is largely responsible for the techniques on building dioramas.

**Edward Hall** of Humbrol Ltd, for information on paints and finishes.

**Robin Harris** for his illustrations and many contributions to the working models section.

**Ted Longshaw** for his inspiring enthusiasm and his contribution to the cars chapter.

**Robert Mogg** and **Peter Walsh** for their assistance in compiling the techniques for the railroads chapter.

**Keith Plestel** of P B Racing Products Ltd, for his specialized knowledge of building and racing radio-control cars.

**Lynn Sangster**, Historex Agent, for his generosity in supplying material and equipment.

**Brian Thomas** for spending many hours showing us how to construct, paint and detail aircraft.

**Terry Wills** for his advice on constructing and painting model vehicles.

**We are also indebted to the following individuals, manufacturers and organizations for their assistance:**

Abrasive Tools Ltd
Airfix Products Ltd
Associated Adhesives Ltd
Astro Flight Inc
George Baker
Bare-Metal Foil & Hobby Co
Beatties Ltd
Bexley Model Boat Club
Bolink Industries
British Model Soldier Society
Bromley Radio Control Flying Club
Cygnets Model Power Boat Club
Bob Denness
DeVilbiss Co Ltd
Chris Donnelly
Dumas Products Ltd
EMA Model Supplies Ltd
Eltham Models
Fox Manufacturing
Neville Guibarra
Ray Habgood
A A Hales Ltd
H G Hannant Ltd
Ronald Harris
Historex Agents
Humbrol Ltd
International Plastic Modellers' Society
Bill Isard
M Jewell
Richard Kohnstam Ltd
A W Lane
Lesney UK Ltd
Letraset Ltd
R Lightheart
MacGregor Industries Ltd
Microflame Ltd
Micro-Mold Ltd
Model Aircraft Ltd
Model Flight Accessories
Morris & Ingram Ltd
National Model Railroad Association Inc
North Middlesex Model Railway Club
Jean O'Grady
P B Racing Products Ltd
Plastruct Inc
Precision Paints Co Ltd
Precision Petite Ltd
Reeves & Sons Ltd
Revell Ltd
George Rowney & Co Ltd
Mike Roper
Sig Manufacturing Co Ltd
Solarbo Ltd
Stirling Models
Tetrosyl Ltd
Trevis Ltd
John Veasey
Wm K Walters Inc
Welling Model World
Gary Wilkins
Cliff Young

Dorling Kindersley would like to thank:
William Furnish
Marlon John
Miren Lopategui
Maria Mosby

All photographs by David Strickland except the following:
Bare-Metal Foil & Hobby Co 79 top and bottom
Charles F Buccola 222 bottom
Historex 102 bottom left; 108 top right and bottom; 141
The Museum of London 157
J N Priest 12 top left
Railway Modeller 161; 184 right
Craig Webb 211 top; 213 top; 216 top, bottom left and bottom right; 217 bottom; 218

Main illustrations by Robin Harris
Illustrations for basic techniques chapter by Hayward and Martin Ltd
Illustration on page 110 by B Sayers

Typesetting:
Contact Graphics
Filmtype Services Ltd

Reproduction:
F E Burman Ltd

| DATE | | | |
|---|---|---|---|
| NOV 1 '84 | MAY 2 2 '89 | | |
| NOV 1 9 '84 | [illegible] | | |
| OCT 16 '85 | OCT 3 '89 | | |
| [illegible] 25 [illegible] | OCT 2 7 '89 | | |
| [illegible] | | | |
| APR 4 '86 | | | |
| [illegible] | | | |
| [illegible] 25 '86 | | | |
| FEB 1 7 '87 | | | |
| | | | |
| NOV 2 3 '87 | | | |
| MAR 1 1 '88 | | | |

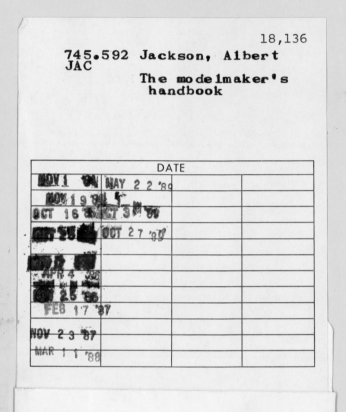